An Oral History of Florida's Pursuit of Gridiron Glory

Peter Golenbock

Legends Publishing
St. Petersburg, FL

A Legends Publishing Company, LLC Book

Published by Aitan Publishing Company
62 East Starrs Plain Road
Danbury, CT 06810

ISBN: 0-9650782-1-3

Library of Congress Cataloging-in-Publication Data
Golenbock, Peter, 1946–
   Go Gators! : An oral history of Florida's pursuit of gridiron glory / by Peter Golenbock.
      p. cm.
Includes index.
   ISBN 0-9650782-1-3 (Hardcover : alk. paper)
   1. University of Florida–Football–History.
   2. Florida Gators (Football team)–History. I. Title.
   GV958.U523 G65 2002
   796.332'63'0975979--dc21
                              2002010004

Readers can reach Legends Publishing Company at froggf@mciworldcom.net

10 9 8 7 6 5 4 3 2

Book design by Mixed Media Enterprises, Inc./Thomas Yu

Manufactured in the United States of America

contents

Contents

Contents

foreword

When I was asked by Peter Golenbock to write a foreword to this book, *Go Gators!*, I didn't know where to start. I had just read it very carefully and realized I had never read a book like it before. It is truly unique.

This book gives a very personal look at Gator football history from the players' standpoint as they were playing the games. It takes you into the lives of these young men coming from very diverse backgrounds as well as into the lives of their coaches.

They answer questions that had never been asked before about why things happened in certain ways and how they felt at the time. I have read things about them that they have never told anyone before. I read some things about myself as a coach that I had never known.

As Gator fans you will want to read this for yourself and relive with them the exciting days of Gator football.

Ray Graves
March 19, 2002

introduction

It all started with an innocent remark as I sat among 90,000 orange-and-blue clad men, women and children at Florida Field. I was the guest of Gary Froid, a football fanatic whose own career as a player at Harvard was cut short by a leg and ankle injury, and a longtime friend and sports connoisseur. Each year Gary bet me lunch at Pepin's restaurant in St. Petersburg over the winner of the Harvard-Dartmouth football game. For a while now, I've been buying.

I grew up and lived most of my life in drab and dreary Connecticut. I didn't realise how drab and dreary until 1989 when I drove down to Florida's Eden, St. Petersburg, to write a book about the men playing for the dearly beloved St. Pete Pelicans of the Senior Professional Baseball League. The league of retired major league baseball players folded after a year and a half, but my wife Rhonda and I had fallen in love with St. Petersburg and with the warmth, charm, and beauty of Florida from the moment we arrived, and we left the north as a memory.

Quickly I shed my Yankee ways. I developed a passion for NASCAR stock car racing and wrote three books about it. I root for the Bucs, not the Giants. I root for the Devil Rays, even when they're playing the Yankees. And I found myself intrigued by the South's love of football. The South couldn't win the Civil War, but they sure could win national championships.

When Gary asked me if I'd like to accompany him to a Florida game, I eagerly accepted. In the South there are two major religions, and one of them is football. I soon found out that in Florida there are more people from the church of Saints Steve and Bobby than any other.

On a spectacular September afternoon, the Gators were playing the University of Kentucky. Florida quarterback Rex Grossman was picking the Wildcats apart, and the Gators fans were whooping and hollering. As an author who specializes in the oral history of sports, the gears of my mind began to spin. I turned to Gary and said, "You know, I ought to write a history of the University of Florida football team."

I knew from my associations living in St. Petersburg that no college football team has a more rabid following. I had always heard about Notre Dame fans, but Notre Dame hadn't had a truly great football team since Lou Holtz coached a ways back. Florida on this day was ranked number 3 nationally, and was throttling Kentucky by the score of 59-31. I've been involved in college basketball games where fewer points were scored. (I can remember a game that Dartmouth played against Bill Bradley's Princeton team in 1965. We held the ball all game long, and we lost 31-17.)

I figured that St. Martin's Press, Putnam, HarperCollins or one of the other big publishers surely would see the logic behind doing a book on the history of football at the University of Florida.

Gary started asking me questions about the book business. I told him it came down to two elements: You have to write a book an audience wishes to read, and you have to let that audience know that such a book exists. If you can do that, you're in business, I told him.

Midway through the fourth quarter, he turned to me and said, "Is there any reason why I can't raise some money for the Gators by publishing a book about them if you write it?"

I pondered the question, but not for long. Gary knows enough people to run for governor. He had been a VERY successful businessman. He is resourceful, intelligent, and he never takes no for an answer anyway.

And so in March of 2001 I began an odyssey, the most ambitious project I have ever entertained, and that's saying something considering some of the mind-boggling projects I've worked on in the past.

I had written an oral history of the Dallas Cowboys, America's Team, and that had been a cakewalk compared to this project. Bob Lilly and Lee Roy Jordan and several of the other Cowboys had had long, successful careers. Lilly and Jordan both played for 14 years. It was typical. I could talk to Lilly and cover a rather wide swath.

But it quickly occurred to me that no Florida player ever played more than four years, and that was only after 1972. Before that freshmen weren't eligible to play on the varsity, and so their careers were for only three years. This book would require an interviewing marathon.

My goal was to interview at least two players, ideally three, for each year of the team's history.

With the help of Red Mitchum, I found Wilber James, who played on the 1928 and 1929 teams, and then I opted to begin the oral narration with players from the 1946 Gator team, when Florida was 0-9 and had nowhere to go but up.

But first I had to find them. Wayne McDaniel, whose job it is to know where most of the alumni live, agreed to help me out. He lent me a book fatter than the Manhattan yellow pages, and after a month of doing my own research and with the help of a student assistant, Josh Christianson, I was ready to begin my search into the soul of the Gator Nation.

Quickly I discovered that there is a network of football-playing alumni who keep in touch on a regular basis, who religiously meet once a year, and who even after as many as fifty years share a fellowship so rare you would think most of these guys are related. I also discovered something else: For many of them, even those players who went on to play football professionally—and many of the men interviewed in this book, if not most, did—their experience at the University of Florida was what defined their lives. For all, their experiences were rich, vivid and immediate, and as it is with all of the oral histories I have written, I am most proud that I have been able to capture these memories between hard covers of this book to save them for future generations of Gator fans. When you get to the end of this book, you will know almost as much about football as the players did. You will also discover the sacrifice, the hard work, the emotional investment, and the end result of all that hard work, whether it was the joy of success or the agony of failure. Without sounding immodest, I like to think that there has never been a book about college football that will allow you to get so close to the emotional action.

It is the story of these men's lives and why they chose to go to Florida, and what happened to them on the gridiron and off. It is a million stories about teammates and coaches and celebrated opponents, and it is about heartbreak and love and success and lost chances.

For all these players the goal has been the same: to win the Southeast Conference Championship. This was the Holy Grail. The players were aware that because of the university's stringent academic requirements, Florida has been at a disadvantage against such schools as Alabama, Auburn, the University of Georgia, and later, Florida State University. But each year at the start of the season, with a clean slate, the Gator players believed that THIS would be the year. And as you will see, for more than forty years, the Holy Grail remained elusive.

Not until the year 1991 did Florida finally attain that goal. Three times before that the Gators had compiled a record good enough for the SEC title, but each time, frustratingly, the school had been placed on probation, and those teams were denied the recognition and the ring.

The triumphs and tribulations of the quarterbacks who played for Florida since 1946 is one theme that runs throughout the book. Beginning with Angus Williams, who came to Florida and then enlisted in the armed forces before returning to play in the late 1940s, I was able to interview just about every major quarterback about his life before, during, and after the University of Florida. If you have ever in your life been a Florida Gator fan, you will get your chance to find out what REALLY was going on in the locker room, on the bench, and out on the field. You will also learn something about these fine men.

In chronological order, I was able to locate Mr. Williams, Haywood Sullivan, who left the team to become a professional baseball player with the Boston Red Sox, Doug Dickey, who today is the athletic director of the University of Tennessee, Bobby Lance, Jimmy Dunn, Larry Libertore, Tom Shannon, Larry Rentz, John Reaves, Don Gaffney, the first Afro-American to play the position; Jimmy Fisher, John Brantley, Wayne Peace, Bob Hewko, Kerwin Bell, Herbert Perry, who left the team to play baseball; Shane Matthews, Terry Dean, and Danny Wuerffel. Dean or Wuerffel? In this book you will hear from both of them.

I sought to interview a number of Florida All–Americans, and to that end I spoke with Charlie LaPradd, Vel Heckman, Larry Dupree, Larry Smith, Steve Tannen, Jack Youngblood, Fred Abbott, John Reaves, Lee McGriff, Scott Brantley, Wayne Peace, Tim Groves, Kerwin Bell, Shane Matthews, Kirk Kirkpatrick, and Danny Wuerffel.

Most of the rest of the players interviewed were All–SEC, but you will find that the handful of players who weren't turned out to be just as interesting. Sometimes the heartbreak of sports is more riveting than the success, and I would not be giving you the complete picture if I didn't include at least a few of the players who didn't end up with the glory they felt they deserved.

By starting with the post-World War II generation, I was able to capture what made their entire generation tick. These men believed in industriously obeying orders, a rule of law and a code of conduct. They did as they were told, they played by the rules, and as you will see, most of these men became as wildly successful in life as they were in football.

It's always amazing to me as I interview for an oral history how much the participants remember about what they have done and seen and experienced, and how strong their emotions remain anywhere from five to fifty years later.

I had the pleasure of meeting Coach Graves and his wife Opal, who has been a figure of grace, beauty and inspiration to everyone around her. The Graves have been very helpful in the publication of this book, and I thank them both from the bottom of my heart.

I also had the pleasure of meeting most of the players interviewed from the Tampa-Lakeland area. To Jimmy Dunn, Jimmy Fisher, Larry Libertore, Larry Smith, John Reaves, David Bowden, Jack Harper, Tom Shannon, and Herbert Perry, whom I met in the dugout of the Chicago White Sox before the end of the 2001 baseball season, I greatly enjoyed our get-togethers. It's part of the great fun of the process.

The rest of the men I met on the telephone, and I truly hope that before the year is up I will have the opportunity to meet as many of them as possible, either at football games or booster club meetings or at book signings. I feel tied to the Gator Nation through the contacts I have made over the past year, and I feel far richer for having done so. One measure of one's success is the friends you make, and so I'd have to say this book has to be a blockbuster, because I've made such wonderful friends in the process. I wish to single out Joe D'Agostino, a warm and wonderful man who loved his Florida family deeply. I regret that we will not get the chance to meet. That I got to know him at all has been a blessing. And if anyone should ever need cheering up, all you have to do is give Red Mitchum a call. Ask him to tell you the one about the guy who married the small-town Alabama girl.

I could talk about each player who favored me with an interview. I will say that the comment I cherished most came from Danny Wuerffel who after we finished after two and a half hours, said to me, "You know, that was the first time I ever talked on the phone longer than twenty minutes, but I enjoyed it." I enjoyed it too, Danny, as will you, the reader.

I have a long list of people to thank for making this book possible. I wish to thank Wayne McDaniels, whose early encouragement and help got the ball rolling; to Josh Christianson and Mike Swals, who helped me with the library and photo research; to Ellen Brewer, Peggy Sills, and Celeste Froid, whose tenacious transcribing made it possible for me to meet my deadline; to Bill Feinberg, Red Anderson, Bill Bunker, George Levy, Kathy Davis, and Paul Bowen, who helped me locate some of the men interviewed in this book;

and to the Gator warriors themselves, many legends in their own right, who took the time and gave the effort to make this book what it has turned out to be: a unique chronicle of fifty years of Florida football. What meant so much to me was that many of these players had no idea who I was and my guess is that they really didn't know exactly what I was doing, but they saw I was serious and had done my homework, and they trusted me with their memories and their stories. I have done my best to be true to your memories.

Finally, I must thank the effervescent Robert Menke, his son Kyle Menke, a future Gator star, and Gary Froid, whom I talked about at the beginning of this ramble. Gary's the one responsible. If you have any criticisms, call Gary. He has broad shoulders. And to Neil and Dawn Reshen, I never can tell you enough, but having you behind me helps give me the strength to write these epics. Also to Merrilee Warholak, who helped with the book's production, and to my wonderful one, Rhonda, and to my haloed son, Charlie, and to our Laurel and Hardy dogs, Doris the Bassett and Mandy the Mastiff, we live a wonderful life in our own Paradise in St. Petersburg. Florida has been berry, berry good to us. And I thank you all for that.

one

The Early Days

The University of Florida and its football team each had rocky beginnings. In 1852 a New England educator by the name of Gilbert Kingsbury founded the East Florida Seminary in the central Florida community of Ocala. A mysterious figure, he changed his name to S.S. Burton as soon as he moved to Florida. (He was one of the first in a long line of transplants to move down to Florida for the purpose of reinventing himself.) Kingsbury /Burton's new institution of higher learning attracted fifty-three students that first year.

But after contracting to build a one-story classroom, he was unable to raise the $925 to pay for it, and the school's board of trustees had to plead with the state legislature for the money.

Even with the emergency funds, the school didn't finish out the year. It was closed in mid-year after Kingsbury/Burton was accused of having an affair with music teacher Anna Underwood. He denied it, but resigned. Kingsbury/Burton then moved to Brownsville, Texas, where he changed his name to Francis Fenn.

The fledgling seminary reopened in 1854 and operated as a military college through the Civil War. After action by the state legislature the seminary was moved from Ocala to Gainesville, the fastest growing city in the state, in January of 1866. The Florida Legislature, meanwhile, saw the need for an agricultural college, and after the federal government gave the state of Florida 10,000 acres and $50,000 in cash in 1872, a dormitory was built to house students. But the school never opened because the Democrats, which swept into office, refused to support it. It wasn't until 1883 that the Florida Agricultural College was re-started, this time in the community of Lake City.

By the turn of the century the student body of the agricultural college had reached 200, and on November 22, 1901, that school played in the first football game ever played in the state of Florida. The pastor of a Lake City Presbyterian church was the coach. An English professor was his assistant.

The Florida Agricultural College lost 6-0 to Stetson University when a sure touchdown was lost when a pass hit a tree stump on the field.

Two years later there was a move to change the name of the school, and in 1903 it became the University of Florida.

In 1905 the seminary in Gainesville wanted to expand. They were offered 300 acres a mile west of the city. That same year the Florida legislature passed a bill calling for a state university to be built on two campuses, with men going to one, women to the other. The bill provided that the men's school be located "at some central point in the state."

Fighting for the men's prize were the two cities with existing schools, Gainesville and Lake City. Gainesville's mayor and council spearheaded a publicity campaign, noting that Gainesville not only was on a rail line, but that the town had "school spirit, good water and a healthful climate." The Lake City paper went on the attack, calling the trains coming into Gainesville "jerk-water" and commenting that Gainesville's water was "not an antidote to Gainesville fever."

In the end money, not a war of words, won the day for Gainesville. When the city agreed to deed 517 acres west of downtown plus make a $40,000 donation, Gainesville won the legislative vote 6-4 and became the official University of Florida. The vote was a unanimous 10-0 that the women's university be located in Tallahassee.

For the first half-century the University of Florida football team mostly struggled. In December of 1912 G.E. Pyle took his team from Gainesville to Havana to play two games. Florida won the first, but in the second the referees failed to call a penalty, and Pyle angrily took his team off the field. The game was forfeited and Pyle was arrested. Before he could go to trial, Pyle and the team snuck out of Cuba by boat and steamed home.

Charles McCoy took over as coach in 1914. In 1916 his team lost every game and was shut out by Georgia, Alabama, Tennessee, and Auburn. Things got better when in 1921 coach William Kline imported five players from the University of Oklahoma.

In 1927 John Tigert became university president. Tigert had starred in football at Vanderbilt and was a Rhodes scholar, and he vowed that Florida would have better facilities and a better team.

In 1928 Florida hired as its coach Charlie Bachman, a Notre Dame player who was picked as coach on the recommendation of Knute Rockne, the legendary Notre Dame head coach. Bachman had coached at Kansas State, and in his first year led Florida to wins in their first eight games. Led by 5'8" 150 pound Clyde (Cannonball) Crabtree, Rainey Cawthon, and Royce Goodbread, Florida led the nation in scoring with 336 points. Among the wins were a 71-6 trouncing of Sewanee and a 60-6 win over Washington & Lee. Going into the final game, Florida had given up but 31 points.

The final game was against Tennessee. No team had scored more than seven points in any one game against Florida. The Vols were led by sophomore quarterback Bobby Dodd, who one day would have a stellar career as the Georgia Tech head coach. Tennessee led 7-0, but then Florida scored to make it 7-6. The extra point was no good as a pass from Carl Brumbaugh to Crabtree misfired. When Florida botched a lateral, Tennessee ran the ball back 70 yards for the winning score. The kick was no good. Florida trailed 13-6.

Florida was certain it would tie the game after it scored a touchdown on a one-yard plunge by Crabtree. But Carl Brumbaugh's extra point try was blocked, and the 13-12 loss would go down in Florida history as one of the first in a long list of "if only" football games.

The mythology is that the loss cost the Gators a trip to the Rose Bowl, but the truth was that Georgia Tech had been invited, not Florida. Coach Bachman had waved a telegram in front of the players and told them the team would be invited if it were to defeat Tennessee, but it was just one of Knute Rockne's old tricks that Bachman had used to motivate his men.

Wilbur James was born in Montreal, Canada, on May 18, 1908. His father worked for a London firm in the mercantile business, specializing in silks, yard goods, and fabrics. When James' mother no longer could stand the cold weather, the family moved to Longwood, Florida, near Orlando.

Wilbur was the captain of the 1927 Orlando High School team. A fullback, he was recruited by Rice University and the University of Tennessee. He chose to go to Florida instead.

Wilbur James: "When I came to the university, I was told by the assistant coaches that if I moved to the line, I would play more. So I went along and started at right guard.

"On offense we had some real speed. Royce Goodbread was on the track team, and so was Red Bethea. Royce was an ideal fullback. He had size and speed. I remember a play that Red once made. He caught a pass to the right, and as the guys were about to tackle him, he turned a somersault in midair with the ball and got away from them. Red, who was a knot of muscles, was a great guy.

"One thing that accounted for the success of the 1928 team was that we had the talent. We had Clyde Crabtree, who could kick with either foot and pass with either hand, on the run or stationary. Try doing that. He was very talented.

"Then we had Carl Brumbaugh, who to me was one of the best quarterbacks in the Southern Conference, not the SEC. And we had Rainey Cauthen, who was a yeller. 'Pass me the ball.' He was captain of the '29 team. He and Dutch Stanley were two of the best ends in the conference.

"That year we KNEW we were the best team in the country. We beat both Auburn and Georgia. We had never beaten either team, and that's what started the interest in football at the university. Beating Georgia was sweet. We played the game in Tampa at the Hillsborough Stadium. They later built Davis Island around it.

"We were undefeated when we faced Tennessee. We were favored to win by two touchdowns.

"Everybody felt we had had an off-day, because we should have won that game. Our running yardage was better, and our passing yardage—we won almost all the categories.

"But in football, you win some and you're going to lose some. We were going to go to the Rose Bowl. It was the only bowl game operating at that time. The Rose Bowl was the only one. Georgia Tech went instead."

Wilbur James' Florida team in 1929 finished 8-2, with losses only to Georgia Tech and Harvard. Grantland Rice, the famed reporter for the New York Herald, covered the Florida-Harvard game. It would be the last great Gator team for many, many years.

In 1930 the Depression hit, and James had to leave college and get a job. George Halas of the Chicago pro team considered him, but he chose to go into business instead.

Wilbur James: "It was hard times. We needed jobs more than anything else. Brumbaugh was with the Chicago Bears, and he told me the Bears wanted me to come up and try out for them, but I was courting Sue, my wife, and we were planning on getting married, and we decided to go on in that direction."

James began selling automobile tires, then moved to the furniture business. After he retired, he and his wife were hired by Florida coach Doug Dickey to be the dorm parents for the football team. He lived in Yon Hall for eight years. At 93, James lives in Gainesville, the Grand Old Man of Gator football.

Bill Mills Sr. was born in Birmingham, Alabama, in 1911. After his dad died when he was three, his mother took him and his older brother to Plant City, Florida, and then she moved the family to Tampa so his boys could get a better education.

Mills wanted to go to MIT, so he attended the Woodbury-Forest school in Orange, Virginia, in order to beef up in math and physics. When he applied to MIT, he was told that the class was already filled but that if he enrolled in another college first, he could transfer after a year.

Mills entered the University of Florida in the fall of 1929, stayed through the spring of 1930, and then attended MIT. During Mills' one year at Florida, he joined a fraternity and roomed with two of Florida's star football players, Clyde Crabtree and Royce Goodbread.

Mills, who today is 91, remembers them fondly.

Bill Mills Sr.: "Crabtree had a knack that he could kick with either foot or pass with either hand, and he developed another knack for starting on a wide end run, holding the ball out in front of him, and kicking it, which was very good for surprise. He was a very fine football player.

"Goodbread was big and husky. They were both great guys. I enjoyed being with both of them.

"That was the last time Florida had a great team for many, many years. The University of Florida did not emphasize the team during those following years, like Alabama and some of the others. I guess the administration and the alumni just weren't that interested, and no one realized that a winning football team could be the great attraction for money raising capabilities. Money was not as loose and free and cheap as it is today, by far. Football was a fun thing."

Back then scholarships went to only the top players who couldn't afford tuition. The football program passed the hat, getting rooters to sponsor individual players. Without an alumni organization, the team could not compete with football powers such as Tennessee, Georgia, Georgia Tech, Vanderbilt, and Alabama.

In 1930, despite the Depression and the end of the Florida land boom, the 22,000 seat University of Florida football stadium was completed in time for the Homecoming game against the unbeaten University of Alabama. Florida lost the game, 20-0.

Florida football remained mediocre up through and after the second world war. One reason was that most of the able-bodied athletes were fighting in the war. Manpower was so short on the Florida varsity that in 1945 Florida's starting backfield consisted entirely of freshmen. Angus Williams, who had starred for Hillsborough High in Tampa, was a member of that starting backfield. The coach in 1945 was Tom Lieb, another former Notre Damer. Williams survived a mediocre 4-5-1 season in '45, but in 1946, after Lieb was fired and replaced by Raymond "Bear" Wolf, he was injured. Rather than lose a year of eligibility, Williams elected to serve in the military.

Angus Williams: "I lettered in four sports, football, basketball, track, and baseball. I could have gotten a scholarship to Clemson, but I was only thinking about going to Florida. Florida was THE school. There was also the University of Miami, but nobody from Tampa wanted to go there. I hate to say this, but we thought of Miami as a foreign country. It's just that the Tampa Tribune wrote everything about Florida, not about Miami.

"My coach my freshman year was an old Notre Dame guy by the name of Thomas Lieb. We called him 'The Irishman.' I really liked him. I was a young kid, so I was kind of in awe.

He'd always say, 'You guys are dressed like champions. Let's see you play like champions!'

"But we had terrible uniforms. We had to tape our pads to our uniforms. We could almost unfold our helmets and put them on our heads. One time one of the players almost got his pants torn off in a game, so we crowded around him on the field while he changed clothes.

"In our backfield that year were ALL freshmen: Fred Hogan from Daytona Beach was the fullback, L.B. Dupree from St. Petersburg was left half, Weldon Wright, who played with me at Hillsborough High, was right half, and I was the quarterback. All the sophs, juniors, and seniors were in the service, and the ones who didn't get into the service, who were 4-F, weren't that good.

"We had a 4-5-1 record that year, and Coach Lieb was fired, and they brought in [Raymond] Bear Wolf.

"In '46 we had spring practice, and it was awhile before Wolf just happened to meet me in the gym. He said, 'You're on scholarship, aren't you?'

"I said, 'Yes sir.' He said, 'What's your name?' and I told him, and he said, 'You played quarterback last year, didn't you?' I said, 'Yes, sir.' He said, 'I want you to go out for tailback. We're going to play the double wing.'

"The draft was breathing down my neck, so I decided to go ahead and enlist and not ruin a year of eligibility. I went into the army, and I spent thirteen months occupying Japan. I was with the MPs in Nagoya. The Fifth Air Force had a baseball team, and I played third base, and when football season came along, I signed up for football and was shipped to Kyoto and spent the rest of the time in the service playing football.

Angus Williams wasn't the only player to leave Florida and join the service in the fall of 1946. He was one of a group of about ten freshman football players who left. Another was Red Mitchum, who grew up poor in Alabama and who's goal was to parlay his football talents into a college scholarship and an education.

Red Mitchum arrived on campus at the University of Florida for summer football camp in '46, knowing that he and every other 18 years old faced an October 1 deadline. If Red enlisted voluntarily before that date, he would only have to spend a year and a half in the military. If he didn't sign up and was drafted, he would be in much longer. While he pondered what to do, he was involved in one of the more unique training camps that the University of Florida ever held.

Red Mitchum: "I went to Florida on June 22, 1946, for summer practice. This was just after World War II. All the veterans were coming back from the war, and everybody thought they were as good at football as they had been four years earlier, when they went into the army. Most of them were just out of high school or they had had a year of college when they left for the war. This same thing happened on campuses nationally: the schools gave them the opportunity to make the team. I don't have a record of how many tried out, but I've heard estimates of around two hundred players. They could still get their schooling under the G.I. Bill, and the deal was that if they made the team, they would get their free meals and free dormitory, and they could spend their G.I. Bill money any way they wanted. It was a good deal, but you had to be able to make the team.

"Only about forty of them made it. Most didn't realize their body was four years older. Some of them quit after two or three days. They'd say to themselves, 'I got my GI Bill, why in the world do I have to put up with some loudmouthed coach holler at me when I've had professionals do it the last four years?' So they packed it in.

"Most of the rest of us were freshmen. Back then they could sign as many freshmen as they wanted to. There was no limit, and so they'd sign eighty freshmen, and then they'd run off the ones they didn't want. And it was a very simple process to run somebody off. You just put them out there head-on blocking and head-on tackling two or three hours, and you did it every day, and pretty soon they say, 'Hey, wait a minute, I think momma will let me come home and I'll eat supper off the table. I don't have to do this.' They'd pack it in.

"I was sure I was one of the players Coach Wolf was trying to run off, but I stayed. Later in life, I was talking with Charlie Hunsinger, who was one of the Florida's greatest running backs. Charlie and I lockered right next to each another. I was much younger than he was, about four years younger because he had been in the service.

"I said, 'Charlie, you know when I came down from Gadsden, Alabama, I was scared to death when I lined up against you guys. I was playing defensive end, and you would come around my end, and somehow, sometimes I would tackle you.'

"He said, 'Red Mitchum, you're at it again.'

"I said, 'What do you mean?'

"He said, 'You've never been afraid of anything. The courage you had to go through what you did inspired me. You stuck it out through the toughest of times. I've often wondered why you did it.'

"I said, 'Well, Charlie, when I was a kid, I worked in the Goodyear tire and rubber plant in Gadsden, in the summers. I saw men who were forty years old who were broken down and looked like they were seventy.' Tire-making was all manual then. If you built truck tires, you did it with your hands. It was hard, hard physical labor. I said, 'I didn't want to go back and do that.'

"They had tried to run me off, but where I was going was a lot tougher than where I was, and I knew that. That's the reason I stayed, and it paid off.

"So during the summer of 1946 I met Jimmy Kynes and Chuck Hunsinger and Angus Williams, who became a close friend of mine.

"They were still drafting 18 year olds. We had until October 1 to enlist. That was the deadline. And a group of about ten of us, Angus, Scotty Peak, me, decided we were going to have to go into the Army to take advantage of a plan where you could enlist for eighteen months.

"And this was something that was done nationally. I met Johnny Karras, from Illinois, who broke all of Red Grange's records, and Doug Moseley, who played center at Kentucky. Thousands and thousands of kids joined the army, and they sent us to Japan and Germany for occupational troops.

"Angus and I became friends, and we took basic training together down in Camp Polk, Louisiana, and then we split up and went to Japan on different troop ships. We both ended up in Southern Japan, but he was in I Corps with Karras and Moseley, and I wound up in the 24th Infantry Division.

"I stayed in Japan for fourteen months. After six months, I was made a staff sergeant. At 18 years old I was the youngest first three-grader in the entire regiment. In 1947 I played football in Japan with the division football team. In a division there are about 20,000 troops. I was chosen to play. I was just out of high school. I was one of the few who hadn't played any college ball. I was 6'3" and about 180 pounds.

"In Japan at ten o'clock in the morning on Thanksgiving Day, I played against Angus Williams' team, and we beat them 21-6, and I caught two touchdown passes.

"It was a ten-team league, and at 18 years old I was able to play in every major city in Japan. I saw all of Japan, but back then I was so young, I didn't know what I was seeing. I could not grasp the history I was going through."

The loss of Angus Williams, Red Mitchum, and the other frosh players to the service didn't make Coach Bear Wolf's job any easier back home in Gainesville. In Wolf's first season in 1946, Florida finished the season with an 0-9 record, worst in school history.

two

Love Brings them Together

One of Coach Bear Wolf's best players was a Miami high schooler by the name of Frank Dempsey. The boy had gone from high school into the Navy, where he flew reconnaissance missions. When the war ended, he decided to go to the University of Florida because it was the only Florida college program where he could play football and get noticed by the pros. He also was recruited by Tennessee, Alabama, Georgia, and Auburn, but his girlfriend was going to the University of Miami, and he wanted to be able to visit her, and Florida was the school closest to her that wanted him.

Coach Wolf had promised Dempsey he could play fullback, but when the boy arrived for the start of practice, Wolf switched him to tackle. Dempsey was so angry he considered transferring, but because of his need to be near his girlfriend, he stayed. Dempsey would go on to play professionally for George Halas and the Chicago Bears and later in Canada.

Frank Dempsey: "I didn't go to Auburn because I had already been there in the Navy. I went up to Alabama and Georgia, but I was in love with a girl who went to the University of Miami and became the Orange Bowl queen in 1950, a beautiful girl, and I wanted to stay close enough, so I signed with Florida—basically because I wanted to be close enough to be able to go home to Miami. Those women are powerful!

"Even though she went to the University of Miami, I didn't go there because I wanted to play pro football, and I didn't figure on Miami doing much. I was sure that Bear Wolf was going to bring Florida back up.

"When I went to see Wolf, I was 230 pounds and could run pretty fast. Wolf misled me. He had said he was going to let me play fullback, but the first day we came out, I was the biggest guy, and they put me at tackle. I wanted to play fullback, and I hated him because he put me at tackle. I didn't like that at all, but that's what happened. So I spent four years playing tackle for the Gators. I played both ways, on offense and defense, my entire career, in all the years.

"But when Wolf told me I'd be playing tackle, I almost left and went somewhere else. Why didn't I? Colleen. I would drive the 350 miles from Gainesville to Miami in my little jeep. It went 55 miles an hour, and you put it to the floor and went to Miami. I took Route 27 down the middle of the state. If you did it at night, the cows and horses tried to get you. Remember, there were no fences back then. I'm giving you all this secret information.

"One night I was driving my jeep, and all of a sudden I'm running in the middle of the road with a whole bunch of horses, and they are bigger than I am! I was blowing the horn, telling them to get out of the way. At 55 miles an hour, they better get out of the way.

"In '46 we certainly didn't have much of a team, I'll tell you. We had a bunch of guys who just started from nothing. And we didn't win a game in 1946. And we didn't get much better as we went along.

"We opened up with Mississippi, and they beat us 14-7, and then we had Tulane beat until the last quarter, and they beat us by six points. Playing football at Florida was an interesting experience. We had all young guys, and a few guys like Charlie Hunsinger, who had played in the Navy in Jacksonville. He was a heck of a good runner. We had H.H. Griffin and another back by the name of Loren Broadus, guys who were little but very fast. Not many of them went into the pros, except Charlie, who was drafted number one by the Bears. He was a heck of a ballplayer, and he and I used to hunt all the time while we were in college. We went anywhere around Gainesville. You could hunt anywhere. Remember, Gainesville was a very small town, only 13,000 people, and 4,000 went to college. Three miles out of town you could start to hunt, a lot of quail, a lot of doves, and a lot of fishing. All the time.

"I had a jeep, and I would wade half the lakes around there chasing gators and trying to get out of the way.

"I liked Coach Wolf. He was a nice guy. I think what happened, he didn't have a strong enough coaching staff. And he wasn't as tough as I later found other coaches. But he was a nice guy, and he did the best he could after starting from scratch.

"In 1947, we finished 4-5-1. What I remember is that we finally won. We weren't a bad team, but we just didn't have enough big time players, and not enough BIG players.

"The big game that year was against Georgia. That was THE team. The game was always played in Jacksonville. Everybody tried to get a seat for that one. There was a lot of hoopla. We lost [34-6] because they had Charlie Trippi, who later played with the Chicago Cardinals. I later played against him when I was with the Chicago Bears. Trippi was a tremendous all-around back. He could pass, he could run, and he could kick. He was bowlegged, the little sucker, and when he came at you, don't go one way, because he could go right by you. Trippi was a very, very talented football player.

"I do remember that in '47 we beat Miami [7-6], and that made my dad happy. And during halftime Colleen was the lead majorette for the University of Miami. She stood in front of everyone else. I never got to see her perform during halftime, because we were in the locker room inside. They wouldn't let me out, and I was too tired to watch anyway. I was resting up for the second half. Later on, in 1950, she became the Orange Bowl queen, and I went to the Bears. She was a singer. She sang on the Ed Sullivan show. She was beautiful, and everyone said, 'How did you get her?' I said, 'Simple. She can't see, and I've got her glasses!' It worked like a charm. Thank God I could talk."

Angus Williams: "I got home from the service in February of 1948. I was playing behind Doug Belden, who was the quarterback, a great passer. But we didn't have any good receivers, so we ended up running the ball a lot.

"The only time I played was when we were getting our tail whipped real bad or when we were way ahead. Finally, Bear called me to go in and play against Georgia Tech, and they were beating the fool out of us, and I said, 'I don't want to go in.' So he sent someone else in there, and on Monday he called me into his office. I told him, 'The only time you want me to play is when we're getting our tail beat. Why don't you send me in earlier in the game when we have a chance of doing something?'

"So he finally did against Furman, and I drove the team for three touchdowns.

"The next-to-last play of the game Furman intercepted my pass, and I went over to make the tackle, and he cut back on me, and another guy hit me, and I tore a cartilage in my knee, and that ended my season. I had to spend seven days in the hospital, and they put it in a cast for thirty days, and I had to spend a lot of time building up my leg because it had atrophied."

Frank Dempsey: "In 1948 we finished 5-5. We were out there to win. Anyone who really is a football player is there to win, and you aren't concerned with anything else. When you step out on the field, you are out to win, and you want to do the best you can. No one ever said, 'We'll just take it easy.' You can't do it. Someone will hurt you.

"Our team needed more beef. I was about 228, and I was the biggest guy out there, and anyone bigger couldn't run, so it was a tough thing. Most of our guys were very small, gutty little devils, but when you went up against really good teams, they had a lot of big guys. Even if you're a tough little guy, you're going to have trouble against tough, big guys."

One of Coach Wolf's "tough, little guys" was a 150 pound speedster by the name of Loren Broadus, who starred on defense and also played running back. Broadus was a such a great prospect that Kentucky coach Bear Bryant, known for his ability to spot talent, heavily recruited him. But like Frank Dempsey, Broadus went to the University of Florida because he was in love with a girl who was going to college in state and he wanted to be close to her. Like Dempsey, Broadus went on to star at Florida for four seasons.

Loren Broadus: "I grew up in Jacksonville. In high school I played football, basketball and ran track. I was All–State in football all three years, and I held some of the track records in the state. I ran 22.7 in the 220 yards and I broad-jumped 23'5.

"I went to Florida because I was in love with a girl. She went to Florida State. I figured I could get an education and keep my love life going too, and so I came to Florida in the fall of 1947. Murphy Hall was four stories. The rooms were rather comfortable, but bare. It wasn't aesthetically exciting but it had everything we needed.

"In 1948, our record was 5-5, but that year we lost to both Georgia and Georgia Tech, which was bad. Today, if you lose to Florida State, you are bad people. Back then the Georgia-Florida game was THE game. If you beat Georgia, you could have a pretty good season. If you lost to Georgia, it was a bad season.

"I thought our coach, Bear Wolf, was a fine human being. He was interested in the individual players. He knew you. He knew your wants, needs and desires. He took a personal interest in you, and yet, on the field it was his intent to develop the team, and the team came first.

"He had a fantastic sense of humor. One time he said, 'I get so tired of seeing homecoming queens crowned.' You know what that means? That we were bad enough that every team wanted to play us at their homecoming. Because at homecoming you want to play a team you can beat.

"I remember him as a man with some compassion, concern for the players, someone interested in the team. I don't remember him as being a great strategist. I don't remember him as being a genius of any kind. Just a fine human being who enjoyed coaching, and enjoyed being with young men.

"My role on the team was as a defensive safety, and usually I was the second running back. I played a lot of minutes. The reason I played defense was that I was fast and I could prevent people from catching passes and going for touchdowns. I could tackle them in the open field and catch them. Most of the time I could keep the people from making a touchdown.

"Our star was [halfback] Chuck Hunsinger, who was large enough and fast enough. He did all he could with what he had, but I don't think he was highly motivated. I'm projecting, but I don't think football was all that important to him. He enjoyed life, enjoyed partying. He was out there and did what he had to do, but he didn't overexert himself.

"Our biggest person on the team was John Natyshak from Pennsylvania. He was 6'10" and reasonably fast. He would come back at 325 pounds and they would have to sweat off about 40 pounds. In shape he went 295. John didn't finish school and didn't go to the pros. You didn't go to the pros like you do now. John had a couple of unfortunate incidents where he didn't end up finishing. But he was a person with integrity. He had borrowed money from some of us, and he went to work at a bar until he could make enough money to pay us off before he left town.

"Another excellent player we had was Frank Dempsey. I remember Frank as being a natural leader. It wasn't that he talked so much, it was that Frank was committed. He was powerful, and you never questioned that Frank was always giving his best. I consider him a man of integrity too. He was a person who wanted what was best for the team, and he gave it.

"We played a defensive game, a slower game in that there was more ground attack than passing attack. That wasn't what the fans wanted. No, the fans didn't want that, but the fact was you didn't score like you do today."

three

Fuller Warren's Promise

When a glib, glad-handing politician by the name of Fuller Warren ran for governor in 1948, Florida was a rural state run by cattlemen and timber barons. As Frank Dempsey related, horses, cows and pigs could roam freely, and if a motorist hit one, he had to pay the owner the equivalent value for it. If the motorist died, his estate was responsible. The flamboyant Warren, who married movie actress Barbara Manning just before taking office, decided it was time for Florida to enter the 20th Century.

Warren had a William Jennings Bryant-like golden-tongued quality. He was adept at turning phrases. As an example, during one campaign in which the local counties were trying to decide whether to allow the sale of whiskey, he was often asked by reporters for his position on the issue. His reply, designed to trap him into taking a position, was ingenious.

He answered, "If by whiskey, you mean the water of life that cheers men's souls, that smoothes out the tensions of the day, that give gentle perspective to one's view of life, then put my name on the list of the fervent wets."

Then he covered his bases by adding, "But if by whiskey, you mean the devil's brew that rends families, destroys careers and ruins one's ability to work, then count me in the ranks of the dries."

While a student at the University of Florida, Warren had run for the state legislature at age 20 and won. After becoming a lawyer, he moved to Jacksonville, where he served three terms on the city council before returning to the legislature in 1939. Though little-known when he ran for governor in 1940, he finished a close third.

World War II interrupted his political career, and when he ran again in 1948, he made several powerful campaign promises that would lead him to victory, including the one to ban all livestock from state roads by forcing farmers and ranchers to fence in their properties. This wasn't as frivilous as it sounds, as Frank Dempsey described. Half-ton cows and massive porkers would lay down on the state roads at night and sleep, and unaware motorists would be killed plowing into them. To pass his bill, Warren had to go up against the powerful Cattleman's Association, which didn't want to have to pay the piper to put up fencing. (The legislature passed his "no-fence" law, effectively removing cattle from the highways.)

He also promised not to enact a state income tax. His recommendation was to tax businesses instead to raise $70 million to pay for the state services needed for the almost one million people who had moved to the state between 1940 and 1950. The highways were in bad shape, the schools were underfunded and closings were threatened, state hospitals were overcrowded, and state universities needed upgrading. Though the cities were growing, the rural-dominated state legislature voted against all fifteen of Warren's corporate revenue-raising plans. Instead, it voted a three-percent state income tax, something Warren had vowed he would veto. But faced with the choice of closing schools and passing the sales tax, he accepted the tax. (Warren forced the legislature to exempt groceries and medicines.)

In addition to paying the salaries of the teachers, he used the tax money to fund the Sunshine State Parkway and the Sunshine Skyway bridge across Tampa Bay. He also had a law passed forbidding the shipping of inedible fruit out of the state and barring the Ku Klux Klan from public places. (Though Warren was credited with doing "the most to bridge the gap between the 19th Century and the mid-20th Century," conservative Floridians would never forgive him for allowing the sales tax, and he failed in his reelection bid.)

He also made a third campaign promise: he would help bring a winning football team and restore pride in his alma mater, the University of Florida. And he would do this by sponsoring a bill through the legislature that would provide for the profits from one day's horse and jai alai wagering to go directly to the University of Florida athletic association for football scholarships.

Warren was elected and the bill passed easily.

Angus Williams: "Getting the pigs and cows off the road wasn't too hard to do. All he had to do was fence. As far as the other thing, improving the Florida football team, the alumni were ready. They were tired of being the doormat of the SEC. So Warren knew what he was doing. He was no dummy. He was just playing politics."

The pressure was building on the University of Florida football program to improve. Coach Bear Wolf knew he had an ultimatum: win in 1949—or else. The newspapers picked Florida to win the SEC. Wolf's starting quarterback that year was Angus Williams.

Angus Williams: "I returned to football in the summer of '49, fall practice, and I ended up beating out Vic Vaccaro and Bob Gruetzmacher for the number one spot at quarterback. Nineteen forty-nine was supposed to be great year. The papers said we were going to be the best team since 1928.

"We started out beating the Citadel 13-0. I threw a touchdown pass to Chuck Hunsinger coming out of the backfield. The Citadel wasn't a good team, but we never took them too seriously, and they always played us tough."

Frank Dempsey: "We beat Tulsa [40-7]. Only 7,000 fans came to the game. They didn't have much of a football team, and we weren't any powerhouse. People weren't going to spend money to see us. Hunsinger scored three touchdowns in that game. He was a power runner. We had little guys on the line, but he got to the hole quick."

Angus Williams: "Hunsinger scored three touchdowns against Tulsa, but he suffered a hip injury, and Loren Broadus replaced him."

Loren Broadus: "I remember going to Tulsa, Oklahoma, and buying these large Stetson cowboy hats. We flew back and landed. I know I had a good game [against Tulsa] because I recall that while the reporters were asking me questions, I had my Stetson on."

Angus Williams: "Our next game was against Auburn down in Mobile, and it was hotter'n Hades. That is the hottest I've ever been. It was so humid and hot, but we always played Auburn a good game, no matter where we played them. I remember they had their big gun, Travis Tidwell, and we had a couple of bad calls against us for pass interference."

Frank Dempsey: "We tied Auburn [14-14], and after that game Coach Wolf decided to institute the two-platoon system. I was happy, because I got to go off for a little while."

Loren Broadus: "Vanderbilt was big. They had an All American quarterback by the name of [Billy] Wade. They were supposed to beat us severely. They were nationally ranked. And we lost in the fourth quarter [22-17]."

Frank Dempsey: "We were ahead of Vanderbilt by a point with only a few minutes left, when they scored. Anybody who plays hates to lose. The guy who tells me, 'It's only a game,' let me tell you, it isn't win or lose, it's win. You're not out there to lose. You're out there to win. You don't like to lose, and if you do, you won't be playing long.

"The next game was a disaster."

Frank Dempsey: "Georgia Tech was in town for Homecoming, and everybody figured we'd clean them up. We had a lot of press coverage back then for a little school. If you're a ballplayer and if you listen to all the hype you'll get killed. Don't let yourself think you're good, because there's a sucker who will tear you to pieces."

Angus Williams: "In the first half I scored a touchdown on a quarterback sneak. I tell you what, the hole opened up so wide that you could have put a truck through there. I really fooled them. They thought I was going to give the ball to Hunsinger. I remember we were leading at the half, and [assistant coach] Dave Fuller told me in the locker room that I had called the best game he had ever seen.

"And then during the half Georgia Tech changed a little bit of their defense, and then they just beat the fool out of us. But I didn't have anybody telling me I should be calling this play or that play." [After Georgia Tech beat Florida 43-14, a howl went up for Coach Wolf's scalp.]

Loren Broadus: "After a defeat like that, there is a period of shock, disappointment, and confusion, and there is an immediate resolve not to let that happen again. And what you have to do, as in all of life, is to take the defeat as it comes, give a little reflection, see what you can learn from it, and then move on to the next game, which we did. We beat Furman [28-27] and then we upset Georgia."

Angus Williams: "Furman, which was a weak team, was next, and all I remember was that the attitude of the players was not good. We weren't fired up. All the talk about Coach Wolf's getting fired just kind of left you in a stupor.

"The great thing we did in '49 was beat Georgia. That was the BEST thing. The Georgia game was THE rivalry back then. The game always was played in Jacksonville, and Jacksonville had a lot of Georgia backers and a lot of Florida backers. We knew a lot of the players on the Georgia team, because Georgia recruited a lot of players from Florida. They had good alumni in the state. For instance, Ken McCall from Orlando, who was the state pole vault champion, a hell of an athlete, wanted to go to Florida, but Tom Lieb didn't show any interest, so he ended up at Georgia and made All-SEC as a defensive back.

"We hadn't beaten Georgia in years, and Georgia was coached by Wally Butts, a great coach. But on Monday of that week during practice we started working on a spread formation that nobody had ever seen before. You have an unbalanced line one way or the other, and you spread them out.

"We had a person playing what we used to call flanker—the right half was the flanker—and the fullback lined up over the tackle, and the halfback lined up behind the quarterback, so I would toss the ball back to Hunsinger, the halfback, and he ran to the open spot, and he could find that open spot. In that game Hunsinger scored three touchdowns, and I scored the fourth.

"I could see how good our attitude was. As a matter of fact Professor Richardson, a money and banking professor whose course I was taking and who liked to bet on games, asked me, 'How are you going to do against Georgia?' I said, 'We're going to beat them.' So he bet a bundle and we won [28-7], and I got a B in the course!"

Frank Dempsey: "From my own point of view, the guys who had been playing together for four years had come to the end. We had been battered and beaten up pretty much by everybody around, and for once we all said, 'We gotta do something. Let's leave with some kind of prestige.' And we all yelled. We all said, 'We going to do something today,' and for once everything clicked. We beat the University of Georgia.

"Charlie [Hunsinger] was running good. [He ran 18 times for 174 yards and three touchdowns.] He kept saying, 'Open me a hole, Dempse,' and I would tell him, 'The guys are beating hell out of me. Run to the other side.' But that day we were getting the holes open for him quick, and he was very quick. If you could get the guy to move for just a second, Charlie would be through there, and once he got through, he was very hard to bring down. He was a heck of a good football player."

Angus Williams: "And after we won, the players carried Coach Wolf off the field. Like I said, the players weren't unhappy with Wolf, and there was so much jubilation about winning that game as big as we did that we just forgot everything. Back in Gainesville, there was a big celebration, though the football players didn't get involved in it."

Frank Dempsey: "After we beat Georgia, everybody in Florida was elated. When we got back to Gainesville, there were people everywhere. It was a real party. Not me, because I was quiet, didn't drink, tried to stand where nobody would see me. Cause Colleen might have found out, so I had to be very careful. She had spies everywhere. Dad-blamed women! It was all right for her to be down there and date, but it wasn't good for me. And I still have her 49 years later. Yep, and the other day she signed an option for another 50, and you know what I got left? A bicycle! Don't laugh, son. It has a flat tire. She owns everything else! But she's worth it. If I get through that 50 on January 27, I'm going to be somebody. I'm going to say, 'I made it. I made it.' I might get a car. I'm hoping."

Loren Broadus: "After we upset Georgia, people were happy, ecstatic. Football became the rallying point for people who didn't have enough excitement in their own lives and who hadn't won much and who needed to identify with winners. When we won, it was 'we.' But if we got the stuffing beat out of us, it was 'they.' And in fact, that happened the last three games of the season."

The players might have saved Coach Wolf's job had they been successful in any of the final three games of the season, but the Georgia win was to be the season's highlight. In 1949 Florida badly lost their three last games to Kentucky, Miami, and Alabama.

Frank Dempsey: "There were three games left in the season, and it would have been fabulous if we had won all three, and we should have, but we played Kentucky—Babe Parilli took over at quarterback from George Blanda, and they beat up on us a little bit [35-0]. They had a lineman by the name of Bob Gain, who I played right in front of the whole game. He was a first-class tough guy, a tough football player. We just couldn't handle them. As I said, Kentucky had several big guys, and we didn't have any, except me."

Loren Broadus: "The next game was against the University of Miami. [A 28-13 loss.] Not only were they much larger than we were, but it appeared to me that they were a little bit more violent. They had a player named September—he was listed at 325 pounds—and I ran the ball, and there was a pileup, and he drew his fist back to crush me, and I turned my head just in time. Then Natyshak said to me, 'I saw that. I'll take care of it.' And the next play the man was out of the game. It wasn't a sweet game, not a nice game. It was pretty brutal. The fact that he tried to ruin my face affecting my thinking about that."

Frank Dempsey: "They were trying to make a state rivalry for the first time, and 55,000 people showed up for the Florida-Miami game. We shouldn't have lost that one either. But that's football. And I got to play my last game in front of my dad and Colleen and everybody at home there. So that was good.

"We played Alabama in our final game, and we played a pretty darn good game against them, even though the final score was 35-13. Remember, you have to have tough people, and we didn't have them. We just didn't have strong defenders. We had a better offense than we had a defense. The other thing is, when you play most of the way most of the time, you're tired. The other teams had more depth, and we never seemed to have depth. I couldn't find any, anyway."

In 1949 Coach Bear Wolf's final record of 4-5-1 would not be good enough to save him.

Loren Broadus: "Our final game was a bad loss to Alabama, and it cost Bear Wolf his job. I didn't have an inkling. I felt sorry for him in the fact that he was doing as good as he could do, but we weren't winning as I think we should have. I would think that every player would think that. And there is only one scapegoat in all of this. The solution belongs to the person in charge, the person responsible.

"But I didn't like him getting fired. I was going into my senior year. And that meant starting over again. So we started over again."

Frank Dempsey: "Coach Wolf wasn't a bad guy. We didn't have the power. You have to have ballplayers. Every team I ever was on that was any good had a lot of power players.

"So they were looking for a different kind of football. I could see they were trying to bring power football to Florida, and in order to do that they had to have some kind of readjustment. They needed a different type of coach."

Angus Williams: "When we read what they were writing about Coach Wolf, our reaction was mixed. He had always been good to us. The football players held a little rally to support him, but we were the only ones who attended. But looking back, I have to say that getting rid of him was the best thing that happened to Florida."

Frank Dempsey and Chuck Hunsinger signed with the Chicago Bears after the '49 season. Former Illinois and Chicago Bears star halfback Red Grange had scouted Dempsey for the Bears and recommended him to Bears' owner George Halas.

Dempsey played for the Bears through the 1954 season. During the off-season he hosted a sports talk show in Miami, and one of his guests was Carl Boyles, the owner of the Hamilton Tiger Cats football team. Boyles offered Dempsey almost twice the salary and a car. Tired of the low pay, he jumped to the Canadian League in '55 and played despite Halas' howls and a lawsuit seeking $150,000 in damages. Because Dempsey was successful in beating Halas in court, he paved the way for hundreds of Americans who desired to leave the NFL for the Canadian league.

In Canada, Dempsey made All Pro, but quit after two years to start his own business in Peterboro, Ontario. He imported guns from all over the world, and later started manufacturing a gun called the Wakefield Mosburg, the only gun made in Canada.

After living in Canada for thirty years, Dempsey retired to Vero Beach, but he had to return to Canada because of higher estate taxes in the states.

Says the former Florida star, "I've led an amazing life."

four

The Final Days of Bear Wolf

Coach Bear Wolf, knowing his days were numbered unless he could dramatically improve the fortunes of his team, made a special recruiting effort before his final season in 1949. Unfettered by restrictions on how many scholarships he could hand out, he and his assistant coaches, led by a top recruiter by the name of Mush Batista, enticed seventy frosh football prospects to matriculate to Florida. But the player who would turn out to be Florida's third All-American was a walk–on by the name of Charlie LaPradd. [End Dale Van Sickel was All-American in 1928 and end Forest "Fergie" Ferguson was named in 1941.]

The stolid, unassuming LaPradd, who had been a paratrooper during World War II, began his football career at Florida after hitchhiking to Gainesville and asking for a chance to play. That he became an All-American was a tribute to his intelligence and desire.

Loren Broadus: "Charlie LaPradd was a fine person. Charlie was well-balanced, powerful, could follow orders very well, knew his place, was smart, and was a good team player. He did his job. If we had had a whole team of Charlie LaPradds, we'd have won more."

Charlie LaPradd: "At that time Florida would take anyone who was over six feet tall and weighed over 200 pounds. Well, it wasn't quite that easy, but that was what the common saying was around there at the time.

"Bear Wolf was the head coach. After I hitchhiked to Gainesville, the coach I went to see a man by the name of Ted Toomey, who had played at Notre Dame. I was asked what my background was, and they gave me a one-year, make-good scholarship.

"I was there as a freshman. We thought we had a pretty talented group our freshman year, until LSU brought a 'B' team to play us instead of their freshman team, and they beat us something like 67-7. Coach Wolf was at Kentucky for the varsity game the next day. I called him and told him what the score was, and he said, 'That's impossible. Nobody can get beat by that much.' Then Kentucky went out and beat them by about the same score. [35-0]."

Among the best of Florida's incoming frosh in '49 were several future professionals, including T-formation quarterback Haywood Sullivan and backs Rick Casares and Buford Long. Sullivan, like Frank Dempsey before him, came from Dothan, Alabama. Tall and lanky and the possessor of a golden throwing arm, Sullivan came to the University of Florida to escape having to choose between state rivals Alabama and Auburn.

Haywood Sullivan: "I had been recruited by Bear Bryant, who at that time was at Kentucky, and by Red Drew, who was at Alabama, but there were such rabid fans in Alabama, if you were recruited by either Alabama or Auburn, you became an outcast from the other half of the city, and that was one of the paradoxes for a lot of the kids. The governor's son, for instance, was a track man, and he went to Tennessee because he couldn't afford to take the heat from the other half of the state if he had chosen between Alabama and Auburn. He ended up going to the Olympics as a runner.

"Bear Wolf was still the head coach, and Mush Batista was the chief recruiter then. He later went to the Air Force Academy and did a tremendous job recruiting out there their first year. Mush was quite a guy. In fact, I didn't know anybody at Florida. But Mush did a great job recruiting, bringing us down there and making us feel we were one of the party already. He was one of the greatest recruiters I ever ran into. He really sold us on the fact Florida was building and that everyone would have a chance to play. The next year, my sophomore year, he left, and we really hated to see him leave and go to the Air Force Academy. But it was a great opportunity for him.

"In '49 Wolf recruited seventy-something players. I remember when I arrived, fourteen of us were quarterbacks. They were starting from scratch, and just about everyone who was already there had been brought over by Wolf from that Naval Base just south of Jacksonville: Frank Dempsey, Bob Gruetzmacher, Dan Hunter, all those guys were going back to school on the GI Bill. They were juniors and seniors going out in '49, and then they brought in a bunch of young guys like ourselves. They were building the program, and it looked very promising for them. Of course, there were great opportunities for me at some of the other colleges, but I wasn't going to go to Kentucky with Babe Parilli pretty much set. Florida State was just starting a program, and frankly had not even become a solid co-ed school. Florida being the mens' college, the land-grand college that it was, was considered the place to go.

"When I arrived on campus, it was a new experience. I had only been away from home one time, and that was to play in the All–America high school game in Corpus Christi, Texas, about two months before. It was the first one played between the East and West. The game later was moved to Memphis. The players I met there went to schools all throughout the country. I felt a little at home at Florida, because being a farm boy, I hadn't mingled with the New York, New Jersey, or California players. The players I met from Florida were overwhelmingly nice.

"We were put in athletic dorms, and I thought the kingdom of the world was right there. So it was a great experience for someone who had never been away from home before.

Bear Wolf had been the head coach when lineman Red Mitchum reported for summer football practice in 1946. Facing the draft, Mitchum and a group of his friends chose to enlist in the Army for eighteen months before returning to school. While stationed in Japan, Mitchum played on the division football team. Upon his return in 1948, Wolf never gave the talented lineman a chance to start. When Wolf was fired at the end of the 1949 season, Mitchum wasn't surprised.

Red Mitchum: "Coach Wolf was an extremely intelligent person. This is harsh to say, but he was at the end of an era in coaching. They ran a double wing when he came there. It was past its time. No one ran the double wing.

"Here's how it worked: the single wing was the formation Tennessee ran until the 50s. It's what they call the shotgun today. Instead of having one wingback—a wingback is someone who lines up behind the offensive end—you had two wingbacks, one on each side. The primary reason was for blocking. You could double team the tackle with the end and the wingback. It was primarily a running offense. That's what Wolf ran in '46, the year Florida lost all nine games.

"Later in '48 he switched to the T-formation. He knew nothing about it, had never coached it before, but he had Sterling Dupree, a man who had played it at Auburn in the 30s with my high school coach, to be his backfield coach. So for two years Bear Wolf ran the T-formation in '48 and '49. We could have used the two-platoon system, but he wasn't aware that that was going on. In '49 he started to use that more, but he never substituted whole teams. He would have several people play both ways. The people Coach Wolf had as assistants were wonderful men, all high character people, but I don't think they were up to date.

"Coach Wolf was a wonderful man with high principles. He taught us a lot. What lingers more than the football is the honest approach to life that he taught us.

"When Coach Wolf was fired in December of 1949, no one ever came to us to talk about it. Players didn't have access to the press back then. Nobody ever talked to the players. You didn't have an opinion. If you had one, who was going to listen to it? We talked to each other."

five
Woodruff Takes Over

After Bear Wolf resigned in December of 1949, he left to coach at Tulane. Wolf's overall four-year record had been 13-24-2. Florida alums were clamoring for improvement.

Gov. Fuller Warren, who had promised a "nationally famous football team in Gainesville," was one of those alums. Frank Harris, chairman of the board of control, was aiming high. He announced that "a big-name coach is being sought."

But getting that big-name coach wasn't going to be easy despite a sudden increase in the football budget. Warren and the Florida legislature were opening the state's wallet to pay the incoming coach as much as $20,000 a year, a huge sum at the time. [Bear Wolf had made $12,000 in 1949.]

Part of the problem was that the University of Florida was known in the sport as a "coach's graveyard." There had never been money in the school's budget for football before. No Florida coach had ever lasted more than seven years. The new man would be the fifth coach in the last thirteen seasons.

Big names surfaced and disappeared. Bobby Dodd, coach of Georgia Tech, was mentioned in an AP story, but the Tech administration insisted he wasn't going anywhere. Frank Leahy of Notre Dame got some ink. The rumor was that he wanted to come south because of his health. Nothing ever came of it.

The university reached out for Jim Tatum, who was coaching at the University of Maryland. In 1949 Tatum's team was 8-1-0 and beat Missouri in the Gator Bowl. Before going to Maryland, Tatum had been fired at Oklahoma for openly paying some of his players after a bowl game. He was once asked, "Is winning over-emphasized in the bigtime [college] game?" His reply was a classic. Tatum said, "I don't think winning is the most important thing. I think it is the only thing." This was years before Vince Lombardi of the Green Bay Packers was supposed to have uttered the line.

But Tatum needed a situation where he would have free reign. He wanted WAY too much control for the Florida administration.

The next announced choice was Red Sanders, the UCLA coach. Florida offered Sanders a long-term contract at $15,000 a year, and he accepted. But UCLA refused to let him out of his contract. So much for the big names.

The third pick was Bob Woodruff, 34, head coach at Baylor since 1947. Under Woodruff, Baylor had fashioned an 8-2 record in '49.

Woodruff had starred on the Tennessee line under legendary coach General Robert Neyland. Woodruff had joined the staff of the U.S. Military Academy during World War II, climbing to the rank of major and helping coach the Glenn Davis/Doc Blanchard national championship Army teams. He was line coach at Georgia Tech and then became head coach at Baylor.

To get Woodruff to leave Baylor, the University of Florida offered him a $17,000 contract, the highest ever paid to a state employee—$5,000 more a year than the Florida governor and the presidents of the two state universities.

During the 12-hour meeting at which he was hired as both football coach and athletic director, Woodruff was given but one condition: beat Georgia.

For his part the new coach and athletic director demanded and received a list of concessions from the administration which he felt would enable Florida football to complete with other SEC schools for the first time in its history.

For the first time Woodruff would build a football organization with specific objectives that would allow Florida to improve its team. What he needed most was a lot of money.

His demands were that Florida:

a) Build the West stands to increase seating capacity at the Florida Field Stadium to 40,000.

b) Borrow $750,000 against future ticket sales to build it.

c) Separate the department of athletics from the rest of the college.

d) Enable the athletic director to answer to only one man—the university president.

e) Reorganize the booster club. The money raised would go to athletic scholarships.

f) Spend more money to hire assistant coaches.

g) Forge closer ties with the Florida High School Activities Association in order to be better able to recruit Florida high school athletes.

h) Hold an annual clinic to be held on campus for high school athletes.

Bob Woodruff had a plan that was universally applauded by the alumni and boosters. For Woodruff the returning football players also had almost unanimous praise.

Loren Broadus: "In 1950, Bob Woodruff came in, and he was in charge, no question about that. We were going to be in shape, period. He was going to be sure that if we lost, it was going to be on ability and not on whether or not we were in shape. So he worked us very hard in pre-season.

"My initial impression was that he was a very quiet, shy person. To illustrate this, after practice one day he turned to Angus [Williams] and me—we were co-captains—and he said, 'Go put on your coat and tie and meet me in thirty minutes.' You didn't ask any questions. You did it.

"We got in his car, and we drove to Jacksonville to the Boosters Club. They had invited him to talk about the team.

"We were sitting there, the show people, and Woodruff got up and said, 'I'm glad to be the football coach at the University of Florida, and I appreciate your inviting me, but it think it's appropriate for the captain of the team to speak on behalf of the team.' The place was packed. There were hundreds of people waiting to hear him speak. And he sat down. Gus got up and said, 'Since Loren is from Jacksonville, I think I'm just going to let Loren do the speaking.'

"I got up and described a game where we had the lead and a minute to go, and the coach sent me in and told me to tell the quarterback which play to call, that I was to get the ball and stay on my feet as long as possible to run out the clock. We were leading by two or three points, they handed me the ball, and I ran around for a while, and they finally tackled me and I lay there as the clock ran, and then we did that again, and the third time this player had me down, and he said, 'I ought to just punch you in the mouth, you little SOB.' And I looked up, and we only had about eight seconds on the clock, and I said, 'You don't have time.'

"That story has been told in different settings. But that's where it began. And after telling that story, I made some general comments about the team, about how we'd do the best we can, and I sat down, and that was the end of it."

Angus Williams: "When they hired Bob Woodruff, he didn't have that big a name, and there were a lot of people who were surprised they picked him. But he brought in a hell of a good staff. He hired Frank Broyles as his offensive coordinator, and I learned more football in one year from Frank Broyles than

I ever learned in football. He was the sharpest guy I knew. He knew everything there was in football. He knew how to coach the quarterbacks, knew the timing, the release, knew how to set the defense to where you could break to the ball when the pass was thrown.

"In 1950 I played a little quarterback, and a lot of defensive half because Haywood Sullivan was a sophomore, and I was the captain of the team, but they wanted a place for me but they wanted to work with Haywood [at quarterback]. And when Broyles worked with him, he threw for over 1,000 yards. And when Broyles left at the end of the season, the next year Sullivan only threw for 600 yards. Then Broyles went to Georgia Tech, who had a kid named Anderson who had been a mediocre quarterback in 1950, and in '51, when Broyles got there, Anderson was named All-SEC. Then Broyles went to Arkansas, and he did wonders. I'm telling you, Broyles had a mind that was unbelievable. He could get the point across too."

Loren Broadus: "Broyles was fantastic, brilliant. I thought Frank was the smartest person on the field at all times. He had wisdom. He was able to work with Coach Woodruff, but his brilliance was his ability to look at a situation, see it, and determine what should be done. He was a good coach and a good motivator, so I appreciated him greatly. At that point he was a young man, but he was very skilled, agile. He could be stern, but in a positive way."

The defense, which was Coach Woodward's specialty, was bolstered by the arrival of line coach Hobe Hoosier. Woodward and Hoosier would bring new, improved strategies to the defense in 1950.

Charlie LaPradd: "When they changed coaches, one of the coaches they brought in was Hobe Hoosier, who had coached at Little Rock Junior College. A boy who had been a year behind me in high school was invited to visit there, and he asked me to go with him, and we went out there. Hoosier was line coach at Little Rock, and he said to me, 'Well, he's too slow, and you're too small to ever play college football.' But they offered us one-year scholarships to go to Little Rock Junior College anyway. The other boy went. He played two years and quit school.

"I ended up coming back home and hitchhiking over to the University of Florida. When Coach Woodruff came in '50, Hobe Hoosier was his defensive line coach.

"The first day of practice, Hobe looked at each one of us and asked some questions. He said to me, 'You look very familiar.' I said, 'Well, I hope you're a good coach because you said I'd never, ever play college football.' We laughed about that for four years.

"Coach Woodruff was pretty young when he came in. [He was 34.] He probably never said ten sentences to me all the time I was there. Evidently he was a very smart person, but he just was not a very vocal person. Ninety nine percent of my dealings were with Coach Hoosier, who was a fantastic guy as well as a great coach."

Haywood Sullivan: "In 1950 Coach Woodruff came in, and a lot of sophomores became starters. I, Buford Long, J. Papa Hall, Sam Oosterhoudt, a little guy from Lakeland, and Jack Nichols from Niceville. Bobby Knight was the most sure-handed pass-catcher in the group, and Don Brown was a very, very close second. Because of the limited plays we ran, we probably threw fifteen passes a game. If they were playing today, they would be in the tops, not speed wise, but maneuverability and great hands. They were real assets. We did well as young kids. About seventy of us from that freshman class survived. We had quite a group. We were really shooting for our senior year.

"We had some great guys coming back too. Charlie LaPradd was our first All–American. Charlie was in the '49 group. He was quite a guy. He was a walk on. Anybody who came out, they put a helmet on him and a pair of shoes and said, 'Let's see what you can do.'

"That season we had tackle Red Mitchum, who was a junior. Red was a person who kept everyone loose with his great stories, and he was always the emcee of a party. He was always telling jokes on himself."

Mitchum had played little under Coach Wolf, but when Bob Woodruff took over in 1950, he quickly recognized Red Mitchum's talent. He saw the determination and drive the youngster exhibited and promoted him to the starting team. Woodruff and Mitchum developed a bond that lasts until this day.

Red Mitchum: "Coach Woodruff had played for Coach Neyland at Tennessee. Neyland was the most influential football coach short of Knute Rockne. He was famous for his Game Maxims, which have been posted in more locker rooms in the South than you can count.

"Here are his Game Maxims, and if you read them and analyze them, they are as appropriate today as they were then on any level of football. If you're successful doing these seven things, you'll win.'

"Number 1, 'Football is a game of mistakes. The team with the fewest mistakes wins.'

"Number 2, 'Play for and make breaks. When one comes your way, score.'

"Number 3, 'If at first a game or a break goes against you, don't slow down or get rattled. Put on more steam.'

"Number 4, 'Press the kicking game. Here is the winning edge.'

"Number 5, 'Lines and backs protect your kicker and passer. Rush their kicker and passer.'

"Number 6, 'Ali-Baba and Oski Wow Wow.' Ali Baba was a thief, so that means make the other team fumble and steal the ball. Oski Wow Wow originated with the University of Illinois, which was an Indian tribe. They got the saying from the Indian word that means 'intercept.' So Ali Baba and Oski Wow Wow means you should recover fumbles and intercept passes.

"The seventh and last rule, 'Carry on the fight and keep it up all afternoon.'

"I remember once talking with Doug Dickey, who played at Florida under Coach Woodruff and who is now the athletic director at Tennessee. Doug said, 'When I went to school at Florida, Coach Woodruff used to tell us those Game Maxims. Then I took a job at Arkansas under Frank Broyles, who had played for Bobby Dodd, who had played for Coach Neyland at Tennessee, and the Game Maxims were on the wall there. When I went to Tennessee to watch my son Daryl play quarterback, I went into the locker room, and the Game Maxims were on the board.' He said, 'If you think you're going to escape the Game Maxims, go north. Don't stay south.'

"Coach Woodruff—he's 80 years old and I still talk to him—was awfully good to me. I started playing in 1950 when Coach Woodruff came along. I started seven out of the ten ballgames my junior year and seven out of ten games my senior year.

When the 1950 team convened it had only one lettered lineman, center Carroll McDonald. Most of the starters were sophomores. Angus Williams was the only starter returning from the 1949 team, and he was moved from quarterback to defensive back to make way for heralded sophomore quarterback Haywood Sullivan.

Angus Williams: "From the start it was clear that Haywood would be the starting quarterback. They intended me to play defense in 1950. It was a gracious thing for Coach Woodruff to let me start the first game at quarterback. I ran the first series of plays in our opener against The Citadel, and we were three and out, and then they put Haywood Sullivan in, and I went to defense.

"I didn't play with the idea that I was trying to star or anything. All I wanted to do was play to win. So it didn't make any difference to me who scored or who did what as long as we could win. Most of the great quarterbacks have a real ego. Evidently, I didn't have a good ego."

But Haywood Sullivan wasn't sharp in his first varsity game, and Florida just did win its opener against The Citadel.

Charlie LaPradd: "We thought we were going to beat [the Citadel] by five or six touchdowns. That day everything they did was right, and everything we did was wrong. It was one of those days.

"We ended up winning the game 7-3. We won on a long punt return by Jack Nichols, who was a super, super athlete. Jack took the ball, and he cut to one side, and he hit the seam in the defense and just turned on the afterburner until he hit the goal post. I always told him he made the touchdown because he was scared somebody was going to hit him.

"Jack would have been the Florida quarterback if it hadn't been for Haywood Sullivan, so Jack ended up playing defensive halfback, and Jay Hall also played defensive halfback. As juniors, they finally got smart and put them on offense.

"At Florida we were short in some areas, and they would switch people around to go both ways."

Haywood Sullivan: "The next game was Duquesne, and in that game I threw three touchdown passes, and that really gave me the confidence to go on."

Angus Williams: "Duquesne came in with the attitude that whether they won or lost, they were going to try to injure us. They had a bad attitude. Very bad. They weren't as interested in execution as they were in hurting us.

"At the halftime the coaches said, 'Now, you have to keep your head on your shoulders, and don't worry about what they're doing, just worry about execution for what you're supposed to do.' And that's what we did. [Florida won 27-14].

Haywood Sullivan: "We had some good games, and we had some bad games. After Duquesne, we played Georgia Tech, and we lost by a field goal [16–13]. Pepper Rodgers, the guy who kicked the field goal, was on the way to the locker room with an injury when they pulled him back out to kick the field goal. That was tough. It was always tough in Atlanta. It seemed to break our back."

Angus Williams: "I had a pass interference call against me, and then they kicked the field goal. What happened was, they sent a guy deep and a guy short, so I got faked out of position by the short guy, and then they threw the ball deep, and I saw it in the air, and I took off and ran like I had never run before—I guess it was fear-speed—and I got to the receiver before the ball did, and instead of tackling him, I just unloaded on him, and the ball hit me on the back of my helmet. Had I looked up, I could have intercepted it. But I didn't know I was going to get there that fast.

"I really felt down in the dumps, but I don't think that play lost the game. I can remember during the game when we were putting the halfback out as a flanker, and he went down and button hooked, and three times Haywood Sullivan threw to three different halfbacks, and all three of them dropped the ball. They were wide open, and they dropped the ball. I almost told the coach to send me in, because I could catch the ball.

"I wish I had. If I had had enough ego, I would have. But it was plays like that that hurt us."

Haywood Sullivan: "It was just one of those things whereby there would be one game that would almost break your heart to lose, and that Georgia Tech game that year affected us as much as anything else. It was tough, particularly when we had almost had it."

Charlie LaPradd: "We played Auburn, which was a good ballclub, it really was, and we beat them pretty badly [27-7]. We were coming on at that time. Every game we were getting a little better."

Haywood Sullivan: "After Auburn, we played undefeated Vanderbilt, a good ballclub, in Nashville. [Vanderbilt was ranked number 13 in the country.] We had a good game that day, not only passing, but running. [Behind Sullivan, Florida won in a resounding upset, 31-27.]

"One of our stars against Vanderbilt was Floyd Huggins, our fullback who came from the Texas. Woodruff had coached at Baylor and he knew people from that area. Floyd was at a junior college, and he brought Floyd in. Floyd was a tough player. We could have utilized him more if we had had more plays.

"Another star in that game was Loren Broadus, who scored two touchdowns, one on a long run. He was a senior, from the older group. Loren was the chaplain of the club. He was very religious, and if we had had a better ballclub and if he had not gotten injured, Loren would have been an All–American. He had the ability and the attitude to have been really great. I thought he would have made a good coach. I do not know what he did after he left school, but I do know he was quite a gentleman."

Loren Broadus: "I know I had a good game against Vanderbilt, scored a couple touchdowns, because I was chosen player of the week by the *New York Times*. I found that out later in the season when someone sent me the clipping."

Angus Williams: "We played them at Vanderbilt, and they were good. They had Billy Wade at quarterback and an end named Bucky Curtis. Bucky was fast, a big end, and he was on my side. I can remember he went out for a hook pass, and just as he caught it, I hit him and as he was going down, he lateralled to the halfback, and the halfback ran another twenty yards, and in the meantime Curtis got up, and the halfback lateralled back to him, and he got down near the goal line.

"I do remember him dropping one in the end zone. The one good thing I did that day was intercepting their last pass play. It was a good feeling."

Haywood Sullivan: "Next we beat Furman, which was one of the good Carolina clubs. At this point we were 5 and 1. We weren't surprised. We were programmed to do what we were supposed to do. I don't think we hardly even knew who we were playing the next week once we were in the ballgame. We took it one week at a time. There was none of this, 'We have to wait until we play Miami.' We always knew whoever we were playing was going to be tough, so we had everything in hand for that week."

With a 5-1 record, all signs pointed for a bowl bid, the first in the history of the University of Florida. The team travelled to Lexington. The frosty afternoon turned into a memorable debacle.

Loren Broadus: "We went to Lexington to play Kentucky, and we had to play in the ice and show, and it was terrible, terrible. We came from Florida into the ice and snow. Oh man, you touch somebody, and you burn all over. Kentucky did a beautiful job that day. They beat the stew out of us [40-6]."

Red Mitchum: "That was the worst day of my life. It snowed all night, and then it started raining the next day. The field was completely flooded, and they thought they had a device that would get the water off the field. They put 1,000 gallons of gasoline on the field and ignited it. All it did was burn the grass off. The water stayed there and caused a quagmire.

"The coaches bought us longjohns. It was a feeling of complete dispair.

"We made the biggest mistake of the day when we started out: we scored first. Jim French, one of our ends, caught a look-in-pass. Our kicker missed a field goal. We had them 6 to 0. Then they came back and beat us 40 to 6. On defense they had Bob Gain, who was All-American, and they had three tackles as good as he was.

"I was playing in front of Bob Gain, and he broke my nose and chipped my cheekbone. Curtis King, who played next to me, came over and looked at me in the huddle. He said, 'Hey Big Red, you look pretty whupped.' I said, 'Well, Curtis, I feel whupped.' He said, 'Well, when we come out of the huddle this time, let's holler something, even if we have to take it back.'"

Haywood Sullivan: "The Kentucky people furnished us with big drums along the sidelines to keep us warm. We had just that year started wearing the old Riddell helmets, the full helmet with the straps, and it was so cold that the steam from your brow and your head would freeze in the top of your helmet, and we were so frozen that we didn't perform at all during the game. Kentucky had a heck of a club anyway. What did they beat us by, 40 to 6?

"Bob Gain, one of their linemen, was in our backfield more than our fullback!"

Red Mitchum: "I've often been asked, 'What's the difference between winning and losing?' Let me give you an example. In 1950 we beat Vanderbilt. When the fans came out to meet us at the air field when we flew back, they took us back to campus in convertibles. My wife was with me, and when we got back to campus, people were screaming and hollering all the way.

"Two games later we went to Kentucky and got clobbered. When we flew back to Gainesville, this time they picked us up in some old yellow school busses, and we had two flat tires. It took us two hours to get from the airfield to downtown. Nobody came out. There wasn't anything but tumbleweeds out across the field. This is a true story. That's the difference between winning and losing.

"I believe honestly, even today, that that Kentucky team was the best college football team I ever saw. I once asked Bear Bryant about it. I got to know him well. He agreed with me. He said, 'Don't tell anybody.' He thought it was a better team than his famous Alabama teams."

The next game was against Georgia in Jacksonville. This was the game Coach Bob Woodruff had promised the Florida legislature he would win. Only one touchdown was scored that day, and it was made by Georgia.

Angus Williams: "The man who caught that pass was named Walston, and he later played for the Philadelphia Eagles. On that play the quarterback ran out of the pocket, and I had the choice either to cover the end or make sure the quarterback didn't run that end, and I was trying to do both, and Walston kept zigzagging, and finally the other defenders got over there, and I got on Walston, and he threw, and Walston made a diving catch and caught it in the end zone."

Haywood Sullivan: "Georgia always was a toughie. We were so keyed up trying to bounce back from that big, big defeat against Kentucky that we were just uptight. Georgia had a good team. The quarterback went on to the pros.

"It was a tough, tough game, not a good game. It seemed like every time we got an opportunity to score, something happened, like a fumble or an interception. They deserved to beat us, because we just didn't perform well. We made mistake after mistake."

Haywood Sullivan: "Then came Miami, which always was tough. Miami was gunning for us. The last part of the season just went downhill." [Florida lost to Miami 20–14.]

Charlie LaPradd: "All I can remember about the Miami game was that the guy playing in front of me was a weightlifter and a state champion, and we beat each other to death. They tried to take me out of the game, but I wouldn't go. I wouldn't go out until he went out. I wasn't going to let him beat me."

Haywood Sullivan: "The final game was a bad [41-13] loss to Alabama. I threw a long pass [70 yards] to Dan Howell, but we got beat bad."

Red Mitchum: "It was terribly disappointing to lose the last four games of the season. I don't know how to explain it to you. I don't even know how to explain it to myself. Like when I came back from that Kentucky game, I had a broken nose and a chipped cheekbone. I got off the plane, and my wife said, 'Did you get to play?' I said, 'I started.' She said, 'Well, I missed the starting lineups.' Well, you're not going to hear anything about an offensive lineman on the radio. What football was about back then was doing the very best you could, and then going to the next game trying to do the best you could. You stayed together. What we had was more like what fraternities seek but sometimes never find—our football team had a togetherness. The only thing that comes close is being in the service, but I don't think it's as close. I served fourteen months in Japan with my fellow soldiers, sleeping right next to them, and I can't remember their names. But I remember every name of the players I played football with.

"Football wasn't life or death. Most of us weren't playing in order to go into the pros, and anyone who went to the pros didn't make much. When Chuck Hunsinger signed with Chicago, he made around $4,000. Frank Dempsey made $5,000. Back then you made more money teaching high school. Nobody made any money in pro football until the 1970s. It was a different atmosphere, a different type of person playing, because their ambitions were not the same. They were trying to get an education, as I said before, to better themselves and their families. It's awfully hard to explain it—I come from a different time.

"And just because we didn't go 10 and 0 has nothing to do with us now. We all wanted to win, of course, or else we wouldn't have played. But you wouldn't want to commit suicide if you lost a football game.

"We were awfully critical of those who criticized us. We felt if you're not for us, you're against us. You didn't have to mouth off. We just stayed within each other and played for each other. That's what we played for—each other. We played for the university and for ourselves and for the coaches. To be praised by the coaches was the greatest thing in the world. We didn't need newspapers, even though we were getting a lot of coverage from around the state. It was the awakening of a new type of football."

Haywood Sullivan: "Our biggest loss came after the '50 season was over. Frank Broyles went back to Georgia Tech. He had great emotions about leaving, but it was his alma mater, and Bobby Dodd wanted him to come back up there. He later became the head coach at Missouri. I've talked to Frank a few times, and I think he knew he was going to be going to Missouri. And when he went to Missouri, he took Doug Dickey, the second quarterback, with him, and then Doug went to Arkansas. There was a great relationship there."

After the 1950 season Angus Williams played in the North-South game in Miami, and in December of 1951 he got married. After he graduated, he worked for Wilson Sporting Goods in Miami. He worked there nine months as a traveling salesman until he rolled his car over on wet pavement. It was time, he decided, to get off the road.

He coached for U. of Florida teammate Frank Lorenzo at Plant High School in Tampa for two years, after selling him some equipment. "He bought a gross of jockey straps only because they were on sale," says Williams about his close friend. From there he coached for four years at the University of Tampa under Marcelin Werda, another Florida guard. By then Williams had four daughters "so I had to go to work for a living." He went into the insurance business, and he became a star salesman and supervisor with Bankers' Life of Iowa. In 1966 he became agency manager, and he retired in 1988. Today he spends six months in the mountains of North Carolina and six months in Tampa.

After playing four years at Florida, Loren Broadus could have become a professional player or a coach at any level of the game. Instead, he discovered he had a different calling, one which he follows to this day.

Loren Broadus: "I was contacted by some pro teams, but I had gotten what I wanted out of football. I coached and taught high school for one year at Andrew Jackson High School in Jacksonville. Then I got an offer to be a head coach at a small college, Georgia Southern, and it caused me to ask myself whether I wanted to do this the rest of my life, and I said no. So I didn't accept the job, and I resigned from my coaching position at the end of the school year and went into business. I stayed in business for five years and then decided I needed to be in the ministry. I took my spouse and child and moved to Lexington, Kentucky, went to the Seminary for a year, ran out of money, so I called the company and went back to work for one year to make enough money to finish up at the Seminary, and then I finished.

"I became a professor at the Seminary. I taught, and I write. I still give lectures and speeches. The writing is something to keep the creative juices flowing. I wrote one book called *Laughing and Crying with Little League.* The second one was *From Loneliness to Intimacy*, subtitled, *Help for the Golf Widow and other Lonely People.* The latest one is called *The Responses to Suffering*, which back then could be the title of your book for the University of Florida football team."

six

Wild and Crazy Guys

Halfback Rick Casares was one of the most talented players ever recruited by the University of Florida. Born in Tampa, Casares moved to Paterson, New Jersey, at a young age after his father died. When he was fifteen, he and his mother got into a battle over whether he would become a professional boxer. Mom won. She shipped him to relatives in Tampa, where he became one of the most highly sought-after athletes to come out of the area. Casares was heading to the University of Kentucky to play basketball for legendary coach Adolph Rupp when his friends and relatives convinced him that if he was going to live in Florida, he ought to go to college in Florida.

Rick Casares: "My senior year we won the city, state, and Big Ten championships, and fortunately I was picked on the high school All–America team. Then I played in the high school All–American game and fortunately was voted the most valuable player. I had a good game, scored a couple of touchdowns and kicked all the extra points and field goals. The four colleges who wanted me for football were Georgia, Notre Dame, Kentucky, and Florida.

"I was going to go to Kentucky. But my family and friends all said, 'We want to be able to come see you play every week.' Everybody I cared about and respected were all University of Florida people. I finally settled on Florida because Pete Norton, who was a great newspaperman for the Tampa Tribune, told me it would be to my best interest if I went to Florida. So I decided to go to Florida.

"At Florida I played on the freshman football team, and it was great. From high school on, all I wanted to do was just keep playing football. To keep playing sports was my goal. I intended to get my degree and become a coach."
Casares' roommate, lineman Joe D'Agostino, was very strong and extremely

quick on the football field. Like Casares, D'Agostino had moved south to
Florida as a boy.

Joe D'Agostino: "I grew up in Cambridge, Massachusetts, and moved to
Orlando in 1946 when I was 12. My father had the gout, and the doctor told
him that our weather in Florida would help him, and of course, it didn't,
because he loved his wine, and wine brought on the uric acid, and the uric
acid brought on the gout.

"I was recruited at the University of Florida by John Eibner, the defensive
line coach. He had played with the Philadelphia Eagles. He was a great
recruiter. He'd come down from Gainesville and talked to my mother and
father. He left me out of it completely.

"But it was my choice to go to Florida. One of the reasons was that my
dad owned a restaurant that he built after coming down from Massachusetts.
It was called D'Agostino's Villanova Restaurant in Winter Park. I figured if I
made the Florida football team, it would be good for him because his restaurant
would get a lot of overflow from the fans coming back from the game at
Gainesville. They would stop and see my dad and say, 'Your son played a
wonderful game.' That helps business out quite a bit.

"My roommate at Florida was Rick Casares for almost the whole time we
were there, until he joined the service for the Korean War. I had met Rick in high
school at a track meet. He went to Jefferson High in Tampa, and we had played
football against each other, and in the track meet I beat him in one of the races.

"Rick was a very complex man. He was a jokester, as I was. One night
I put a dead rattlesnake under his newspaper, had it coiled up, and when he
got up in the morning, he saw the rattlesnake and jammed himself back and
hit his head on the railing of the double-decker bed. He was quite upset with me.

"That evening I was sound asleep, and he tied me head and foot to the
rails of the bed and painted me with aluminum paint. I mean, ALL OVER.
We used to do things like that to each other. It was an awful lot of fun. He
never got angry.

"It took quite a long time for the paint to wear off. The players found
out about it, and they thought it was a big joke, because they knew we were
jokesters. It was good for team morale."

Rick Casares: "Did Joe tell you the story about his putting analgesic balm
in my shorts? I put my shorts on for a workout, and of course, analgesic balm

gets in your privates, and I was on fire. So I ran into the shower, which is the worst thing you can do. I knew who had done it, knew it had to be Joe.

"I saw him laughing, and he took off, and he ran and locked himself in our room. Haywood Sullivan and Bubba McGowan roomed on the same floor, and they were avid hunters, and I knew they had a shotgun in there, so I ran in there and I said, 'Give me that shotgun.' Cause Joe had locked himself in the damn room. And so I got the shotgun, and I said, 'You better open this door.' And he said, 'No, you're going to hurt me.'

"I said, 'You better open this door, or I'm going to shoot it off.' He said, 'I'm not opening it.' I said, 'Get out of that room, because I'm going to shoot this lock off.' And I did. I shot the lock off, and I went in there and I grabbed him, and then he got out on the ledge outside the window, so I locked him out there. He was in his shorts right across from the girls' gym. And I left him out there for a couple of hours.

"Joe was always doing little stunts like that. Yeah, that's right, he did. He was good. I loved Joe. To this day we're close. But he was like a little kid. He was devilish. He was a really funny guy."

Haywood Sullivan: "Rick was a fun-loving guy, and every time he did something it was magnified, right or wrong. He would get in some trouble. One time he took his roommate and held him down on the bed and shot around him with a pistol. He just made D'Agostino's life miserable by just aggravating him, but he loved him, absolutely loved him, and that's the reason he picked on him, just for show."

What was amazing was that Rick Casares managed to survive his college years. The closest he came to disaster was a car accident one rainy night in Gainesville.

Rick Casares: "I had been to a fraternity house party, and the band was a black trio, three black fellows, and at the time I was pretty broad minded— I've always been that way about black guys and myself, and I was taking the three guys home, and it was raining like the dickens, and we were going down the streets of Gainesville, and I could hardly see, and I was peering forward, and it was raining so hard, and in the middle of the street there was an island with a tree, which I was unaware of, and while I was looking, I ran into this tree in the middle of the street and smashed up my Buick. My face hit the steering wheel, and I broke my nose. Fortunately, I was going slowly. It stung me, and I could hear one of the band members say, 'Rick's dead!' And they took off. Cause at that time they didn't want to be caught with a dead white guy in the car.

"The police came, and I went to the hospital, and they set my nose. I wasn't hurt badly enough to affect my football, though."

Red Mitchum: "I remember Rick did crazy things. He used to hold D'Agostino out the window by his feet. And one time D'Agostino was asleep, and Rick painted him all over with mercurochrome—ALL over him—turned him red.

"They did a lot of hunting back then, and they kept guns in their room. Loren Broadus and Jim Yancey were the best hunters. Jim would go into a neighborhood where he knew people who had bird dogs. He would coax a bird dog into their car and take him out and hunt with the dog. Then they'd bring him back and let him out where he picked him up. They never stole the dog, just used it.

"Of course, Rick and Joe also were hunters. The girls' gym was right across the way, so if you wanted to test fire, you fired into the girls' gym. The campus police finally stopped that. They had a raid and stacked up the weapons in front of the dormitories. They didn't punish anyone. They just made them take their rifles home."

Rick Casares: "The thing is, I loved guns. Bull York, who was from Fernandina, was an amazing specimen. Bull was about six foot, 270 pounds, the widest and thickest guy I ever saw. He played fullback for Fernandina, but Coach Woodruff moved him to guard. Bull was something else to see. At that time nobody was big, except Charlie LaPradd, one of the few who weighed over 210 pounds. Bull could run. But Bull would find a gun, and would bring it to me to shoot. I used to shoot them out of the window up in the air. I had a reputation for that. (Heh heh heh.)"

seven

A Win over Alabama

Haywood Sullivan: "We opened up the 1951 season against Wyoming. They were a pretty good ballclub, but it was a good start for us. [Florida won 13-0.] Some of those schools could jump up and hit you in the nose pretty good.

Rick Casares: "We had a great defense and Charlie LaPradd led it. Charlie was one of the oldest players on the team. He had been in the service and was a big, tough guy He was an exceptional defensive tackle, a true All-American."

Charlie LaPradd: "They had a coach out there who knew Woodruff, and they worked out a deal, on a one-year basis, for Wyoming to open the season in the Gator Bowl. On the first play of the game a guy swung an elbow at me and cut me above the eye. We had on white uniforms, and I was bleeding all over everything. They took me over to the sideline, and the crazy doctor we had at the time put clamps on it.

"When I came out, Woodruff said, 'Well, you know, I meant to tell you about that guy. He's real bad about throwing elbows.' I said, 'Thanks, coach.' Then he said to the doctor, 'Go back inside and put stitches in that eye. That boy can't play with those clamps in there.' I went back in the locker room, and he took out the clamps and stitched it up. Then I came back out and went back into the ballgame."

Haywood Sullivan: "After Wyoming, we beat The Citadel [27-7]. Back then in any game when you got a couple of touchdowns ahead, very, very few clubs would run up the score. It wasn't there to do, because the offenses were not built that way. You went to your defensive strategies. You didn't have the offensive fire-power that you have today, the scatbacks and all the sophisticated plays that they use to score 50 or 60 points.

"People respected other teams. You didn't want to embarrass anybody too much, so if you had a comfortable margin, you didn't want to show the other side up.

"The next game was against Georgia Tech. They were just too good for us. [Florida was shut out 27-0.] Plain too good for us. That hurt."

Charlie LaPradd: "It was one of those days when you couldn't do anything right. Georgia Tech had a big name. You always looked up to them as being somebody you almost couldn't beat."

Rick Casares: "Georgia Tech had the fastest linemen I had ever seen. We were dazzled by the speed of their defense. It was the most speed we had ever seen. It seemed like they were flying."

Haywood Sullivan: "Then we flew out to California to play Loyola of Los Angeles. We didn't fly all the way. There were no jets. We stopped in Texas and worked out at Rice University.

"They had a quarterback by the name of Don Klosterman. They were building up Loyola as one of the top ten teams in the country. The game was billed as a citrus game, California against Florida. A lot of chambers of commerce were involved in this one. We played in the Rose Bowl, and it was quite a ballgame. If I recall right, they threw 66 passes against us, and Klosterman must have completed fifty percent of them, and we beat them 40-7. It was just one of those games where you lay back, lay back, and boom, we capitalized on everything. That game was one of the highlights of that year for us. We went that distance and played that well."

Charlie LaPradd: "That flight was a new experience for me. It was the first time I ever landed inside the plane. That's a true story, because in all the rest of my flights, I had jumped out.

"The only thing I remember outside the game itself was spending the whole game looking at [movie actress] June Haver, who was sitting on their bench. But we beat them pretty bad. Klosterman was the only thing they had going for them."

Joe D'Agostino: "They took us to a couple of movie studios, and we met Virginia Mayo, who was very gorgeous. We loved it at the studios, saw how pictures were made. And then back on the bus.

"The president of the university came with us to California. We made a stop at Tijuana, and everyone got off the bus, walked around and looked at the culture. We had a few hours, and we were told if anyone was not on the bus, they would have to find their way back home. Turned out the people who were late were the head coach and the president of the university. For them we waited.

"We won the game easily. They had huge players, but they were slow."

Rick Casares: "I had one of my best games as a running back against Loyola. Coach Woodruff alternated the running backs a great deal, which was difficult for me. That night I had a great game running. It was the beginning of my long-range touchdowns and caused the coaching staff to give me different plays for long runs, instead of just inside stuff.

"Our next game was against Auburn at Auburn, and it's one experience I've never had since. We stayed overnight there, and the Auburn fans stood outside our hotel, and you could hear them for hours hollering 'War Eagles.' It sounded like we were at a rock concert. It was the greatest show of spirit I've ever seen. They were out there until about two in the morning screaming 'War Eagles' and raising cain. Nobody broke them up, either."

Charlie LaPradd: "In that Auburn game I scored a touchdown on a blocked kick. They were down about their 20 yard line, and one of our guys blocked it. I was right there, caught the ball, and ran on over for a touchdown.

"A good friend of mine's grandmother, who was in a rocking chair, was sitting at home listening to the game. She listened to every game I ever played. Shirley, her daughter, told me that when I scored the touchdown, she fell out of her rocking chair. But it turned out to be a very, very bad loss." [Auburn won 14-13.]

Haywood Sullivan: "They beat us in the last two minutes, just like the Georgia Tech game of the year before. I was very despondent after that game, because there were so many people from my hometown who were up there. After the game, we knew we should have won, and we didn't, and it was a big letdown again, just like the Georgia Tech game the year before.

"We came back and beat Vanderbilt [33–13]. Vanderbilt didn't have a bad ballclub. We got to run more in that game because they had a good pass defense. We ran quite a bit, and I scored a couple of touchdowns in that one.

"Our next game was against Kentucky and Babe Parilli again. They were a good club, and Parilli was just an outstanding player. [Florida lost 14-6.] He threw two long touchdowns. He had some great, great ends, and they had a lot of talent and a well-coached ballclub.

"Georgia was next, and we lost [7-6] when Florida missed the extra point. We try to forget those things, and after this period of time, it's lucky we have. But I remember we moved the ball from the 20 yard line to the 20 yard line, but they just dug in. As you go over these games, you can see that a break here or a break there, we could have had a hell of a season either one of those years.

"We then went to Miami, and got beat [21-6] by a good club in the Orange Bowl. The most vivid thing I remember about that game was the field itself. The Orange Bowl was like playing in a sand pit. They would play high school games in it on Wednesday night, Thursday night, and then the big high schools would draw 40,000 on Fridays. The field was just worn out, and we just didn't get going.

"Miami has always had a good program. They recruited big time from up in Pennsylvania, and they had some tough, tough kids."

Haywood Sullivan: "The game I remember most was our final game. It was Alabama's Homecoming game, and they were heavy favorites. All the people from Dothan who had been at the Auburn game, who had been disappointed by our loss, all seemed to gather for this game in Tuscaloosca. We had a great day. [Florida won 30-21.] It was the highlight of all the games we ever played, coming back after losing the three we did the way we had.

"In the first quarter I threw a touchdown to Jim French, a veteran, a nice guy. He was more of a blocking end, and I didn't throw to him much. And Buford Long scored two touchdowns that day. Buford could run. You get him outside, get him loose, and he was pretty tough to catch."

Charlie LaPradd: "I can remember in that game I was following the play out to the sideline, and when I made the tackle, the runner twisted and landed on me and crushed my collarbone.

"I went in, and they x-ed a piece of tape across my chest and around my body, and I went back out and played. Come to find out I had a fractured collarbone. That was a good ballgame, a very good ballgame."

Joe D'Agostino: "Charlie LaPradd was extremely tough. It took two or three men to get him out of the way. He wasn't nimble on his feet, but they couldn't move him, because he was so good. He was our team captain, and he kept up the spirit on the line. He'd come up and down the line, hitting us on the butt and telling us to get with it and play hard, and we all loved him. I do today."

Charlie LaPradd: "In that [Alabama] game Rick [Casares] kicked a field goal from a very tough angle. The funny thing about that was Rick never practiced kicking, but he had been an extra-point kicker and field-goal kicker his whole career. We had somebody else kicking, and he had missed a couple, so we had Rick kick it. And of course, he did what he was supposed to do. Then a fellow by the name of Bill Wester, a defensive halfback, intercepted an Alabama pass and ran it back to the one yard line. On any other team in the country, probably, Billy Wester would have been playing first team. But because we had Jay Hall and Buford Long, he was playing second team. So they put him over on defense. And after the interception, we scored from close in."

Haywood Sullivan: "I scored from the one to make the score 30-21. For the next three or four days all of us enjoyed the fact that we had beaten them. I had a lot of fun with a lot of the people I knew from Alabama, who had given me hell about the Auburn game. I had a chance to get back at a lot of them."

Joe D'Agostino: "It was a lot different than today. If you won a game, you were all elated, of course, but we didn't do any jumping around, screaming or hollering. We just went into the locker room, changed clothes, and got on the bus. It was nothing like the way they put on a show today. You never did that. There was no whooping and hollering if you scored a touchdown. That's why people my age feel 'eck' about today's football."

After finishing the season 5-5 in 1951, everyone was looking forward to a spectacular 1952 season, one that would feature Haywood Sullivan at quarterback and Rick Casares at fullback. But the fortunes of that '52 squad would suffer a crippling blow when in the spring of 1952 Sullivan starred in the NCAA regional baseball finals at Kannapolis, North Carolina. Duke University, led by shortstop Dick Groat, went on to defeat Florida, but Sullivan was so outstanding a prospect that the Boston Red Sox offered him a signing bonus of $75,000 to play professional baseball. It was an offer he couldn't refuse.

Haywood Sullivan: "The circumstances surrounding my decision not go back to school for another year was this: I had just gone through a mandatory ROTC program at the university. I was in the Air Force ROTC, and if went back to school, I was in line to be commissioned. The Korean War was on, and under the circumstances I would have had to spend four years minimum in the military service after getting the commission.

"Furthermore, the recruiters let me know that in the upcoming winter meetings, baseball was going to change the bonus rule to read that if any kid signed professionally for more than $6,000, he would have to spend two years on the major league roster. They were trying to discourage big bonuses, and this was the way they were going to do that, because teams weren't going to flood their rosters with kids. So if I played another season at Florida and waited until the football season was over, that meant it would be almost impossible to receive any kind of money for signing.

"The Red Sox offered me quite a bit. So did Cincinnati and Detroit. The scouts were after me.

"My family didn't have any money whatsoever. I would have had to wait four more years after that last year to even consider signing with professional baseball. And who knows what would happen in those four-plus years? It was a dilemma for me to leave school and leave the team, but with the amount of money being offered it was a no-brainer.

"I often hear the comments, 'Where could we have gone? What bowl could you have gone to?' And you never know those things. But I could have gotten hurt in the first game. Or we could have had a lousy year and I would have gone on to the army and gotten killed. Who knows?

"I resigned a possible military commission and signed with the Red Sox in June of '52. I went to Albany, New York, and played the rest of that year, went back to spring training with the Red Sox, and after helping coach the freshman team at Florida during the winter, I went to spring training, and that's when I was drafted into the service and was there when Rick Casares was drafted at Fort Jackson."

Red Mitchum: "We had a nickname for Sully. Instead of Haywood, we called him 'Hard Wood' Sullivan. He's a pretty good singer. He sang bass for us in the quartet. The other two people were Don Brown, who ended up as a coach at Florida, and Bubba McGowan. Bubba and Sully played high school football together at Dothan. He and Sully were best of friends.

"You know the first thing Sully did when he signed with the Red Sox? He went home to Dothan, Alabama, and bought his folks a house. He signed for $75,000 in 1952, which was a lot of money. He was the highest paid catcher ever to sign. He took that money—his daddy was a salesman in a furniture store back in Dothan—and he bought them a house. I think that shows right there the character you have in football players."

Joe D'Agostino: "Haywood is one fine person. He was as pleasant as could be. He was a deep Southerner, but he was not a redneck. He got along with everyone and had a wonderful sense of humor, was a wonderful presence on the field.

"The reason we didn't do better, even with Haywood, was that the recruiting wasn't the best. We didn't have all the right-type players.

"When he signed with the Red Sox, the other players understood. They gave him A LOT of money. And we also knew that playing baseball, he wasn't going to get hit as much, wasn't going to get bruised and banged up and carried off the field."

Haywood Sullivan: "When I was playing football and baseball, one outstanding thing I remember was the great camaraderie we had with the university staff, with Dean Beattie and Dean Brady and J. Hillis Miller, the president of the university who started the first medical school. They named the medical school after him, which has since been changed to Shanns. President Miller never missed a game, and very, very few practices. You'd always see him sitting on the sidelines watching practice every day. So would a lot of the staff. The old professors were a great group of people."

.ed Mitchum: "When I was a senior [in 1951] I was walking off the field .ı September when Marshall Crysler, a former president of the university and a boy named Bill Henry, called to me and said, 'Red, the Blue Key organization met last night, and they voted you to emcee the Gator Growl.' That's a student function at Homecoming. They fill the stadium for it. More people went to Gator Growl than went to the football games. They said, 'We went you to emcee Gator Growl. You'll be the first student in the history of Florida ever to be the emcee.'

"In those days if you did anything away from football they had an expression: 'You don't have your mind on the game.' The notion was that you cared more about doing other things than playing football. I can remember the story they told about one player they made run laps because they found books in his locker!

"I said, 'Marshall, I would love to do it, but I'm just barely holding onto my starting job as an offensive tackle.' I told them I really felt wonderful that they had asked me to do it, but I couldn't.

"I went to get my mail in the athletic department, and I found a note in my pigeonhole box asking me to come see Coach Woodruff the next day at one o'clock. I couldn't figure out what I had done. I hadn't been in any fights. My grades were fine. I knew I hadn't cut any classes. One time I made a comment to my money-and-banking professor. We were talking privately, and he was telling me how much smarter he was than I. I said to him, 'If you're so smart, how come you're not rich?' He laughed. But I thought that maybe he had turned on me.

"So I went in to see Coach Woodruff, and he said, 'Sit down, Red.' I figured I was in trouble, because the few times I had been in the head coach's office I had never been asked to sit down.

"He said, 'I understand that Blue Key was asked you to emcee the Gator Growl.' I said, 'Yes sir, but I'm not going to do it because I have my mind on the game, and I know that's the most important thing to me.'

"He said, 'Well, just a minute. Let's think about it. Number one, it's quite an honor for them to select a football player to emcee a function like that which will have over 67,000 people in the stands. Another thing, what would it look like if the boys who are coming up here in the future see that we encourage our football players to do other things? It would let them know that we want our football players to be well-rounded, educated men. And another thing, it would help us with recruiting if you did this.

"Another thing,' he said. 'The president of the university called me two days ago and said you WOULD emcee Gator Growl.'

"I said, 'Coach those other things don't seem so important to me.'

"He said, 'No, they're not, Red, but they sounded good, didn't they?'

"And that was probably the biggest thing that ever happened to me because I was able to get my name out among more people in one night. That helped me in business to meet people in the future. 'Yeah, I remember you, Red. You emceed Gator Growl.' And it was a tremendous help to me because I have been in selling all my life. That was my major—sales and sales management and marketing. If people feel like they know you, they trust you more. If they trust you more, they're more likely to do business with you.

"I think people get misunderstood in life because they do something to get their name known, and they feel, 'Well, the public owes me because they know me.' That's not true. People may want to meet you because you're famous. But after they meet you, if you're not acceptable, you won't achieve.

"Coach Woodruff taught me, "Red, if you're going to speak, don't ever tell any risqué stories.' Over the last 35 years I've averaged making fifty speeches a year all over the United States.

"When I was going back into the Army during the Korean War, Coach Woodruff called me into his office. He said he wanted to see me before I left. I've never been so amazed in my life at what he said.

"He said, 'You know, Red, I had to play you because you reminded me so much of myself.' He said, 'You didn't have great ability, but you tried harder than anybody I ever coached. I know you knew all the plays because I heard an assistant coach many times ask you what the assignment was—not for your position but for someone else's, and you knew it. That always impressed me. I know that you'll do well.'

"He went on, 'A lot of my boys, I worry about them having a job when they get out of school, but I don't worry about you. I know you'll do well. In fact, I've always wanted to be nice to you because I might be working for you some day.'

"He finished, 'I just wanted to tell you. I knew you didn't have a father when you were young. I knew all about your history, and I'm so very proud of you and what you've been able to accomplish.'

"Now he calls me 'Son.' I have three children and seven grandchildren in Ocala. They all have degrees. Not that there's anything wrong with a cotton mill background, but I escaped from that and was able to give through going to college, through playing football, my three kids degrees, who in turn have three in college now.

"People wonder, what held all you misfits together? You didn't win a game in '46, and for four years you were 5-5 and then in '51 we lost three ballgames by nine points. Kentucky beat us 14-7, Auburn 14-13, and Georgia 7-6, and with those three wins, we would have gone to most any bowl in the nation. But what held us together?

"It was the character of the people. And what we were seeking then wasn't the ability to play pro football. A lot of us may have wanted to coach, and some of us did, but it was the friendships you made and the character of the people that were most important. Who they were and what they were and what they stood for, because what they came to Florida for was to get a degree.

"All of us were Depression children. All of us were raised with one foot in poverty, and the other seeking to find a step out of it, so it drew us together.

"When people would say to me, 'Mitchum, you haven't done THAT well,' I'd say, 'You should have seen where we started from.

"See, it might be hard for you to understand: All of this feeling we have for each other, we never have to say. Nobody ever talks about it. But I don't think you will find any university in the nation that has a camaraderie among its former football players the way we do at the University of Florida."

eight

Haddock, Dickey and Lance

One of the starting backs in 1952 was a Navy veteran by the name of Tommy Haddock. Haddock had been recruited by Florida head coach Tom Lieb back in 1946, but by the time Haddock arrived in Gainesville, Lieb was out and Bear Wolf in. When Wolf refused to offer Haddock a scholarship, he joined the Navy and flew fighter jets. During the Korean War he patrolled the Mediterranean Sea on a carrier.

In the spring of 1952 Haddock was discharged from the Navy, and he returned to Florida, where twice he was told he couldn't play football because he was too old. On the way out for the final time, he ran into Charlie LaPradd, who knew how good Haddock was. LaPradd, who was highly respected by everyone, convinced the coaching staff to change its mind about Haddock, who became one of the rotating group of halfbacks in '52.

Tommy Haddock: "I graduated high school in 1946, and it was a funny time. Tom Lieb was the coach at the University of Florida, and he or one of his scouts had seen me play my last couple of games. They told me they wanted me to come to Florida on a scholarship.

"Well, he got fired after the season, and Bear Wolf came in. He was a single-wing coach, and he told everyone to come down on tryouts. When he saw me, he told me I was too small. I weighed about 160. He said he wanted me to come out on my own. Well, I had no means of doing that. I couldn't do that. So I said, 'Well shucks, I'll go home and see what else prevails.'

"I needed a scholarship to go to college. I had to come up with something on my own. Anyway, I wanted to do two things when I got out of high school. I wanted to fly a Navy fighter plane, and I wanted to play football at the University of Florida. I decided to try the Navy flight deal.

"In the spring of '52 I got out of the Navy, and I went down to the University of Florida to see coach Hobe Hoosier, the defensive line coach, who shuffled me to a guy by the name of Dick Jones, the head recruiter. They had three weeks to get ready. I told him I hadn't played in a couple of years, and he told me I was too old.

"I said, 'Coach, I don't want you to give me anything. All I want is an opportunity to put the pads on and see whether I can make this ballclub. If I didn't feel I could make it, I wouldn't be bothering you. I've got a Navy scholarship. I'm not asking you for a scholarship. The Navy's paying my way.'

"Anyway, he said no. I told myself, I guess it's just not in the cards. I went home, and about two weeks later I ran into a fellow by the name of John Patsy, who was a reserve guard on the Florida football team. We got to talking, drinking a beer, and he asked me what happened. After I told him, he said to go back there and make sure I get to see Coach Hoosier. So I did. But they sent me to see Coach Jones, and he wouldn't let me see Coach Hoosier. And again, Coach Jones said no. I told him, 'I promise I won't bother you again, coach.'

"As I was walking out the front door of the old gym building down the stairs, Charlie LaPradd was walking up. I had played one of my last football games against Charlie. He played at St. Augustine, which is about thirty miles down the road from Jacksonville Beach. They had a big ballclub, but we ended up beating them, and Charlie and I became good friends.

"He said, 'What are you doing here?' I said, 'I'm just trying to get the chance to come out and play some football with the team.' And I told him what happened. He said, 'I'll tell you what. If you can still run that ball like you used to, I'll get you a chance.' And he went in and saw Coach Woodruff.

"Charlie came out and told me to come out the second day. The first day they were going to take pictures. The second day, he said, 'They'll put you in pads.' And when the season started, I was playing. When Charlie got me the opportunity, that's all I was asking.

"The problem was Dick Jones. I don't know—I have always held it against him. That's just the way life goes. It was a great motivation—the fact that he had told me that I couldn't do it. I knew that I could. It was very motivational. To have a friend like Charlie LaPradd was the best thing."

Another new member of the team in 1952 was a 6'4", 190 pound athlete by the name of Doug Dickey. Dickey had gone to P.K. Young high school in Gainesville and had starred in football, basketball, and baseball. Though unrecruited, he was known to the coaching staff. After being asked to try out for the team by assistant coach Dave Fuller, who was also the baseball coach at Florida, Dickey quickly established himself as an excellent defensive back. Then in 1952 the college rules changed, and players had to be able to go both ways. Dickey was an outstanding defensive back, and the coaching staff would have had to bench him unless they also used him at quarterback. The unheralded Dickey rose from the seventh QB on the depth chart to become the starter.

Doug Dickey: "Colleges didn't recruit me after high school, probably because P.K. Young was a little school. I did have a scholarship offer from Ohio University, I could have gone up there, but I just decided to stay home and play for Florida. It was a time—Woodruff had come—it was exciting. I thought it would be a good place to be. I thought I was going to be a teacher, and I thought having a Florida degree to be a teacher would be the right thing to do. With my family background, that's kind of where I was headed— we're all preachers and teachers.

"I was working on the grounds department at the University of Florida for the summer, making a little money and getting ready to go to school. I was going to walk on in basketball and football. Another kid and I had actually tried out in baseball with Coach McAlister, but he didn't offer us anything.

"Dave Fuller, one of the assistant football coaches at the university, was also the baseball coach. He called me up and said, 'Look, we have six or seven quarterbacks out here, but I think you're as good as any of these guys. Why don't you get off the grounds department truck and come out for football?'

"This was the fall of 1950. I went as a walk-on. I remember getting in line—I was the seventh-string quarterback.

"I didn't even know how to put my hip pads on. One day I was trying to get dressed to go out for practice, and they were wearing equipment I had never seen.

"After a month or two, I ended up being a defensive back. I was about 6'2" and about 170 pounds. I remember playing a freshman football game against Tulane. Max McGee was playing against us. We rode the train to New Orleans, lost the game something like 35-14, and came back. I don't remember much about my freshman season other than that game.

"One of the members of my freshman class was Rick Casares, a fullback on our team. He and I played football, basketball, and baseball. He also threw the javelin on the track team. He was a four-sport athlete at the University of Florida, though he didn't play much baseball. He could play anything, do anything.

"The first semester I lived at home. Like I said, I was a walk-on. I got a half of a scholarship my second semester, and I moved into the athletic dorm with Rick and Joe D'Agostino my second semester. After that, I got on scholarship and lived in the dorm from then on."

When Haywood Sullivan took the $75,000 bonus from the Red Sox, Coach Woodruff was stuck for a quarterback. In 1950 Sullivan had set nine Florida records including best passing average (50.3%), most yards running and passing (1,170), and passing average for one game (7 for 7 against Kentucky).

The day Haywood Sullivan announced he was signing with the Red Sox and leaving the football team, Coach Woodruff and his staff put in a call to Nashville, Tennessee, where it summoned from his graduation ceremony 18-year-old Bobby Lance. Though Lance was only a freshman, in 1952 with all the soldiers off to the war in Korea, the NCAA decided that for the one year freshmen could play. Lance remembered how humbling it was for an 18-year-old to play on this team of veterans.

Bobby Lance: "I ended up going to the University of Florida because of Dick Jones, their great recruiter. Dick had been a hell of a recruiter at Georgia Tech, and my brother had signed with Georgia Tech, so Dick knew the family, and he saw me play, and he moved on to Florida with Bob Woodruff. So Dick Jones recruited me. He was the reason I went to Florida.

"I visited the campus and met the players. I don't see how anyone who's recruited can see the campus and the beautiful girls and the weather and not go to Florida. I was ready to get away from all the bad weather. And though it sounds corny, it was love at first sight.

"I was lucky as hell. It was graduation day, and I was on the stage getting my diploma at Dobbins-Bennett, and I got a phone call. They said, 'You have to get to Gainesville right now.' So I didn't have much of a graduation ceremony. I got on the next plane and headed to Gainesville.

"What had happened was good news, bad news. Florida had a great, great quarterback named Haywood Sullivan, and he was going to be a senior. But that day he signed with the Boston Red Sox for $80,000, which was a huge amount of money back then. The only quarterback we had behind him was Doug Dickey, who was about like me, a very average quarterback. Fred Robinson had a pretty good arm, but with the type of offense we were running, they needed a runner, not a passer. Fred had a fine arm, but throwing the ball wasn't in vogue. His arm was so much better than ours it was a joke. Fred should have gone to Georgia, where Wally Butts had fabulous pass patterns. It was a damn shame the limited time he got to play. He was a passer. The rest of us were runners.

"They were even thinking about putting Rick Casares at quarterback, which would have been a total waste of his talent. He was the best fullback in the country.

"I hustled down to Gainesville. I was lucky as hell, because all the boys were coming back from Korea, and they decided that freshmen could play. So I was able to sit on the bench freshman year with the varsity. That was 1952, the Gator Bowl team.

"Thinking back on it, it was pitiful. I'm looking at Charlie LaPradd, All-American, a paratrooper who was 25. I'm looking at Joe D'Agostino, 24. Reed Quinn was 26. And here's this little ole 18-year-old freshman. And I was thinking, What in the hell am I doing here?

"But we would have won the National Championship in '52 if Haywood had stayed, because he was a great, great quarterback, and the rest of us were average. Still, no one held it against Haywood. He was dirt poor from Dothan, Alabama, and I say dirt poor with all the respect to his mother and daddy. They couldn't help it. They didn't have any damn money. And he got $80,000 from the Red Sox, and much later on he befriended Mrs. Yawkey. Sharpies were trying to screw her out of her Boston Red Sox stock, and Sully sold his part for $52 million. Hey, he ain't poor now! But just a damn fine person, and one thing about that Gator Bowl team, Buford Long, who later played with the New York Giants, played three sports: baseball, track and football. Casares was All-SEC in football and basketball. Papa Hall had the world record in the high jump, 6'11 3/4," and back then we scissored. There wasn't any Fosbery Flop. The point I'm getting at is that those guys were all two- or three-sport lettermen.

"The rest of us were boys, and Rick [Casares] was a man. See, at age 16 he was New Jersey heavyweight boxing champion. A bad ass. And at one time in basketball he held the Coliseum scoring record with 32 points. He was great in baseball and in track, and God, he was one of the most modest people I've ever been around in my life.

"This was unheard of in the '50s, but Rick's mail would come in, and there would be pictures of nude women inviting him over for, you know, whatever. Imagine! My God, we would all hustle over there to help him open the mail!

"He was from Ybor City, and I remember he invited us to go with him to a nightclub there, and I knew we were in good shape when we walked in, and the girls were up there dancing, and they said, 'Hey, Ricky, hey.' And I said to the other guys, 'Boys, I think we've just struck gold.'

"He was just a master with women. He was so charasmatic. He was handsome, kind of a Greek type of guy, and he was so damn modest, and he could do all those Latino dances. He could walk into a place where no one knew who he was, and suddenly, here come the ladies. He was unbelievable.

"His roommate was Joe D'Agostino, God bless his heart. My friend, Larry Davis, who played against him, said, 'I know when they put me in there to block him, I haven't blocked him yet.' I said, 'Larry, nobody else in the Southeastern Conference has either.'

"What I recall as a young person was how unbelievably kind Joe and Rick and Art Wright, and Curt Haygood were to me. Just unbelievable people. And Sully came back to Florida in the off-season to coach, and the $80,000 didn't affect him one iota. He was terrific."

nine

The First Bowl Victory

With Haywood Sullivan on his way to the baseball major leagues, in 1952 Coach Woodruff had two viable choices. One option was to use weak-throwing but smart Doug Dickey at quarterback. The other was to shift Rick Casares from to fullback to quarterback. The drawback was that if Woodruff did that, he would lose perhaps the best running back in the country—Casares.

Casares, for one, knew exactly what he wanted to do.

Rick Casares: "I wanted to be a running back. Coach Woodruff started me at quarterback against Stetson, and in fact I threw three touchdown passes, and we won the game easily, but after the game was over I felt like I wasn't even in the ballgame. I was handing off the ball, and when the game was over, I felt like I hadn't even been in the game.

"If we had been smarter at the time, they would have made me a running quarterback. That would have been different. But Haywood had been a drop-back quarterback, and that was the formation we were using. I talked to Coach Woodruff about how I felt, and as I recall, that's when they started using Doug Dickey at quarterback."

Dickey may not have had a strong arm, but he was a brilliant strategist who called a fine game.

Red Mitchum: "[In 1952] they had gone away from platoon football, and you had to play both ways. Doug was tall at 6'4", weighed maybe 190, and he was extremely smart. They moved him to quarterback, and he did an outstanding job. He didn't throw the ball especially well. He was a catcher just like Haywood Sullivan. I told him the reason he could throw a baseball better than he could a football is because you can't throw a baseball end over end! But Doug did a great job of calling the plays and moving the ball, and he had the respect of everybody."

Joe D'Agostino: "Doug just wasn't the passer Rick was, but he had a very smart intellect."

After the Stetson blowout, Florida went to Atlanta to play Georgia Tech.

Tommy Haddock: "We were tied with only a few seconds to go when Pepper Rodgers kicked a field goal. [Tech won 17-14.] I do remember we were really dejected. [It was the second time in three years Tech defeated Florida on a last-second field goal.] But Coach Woodruff said to hold our head high, because we had played a good game. We played an outstanding team. We played them in their backyard. We played them off their feet in their backyard. The fact was, they won, but that's the way the ball bounces sometimes."

Doug Dickey: "The coaches weren't happy with what happened at Georgia Tech. They thought they were wasting Casares playing quarterback, so one day they called me and said, 'Come over here on offense. We want you to play quarterback. We're going to put Casares back at fullback.'

"I wasn't real happy about it at the time. I was the first-string safety man. I liked the guys I was with and liked my coach. Also, I never thought I was that good a player, but at the same time they wanted me to do it—they wanted me to call the plays. Back then the quarterback called all the plays. I could call the plays better than Casares could, and he could run the ball better than anyone else we had. That was part of the deal. I didn't have to do a lot of passing. What they wanted was for me to get the running game going with Long, Hall, and Casares. We had enough defense to play pretty well. So we were able to take Florida football to another level."

Rick Casares: "That year I was always getting moved around. I really wanted to be a running back. We never could get into a groove that year."

Doug Dickey: "The next game was against The Citadel. Johnny Rauch was the quarterback coach, and he started working with me every day. We beat

The Citadel [33-0], and then we beat Clemson [54-13]. We had a really good running game. We had backs who could run, and we had some second-string backs that weren't bad—Sam Oosterhaudt, Kent Stevens, and Tommy Haddock, people who were pretty dad-gum good. We were able to run the ball. I may have thrown a jump pass or two. I may have thrown a flat pass or two. I threw a touchdown pass somewhere along the way."

Rick Casares: "Poor Citadel was always outmanned. Their recruiting was difficult for them because they were a small military school. They really couldn't attract very much quality to play.

"Even though we beat Clemson so badly, I never was really happy, because we had so many running backs. You'd play most of one game, and I felt I had done well, and the next game I wouldn't start. We had about eight quality backs, and Coach Woodruff would rotate us. You'd get in a groove, and then you wouldn't play that much, which really was disheartening."

After the Clemson game, the University of Florida was ranked in the top ten in defense for the first time in memory. The defensive players reveled in their new-found and short-lived status.

Joe D'Agostino: "For many years our team had had no recognition, and in 1952 at one time we were seventh in the nation defensively. It was incredible. We got our recognition in the Jacksonville and the Miami papers. But their thought was, maybe this was just a fluke. The players didn't pay attention to the papers a bit. Not one bit."

It turned out to be shortlived as feared. The next week Florida was pounded by Vanderbilt by 20 to 13.

Tommy Haddock: "I injured my shoulder in practice the week before the Vanderbilt game. I went over a pile and landed on my shoulder. It just separated. I am bothered by this shoulder so bad now it's unbelievable. I still feel that the old physician, who was our team doctor, was partly to blame for what I have now, because he didn't know what the heck to do."

Bobby Lance: "The game was played in Nashville, and I remember it was colder'n hell. Everybody about froze to death."

Just as unexpectedly, in the next game Florida pulled the upset of the season. In his second try against the University of Georgia, Coach Woodruff came away with a 30-0 rout. The move to make Dickey the quarterback so he could return Casares to running back proved to be the right one. Dickey did an excellent job running the Florida offense, and Rick Casares had a career day. He carried the ball 27 times for 108 yards and a touchdown, and he kicked all the extra points and a 24-yard field goal.

Joe D'Agostino: "On the first play Arlen Jumper and a Georgia end by the name of Harry Babcock got into a fight. Both of them were thrown out. Arlen was from Texas, had a Texas attitude. The other guy was bad-mouthing him, and he was going to stop it right there and then. And boom, they just got into it."

Tommy Haddock: "Rick Casares ran for over a hundred yards and a touchdown. They finally got around to putting Rick back where he should have been—at fullback—instead of playing him at quarterback. What can you see other than Rick was just a heck of an athlete. He was a big guy, a powerful runner. He was an outstanding all-around athlete."

Rick Casares: "That Georgia game and the Loyola game stand out as games where I did a great deal. Besides the excitement leading up to the Georgia game, I particularly liked to beat Georgia, because I didn't really care for Wally Butts.

"I was recruited by the University of Georgia, and when I was there I saw one of their practices. I thought Coach Butts was really rough on his players. I didn't like the way he treated them. He was renowned for being a really tough coach. He was abrasive. I didn't like his style, and I quickly wrote off Georgia after visting them and seeing that.

"And when I went to the University of Florida, I really wanted to play well against them, cause of the rivalry and Coach Butts."

Joe D'Agostino: "We were really elated that we beat Georgia. We went into the shower, and we showed a lot of emotion, because they had beaten us so badly for so many years. But that was it."

Tommy Haddock: "In the next game we beat Auburn, and then we lost to Tennessee [26-12] and a big guy named Doug Atkins. They were a good team."

Joe D'Agostino: "Atkins was a six foot ten end. He was real tough. We put Andy Kozar, their All-American halfback, out of the game. We were all tackling him, and I caught him in the ribs, and that was it. Out he went.

"Atkins was very mean, a very good defensive end who deserved all the accolades he could get. He was disruptive, very hard to stop. I thought to myself, Thank goodness I'm on the defensive line!"

Next came a crucial game against seventh-ranked Tennessee.

Charlie LaPradd: "The only speech I remember Coach Woodruff ever making, and everybody will remember that one, was one he gave before the Tennessee game when we went up to play them.

"Before the game started, we were all in the locker room, and he was giving us a pre-game speech. He said, 'Boys, above all things, just remember, we're not beat yet.'

"The players turned around and looked at each other. We said, 'What the hell is he talking about, 'We're not beat yet'? We're not even on the field. You talk to anybody who played at that time. Everybody still talks about that."

Doug Dickey: "In the Tennessee game, physically they were stronger offensively than we were defensively. We couldn't keep them down enough. We broke a long run early, got another score, but that was it. [Florida lost 26-12.]

"But that season we finished up strong. We started by beating Miami badly [43-6].

Joe D'Agostino: "We carry memories with us. Art Wright played defensive guard, right next to me. He was the most underrated player at the university.

"One of my most vivid was that the referees kicked Art out of the Miami game. Art asked the referee, 'Am I out of the game?' He said, 'Yes, you are. Get off the field.'

"So Art ran back to the line and sucker-punched the guy who had instigated the business that got him kicked out of the game. Art wasn't going to go whimpering. He went up there and popped him and came off the field."

Doug Dickey recalled the strength of the Florida offense.

Doug Dickey: After Miami, we had a good game with Kentucky at home [a 27-0 win]. That was the year when we were high-powered offensively, and if the defense would get us anything at all, we'd get some things done running the ball, and I threw just a little bit. Freddie Robinson, who played behind me, could throw the ball pretty good, and so he would play some, and I would play some, and we got the offense going pretty good. There wasn't a lot of imagination to it. It was like, 'Do you want to run to the left or to the right or up the middle, or do you want the trap or the double whammy?' I'd study the defenses with the coaches, and I tried to call the plays. I guess they liked my play-calling ability. Anyway, it worked."

Tommy Haddock recalled the strength of the defense.

Tommy Haddock: "Great defensive players have a way of contributing to fumbles, and we had a damn good defensive ballclub. We had some guys who could crush you, like Charlie LaPradd, who was number one, and Joe D'Agostino, who was very good. Joe was a quick, good-rushing nose guard. He had the ability to move and the quickness. Bubba Ware at linebacker also was awfully good. We had some good guys who could play ball."

Doug Dickey: "After we beat Kentucky in Gainesville [27-0], Florida was invited to play in a bowl game for the first time in its history. Everybody was very excited."

Not everybody, not at first. The seniors, who were counting on winning the National Championship before the defection of Haywood Sullivan, were so disappointed that their initial vote was to skip any bowl game and go home. Their reasoning: If we can't play in the Sugar Bowl, we don't want to play anywhere.

Bobby Lance: "Charlie LaPradd and the other seniors got together, and they voted against going to the Gator Bowl. They said, 'We don't want to play in that. We should be playing for the national championship, so we're not going.'

"It's the damn truth, and if anyone denies it, they are a damn liar. I guarantee they voted against it. Then Woodruff and them took another vote and said, 'Everybody voted for it. We have to play.' But nobody knew where the 'yes' votes came from. I hate to be pinning this vote talk on you, being a Floridian. It was like the George W. Bush election."

After Woodruff rallied his troops, the excitement of playing in Florida's first bowl game grew.

Rick Casares: "There was a great deal of excitement among the guys, including myself. It surprises me, even thinking about it now, how excited we all were to be going to a bowl game."

Bobby Lance: "We trained at Ponte Vedra, which was very lavish. We stayed at The Inn, a posh place. I remember several years later Vanderbilt played in the Gator Bowl, and they asked me, 'Where did you train?' I said, 'Ponta Vedra.' They said, 'We stayed over at the Days Inn.'

"And what pissed me off, Rick Casares pleaded with Woodruff to let him play in the Gator Bowl basketball game the night before the football game, and Woodruff said, 'Oh no, if you got injured, they'd run me out of the state of Florida.' I wished he had let Rick play in both of them. It would not have bothered him. He could have played ten football games in a row and said, 'When is the eleventh one?'

"But Tulsa had a damn good football team, and I got to sit on the bench, and I was thrilled to death. I still have my program."

Joe D'Agostino: "We went to the Gator Bowl. There were a couple of other bowls we could have gone to, which we had wanted to, but Coach Woodruff decided that Jacksonville was better because it was closer, and to get us to go there, he told us that after the game we would take a cruise to the islands, but after the game nothing occured. We just all went our separate ways. And that disappointed us."

More disappointing was the serious hamstring pull that quarterback Doug Dickey suffered before the Gator Bowl game against Tulsa. Nevertheless, Florida won 14-13. J. Papa Hall was the star of the game, as he ran 94 yards in 17 carries and caught two passes for 66 yards.

The game should have ended in a tie when Rick Casares missed the extra point after the second Florida touchdown, but Tulsa was whistled for being offsides. Casares got another chance, and this time he kicked it through for the winning point. For the first time in its history, the University of Florida was a bowl winner.

Doug Dickey: "I can remember the last practice before we went to the Gator

Bowl, we were running wind sprints. I pulled a muscle in my hamstring, the worst injury I've ever had in athletics. My leg turned black and blue from it, and I really couldn't play in the game. I played a little bit, and Freddie Robinson played most of the game. I threw a screen pass to Jay Hall, and he went down to the one-yard line, and he scored. I couldn't hardly walk, much less run, so I didn't play much. I didn't get to participate as much as I would have liked to in that game."

Bobby Lance: "Tulsa had these huge players, and they were all ganged up to stop Casares, and along comes Papa Hall, who was a world-class sprinter. Good God, he ran a legitimate 9.6. Jay was a big man, 6'1", 180 pounds then, plus he had those high jumping skills. He's one of those guys whose legs look like they start under his armpits. Jay had phenomenal speed."

Rick Casares: "I wasn't used much in the game, surprisingly. That was Coach Woodruff. I was unhappy. If I had to do it over again...I shouldn't say that because of the guys. I loved the guys. We were really close. It's what's great about team sports."

Tommy Haddock: "Winning the Gator Bowl meant a lot to us. It just made us very proud. We felt like we had accomplished something. We had talked about wanting to go, and there weren't very many bowls at that time. It was a big honor for us to be invited to the Gator Bowl. Of course, the Gator Bowl committee had always wanted the opportunity to invite the Gators to the Gator Bowl. It was quite nice. We had a good time. We played Tulsa, who was the scoring champions of college football that year.

"We did what the coaches told us and worked hard and wound up beating them by one point.

"At the end of the game we tied the game on a touchdown, and then Rick [Casares] lined up to kick the extra point, and he missed, and I was holding, and I remember how disappointed I felt, but Tulsa was offsides, and I remember when I found out it was against them and that we'd get another chance feeling back on top of the world, and after we got another shot at it, this time he made it. We were a happy bunch of guys."

Doug Dickey: "We beat Tulsa, and we were all excited. We had a big banquet and I got a wallet or belt or something from the Gator Bowl as a prize. But what we reflect upon is that we were the first team. I played on the first high school eleven-man team, the first bowl team for Florida—those things have been firsts in my life—you think of the special moments, and that was one of those special moments."

Doug Dickey: "This was the best Florida season since 1928, and Coach Woodruff gets the credit for that. He recruited a lot of us. Bear Wolf had signed that earlier class. Coach Woodruff signed my class, which was the first class, and there were a bunch of walk-ons too. Coach Woodruff went after the numbers game really good and knew how to deal with that. But he had a really good coaching staff, Hank Foldberg, Dale Hall, Johnny Rauch, and John Eibner, a good offensive line coach who had been a pro player. Some of the coaches—Hobe Hoosier and Johnny Mauer—used the Tennessee-style defense. He didn't have enough defensive coaches, like we do it today. But it was a really good group of men who we played for. They got something done. They set a new standard in Florida athletics."

Tommy Haddock: "Coach Woodruff was a great guy. He was a very quiet individual who was big on delegating authority. During the '52 season the guys who did the strategy and the substituting were Hank Foldberg, the line coach, and Dale Hall, the backfield coach for the offense, and for the defense Hobe Hoosier, the defensive line coach, and Coach Mauer, the defensive backfield coach. Mauer was in the press box, and Hoosier was on the field. Coach Woodruff would have a say so once in a while, and then they'd do what they thought they needed to. But when they talk about who at Florida was the one who started the modern era, you need to go back to Coach Woodruff, because he really did."

ten

A One-Platoon Disaster

Tommy Haddock: "The thing that hurt us in 1953 was that we were geared for two platoons, and that year the NCAA knocked out the two platoons and made it a single platoon. Everybody had to go both ways. If you started a quarter and came out, you couldn't go back in until the next quarter. That was a killer. Oh, it KILLED us. It hurt us bad, just really bad.

"It hurt me more than anybody because Coach Mauer thought I was too small to play defensive halfback. They primarily let me play when we had the ball. They'd leave me in to play a little defense, and I could run. I didn't get burned too bad."

Doug Dickey: "Going back to one-platoon football was bad. General Neyland [at Tennessee] probably put that sucker in. It was a cost-containment move. Teams had so many players. The big teams were trying to travel and it cost too much. It was a dumb thing. It was horrible to have to go back like that.

"So basically what we did was put the defense on the first string. I was the only guy on the team that played both ways, so I became the quarterback for the first string. Because the defense was going to go out there first, and so we tried to play the best offense we could. Behind me I had Larry Scott and Bob Davis, who had been defensive halfbacks the year before. We didn't get much done, and then the next group, which had more of the offensive stars from the year before, they came in, but all of our offensive stars were gone.

"The second team had Bobby Lance at quarterback, and behind him were Freddie Robinson and Harry Spears. I lost my punting job. Spears could punt, so he punted in my place.

"Also Rick Casares had had a car accident during the summer and got hurt and didn't play much, just two or three games. And in the summer I sprained an ankle, and in the fall I suffered a rib injury. It was not a good year for me, though we had a big win against Georgia."

Joe D'Agostino: "We opened the season losing to Rice [20–16. Florida was ranked 15th in the country, Rice 12th.] Dickie Moegel scored three touchdowns against us. It was the first game I had to play both ways, and it was terrible.

"For some reason the coach wanted us to run sweeps that game, and after you've run two or three sweeps in the row and you then go back on defense, you're tired. So I don't think it was used very properly."

The next game, played in Gainesville, was against third-ranked Georgia Tech. The result was a memorable 0-0 tie in unforgettable weather conditions.

Bobby Lance: "We played the game in a hurricane, but back then it didn't stop the game. You couldn't have had a dry ball if you had 6,000 balls. There was six to eight inches of water on the field. What the official had to do, he put his foot on the ball so it wouldn't float down the field. Even as great as Rick was, his punting average that day was about four yards. So finally someone beat on Woodruff's head and said, 'Heyloo, this ain't worth a damn. Just run a quarterback sneak on fourth down.'

"[Georgia halfback] Bill Tease was going around left end, and Curt Haygood tripped him, and that preserved the tie. Because a 0-0 tie against Georgia Tech was a hell of a win. Tech was a much better football team. No question about it. They were better."

Joe D'Agostino: "We stopped Georgia Tech maybe five times inside our fifteen yard line. We were just tough. We got across the line faster than they could hit us. We hit them first. We disrupted their rhythm, stopped them from scoring.

"Rick Casares saved the game with a long punt to get us out of danger at the end of the game. It was joyous to play with Rick."

But Rick Casares' college football career ended after the Georgia Tech game when he was drafted into the army.

Bobby Lance: "During the summer Rick got into a tragic car accident in Tampa. He was driving a woman's Cadillac convertible, and it ran off the causeway, and she died, and he was beat nine ways to hell and back. It was a tragic accident.

"They sent him to the army to Fort Jackson."

There was another reason as well. The Korean War was on, and some parents of soldiers were outraged that athletes, both pro and amateur, were getting preferential treatment. Casares got his notice to report after the Georgia Tech game.

Rick Casares: "There was a big, nationwide investigation going on into the preferential treatment of athletes. I was told that someone on the Tampa draft board didn't like that I was going to school. I didn't think there was any way they could draft me. My grades were good. But they were able to do it. And what's unbelievable, I had a slight separated shoulder. I couldn't lift my arm all the way up. When I went for my physical, the first doctor wouldn't take the responsibility for passing me. He sent me to an Air Force doctor, who declared me fit to serve.

"At the time I was heartbroken, but it turned out to be the best thing that ever happened to me. Instead of going from college to the pros, I went to Fort Jackson in Columbia, South Carolina, for eighteen weeks of basic training, which was murder."

There to greet him was his old teammate, Haywood Sullivan.

Haywood Sullivan: "Rick went into the Army, and when he came into the Army, I was there at reception, to receive him.

"See, I signed to play professional baseball after the '51 season. Rick was still in school, which would have been our senior year, and I was already in the army when he was forced to join up. He was drafted into the Army, and I was at the reception center at Fort Jackson, South Carolina, when he came through. I got him on the football team up there."

Rick Casares: "I liked being the army. I was one of their best soldiers. They thought I would be one of those goof-off jocks, but I had gone through ROTC, and I knew the basics. I was an officer, so I knew all the hand maneuvers with a gun and the marching maneuvers, and I was good with a gun. My company had me marking targets, I shot so well.

"I was in the army two years. I played football in the army, went both ways. I played fullback and linebacker and made the all-service team, which was all the services. I never left Columbia, South Carolina. We had a general who was crazy about athletics. We had the best football, basketball, and baseball teams in the whole Third Army, because he kept everyone there.

"In the army I got bigger and stronger and faster. The Chicago Bears drafted me in 1954. I was a Floridian, and it was cold as hell in Chicago, but I loved it. I had a Jersey interior. I loved the cold weather, and I was never hard to get along with, and I believed in working harder than anybody, and I fit right in."

Bobby Lance: "I had some friends up in Fort Jackson with Rick. They said, 'The things he did sportswise were unbelievable.' Paul Brown, the coach of the Cleveland Browns, once said to me, 'He was the greatest fullback I've ever seen come out of college.' I said, 'Then what happened?' He said, 'Along came Jim Brown.'

"But I once looked Rick up in the Bears' media guide, and he had a [12-year] career, and his accomplishments were big. I remember talking to Bill Wade, who went to high school with me at Montgomery-Bell Academy. Bill played 13 years in the NFL, and on the Bears he played with Joe Fortunato, Richie Petitbon, and Doug Atkins, and he said that Rick Casares was the greatest athlete he had ever seen."

In 1956 Rick Casares scored 14 touchdowns for the Bears. That year he led the National Football League in rushing with 1,126 yards and was second in scoring behind quarterback Bobby Layne. More important to Casares, he led the Bears to the title game against the New York Giants. He would go on to a stellar pro career, scoring 360 points in his twelve-year career.

After football, Rick married a woman whose father owned the Tampa Bay dog track. He is still involved in the running of the track today.

The loss of Rick Casares was a blow to the Florida team. Haywood Sullivan, who was helping Woodruff coach the backs, recalled how fortunate the Gators were to have a deep group of fine backs behind him.

Haywood Sullivan: "We had Buford Long, Fred Nichols, and Sam Oosterhoudt and three or four others, a pretty dern good backfield. Our backs were as good as anybody in the conference. It was a matter of our offensive line doing the things they were supposed to do."

After a 26-13 loss to Kentucky, Florida thrashed Stetson by the score of 45-0. The offensive highlight came in a 60-0 walloping of The Citadel.

Tommy Haddock: "The first team, which was the defensive team, went in and after the first quarter the score was 0-0. In the second quarter the offensive team from '52 was in, and we moved the ball pretty good on them. Dickie Allen scored three times in that quarter. Dickie was a pretty good little quarterback. He could throw the ball well."

Bobby Lance: "Dick Allen was a damn good quarterback, a good athlete from Atlanta. Tommy Haddock had come back from a military career. He was a very small man from Jacksonville, but just as tough as a knot, and it was a real thrill for me whenever Tommy scored, because he wasn't a frontline player like Papa Hall or Buford Long or Rick Casares, but he was a phenomenal person. On any sports team you always have a favorite. There were some people who I played with, if I never saw them again, that would be fine with me, because all they thought about was their selves, and that don't do nothing for me. But Tommy, whenever he scored, it just thrilled me to death."

The next week Florida played LSU in their Homecoming game. The game ended in a 21-21 tie.

Joe D'Agostino: "Curt Haygood was supposed to start in my place because I was hurt. I had separated my shoulder, and they put my left arm to my chest and wrapped it, so I only had one arm.

"Curt had invited his parents and all his friends up to the game because he was starting, and I was so happy for him, because he really had worked very hard for all those years.

"We were downstairs before we were to go out onto the field, and I was half asleep, because I knew I wasn't going to play, and Coach Woodruff looked at me and said, 'How do you feel?' I said, 'Oh, fine.' What else are you going to say? He said, 'You're starting.' And Curt's mouth dropped. My mouth dropped. I was so bitterly disappointed for Curt. It was a rotten thing to do. I loved Coach Woodruff, but I thought he did a disservice to Curt. He did get in. He played some. But he didn't start, and that was a bad move.

"I played an awful lot of that LSU game with a bad shoulder, and I shouldn't have. I should have faked an injury, but I'm not the sort of person to do that. That's not the way you do things."

Bobby Lance: "I do recall we were damn lucky to tie them. I really did think LSU had a better football team than we did."

After the tie with LSU came a 16-7 loss to Auburn. Though Florida's Mal Hammack KOed Auburn's star quarterback Vince Dooley, Florida still wasn't able to win the ballgame.

Tommy Haddock: "I remember in the Auburn game, Macky Hammack, who was playing linebacker, hit Vince Dooley, the Auburn quarterback, and we thought he had killed him. Macky just absolutely crushed him, knocking him out of the game. That was the reason I always thought that Macky would have played linebacker in the pros. He played for the St. Louis Cardinals, but they made a running back out of him."

The Florida record stood at 2-3-2 when it faced Georgia in the Gator Bowl. Once again, it was time to play THE GAME, the one Coach Woodruff had been hired to win, and for the second year in a row, he did what he promised to do as the Gators won 21-7 in a nationally televised game.

Doug Dickey: "The highlight of the season was the Georgia game. I remember [Georgia coach] Wally Butts had made the quote that I was the only knuckleball quarterback in college football. Well, somehow I managed to throw a touchdown pass. The guys kidded me afterward. They said, 'When you threw it, I thought it was going out of the stadium, but it finally came down.'

"I remember knocking down a [Zeke] Bratkowski pass in the end zone late in the game to prevent a touchdown. We managed to carry the day. That was the main moment of the year for that team.

"We had a 3-5-2 year. We tied two games [Georgia Tech 0-0 and LSU 21-21], and we had a couple of tough losses [Tennessee 7-Florida 6, Miami 14-Florida 10.]"

As a capper to a disappointing year, Florida lost the final two games of the season to Tennessee and Miami. What Bobby Lance remembers above all else in the Tennessee loss was the ferocity of Mal Hammack.

Bobby Lance: "We were 3-5-2 in '53, but we didn't have a bad team. After those horses left [J. Papa Hall, Buford Long, and Rick Casares] there was a meltdown. That was the year Mal Hammack came in from junior college. There were few people I ever played with who equalled the courage of Mal Hammack. Mal was BAD news. He could knock your ass off. He played 13 years on special teams for the [Chicago and St. Louis] Cardinals. To play special teams you have to be insane. I used to hate to run down on kickoffs. I'm a nice guy, and I could get the hell knocked out of me. But Mal was a very different person, on the same vein with Casares.

"I remember the Tennessee game. They had a great big tackle by the name of Darryl McCormick. He was a huge man for that day, probably 220. I caught a punt, and Mal was back there blocking for me, and he hit the guy. Mal didn't weigh but 195. But when he hit the guy, his eyes looked like a Las Vegas slot machine. Mal knocked him out. I will never forget it.

"Mal was one of these guys: they said Rocky Marciano could hit you with a six-inch punch and nearly tear your head off. Mal had that ability to explode.

"I remember Coach Woodruff would say, 'We're going to scrimmage today,' and he'd name who was on which team, and I just prayed I was on Mal's team! I didn't want him knocking my ass off."

Against Tennessee, Florida led 7-6 with only minutes to go when Pat Shires kicked a 9-yard field goal for the Vols.

Joe D'Agostino: "Any loss is disappointing, but when you go so far as to think you have the game won, and you're fighting hard to make sure you win, and then you lose, it's very, very disappointing. And against Miami we were winning late in the game, and they scored twice to beat us. We finished 3-5-2. It wasn't very good, was it, though I must say that the defense only allowed 11 points a game. We did have a fine defense."

Doug Dickey: "It was a weird year. I had an injury or two, Casares didn't get started then left, and for the coaches it was a mix that wasn't good. Things just didn't come together right, with the linemen groups trying to play both ways."

Bobby Lance: "With the material we had, it was almost absurd not to be undefeated, but we did lose Haywood Sullivan. Let's say if the [2001] Florida team had lost Rex Grossman, there might have been three more losses. I would say Coach Woodruff was a 'good' coach. We didn't have a 'great' coach like Steve Spurrier."

After Joe D'Agostino graduated, he returned to his parents' restaurant in Orlando for a few years. Injuries from football then began taking their toll. He got his knee fused. He had his knee joint removed. Later, doctors took out a shoulder joint. In 1976, he was disabled.

Says D'Agostino, "Left me pretty much with nothing to do. and that's what I've been doing since 1976. Other than that, I'm in good health."

After Doug Dickey graduated, he had a one-year ROTC commitment. His wife was pregnant, and he wanted the baby born in Florida, so in the fall of 1954 he took a job as assistant football coach, head soccer coach, and head swimming coach at St. Petersburg High School.

In 1955 Dickey entered the army and became a pilot. He was assigned to Fort Carson, Colorado, where he was assigned the task of running the rifle range. He knew the athletic director of the base, and told him he could do a better job coaching the football team than the person doing it at the time. He was given the job.

In the fall of 1957 Dickey's team won the All-Army championship. Fort Carson was selected to play Fort Dix, New Jersey, in the Satellite Bowl in Cocoa Beach, Florida. Fort Dix also had pros. When the Fort Carson quarterback went AWOL, Dickey had to suit up and play. He threw two touchdown passes, and Fort Carson won the game. When he returned to the base, the general told him, "Listen, if there's anything I can do for you, call me."

Two months later Dickey received a call from Arkansas coach Frank Broyles, who had an opening for an assistant. Dickey told Broyles he owed the army another year of service, but he said he'd make a phone call. He called the general. He told him, "Listen, we're not at war with anybody. How about getting me out?" They said he could if he joined the Arkansas national guard. It was the start of the long, distinguished career in football, including a stint as head coach of the University of Florida from 1970 through 1978.

Doug Dickey today is athletic director at the University of Tennessee.

eleven

An SEC Championship Slips Away

Coach Woodruff realized that the team needed to bolster its coaching staff, and to that end in 1954 he brought in two former Army coaches, line coach Hank Foldberg and backfield coach Dale Hall, who had been the fourth back in the famed backfield of Doc Blanchard, Glenn Davis, Arnie Tucker, and Dale Hall.

Bobby Lance: "Foldberg and Hall were extremely bright. The linemen worshipped Foldberg. He was a great, big man who had been an All-American at Army. He was a phenomenal line coach. The linemen were not afraid of him exactly—perhaps respect would be a better word. But he didn't allow any grab ass. He was all business and a hell of a coach."

One of the emerging stars on the Florida starting lineup was a sophomore running back by the name of Jackie Simpson. A broken field specialist, Simpson came out of Miami to become one of the greatest backs in Florida history. He was elected into the University of Florida Hall of Fame in 2001.

Jackie Simpson: "I was recruited by Florida, Florida State, Tennessee, and Georgia. I chose Florida because I had a couple of friends, Ray Brown and Larry Dyal, whom I had played with in high school and who were a year ahead of me. Also, I liked the atmosphere of Gainesville. I just wanted to be a Gator, I guess.

"When I enrolled in 1953, freshmen were allowed to play on the varsity. That year the NCAA switched to one-platoon football. Once you came out, you couldn't go back in until the next quarter. I thought it was a stupid rule myself. I didn't like it.

"The first couple of years Coach Woodruff had two teams. He called one the orange team and the other the blue team.

"The highlight for me that first year was just making the varsity team. I thought that was pretty big. I remember in '53 we played Stetson, which was a very, very small school. That was the first game I got to play in a lot. I scored four touchdowns, but two were called back. Twice somebody was offsides.

"In '54 we still had the orange team and the blue team. Some of the better players went both ways. We opened the season getting beat by Dickie Moegel and Rice [34-14]."

Bobby Lance: "I started the Rice game at quarterback, and as I recall, I played poorly. Back then the quarterback called all the plays. I don't want to make us rocket scientists when we weren't. You had a pattern you went by, but basically you called the whole damn thing.

"I played poorly against Rice. I remember I came over to the sideline, and Woodruff said, 'You've called the last ten plays to the left. Do we have any that go to the right?' In other words, Dumb ass, wake up here, pal."

Jackie Simpson: "We went to Georgia Tech, which was ranked fifth in the country, and we beat them 13-12. We got up for the game. It was a very tough game. It wasn't like we beat them at home; we beat them there.

"Doug Dickey was our quarterback. He was a big guy for a quarterback. He was good. He was very intelligent. That's why Woodruff liked him. He would call the plays most of the time.

"In that game I scored a touchdown on a sweep, and I broke off a long run, a fifty or sixty yard kickoff return. Some guy just caught me by the foot."

Bobby Lance: "Jackie Simpson was an All-American at Senior High in Miami. He was a very gifted, an excellent defensive player, and a phenomenal open-field runner and an excellent punt returner. Jackie, and the other back, Jim Rountree, were unbelievably modest. Jackie was a phenomenal person.

"I remember in the Georgia Tech game, I came over to the sidelines. My foot was killing me, because someone had stepped on my foot. My shoe was ripped. We taped up the shoe, and I went back into the game.

"Also somewhere during the game, somebody took his fist on a play I ran and rammed it into my face and broke my nose. We wore those itty bitty face masks. I had blood everywhere.

"I scored a touchdown on a quarterback keep from seven or eight yards out—an option to the left—and that put us up 12-6, and then Dick Allen kicked the extra point to make it 13-6.

"Tech had damn good kickers, but we won when Bill Tease missed an extra point. Really, Tech should have won, but they missed both extra points.

"After we won, we flew back to Gainesville, and when we tried to land, they had trouble getting the students off the airfield. Finally we got our ass off the plane, and down at 13th Street they started a bonfire and burned up a traffic light! So it was pandemonium because it was a huge upset.

"So I remember the bonfire, my broken nose, and one of the few touchdowns I scored. And my dad was in the stands, so that was a big deal. But quite candidly, Tech had a better team than we did."

Jackie Simpson: "In the next game we beat Auburn 19-13. Bobby Lance had an 84-yard run. Bobby was a good runner. He was fast for a quarterback. We really didn't throw a lot. Recently I was looking at some statistics. We may have thrown the ball seven or eight times a game—that's nothing."

Bobby Lance: "The next game we lost to Clemson [14-7]. Clemson had these tough-ass country boys, and they threw me out of bounds and dislocated my shoulder, and as I was lying there trying to recover, they were spitting tobacco juice in my face and kicking me. Horrible sportsmanship. I went out of the game and didn't come back."

Jackie Simpson: "Then we beat Kentucky [21-7]. We needed to beat LSU to lead the SEC, but they beat us pretty good [20-7]."

Bobby Lance: "What I remember most about the LSU game was the dumbest thing I've ever heard in my life. We were in the locker room before the game, and everybody was in awfully good mental shape, paying attention.

"Woodruff said, 'Be quiet just a minute.' He said, 'You have to realize that even if we lose this game, we'll still be tied for the SEC title.' I thought, What in the hell is this man thinking? And we didn't disappoint him. We went right out there and lost.

"The other thing I remember about the game was that LSU knocked Curt Haygood out. He was laying down at the end of the field, and finally someone said, 'You know, someone is laying down at the end of the field, for God sakes. Go see if he's dead.'

"But the thing I remember most was that absolutely horrible thing that Woodruff said before the game. In retrospect, he was trying reverse psychology, saying, 'Just go out and play. Don't worry about it, because even if we lose, we're going to be tied for the lead.' He was trying to relieve the pressure. But if it had been me, I would have had a different type of talk.

"And that day we played awful. I played awful. I stunk up the joint, but I had a lot of company."

Jackie Simpson: "Next was Mississippi State. It was Homecoming. We played a sloppy game. [Florida fumbled nine times.] In fact, I had just gotten out of bed with the flu. I fumbled on the goal line. Buster Hill, our offensive tackle, landed on it, recovered the fumble, and we beat them 7-0.

"Georgia was next. If we beat them, we would have won the SEC championship. [Florida lost 14-13]. Then we beat Tennessee [14-0] in Knoxville. Ray Brown, whom I had gone to high school with, scored a touchdown on a long [70 yard] pass [from Dickie Allen]."

Bobby Lance: "Raymond had good hands. It was the only touchdown he scored in his career, but I'll be damned if I know why. He was a very tough individual.

"What I remember about the Tennessee game was that I dislocated both of my big toes, and they put splints in my shoes, like tongue depressors, and I had to run on the sides of my feet. It wasn't one of my better memories.

"I don't know why they didn't score. Tennessee had a damn good team. But Coach Woodruff had been a Tennessee guy, and Hobe Hoosier and Johnny Mauer, and they were thrilled beyond words to go up there and beat their alma mater."

And so although the 1954 season ended with a 5-5 record, the year wasn't as disappointing as the record may have indicated. All five wins came against SEC teams. The next year would be a disappointment.

Jackie Simpson: "In 1955, my junior year, we won the opener against Mississippi State [by 20-14]. State led 7-0, and Bobby Lance, the quarterback, called a trap play going up the middle. I got the ball, and it just broke clear. I scored on a 49-yard run.

"Then later on in the game, when they were driving down to score on us, I intercepted the ball on the goal line and ran it back a hundred yards. That was great.

"I can close my eyes and picture it—it was in the right hand corner of the end zone in the South end. The end came out and ran what you call a square-out. He's supposed to come down and plant his foot and run a square-out to the sideline. The quarterback let the ball go, and I saw it coming so I just went in front of him and took it. I went a hundred yards. I didn't really have that many people to beat. For one thing, we were over on one side, and he threw to the other side. They said there was one guy chasing me, supposedly one of their sprint guys on the track team. I had the angle on him, so he didn't get me.

"I held the record for just one year. The next year Joe Brodsky tied it. He went a hundred yards against Mississippi State the next year. In fact, he set a record that game for the most yardage after he intercepted three passes in one game."

Bobby Lance: "The only thing I remember about his 100 yard interception and runback was that he yelled, 'I got it,' and I went and blocked the guy they were throwing the pass to. Quarterbacks aren't usually very good blockers—I probably made three blocks the whole time I was there—and that was one I made, and Jackie ran down the field and scored."

Jackie Simpson: "Our next game was against Georgia Tech, and I thought we should have won the game. I had a pretty good game. I had about 90 yards rushing, but we had chances to beat them and we just didn't get the job done. [Tech won 14-7.]

"And then we got shut out [13-0] by Auburn up at Auburn. I had a 65 or 70 yard run, and I got knocked out of bounds. Maybe if we would have scored on the play, we might have been in the game."

Bobby Lance: "All of us stunk up the joint. But Auburn was a horrible place to play. You stayed in this country hotel, which was four stories, no air conditioning, and the bastards rang cow bells all night long to keep you awake. You couldn't call the police. They were probably down there encouraging them.

"I didn't like to play Auburn. They were like Clemson, terrible sportsmen and dirty players. Florida has never ever been a dirty football team. It's just not the character of the school."

Jackie Simpson: "We then beat LSU [18-14]. Jim Rountree had a great game. [On one play Rountree took a handoff from Bobby Lance and ran 59 yards for a touchdown.] Rountree and I started out together as kids. We played Little League football together. Then he went to a different high school, Miami Jackson. He was a great runner, played both ways. He could catch the ball. He could throw the ball. He was just a super athlete."

Bobby Lance: "I remember Jimmy running. Jimmy was a very gifted runner, and he and Simpson were hellacious boxers. Damn, hell, I was down at Jacksonville Beach one night, and someone said to me, 'There are two guys down here who kill people.' I said, 'What are you talking about?' He said, 'Two little bitty guys.' And I went over there, and some sailors had jumped them, and Jackie Simpson and Jimmy Rountree had knocked out four or five of them. I mean, there was blood everywhere. They just loved to fight, and they were damn good at it.

"To get to the scoring line, Jimmy would run over half the people on the football field."

Jackie Simpson: "Joe Brodsky also was really good, but he was hurt a lot. He had a couple of bad injuries. We had good athletes at Florida. I don't know why we didn't put it together. We should have been a lot better than we were."

After Florida shut out George Washington 28-0, they lost to Kentucky 10-7, when a substitute quarterback named Delmar Hughes kicked a field goal with 34 seconds left in the game.

Bobby Lance: "As far as Hughes having a broken nose, they accused Coach Woodruff the play before of ordering a player by the name of Weldon Lockhart, who kicked Hughes in the face with no mask and broke his nose, to do it. That was totally untrue.

"Against Kentucky I scored a touchdown from 14 or 15 yards out, and later in the game at a critical point, I gave the ball to Bob Visser and pulled it out, and I ran seven or eight yards for a first down, and the referee blew the whistle and ruled the play dead. I was cussing out the officials. Nowadays they would have thrown me out of the game.

"I said, 'I'm up here with the ball. It's a first down.'

"He said, 'You need to shut up.'

"I said, 'You need to shut up, because after the game I'm going to stomp the hell out of you.' So they beat us, and we were a much better team than Kentucky, but we didn't win."

Jackie Simpson: "The next week against Georgia, I played, and we won [19-13] when Jim Rountree had a big game. [He scored twice.]"

Bobby Lance: "I remember that one well. We were behind 13-0 at the half. We hadn't scored. And Woodruff had worked us like dogs that week. I got up in the locker room during halftime and said, 'What are we doing, guys? We haven't scored a touchdown. We're laying around. We worked our asses off all this week…and everyone started yelling, 'Yeah, yeah, this is awful….'

"So Georgia kicked off, and Jim Rountree took the kickoff and went 80 yards and scored, and from then on it was all downhill. As soon as he made that great run, that was it. We were going to beat them. Jim was the ignition that got it started."

Jackie Simpson: "Homecoming against Tennessee was next, and we didn't do anything. Tennessee had a good football team. They had Johnny Majors. We just didn't show up. [Florida was shut out 20-0.]"

Bobby Lance: "Johnny Majors was the tailback for Tennessee, and he had a fine game, and there was a boy from Gainesville named Bronson who played fullback at Tennessee, and that pissed us all off because we couldn't score a touchdown at Homecoming and some guy from Gainesville beat us!

"Johnny Majors was the star of that game. You could never get an angle on him. He was like Tony Dorsett. Nobody ever hit Dorsett because he was angling you all the time. You couldn't hit him head on. Son of a bitch, Johnny was amazing. He was 165 pounds, but he had unbelievably large hands like Julius Erving. He was one of the greatest punters ever to play in the SEC, and he wasn't bad at passing either. He would have made a hell of an option quarterback.

"Johnny was a nice man who was treated horribly by the University of Tennessee. Horrible. I live in Nashville, and these bastards, if you beat them, every sports page has a mile long excuse. I get awful tired of hearing about the Big Orange."

Jackie Simpson: "We then lost to Vanderbilt [21-6] up there. We got to the two-yard line when the gun went off for the half."

Bobby Lance: "I played in that game, and we were going in on the four yard line—I almost had a gimme touchdown—and I fumbled. I played a horrible game in front of my parents and a lot of relatives. It was a freezing cold day, and we were absolutely awful, and the morale on the team on a scale of 1 to 10 was maybe a 2.

"I hate to say it, but I swear to God I think everybody about gave up. We had zero emotion. Including myself. It didn't look like anybody gave a damn. If it works, fine, if it doesn't, the hell with it, let's go back to Gainesville. We're freezing to death.'

"It was a horrible senior season."

Jackie Simpson: "In the last game in '55, we lost to Miami [by a point, 7-6. Florida was a four-touchdown underdog.].

"We were heavy underdogs that day, and we played well. I almost broke a punt for a touchdown, went about sixty yards, but some guy got me or we probably would have won the game."

Bobb Lance: "The only player on our team who was unbelievable that day was Jackie Simpson, because he had had a hamstring pull and had it taped, and they shot him full of Novocain, and he damn near scored at the end of the game. Had he had his regular legs, he would have scored, and we would have won. No question about it.

"I just remember the heroic thing Jackie did. A hamstring pull is painful, but he played through that pain and was one tough-ass. And I'll be frank, I was absolutely delighted when that damn season was over, because it was just miserable."

Jackie Simpson: "We finished the season 5-5. I liked Coach Woodruff. He was a good coach, though he was probably a little too easygoing. We had some guys—Rountree, Brodsky and myself—who could catch the football, but they would never swing us out of the backfield and throw the ball to us. I could never understand that. When you only throw the ball seven or eight times a game…. But back then none of the schools really threw much.

"And you didn't go to the quarterback and say, 'Hey, throw me the ball.' You just didn't do it. I just felt that maybe we were a little too old-fashioned. I could throw the football, but in '56 I threw one touchdown pass, to Rountree, against Auburn. But Coach Woodruff didn't let us throw the ball much. Rountree could throw it too."

Bobby Lance: "In my judgment during the years I played at Florida, basically the teams had bad attitudes. They didn't present themselves as winners. If we lost one game, everybody sulked around. Well, damn, get on with the next program. And I think it gets back to coaching. When Steve Spurrier came to Florida, he said, 'I can't believe the way these players think. Gosh, I hope we can make third in the SEC. Wouldn't that be wonderful?' He said, 'What are you talking about?'

"We never had that killer instinct of 'Gee, we're tops in the SEC. Let's knock their asses out today.' I don't think we had that attitude. It's a horrible admission, but it's the damn truth."

After graduation Bobby Lance was drafted by the Green Bay Packers in the sixteenth round. Before heading north to Wisconsin, he first had to fulfill his duties to the armed forces. He went to the Brook Army Medical Center, where he played on the base football team along with Harlan Hill, the great receiver for the Chicago Bears.

He arrived in Green Bay and played the exhibition season with Paul Hornung, Jimmy Taylor, Bart Starr, Jerry Kramer and Ray Nitschke.

Bobby Lance: "I didn't make the Packer team. There are superstars in the NFL and the next level are the great players. I was a good player, and there is no room for good players in the NFL. No way. Then, now or ever. Wasn't no room for a good ole boy. Sent his ass back home."

A little lost, Lance decided to go back to school, and he got a master's degree in banking from Northwestern University. For the last thirty-five years Lance has been involved in mortgage banking and real estate.

"I like to buy land and get it zoned and resell it," he says. "I have a nice lifestyle."

twelve

Dunn and Heckman

Jimmy Dunn, one of the finest quarterbacks ever to perform at the University of Florida, came perilously close to going elsewhere because the Florida brain trust thought him at 5'9", 133 pounds too small to play in the SEC. When Florida State offered him a one-year, make-good scholarship, Dunn accepted.

But Florida got lucky. Frank Lorenzo, who had played for Florida in the late '40s, was head coach at Plant High School in Tampa, and he was named the coach of the South All Star High School team. Lorenzo chose Dunn to quarterback his team, and since both were from Tampa, Lorenzo was able to work with Dunn for six weeks before the game, and after Dunn was chosen to start, he went out and played magnificently in a 14-0 victory. Dunn scored both touchdowns.

When Coach Woodruff offered Dunn a four-year scholarship, he switched schools. FSU coach Tom Nugent was furious, and rightly so. The quick and resourceful Dunn went on to lead the Gators to three winning seasons beginning in 1956.

Jimmy Dunn: "The first time I ever saw my name on a depth chart, I was fourteenth. That's how many quarterbacks were lined up to practice. Fourteen teams lined up. I got up to the top ten because guys quit. For a while I was running eighth and ninth, and when the '56 season began, I was fourth.

"We came through spring practice, and they told us that four or five quarterbacks were going to travel. I remember seeing my name—I was third on that list. I was behind Dick Allen and John May, and when spring practice was over, they brought Harry Spears back from the service, and I was fourth. Harry had started for Florida two years before. He spent two years in the service, and he had another year of eligibility at Florida, so they went and got him out. He was in Germany, and he didn't arrive in Gainesville until August. So automatically he went ahead of me. In fact, he also took my number 12, which I had worn when they took all the pictures, and all of a sudden Harry bounced into town, and he was number 12. So I ended up with 14, which was better anyway.

"I was friendly with the other quarterbacks. John May was a big, strong guy. He could throw the ball, and he could punt it. I was surprised the day he told me he was going to drop out and go do some other things. Had he stayed, I never would have played ahead of him. That was the only reason I got to play. Harry was back, but he hadn't spent enough time on the practice field while he was away. He could still throw the ball, still could kick it and he was a good athlete, but he couldn't run, and the quarterback had to be the safety man on pass defense, and he couldn't play defense like they wanted it played. I could. The coaches told me that I should line up sixteen yards deep and, 'Don't let anyone get behind you.' I can honestly say in the three years I started, no one ever got behind me. I didn't make many tackles—that was not my responsibility to tackle people in the off-tackle hole—but NO ONE got behind me except one time against Georgia in '58 when we were in a goal-line situation from about the five-yard line and Fran Tarkenton threw it over my head for a touchdown. But I was playing corner, trying to stop the run. I wasn't upfield.

"On offense they didn't want me to do much. The offensive schemes had been cut way down because everybody had to practice on defense. Everybody had to practice the kicking game, and everyone had to play offense. So the game itself was really simple. It was run off-tackle three yards and a cloud of dust and then punt the ball.

"I could get the ball from the center, and I could hand it off to one of the running backs, and I did have a little ability kicking it. I didn't have a strong leg, but I did better kicking it out of bounds. We also had Bobby Joe Green, who was a classic punter. He was All-Pro in the NFL. We had him, and we concentrated on defense—that was the personality of our team."

One of the young lineman who stood out during practice before the 1956 season was a raw-boned kid out of Allentown, Pennsylvania, by the name of Velus "Vel" Heckman. A 200 pounder, Heckman had wanted to go to the University of Miami, but he was rejected for being "too small."

Heckman could have gone to a number of northern colleges, but the PA announcer at his high school football games had gone to the University of Florida, and he touted Heckman on the Gator coaching staff. When assistant coach John Rauch liked what he saw, Heckman became a Gator. He would go on to become a consensus firstteam All-American at defensive tackle.

Vel Heckman: "I wanted to go to the University of Miami because I had three of my buddies playing from high school playing at Miami. But Miami turned me down—told me I wasn't big enough to play big-time football. I ended up going to the University of Florida because our play-by-play announcer, Ernie Stigler, was a Florida grad. He graduated from Florida in communications. He was a crippled guy, but he was the one who told them to come up and look at me. Johnny Rauch, who ended up the Buffalo coach in pro football, recruited me. He came to Allentown, and he looked at game film, and he liked seven of us. He looked at grades, and he liked three of us.

"My dad owned a seafood business, and on Friday I would stay home to work for him. Coach Rauch wanted to know where the business was. The store was in the front, and in the back was a big workroom with walk-in freezers. My dad did wholesale and retail. John came in the back door. Nobody was back there but me. I was in the cooler getting two sacks of clams.

"He walked into the back, and all of a sudden I pushed open the cooler door, and it came flying out, and out I walked with a bushel of clams in each hand, without my glasses on and a cigar in my mouth. I was 17.

"I went over and set those clams down, picked up my glasses, and said, 'Can I help you, sir?'

John said, 'I'm a coach at the University of Florida. I'd like to talk with Velus Heckman.'

"I said, 'You've got him.' Then I said, 'Wait a minute, let me get my dad.' I ran in the front, got rid of my cigar, and brought my dad out.

"They flew us down to see the school. Academically it was sound. Their facilities were very adequate. But the big thing was that Miami had turned me down. When he said, 'Our big rival is Miami,' I said, 'I'll sign.' I had other scholarship offers, but I decided Florida was where I wanted to be.

"I could have gone to the University of Maryland. They were the top football team in the country in 1954.

"Several schools didn't want me, including Notre Dame, Syracuse and

Penn State, the only three predominant schools in my area. Rutgers wanted me, and Wake Forest, North Carolina State, Virginia, and the Naval Academy—I turned that down. I said, 'I sure as heck don't want to be a military man.'

"When I got to Florida as a freshman, everyone would talk, and this one was All-South and that one was All-State and this one was All-American. When they asked me, 'What were you?' I'd say, 'All-Allentown.' They'd say, 'How many teams did Allentown have?' I'd say, 'One.'

"The great opportunity for me was that I improved each year. I did not top out in high school like a lot of kids did. I think my improvement came because of desire and because of good coaching: Hank Foldberg, John Eibner, and Hobe Hoosier."

Heckman had a difficult time freshman year and twice left school and returned home. But Coach Woodruff saw that Heckman had the potential to be a star player, and twice he had him brought back to Florida.

Vel Heckman: "Two times I quit, and twice they came back and got me. After staying my freshman year in '54-55—I actually red-shirted myself, which actually made me a better football player—in September of '55 I ended up going back home to Pennsylvania to go to work. I was just dissat-isfied.

"They came back and got me. Dick Jones talked me into coming back. And after spring practice, even though I was first team, I wasn't doing well in school, and I just said, 'To hell with it,' and I quit again. John Eibner was one of the coaches. Years later John and I were drinking at a Boosters' Club meeting, and he said to me, 'You know that summer of '56, we'd have coaches meetings. The last meeting we had in August, Woodruff said, "Damn, if we had one more tackle, we'd be tough this year." He looked at Eibner, and he said, 'Go get the S.O.B.' That was me.

"Eibner told me, 'He didn't even say your name. I just went and got a plane ticket and flew up to Allentown.' He spent about a week with me, and finally I decided to come back. That straightened me out. I came back to study. So I'd say Woodruff's patience with me was what may have helped me become a football player at Florida and then also to graduate.

"When I began playing varsity in 1956, a lot of us felt that Woodruff was too defensive-minded. We felt like we needed to expand our offense more, but there wasn't a hell of a lot we could do about it. Woodruff was brought up under General Neyland's rules of football, and he wouldn't change. He believed that defense won ballgames. The idea was to keep it close and let the other team make mistakes. That was his attitude. I would say that Woodruff went by Neyland's book paragraph by paragraph. We respected the man a heck of a lot. Woodruff was a good man. Very fair. He helped me a lot."

thirteen

Platooning

Vel Heckman: "The way it worked, Coach Woodruff handled it as a two-team system. The rule was if you started a quarter and came out, you could go back in the same quarter. But if you didn't start the quarter, if you came in and came out, you couldn't go back in that quarter. So what he did, he had a first team. We'd usually play the first seven or eight minutes of the quarter. Then he would put the second team in. If they did well, we wouldn't even go back in that quarter. But if they got in trouble, he could put the first team back in.

"There's no doubt about it, players got tired going both ways. The coach who got ahead of that system was Paul Dietzel at LSU. While everybody else was playing two teams, Paul was playing three teams. He had a team like we had that went both ways, and he had an offensive team, and then he had a defensive team, which he called 'the Chinese Bandits.' So he was playing 33 guys against our 22 in a quarter."

Jimmy Dunn: "What the coaches did was play the first team for six minutes, put the second team in for five, and then put the first team in to finish the quarter. Or you could substitute individually. The punter would start the game on offense as a receiver so he could punt more than once a quarter. Bobby Joe Green would start at receiver for us, run three downs, and kick the ball. Then we'd go play defense, get the ball back, run three more plays, and Bobby Joe'd kick again. If we had field position in the middle of the field, I'd punt it. I would kick the ball out of bounds. That's what the rules forced you to do. If the ball was inside our twenty-yard line and it was third down and more than six yards to go, we would often punt.

"We ran a very conservative offense, and it was obvious—no secret—that it drove our offensive coach Hank Foldberg crazy. He didn't hide his feelings or emotions. You knew.

"I would say that Coach Foldberg was not my biggest fan at the time. He thought Florida could have done some things offensively with someone else in there, and I'm sure he was right. I'm sure there were a bunch of times when he cussed me out.

"I didn't have the arm to throw the ball 35 or 40 yards downfield. I couldn't do that. I was as big as I ever was going to get. Doc Langford did everything in his power to make me gain weight. They gave me milkshakes and eggs and black strap molasses. I would go into the dining hall three times a day, and a lady named Ma Swain looked after the training table of the players. She would make me these milkshakes. They gave me booklets for me to go get food supplements. I drank them and drank them. They invested probably a hundred dollars in exotic weight-gaining drinks. Doc would weigh me once every two weeks. I didn't gain one ounce.

"He said, 'That's it. No more drinks for you.' They said, 'That's as big as you're ever going to get.'

"But the other quarterbacks couldn't play pass defense. They would have had to get in some scoring contests to win with someone else in there, because the ball would have gone over the other quarterbacks' heads for touchdowns on defense. They couldn't return punts. They couldn't return kickoffs. I was playing because I had more speed than other guys."

When the 1956 season began, Florida was optimistic. In addition to sophomore Jimmy Dunn, who Coach Woodruff once called 'the best player I ever coached,' and star lineman Vel Heckman, the team boasted four pro-quality backs, Jackie Simpson, Jim Rountree, Bernie Parrish, and Joe Brodsky. In the 26-0 win over Mississippi State in the season opener, Brodsky intercepted three passes, including one he ran back 100 yards for a touchdown. When he reached the end zone, he passed out.

Jimmy Dunn: "In our opener against Mississippi State, Joe just ran and ran and ran. He was exhausted. Joe was a linebacker, and [Mississippi State quarterback] Billy Stacy tried to throw it out in the flat, and Joe went underneath and caught it and he took off. For a big guy, Joe could run good. Stacy got caught up in traffic. Anyway, after running a hundred yards, Joe was exhausted. It was over 100 degrees in Starkville that day.

"I didn't get to play until the fourth quarter. And I was sitting over there getting some sun and watching everybody play until it was out of hand. Back then, if you led by ten points, the game was over. Not many teams caught up when they were ten points down.

"I remember I led a drive downfield, and we scored the fourth touchdown. [Florida won 26-0.] I remember holding for the extra point and catching a punt. And I remember watching Billy Stacy, and I thought he was pretty good. He was a sophomore too. I was thinking how much better he was than I was. He was bigger, stronger, and faster, and starting the game."

Vel Heckman: "Stacy was the quarterback at Mississippi State. Just as he threw the ball, I hit him. I don't know if I deflected the pass or not, but I remember Joe running, and I'm laying on top of Stacy, watching him go down the field."

Jimmy Dunn: "Clemson was next, and they were very, very good. I was surprised by how good they were. They went on and played in the Orange Bowl. I got to play in that game, and I did a couple of things pretty decent. I wasn't doing anything great, but I wasn't doing anything bad." [Florida and Clemson tied 20-20.]

Vel Heckman: "Clemson had a very good football team that year. I was playing first team, and John Barrow was the guard next to me. I was a tackle.

"Clemson's first team was giving us a fit. Every time our second team would go in against their second team, our second team would do a better job than we would. Our fans were booing us. John and I came out and were sitting there on the bench. I looked at John and said, 'Hey, John, the way things are going, I think I'm gonna try real hard next week to be on the second team.' We laughed."

Jimmy Dunn: "We played Kentucky, in the rain. [Florida lost 17-8.]Harry Spears started [at quarterback], and they sent me in late in the game and I threw Bernie Parrish a 35-yard touchdown pass. More than likely, I hit a seven-yard pass, and Bernie ran the other 28.

"By his junior year Bernie was probably the best all-around football player in the SEC. My sophomore year we had a couple of other backs, Jim Rountree and Jackie Simpson, who were good players. They played in the NFL or Canada as defensive backs."

Vel Heckman: "Against Kentucky, Jimmy Dunn came into the game and played quarterback, and he threw a touchdown to Bernie Parrish. Jimmy played first team with me for three years. He was a fine, young man, and an athlete. Jimmy weighed 140 pounds. Jimmy had all the mechanics. It's a shame Jimmy wasn't bigger. Jimmy was a great out of bounds kicker. He could punt that ball out of bounds.

"Bernie was also a fine athlete. Bernie, Don Fleming and I roomed together in Murphy Hall our junior and senior years. Bernie most likely was the best overall athlete I've ever known. God, he earned twelve to fifteen letters at the University of Florida. Bernie did not play football his freshman year. He came from PK Young High School. Woodruff didn't give him a scholarship his freshman year. He was playing basketball and baseball."

Jimmy Dunn: "Our next game was against Rice, my first start at quarterback. Rice was led by Frank Ryan and King Hill, two NFL quarterbacks. They had a receiver named Buddy Dial. They were the number one passing team in the country.

"When they came into Gainesville, they were about 13 point favorites, which was BIG. That's like 25 points today, and we shut them out 7-0.

"We had a six-man line, three deep, and we were told, 'Don't let them stay as deep as the deepest.' They couldn't handle our pass rush and our zone defense. We kept everybody in front of us, and they caught the ball, and we went and tackled them. Nobody got behind us.

"They moved the ball from their twenty to our twenty, but they couldn't get any closer. We got a break and scored and kept them out of the end zone, and so back then, you see, the passing teams really didn't do that well. They couldn't execute like they needed to against the good defensive teams.

"We had good defensive backs. In that game Bernie Parrish, Jackie Simpson, and Jimmy Rountree were playing defensive corners, and I was lined up playing safety, but I had a supporting cast.

"That was my first start as a Florida quarterback, and a newspaper reporter wrote an article saying I had started because I could run, that I could play pass defense against the leading passing team in the country.

"Joe Brodsky scored a touchdown, and we beat them 7-0."

Vel Heckman: "Rice had a heck of a football team. They had Frank Ryan and King Hill, and that was basically the first era of college football that we had to play against a lot of passing.

"In that game Woodruff made a crucial move to help the defense. Larry

Wesley was a senior tackle, and I was a sophomore. He played behind me the first two or three games. For the third game he moved me to second team and Larry to first team because Larry was a great defensive football player. He wasn't much of an offensive player. That's why I was in front of him—I played better both ways. But Larry, who was 6'3", was a hell of a pass rusher. We tackles played hands-up at the ends. Larry rushed from the outfield. Larry was drafted by the New York Giants, who were national champions, and he was the last player cut.

"So in the Rice game I played with the second unit. Like I said, most of the time the second unit got in at least 24 to 28 minutes in a game. I felt like it was a demotion, but as I look back on it, Woodruff made a good move. 'Cause Larry played a hell of a football game."

Jimmy Dunn: "I remember going up to Nashville. Vanderbilt had a big guy named Phil King, who became a running back with the Giants in the NFL. They tried to isolate him on me. He was about 6'4", probably 225, which made him bigger than most of the linemen we had. They'd take him out of a slot and run him down in the middle of the field and have him curl in front of me on key third-down plays.

"They were able to do that a couple of times. I weighed 140 pounds and I was bouncing off him like throwing a rock up against a wall. It was third and seven, and I remember Jim Rountree saying, 'The next time they are in that formation, I'm gonna come play safety and you play corner.' They threw it to Phil down the middle, and Rountree nailed him upside the head, and they never ran it again. Jim wasn't doubting how good I was or whether I had the ability to stop the guy, he just knew I was outmanned. [Florida won 21-7.]

"We beat LSU over at LSU [21-6]. Jackie Simpson scored on a 49-yard run."

Jackie Simpson: "Against LSU, I scored a [49-yard] touchdown on a punt return. I remember it was a low kick, a line drive. I caught it on the run and kind of caught them napping. In fact, I went straight on up the field."

Jimmy Dunn: "Then we played Auburn in Gainesville. [Florida won 28-0.] We hit three home runs against them. We had a blocked kick, and I ran an option play for a touchdown—58 yards on an option play. We would fake off tackle, and then we would take it out to the next man and either keep it or pitch it. This time I kept it, and I can remember cutting back against the grain, and we had a lot of blockers. I remember Bernie Parrish made a great block. Don Fleming made a great block. Nobody even touched me. I remember I kinda tripped and fell into the end zone."

Jackie Simpson: "That [Auburn game] was the one in which I threw my one touchdown pass. They pitched it out, and I acted like I was running an end sweep, and I stopped and threw it to Rountree for a [53-yard] touchdown."

Jimmy Dunn: "I started against Georgia [Florida won 28-0, the fifth straight win in games that Dunn had started.]. Brodsky again played a great game, intercepted two passes to set up touchdowns, and he ran for a long touchdown.

"Brodsky was a VERY good football player. He was a good linebacker and a good running back and he had good hands—he could catch the ball.

"Joe went on to have a very good coaching career. He was one of the few coaches to win a national championship as a high school coach, won a national championship on the coaching staff of the University of Miami, and won the Super Bowl with the Dallas Cowboys. Joe lives in Miami. He and his wife are taking cruises."

Jackie Simpson: "I remember we were playing Georgia in Jacksonville. The half had ended, and we were running off the field into the locker room, and our cheerleaders shot off one of our small cannons, and it must have been pointed the wrong way, because it went off and blew a hole in Coach Woodruff's pants! I was jogging behind him. I saw him reach down and pick up the cannon and take it away from them, and I know he never did give it back to them. The thing I laugh about is, how would you like to be in the dressing room, and if you're playing a bad game, all of a sudden you see your coach coming in there carrying a cannon—what are you thinking? Right 'Golly, have I played that bad?'"

Jimmy Dunn: "We only had two games left in the season, Georgia Tech and Miami. I remember Coach Woodruff came to me the day before the game, and he said, 'I want you to work out with the orange team.' The first team was the blue team. He said, 'I think Harry has more big-game experience than you do. I think it will be better for us.'

"I couldn't understand it. We'd just won five games in a row. We were six and one. I felt those five wins were all big games. The Florida-Auburn game was big. The Florida–Georgia game was big. And Florida–LSU certainly was big. But I didn't say anything. Shoot, I wouldn't have said a word to a coach. It wasn't nothing but 'yes, sir' and 'no, sir.'

"I was disappointed. I don't know how the other guys felt. But after becoming a coach and seeing what happens in practice with teams and knowing the importance of continuity, I think if you are in a good rhythm, you shouldn't try to fix it. And the change killed us.

"I played with a different group. Spears played with the first group. I switched to the second group. But I wasn't playing with the guys I'd been playing with." [Florida lost to fifth-ranked Georgia Tech 28-0.]

Vel Heckman: "Georgia Tech was a great, great offensive football team. Tech ran an unbalanced line, and we had problems playing it because in our offensive scheme we didn't overshift enough."

Jackie Simpson: "I got a blood clot in the Georgia Tech game, and I missed the Miami game. We lost a lot of games we should have won. Like I said earlier, we had some good football players, and when I look at the guys we had, I would think, how could we not win more games than we did? It just didn't happen."

Jimmy Dunn: "Miami was our last game. The Georgia Tech game kinda let the air out of us. If we'd have played them decent, I believe we'd have played better against Miami. If Brodsky and Simpson hadn't gotten hurt, I think it would have been a different story too.

"Miami was a great football team. Don Bosseler, their running back, became a star in the NFL. We made a couple of mistakes in the kicking game. They blocked a punt. They just outplayed us. They were better than we were. [Florida lost 20-7].

"We finished the season 6-3-1, but there weren't many bowls back then. I guess we just didn't have a good enough record. We didn't have a good enough team."

Vel Heckman: "So we finished the season 6-3-1, which for a Woodruff team wasn't disappointing at all. We played some good football teams. From 1952 to 1956 Florida became a football power—to a degree. We were constantly in the Top 25, which before that was unheard of. Woodruff made it so that we were now a respected football team that had to be handled that way, instead of a doormat."

At the end of the '56 season Jackie Simpson played in the prestigious North-South Shrine game. Len Dawson and Tommy McDonald played for the North. Sonny Jurgensen QBed for the South. Simpson played defensive back and made an interception.

He was drafted and played in the service for the 82nd Airborne in Fort Bragg, North Carolina in 1957, and in 1958 he joined the Baltimore Colts. His salary was $10,000. That year the Colts defeated the New York Giants for the NFL championship in one of the most memorable NFL games of all time. His winning share: $4,200 and a championship ring. The Colts repeated again in '59.

After two seasons Simpson joined the Pittsburgh Steelers with quarterback Bobby Layne. His most vivid memory was letting the maverick Layne borrow his Thunderbird when he was sick in the hospital. Layne wrecked it. And then had it fixed.

After football, Simpson owned a lounge in downtown Miami, entered the roofing business, and worked for a company called Carribean Parking Systems. He is retired and living in Pensacola.

fourteen

A Year on Probation

Jimmy Dunn: "In 1957 the football team was placed on probation, because of illegal recruiting of a baseball player! If it had been a football player, it might have been different. No, the coaches shouldn't have done that, but it seemed most unfair to be on probation because of the illegal recruiting of a baseball player. Coach Woodruff was the athletic director, and they penalized him and the whole sports program.

"They didn't do anything to our scholarships, but for one year we couldn't go to a bowl game and we couldn't be on television and get television revenue. It was just a financial thing. No bowls and no TV.

"From what I understand—it was common knowledge—Coach Woodruff allowed the recruiting violation after a peer group told him it was okay because 'Everybody was doing it.' And then one of those peers turned him in."

Vel Heckman: "I'll tell you that story. All the universities were doing this: like with me, Florida gave me two round-trip tickets to Pennsylvania a year. They paid my way to come to school and to go home at the end of the year. That was all they were allowed to give me. But then at Christmas, they gave me another round-trip ticket. All the colleges did that with their out-of-state athletes. They were all doing it.

"Bobby Dodd, the coach at Georgia Tech, was a good friend of Woodruff's, and before an SEC meeting, Dodd cornered Woodruff and said it was going to be brought up. He said, 'Let's all admit we are doing it, and it won't be that bad on us.' Dodd asked Woodruff to do that, and he did, and none of the others did. And they put us on probation. Now that was the story we heard back in those days. We could all accept that, knowing Woodruff. He was a good, honest man, and here his buddy talks him into coming up and admitting this, and then they all back out and don't say anything. So that's why we were put on probation.

"And after that, they quit giving us the plane trips."

Jimmy Dunn: "We were supposed to open the '57 season against UCLA, but it was cancelled when the Asian flu swept through our team. It would last six or seven days, and guys would drop fifteen to twenty pounds. They just said we weren't healthy enough to go to California to play."

Vel Heckman: "All of us got the flu. Must have been 45 per cent of us who had it. The infirmary was full of people, and it was disappointing we didn't get to play UCLA. Missing that game, losing the opportunity to go to California, was crucial to our season. I think if we had played that game, it would have added more to our season."

Jimmy Dunn: "As a result of the UCLA game being cancelled because of the flu epidemic, our first game was against Wake Forest at home in what was almost a hurricane. Rain was coming down parallel almost, pushed by a 30-mile-an-hour-wind.

"Because of the conditions, we played a defensive game, playing for field position and hoping for turnovers. It was so bad that a couple of times we punted the ball on second down!

"We didn't want the ball, because it was impossible to do anything with it, and we didn't have the talent to throw it.

"Our talent in '57 on that kind of field team was to play defense. We got field position, and once we got in four-down territory, we had enough running talent that we could get it into the end zone.

"Jim Rountree starred in that game. I remember the first time I saw him play was in the High School All-Star game in Gainesville. He was a year ahead of me, and he was a quarterback for Miami-Jackson, and I saw him run 95 yards for a touchdown. They couldn't tackle him.

"Jim had great skills as a runner. He could run outside, and he had great hand-eye coordination that allowed him to catch punts as good as anybody I've seen. The ball never touched his body when he caught a punt. He just grabbed it with his hands. He was also a good passer, and we used the halfback pass a lot with him. He could run with it, throw it, and he could catch it, and back then, as you know, the rule was that everybody had to play both ways, and he could play defense. He was an outstanding defensive halfback. Back then we were defensive halfbacks. Today we're corners. So he was a corner, and he went on to be corner in the pros.

"We were just better than Wake Forest, and we blocked a couple of kicks. We won it [27-0] on defense, with the rain and being at home."

Vel Heckman: "We beat Wake Forest easily in the opening game. They were easy.

"Our next game was against Kentucky, who we hadn't beaten in forty years. That was my coming-out game as a football player.

"In August I suffered a shoulder separation. I don't know how I did it. It was slight, but every time you would push on that damn bone, it would hurt like hell. For the first seven games I played with Novacain. Nobody said I had to take it, but I asked for it because it hurt so much I couldn't practice.

"Kentucky had a tackle named Lou Michaels, an All-American. Lou was 6'3", around 265. When we were on offense, Lou played me head-to-head.

"John Eibner scouted Kentucky. I would ask John about the tendencies of the guys I had to play against, whether they had anything wrong with them. John and I would sit and watch game films, and we noticed that when Michaels was going to his right, he put his right foot back a little in his stance. If he was going to his left, he'd put his left foot a little bit back. John and I decided I'd just take him the way he wanted to go.

"That did a lot to help our game, because we were able to run off tackle quite a bit in that game. Normally nobody ran against Michaels.

"And after that game, some of the teams started shying away from me. Your good teams wouldn't, like Auburn or LSU, but most of the other teams, the average teams, would not run my way.

"We played a real good football game. The Kentucky win was huge, very, very huge."

Jimmy Dunn: "The unusual thing about the Kentucky game was that I was sick as a dog the week before the game. We had had to cancel our first game against UCLA because of the Asiatic flu. We did not have enough players to go out there and play. The bug was going around. We had guys in the infirmary, running high fevers, throwing up, but I didn't get it. By the week before the Kentucky game, I got it and got it bad. I did not go to practice one day. All week I was home in bed. I had a fever and I was throwing up. I never left my apartment, and they came and picked me up on the way to the airport to go to Lexington.

"When we got to Lexington, I went straight to my hotel room. I did not leave the hotel room, did not work out with the team until the night of the game.

"I started, and I played pretty well. I threw a little wobbly pass to Rountree, and he caught it and ran for a touchdown, so they give me credit for hitting a touchdown bomb, but in reality... I also remember that in that game Bernie Parrish took a handoff at our own 35 and ran twenty yards for a long gain.

"Bernie was our biggest and best running back. We had a bunch of little guys playing in the offensive backfield that were put there because the rule said that you also had to play defense. Se we had little defensive corners, Don Deal, Don Lucy, Doug Partin, me, little bitty guys. Bernie Parrish played fullback, and on defense he played linebacker. He and Rountree were the only runners on our team would had the strength and size to run off tackle. Bernie reminded me a lot of Rountree. Both of them played corner in the NFL.

"And then two plays after Bernie's run, I ran 32 yards for a touchdown. Some things stand out, places you play: at the time the lights weren't very good at that field in Lexington. It was an old stadium, and it seemed like it was dark, and I swear I ran about fifteen yards before anybody saw that I had the ball and was running. Because a giant hole opened up, and I was just running through it, expecting to get knocked upside down any second, and it never happened! And so I just kept running, and I swear it was because they chased the halfback on the pitch and nobody saw me. All of a sudden I was in the end zone. So it was not a great run. All I did was go down the line of scrimmage, plant my foot, and ran a straight shot into the end zone.

"We beat Kentucky that day 14-7, and it was a big game for us. It showed us that we did have a good team and we could win on the road. It took a monkey off our backs. It showed everyone the Florida Gators could go and win against a good football team."

Vel Heckman: "Our next game was a [29-20] loss to Mississippi State, which always was a tough football game for us. They had Billy Stacy at quarterback and they had tough linemen. Georgia and Mississippi State had the toughest linemen. It was always a very physical game against those two teams. You could see it by how banged up we were after the game. We were winning after three periods, but they scored a field goal and touchdown to beat us."

Jimmy Dunn: "They had a great quarterback in Billy Stacy, and they put some other people with him, and they were very good and beat us. They deserved to win. We turned the ball over a couple times. I fumbled. That was the game in which I intercepted a pass and in running it back, I fumbled. I went from hero to goat."

The highlight of the 1957 season was a 22-14 victory over 10th-ranked LSU, led by Billy Cannon, one of the greatest athletes ever to come out of the SEC.

Vel Heckman: "We won the game on a pitch out from [Jimmy] Dunn to Bernie [Parrish for 27 yards.] In our offense the way things went, Bernie his junior year was good for from 150 to 200 yards running and receiving."

Jimmy Dunn: "Playing LSU was big time. Cannon was a great player, and he had a lot of help. That team the next year won the national championship.

"Cannon was the best athlete for that ten-year period of time maybe in the country. We had had a shot at him when he was coming out of high school in Louisiana. He had some family in Florida and was being recruited by the Gators, but we didn't get him.

"Billy Cannon was a guy who could win a game single-handedly. In fact, he won the 100-yard dash in the SEC track meet, and he also won the shot put! That's the kind of athlete he was. And he had great hands, which was evident later in his pro career, because he ended up starting at tight end for the Raiders after his running back career was over.

"That day we stopped him. Our whole defense was built around stopping the run, and if the eight guys up front could get the run stopped, we had three guys with better than average speed in the secondary to stop their passing game. Really, the coaches didn't have that much time to work on a sophisticated passing game. It was play-action or basic routes, because you only had half as much time to work on it as you have today, so the pass defense usually was made up not by the schemes but by individuals who had speed and who could play a zone and react to the ball, and that was what we had."

Florida also had Jimmy Dunn, who hit Louis Pelham with a 26-yard pass and then ran in for the score to give the Gators a 15-7 lead at the end of the first quarter. The clincher came when Dunn pitched out to Bernie Parrish, who ran 27 yards to paydirt on a sweep.

Unfortunately for Florida, the next game came against the team that finished number one in the country, Auburn.

Jimmy Dunn: "We played Auburn at Auburn, and they killed us [13-0], and it could have been worse.

"Auburn completely dominated us down there, and we couldn't get back to the line of scrimmage. They ended up winning the national championship, and the next year LSU ended up winning the national championship, and at the time these were the teams we had to recruit against and go up against. It was the best football in the country, even though it wasn't as exciting as it is today. But it was exciting at the time because everybody was accustomed to seeing this chess match. We went for field position, kicked the ball, and scored when we could. It was close knit and whoever made a mistake—blinked—got beat.

"This is what Woodruff coached, and this was what the rules mandated, because any team that tried to do any different didn't have enough time on the practice field to execute an offensive passing game and also execute the defense to stop the other team's offense and to work on the special teams."

Vel Heckman: "In that game if we would have run a halfback dive play more, we'd have done better, but that was not in our offense for that game. Look at our statistics: our biggest gain that day was for 13 yards. I said to Jimmy, 'Run a damn dive play behind me. I've got the damn linebacker playing head-up on me.' Jimmy called a dive, and Roundtree ran for 13 yards, and we never ran it again.

"The coaches didn't feel like that play would go, and that was the only damn play we made any yards on. And they wouldn't let him run it again. They told Jimmy the play was not in our offense for this game. I was upset that game because of it."

The loss to Auburn was the last game Florida would lose the rest of the year as they finished out the season with three wins and a tie. In the Georgia game, Florida held their rivals to one first down and 26 yards rushing in the first half on the way to a 22-0 rout.

Jimmy Dunn: "That was the most we could ever hope to beat anybody, and we completely had them outclassed that day. That was a rout. That was like the Gators beating someone 50-18 today. Georgia had some good running backs and good linemen, but our defense was better."

Vel Heckman: "You've got to realize that in '57 we had a damn good line that year with Charlie Mitchell and me. Charlie was All–SEC that year. We had some good football players and played some real good defense. The outstanding player on defense that day was Hal Boney from Jacksonville. He got fired up for that game every year.

"I'll tell you what I remember most about playing Georgia: the week before the game all the guys would get all fired up. I came from Pennsylvania, so to me it was just another football game. And it used to piss me off. All three years against Georgia, the Jacksonville boys would get all fired up. You'd have thought they were playing in the damn Super Bowl. It just used to make me mad. I would say, 'Hell, why don't you like that every game? We'd go better.'"

In the 14-7 victory over Vanderbilt, Bernie Parrish scored both Florida touchdowns, one on a 45-yard run, the other from 23 yards out.

Jimmy Dunn: "We didn't really outclass anybody that year, and except for Georgia, nobody really outclassed us, except for Auburn. Other than that, we were pretty much in every game. If we ever got eight points ahead of anybody, we'd kick the ball on third down and sit on it, because we knew they couldn't catch us. It was a different mentality. Vanderbilt was very physical, and we got beat up, but there were as many or more of their guys who got hurt as ours."

Vel Heckman: "We beat Vanderbilt even though they had big, strong running backs, and the next week we traveled to Atlanta to play Georgia Tech. The game was played in the drizzling rain. We were snake bit that game. We had a better football team than they did. Let's put it this way: it was a Bobby Dodd football team, at Georgia Tech, and it was on national TV, my first experience on TV. They even sprayed the field green because it was on TV. At the end of the game we had green dye all over our uniforms."

Jimmy Dunn: "It was cold and raining, and we scored a touchdown, and we got it called back. It was a halfback pass. I got the ball and pitched it to Bernie, and he threw the ball to Rountree, and the play went for a touchdown, but one of our linemen was called for being down field, so they called it back. It was the kind of penalty, if it had been in Gainesville, it would not have been called. It was somebody just searching: 'Please let's find something to bring back that play.' And after he searched around, he saw that our lineman was about two yards down field from where he should have been, and I honestly believe that he had drifted down there AFTER the ball was already in the air, when they play was basically over.

"In this game with Georgia Tech in the rain, we couldn't move the ball, and they couldn't move it. The ball was staying between the 30s.

"One time we got them backed up and we made them quick kick, and those were the big plays in the game: the quick kicks. After the third quarter, they kicked it to us, and we had the ball about midfield, and on second down they called us for holding, so now we had second down and 25 to go. It was physically and mentally impossible for our football team to make twenty-five yards and get a first down. I knew we were going to punt the ball, and I was the punter. So on second down and 25, I called a quick kick, and Bernie kicked the ball out of bounds on about their ten.

"Harvey Robinson, our offensive backfield coach, a great football coach, had been at Tennessee with General Neyland. After the game he said that was the best play I had ever called—a quick kick was the best play I had ever called! I did make a couple of big runs, and I thought maybe he might allude to them, but no…. But that was the times, and that was the way the game was played."

Vel Heckman: "I also remember Bernie broke loose for a touchdown and squeezed the ball too tight, and it shot up in the air, and he turned around and got it, but he got tackled and didn't score. With the score 0-0, Bernie tried a field goal at the end of the game, but it fell just short.

"Really, to us, we felt like we were out-officiated, and after that game we were very disappointed because of that. Like I said, it was Georgia Tech AT Georgia Tech, Bobby Dodd was one of THE coaches in the country, it was on national TV, and they just weren't going to let us beat them. We all felt like that after the game. We felt like we won the football game but we got out-officiated."

The last game of the '57 season was a 14-0 win over an excellent University of Miami team.

Jimmy Dunn: "Miami was close to where they are today—they played extremely well back then. They had a lot of good players including Don Bosseler, who ended up having a great career with the Washington Redskins. Miami was a top-rated team."

In the game Dunn scored from the one, and Ed Sears scored the other touchdown from the one. The defense, marvelous all year, completed its fifth shutout. One of the stars was Vel Heckman, who played with a broken finger.

Vel Heckman: "In the Georgia Tech game I broke the end of the tip of my finger off my right hand, and the doctor put it in a cast. On Monday I went to a specialist in Jacksonville, and he wanted to put the cast back on. I told him I had a game on Saturday and I couldn't be in a cast if I wanted to play. He said, 'Well, then you're not going to play.'

"Our last game was against Miami, which was for me like the Georgia game for the Jacksonville boys. The break was from the nail on out, broken just below where you see your nail.

"I said to the doctor, 'I heard you can wire them up. If you can't, then cut the finger off.'

"He said, 'We'll try.' In his office he drilled two wires through my finger, down the bone, pulled the finger together, and bent the wires to hold it in place. By that time my finger was as big as a fat cigar, so in the Miami game, I played with Novacain in my hand. Like I said, I would have played if he had had to cut my finger off.

"We shut them out in the Orange Bowl, even though Miami had a heck of a football team. We finished the season 6-2-1, and the only reason we didn't go to a bowl game was because we were on probation."

fifteen

The First Florida State Game

Vel Heckman: "Nineteen fifty eight was going to be our year, but then Bernie Parrish signed with the Reds, and that hurt us. Bernie could have played any position he wanted to, but mostly he pitched and played third base. He could do anything. We encouraged Bernie to sign the baseball contract because it was a lot of money. Bernie signed for $40,000. Pro baseball paid so much more than pro football. When I signed with the San Francisco 49ers, I signed for a $1,500 bonus, and a $8,500 contract. I had the biggest salary/bonus of any rookie.

"Bernie went to pro baseball in the spring after the semester ended in '58. Cincinnati sent him to AA ball. Bernie felt he needed to be higher. The next year Bernie played well in spring training, and he felt they should have promoted him to Cincinnati. They sent him to Triple A. You've got to know Bernie: he went out to Triple A and then all of a sudden, he said, 'To hell with you all. You're not gonna let me go to Cincinnati? You're going to make me wait a couple of years to go to Cincinnati?' So he quit. The Browns had drafted him in '58. He called Paul Brown and tried out for football."

Jimmy Dunn: "If Bernie had come back and played with us in '58, we had as good a chance for that period of time in Gator football to win the Southeastern conference.

"We had some speed, and we had good defense, but without Bernie, we didn't have any punch. We had a pony backfield, and it was hard for us to make third and one, because no one had the size and strength to run off tackle. Bernie Parrish had that.

"Several games in '58, my senior year, we came close, and if Bernie had been there, he would have been the winning edge. He was a great athlete.

We needed him. But nobody could blame Bernie. He got a great offer to go play professional baseball, and it was more money than any of us had ever seen.

"Bernie had made a lot of friends in Gainesville, and it was not an easy decision for him, but it was too much money for him to turn down. He could have taken a chance. The same money would have been available to him the next year, but he might have gotten injured or the circumstances might have changed, and there was no reason for him to wait."

With the departure of Bernie Parrish to pro baseball, a Texas import by the name of Don Deal got the opportunity to start for the Gators in the backfield in 1958.

Don Deal: "I was 5'9", 155 pounds, and in those days in Texas there were a lot of guys of my size and ability, and I had a partial track scholarship and partial football to go to SMU. When I had the chance to go to Florida, I jumped at it.

"I arrived on campus in the summer of 1955. The scary thing was that back then there was no scholarship limit, and when I walked in that first day there must have been 70 or 80 guys on the freshman team. I remember the coaches saying, 'Everybody who was All-American stand up,' and a lot of guys stood up. 'Everyone who was All-State stand up.' Everyone stood up.

"Then he told the front row to stand up. He said, 'Those will probably be the only ones who will still be here in four years.'

"I played my freshman year. I was on the team with Jimmy Dunn. We had a great time. That was a wild bunch that came in from all over the United States. We didn't go to many classes, but we had a great time.

"I got in some grade difficulty and had to go into the Marines. I needed to do that. The coaches said I needed some time to mature—this was for academic reasons. I was in the Marines for six months, fought the battle of California. Joining the Marines from Texas, I didn't have to go to Paris Island. Instead I went to Camp Pendleton in San Diego.

"When I returned in '58 I had put on some weight and got a lot stronger. I was 5'10", about 185 pounds."

Jimmy Dunn: "We opened the season with a big [34-14] win over Tulane. They had a back, Tommy Mason, who was a great football player, and I enjoyed playing against him.

"I didn't do anything outstanding in that game, and though I've never seen it documented, I believe I scored the first two-point conversion in the history of college football.

"After an early touchdown, I was holding on the extra point, and I mishandled the snap, and I ran for two points. I didn't think about this for twenty years, but it occurred to me we were in the Eastern Time Zone, it came fairly early in the game, and it didn't happen very often, and I never saw anything in the papers about anyone else scoring on a two-point play. It has to be one of the greatest all-time trivia questions: who scored the first two-point conversion in college football?"

Don Deal: "I wasn't the starter in that first game against Tulane. Back then the substitution rule made you play what amounted to two starting teams. You had to go both ways. One team would play the first eight minutes of a quarter. Then the next team would go on. So you had to have twenty-two guys. It was a crazy rule.

"Micky Ellenberg was the second-team quarterback. I came in in the game, and I had a 67-yard run, and we ended up beating them pretty good."

Jimmy Dunn: "We had four tough losses in '58, including a tough one [14–7] to Billy Stacy and Mississippi State. Stacy was too good for us. He was a great football player. We scored our only points when Don Lucy intercepted a Stacy pass and ran it back for a touchdown.

"Lucy was a running back and a defensive back from Daytona Beach, a real good player. He played with Don Deal and Doug Partin. Simpson, Roundtree, and Parrish all were gone in '58. See, in '58 we were little. We really were. I was the tallest player in the backfield. I was 5'10". Deal and Lucy and Partin were 5'8". And they weren't heavy either. They were 165 pounds. Remember the Four Horsemen of Notre Dame? We were the Four Shetlands!"

Vel Heckman: "We flew out to Los Angeles in a charter plane to play UCLA. We flew from Florida to Dallas, Texas, changed pilots, and then we flew to L.A.

"They hyped the game pretty good. Woodruff took baby alligators out there; they were about a foot long. UCLA had the Bruin girls, a bunch of pretty young ladies who met us when we got off the plane. They were all dressed in powder blue outfits. They had oranges for us, and we handed them alligators, which was very unusual. Nowadays the animal people would be going crazy. We went to Disneyland, which in that period of our lives was very, very unusual. We even ran into a couple movie stars, though I forget who they were.

"I have a funny story to tell you. Vic Miranda, an Italian boy, had a little darker complexion. We didn't have any blacks playing for us at that time in the South. We flew in.

"Vic was a buddy of mine, as were Oren Genimore, Pat Patchin, and Don Fleming. Oren and Pat were from Steubenville, Ohio. Don was from Shadyside, and I was from Pennsylvania. Vic was from Miami, but he hung around with us.

"The coaches told us that when we flew in they were going to have the UCLA girls there, and we were teasing Vic that several black girls would be there to meet him. Lo and behold, when we landed, three of them went right to him.

"During the game one of the black players for UCLA said, 'Miranda, what are you playing on that white boys team for? You're blacker than I am.'"

Jimmy Dunn: "The Coliseum had been converted to a baseball diamond for the Dodgers. They had just come from Brooklyn, and so the left field stands were very short, maybe 250 feet down the line. The baseball diamond was cut into the football field, which ran toward right field. The Coliseum was a BIG place. It was about 800 feet to right field, and 250 feet down the left field line, and all of us were standing at home plate and seeing how close that was, but it did have a big screen. They had not completely removed the pitcher's mound for our game. The clay from the cutout was still on the field for the football game.

"I remember Bob Milby hit a draw play, and he was running up the middle of the field, and he was by everybody, and there were a couple guys chasing him. When he hit the dirt of the infield, he slowed down, and this kid from UCLA ran off the grass and tackled him. If it hadn't been for that dirt, he'd have run the other thirty yards for the touchdown. But playing in that dirt, we'd run a play and everybody would come back to the huddle covered in red mud."

Don Deal: "We flew out to California to play UCLA. That was quite a trip. We went out on a Thursday. None of us had ever been to Disneyland, of course. We went to the Rose Bowl and did the whole tourist thing. It was like a homecoming for me, because the year before I'd been out there with the Marines. When I got to the stadium, there were four or five guys I had been in the Marines with at the game. As I look back, I thought that was one of the turning points of Florida football history—to go out there and beat a team like UCLA [21-14].

"I had a real good game. I had a lot of yards and broke a long run for 67 yards.

"We were moving the ball pretty good that day. I had a handoff from Jimmy Dunn around the left side, I got off-tackle and got into the secondary, broke outside and then broke down the sideline. It was a footrace then.

"I think for everybody beating UCLA was the highlight of the season—to go out there and beat them.

"Jimmy was a magician. He weighed 147 pounds and was tough as nails. He had a lot of running ability, was quick. It was amazing the skills that he had."

Vel Heckman: "We tied Vanderbilt in the last seconds of the game when Jimmy threw a touchdown pass [to Dave Hudson]."

Jimmy Dunn: "We were behind 6-0, and we were running our two-minute offense, which was not very sophisticated. Dave Hudson was a tight end and also a defensive end, a very good football player out of Pensacola. He was a sophomore, a very good prospect. He could catch the ball and run with it, and with only seconds remaining in the game, I was able to hit him with a short pass to tie the game."

Vel Heckman: "We would have won it, but Tom Moore, a safety and one of their big running backs, blocked the extra point. Moore was just as damn big as Phil King."

Jimmy Dunn: "Back then the extra point was not as automatic as it is now. We didn't have kickers. We had players who kicked the ball. Our center, Joe Hergert, was the kicker. Billy Booker was a better kicker, but for this kick Billy was dead. He couldn't come back into the game.

"See, when you started the game, you could only go back in one time in the quarter. And if you started, you could only go out once.

"We had a specialist punter, Bobby Joe Green, who was a great punter. Bobby Joe had enough talent that he could play end. So if Bobby Joe doesn't start the game, he can only punt one time in the quarter. With an offense that was going three and out a lot, we punted more than one time in a quarter, so Bobby Joe would start as a receiver, play split end, we would run our three plays, and Bobby Joe would kick, and then he'd go out of the game and he could come back in once a quarter and kick, so he had to be a player. But we didn't have a field goal kicker or an extra point kicker who was in his class. So our field goal kicker at the time was Joe Hergert, our center, and he was just a big ole lineman who kicked straight ahead and punched it through the uprights. The extra points and field goals were not automatic."

The next game was a heart-breaking 10-7 loss to number one LSU. Florida led until the final three minutes of the ballgame.

Don Deal: "LSU was one of the top teams in the country. They had the Chinese Bandits special team, a big, old tackle named Bo Strange, [All-American halfback] Billy Cannon, and all the horses out there. It was a big game for me because that was the only game my dad ever saw me play.

"Corpus Christi is a long way. He worked in construction all over the country, and it was just tough for him to get to Gainesville. The LSU game was in Baton Rouge, and my parents came, and they were amazed. That was the first time they'd ever been to a big-time college game. Of course, all the LSU fans were doing what they were renowned for doing—drinking and raising cain. Mommy didn't understand what this college football was all about. She kind of thought maybe I was in the wrong place and doing the wrong thing. She had never seen anything like that. She didn't know things like that existed.

"The LSU game was a big deal. It was exciting. They had the tiger sitting right outside your dressing room. As you walked through, the thing would snarl at you.

"We played them tough. We had a shot to win. We had a pretty good football team, just a tough bunch of guys. A good bunch of players."

Jimmy Dunn: "We played in front of their crowd, and our team played extremely well and moved the ball on them on offense, and we maintained our field position.

"When Bobby Joe couldn't kick, I was the punter. My specialty was that I could kick the ball out of bounds. So if I was in the game and the ball was inside the other team's fifty yard line, I'd punt the ball. They didn't waste Bobby Joe's kicking ability to kick one 35 yards. They wanted him for the longer ones.

"But against LSU twice I kicked the ball out of bounds inside the LSU five. So we had the field position, and it took them pretty much the whole game to recover from that."

Don Deal: "The score was tied [7-7] with a few minutes to go. They marched down to the twenty, and on fourth down [Tommy Davis] kicked a field goal to beat us.

"We had a couple of chances. Back then it was more of a punting game. There weren't many high-scoring games. Nobody threw the ball all over the field like they do now. A touchdown and a field goal was a lot of scoring."

Jimmy Dunn: "They were good, but we had chances to win that game. We had a couple of big plays late, where we were inside their ten yard line, and we got a penalty. Then we got sacked for a loss, and that put us out of field goal range. That's a game we should have won.

"It was like that with our team. We were there, but we were just not quite good enough. That's how close we were to being one of the best teams in the country. We were in the top fifteen, but with a little help, we could have been in the top five. The guy we needed was Bernie Parrish."

Don Deal: "Auburn, the national champs in '57, was next, and again we had a chance to win. I had a pretty good ballgame that day. I had one run over forty yards, and I intercepted a pass and went downfield. We got down close but we were only able to score on a field goal. Auburn only scored two field goals."

Vel Heckman: "We ended up getting two tackles hurt in the LSU game, so we were going to have to play third-teamers against Auburn. We had one I felt was a pretty good football player, but I didn't feel the other one was that good. I went and talked to Woodruff, and he agreed to let me play on both teams. So I played right offensive tackle with the first team AND left offensive tackle on the second team. And I stayed in on defense. I just came out on some kicks. In '58, my senior year, I played 58 minutes in the Auburn game and I lost 19 pounds. They beat us 6-5. After the game Shug Jordan said that Woodruff messed them up by playing me at different places on defense. That was another game that helped promote me.

"We could have won the game. It was 6 to 3, and we had them in their own territory at their 15 yard line in the last couple minutes of the game, and they took a safety so they could punt out of the hole. And then we marched down the field to the Auburn ten with three minutes left, and we tried for a field goal, but didn't make it. Auburn was the number three team in the country that year. It was our last regular season loss that year.

"That day [against LSU] I played one of the best games I ever played, and I didn't know it until after the game. Paul Dietzel, the LSU coach, came into our locker room to meet me. He came up and shook my hand and said, 'Vel, that's the best tackle play I've ever seen.' Later on, I made All-American, and he was on the All-American trip to New York I went on, and he congratulated me again. At the end of the season I played with some of the LSU guys in the Senior Bowl, and they said that they had tried to trap me, and I had put two guards out of the game. As I said, if you do your steps right, drop your shoulder and throw the forearm.... But the LSU game was one of the games that helped me become an All-American."

Don Deal: "The score was 6-5 at the end, and Joe Hergert tried a long field goal and didn't make it. But it may have been our best game of the season. We played super. Our defense played outstanding. They had been national champs. They had a lot of big names, big guns. It was one of those games where you felt brokenhearted, because you had a chance to win.

"Those were two SEC games right there—LSU and Auburn—if we had won them, they would have been big, big wins for Florida at that time."

After the disappointing loss, Florida then met Georgia. Bob Woodruff had been ordered to beat Georgia by the administration and the alumni, and after nine encounters, Woodruff's record was 6-3, including the 7-6 squeaker in 1958. Georgia scored first and missed the extra point, but Florida won when Jimmy Dunn ran an option play to the left, cut back to his right and ran 76 yards untouched for a score. Billy Booker's PAT was the game winner.

Jimmy Dunn: "They played a lot of high school games at the Gator Bowl, and this time of year the field got soft, and it was wet, and we couldn't do anything. We had those little, bitty backs, and we couldn't do ANYTHING. We had very few first downs. We didn't have anything that resembled a drive at all. But we were playing defense. They were moving the ball. They were making first downs. They ran against us better than anybody had all year. They had a lot of chances to score. Three or four times they were inside our ten, were whipping us bad.

"On this particular option play, it was wet and the ground was soft, and these big linemen were getting slower and slower, so when I ran this play, I got through the first line of defense, and then I was out where the little guys play, and we had some great downfield blocking. We were down there rolling at the defensive backs. I didn't break tackles or run over people. I was just following where my blockers were. But it WAS a giant play in the game, because I don't think we had even been in their end of the field.

"And then Billy Booker kicked the extra point. Billy had a cast on his arm when he kicked it. People used to say to Billy that I won that game, and Billy would say, 'No, Jimmy tied it. I won it.'

"So that made it three straight wins over Georgia for us. It was a great accomplishment. Also, we won bragging rights with the Georgia guys, many of whom we knew and saw every year. We had some Georgia players, and they had Florida players. It was built up in the press and had national implications, the largest cocktail party in the country. That was its reputation."

Vel Heckman: "Then the next week we beat Arkansas State 51-7, and twelve of us didn't even play, which made me mad. Here I was being pushed for All-American, and here's a week I didn't play. During the game I tried to get Woodruff to play me, but he said no. I'll never forget, in the second quarter we were ahead by three touchdowns, and he said, 'Heckman, get in there.' I said, 'Like hell.'"

Don Deal: "A bunch of us [starters] didn't get to play against Arkansas State. The biggest thing we did that game was help move the bandstand out at halftime for the bandleader so they could play."
The next game was the inaugural game between Florida and Florida State University. For years Florida State had pushed for the game, but Florida had refused to put the former girls' school on the football schedule. After an act of the state legislature, in 1958 the first game between the two schools was scheduled on November 22, 1958. Florida won 21-7.

Vel Heckman: "You know the legislators forced us to play them. Florida didn't want to play them. It started a great rivalry—which is great.

"Tom Nugent was their coach. They had a good football team. They took the opening kickoff and returned it to the three-yard line. But in my mind they had eleven good players, and we had twenty-two."

Jimmy Dunn: "When I was at Florida as a student, neither I, or any of us, understood why we didn't play FSU, or today why we don't play the

University of Miami. From what I read, there was no advantage for Florida to play FSU. Everything was in FSU's favor. If we let them play us, it would give them credibility in recruiting, and it was a game you could possibly lose, and we were expected to win, so there was nothing to gain by playing FSU.

"So someone from FSU went to the legislature. Why not? Why not do everything possible to help your program? If the role had been reversed, the Florida people would have done exactly the same thing. The game was coming. This just brought it on two or three years earlier. It WAS gonna happen. Two big schools in the same state have got to play each other just for the recognition and to give the high school players a choice where to go to school. I just happened to be there for the first one.

"Our team knew 90 percent of their players and vice versa. It was a lot bigger game in the media than it was between us. It means a lot more today than it did then. We knew we had to play our best, because they were good. They did a lot of things we had not seen. They were in a four-man I formation. They had motions. They had tricks plays we hadn't seen. We worked hard in practice, because we didn't know what to expect.

"We played a pure vanilla kind of football. Everybody lined up and ran off right tackle.

"I remember Jack Espenship ran back the opening kickoff, and I made the tackle. I was the first Gator ever to tackle a Seminole."

Don Deal: "FSU scored first. Then Dave Hudson blocked a punt, picked it up and ran in to tie the score.

"Jimmy Dunn took care of the rest. We beat them [21-7]. Everybody was fired up."

Jimmy Dunn: "We should have won. We were expected to win, and we won. If we just went out and did what we were capable of doing, we knew we'd win the game. Don't do anything stupid, don't turn it over and don't throw a lot of interceptions and kick the ball good and cover, and good things will happen, and that's the way it worked out.

"Lee Corso was the defensive backfield coach, a personal friend of mine. He tells me the reason we won is because his pass coverage was so good, I had to run the ball. He said his defense had everyone else covered. He said, 'If I hadn't covered them so well, you wouldn't have run so much. You just ran, and we couldn't catch you.'"

Vel Heckman: "We then beat Miami again [12-9], so I ended up with a 2-1 record against Miami, which always made me happy."

Don Deal: "Miami was a throwing team. They threw the ball a lot. In between the thirties, they did a lot of damage. Our defense got tough and kept them out of the end zone."

Jimmy Dunn: "We played Miami in Jacksonville in the Gator Bowl. Right at the end they had us backed up, and we stopped them inside our five, and I remember giving them a safety, and then we punted the ball out and held them."

Don Deal: "After beating Miami, we were invited to play Mississippi in the Gator Bowl. It was back and forth. We lost because we never could get into the end zone. Ole Miss had a heck of a good defensive football team. Every time it was third and three, they held us to short runs, or we would punt the ball."

Vel Heckman: "Other than the major bowls, the Gator Bowl was a very important game. If you didn't go to the Orange, Rose, Sugar, or Cotton, then there was the Gator. So I'd say it was the fifth-most important game in the country. The conferences had deals with four of those bowls, so if you got picked for the Gator Bowl, it was a pretty important game.

"We lost 7-3. It was frustrating. We kept moving inside their ten, but then we didn't score. There was a fumble or interception. We had a better team. We just blew it. We blew it."

Jimmy Dunn: "There again, we didn't have the power to get the ball in the end zone when we had to. We got it to the 3, to the 5, to the 15, and we didn't score. We could get it down there, but when we got into four-down territory, where all the defensive backs were up playing in that box, we couldn't make an inch. No Billy Cannon. Or no Bernie."

Vel Heckman: "In '58 we most likely would have won the SEC and the national championship if Bernie had not signed his pro baseball contract. Woodruff lost his job after '59, and if we would have had Bernie, Woodruff never would have lost his job. Cause in '58 we lost to Auburn, which was the top team in the country the year before. We lost to them 6–5, and they were number three at the end of year. We lost to LSU, the number one team in the country, 10 to 7. We lost to Mississippi State 14 to 7. We would have won those games with Bernie. He was so great on defense too, which became evident when he joined the Cleveland Browns."

Jimmy Dunn: "The Mississippi game was our last game, and when it was over and we had lost, we still felt we were the better team. We did not execute. We couldn't punch it in. We were better than Ole Miss, and we should have won that game, and we didn't do it.

"And after my senior year ended, the only interest from the pros was from the Canadian League. I needed another quarter of school to graduate. I had to intern somewhere, so Coach Woodruff told me I could come back and be a graduate assistant on his staff, and I could go intern. The college got me an internship at a junior high school in Gainesville during school hours, and then I coached the freshman football team in the afternoons.

"I enjoyed football. I thought about the game a lot. I enjoyed the competition of trying to put together a team and going to play someone else."

Jimmy Dunn would coach under Bob Woodruff and Ray Graves, under Doug Dickey at the University of Tennessee, and under Steve Spurrier with the USFL's Tampa Bay Bandits. Today Jimmy Dunn is the coach of the Charleston Swamp Foxes in the Arena Football League.

Vel Heckman, Dunn's teammate, in 1958 was named to the All-American team. He would go on to play pro ball, but only for a short time. His heart wasn't in it, and he returned home to Florida, where he coached high school ball and then went into business.

Vel Heckman: "So in '59 I went out with the 49ers. I had no idea the difference between college and pro ball. I signed for a $8,500 salary. All the guys I spoke with had off-season jobs. You had to rent your own room in Frisco. You had to pay for your own food.

"To give you an idea how close-knit the veterans were back then, only an average of one and a half rookies made each team.

"I was an offensive guard, and after an afternoon of one on one blocking about Leo Nomellini, our defensive tackle, that night Y. A. Tittle and John Brodie took me out for drinks. This was during the second week of practice.

So I had the team made. After four weeks I was playing first string for them, but I ended up getting banged up some and got disheartened. I just left. I didn't get cut.

"I came back to Florida and coached the freshman football team while I worked on my degree.

"I coached Florida in '60, then coached at Florida Military Academy, which was a college team in '61. In '62 I ended up the high school football coach at Lake View High School in Winter Garden, Florida. I was head coach and athletic director until 1975. Then I quit teaching and went into the specialty advertising business. I've been doing that ever since—selling promotional products.

"I had no regrets [about quitting pro ball], because I can walk and run and I'm 65 years old. I have too many friends [who played pro football] who have had knee replacements, hip replacements, and no pension."

sixteen

Woodruff Goes for a Tie

Don Deal: "Nineteen fifty nine was kind of a funny year. We never could get anything really good going. We started out good enough, beating Tulane [30-0]. Dickie Allen was the quarterback. He was a pretty flamboyant guy. He threw the ball around pretty good. He didn't have the running skills Jimmy Dunn had, but he could throw it.

"I also remember the great year Bobby Joe Green had. He came from Oklahoma. Don Chandler, a great punter, a great athlete, had played at Northeast Oklahoma Junior College in Commerce, Oklahoma, which was renowned for having great punters. Bobby Joe Green played at the same school. He was one of the greatest athletes I've ever seen. He could run a 9.6 hundred, and he could high jump 6 foot 10. In fact, he and I started the ballgame. He was at one halfback, and I was at the other. He could just do it all. He was a great athlete, and he could punt the ball—he did it for nineteen years in the pros.

"And in the Tulane game he did one thing that was the last time it ever happened in a college football game—he drop-kicked the extra point.

"We scored against Tulane and lined up with ten men on the line of scrimmage, and he was back there by himself for the extra point. And he drop-kicked it!

"They just wanted to see him do it. Because on kickoffs, he could drop-kick it out of the end zone.

"I can remember he and I would work out together. I would get at the top of the stadium, and he would punt, and I would tell him whether the ball was above the top of the stadium or below. He wanted to hit it above the stadium every time, and did.

"After beating Mississippi State and Virginia, our next game was against Rice in Houston. That was kind of a homecoming for me because Houston and Corpus Christi are not too far away. This was a controversial game.

"Like I said, every game was low scoring. It was back and forth. We played pretty well. I scored once in the game on a short pass.

"They had a couple of big running backs, and with about six minutes to go, the score was tied, and the coaches decided to play for the tie, instead of playing for the win.

"The players weren't real happy about it. We were playing in Rice Stadium—it's huge, where they held a Super Bowl game, and it was one of those games where you thought you had a chance to win and thought we should have won. To go home with a tie just wasn't satisfying.

"No one said anything, but you are just not happy with the situation. In your heart you know at least you've given it your best shot. I know one of the great coaches once said, 'Avoid losing,' but there is a point where you have to try to win the ballgame.

"But of course we were looking at things from our perspective. The players don't understand the pressures that coaches have on them from the alumni."

Florida proceeded to lose its next four games in a row.

Don Deal: "The next week we lost to Vanderbilt [13-6]. We might have had a letdown because of the Rice game.

"LSU shut us out [9-0]. Our offense didn't do a lot all day. Their defense shut us down, and it was just one of those days when you just couldn't get anything going. We played them at home. That was embarrassing.

"We then were shut out by Auburn [6-0]. That was a heck of a football game. There again, David Hudson, who never missed the ball, dropped one in the end zone, or we'd have won 7-6. It was raining that day. We must have punted on third down five times. It was just a tough, gloomy day in the rain, but it was one of the better games that everybody played. Auburn was great. We played good, and we ended up on the wrong end of the stick.

"And then Fran Tarkenton and Georgia beat us [21-10], and we finished the season winning our last two games. We beat Florida State [18-8], but by then we could tell that Coach Woodruff was in trouble. The press was coming after all the players. They were coming around, and that wasn't good. Everybody was kind of down. Everyone had high expectations when the season began, and when it doesn't go right....

"It was to me a sad situation. I liked Coach Woodruff. He did a lot for me—getting me back on the track academically. Coach Foldberg was a good, personal friend. I sure didn't want to see anything happen to them. I knew their families.

"The final game was against Miami. Everyone told themselves that if we beat Miami, then the coaches would get to stay. I can remember during the game I caught a pass and scored, and it put us in front, and Coach Robinson, who was the backfield coach, came over to the sideline and said, 'Hey, you saved the game. You saved our jobs.'

"We ended up winning the game, and we all felt good. We were all fired up. We thought everything was going to be fine, that we'd go into the next season and everything would be okay for them. And then it wasn't. Why? The players didn't know. All we did was read about it the paper. I didn't have a whole lot of input in that."

Jimmy Dunn: "In 1959 I was interning at a junior high school. By then, the Florida football program had come to a certain point, and we couldn't get over that hump. If we could have won one or two more games during any one of the three seasons, or if we hadn't been on probation and if the UCLA game hadn't been cancelled, we'd have finished 7-2-1, and that would have put us second in the SEC and would have put us in the Cotton Bowl. Any combination would have saved Woodruff's job. I think one more win in '58 would have saved him. If we had beaten Ole Miss in the Gator Bowl in '58, I think it would have saved him.

"But maybe not. There was a group of people who thought we should have been more explosive. But nobody was that way. When they changed the rules calling for one-platoon football, he knew how you had to play the game. It had to be field position, kicking, had to be defense, and any time you had left over you did safe-type plays so you wouldn't turn the ball over.

"And the fans are only happy with this kind of football when you win. When I was coaching at Tennessee, we played the exact same kind of football, but those fans were coached to understand and appreciate the defensive game by General Neyland. When the Tennessee fans were asked in a newspaper poll to pick the top ten games, we had just had a 37-34 shootout with UCLA. It was a great, great college football game right down to the last play, but that didn't even make the top ten. The game that won was a defensive struggle against Georgia Tech that Tennessee won 6-0. So their fans were coached to appreciate field position, kicking, and defense.

"Those were the things we did very well. Auburn was national champions, and they won games 7-6. That year they won five games by less than five points. So it wasn't by how you scored or how you won, it was just if you won or not.

"Coach Woodruff wasn't a real sociable type guy. He was kind of standoffish. He spent all his time with people he cared about rather than try to make friends with people who weren't in his inner circle. But he was a super guy. He'd do anything for you. He really enjoyed his players.

"And he told me that for him to stay he had to get rid of some assistant coaches, but he wouldn't do it. He wouldn't fire them. They just wanted him to make changes in the staff. But those guys had been loyal to him, and he was extremely loyal to them. He wouldn't have any part in firing them, so they decided to make a change.

"He went back to Tennessee as coach and after one year took over as athletic director.

"His replacement was Ray Graves, who was a well-known football coach in the South, a defensive coordinator at Georgia Tech. He had been with Bobby Dodd a long time, had been a great player at Tennessee. Ray had a great reputation as a football coach and recruiter in the south.

"I'm sure they brought Ray in to hire offensive-minded people, and that's what he tried to do. He put together a great coaching staff, including Pepper Rodgers, Jack Green and Gene Ellenson. He kept some of the guys from the old staff, Hobe Hoosier and Johnny Mauer. They were all good recruiters, and Ray was more sociable to the alumni and to the public than Woodruff. Ray was a PR kind of guy and a good football coach. He hired good people."

Ray Graves: "Bobby Dodd pretty much told me, 'When I retire, you will be the head coach at Georgia Tech.' In 1957 Bobby was offered the Florida job. I came to Gainesville with him. He was fishing a lot, and he came down to talk about the job, and we fished the lakes around Gainesville. The AD, Coach Alexander, told me, 'If Bobby takes the Florida job, you can have the Georgia Tech job.'

"I don't know why he didn't take the Florida job. He liked Georgia Tech, had been there a long time. Florida wasn't as bright an opportunity to recruit. At that time Florida wasn't winning too many ballgames.

"Anyway, he came back to Georgia Tech and stayed, and Woodruff, who was the Florida coach, recruited his son, and in 1959 Georgia Tech played Arkansas in the Gator Bowl, and at the dinner that night after the game, it became clear that the big name Notre Dame coach that Florida wanted wasn't going to come, and Dutch Stanley, the head of the search committee, told me he wasn't coming, and Dick Stratton, who was also on the committee, said to me, 'Listen, come out here and let's talk a minute.' I went into a little office, and he said, 'Why don't you apply for the Florida job?' I said, 'I don't know. I'm pretty well set at Georgia Tech.' He said, 'It might be a good opportunity.' I said, 'Nah, I'll pass.' He said, 'Will you think about it?' I said I would.

"The next week I went to the NCAA meeting, and Dutch Stanley talked to me. I said, 'I'll go back to Georgia Tech and talk to Bobby Dodd,' and I did. Bobby said, 'Bobby Jr. is down there, and they just had a good freshman class. They have Lindy Infante, and they think they're going to be pretty good.'

"We talked about it, and Bobby said, 'I'm going to coach another eight or ten years. Why don't you go down there and find us some good lakes to fish? They you can come back here if you want to. Bobby's down there. It might be a good deal.'

"So I called them and told them I'd take the Florida job. I met Dr. Reitz at the Holiday Day in Gainesville. All he said was, 'I want you to graduate the players and play within the rules. That's all I'm asking.' [During the Ray Graves era over ten years, 94 percent of his football players graduated, and 56 percent of them went on to get a graduate school degree.] Dr. Reitz was a good president to play for. He was a big booster of mine. Our birthdays were the same, December 31. He also said, 'You'll make $17,000. That's what I'm making now. I have a house and a car, but you get a car, not a house. You'll never make more money than I make.' And we shook hands, and that was it. Dr. Reitz went on to make $19,000 and then $25,000, and that's what I made as athletic director and football coach for ten years, and after that I was athletic director.

"When I came to Florida after Woodruff left, they said, 'What are we doing bringing another defensive coach from Tennessee down here?' Woodruff once kicked on third down against Rice. I said, 'Listen, I was a defensive coach, and I had a pretty good defensive reputation there, wrote a few articles, but I'm going to tell you this: the offense I put out there is the one I don't want to play against. I'm going to make them defense us the width of the field, and I'm going to put men in motion, make them make decisions after the ball is snapped, which gives them a chance to make mistakes on defense.'

"I said, 'That's the kind of offense I'm going to put in. I hope I can recruit the players to make that offense effective.'

"That was the way I started. At a couple of Quarterback Club meetings I told them, 'Out of Graves will come the ressurection of the Florida offense.'

seventeen

Larry Libertore

When Ray Graves arrived at Florida, his intention was to start his mentor's son, Bobby Dodd Jr., at quarterback. But after he arrived he soon saw that the boy didn't have the athletic ability needed for the position. Graves moved Dodd Jr. to defensive back, and he gave the job to a diminutive whirlwind of a runner by the name of Larry Libertore. According to Ray Graves, "Larry was as slick a quarterback running the option as anyone."

Larry Libertore: "I heard from most colleges. But I was 5' 8 1/2", and I weighed 132 pounds. I had wanted to go to Ohio State or Notre Dame, cause I grew up there as a young person. In Ohio, you never heard of a school in Florida.

"I narrowed my choices to the University of Miami, Florida State, Tennessee, the University of Georgia, and Florida. Some of the schools came to see you instead of you coming to see them. I remember the scout from Tennessee when he actually saw me. I could see what was going through his mind: 'How could he even PLAY football?' Because I was really small, even then.

"My high school coach convinced me that I didn't want to leave the state of Florida. He said, 'You plan to live in Florida. You're going to make it your home and your family and friends will live there. You don't want to graduate from a school where you're not going to live?'

"That argument made sense, and at the time he also discouraged me from going to Miami or FSU. I didn't know it, but he had made an agreement to coach at the University of Florida.

"I signed with Florida for a couple of reasons. I wanted to play quarterback as early as I could. I would have had to wait until my junior year at Miami because Fran Curci was there ahead of me. At FSU, they were just beginning to put together their program, so I didn't want to go there. The fact was, I was going to stay in the state of Florida, Florida recruited me heavily, and they were really nice to me.

"I played most of the time as the quarterback on both the freshman and red-shirt teams against the varsity. And no question about it, practice was much harder than the game. If you could play every day in practice—I was the other team's quarterback for two full years—and I was quite successful at it. They would tell the defense what plays were going to be called, and I still did well.

"The first two years I was under Coach Bob Woodruff. As a freshman or sophomore, we didn't have much contact with the head coach. But my recollection of Bob Woodruff was that he was a fair man. He was definitely a defensive coach. Most of their direction appeared to be aimed at a strong defense. That bothered me to a degree. Jimmy Dunn, who was from Tampa, was the quarterback. He was a senior my redshirt year. They were running the option, and I wanted to be an option quarterback.

"The coach I was closest to my redshirt year was John Eibner. He was a great guy. I think he got a kick of me being the quarterback and running plays. He was motivated to succeed against the varsity defenses. So I was close to him.

"After the '59 season, they brought in Ray Graves, and I was devastated. Here I am, I haven't played a down of varsity ball. I'm 135 pounds at a major college, and there are eight or nine quarterbacks there. They bring in Ray Graves from Georgia Tech, who didn't know me from Adam, hadn't recruited me. I really strongly considered changing schools. I would have gone to Miami or FSU, just to go somewhere. I was really concerned I wouldn't play. Because once again, everyone else made an issue of my size. It was just, would I get a chance? I didn't know.

"Graves and his staff came in right before spring practice and began interviewing players. The first thing they were trying to do was eliminate some scholarships, get rid of some players, and I went through that, and when spring practice started, I was the sixth or seventh-team quarterback. Then I began to move up.

"I had somewhat of a successful spring practice and by midway I was playing first or second team quarterback and playing a little on defense and returning punts a little. I was then quite enthused to go into my next year.

"I was a natural quarterback from the stand-point of footwork, hand-work. It was a God-given thing. And I had a decent arm. I could throw long.

Could I have thrown 30 or 40 times a game like they do now? Probably not. But no team did that then. Most of the time we threw seven or eight, and only when they needed to. I don't know what reason it was, but I felt that when I needed to do something, I could do it.

"When we started in '60, most players were playing both ways. We had limited substitution, so I would leave the field, and they'd put a linebacker in. Or at times on first down I'd stay in and play safety, and the center would go out and they'd put a linebacker in. I also returned all the punts that year.

"Something else I'll share with you: in 1960, my sophomore year, I ran the ball more than any back in the Southeastern Conference. People would say, 'He never got hurt because he was so quick and they never could catch him,' but that isn't true. I only scored three touchdowns all year, so what happened the rest of the time? I took my share of hits.

"In games, it got to the point that the defensive player would rather that I pitched it than kept it. So they didn't even care, they just went after me every time. So there were plenty of times when I went back to pass, got rid of it, and got hit. And when we started winning, I started getting publicity, and the other schools began to resent a quarterback being successful at 135 pounds. It was kind of insulting to them. And I think the coaches of the other schools played that up. So the defensive coaches went out of their way to make my life difficult whenever they could, and the more the game went on, or if they missed a tackle, the madder they would get. So if you're the quarterback, and you have your hands on the ball, you're going to get it, whether you have your eyes open or not. But I enjoyed it. It was a real challenge to me.

"I can remember in 1960 the look on the face of the players in the huddle of the excitement and the enthusiasm when I would call the play. When it was third down and two yards, and I'd make the first down to keep the drive alive, or if I completed a pass third and nine, back then it was a real accomplishment, because everybody in the stands knew you were going to pass.

"One of the gifts I had was the ability to do the little things to keep a drive alive, and when they piled on, I didn't get hurt. They were always piling on, and that kept the offensive line on my side, kind of like the big brother, like the guys in the neighborhood watching over you. And that caused us to play better. It's hard to explain, but when they saw this 135 pound guy returning a punt, what looked like suicide, the other guys would say to themselves, 'I'm going to do everything I can for this guy.'"

eighteen

A New Era

When Coach Graves came to Florida, the varsity players were apprehensive. All they knew was that he was a defensive expert. But what of the offense? Graves brought with him an offensive mind by the name of Pepper Rodgers, the same Pepper Rodgers who twice as a player had beaten Florida with last-minute field goals. Now Florida had Rodgers, and very quickly he won the players over with his offensive genius. One of those players was highly recruited back Lindy Infante, who years later would go on to coach the Green Bay Packers.

Lindy Infante: "I was born and raised in Miami. I went to Miami Senior High School. In those days you didn't have to go to the school that was in your neighborhood. You could go anywhere. Miami Senior High was THE place to go at that time. Miami Senior had a track record. It was a football factory. We had over 4,000 students. We had well over a hundred players on the football field. Otis Mooney was the head coach. If you lost a game during the season, you had a bad year.

"I got lucky and had some schools after me. There were quite a few, but when I got through I narrowed it down in my own mind to either Georgia Tech, Georgia, Miami, or the University of Florida. I wasn't planning on going away from home. So when it was all over, it was basically a no-brainer. I just felt the University of Florida was the place for me. I was from Florida, and I had a lot of friends who were going to the University of Florida, not all football players, just buddies of mine. Of course, at the time you read about it, heard about it, you couldn't avoid it. And even though the University of Miami was local, it recruited mostly from out of state. Florida was predominantly an in-state recruiting school, which was more to my liking.

"The guy who actually recruited me was Hank Foldberg. He was a very impressive individual. He was a very big, impressive guy.

"At the time the colleges were recruiting me, I was living with my sister. My mother and father had been divorced when I was young, and when my mother passed away, I went to live with my sister, who was eleven years older than I was. She had her own family. So she took me in. But the recruiting got to the point where one of the universities that I talked with offered me clothes and free trips home and things of that nature. So I thought I was a hotshot guy, and when Hank Foldberg came to my house, we were sitting and talking, and I remember Hank saying, 'If you come to Florida, we'll give you a room, books, board, tuition fees and fifteen dollars a month for laundry.' That was what was allowed at the time.

"I looked at him and said, 'Is that all you give me?' I didn't mention the school, but I told him what they were offering. He was a big, very impressive guy, and he looked right across at me and said, 'Let me tell you again: We'll give you a room, board, tuition fees and fifteen dollars a month for laundry, and that's it.'

"I said, 'Where do I sign?' And that was it. I said to myself, To heck with the other stuff, this is where I want to go.

"After my freshman year Coach Woodruff was fired. I don't even remember it being a factor, to be honest with you. As freshmen, you were around the varsity and varsity coaches, but only when there was a scrimmage or when they needed somebody to tackle or somebody to knock down. You were there if they needed somebody to line up and beat 70-0 in a scrimmage game. But it was just a transaction in football, and whoever came in, we were going to go play for him as good as we could. I know I liked Bob Woodruff what little I was around him, but I certainly liked Ray Graves, and we've been friends ever since.

"And with Graves came Pepper Rodgers. We became more innovative on offense, did more things."

Some players were in awe of offensive coordinator Pepper Rodgers. Others were equally impressed with Graves' defensive coordinator, Gene Ellenson.

Don Deal: "We didn't know Ray Graves when he was hired. We were apprehensive, just like anybody else. Everybody is afraid of the new. You worry, 'Am I going to fit in,' or 'What do they have in mind?' or 'Who are the new coaches?' But then again, it's a new start for a lot of people, and you look forward to going into spring practice. It was pretty combative.

"With Ray Graves in charge, the offense changed a little, and we had some pretty good guns coming back. We knew the defense was going to be good. Graves was the defensive guru. And Pepper Rodgers was a different kind of an offensive guy.

"Pepper was a free spirit. We'd never seen a coach who drove around on a motor scooter. He liked to throw the ball around a little bit.

"And you can't forget about Gene Ellenson, who was Graves' defensive coordinator. Gene was an important ingredient in our teams. He was the kind of coach everybody wanted to play for. He was exciting, and he could motivate the moon to turn off.

"Though Graves was known as a great defensive coach, Gene was the catalyst who pulled everyone together. He was just an amazing man. All of us who played under him would flock to him. He was just something else. Gene Ellenson was the go-to guy.

"Our quarterback in '60 was Larry Libertore. To me, Larry was Jimmy Dunn all over again. Same size—about 145 pounds, a fiery kind of guy, liked to have a lot of fun. He was kind of a little jitterbug. He could turn a missed tackle into a 60-yard run. The other quarterback, Bobby Dodd Jr., was more the drop-back kind of thrower. His dad was head coach at Georgia Tech. Bobby was a gentleman, a real smart guy with quite a lot of ability.

"Why Bobby Jr. went to Florida instead of Georgia Tech nobody knew. Bobby had been recruited by Coach Woodruff. Of course, Ray Graves had coached for Bobby, and he had a lot of respect for Ray. I imagine it was kind of like why my son didn't want to go to the University of Florida. He just wanted to get out of town. That happens a lot. We had a lot of guys from Georgia.

"In 1960 they modified the substitution rule, allowing one player to be a wild card, to come in and out at will. And if it was a drop-back situation, Bobby played quarterback, and Larry would come in and run the option play and scramble.

"The idea was to not have your quarterback playing defense. The quarterback also was the safety, and so sometimes the coach picked a guy who wasn't as good a quarterback but who played defense better, and that could make things tough. As a coach you tried to have two good teams and balance them out. Sometimes the second team would actually be a better offensive team than the first team. In fact, some coaches liked to load up their second team, knowing you were also bringing in a second team. As a result the strategy often was the way you substituted.

"In '60, we had a good bunch of backs—at the beginning of the season everybody seemed to be getting hurt—including me, and Lindy Infante, who had played high school ball in Miami, was promoted, and he was just an all-around, real good back. He could run, catch, block, and we also had two young guys, Bob Hoover and Dick Skelly, who were the prototypes of the big running backs that everybody is going after now. Both of them had a world of talent.

"I missed the first two games that year with a bad ankle injury. Doug Partin played in my place. Doug was our little cattleman. His dad owned a big ranch down in St. Cloud. Doug was tough as nails. He rode bulls.

"One thing I remember, Doug always had a chaw of tobacco. In one of the games, he got hit and swallowed the tobacco, and if the trainer hadn't known he had tobacco in his mouth, he probably would have choked to death.

"In our first game against George Washington [a 30-7 win], Doug had a long [60-yard] touchdown run. And Larry threw for two touchdowns, and fit in very well, 'cause we started running an option-type offense, and that fit into Larry's talents to a tee."

Larry Libertore: "We beat George Washington in the opener in the Gator Bowl in Jacksonville. After two years in college, it was exciting to get to the first game. I can remember they always had trouble getting equipment to fit me because I'm so little. Your game uniform is different from your practice uniform, and when I put my game pants on, they came down to my ankles, and the thigh pad was over knees. I had to tape them up. I remember that it was kind of awkward. But I also remember it to be exciting. You need a game like that realize how much you need to learn and how inexperienced you are and to get the butterflies out of your stomach. But I loved after minutes of it. It was a fun evening."

Lindy Infante: We opened against George Washington, and Doug Partin, who was senior, made a 60-yard touchdown run. After that, Doug got hurt, and in fact that may have been why I got to play a lot more that year.

"So I got to play against George Washington in my first varsity game, and I don't know if any athlete past or present can put into words to explain to people who haven't been out on the field in front of a big crowd… I certainly don't have the kind of words that can explain to somebody the feelings you have when you're out there. It's exhilarating. It's exciting. All of us, we just lived and breathed football. We felt we were put on earth for football. So when you get the chance to get out there and perform early in your career, I can't imagine anyone NOT being nervous. I'm sure I was apprehensive and nervous, but I was also exhilarated and felt a sense of accomplishment, a sense I had arrived. You are somebody now, because you have been out on the field. It was special."

The second game of the season was against Florida State University. Before the game a group of young men approached end Jon MacBeth with an offer of money if he would play at less than his best. MacBeth immediately reported the bribe to the coaching staff.

Lindy Infante: "That was such a big game, and I guess some gamblers thought they were going to get rich on that one. Because they felt all the money was going to be riding on Florida. I don't remember the point spread. None of us ever paid any attention to it. But we were supposed to win the game by a big margin, and a group of guys approached Jon MacBeth about shaving points, maybe fumbling here and doing something that would keep the score close. Jon, certainly to his credit forever, went to the coaching staff and told them about it. One thing led to another, and before the game they arrested the guys who made the bribe."

Don Deal: "It was kind of a scary deal for Jon. They gave him security, the whole nine yards. What I didn't understand was why they picked Jon out. Jon wasn't carrying the ball that much. None of us got many carries because we were playing defense half the time. The other half of the time, because there were two teams, you weren't even on the field. So if you get to carry the ball three or four times a series, that's a lot. So the impact of one player in a scheme of two different offensive teams was small. He might have hurt the team by doing something on defense—missing a tackle, say, but Jon was very intense. He would never have done anything like that. He was our law man.

"In the end we won the FSU game 3-0—on a Billy Cash field goal."

Larry Libertore: "We found out about the bribe attempt after the game. We were kind of astounded that that stuff even went on. None of us had ever had any experience with anything like that before. We were all proud of Jon for what he did. We were sitting around saying, 'Boy, that takes a lot of courage to do that.' Because when you start dealing with gamblers and bookies and people losing a lot of money, your life is on the line.

"We won the Florida State game 3-0, but it wasn't very much of a contest. Bill Peterson had just come there as head coach. At that time it was huge for FSU to play us or Miami. For Florida, the big games were in the Southeast Conference; Georgia Tech and Auburn were the big games. So it wasn't like we got up for the FSU game. I would say FSU was sky high to play us where we were just average. So they played on a more intense level than we did.

"Billy Cash kicked a field goal to win the game. They just played way over their heads, and we played mediocre. Not taking anything away from them, but that's the way it was."

The next ballgame was against Coach Ray Graves' old school, Georgia Tech. The last time Florida had beaten Tech was back in 1954. Graves used both Bobby Dodd Jr. and Larry Libertore at quarterback.

Ray Graves: "I had to play Bobby Dodd in Gainesville in our third ballgame, and we lucked out. We changed our luck around. The game was covered nationally. There was a lot of interest in it since Bobby Jr. was our quarterback, and Bobby Dodd was my old ex-coach. We beat Georgia Tech 18-17. We went downfield and scored with about a minute to go, and we went for two and made it."

Don Deal: "I finally got to play—against Georgia Tech, the tenth-ranked team in the country. We were losing by a touchdown [17-10] with five minutes left in the game, and we had the ball on our own ten yard line. What happened next was amazing!

"There are days when you go into a game, and everything has to fall into place for you to win, and that day, well it did for us. Everything just happened the way it was supposed to happen—like it was scripted."

Larry Libertore: "We proceeded to move down the field, moved up to about the 40 yard line. I passed on a couple of third down situations for first downs. Then they took me out for a play. Bobby Dodd came in, and he went to his left and threw a pass back across the field to Don Deal, and that took us down to the 25." Then I went back in, and we ran a trap play, and we ran an option off tackle—I gave it to the fullback, Don Goodman, and he ran it down to around the two, and they put Bobby Dodd back in. I can't comment on why they did that. Usually when you're in a successful drive you don't change players, but the coaches did what they thought was right.

"So Bobby went in and they ran a couple of plays, and on third down there was a mishandling in the backfield, and the ball ended up on the three yard line. It was fourth down, and they put me back in the game.

"We ran the option to the right. I had nowhere to go, and at the last split second, I pitched it to Lindy and he was right smack on the out-of-bounds line, and he just made it into the end zone, and that made it 17 to 16."

Lindy Infante: "To be frank, when we called the play, I said to myself, Larry is going to keep this thing. Because Larry would much rather hang onto it and run with it, not selfishly, but he was such a good runner he could make things happen when he had his hands on the ball.

"So the play was called, and the play was in progress, and the last thing on my mind was that he was going to pitch it to me. And when he did, to be honest, it kind of caught me off guard. We were running out of field, and when the ball came toward me, I kind of reached out with one hand, stopped the ball, got it under control, and headed for the pylon.

"Luckily, I eked it in. I always kid people when they ask me about it. I say, 'Oh, it was a brilliant run for a touchdown.' I don't tell them it was a four-yard no-brainer where all you had to do was get it to the corner of the end zone before anyone tackled you.

"A few years later I met the defensive player who tackled me on that play. I wish I could remember his name. He said, 'I swear I stopped you.' I said, 'No, you didn't.' There's a photo of it. To me it shows that I just barely got it in."

Don Deal: "Graves went for the two-point conversation to win the game. The way the game had gone, there was no way we could have gone for one.

"It wasn't a conference game. Bobby Dodd Jr. was playing. It was a game we had to win, and we just kind of felt like we were gonna win it. We knew we were gonna win the ballgame—it was fate.

"Libertore took the snap, he faked to the fullback, and Jon MacBeth— Honest Jon—went through the line, and Libertore hit him, and we won the game 18–17."

Larry Libertore: "Pepper Rodgers and I had already decided what the two-point play was going to be. It was already decided: a fake to the fullback, Jon MacBeth, and I either keep it or pass to him. It wasn't a play we had used before.

"I came out as the quarterback going toward the fullback. In the belly series you put your hands and the ball in their stomach. You hope the defense will tackle him. You pull it back out. In this case you hoped they wouldn't tackle Jon, because he was the pass receiver, and he was the only one. So I pulled it out of his stomach, and of course, I had the option of running. I started to run, and I started to turn toward the goal line. I wasn't that far away, but I could tell that it would be a miracle to get through and get in, but I had no choice, I had to either keep it or pass it, and just as I was able to turn up the field and run, I popped the ball to him. He caught it, and we won 18-17.

"It was fantastic, because we won and it was a big game. It was a big deal, and we enjoyed the moment."

Ray Graves: "Everybody asked, 'Why did you go for two?' I didn't have any choice. The team was a two touchdown underdog, and we had a chance to win a game instead of a tie. I couldn't have looked them in the face or walked into the dressing room if I hadn't. If we went for two and didn't make it, they played good enough to win, so that was the easiest decision I ever had to make. "The win gave us confidence that 'we can win at Florida.'"

Don Deal: "I tell you it was very fulfilling. Everybody was starting to feel like, 'Hey, we're not half bad.' Of course the coaching staff and everybody feels pretty good when you beat what we considered to be a pretty powerful team."

Lindy Infante: "At the time winning the game was significant. We were just happy to have won. It was really a big game on that 1960 team, because the win catapulted us to being a pretty solid team."

Larry Libertore: "When I hit Jon with a pass, and we won the game, I would like to think that was the turning point for major big-time for the Gator football program. Because we had, for the first time offensively won a big game we weren't supposed to win.

"With five minutes to go we had been way down at the other end of the field. It used to take you four or five minutes to go the length of the field. Now they do it in two plays. But to sustain a drive and get down to the goal line against Georgia Tech, which had a quality football program, to be successful in that game led to the beginning of a new era for Gator football."

nineteen

A Big Win in the Gator Bowl

Larry Libertore: "Of course, you're going to ask me what happened the week after the Georgia Tech game against Rice in Miami in the Orange Bowl. It's one of those things they do to satisfy the alumni and to broaden the name of the school. And for whatever reason, all of us, the players and coaches, took this game for granted.

"Rice outplayed us and outcoached us. I remember that every play I ran as a quarterback, they were waiting for us like they knew what we were going to do. Of course, the coaches called most of the plays so your hands were tied. It just didn't seem like anything we did worked. Nothing. [Rice won 10-0.] So you shake it off and go on to the next one and learn a lesson from it."

Don Deal: "When Rice played us in the Orange Bowl in Miami, we had had some players hurt in the Georgia Tech game. We were down to about two running backs. Lindy got hurt. I was about the only one left. Everyone got hurt at once, and that does happen. We were switching back and forth from right to left just trying to get two backs into the ballgame. We just couldn't get anyone well and couldn't get anybody going against Rice."

Larry Libertore: "We played Vanderbilt. Back when we played in the SEC, those were big games, even with schools like Vanderbilt and Tulane. Perhaps we were better, but when you play those rival teams in your conference, they always play above what they would play. So it was a tough, tough game, but we got back on track with the option play and some passes and turned it around.

"Late in the game, we called an option play to the right. I kept it. There was a little bit of space. I ran up and then cut back against the grain. I remember the safety man had an angle on me. I can see this guy gaining on me cause his strides were bigger. He got me around the twelve yard line. [Libertore was credited with a 58-yard run.]

"We were fourth and six. The coaches called for a fake field goal. We lined up to kick a field goal, and I held, and I rolled out to the right and threw it to Don Deal for a touchdown."

Don Deal: "We shut out Vanderbilt [12-0]. Larry had another big game. He was as quick as a cat. If somebody didn't tackle him, he was gonna go. He was one of those jitterbugs with the big heart like Jimmy Dunn.

"We had a fourth and six, and Larry threw me a short pass for a touchdown. When you have a quarterback like Larry who gets hot, running and passing, it's just hard to contain him.

"We played LSU at Baton Rouge. That was a big game for us. Playing at Tiger Stadium at 7:30 at night with all the crazy Cajuns screaming and hollering out there—it's an amazing thing. It's like visitors coming to the Swamp. To go to Tiger Stadium, that was a big deal.

"And on the very first place of the game, Larry took three steps to his left, cut back, and ran 66 yards for a touchdown. It was amazing we got that kind of start."

Larry Libertore: "Against LSU, the very first play of the game was an option play. As unusual as it was, there was nobody to pitch it to. So it was an option with no pitchman, which means it was a keeper. I ran the option to the left. Tiger Stadium was loud and noisy. I saw a little opening, and I cut into the opening. I reversed my field. I went the rest of the way for a touchdown. Sixty six yards, and I think everybody in the stadium was stunned. And the strange thing was that at the end of the first half, we only made a total of seventy yards."

Lindy Infante: "Larry and I roomed together our sophomore year and got to know each other quite well. He was a fun guy. We had something in common—we were both from Miami. I respected him as a person. We got along well together, had a lot of fun together. When you room together, you create a bond, and we were around each other when we were trying to study, though I'm not sure I did a lot of that at that point in time. But really, you become friends forever."

Don Deal: "Billy Cash won the LSU game when he kicked two field goals—he was the money guy. Everybody had a lot of confidence in him.

When he was going to kick with the wind you had the feeling he was going to make it—and we won the game [13-10]."

Don Deal: "It was a fun game, and everybody played well. Afterwards Coach Graves let us have a little party—a little down time. He turned us loose on the city of Baton Rouge."

Lindy Infante: "One story about the LSU game: It was just before the half and I ran the ball and made a short run. It wasn't anything spectacular, and I fell to the ground. LSU had a reputation for hitting you with their helmets, and one of the players speared me right in the middle of my back as I hit the ground.

"Everybody who has ever played football gets the wind knocked out of him, and that was my first sensation. I got up. It was third down, and I went back into the huddle. I was having a real tough time breathing. We punted the ball, and then we turned around to play defense.

"I was on the defensive left side as cornerback and I was still having a lot of trouble breathing. Usually your breath comes back relatively soon, but this wasn't happening. So they ran a pass, and I had to cover a guy down the field, and I couldn't run. He ran by me.

"Right after the play I ran over to the sideline to Ray Graves, and I was gasping. 'I can't breathe. I can't breathe. You've got to get somebody else in there.'

"There was a goofy substitution rule that if you started a quarter, you could only be replaced one time that quarter. So by my leaving the game for a second time, it cost us a five-yard penalty. So everybody was mad at me because I had come off.

"I went to the bench, and I still couldn't breathe. They took me in the locker room, and at the half I'm still having trouble breathing, so they take me to a hospital in Baton Rouge and took x-rays. Nothing was broken, but I had a badly bruised back and that was causing the pain and keeping me from breathing. They sent me back to the stadium about the time the game was over.

"We had won the game, and everybody came in and was celebrating. We go back to the hotel room. Ray Graves was so excited he told everyone, 'No curfew tonight. Go out and have a good time. We'll see you in the morning when we fly out.'

"I couldn't do anything. I went up to my room and finally had to call the trainer who got a doctor. They gave me a pain killer to help me through the night.

"We got on the plane, flew back to Gainesville, had our Sunday meeting. Then on Monday we were back out on the practice field. I was still having trouble breathing, but I didn't want to lose my starting job. My chest was strapped up, and I was out there. I ran three or four plays, but I couldn't do anything.

"About this time an ambulance comes out onto the field. A doctor comes over and says to me, 'Get in the back.' I laid down. I still had my practice gear on.

"I said, 'What's going on?'

"He said, 'We have to take you back to the hospital.'

"Three or four doctors were there to meet me. They took me into a room and I wanted to know, 'Can you tell me what's going on here?' They were cutting my shoulder pads off with scissors. The doctor said I had had a birth defect. He said, 'Your lungs have bubbles on them, and you got hit so hard your left lung collapsed. Your left lung is lying on top of your stomach. We have to be careful, because if your other lung pops, you'll be dead.'

"I said, 'What about football?'

"He said, 'You'll never play football again. You're done.' He said that with any luck I would be back on my feet in six months. 'After that maybe we can get you into a wheelchair. In a year you'll be able to walk, but you'll never play sports again.'

"Of course this devastated me. They put me in the infirmary, and that's where I was supposed to lay for six months.

"I called my sister back in Miami. I said, 'I can't stay here for six months. I'll go crazy.'

"A couple days later they put me on a train, because they said the altitude of an airplane would have killed me. I get on a sleeper car, and they gave a porter twenty-five bucks to check on me every so often. I get to Miami. My sister had a hospital bed put in one of the rooms. This was on a Wednesday. I'm all set for six months convalescence.

"The next day I still have some pain in my neck and shoulders, but I am breathing better. I told my sister I wanted another opinion.

"I go to our family doctor. I actually drove myself. They x-rayed me, did a couple tests, and the doctor comes back and says, 'I don't know where they got that diagnosis. I'll tell you what happened. You got hit so hard your left lung popped. You have a hole about the size of a quarter in the bottom of your lung. But the hole was sealed already, and your lung already is about halfway filled with air. The pain you are feeling is the air that was in your chest cavity working its way out of your body. As soon as that gets out and your lung fills back up, you can go back and play.'

"I said, 'When will that be?'

"He said, 'Next week.'

"So I went back to the university the next Monday, practiced, and I was fine. I went from being dead to going back onto the practice field in two weeks. I pulled a muscle in practice that week after I came back, so I missed the Auburn game, but I came back to play against Georgia.

"I don't know if you can fathom the highs and lows of that week and a half period. To all of us back then, football was THE most important thing in our lives, just about next to family. To have been told so bluntly I would never play again, it was crushing, a devastating blow. Then within about four days, to find out I could play! It was the thrill of victory, the agony of defeat, all wrapped up in one week and a half.

"I was out on the field playing against Fran Tarkenton and Georgia. Tarkenton was a halfway legend at that time already. You really enjoyed playing against guys like that."

Going into the game against fourteenth-ranked Auburn, Florida was 3-0 in the SEC, 5-1 overall.

Don Deal: "We couldn't get a whole lot going in that game. I don't know if it was their defense or our lack of offense. But Auburn always was a tough team. They were known for being a tough defensive team. You can see the scores in the past when we played them—6-5, 6-0. In '60 we lost on the field goal [10-7.]"

Larry Libertore: "We were tied 7-7 at the half, and we lost on a field goal. Auburn was a big, fast football team, one of the larger teams like Georgia Tech. They were really quality, and we struggled. They stopped our option play, made it difficult for us. They overloaded their defense on the side where we wanted to run, and that made them even harder to block. So we lost that game to Auburn, and had we won that game, we would have won the SEC championship for the first time in Florida history. It would have been a major accomplishment. At the time we didn't even realize how close we had come. Maybe I was just naive. But I can't remember at all during that time even knowing we were in the running to win the SEC."

Don Deal: "Our next game was against Fran Tarkenton and Georgia. We won the game [22-14], and I remember that chasing Tarkenton down was quite a feat in itself. Again Patchin and Miranda made big plays. The defense made big plays all game long. I also remember that our offense monopolized the ball and took a lot of time off the clock. We didn't throw a whole lot. I can remember we just ran it and ran it and ran it and ran it and ran it and finally we scored. We kept the ball away from them. Bob Hoover had a big ballgame. And our defense made the plays."

Larry Libertore: "I started the game against Georgia. They fumbled the kickoff, and we took it in for a touchdown. We were ahead 13-0 when I returned a punt. I was running down the side-line, and I pulled my hamstring so I couldn't go back in there. I was done. Bobby Dodd went in. Tarkenton was Georgia's quarterback, and he could really throw the ball. But we had scored the first two times, so we had the advantage. We did have a good defensive team.

"I didn't start against Tulane because we weren't sure if I could. It was Homecoming. When I went in, the coaches were pretty smart. The first play we ran was a trap. It made it look like I was going to run the option. Tulane must have thought I was going to go wide. Boy, there was a hole a mile wide up the middle. Bob Hoover went right down the middle all the way and scored a touchdown. I just handed him the ball. [Florida won 21-6.]

"We played Miami. This was an unusual game, because we called all the plays from the line of scrimmage. I'm sure it was Pepper Rodgers' idea. Maybe we should have done that against Auburn. Even though we went into a huddle, we didn't call the plays in the huddle. We'd go up to the line, and when I'd see how the defense stacked up, we'd go the opposite way. I thought it was really innovative. We used colors or codes. If blue's a live color to change the play, and you say 'green,' they don't know. If you say 'green,' or even if you don't say anything, you just call the play at the line. They don't know whether you've called it in the huddle or not. And they don't know our plays anyway. We had never done that before.

"We practiced it all week, and it was successful that day. We should have done some of that against Rice and Auburn. It was a big win."

After Florida beat Tulane, Florida met Miami in front of 61,000 people at the Orange Bowl.

Lindy Infante: "It was always fun to go back home and play because you had so many friends and buddies down there. Many of my friends did not go to college. They were working in Miami."

Don Deal: "That game was a kind of homecoming for all our Miami guys, especially Larry, who had a big ballgame. Larry had one of those great years. Larry had some big games against Miami. [Florida won 18-0.] And so we were invited to play in the Gator Bowl against Baylor, which had the big running back, an All-American, Ronnie Bull.

"We won the game [13-12] on Billy Cash's extra point, and Larry was the MVP of the game. There were no long runs in the game. It was just one of those real physical games. The guys in the trenches won the game.

"We finished the year 9 and 2, and everybody was real pleased. We were a field goal from winning the SEC."

Larry Libertore: "We were invited to play Baylor in the Gator Bowl, which was as big a deal as it could have been at the time. But I don't think any of us as players saw the significance of what we had accomplished. We played week in, week out. We did our jobs and went home. It was nice to win, but I don't think we really felt the significance. The newspaper reporters weren't there interviewing you. It wasn't on TV.

"Everything was low key. It all revolved around the coaches. Very little revolved around us players. On Saturday afternoon most of the time, if there was an SEC game, it was usually Ole Miss, cause they were the big team, or whoever they played that week. We hadn't been on TV."

Lindy Infante: "It was special. Any time you go to a bowl game, it's special. You know you're on television. That's a big deal. Back then TV games were few and far between, not like today where every game, every week, you're on television somewhere. When you're on TV, you can say to friends, 'Hey, I'll wave to you.'

"And up to that point our record in '60 was the best in the history of Florida football. It was exciting to be part of that. Our class was a pretty solid class and there were a lot of great seniors on the team. We complimented each other pretty well. We certainly weren't a national power, but we were a good football team."

Larry Libertore: "What I remember about the Baylor game was that nobody expected us to win. They came from the other end of the country.

We scored our second touchdown on a fumble recovery, and Billy Cash kicked the extra point to win it. And after the game I was awarded the MVP, which was nice, but again, the award didn't mean anything close to what it means today. In the scheme of things, how important was that award? I didn't even know that I deserved to win it, so the fact that I won was nice. But any time you win an award like that, it's the result of the whole team, of everybody else doing well."

Don Deal: "That '60 bunch was real tight. Everybody did a lot of things together—a lot of off-the-field stuff. But again, everybody was a student too, a student first. What's amazing is that almost that whole team graduated and did well. Gene Page is a doctor, Pat Patchin is an engineer, and Vic Miranda did well in the insurance business. The whole team has had a lot of success after college.

"After the season I was contacted by some pro teams saying they were going to draft me. Green Bay called me. But I didn't get drafted, and that kind of hurt a little bit. I had a chance to go into business in Gainesville, to become a partner in a bar called the Gatorland Lounge, and that's what I did. But after a year, I got married, and I got out of that, and went into high school coaching. I became an assistant coach at St. Pete High School and taught drivers' ed. I stayed there six years and went back to the University of Florida as a graduate assistant coach, and stayed there for six years. In 1966, when I came back into coaching, Dr. Cave, who invented Gatorade, also invented something called 'Hoppin' Gator.' It was similar to Gatorade, but it was a beer that was supposed to get into your system faster with electrolytes. I don't think they sold very much of that.

"I went to Southern Mississippi for two years and came back over here to Fort Walton and got back into the school business. I went to a middle school as a head coach and dean. Then I moved to Waxahachie High School where I was vice-principal until August of 2001."

twenty

A Lean Year

Ray Graves: "Six or seven players from 1960 didn't have enough credits to get into the university college, so they dropped out. I lost my big tackle from Miami, and three or four other fine football players. They went to junior college and worked for a year. So in 1961 we had trouble, but we recruited pretty well and came back."

In part to make up for the loss of his seniors and his ineligible players, in '61 Coach Graves started using the three-platoon system, inaugurated by Paul Dietzel at LSU. The idea was to tire out the opposition with numbers.

Larry Libertore: "In 1961 we had three different teams instead of two. One group was the passing group. My group was the option group. I forget what the third one was. The theory was that we wear out the other team. I assume this was Pepper Rodgers again and all his innovative ideas. All the seniors left over from Bob Woodruff had left, and what they were trying to do was get as many guys to play as they could, cause if you have a lot of players and they don't play, they tend to lose interest. So from a theory standpoint, it makes sense. But in practicality it wasn't as successful as they had hoped it would be.

"You can look back and say they should not have split us up. Of the three teams, perhaps they should have played the best eleven. We weren't successful in '61. The other teams began to catch up with us a little bit. They began to know what we were doing. We lost a lot of players. We were in transition.

"We started the '61 season beating Clemson [21-7]. Lindy Infante scored three touchdowns, two of them on passes from me. Lindy was a tremendous athlete. He was from Miami like me, and we became good friends. He was dedicated and conscientious, a guy you could count on not to fumble when he had the ball, to be where he was supposed to be, and to do those things that were important in a football game. That was a good game for the University of Florida, for him and for me."

Lindy Infante: "I scored three touchdowns, but quite frankly none of them were spectacular. I'm sure any of our backs who had their hands on the ball would have scored the same three touchdowns that I did. It wasn't anything to write home about. It was fun to see your name and picture in the paper and have it say you scored three touchdowns, but it wasn't something where I said, 'Boy, I just lit the place up that day.'

Larry Libertore: "Then Florida State tied us [3–3], and they were just more ready than we were. I think we had more athletes, better athletes, but they came ready to play more than we did.

"We both played hard, and Florida State was coming on. Our team was not as good as the team we had the year before. That was the first time Florida State had tied Florida. They never did beat us while I was there, but they did tie us.

"We beat Tulane [14–3], and then we went out to Houston to play Rice, and they just outplayed us [19-10]. They were lankier, faster, a different style of player than the stronger, bigger players in the SEC.

"We beat Vanderbilt [7-0], and during that game I was injured. We ran an option play, and I had already pitched it. I was standing there, and a guy hit me from behind with his helmet right in the lower part of my back. It really hurt me, and I played some more in that game, even though it hurt."

Lindy Infante: "We went to Vanderbilt late in the year, and it was cold. We're from Florida. We're used to 95 degree weather every day. We went up to Nashville, and we felt we were in the middle of the Antarctic. It was something like 35 degrees. To us that was, 'Boy, what are we going to do playing in this cold weather?'

"In the locker room before the game everybody had on thermals or long johns, sweatshirts under the jerseys. We went out there and played, and by the time we got into the locker room at halftime, guys just shed everything. Because it wasn't nearly as cold as we had perceived it to be. Once we started playing and sweating, all of a sudden we started suffocating because of all the junk we had on our bodies. After halftime we went back out there and played in our normal gear.

"We won the game on a pass from Larry to Tom Smith, a tight end, and then he hit me with a pass for a touchdown."

Larry Libertore: "On the way home from Nashville and the next day, right where my belt is and lower looked purple and almost like a basketball, about a foot around, and it swelled up. I could hardly walk. I couldn't wear my belt. It wouldn't fit around.

"I went to the training room, and it didn't seem to be getting better, so they put a needle in to drain it, like you would drain a knee, but the fluid was like putty. You could just push your finger into the area. It was pretty serious. I didn't start against LSU at home because they weren't sure whether I could play or not, but I did play, and I remember running an option play, and I pitched it out, and the safety intercepted the pitchout and ran for a touchdown. The guy was kind of hiding behind the linebacker, anticipating what we were going to do. He picked it off and went all the way.

"In the newspaper they said, 'If you live by the sword, you die by the sword.' It's true, you know. We were successful with the option, and we lived by it. That was a play where they outcoached us. We lost [23-0].

"Against Georgia Tech, they began to think they might need to pass a little bit more, and they brought in Tom Batten, who was a better passer, but we got shut out [20-0]."

Georgia was the next opponent, and coach Ray Graves decided to replace the banged-up Libertore with drop-back passer Tom Batten. Given a rare start, Batten played heroically, throwing for three touchdowns in a 21-14 victory over Georgia.

Lindy Infante: "The Georgia-Florida game has always been big. Way back then it was called 'The World's Largest Outdoor Cocktail Party.' Those Georgia games are special. They were fun because, as I said before, you're playing against high school players you've played against before. And of course, there was the natural rivalry between the two.

"Tom [Batten] was one year ahead of us, but he red-shirted. He was more of a drop-back quarterback, not a runner, scrambler guy, but a pretty good thrower. Against Georgia, Tommy threw for three touchdowns, to Bob Hoover, Ron Stoner, and to me. On the touchdown he threw to me, I got myself fairly open in the end zone, just a routine, sterling catch.

"In the three years I was there we didn't lose to Georgia. And then [in a 32-15 loss to] Auburn, I had a 50-yard run. We were coming out of the south end zone at Tiger Stadium, and I ran a play over to the right side, and I went through the line of scrimmage and hit a nice hole and got up in there. A defender broke down right in front of me, and I made a little move. He missed me, and I went 50 yards. I didn't think it was anything outstanding.

"After the ballgame I remember the quote in the paper. They asked him, 'How did you miss Lindy out in the open field like that?' He said, 'Well, you know what, I lost him in the sun!' The way the stadium was configured, the sun was kind of low coming out from behind where I was running. He swore the sun blinded him and that was the reason he missed me. I always thought that was a classic statement.

"But what I remember most is that they beat us 32-15."

Larry Liberatore: "Our season ended with losses to Auburn and Miami [15-6], and I ended up playing defense in that Miami loss."

In the loss to Miami, Lindy Infante suffered a concussion.

Lindy Infante: "I went to tackle somebody, and I got kneed in the head. I remember waking up and when I really realized where I was, I was in the hospital. That was the ballgame in which George Mira was quarterbacking for Miami. Mira was right-handed, and on a pass play he got tied up somehow, and he switched the ball to his other hand, and he threw a touchdown pass with his left hand. I was in the game at the time, because I remember the play."

Larry Libertore: "Then our season ended. It was a pretty sorry [4-5-1] season."

twenty-one

A Devastating Loss to Duke

The year 1962 marked the debut of two of the University of Florida's celebrated players, halfback Larry Dupree and quarterback Tommy Shannon. Dupree was an exciting runner from a tiny town in northern Florida. He was in awe when he arrived. By the time he graduated, everyone was in awe of him.

Larry Dupree: "I grew up in a little town called McClenney, Florida, up in the northeast corner of Florida about six miles from the Georgia line. I played football with the local school team, Baker County High School. We were a small school, so we didn't get much notoriety living right here next to Jacksonville, so nobody knew we were out here.

"Ray Graves had just come to Florida. It was his first year, and it looked like he had a great program going. He was going to play some wide-open football. Also, I had grown up in Florida, and down deep, I knew I wanted to live in Florida. I told myself that the smart thing was to go to Florida.

"And it was a great decision for me. When I arrived at Florida I wasn't a heralded player, but I had some good opportunities and some good breaks. I wound up having a very good career, and tons of friends, and Florida was a great place to go to school.

"I remember when I first came out for the freshman year, Florida had signed 45 kids. They had some great players. I wasn't very high on the list when I started out. The freshman team had some great backs, Allen Trammell, Allen Poe, and David Hires. But about the second week there we scrimmaged the varsity, and I broke a couple of long runs, and then I started moving up very fast, and I never played on the second team again.

"I felt like a dummy. You've got to imagine it: I came from a town of

2,400 people, never had been anywhere in my life, and all of a sudden I couldn't understand why people were staring at you when you went to restaurants or was out in the community. My first thought was, 'I've done something wrong.' I didn't realize why they were staring at me. It took me a long time to understand that I had made a name for myself, and everybody wanted a look. They thought you were a little different than a normal human being would be, although that's not true.

"It was like going from the country to a fairy tale. It was Alice in Wonderland. Lots of these kids had been around a lot more than I had. I was very uneducated as far as travel or anything else. Everything that happened was new to me. But it was a great career. Golly, I wouldn't change a thing if I could go back and do it again.

"It's a great school. That was a great era. Ray Graves was a great man. He's a guy who cared. A lot of people who coach, and this is true out of football as well, they only care if you can accomplish what you want them to accomplish. Ray Graves was different. He cared for us as individuals.

"I can't tell you the number of times I went and hung my head on his desk, and he helped me. Like, golly, what have I done here? I tell you what, he was just like an old dad. He would get right down and help you. And not just me. It was the same with all the guys. Most of the guys I still have contact with have great respect for him. Occasionally on a Sunday morning I'll get a call from him. He'll just say, 'I wanted to call and check on you and say hello.' There's not many coaches around the country that would do that. And I'm not the only one he does that to. He loves all those guys, and deep down, we all have a great love for him too. He was a giant part of our lives. He had a lot of influence in what some of us became later.

"I think football is a great sport. I do love football. It's an opportunity to be something that you can't be any other time in your life. It's a great team sport. It teaches you to respect other people. You can line the town drunk's son up by the doctor's son—it makes no difference out there, one of the few places where it's that way.

"In football you can get on that field and become just about what you want to become. You can be a monster in disguise. But if you're ever going to do well, you have to put heart and soul in it.

"My sophomore year we had a talented group of freshmen that came up. A lot of these guys did very well at Florida. I was in the same class with Tommy Shannon."

Tom Shannon: "I was born in Boston and lived there for ten years. I played the first couple of years of Little League baseball in Malden, Massachusetts. My dad was with the United States Customs Service, and he was transferred to Miami, and then I went to Archbishop Curly High School in Miami.

"I was recruited reasonably heavily by Miami, but I decided I wanted to get away. I had always gone to a small Catholic school. I wanted to get my education out of Miami. When I went onto campuses like Georgia Tech, Auburn, and Florida, you're walking on red-brick ivy-covered campuses that are just spectacular. Miami had a very commercial, almost inner city look to its campus. I had been around Miami's campus a lot. From a little kid up, Miami was in our back yard. And Miami didn't recruit that many Florida kids then. Miami was a big recruiter in Pennsylvania, the coal-mine type of deal that Andy Gustafson used to do.

"The fellow who recruited me for Florida was Jim Powell, who was on Ray Graves' staff. He had formerly been at Edison High School, and after I enrolled at Florida, he returned to Hialeah High School. He just wanted to be a high school coach. He wanted to work with kids and help mold character. And he went on to have a fantastic career. He was one of the all-time great people I'd ever met. He was very, very instrumental in my coming to Florida. Of course, when you met Coach Graves—when you walked into his office it was like walking into the governor's office. He had the state of Florida flag on one side and the United States flag on the other. You're in this humongous, very impressive atmosphere. So I instantly fell in love with the University of Florida.

"And when I arrived on campus as a freshman, I was in awe. Of course, there were a lot of former high school players playing at Florida who I looked up to. I grew up in the Edison Park area. If I hadn't gone to Catholic school, I'd have gone to Edison. Bobby Hozack, Larry Travis, and Larry Libertore, one of my heroes in life, had gone there. Even though they were older than me, I'm sure they remembered me from winning the national Pony League championship in baseball. We won the state championships five years in a row, went to the baseball finals three times, and we won it once.

"We had a great crop of freshmen. Jerry Newcomer, who came out of Miami Senior High, was my roommate, along with Barry Brown, who came from Ann Arbor, Michigan. We lived in Tolbert Hall and really enjoyed the experience. Of course, your freshman year is pretty much relegated to holding bags and being a blocking dummy.

"Mississippi State was my first varsity game [in 1962], and I started at safety. In fact, I was the guy who held his hands up when they did the kickoff as the team ran down the field. Then I was the safety going down the field.

"I'll never forget it because Mississippi State had a world class sprinter, Odie Burrell, and he was quick. He broke loose up the middle, and I was the trailing safety, and man, it was like 'magic moments in sport.' The guy was juking and running up the middle of the field, and all I could remember was when you're making an open-field tackle, it's not head to the bellybutton, it's face mask to face mask. You've got to take him down.

"I met him at the 40-yard line, and he put me in the third row. I realized it was 'Welcome to college football.'

"I staggered off the field. I was supposed to stay in, but I got hit so hard I had to leave. I remember Coach Rodgers saying, 'Get back out there.'

"That was spectacular. That was 'magic moments.' And we did win that ballgame [19-9]."

Larry Libertore: "In '62 I was back at starting quarterback, and in our opener against Mississippi State I had as good a football game as I've had. It was a solid game. I was healthy again."

Tom Shannon: "The second game we went back home to play Georgia Tech. I started that game on defense, and I was returning punts. That day we were shut out [17-0.]

"When people ask me about the best coaches I ever played against, of course there was Bear Bryant of Alabama and Shug Jordan of Auburn, but of those who might have been the best, I will tell you, by far I thought Georgia Tech's Bobby Dodd was the best strategist we ever played against. He would kick on third down. He was the master of the quick kick. He would keep you backed up at your own goal line. You're not supposed to make any mistakes, but you do— fumbles, interceptions, miscues on the exchange—and if you did that, you were in your own territory. And Bobby Dodd always had a great field goal kicker. Remember Billy Lothridge? And Ted Davis? They had a great football team."

Larry Libertore: "When Georgia Tech shut us out, they shut down our basic option offense. Some teams were strong enough and smart enough to do that. And when they did, we didn't have an alternative.

"By the time I was a senior, it became obvious to me that the other teams were ahead of us with regard to what we were doing offensively. I did have some disagreements with the coaching staff about it, because I would come under center, and the linebackers would call the play we were going to run. I mentioned that to the coach, and he would say, 'Oh well, all teams know what you're going to do, and you've got to be better than them.'

"I hurt my knee at the end of the Georgia Tech game. I was covering a punt. I stopped because the fellow was already tackled, and my knee went out from under me. So I was not able to really do much against Duke, and I didn't play in the game at all.

"And I remember, right before the Duke game, it was like I wasn't even on the team. When I'd go out for practice, I wasn't on the varsity, wasn't on the B team. I didn't do anything. I just stood there. That was a really empty, hurt feeling."

Ray Graves: "After Tom Shannon beat out Libertore, I told the Quarterback Club in Daytona, 'I'm not starting him because he's left-handed. I'm starting him because I'M left-handed.'

"Steve Spurrier inherited something I did: We would grade these boys every game, and if in two games one player outgraded another player, he'd move right on up, and he knew that's the way it was going to be. Tommy was executing our offense a little better, so we moved him up, and that was a tough one, because Larry was devastated. But Larry was so much of a team man that I put him on defense, and he played his heart out. Larry did whatever you asked him to do: put on the other team's attack in practice if they were running the option. He was a pleasure to coach and have as part of the team, and a few years later when Steve Spurrier beat Tommy Shannon out, Tommy did the same thing. He played defense and he was a team player. Tommy and Steve are still best of friends."

Larry Libertore: "They inserted Tommy Shannon as quarterback against Duke, and he had a pretty successful game even though we lost [28-21]. Coach Graves was really upset, because we were expected to win that game, but every time we would score, they would score. Duke was successful throwing the ball, and I remember thinking that I wouldn't mind playing defense, but I was hurt and I didn't get in."

Tom Shannon: "On Tuesday before the Duke game, Coach Graves called me into his office and said, 'We're thinking about starting you this week.'

There are a lot of players on the team, and I figured he really didn't know who I was, because I HAD started the first two ballgames.

"I said, 'Coach, I'm already starting.' He said, 'No, I don't mean on defense. I'm thinking about starting you on offense.' Of course, I had heart palpitations, and my mouth dropped open. Larry Libertore, the quarterback, was one of my heroes. Graves said, 'Larry's so beat up, he's black and blue, and he's going through this injury time.' Course, there were two other guys who I really admired a lot, Tom Batten and Bobby Dodd Jr., the other two quarterbacks on the team, and I really hadn't thought much about starting with them around. I really felt I was their junior. I really didn't understand what ability, if any, I had on offense. I was really enjoying defense. I loved coming up and playing a linebacker kind of safety.

"But as it turned out, Coach decided to start me at quarterback against Duke the following Saturday. Of course, that's history. You know what happened. We were up 21-0 at the half, and we lost the ballgame 28-21.

"The star of the first half was Larry Dupree, who had the greatest moves I've ever seen in football. I had the ability to hand off to him and look back, and his butt could go sideways faster than it could go forward. He had an instinct for breaking loose and making the big play. Larry Dupree was one of the gutsiest people I ever met in life, a really, really fine person. A country boy from Baker County High School in McClenney, Florida. In the Duke game, I handed off the ball to Larry, and he took it 76 yards. I remember it like it was yesterday. He went off the left side and went all the way."

Larry Dupree: "I have to be truthful with you: I'm one of those guys who doesn't remember anything until I'm in the end zone. At that time I didn't know who Mike Curtis, one of the great NFL linebackers, was. He was the middle linebacker for Duke. I remember him, because the first time I carried the ball, he took a pretty good shot at me, but I didn't go down. I went to one hand, and I got up, and it was nothing but green pastures all the way to pay dirt.

"One of the funny things that happened—I don't remember it but I saw it on the replay that we watched over several times—how many times have you ever seen a quarterback out front leading the back for a 70-yard touchdown? Well, it was a quarterback named Tom Batten who actually did that. He ran stride for stride with me. The guy he blocked was the son of the great [Oklahoma football coach] Bud Wilkinson. Those are the little things you remember. I was a whole lot more impressed with those people than they were with me.

"We led Duke at the half 21-0, and then in the second half I got nailed with my foot planted, and I hyperextended my knee. I think I could have played, but they didn't want to take a chance. For me to sit on the sideline, that was the worst thing. I'd never sat on a sideline in my life.

"You've got to understand that in high school I never came out of a game. I played pretty much all the time on the freshman team. I didn't play a lot more than first two games sophomore year, but I knew that once they gave me a chance, and if they gave me the ball fifteen or twenty times a game, I could do something. So sitting on the sideline was tough, very, very difficult. I felt like being the little kid who ran up to the coach and pulled on his shirt saying, 'Hey, coach, let me play.'

"But they didn't want to take the chance I would hurt myself worse, and that made me feel good about Florida. I said to myself, Hey, they care about my well-being. I guarantee you that some coaches would have played me, buddy. I'd have gone until I couldn't go any more. A lot of great players have been ruined that way."

Tom Shannon: "So we led at the half 21-0. Then two things happened. It narrows down to about two plays. If you recall, the first team to run the Lonesome End was Army with Bill Carpenter. And Duke employed the lonesome offensive end. He was a guy way to hell out on the other side of the field. Now it's called the single wide out. But it was new then. They would signal to him what play to run, and he would be one-on-one, just running a deep route.

"Duke had a great long-throwing quarterback by the name of Walt Rapold. And I can tell you exactly what happened, because Hagood Clarke was playing defensive halfback, and as this lonesome end was going deep, it was evident that the sun impeded Hagood's sight. You can see it in the film. There was no physical reaction. Hagood didn't even try to put his hands up because you could see him looking up, but the ball went right over his head, and the guy caught the ball in his gut and fell into the end zone. So it was a heavy sun that day.

"Duke caught two long bombs in the same direction. If there's a reason for an excuse, that would be it.

"In the second half we couldn't seem to crank up the offense—no excuse. We don't know what we did there. They probably made some adjustments during the half, and their coach was a great coach. His backs were Jay Wilkinson and Mike Curtis, who later was one of the all-time great linebackers in the pros.

"So we didn't score in the second half, and we lost 28-21, and I was so overwhelmed at having started the ballgame and having that great first half, and then overwhelmed at losing the ballgame. I wasn't used to that. So I was probably buried back in the dressing room somewhere."

Lindy Infante: "Everybody was down after that one, because we felt we were going to be a pretty good team. We had some young guys coming up. A lot of us were seniors. Then we started to have some injuries, and it took it's toll. All I remember is the feeling after the game. The locker room was really depressing. We thought we had won, and we let it get away."

Larry Dupree: "After the game Coach Graves and the coaching staff were at the lowest point I'd ever seen them. That was a bitter, bitter loss. I was a sophomore, so it didn't hurt me like it did some of the upperclassmen. I was still looking at two or three years with an opportunity to play. For the seniors, this was it. I was young, 18 years old, and I hated it, but I had another chance to do something the next week, and I was ready to go."

twenty-two

A Big Gator Bowl Victory

Larry Dupree: "After the loss to Duke, they shuffled some of the personnel around. Tommy Shannon and I both started after that. Tommy was a brash young guy with a lot of confidence, didn't throw the best pass I've ever seen by any stretch of the imagination, but he was very accurate. If there was a receiver open, he seemed to be able to find him. Tommy meant a lot to the football team because he gave them some new leadership. Some of the younger guys began to make their presence felt. The seniors realized, Hey, we're not going to be able to run them away. They're here, and they're going to move in and stay.

"Back then the underclassmen had to earn that right. It's not that way any more, and there are good things you can say about that too. I always had a lot of respect for the older players.

"But I arrived on Monday for practice in full gear ready to go, and we were playing Texas A&M, coached by Hank Foldberg. That was a big ballgame for them, and we killed them [42-6]. The team started to come together with the new additions, and we were finally accepted. It was, 'Hey, these guys can help us win.' It seemed that the whole attitude changed after that. I was just so excited to be there."

Larry Libertore: "We overwhelmed Texas A&M, Hank Foldberg's team, on Florida Field. We were just a better football team in every which way in that game, and then we clobbered Vanderbilt [42-7], and Larry Dupree ran for a long touchdown. Larry was one of those players who could stop and start and turn. He had decent size, decent speed, and a lot of agility. He was another natural. It was a pleasure to watch him run. Lindy Infante was a straight-ahead, slashing runner, whereas Dupree had a lot of hip movement, a lot of moves."

Tom Shannon: "Weird things happened against Texas A&M. We scored 42 points against Hank Foldberg, who was a great coach. Then the next week we played Vanderbilt at home, and we scored another 42 points. All of a sudden, everyone was saying, 'Jeez, we must have found ourselves a starting quarterback.' But I didn't have that much to do with it. Lindy Infante did. Certain plays just turned out. Lindy ran a great reverse. You throw a pass, and all of a sudden there is an alleyway, and it's complete. I'd think, Wow, this is all right. So things seemed to work out.

"And Larry Dupree had a great game against Vanderbilt. He really broke out in '62. His sophomore year was the breakout year of all breakouts.

"We had some pretty good running backs while I was there. One reason they were able to do as well as they did was Pepper Rodgers, our offensive coordinator. He was a real cutting-edge coordinator. He went to wide-outs early, went to the men in motion. We were one of the first teams in the country to do that. He would be invited to all the NCAA football coaches clinics to talk about offensive strategy. He studied and seemed to understand how to spread out the defense. And as a result we were able to run the ball better."

Larry Libertore: "After I recovered from my knee injury, I didn't play quarter-back any more. Against LSU I played defensive safety the whole game. I found out about it when the depth chart came out the week before the LSU game and I wasn't on it. I remember going to see Coach Graves in his office. I was really upset. I said, 'How can someone who has played as much as me go from first string to no string?' He said, 'Well, you're hurt. We think you should take some time off.'

"I said, 'I'm not going to do that. I'm not going to go away.' At practice I stood around. I didn't do anything. It was very devastating for me to lose my starting quarterback job, and not from an ego standpoint. I just really loved to play, and I wanted to play. In my mind I still had the same talents I had when I was successful. It didn't make any sense not to be playing any more.

"Tommy Shannon was my closest friend, and he felt bad. It wasn't his fault. It wasn't anything personal. Actually, even when I was playing quarterback, I wanted to play EVERY PLAY. I didn't ever want to come out. Some players are happy to get off the field and rest. I wanted to play all the time. I remember in my early years when I told the coach I wanted to return kick-offs too, he said, 'You have to let somebody else do something.'

"One thing I have to say, and I'm not shy about saying this, is that from the time I went to play defense, Pepper Rodgers never acknowledged me as a player on that team again. None of the other coaches were that way. I went from being his quarterback to a person he hardly even said hi to when he saw me. That hurt. That really hurt. Because I didn't know why. There was never really an explanation. My name was just left off the board.

"So what they did was let me play safety. And I played safety every game the rest of the season.

"I said, 'If I'm good enough and healthy enough to play defense, how come I can't play quarterback?' They said, 'We don't think you move as quick as you used to.' I'm sure they felt that way. But for whatever reason, I was very hurt at the time."

Tom Shannon: "We played LSU, led by Jerry Stovall. That was Paul Dietzel's team. [LSU was ranked sixth in the country.] They were big weightlifters, big aerobic guys. Remember when they had you pressing against an immovable object? That was the beginning of isometric weight lifting. They were studs.

"That was like throwing the Christians to the lions. When you ran onto that field in Baton Rouge, it was one hundred percent enclosed and double-deckered. It was an eight o'clock game, and people there had been drinking since three in the afternoon. They put a tiger in a pen outside our locker room. The windows were open, you're in the dressing room, and you get this echo. I think they put an electric shocker on his butt, because he would go rooooaaarrrrrr. Here you are, putting on your pants, and holy samoles. I'll never forget it.

"Lindy Infante broke his leg in the first half, and here we were at halftime, down 20-0, and I remember being in the john, and I could hear Lindy screaming from his broken leg. He was the captain of the team, one of my heroes."

Lindy Infante: "I just planted my leg. My cleats got stuck in the grass the wrong way. I dislocated my left ankle and broke the lower leg at the same time. Two days later they operated. They had to reattach all the ligaments in my ankle and put me in a cast for eight weeks, and I was done."

Tom Shannon: "I remember it was halftime, and we were down 20-0 to LSU. We were just getting absolutely bombed. Every time I turned around, the defense was all over us. Freddie Miller, their All-American defensive tackle, was playing with a broken nose. There was blood everywhere. And Coach Graves at halftime said, 'They put their pants on the same as you do, one leg at a time.' And I was looking at myself, thinking, There is no way they put their pants on the same way we do, coach." [Florida lost 23-0.]

Larry Dupree: "Losing to LSU was the lowest point of my career thus far. What happened, I ran into a great football player, a guy named Jerry Stovall. If I got on the corner with a defensive back, there weren't many people I couldn't shake. Stovall was a senior, and he gave a sophomore a severe lesson that 'You don't know it all, Bud.' I'll tell you, he humiliated me. He ate me alive. Stovall was a really great football player who impressed me as much as anybody I ever played against.

"I had a rude awakening playing LSU. I had probably gotten my confidence a little too high, and Stovall brought me back to earth. And when we played Auburn the next week, they had a fullback by the name of Tucker Frederickson. Tucker and I had been on the same All-State team. We'd played against each other in high school all-star games. He was much sought-after. Everybody wanted Tucker.

"And that week I worked harder preparing for a game than every before. Everything I did, I tried to magnify it. If I had to run ten yards, I ran twenty. If we ran sprints, I ran twice as many. Auburn was a very good football team, and we just went in and dominated them [Florida won 22-3]. Physically we won the war. I had a really good run against them. It was an off-tackle play, where all of a sudden you look back and everything across the grain is wide open. They had a back at the corner by the name of George Rose, who was a great sprinter. I knew he was on the corner, and we were running at him. When I broke through the line, I knew he was going to come out smoking, and I had to zig and zag a couple of times, and I ran to the corner, dove, and made it. That put the cap on the ballgame for us. We pretty much had control at that point. After the game it was easy to walk up to Tucker and say, 'Hell, good to see you again.'"

Tom Shannon: "Auburn had some of my best friends, Tucker Frederickson, George Rose, Mickey Sutton. Tucker and I traveled on a couple of recruiting trips together. Actually, when I left Tucker the week I committed to Florida, he had told me he was ready to commit to Florida. A week and a half later, he committed to Auburn. Probably the main thing was that Tucker's dad was a veterinarian, and Auburn had a great vet school. Today Florida has a fantastic vet school. But Auburn had some great athletes. No argument, that was some rivalry for us in those days.

"Tucker was one of the running backs. Jimmy Sidle was their quarterback. We played a real great game against them, though. I remember talking to Tucker after the ballgame. He actually came into our dressing room after the game. He said to me, 'Jeez, looks to me like maybe I went to the wrong school.'"

Larry Libertore: "I made 13 tackles against Auburn, and I was Defensive Back of the Week. So I don't think I had lost any of my ability. Of course, it was easy for me to play safety. I pretty much could tell what they were doing on offense all the time. But I kind of lost enthusiasm for the overall picture. But I wanted to play, and I played. We went on that year to have a good enough season to play in the Gator Bowl."

Larry Dupree: "The next week was a big ballgame for me. We were playing Georgia in Jacksonville, and every relative I had in the state of Georgia was going to be there doing something they'd never done in their life—root for Florida. Everyone in my hometown who could get a ticket was there. If you'd have wanted to rob the bank, it would have been no problem at all. So this was a special game for me. I was coming home within thirty miles to play in a stadium that I'd watched ballgames as a kid and dreamed of playing in.

"And it was an exciting game, a very physical game—Georgia was always very physical. They are going to stand up and hit me. But I had a good day. I ran for two touchdowns. The substitution rule didn't let you just run guys in and out like today. You had an offensive team, a defensive team, and a both ways. Our defensive team was on the field against Georgia's number one offense. They caused a fumble, and we got the ball somewhere around the fifty. They sent Tommy and me into the game with the defensive unit because we've got to run one play before we can get those guys out of there. We're in the huddle, and all these big linemen who never get to block anybody, they were going to get one chance, and they were very excited. They said, 'Hey, we're gonna score.' And we did, on the first play, boom. They did the job, and I just ran. They had everything laid open for me. I only had one guy to beat. They had done everything else. And when they got to the sideline, that was an excited unit. They had gotten a chance to score a touchdown offensively. That was a fun ballgame. I enjoyed it. When I look back, that's one of the ones I really like to remember.

"We won [23-15], and it was a crucial time for me and for our team. That was a great, great win for us."

Tom Shannon: "Larry Dupree had a big day, ran for 111 yards. If he was hot, I was just gonna give him the ball. That was the deal. We'd run him 30 times. And that was in the days when you didn't do that. But once he really got the 'mo' going, there was no reason not to give him the ball.

"One of the stars of the FSU game was Hagood Clarke, who was a walk-on. He and Allen Trammell both. Hagood had gone to a thirteenth year at a prep school and Alan did the same thing, and they walked on at Florida. But Hagood was a spectacular athlete. He went on to play for years for the Buffalo Bills. And Allen was probably just as good an athlete. He was a spectacular baseball player. He once hit a ball over 500 feet in an SEC game. He was also a great punt returner and defensive back.

"We won the Florida State game 20-7. It was important. Sure it was. It was a rivalry even then. My freshman year the score was 3-0, then it was 3-3, a tie. There already was a great rivalry going on.

"I remember in '58, I followed them. Jimmy Dunn was our quarterback. Vic Prinze played for FSU, and everybody says Burt Reynolds played football for them, but I really don't remember Burt Reynolds playing football there at FSU. Eddie Feely was a quarterback out of Gainesville High School, played for FSU. A lot of kids I played with and against in Miami went to FSU. They had a lot of great athletes."

Larry Dupree: "The next game was against FSU, and before that game we learned the first lesson in 'how to keep your mouth shut.' I think Tommy got a little carried away. He went on Coach Rodgers' TV show and said something about 'a bunch of Florida rejects.' It wasn't quite that crude, but that was what he meant. That made it rough on everybody, and I don't think Tommy ever made that mistake again.

"At the start of the game these guys had extra fire in their eyes. 'Reject!' I mean, I don't know how many times I got nailed in the head, and the guy said, 'Reject!' I wanted to say, 'Hey, guys, I didn't say that.

"Tommy was a great player and a great guy, and a great, great friend of mine. I mean, I loved the guy. We've all done something like that once or twice in our life when we should have had better sense. After you say it, you say, 'Why did I do that?' I'm sure Tommy had a lot of people asking him why he did that—a lot of the coaching staff."

Tom Shannon: "Florida and FSU didn't have a hatred for each other as much as we wisecracked at each other. I remember they made a big deal of me going on the Pepper Rodgers Show on TV and saying that nobody who went to FSU had been recruited at Florida, and the guys who were recruited by both Florida and FSU chose to go to Florida. I also said that the difference between Coach Graves and Coach Petersen was like big league versus little league. Coach Graves was big league. Coach Peterson had an office under a poorly built high school football stadium. You walked in the Florida Field, and it was, 'Oh, my God.' It was stable, concrete, big time football. Florida State in those days was still just breaking in. So it was interpreted that I said that Florida State has Florida rejects.

"The other thing I said was, 'Well, jeez, their offensive team wears a certain color socks and their defensive team wears a certain color socks.' I said, 'That should really make a difference, what color socks you're wearing.'

"They showed the show to the FSU team. They were staying at the Holiday Inn in Ocala. Needless to say, once the game began, I never heard the end of it. Jim Cosey, one of my best friends from Edison, was playing defensive end at FSU. Boom, he hit me with an elbow in the mouth and tried to bite me. He said, 'Does that feel like a Florida reject?' And they were pinching a little extra hard in the pileups. I understood that, but it didn't really make any difference. Most of us belonged to the same social fraternity, and at Christmas we all partied together the same way we had always done before."

Larry Dupree: "FSU led at the half 7-6, and it was tough. I got beat up bad in that ballgame. These guys put a whuppin' on me. And then Hagood Clarke ran back a punt for a touchdown. Hagood was a year ahead of me. He was one of those guys you always want on your team. He's a guy sometimes you don't notice, but when the chips are down and you need the big play, the guy would do it. He was such a gentleman off the field, and such a tough guy on it. I always had great respect for him."

Tom Shannon: "We finished the season with a 17-15 loss to Miami, a great football game. I remember Miami always covered the opening kickoff with fire in their eyes, yelling the most distasteful four-letter or multiple cuss words. Walt Kachefsky, one of their defensive coaches, had a great ability to fire them up before coming out on the field, all blood and guts. And Bob Hoover took the ball, and they came down the field, and it just looked like a wreck on the kickoff return. Bob suffered a broken leg.

"And I remember our first handoff was to Larry Dupree, and he fumbled the ball on the exchange. And they went right in and scored. With five minutes gone in the game, we were down 14-0. Here we were in the Orange Bowl, where I grew up, watching Miami High-Edison games as a kid and always in awe. Fifty five thousand went to that game on Thanksgiving. Here we had 65,000 and I was having that Christians to the lions feeling again.

"So we were down 14-0, and we had to battle back. And we did. We chipped away and we went right down and scored, and we went for the two-point conversation, and that year we were successful something like eleven times, and so we went up 15-14, and I'm thinking we're going to win this ballgame.

"Our defense played a great, great defensive ballgame. I was on the sidelines, and I remember George Mira had fourth down, and he dropped back to pass. Frank Rhinehart, their left end, was blocking on the play, and he got knocked down in the backfield. As he was getting up, he looked up. Mira had thrown a dart to the right, and Freddie Pearson or Antoine Peters jumped up and blocked it, and the ball got hit in the air and came back over Mira's shoulder as an incomplete pass. Rhinehart, who was getting up, caught the ball and ran for a first down. Otherwise the ballgame was over. It was a miraculous play. It obviously couldn't be planned. It was God's will.

"After Rhinehart ran for a first down, they ended up kicking a field goal, and they beat us 17 to 15.

"I remember in that ballgame I threw one of my best spirals I ever threw—I was not famous for my spirals—Sam Holland was deep down the middle of the field. He was fifteen yards deeper than Nick Spanelli, who was covering him. He had beaten Nick on a deep post, but instead of completing the post, he straightened it out, running directly away from the ball, and it was right over the top of his head. I was watching from the ground, because I had been knocked down, and I could see the ball go right between his hands. He hit the ground at about the midfield stripe. It would have been a 75-yard touchdown pass, but it was not to be."

Ray Graves: "When I left Miami, I was really sick. Sam Holland had gotten behind the defender, and Sam dropped a touchdown pass for a win. Tommy has never let Sam forget it.

"I was on the way up to Valdosta when I called the Gator Bowl committee—if we had beaten Miami we would have gone to the Gator Bowl. They said, 'No, we're going to take Clemson.' I said, 'Clemson? We have the same record they have.' I talked to a couple of people on the Gator Bowl committee. I said, 'Listen, if you give us a chance, I promise you I won't embarrass you.' I was really grasping, but we finally got the bid, and we were challenged. I had Gene Ellenson, my motivator, make two or three speeches to get them fired up for this game, because we had asked for the chance.

"We went over to Daytona to practice, and some of them got Confederate flags. We were playing Penn State, and it was the Yankees against the Southerners. Penn State had won the Lambert Trophy, and they were ranked fourth in the country, and we weren't ranked. So it was the north against the south, and it was a lot of fun. And then they went out and played a great ballgame."

Larry Dupree: "Back then it was a big deal for Florida to get in a bowl game. They'd been a mediocre team for many, many years. There was new hope there. There was Coach Graves. And he had some pretty good assistant coaches with him. Pepper Rodgers went on to have a great coaching career. Guys like Ed Kinsler, Jack Green went on to Vanderbilt. Coach Green was a great All-American from Army. He played with Doc Blanchard and Glenn Davis. I liked to be around him, just because he'd been around those guys.

"I just think that was some exciting times at Florida. It was the start of something at Florida. There was new hope. We had beat some teams we hadn't been able to beat much before."

Larry Libertore: "Even though we were 6 and 4 after we lost to Miami, we were still invited to play Penn State in the Gator Bowl. Penn State was not a team we were very much aware of. In fact, some of the seniors almost would have preferred not to go to a bowl game. We were tired from the season, and we couldn't go home, had to stay on campus and keep practicing. Some of the seniors were ready to move on with their lives. I remember the coaches had to use persuasion with some of the leaders on the team to say how important it was to the players and the team to go to the Gator Bowl, and they were successful doing that. They said they were going to try to make our experience on campus more exciting. They said, 'We'll try to give you a little more time to yourselves.' Because when everybody leaves campus and you're practicing over the holidays, it's pretty bleak. Our season had just been average, and it was hard to get enthused.

"And their strategy was to prepare us like we were playing the Green Bay Packers. They told us, 'You shouldn't even be in this game. There is no way you can compete with them.' They got us riled up against Penn State the same way FSU got worked up when they played us.

"I suspect Penn State told themselves, They're not that good. They're from the South.' And in that game we were very well prepared, and we played hard, and won won [17-7]."

Tom Shannon: "When we were invited to the Gator Bowl, we kind of semi-backed in. We were 6 and 4. We went to the Gator Bowl because we were a team that could bring a crowd. The team they invited to play us was Penn State, the Lambert Trophy winners. They were 9-1. They had Pete Liske at quarterback—he played twenty years in the Canadian league. They had Junior Powell, and their all-world running back, Roger Kochman. We were seventeen point underdogs.

"They were really a good football team. They had an All-American defensive tackle, Chuck Simansky, who was spectacular. A lot of those guys went on to play in the pros. And their head coach, Rip Engle, was really spectacular, and Joe Paterno was one of his assistants.

"The way I remember the story, Penn State was upset they had to play in the Gator Bowl, because they were holding out for the Cotton Bowl, and they didn't get invited. I don't know that they took us as seriously as they should have, because we were 6-4 and appeared to have 'backed' into the bowl.

"We opened the scoring on a 43-yard field goal by Bobby Lyle. Bobby was a big guy. He was a real good tackle and a real good field goal kicker. He did all our kicking off, and he really boomed kicks.

"We drove down toward their goal, and it was fourth and seven, and I rolled left. I pumped the ball, and the defensive guy jumped, and I ran around him. At about the two yard line, I took a heck of a hit in the head, but we made the first down.

"My head was not clear. I attempted to call a play, and it took a little longer than it should have. I tried to put a man in motion, and we ran out of time. So we got a five-yard penalty back to the seven. First and seven.

"Everything cleared up, and I called a typical rollout to the left. Being left-handed, rolling left was the best way for me to go, although we could roll both ways. Larry got open and just kind of turned, and I can still see him— he was open, and I kind of laid it in, and he just turned around, squared his shoulders and caught the ball in his chest for a touchdown. Larry was one of the greatest football players Florida ever had."

Larry Dupree: "Sometimes you play a team, and you are just waiting for them to erupt. You know they're capable of it. That day we had some great plays by individuals. I think we had emotion on our side, which helped us a great deal. They probably were a little overconfident. They figured, Here's a 6-4 team playing us. What are we going to gain by this?"

Tom Shannon: "On the first play of the fourth quarter we were on the left hash mark, and it was third and one on their 19-yard line. My rommmate, Jerry Newcomer, was in the running back position. I hand faked to Jerry because they were coming up to stop the first down. And Hagood Clarke ran a post to the flag.

"I just laid the ball up in the air, and he was open, and he made a great catch. We won the ballgame on two touchdown passes, and based on that, I ended up getting the Most Valuable Player in that game. We won 17-7."

Ray Graves: "We just played a great ballgame offensively and defensively. I remember our end, [Barry] Brown, went down on a pass, and he fell down, and then the defensive back left him, and he got up and caught a 15-yard pass. After that I thought, Somebody up there thinks we ought to win this ballgame.

"It just shows you: the team that comes and wants to win more than the other—you can tell right quick after three or four series that one team has come to play and the other is just there. Morale is so important. It decides a lot of games.

"We came to play. We wanted to win. We weren't that good, but Penn State figured they could beat us, and they weren't that fired up about coming down for this bowl game. And about five years ago Tommy Shannon was elected into the Gator Bowl Hall of Fame."

Larry Libertore: "We definitely had an excellent game against Penn State and shocked them completely. I played a few plays on offense, but mostly played defense and returned punts.

"I was happy. I was not unhappy. I was just disappointed because I really wanted to play quarterback. But you have to understand that playing college football back then wasn't very glamorous. You had to be up at breakfast every morning at 7:30. You went to class in the morning, and as a quarterback I had meetings until practice. And the practices were a lot longer than they are now. You might practice for two and a half hours. You run plays over and over. You run sprints. You run drills. You have tackling drills and blocking drills. That prepares you for the game, but it's a lot tougher than the game. The game is a pleasure.

"And you might have a couple of meetings at night. So you were tired and beat up all the time. Then the season was over, and before you knew it, it was time for spring practice. Most of the players didn't have any money or a car. Plus you had to go to school and were tired, and it's hard to study. School's a big letdown after you've played football on a Saturday afternoon, unless you just love to study and you know what you want to be. By the time you go back to your dorm room at night to study, everybody else has studied all day, and they are partying. So everybody in the dorm is happy, and you have to study. You're so tired you can't keep your eyes open.

"A lot of the players didn't like the routine, the discipline, the whole scene. It was kind of demeaning. I just liked every bit of it. To me, it was the biggest challenge. All I ever wanted to do, even in grade school and high school, was to play quarterback in college. That was my goal in life. Or to play defense, or return kickoffs, punts, whatever. I just loved it, but for most of the players it wasn't their whole life. They were there and they made the effort, but in the scheme of things it wasn't that important. To me it was the most important thing you could do.

"I probably was at odds with some of the players, not knowingly, but because of my attitude about wanting to play all the time. 'Cause I was gung-ho, and they weren't. I might have come across as 'I'm better than you,' which never was my intention. It was just that I just loved to play the game. I must have a screw loose.

"I would have liked to have gone on and played wide receiver or punt returner in the pros, but there was no interest. My guess is that my size had a lot to do with it. The other thing was that there weren't any pro teams in the South, no Atlanta Falcons, no New Orleans Saints, no teams in the South [except Dallas].

"My senior year I interned at Gainesville High School, and I determined I didn't want to coach. Maybe I was burnt out a little. But the students would constantly challenge me. 'I can throw the ball farther than you. I can run faster than you.' I just thought, 'Do I want to do this?' I didn't think I wanted to.

"I went to see Gene Ellenson, who everybody on the team loved. He said, 'If you don't have that burning desire, go try something else, and if that doesn't work, you know you can always coach.' I thought it was good advice. He was honest.

"Scott Kelly, who was running for governor of Florida, wanted me to come work for him. He pursued me. I was so involved in football and finishing school that I really wasn't into politics. Scott had gone to the university. He had been a former mayor of Lakeland, and he served in the state Senate. He was 35 years old, a big sports fan, and when he pursued me I didn't even know what he wanted me to do. When I took the job there was only one other person working for him, a really talented guy who wrote his speeches. He took me around and showed me what he was doing. His job was to organize people and get out the vote for Scott Kelly. One day he said, 'I gotta go.' And he left me up in Pensacola and said, 'You're on your own.'

"And that was when I discovered how fervently the people of Florida feel about Florida football. I had no idea. I would go into Panama City, Pensacola, Quincy, every city in Florida, and I'd call up people on behalf of Scott Kelly, and the people would say, 'Oh man, I sure would love to meet you.' They wanted to meet a quarterback. They invited me to their homes, happy to host a dinner. And Scott would come, and if we had forty people, every one knew I had played quarterback at Florida.

"I didn't have a clue. But Scott Kelly was a smart man. He knew. It was such a eye-opener for me. People would remember plays. They'd say, 'I remember when you scored....' They remembered things I couldn't believe. It was such a feel-good feeling.

"So I was traveling around the state, and for the first time had a little bit of money in my pocket. Because I was getting $100 a game playing for a pro team in Orlando. I played for two years as a wide receiver. We played Saturday nights. It was a really pleasant time in my life.

"I was in heaven. I didn't have to go to classes, and I was getting paid to play pro football. As quarterback, you have to know everything. As wide receiver, I didn't have to worry about a thing. You just go out and catch a pass. It gave me a new perspective of the game. As wide receiver you don't worry about what your defense does. You don't worry about play calling.

"Then I started a team in Lakeland and went and got stock-holders, and I signed all the players. I got some from my Orlando team and some from the University of Florida—I got Jack Harper and Jack Katz. The first year I was the coach, I played quarterback half of the time because I couldn't find a quarterback, and I could do it. I knew the system. The second year Buford Long came along as coach, and I played wide receiver again.

"And after I started this team, I got into the real estate business. It's been a fun business. I've enjoyed it."

Senior Lindy Infante left Florida with no intention of coaching. He wanted to be an architect. But life can be funny. Infante started coaching in high school, came back to Florida, and ended up having a 17-year pro career that would eventually bring him the head coaching job of the Green Bay Packers.

Lindy Infante: "After I got out of the cast, my leg looked like a refugee's leg. It was atrophied, and I had a lot of rehab I had to go through.

"Luckily, I still got drafted by the pros. Back then there were two leagues, the AFL and the NFL. The Cleveland Browns drafted me and so did the Buffalo Bills, as a defensive back. I signed a contract with Buffalo and went up there to training camp. I broke a toe in their camp, and was the last cut. I went to Hamilton, Canada, and played three or four games. I decided I wanted to be an architect, and I came back to the University of Florida and enrolled in architect's school.

"Both Buffalo and Hamilton wanted me to come back to the next training camp, and I said no. I did another semester in architecture school, and I made the best grades I ever made. I was really interested and involved.

"But I had started as an education major, and there was a policy that if you didn't finish your degree within a certain amount of time, you started to lose credits. I had to decide whether to finish in education or to stay in architecture and not get my education degree. All I had left was my internship, which was one semester at a high school some place. So I decided to take a semester off from architecture, go intern to get my education degree, and then come back and finish architecture. That was the plan.

"I interned at Miami Edison in the physical education department. While I was there they let me teach architectural drafting. The football coaches asked if I wanted to help in the afternoons, and I said sure. I didn't have anything else to do, so I went out in the afternoons and helped them coach the football team.

"Then as soon as the semester was over, it turned out that Miami High had a job opening, and they called me to come up and teach math and coach the offensive backs on the football team. I wasn't sure. My girlfriend at the time, who is now my wife, and I were about to be married. I went and accepted the job. I told her, 'I'll do one semester here at Miami High and then coach the football team, and then I'll go back to the University of Florida.' That was the plan.

"It was my first coaching job where I was getting paid—six hundred dollars a year—a pretty big deal on top of my $3,000 salary. I thought I was in high cotton. That year we went 12-0 and won the state championship and got voted the national champions.

"I thought, 'This is fun. This coach stuff is easy.' The next thing, I got invited back to the University of Florida as a teaching assistant, which I did. Then Billy Kinard left as coach, and I got hired. That led me into coaching. That was the end of architecture.

"I coached seven years at the University of Florida. I coached three years at Memphis State University as offensive coordinator and assistant head coach. While I was there at Memphis State, the World Football League had a team called the Memphis Grizzlies. They were using our practice facilities. So I would go out and just listen in while they practiced. I was intent on learning and listening. They were nice enough to let me hang around and watch— not teach or coach—just watch. I would stick my head in the huddle.

"John McVey was the head coach. Bob Gibson was the offensive coordinator. Bob got a job with Charlotte in the WFL, and I went to coach with him for eleven weeks, until the league folded. Then I got a job at Tulane University in '76, and in the interim Bob Gibson got hired by John McVey, who got the head job with the New York Giants.

"It was kind of ironic. A bunch of us were sitting in my office at Tulane University. I had coached college ball for twelve years. Somebody asked me, 'Do you think you'd ever like to coach professional football?' I said, 'Absolutely no way. No one could pay me enough to coach professional athletes. I don't have any interest in doing that.'

"About ten minutes later the phone rang. It was Bob Gibson of the Giants. He said, 'Lindy, our receivers coach just resigned. I told John McVey about you. John knows you. He'd like you to come up and coach the receivers. Would you like to do it?'

"I said, 'Golly, Bob, I don't know. I hadn't even thought about anything like that.' We had just gotten through talking about it. A couple of my coaches were still sitting in my office. I said, 'For how much money?' He told me, and it was almost double what I was making. I said, 'When do you want me there?' And that was it.

"I coached fourteen years in the NFL. I did a year with the WFL. I did three years with the USFL. And you know what? I enjoyed them all. I really did. Ninety five percent of the professional athletes were good guys, fun people to be around, fun to work with. Ninety five percent of them are going to give you everything they got. And the ones you unfortunately read about too much in the paper are the other five percent."

twenty-three

An Upset of Alabama

O ne of the most talented backs to play at the University of Florida was one from Lakeland by the name of Jack Harper, who had taken his high school to the state championship and who was wanted by most of the top schools in the Southeast.

Florida State even offered to give Harper $200 a week during the summer to rent umbrellas on the beach. But Harper had a girlfriend in Lakeland and wanted to be close to her, and the closest top Florida school was in Gainesville. It was also the golden era of the space program, and he wanted to study at Florida to be an astronaut.

Quickly, he lost the girl and the desire to go up in space, but Jack Harper became a star for Florida on the football field.

Jack Harper: "I had around 20 to 25 offers to go to college. Alabama was the first team to talk to me. That was the years they were winning national championships under Bear Bryant. I was amazed when my junior year a representative from Alabama, an assistant coach, came and talked to me about signing with Alabama. And everybody else too—Georgia Tech, Tennessee, Vanderbilt, all the SEC teams, Miami, Florida State, just a lot of them.

"I picked the University of Florida because it was closest to Lakeland. I had a girlfriend in Lakeland, and that was the number one reason I went to Florida. The other reason was that it had a strong alumni backing. Also I wanted to go into aeronautical engineering. That was about the time the space program started. I'm really not that smart a person. I have pretty good common sense—sometimes—but academically I wasn't that smart.

"When I arrived at Florida, it was pretty hard. Freshman year I was in awe just being at the university and pretty naive about everything. I don't remember much about freshman year except that school was hard. It was a real difficult environment for me.

"I think football at the college level is the hardest football to play. It's a lot harder than the pros were. When I played I ran, I had to return punts, I had to return kickoffs. Basically I was involved in every offensive situation. My freshman and sophomore years they didn't have the platoon system. You played both ways.

"Freshman year we played other freshman teams. But what I remember most about that was my freshman year we first had Gatorade. We were guinea pigs for Gatorade. They would stuck us with a needle before practice and stick us with a needle after practice. I thought, and so did most of the other players, that that was all in what you did in college. I didn't know I was part of the development program for Gatorade—hopefully Gatorade will send me a big endorsement check. But I didn't get anything out of Gatorade. I just remember I was a guinea pig.

"I didn't know if I was good until I got to the pros. Then I knew I was good. I had no idea I was a good football player until I walked into the training camp of the Miami Dolphins and saw what was there and I knew I could make the team. Why it took me that long, I don't know.

"My first game was against Georgia Tech at Grant Field in Atlanta in September of 1963. I was a sophomore. It was supposed to be a grudge match between Coach Graves and Bobby Dodd, supposedly because his son never became the starting quarterback, but I didn't keep up with stuff like that. I wasn't engrossed in who was playing for what team and how they were doing. Something was going on, but I didn't know it. I was a sophomore, and I was playing in front of a huge crowd, and you're in awe of everything. I played 42 of the 47 minutes. I played both offense and defense. It was raining and in a mud hole. We didn't lose by much [9-0], but we did lose."

Larry Dupree: "The '63 season opener against Georgia Tech in the rain in Atlanta was a miserable, miserable day for the Florida Gators. It was for me. It was kind of the way Coach Dodd coached. I always heard he had such a different attitude about coaching. Back in those days the hard-nosed way of coaching was prevalent throughout the country. But Dodd was a guy who wasn't that way. He was more like Coach Graves—well, Coach Graves had spent time under Coach Dodd. But when we played Georgia Tech, you felt that even though we had beaten those guys up, for some darn reason they got more points than we did. We would have felt better playing on a dry field. And they had Billy Lothridge. But had it been dry, maybe we would have given them a better ballgame."

Tom Shannon: "Losing to Georgia Tech in the rain in Grant Field in Atlanta was really a frustrating experience. I got knocked down more times in that ballgame without a block, looking the other way and just getting killed. I think Ted Davis and Billy Lothridge made All-American that day. Every time I turned around, they were in my face and they knocked me back. Thank God it was raining. I remember Lothridge saying to me, 'Hey, your left hand hasn't hit me all day long. I feel bad.' He kept coming in full speed and just crushed me.

"Actually we were in the hunt until Bruce Bennett, a great athlete for us, fumbled a punt."

Larry Dupree: "We tied our next game against Mississippi State [9-9]. Later in the game Tommy [Shannon] threw a pass to Randy Jackson, and Randy dropped it. We actually should have lost that game, but the holder for Mississippi State dropped the snap, and they didn't convert the extra point. Boy, you talk about low. That was the low point for me in Florida football.

"First of all, we went up and performed miserably against Georgia Tech. We just weren't happy with ourselves. We felt like we had more to do with losing the game than they did. Then you know you should beat Mississippi State. You've GOT to beat Mississippi State. If you don't, you're not playing for a championship any more. You put yourself out of it that early. It was a low point. It was a tough point."

Tom Shannon: "What I remember most about the Mississippi State game was calling three straight quarterback sneaks on the one or two yard line, and each time their All-World linebacker, Justin Canale, who was also their kicker, a blond-headed, flat-top, big stud guy, tackled me with his helmet and really bruised me.

"I remember looking over at [offensive coordinator] Pepper Rodgers, and he was in the squat all three times. It was quarterback sneak, quarterback sneak, quarterback sneak. And I promise you on my rosary beads that I was over that goal line by at least a half a length two or three times and getting thrown back each time. But they didn't call it a touchdown, and they spotted it on the one-inch line.

"I remember being over on the fourth down play and running off the field and saying to the coach, 'I was in two out of three times.'

"When the game ended, which was shortly thereafter, Justin Canale came over. We walked off the field together. He said, 'If it's any consolation to you, you definitely were over. We thought we lost the ballgame and can't believe those referees didn't give you guys a touchdown.'

"We were lucky because they missed the extra point—the holder dropped the snap. So we could have lost it. But we should have won by a touchdown whether they kicked the extra point or not.

"So we tied that game when we should have won it. And if we would have won that game, we would have been 7-3, instead of 6-3-1, and we could have gone to a bowl game. That game cost us a bowl that year. Cause two weeks later we beat the number one team in the country."

"The next week we played the Richmond Spiders [a 35-28 win]. We played it in Gainesville. A lot of times a school like Richmond will say, 'We'd like to come to your stadium, even though it's our home game, because you get a bigger crowd, and you give us a guarantee of $600,000 for the week.' We kind of use it as a good practice week. Although we found ourselves down 10-0 after the first five minutes.

"We fumbled the kickoff. Then we turned the ball over, and they scored a field goal and a touchdown. It was 10-0 before we could turn around.

"But there wasn't any consternation. I remember Pepper Rodgers looking at me and saying, 'Look, we're going to score more than ten points in this ballgame. Just take your time. We don't have to get it back quick.'

"I remember having a pretty good game. I hit Hagood [Clarke] four or five times over the middle. We had a good game plan. We knew what their weaknesses were.

"They had a big, ole tall, lanky guy at quarterback who could throw the football into the stadium. He had a great arm, and our guys probably underestimated him on the defensive plan, but we scored 35 points, so we deserved to win."

Larry Dupree: "Richmond was ahead of us 10-0, and they had no business being on the field with us. Now it's three games in a row that we're playing badly. What do we have to do to put this thing together? Are we capable of putting it together?

"There was some finger pointing. No one really knew what was wrong. What are we gonna do to straighten this out? We're facing the possibility of getting our brains beat out.

"But then we did some soul searching and said, 'Hey, we're better than this. It's a matter of getting focused and doing what we're supposed to do. And we came back at beat Richmond.

"We knew we were well-coached. We had great coaches, and we knew that. In that game we knew if we were going to have any chance against Alabama [the next week], we had better get our stuff together. I recall at halftime that was said to a lot of people. And then we came out and did what we had to do. And then we had a great week of practice going to Alabama.

"People's attitudes were good. Hey, this is an opportunity for us. We're getting to play [third-ranked Alabama] what is probably the premier football team in the country. Bear Bryant was already a legend. Joe Namath was the quarterback."

Tom Shannon: "We played Alabama in Tuscaloosca at Denny Stadium against Joe Namath. Yep, that was big.

"When you played Alabama, first of all, the most awesome thing is you're playing against one of the all-time great coaches of the world. Bear Bryant, to me, was the ultimate coach. Although I felt that Bobby Dodd was the ultimate strategist, I think Bear Bryant was the ultimate guy who used his players according to their talent. He didn't force them to play his game plan. If he had a drop-back passer like Joe Namath, he'd use a drop-back offense. When he had Steve Sloan, he wouldn't make him be a drop-back quarterback. He knew Sloan was a roll-out guy, so he would go to the option when Sloan came in. He was flexible enough to recognize their ability, and he would alter his game plan and his system to fit the ability of the quarterback.

"Joe Namath had probably the quickest release in football. But Namath, in my estimation, would have been ten times the quarterback if he had come later in life, because today's system is wide-outs and men in motion. In those days a lot of times we were running the T-formation, three backs in the backfield with a man in motion. For us to have one wide-out was a big deal. You never saw double wide-outs and a man in the slot in those days. Joe was a prolific passer for his time. But he didn't throw nearly as much as the quarterbacks six or seven years later.

"Joe had one of the quickest releases, one of the strongest arms, and terrible knees. Joe had bad knees all the way through his career. I remember him getting carried out of the ballgame and coming back in.

"I really enjoyed playing that football game. The flats were open all day long. We could complete a pass almost any time we needed to. I remember Larry Dupree running a student-body right, as we called it. I threw a block, got out front of the play, and got hit in the head by someone's knees. It was fun.

"They had fantastic talent. Do you remember Paul Crane, the center? Mike Fracia, Benny Nelson was the running back, Joel Hurlbert was an All-American cornerback, number 16, and of course Namath.

"I'll never forget the look in his face when we did a fourth and one fake on him down on their six yard line. Allen Trammell was absolutely slap-ass wide open and dropped the ball. Another time I hit Trammell in the flat. He turned it up, running down the field, looked like he was breaking loose, and they tore the ball out of his hands.

"We should have won that game 23-3. We could have easily kicked a field goal and scored another touchdown, and Bear Bryant acknowledged that after the ballgame. I understand he was so upset they had lost to us that he practiced them Sunday morning after our game at seven in the morning. He was really pissed. And his quote in the paper was, 'We're just lucky we didn't get beat by two or three touchdowns.' That was really the case.

"Namath was frustrated. Our defense that game, Jimmy Morgan, Roger Petty, Frank Lasky, and Jim Pearson were in their backfield all day.

"I remember we were running out the clock. We were in the huddle, and we were screwing around. Even though it was a 10-6 game, we knew we were going to win it. Our defense played so well there was never a risk of losing the ballgame. All I had to do was make sure I didn't fumble, so I was just taking the ball and dropping to a knee. And even when I was down on one knee, they were hitting me. I remember Dennis Murphy getting in a scuffle because some guy was piling on me. They knew the game was over, but they were doing everything they could, and we were just running out the clock. And I was yelling colors that didn't mean anything. 'Pink 27,' Everybody was laughing in their stance. I'm taking the snap. It was almost adding insult to injury, but it was fun.

"When the game was over Namath came over to me and gave me a big hug.

"It was a sellout crowd in Denny Stadium in Tuscaloosa. We were on Alabama's campus, and until his very, very last football game against Southern Mississippi [in 1982] when Reggie Collier was the quarterback, this was the only game Coach Bryant ever lost at home. So that was a BIG deal for us.

"After the game I remember sitting in the locker room and breaking down crying. Because we had been under such pressure. We almost got beat in Richmond. We got tied by Mississippi State. We lost the Georgia Tech game. We had thought we were going to have a really great football team. I remember before the season being picked in Street and Smith magazine as 'the quarterback to watch,' alongside Roger Staubach, Joe Namath, Tommy Myers from Northwestern, and Craig Morton at California.

"Our expectations had been so high, and then to come out and lose to Tech and get tied by Mississippi State, and then play poorly against Richmond. It was adding insult to injury, so after we beat Alabama, we felt, 'Hell, maybe we're coming out of it. We've got a hell of a defense. We can really win these ballgames.'

"The other thing I remember is returning to Gainesville after the game. We had to circle the airport for 45 minutes, until they could get the crowd of 10,000 people off the landing strip and off to the side so the plane could come in. And then they allowed them to come out to the plane after it shut down all its engines.

"I remember the door opening and this massive throng of people. The crowd noise was incredible. We got off the plane, and it was the greatest welcome anybody could ever have had. You were literally fighting your way through the crowd. Everybody was shaking your hand and grabbing hold of you. 'How are you doing?' 'Good to see you.' Neat stuff. Magic moments in sports."

twenty-four

Dupree's Great Day

Tom Shannon: "After we played Alabama, we beat Vanderbilt 21-0. It wasn't much of a ballgame. Allen Poe had a big game at running back. Allen was from Tampa, a real studly little athlete. I remember against Vandy hitting him on a quick look-in pass for a touchdown.

"Our other halfback was Jack Harper, who had a great day. We called him 'Lazy Jack,' because he didn't like to practice too much. He was very happy-go-lucky, had fantastic ability. I felt he had the same ability that the great Cleveland runner Jim Brown had. They said Brown could give you a 'dead leg,' lean your way and then you'd go to tackle him, and his leg would be limp and he'd hip right by you. Jack Harper had that move. It was natural for him. He would shake right in, didn't look like he was very fast, and he could go from zero to forty real quick. Later on Jack went to the Miami Dolphins as one of the big running backs with Larry Csonka and Jim Kiick, and he may have been a better back than Jim Kiick.

"Jack was kind of a loner. He would go down to the woods. He liked to hunt and fish a lot. He would go down into the Everglades for days at a time. It's hard to understand when people want to be a loner, but not everybody is cut out to be 'Mr. Personality.' Yet today he's got a great personality."

Unfortunately for the 1963 Gators, success came to a screeching halt with back to back shutouts at the hands of LSU (14-0) and Auburn (19-0).

Tom Shannon: "Our Homecoming game was against LSU, and it was very frustrating. They had a great defensive end by the name of Billy Truax. Today I can still feel where he cracked two of my ribs. We would drive down the field, but we just couldn't get it in the end zone. I remember getting down to their six yard line a couple of times and not being able to push it across. I had the opportunity to throw two or three balls deep to the outside, but we had some dropped balls, and that was disappointing. LSU was a great football team, not typical of who you'd want to play on Homecoming."

Jack Harper: "I remember that game because that was when I really got to feeling bad. I couldn't understand why I was always tired and wasn't in shape. That was the first game when I just couldn't understand why I was out of shape."

Tom Shannon: "After LSU we had to go to Auburn. In those days going to Auburn was really tough. Florida hadn't beaten Auburn at Cliff Hare Stadium in a long time and continued not to beat them there for a long time. It was a tough place to play.

"That was one of those years where we got caught in the middle against LSU and Auburn. LSU was a top-notch team, with its 'Chinese Bandits' and the 'go team,' and Paul Dietzel, and we have to go up to Auburn, where Florida never wins. Those are two games right there you're literally almost giving away. And we lost to Georgia Tech—not a bad team either. Those were our only losses that year. Not bad."

The better teams finish the season on a winning note, and this '63 Florida team won its final three games. The Georgia game was played in Jacksonville on November 7. Tragedy struck just before the game when Larry Dupree's wife Denise, nine months pregnant, lost their child.

Tom Shannon: "Larry was not going to play. The night before Larry was in the hospital with Denise all night long. The baby was born dead. The Friday night before the game we would always get together, particularly if it was a home game or one in Jacksonville. We were watching a move before the ballgame.

"Larry walked in. The coaches called 'time out.' It was a very somber, tearful moment, as Larry explained to the team that the baby was born dead.

"He had still not made up his mind whether or not to play in the game. He said, 'And whether I'm there or not,' my heart's with the team, and I'm going to do the best I can, and I'm going to do what my conscience leads me to do.' We were concerned that if he played, he might not be able to finish the game because he had gone about 48 hours without sleep.

"On Saturday we went to Jacksonville, not expecting to see him. We went into the dressing room, and he was already sitting there, fully dressed. He has his uniform on, and he has his chalk under his eyes, and he just looked at me. I'll never forget the look in his eyes. It was a very, very emotional time. Here was a guy who had just lost his baby, and he said, 'I'm not here to waste my time. I'm here to win a ballgame.'"

In the Georgia game Dupree ran for a 65-yard touchdown, only to have the officials say he stepped out of bounds a few yards short of the goal.

Tom Shannon: "I remember giving him the ball time after time. He just kept saying, 'Give me the ball.' Needless to say, he broke loose down the right sideline, one of the best runs I've ever seen in my life. They say he stepped out of bounds. I was watching him from behind the whole way. I've always said I had the opportunity to watch the best hips that ever ran for Florida.

"I NEVER saw him step out. I don't think the referees cheat. I think they sometimes are overzealous.

"Anyway, late in the ballgame, as we were driving against Georgia, we got down to the goal line. Everybody in the huddle was saying, 'Give the ball to Larry.'

"I remember Larry Bechman looking at me. Larry was a great leader on our team. He said, 'We've got to give it to Larry.'

"I said, 'Don't worry about it. We have it under control.'

"Georgia was expecting us to give it to Larry, and we gave it to him off right tackle. I'll never forget watching him get hit and stop, and I saw his knee go down, but not hit the ground, and his calf kicked in to where it looked like it exploded, and he ran right over the guy into the end zone. His determination was incredible.

"After the ballgame was over [Florida beat Georgia 21-14], we lifted Larry up on our shoulders. One of the best compliments I ever received in my life was when his next son was born, and he named him Shannon. Shannon Dupree is proably 30 years old now. We're getting old."

In the Georgia game, safety Bruce Bennett, who would go on to be named All-American two years later, intercepted a pass and scored a crucial touchdown.

Tom Shannon: "Bruce came out of Valdosta High School and was touted as a fantastic quarterback. He played his freshman year, and the next year lined up as backup to me. But he turned out to be one of the best safeties Florida has ever had. He was a very, very nice guy and a hard-nosed football player. He had a knack for knowing where the football was going, so he was our 'Johnny on the Spot' with interceptions. And he loved to come up and hit."

There was a week off between the Georgia and Miami games. Miami was scheduled for Saturday, November 23, 1963. On the afternoon of the day before, President Kennedy was assassinated in Dallas.

Jack Harper: "I was in the parking lot when I heard about it. It seems like I was in a car and heard it on the radio, though I don't know what I'd be doing in a vehicle sophomore year, 'cause we didn't have any cars. We either had to walk or ride our bikes. I remember I was right at the north parking lot there next to Murphy Hall, where I stayed in our nice, un-airconditioned dorm rooms.

"The things you do…you're practicing, you've got mono, you're getting the hell beat out of you. It's hot, you go home and it's hot, and you have to go to class at seven o'clock in the morning. You practice for three and a half or four hours a day, and then you have to go home and live in a 95 degree dorm. It was a great deal. It was just the absolute… some of the worst days of my life."

Tom Shannon: "I'll never forget going back to my dormitory. In those days they had maids go around the dormitories and clean the rooms. Our maid was in our room. She was Afro-American, and she was crying, 'Oh my God, they have shot President Kennedy.' They had not yet announced that he had died. I remember sitting close to the television set.

"Everybody was in tears. I remember going right over to the Catholic Youth center, which was right across the street, going over there to pray immediately. That was just such a personal affront to everybody, whether you agreed politically with John F. Kennedy. This was the guy who we chose to be the leader of our country, and somebody had shot him.

"And after praying, I went over to the athletic department to find out if we were going to make the trip to Miami. The word went out that we were going to go, though we didn't know whether we were going to play the game. We wondered whether it should be played.

"In the end, of course, they said, 'John F. Kennedy would have wanted you to play it.' We decided to play it in his honor—to dedicate the game to him and play it in his honor because he was an athlete himself.

"And the game turned out to be a GREAT football game. We played against George Mira again. Our preparation for the game was superb. I remember suckering them with reverses. They had a very fast-moving, fast-reacting defense. They were so quick that sometimes if you had false-direction plays, they would play themselves out of position.

"I remember giving the ball to Hagood Clarke on a reverse. I got killed, and I was laying on the ground watching him go through the hole, and watching him run down the field. I was yelling, 'Go, Hagood, go.' He went for a 75-yard touchdown.

"Harry Fersch played defensive tackle for Miami. He and I had played football together at Bishop Curly High. I was laying on the ground, and he said, 'I got you, didn't I?' I said, 'Yeah, you got me, but look down the field right there, baby.'

"When I got up, I said, 'Harry, look at what you just did. You came out of your tackle slot, and he went right through it.'

"That game was a great strategic ballgame. That was the best play selection game I ever played in my life. I remember on a lot of plays saying to myself, That was a spectacular play call against these guys."

Jack Harper, suffering from mononucleosis, suffered through the humiliation of poor performance. Worse, he didn't know why. Finally, after a terrible practice, he checked himself into the hospital. Tests came back saying he was infected with mono. Harper was thrilled. At least now he knew there had been a reason for his subpar play. He would miss the final two games of the season against Miami and Florida State.

Jack Harper: "I got to where I hated football. I didn't know what was wrong. I was back in the days when you really had no rights. You had the right to play football, and you had the right to get your butt kicked. Coaches didn't mind kicking your butt. They didn't mind screaming at you.

"My sophomore year you didn't get to drink water during practice, because they didn't supply it. But they would bring a bucket of water out onto the field. You would get a towel, and everybody would suck on the towel. That's how you got your liquids back into your system! You had to suck on a nasty old towel.

"So we went to Miami that year. We were having practice leading up to the game. I had never seen Ray Graves. He was usually sitting up on this tower with his cigar watching the guys. But we were running a sweep play, and I fumbled a couple of times. Every practice was getting harder. Day in and day out, it got to be harder and harder and harder. I just thought I wasn't in shape. So that afternoon I fumbled some, and Graves came running at me, and he says, 'Harper, if you fumble once more, I'm gonna run your ass until you drop.'

"I was trying to do the best I could. I didn't know there was anything wrong. So on the next play, I fumbled, and he ran at me and grabbed me and said I wasn't trying hard enough. He said, 'Get your butt running around the field.' So I made two laps around the gigantic practice field. Every step was killing me, and I didn't know what was wrong. I came off the field, and I just felt terrible.

"I went to the trainer, Jim Cunningham, and told Jim I was sick. He sent me down to the infirmary. That evening I talked to a doctor, and they took some blood samples. I had strep throat, glandular fever, and mononucleosis. Apparently I had had mono for months and was getting over it.

"I was so joyous when I found out there was something wrong with me! It wasn't just me being lazy. That was the name they gave me that year—'Lazy Jack.' Every step was very hard for me. I'd be crying at the end of practice because of the wind sprints.

"Pepper Rodgers called me into the office—he was one coach I did admire—he said for me to dress in shorts and that I would play on Saturday.

"I had no intention of playing any more football that year. I went back to the doctor and said, 'What can happen?' He told me I had an enlarged spleen because of the mononucleosis and if I got hit there, I would be in serious trouble. He said, 'I don't want you playing.' So I didn't play in the Miami game. I went hunting over in Chiefton.

"I don't think we were emotionally and mentally prepared the way we should have been through a lot of the University of Florida. I think we were better than we showed—better than our records. I don't know if it was a motivational thing or a coaching thing. But we were better than we were. Where the fault lies, I have no idea. I just think we were better."

The final game of the '63 season was against Florida State, a game that quickly was becoming a lightning rod for this football-crazy state. Though the Gators won the game by only 7-0, the players never doubted the outcome.

Tom Shannon: "I will tell you that though it was a 7-0 ballgame, I don't think we ever felt we were gonna lose. I don't think that was overconfidence. I just felt like we thought we could control the ball. I knew we could throw a seven-yard pass in the flat any time we wanted to. I remember just rolling right and rolling left and hitting guys in the flat.

"I didn't really get the ball downfield a lot, but we controlled the ballgame.

"In that game I gave Larry Dupree the ball time after time after time. [Dupree carried the ball a then-Florida record 31 times .] With Larry running the ball thirty plus times, you felt like you were in control. Obviously, if they had thrown a bomb, we could have lost, but they weren't bomb throwers then— not until the next year when they had Steve Tensi and Fred Biletnikoff. In '63, Tensi and Biletnikoff were playing defense.

"We had hoped we would get a bowl bid at 6-3-1. We had gone the year before with a 6-4 record, and we thought we had a better football team. If only we had beaten Mississippi State.

"LSU was a better team, and Auburn was better at Cliff Hare Stadium, and maybe Georgia Tech was better. We gave away the Mississippi State game, and that was the difference. We beat Miami. We could have been invited to the Orange Bowl. I think Miami was considering us. But we didn't get it."

twenty-five

The Coming of Steve Spurrier

Going into the 1963 season Coach Ray Graves had recruited six of the best quarterbacks the state of Florida had to offer. He and his staff were loaded at the position. Graves then received a phone call from his brother Edwin, who lived in Knoxville, Tennessee. Edwin called to tout his brother on the talents of a boy who had just led his underdog Johnson City High School team to a resounding 27-10 win over Knoxville's Central High, the perennial powerhouse. The quarterback Edwin Graves wanted his brother to pursue was a kid named Steve Spurrier. Though Graves already had his quota of quarterbacks, he trusted his brother's judgment enough to go after one more.

Ray Graves: "I'll tell you why I signed quarterbacks. Quarterbacks are the leaders. I always recruited looking for leadership and athletic ability. Quarterbacks usually were the best athletes on the team. They could play three or four positions. Like Dick Trapp. He was a quarterback, and he turned out to be a pretty good wideout.

"My brother called me and said, 'Have you heard about this Spurrier?' I said, 'No.' I had never heard of him. He said, 'I think he's a pretty good athlete. Everybody is talking about him here that he's one of the best quarterbacks in the state. He just beat Central High. He does everything. He kicks field goals, extra points, he punts, and he passes. He's an all around athlete.' He said, 'His father is a preacher up in Johnson City, and our dad was a preacher. Maybe you have something in common to help get his attention and to recruit him.'

"That was the first I heard about him. I wrote and called him. The first time I met him he was playing baseball in Greenville, Tennessee. I talked to him and got him down for a visit. I tried to tell him what we were doing offensively, gave him a look at some of the movies.

"I said, 'We just bought the golf course.' He said, 'I'm interested in golf. I've started to play a little.' I said, 'Let's go down to the golf course and hit a few balls.' A few years ago I talked to Steve. I said, 'Honestly, tell me, did the sunshine and golf balls have anything to do with your coming to Florida?' He said, 'That didn't enter into it.' To this day I don't know what sold him on Florida.

"While he was visiting, he got sick. He had the flu, a little fever, and we took him to the hospital. I sat with him a long time. I'd do that. I had a good feeling about him.

"I talked to a lot of other coaches. I asked, 'Why isn't Tennessee after him?' They said, 'Because they're playing the single wing, and he isn't interested in Tennessee.' Ohio State was calling him every night. Johnny Vaught of Mississippi had his ear, because they were winning everything over there. If he hadn't come to Florida, maybe he would have gone to Mississippi.

"I think we sold him on the offense and maybe on the challenge. We showed him, and he said, 'I can execute that.' And we got him as a freshman, and he had a good freshman year. He played on the scout team. He didn't practice as well as he played in games. He practiced methodically. Looking back, he was always thinking on the football field. He could think while he was under pressure."

Steve Spurrier was a Floridian by birth. His father, Graham, was a nomatic Presbyterian preacher, and the Spurriers were living in Miami Beach when he was born in 1944. He was named Stephen after the first Christian martyr.

His parents had met in Charlotte, North Carolina, as members of a Christian youth group. The preacher's first pulpit was in Eudora, Arkansas, the next was in St. Albans, West Virginia, and then came the stop in Miami Beach.

When Steve was three, the family moved to Athens, in East Tennessee. Five years later, in 1952, they moved again, to the Tennessee town of Newport, a hamlet so small it didn't even have a Little League.

His parents went on a retreat in Montreat, North Carolina. While they were there, Sid Smallwood, the athletic director for the Johnson City school system, saw Steve and his older brother Graham playing baseball. He saw their skill and decided to convince Reverend Spurrier to move to Johnson City by letting him know that there was a Presbyterian church in town that needed a pastor.

The Spurriers moved into a house behind the Calvary Presbyterian

Church. Immediately, Steve impressed everyone with his abilities in basketball and baseball.

Even in the ninth grade he was a talented field goal kicker, but because of his size, he didn't play in the field until his junior year in high school. The coach let him play quarterback for the first time in the final game that year.

Spurrier was the kind of kid who practiced long after everyone else had gone home. At age 11, Santa Claus gave him a kicking tee, and he would practice for hours in his backyard kicking a football over a tree limb. He forced his older brother Graham to play catch with him for hours on end. He would go on to become an All-State selection in football, basketball, and baseball.

Prior to his senior year, Spurrier dislocated his shoulder, but played anyway. The University of Alabama offered him a scholarship, but at the time 'Bama had legendary quarterbacks Joe Namath and Steve Sloan, and Spurrier didn't want to have to wait his turn.

Thanks to Coach Graves' sales job and his friendship, Steve Spurrier decided to go to Florida. Tommy Shannon was Florida's starting quarterback at the start of the 1964 season, Spurrier's sophomore year.

Tom Shannon: "Behind me was a kid by the name of Steve Spurrier. I think at one time Steve had signed with Alabama. He was going to go to Alabama. And then at the 90 yard line, he decided to come to Florida. But we didn't know much about him other than he was a great athlete, a football, basketball, and baseball guy out of Johnson City, Tennessee.

"He played against the varsity a little bit his freshman year, but we actually had a great B squad quarterback in Wayne McDaniel. We also had Kay Stephenson, a great quarterback. Kay went on to play backup quarterback to Jack Kemp at the Buffalo Bills. Kay threw the prettiest pass I ever saw. Bud Williams could really hum the football, but we were a team that didn't drop back. We rolled out, ran the option, and you had to have quicker feet.

"Timing in life is everything, and if they had come a little later, all those guys would have played, and I'd have stuck to defense because I didn't have the arm Kay Stephenson had. But Kay didn't have the feet I had. I was a scrambler and could run a little bit, and that's how I ended up playing.

"So as I began my senior year, we had Steve Spurrier coming in. He was a better drop-back passer, had a little stronger arm, was a couple inches taller, had great leadership skills, and was savvy about football.

"Something else happened that was big. I didn't play spring football. I played baseball. And that allowed Steve Spurrier to run the varsity between his freshman and sophomore years and to get all the reps he needed to get, versus senior quarterback Tom Shannon being there in the spring. That, as much as anything, was what allowed Steve to develop and allowed Coach Graves and Coach Rodgers and Fred Pancoast to work with Steve a lot more than they normally would have if I had gone to spring practice that year.

"Looking back, I wouldn't have done anything differently. I wouldn't have given up baseball for that. But my point is that when Steve didn't have to split time with the senior quarterback during spring practice, it was very much in Steve's favor.

"I must tell you, though, Coach Rodgers and Steve and I sat down and talked before my senior year, and Steve's attitude was, 'I don't need to start. Tom's the senior quarterback. I'd just as soon be on the sidelines and watch what's going on and adjust to it and get a chance to come into the game.' That was very friendly, very acceptable, versus today when a freshman comes in, he doesn't care whose job he's taking; he wants to start.

"Steve and I were roommates on the road. We had a mutual respect for each other. We recognized him as the great talent he was going to be, though we couldn't have predicted he would win the Heisman Trophy and go on and have a great professional career as well.

"From the first, I saw that Steve had a very, very good sense of values. He's very compassionate and extremely family oriented. He's as honest as the day is long—he would never cheat at recruiting, and he can't stand to be cheated against. If he thinks someone else is doing some illegal recruiting, he gets on the phone and says, 'Hey, guys, let's don't make this an uneven field.' He just won't put up with anything less than excellence. He's a hard taskmaster, but he's extremely sensitive."

Jack Harper returned to Florida in 1964 to play his junior year, despite his bout with pneumonia and depression. It was only his integrity as an athlete that impelled him to finish his senior year.

Jack Harper: "Football started up again my junior year. It was so difficult. No matter how hard you try to get in shape, there's nothing like going and having somebody push you rather than your pushing yourself. You'd come out of two-a-days, and your muscles were so sore, you couldn't move.

"Why didn't I quit? I guess it's not in me to quit. What else did I have going to me—absolutely nothing. No, quitting was not an option. That never entered my mind, cause you just had something to do, and you had to do it. Gosh, after being put up for a scholarship and playing and doing somewhat well in my sophomore year, quitting was never an option."

Tom Shannon: "Our first game in '64 was against SMU. I thought we had a game plan against SMU that was terrific. They were expected to have John Roderick, a world-class sprinter, who didn't make the trip. He had gone down to Mexico during the summer and ended up with a bad, almost deadly, case of dysentery. So we beat SMU pretty handily.

"Steve came into the game in the second period, and on his very first pass, he hit Jack Harper for a 57-yard touchdown. It was a great coming-out party." [Florida won 24-8.]

Jack Harper: "That was a screen play. It was a pass of one yard, and then basically I went and did my job. If you go and score a touchdown, it's no big deal. You just go ahead and get ready for the next play. It wasn't no big deal. It's more of a big deal now, because I can look back and say, 'I caught Spurrier's first touchdown pass.' Spurrier is such a celebrity and such a nationally known person whereas Jack Harper is still a little dirtball down here in Boca Grande grubbing around for a living. Now I say the older I get, the better I was in football. 'Oh yeah, I caught Steve Spurrier's first touchdown pass,' which was a screen pass to me. He didn't really have anything to do with it. I did it all. I went around 15 or 20 of their players and scored, but that was just what I was supposed to do. But now as you get older, it's kind of a big deal. I'm the only guy who's ever caught a touchdown pass from both Steve Spurrier and Bob Griese—that's my claim to fame. That's about it. When people start talking about the Gators, I just kind of go along with them. It's still just what I did, and the good Lord gave me the ability to do it, and I did it, and now I'm doing this.

"Steve Spurrier was a good quarterback, but I really didn't know how good he was. Not being a student of the game and not being able to compare him to anyone else, I couldn't really tell how good Steve was. I know he liked to get in the huddle and he would make up a few plays. The only thing bad about Steve Spurrier was he threw the ball to Charlie Casey more than he threw it to me. He missed it there. He should have been throwing more to me than he was Casey."

Tom Shannon: "When we played Mississippi State, I was a little disappointed because I thought we left our game plan. They had a team like FSU—I just felt that any time we rolled out in the flats we could beat them. They were in a six-man line; they were weak in the flats. Every year we could wear them down throwing in the flats. We were a control team. We weren't going to throw bombs. In those days, no one really did.

"But in that game we left our game plan, and we were very fortunate at the end of the game when Steve came in. He threw some down and outs that got us down the field, where Bobby Lyle kicked a field goal to win the ball game.

"But after the game I was upset we had left the game plan that always beats Mississippi State or at least keeps us in the hunt. It was the beginning of the era of mixing quarterbacks, and I felt like it caused some lack of execution on the field. Guys were kinda running into each other a few times during the ballgame. Some things happened that weren't indicative of the disciplines we had up to that game. We left our disciplines and played ragged, but we pulled it out in the end.

"We were supposed to play LSU next. They were predicting that a hurricane was going to strike Louisiana that weekend, though. We went up to Jackson, Mississippi, and spent the night to see whether the hurricane was going to hit. And it did hit, and we went back home. They delayed the game until the last game of the season.

"Next came Ole Miss. We had a good game plan. They had Stan Hindemann, a huge lineman who played fantastic football. Matherly was their quarterback, and he ended up more famous as a country singer and songwriter. Man for man they ranked up there with the best as far as their personnel was concerned. They had a great athletic team in 1964, a strong, fantastic football team.

"And we beat them 30-14, and the next week we beat South Carolina [37-0], and their quarterback was Dan Reeves. We had a great ballgame against South Carolina. At this point we were still trying to stay with the senior leadership program, although the baton was being handed to Steve pretty rapidly. He was getting more and more playing time, and his talent was really coming out."

Florida won its first four games of the '64 season, but its toughest opponent, Alabama, again led by Joe Namath and backup Steve Sloan, proved too strong. Alabama won a close battle, 17–14. What marked the game was that Steve Spurrier started and played right to the end. Senior Tom Shannon spent the day sitting on the bench.

Tom Shannon: "I did not play in one play of this ballgame. That was very hard. Cause we had beaten this team the team before [with Shannon at quarterback]. Before the game and after the game Joe Namath came up to me and wanted to know, 'What in the hell is going on?' I said, 'Well, we have got kind of a phenom here. The guy's a good athlete, but I don't know why I'm not playing because I haven't thrown that many interceptions or made that many fumbles.' There seemed to be a lack of interest in playing the senior at the time, which hurt us because at the end of the football game we made some sophomorish mistakes."

Late in the game Florida was on the 7. Shannon stood on the sideline while the inexperienced sophomore called the plays. When Spurrier, perhaps a little flustered by the pressure, thought he was on the 2, not on the 7, he called a play that was stopped at the line of scrimmage and caused the clock to run down. Shannon could only shake his head and wonder what might have been.

Tom Shannon: "He handed off to Johnny Fiber, our fullback, against the number one defense in the United States with time running out. I don't know if it cost us the ballgame, because we don't know whether we could have scored a second touchdown, but if we had just rolled out and thrown the ball into the end zone, you would have had a chance to win and stop the clock if it's incomplete. If you call a roll-out, you don't get caught on a running play up the middle and you certainly don't get tackled with the football in your hand. You roll out one way or the other and stretch them out, and that's what we were good at. And we were really good on two-point conversations. We would run roll-outs and stretch them, and Floyd Dean, Lynn Matthews or Randy Jackson would get open in the end zone. That was the play I would have liked to have seen run at the time.

"It didn't seem that Coach Graves or Coach Rodgers sent in any play. They put the pressure on Steve, under the heat with the clock running down. It forced Jimmy Hall literally to be running onto the field and kicking as the clock was running out. And there were only ten men on the field when he did it. Again, it was an absolute lack of discipline. We lost our discipline in the Mississippi State game, and we lost our discipline which led to this loss. We could have won this game. We were down 17-14 on their 7 yard line, with twenty seconds to go and a chance to put the ball into the end zone. And running a running play right up the middle cost us this football game.

"There were no recriminations. We came out of there saying, 'Didn't Alabama win the national championship this year?' I think they did. They beat Oklahoma in the Orange Bowl to win the national championship. So we played a hell of a football game against a hell of a team on their turf for the second year in a row. So here I was, a senior quarterback standing on the side-line for the ballgame, and the way I felt about it was, 'That's fine. It's in the books.' I crossed over that line back in the Mississippi State game. This was a maturing experience for me.

"On the way home on the plane I remember helping to serve the meals. I was not upset at all personally. I was upset we didn't win the football game, because I thought we had a great, great football team. Beating the national champions certainly would have been a gigantic feather in our cap. We could have gone to a bowl. By the way, that five-yard field goal would have tied the game."

Ray Graves: "Steve's mistake cost us the Alabama game. He thought he was on the two when he was actually on the seven. He thought we had scored on the play. And it cost us the ballgame. But there's not much to say. I never talked to any player about a mistake he made during a ballgame. You look at the films, and you try to criticize them at that time.

"But once Steve became the quarterback, he was our man, and I always had confidence in him. In the huddle Steve would challenge the receivers and give everybody confidence that, 'Hey, this will work.' And they believed it. The offensive line, boy, I'll tell you, they protected him. They worked hard for him and gave him good protection.

"He was the only quarterback I coached who I gave free hand to call a check-off on any play we called from the sideline. Usually we signaled and didn't give the quarterback a chance to check off a play on the field. After a while I had every confidence in Steve, because he would check to a better play than the one we called on the sideline.

"If you have a quarterback who can do that, you give him free reign, because the players on the field have more of a feeling for the game than you do on the sideline. He was a player who would even check off after the ball was snapped, just by hand signals. Charley Casey and he were pretty close.

He would stay out after practice and work on routes with his receivers. I can see them out there now. Casey would out there. Richard Trapp was out there. Steve was a coach and a player out on the field. He gave confidence to everyone—the players, the coaches, and the fans that we were going to win."

After losing to Alabama 17-14, Florida defeated Auburn , 14-0 at Florida Field. The next game was against Georgia, a 14-7 loss. The key play came when Georgia field goal kicker Bobby Etter picked up an errant snap and ran the ball in for a touchdown.

Tom Shannon: "I remember watching Etter pick it up. He ran down the left side. My roommate, Jerry Newcomer, was the cornerback, and he was making sure it wasn't going to be a two-point conversation or a fake and so he laid back until he could make the tackle, and Etter ran it in.

"We never should have lost that ballgame. We had a superior football team. There's no way we were supposed to lose to Georgia. Again, Georgia was a team you could throw against in the flats all day long or you could run traps all day long. We didn't run that game plan. We seemed to go away from what worked against these teams to match the talent of where we were, and we didn't get there."

Next came Florida State, a team that had never defeated Florida. After the Georgia defeat, Coach Ray Graves gave Tom Shannon the opening nod at quarterback.

Tom Shannon: "The first time we had the ball we drove it down the field. Everything we did was right. I threw the ball, and people caught it. We drove it right down to the one-yard line, and on the one, the snap was fumbled, and it went between my legs. I fell to my knees. The ball was behind me, and I didn't see it. I remember their defensive end, D'Allesandro, recovered the fumble on the two yard line. I remember Coach Graves being upset with me because we fumbled the ball. To be honest with you, I don't know how I ever got back into that football game. I remember telling Coach Rodgers, 'I never got the ball snapped into my hand.'

"The replay showed that the ball was snapped into the inside of my left thigh pad. I guess Bill Carr dropped his tail as he was firing out, and as he did the ball didn't get snapped back up to where my hands were. The coaches couldn't see it, but if you watched the film, you could see the ball actually turning as it came off my thigh pad. It was behind me. We had called a quarterback sneak, and I called 'Hut, go,' and I never got my hands on it.

"I remember going to Coach Rodgers at halftime. I said, 'Coach, I'm hot. Everything I'm doing is right.'

"He said, 'Well, you fumbled.' I said, 'I didn't fumble. I'm telling you the ball didn't hit me in the hand.' When the game was over, he came over to me and said, 'You were hot, but Coach Graves just didn't want to put you back in the ballgame.'

"At that point we had all crossed over that line. It was a matter of their not thinking you had the talent, and the judgment was made. But as it turned out, I started the next week against Miami and started against LSU and had a great ballgame."

Jack Harper recalled a defeatist attitude before the FSU contest.

Jack Harper: "I remember distinctly in the locker room there was an air of defeat prior to the game. I remember I had it within myself to say something that would change the atmosphere. If someone would have just gotten up and told everybody what was going on: 'We are not mentally and emotionally ready to play this game. We are going to get our asses beat unless we change right now, right here.' I remember very distinctly I needed to do that, and I didn't do it. We should have won that game.

"We outplayed Florida State, and we lost that game [16-7]. To this day I wonder why I didn't say something. Mainly, it was because I didn't consider myself a leader. I wasn't a leader of the team. I was a loner of the team. I heard that there were bets in the stands that I would be the last man out on the field when they say, 'Here come the Gators.' And people used to win money betting on me, because I was always the last guy out of the chute. I was the last guy all my junior and senior years. I figured, if you can't be first, you might as well be last.

"But I hold myself accountable for losing that Florida State game. I was so fired up that I scored, but that was one of those games I was just pissed off through the whole game, and we lost. If only I had said something. If only SOMEONE had said something."

Tom Shannon: "We beat Miami 12-10, and it was a great victory. In the game Larry Dupree scored his final touchdown of his career, and that was another thing: For some reason Larry Dupree was not used much his senior year. But he carried so much respect that the two All-American running backs in 1964 were Gale Sayers of Kansas and Larry Dupree of Florida. Unfortunately, he fell out of favor. Something was going on where they thought Johnny Fiber, who weighed 225, should play. Dupree wasn't that big. He was a quick fullback, more of a scatback. Larry had speed. We never could figure out what happened to Larry that year. I don't think the coaches felt they owned us any explanations, and they really didn't. But Larry and I both made up our minds we were going to tough it out. It was a reasonably interesting maturing year for both of us."

After the 12-10 victory over Miami, the Gators made up the LSU game at the end of the season. They would win it in an upset, 20-6, to complete a 7-3 season.

Jack Harper: "We went out to Baton Rouge, and it was cold. I don't know why, but I enjoyed that game. It was one of the memorable games I played in. We beat their ass. All I remember is that we went into the game with absolutely nothing to lose, and we were prepared, and everything we did, we did right, and we just beat the crap out of them. We were just a better ball team, especially that night."

Larry Dupree: "In 1964 our last game was against Sugar Bowl bound LSU. We played the game last because we were supposed to play them the third game of the season, and we got hurricaned out. Hurricane Dora came through and washed out the game, and it was scheduled at the end of the regular season on December 5. It was an extremely cold day, and we beat the britches off of them. We beat them worse than the score indicated [20-6]. I mean we just physically manhandled them. It was some of that 'we're going to show you' attitude. We physically beat them up.

"I'll tell you what—we made the Sugar Bowl committee look very bad. Graves wanted the committee to know we were a darn good football team, that we'd represent the conference well. He told them, 'We've got a very good chance of beating LSU. They had to take LSU or us.

"The Sugar Bowl committee picked LSU. New Orleans was right there. Picking LSU was a popular choice—bring in the home team. So beating SugarBowl-bound LSU was a great, satisfying win. Since we weren't going to get to play anywhere, LSU was our bowl game."

Tom Shannon: "The final game of the season was the makeup game against LSU in Baton Rouge. LSU went into this game 7-2. We were 6-3. The teams we had lost to were Alabama, Georgia, and FSU, good teams. The first two we never should have lost. We could have gone into the LSU game with one loss. I remember Coach Graves saying, 'If you beat these guys, there's a very good chance you'll get an offer to the Sugar Bowl.' Because they were holding open the Sugar Bowl for LSU.

"It was cold as hell. That was the coldest I ever remember playing in. We had muffs on the sideline for our ears and hands.

"Steve had a mild sprain of his ankle in the Miami game, and I remember starting that game and running some options that worked very well, pitching the ball to Depree and handing off to Graham McKeel quite a bit. I thought Graham was one of the great up-and-coming backs. I remember getting to the goal line. I threw a jump pass to Charlie Casey on the two yard line. Then we gave the ball to Graham a couple of times. He said to me, 'Why are you doing this to me? I'm too young.' The second time Graham jumped over the top of the pile for the touchdown.

"I also remember calling a fullback draw and running a quarterback sneak instead. Because they came out, and they had no linebacker. I ran about 25 yards, just ran right up the gut. We had a very, very good game against an excellent team. We beat them 20-6.

"I remember Pepper Rodgers coming to me in the dressing room afterwards and saying, 'I'm really, really happy you had the opportunity to finish your career with a great ballgame.' So I was very happy.

"During the season Dupree and I got together several times, and we talked it over. We said, 'Hey, let's finish this season. Let's make up our minds we're here to graduate and get a degree. Let's finish it with strong leadership. There are kids counting on us; we're seniors.' And the sophomores, Spurrier and Fiber had really good years the way it turned out. Again, we didn't know Steve was going to win the Heisman two years later. Obviously that made the coaches look prophetic, because they recognized the talent.

"And after the season, I got several letters from the Oakland Raiders about coming out and playing defense. In those days Al Davis was really enamored with Florida football. He ended up bringing Pete Banaszak from Miami. He brought Fred Biletnikoff from FSU. Jim Otto already was from Miami, and Bill Miller was from Miami. So there seemed to be a very strong Florida contingent out on the West Coast. In those days the AFL was a separate league from the NFL. But my concentration really was on baseball. In between my senior year and a fifth year, I played in the Basin League in South Dakota, with a lot of guys who went on to the major leagues, Ted Sizemore, Reggie Jackson, Sal Bando, and Rick Monday, all from Arizona State, had played there the year before. It was a stopover place after you'd been drafted.

"I played first base and actually led the league in batting right up until the last week, when Ted Bayshore from UCLA beat me out. I came back to Florida, went through a fifth year, played baseball, and graduated.

"I took a job with Larry Dupree working together in graduation supplies. We worked for a company called the Jack Williams Company. We were franchise reps for the state of Florida. We traveled the state selling school rings. At the time Mr. Williams had about 75 percent of the state of Florida. He had been around a long time. It was a very good opportunity for us.

"Then I got married, and I got a call from Jerry Atwell, who owned the Montreal Alouettes football team. He lived in Fort Lauderdale, even though the team was from Montreal. It was two years after I left Florida, but he wanted me to come to the Alouettes and play backup quarterback and start at safety.

'I went up there and made it through the first couple of ballgames, and then my knee went out. In those days if you tore your ACL, you had a 50–50 chance of ending up with a stiff knee. That's what ended Larry Dupree's pro career with the St. Louis Cardinals. Bouncing back from an ACL literally didn't happen, so I never even bothered to have it operated on. We just packed it up and came back home. That was it for football and baseball. I moved to Tampa in 1968.

"I had graduated from business school, and I went to work for Watson and Company, architects and engineers. Mr. Watson wanted someone to assist him as he grew. He was a Florida fan, a gigantic alumnus. I went through psychological testing for three days. My wife and I stayed at his guesthouse for about a month.

"I worked for Mr. Watson for two and a half years before I went to work for one of our clients, a homebuilding company that had 1,200 acres under option in the Carrolwood area of Tampa. It was all farm land. So I got into the development business around 1970 and was in it until 1994, when I went into the franchise business for the Outback Steakhouses. We own 53 Outbacks and growing. We're having fun. My wife Kathy and I are out in

California five months a year. We own our home here in Tampa, and we rent a home in San Diego."

Larry Dupree should have been a longtime pro star. The St. Louis Cardinals were so high on Dupree as a running back that they traded away their all-pro star John David Crow to make room for him. But in light practice early in his first training camp, he made a misstep and heard a loud 'pop.' His pro career was over before it began.

Larry Dupree: "I wanted to play pro ball, but it wasn't life or death for me. I went to the St. Louis Cardinals. I played some exhibition games for the Cardinals, went down with a knee injury, and never came back from it.

"We were at Lake Forest, Illinois, practicing. It wasn't in a game. It wasn't even a live practice. In fact, it was against a dummy. I just stepped wrong.

"We were working on getting the back out of the backfield. Boy, I'm tell you, it was like somebody shot my leg off. Then boy, after that it just continued to get worse. I couldn't get full extension of my leg. No matter how hard I worked, I never got rid of the tenderness there.

"They flew me back to St. Louis to a Dr. Reynolds. He didn't give me a lot of encouragement. He didn't say quit, but he said I'd have a lot of problems. Back then when you tore a cruciate ligament, it was only so many hours before the thing starts to deteriorate, and then you've got to take some other part of the body and try to make a ligament. Today, I'd have missed a season. I wouldn't have missed the rest of my career.

"I lived on quickness. I was quicker than most anybody I played against. Then all of a sudden, you don't have that step any more. Instead of being gone, you're caught in between. You've had it all your life, now all of a sudden it's gone and there's no way to get it back. I went through spring training trying to get it back, but I just was never the same.

"It wasn't hard for me to go do something else. Football wasn't life or death for me. You can't go into that game thinking you're going to die there. We know it's short-lived. You're kidding yourself if you don't have yourself prepared for that at any time. That was a chapter in my life that I enjoyed, but it was time to go into something else.

"For a number of years I was in the construction business. I was in the automobile business a number of years. I'm retired now. I have some health problems. I had back surgery, open heart surgery. That humbles you about life. For the first time in your life you realize, 'We're not talking about some-body else. 'It's me, and I could die.' Your body feels death, because they do stop that heart while they're working on it.

"I went and had a test one afternoon, and the next morning I was on the table. I have felt so much better since it was done. I had been having chest pains. I didn't know how bad I felt. Luckily my wife prodded me to go to the doctor. I had no heart damage. I did not have a heart attack. The doctor said I probably would have had one within thirty days. God was looking out for me.

"It is tough to get over. I am still physically weak. My diet had to change, and that's been tough. I grew up in a little country town that took pride in its great cooks. I can only eat fried chicken occasionally. Now the big thing is the salt. I have to learn to do without the salt. I'm getting used to that. I use a lot of black pepper."

twenty-six

Steve's Go-To Guy

One of Florida's star receivers during the Steve Spurrier regime was a wideout by the name of Richard Trapp. What made Trapp's story so amazing was that he didn't begin playing football until his senior year in high school. He didn't start until the middle of the season, when a back got hurt and the coach needed a replacement. The first time Trapp ran with the ball he scored on a long touchdown. Despite his lack of play, Trapp was not overlooked by Coach Graves' staff. He was offered a scholarship, and during his junior year in 1965 became Steve Spurrier's favorite target.

Richard Trapp: "Coach Graves was the one who recruited me from Florida. He's a heck of a man. He really is. I was born in California, and I had lost my dad to cancer when I was about four years old. In fact, that's why we moved to Florida. It was my mom, my older brother, and I, and we moved to Bradenton to live with my mom's brother and to start all over again. So I didn't really have a father figure, and Coach Graves became one.

"He was an impressive man. Couple that with the fact that he was going to let me play baseball also, and also that Gainesville is closer to home than any other school. And I was a Gator fan. Put all that together, and I went to Florida.

"My sophomore year, I made the varsity, and that year we started having a very good team.

"I didn't play very much the first few games. We had Charlie Casey, who was an All-American receiver. We had a couple of other good receivers, Jack Harper and Paul Ewaldson.

"Our quarterback was Steve Spurrier. I didn't really run around in the same circles with him. He was a year ahead of me. He was dating Gerri, so he was pretty much a homebody—maybe not homebody, but he had a steady girl friend. And I was single. So I didn't run in the same social circles with him. But on the football field, he was certainly someone you looked up to. He was talented and very prepared, and he took the game very seriously.

"My sophomore year we had at least ten players who ended up playing in the NFL. All the way from Barry Brown to Larry Gagner to Jim Yarbrough to Charlie Casey to Allen Trammell to Spurrier. And Bruce Bennett, a little guy from Orlando, was voted on the All-Century team as the best defensive back in the history of Florida. We had Glenn Matthews, Bill Carr, our center, and Jack Harper, who was with the Miami Dolphins, and Harmon Wages.

"Our problem—which is not a problem any longer—was not that we didn't have any excellent athletes—our top 22 could play with anybody—but it dropped off quite a bit after that, and we didn't have the depth of the top teams."

The opening game of the 1965 season was a 24-14 win over Northwestern.

Jack Harper: "I had finally decided I didn't want to play running back any more. I was getting the hell beat out of me. My body was already beat up. What I wanted to do was play wideout receiver, and they accommodated me.

"I played a guy named William Buckner, and that was really the first time we ever played against a black player. I played wideout receiver, and I caught one or two passes. But it was absolutely the most boring, easy football game I ever played, because I did nothing except run pass patterns. I wasn't involved in blocking assignments or in carrying the ball or getting the hell beat out of you every play, which is what I was used to. So when I came out of that game, I thought it was a big waste—I was very disappointed in myself because it was not a gladiator-type position."

An 18-13 loss to Mississippi State followed.

Jack Harper: "I had heat exhaustion at halftime. They packed me in ice and gave me fluids. I couldn't move."

Florida defeated LSU and Ole Miss, then led Auburn 10-0 at the half before losing that game 28-17.

Jack Harper: "That game ticked me off. We should have won that game. I remember one guy [Bill Cody of Auburn] made an interception and scored a touchdown. I remember I almost ran him down on the three-yard line. I tried catching him for eighty yards. That game sucked."

Florida rebounded with a 14-10 win over Vince Dooley and the University of Georgia. Jack Harper, the reluctant hero, caught the game-winner on a long pass from Steve Spurrier.

Jack Harper: "I scored the winning touchdown in that game, and that's what most people remember about me. I didn't know where I was, but I looked up and the ball came down. I grabbed it and fell backwards and happened to be over the goal line, which scored the touchdown. That's what most people remember. I remember that. I remember I was mad in that game. You just finally get charged up, and you get mad, and you want to win, and you want to scream and holler and get everybody motivated and go for it. Once the game started, I got into it real well. I know I got a penalty forearming tackles while I was running the ball. You are trying to knock people off of you who are trying to hit you.

"We won there right at the last. Yeah, Spurrier finally threw me a pass."

The next game was a 51-13 romp over Tulane.

Jack Harper: "Before the Tulane game, the referees came in, and I guess they thought we were acting silly. They came in and said, 'You guys better be a little more serious about the game. They've got a good football team.' We didn't pay them any attention, and I guess for good reason. We just kind of beat the crap out of them. In that game I went to the left, and I stopped and went the other way and lost ground, but I scored a touchdown."

After the win the Gators accepted a bowl bid to the Sugar Bowl, the first time the University of Florida had ever been invited to the prestigious New Orleans bowl game. After Florida lost to Miami 16-13, the Sugar Bowl committee began to get nervous. Next up was Florida State.

Jack Harper: "I hate FSU. And I made two great catches in that game—one for a touchdown, and one was a short pass that Spurrier threw. It probably was the luckiest catch I ever made. The ball was coming down over my left shoulder, and I was running. I just happened to stick my arms out over my left side, and the ball hit me and fell in. Then I went in the end zone. The good Lord was with me on that catch. It just stuck."

Florida met Missouri in the Sugar Bowl. At the half, Missouri led 17-0.

Jack Harper: "I think we partied too hard on Thursday night prior to the Saturday game. I know I did. We were in New Orleans and on Thursday we partied a lot and had a pretty good hangover. And on Friday we had to go to practice, and they had two or three events scheduled, so it was kinda bad not getting much sleep and rest after partying most of the night.

"I spent most of Friday talking to the pros. I remember Coach Eibner was the offensive line coach, and he said, 'Hey, the Miami Dolphins want to talk to you. I'll talk to him for you and see what they can do.' The Dallas Cowboys, the New York Giants, and Miami were all talking, and Miami offered me a $10,000 signing bonus—nothing like what Charlie Casey and the rest of them got. They got $60,000, $70,000, $80,000. He told me what they were offering, and the only reason I settled with Miami was that it was in Florida. I didn't think I wanted to go to New York, and I didn't know anything about Dallas. I didn't even keep up with who was winning in the pros in those days. I just figured Miami would be close to home and I could stay in Florida.

"So I committed to Miami for a $12,000 signing bonus.

"On Friday night we were to see a wonderful show, Sound of Music. What a great show to be picked to go see prior to a football game! I have never seen the whole show, and I never will see it. 'The hills are alive...' Oh my God. I got up and left the theater and tried to get some sleep and tried to get ready for the game.

"I really wasn't prepared for the game. And I never did get much sleep.

"I remember the game. They had a tough football team. Our football team kinda dried out the first half. And I fumbled a dad-blamed punt. The ball came down out of the sun, and the guy on the Missouri team came right by me, hit my shoulder, the ball hit me, and they did not call interference. And they recovered the fumble."

Richard Trapp: "My sophomore year I ended up playing quite a bit in the Sugar Bowl. We were down 20-0 to Missouri in the fourth quarter, and nobody thought we had a chance to win the game.

"Coach Graves just wanted to put some points on the board, so he put me in, and Spurrier was our quarterback, and I caught five or six passes, and we ended up scoring three touchdowns and should have won the game, but after every touchdown Coach Graves went for two, and we didn't convert on any one of them, and so we lost the game.

"The first time we went for two, I don't remember anyone second-guessing it. Obviously, hindsight is always better than foresight. Certainly we could have gone for the extra points, but we ended up making it a very exciting game."

Jack Harper: "The thing I remember most is that final two-point conversion try at the end of the game where I told Spurrier, 'I am going through the line. I will be open. Just throw me the damn ball.'

"And, of course, he had Charlie Casey on his mind, like he always did, and that was basically it. I told him in the Sugar Bowl game that I'd be open through the line. We were down 18 to 20, and all he had to do was throw it to me—I just went through the line and faked a run, and I was standing there with no one within three yards of me. All he had to do was throw it three yards, and we'd have tied them, and I'd have been a hero, and he'd have been a bigger hero. And of course he winged it to Casey."

Richard Trapp: "After the game there was a lot of second-guessing. I do think the players liked and respected Coach Graves. So the second-guessing was more a lament like, 'I wish we had done this or that,' rather than criticism.

"Really, winning or losing a bowl game is not that important, unless you're trying to be number one. It's not as important as playing a good game. That was a big game for us. It was the first time we had ever played in the Sugar Bowl. It was just a great experience. We ended up making a very good game of it, and if I remember right, it was the best game played on New Year's Day.

"We finished the '65 season 7-4 and we went to the Sugar Bowl for the first time, but at the end of the season we felt we should have been better than we were. We had Spurrier, who came off his best game in the Sugar Bowl, who had broken all the Sugar Bowl records that year, coming back, and we had Larry Smith, a very highly touted running back who was on the freshman team, coming up, so we had a lot of aspirations."

Jack Harper: "After the season ended, I got half my bonus, $6,000, from Miami, and I was the richest man in the world. And during the summer I refereed back in Lakeland, and I spent a lot of time over at Anna Marie Beach at Stanley and Shirley Sargeant's house. Best summer I ever had. Fishing and trying to cast net mullet and being able to go out with them on their big boat grouper fishing, and living in their guest room. My earliest memories are going over to Anna Marie Island, with the waves and the smell and the sea.

"Then I showed up at St. Pete Beach, where the Dolphins had their training camp. We stayed in the Dolphin Motel. I told one of the coaches I wanted to play wideout, because my both my shoulders were tore up, gone. My rotator cuff would dislocate and pop out and pop back in any time I got hit. It was very painful. And I had no upper body strength because of the pinched nerves in my neck.

"I remember the first morning I went out. There were eighty rookies in camp. I looked around and said, 'I can make this team easy.'

"I was a wideout receiver, and I was to go downfield even though the play wasn't coming to my side, and this Bill Buckner from Northwestern, one of the first blacks we ever played against, he just sat up and I hit him, and it seemed like everything in my back broke. I finished practice and went in, and the trainer said to dress out in shorts the next day. And I did that on Friday, and on Saturday we had a scrimmage, and I dressed in pads, and I never got in. I never got to play. On Saturday afternoon I was cut. So I was very disappointed. I went back to Lakeland."

Jack Harper played for the Lakeland Brahmans in the North American Football League. His pay was paltry. The team played on Saturday nights.

Jack Harper: "It was the most fun, most wonderful football I ever played in my life. Buford Long, from the Giants, was our coach. You got paid two hundred dollars, and there was very little hitting. We played for the championship against St. Pete, and then I got to go back to the beach. It was just a really enjoyable time.

"After that Joe Thomas, who had signed me in Miami, recruited me as a free agent. I told him I hadn't received my other $6,000. He asked if I would like to try out the second year. I said sure."

Harper played another season with the Lakeland Brahmans. John Stofa, cut by the Dolphins, was the quarterback, and the backs were Harper and Larry

Libertore. When Harper returned to the Dolphins, this time it was as a running back, and this time he made the team.

He played through 1967, and in '68 he seriously hurt his neck and shoulders, and when he couldn't pass the physical in 1969, he retired.

Harper got his real estate license, returned to Lakeland and started developing property. In 1972 a friend convinced him to buy a condo in the seaside community of Boca Grande. After the marina burned down in '75, Harper bought the property and started to rebuild it.

Harper began a tarpon tournament which has become world famous. It is his twenty-fifth year, and his plan is to televise the tournament and award the winners a million dollars in prizes.

Said Harper, "It's gonna happen, if…if…if I can just keep it going. If I don't get so stressed out with life's everyday problems, people quitting on you and…. "

twenty-seven
Spurrier Wins the Heisman

In 1966 Steve Spurrier was the Florida quarterback. The job was his, and no one was going to take it away. Behind him was a sophomore, Larry Rentz, an outstanding high school athlete who as a senior had led Coral Gables High School to the mythical national championship.

Larry Rentz: "My first name is Ralph, not Larry. It's my preferred name. I don't particularly care for Ralph so I chose Larry. I grew up in Coconut Grove in Miami. I've lived there all my life.

"Quite a few colleges recruited me. I never counted them. Of course, there was the University of Miami, Georgia Tech, all the schools in the southeast, Notre Dame. It got so cumbersome, with all the mailings and the phone calls that my mother wisely declared a moratorium. My dad had died when I was a young kid.

"My mom, my uncle Frank and I sat down and narrowed it down between the University of Miami, Florida, and Georgia Tech.

"I got a full scholarship. Florida did something very creative. They gave me an all-sport scholarship, so that meant I could play any sport I wanted to. I was told that was the first one ever offered.

"I chose Florida, not based on athletic programs, but based on the school and campus and that I was planning on living in Florida. I didn't go to the University of Miami because I thought a little experience away from your hometown might be corrective.

"In those days, in 1965, freshmen were not allowed to play on the varsity. Three of us roomed together in Murphy Hall, myself, Larry Smith from Tampa, and Allen Brown, a defensive end at Coral Gables High School.

"I guess I was most impressed with the size of the school. Most of the players were on scholarship, either full or partial. There were a couple of walk-ons. Of course, everybody was biggesr and faster and stronger than in high school. So it was an awakening.

"I had a good freshman year, two games in particular. One was against the U of M in Miami in the Orange Bowl. David Teel was their quarterback, and Ted Hendricks was their defensive end. But our defensive backs were short, so they switched him to offense, and he caught something like fifteen passes. It was quite a game. There were about 50,000 people in the stands. We'd score. They'd score. We'd score. I think the score was 41-38. There was a lot of scoring.

"Nineteen sixty six, I was a sophomore. That was Steve Spurrier's senior year. That year he won the Heisman Trophy, so before the season I spoke to Ray Graves and said I would be glad to play free safety on defense instead of sitting on the bench behind Steve.

"We beat Northwestern in the season opener, 43-7. They had a tight end—I can't remember his name—who was huge and mouthy. He was about 6'8" and 250 lbs. The free safety has to cover the tight end a lot of times, and he and I got in it. He was a trash talker, and he was bad-mouthing our defensive backs.

"Steve always impressed me. He always seemed to get the job done. He always was cool, calm, and collected. I never saw him frazzled.

"Steve probably knew the offense better than our coaches. He always seemed to be in control of the situation. To be honest, he didn't impress me as being overly athletic, but he had a smoothness about him that was uncanny. I've seen a lot of other athletes who had more raw talent but weren't as successful. So a lot of it is between the ears."

Larry Smith, who had battled Rentz in high school, was another outstanding sophomore to join the varsity in 1966. At 6'2" and 200 pounds, he was a hulking presence who his teammates recall didn't speak very often.

Larry Smith: "I was born and raised in Tampa. I played for Madison Junior High School and then at Robinson High School. My junior year the team went to the state championship final game. It was the first playoff game ever held, and we lost to Coral Gables in a very close game.

"My senior year our team was not as good as the year before, and we didn't quite make the playoffs, but I made All-State and All-American and was heavily recruited. I took trips to Duke, Vanderbilt, Florida State, Auburn, and Miami, as well as the University of Florida. All the coaches were very impressive, but my father had gone to the University of Florida, and I had been going to University of Florida football games since I was a young man, so I would say it was a pretty strong pull. And I was very impressed with Coach Graves and his wife Opal. They were very nice and gracious people. They came in and told my folks that they were going to take care of their son, and they meant it, and that came through.

"I came to Florida in the fall of '65. We had our own freshman schedule. Mostly what we did was go out and practice with the varsity and get beat up every day. So you sort of learned the hard way, but that was the way it was done.

"We didn't have that large a squad. We had four or five scholarship backs, and we had a lot of walk-ons to fill out the squad.

"My sophomore year was 1966, the year Steve Spurrier won the Heisman Trophy. What I remember about Steve was that he was a good player, and everybody looked up to him. He was always extremely confident and composed. I got to play in the first game of the season against Northwestern. That was sort of exciting."

Richard Trapp: "I started the first game of the '66 season against Northwestern. And that first game I scored a couple of touchdowns. Very quickly it became obvious that Steve and I had good timing together. He has said that he really liked throwing the ball to me. A lot of it is timing and knowing what you can expect from the other guy.

"And I really liked working with him. You had the feeling that if you could get open, he was going to get the ball in there to you.

"Steve was someone everyone looked up to. To this day he's a very loyal, faithful individual. If he's a friend of yours, he's a friend of yours. If you don't know him, you may not like him because of some things he says. He says what's on his mind basically. He did back then, too. If that's the worst thing you can say about somebody, that's not too bad.

"I admired him. Absolutely. He was well-grounded. His father and mom did a good job with him. He was pretty stable and more mature than a lot of us at that age. His senior year he married Gerri—what a nice lady she is. You just had a lot of confidence in him. You thought you were going to win any game, that you had a shot at winning as long as he was in there.

"Everybody felt very fortunate to have Steve on the team. He just made the team better, and I certainly learned a lot and he feels the same way. On Father's day weekend each year all the players on the team get together in Crystal River at the Plantation Inn. We've been doing it for the last 30 years.

"So Northwestern was the beginning. We beat them pretty had, and everybody had a really good feeling. That was a great start for a season.

"Our next game was against a tough Mississippi State team, and we beat them pretty badly [28-7], and the first few games we didn't have any trouble at all. We beat Vanderbilt [13-0]. We didn't play a very good game, and Coach was not happy with our play. But the main thing was, we still ended up winning.

"Florida State came next. The build-up for the game was very exciting. A program is built over a period of time, and we were building a program. We really felt we were at a critical juncture what with what Spurrier was doing and the talk of his winning the Heisman Trophy and a lot of talk of how 'Florida is on the brink of becoming an elite football program.'

"And back then FSU was also making great strides in their program so winning that game was certainly very important to them.

"And we were ahead by five points with less than a minute to go in the game. They had the ball around midfield, and their quarterback, Gary Pajcik ran to his right, and he threw a pass toward our end zone to Lane Fenner. Bobby Downs and Larry Rentz were our two defenders. The question, of course, is how they allowed him to get behind them. I don't know if there was a mix-up or what. But I was standing on the sideline, and when the pass was thrown, everybody stood up, and I actually couldn't see the end of the play. I remember everybody in the stands was jumping up and down, and I couldn't tell if it was because we stopped them or because they had scored a touchdown. I didn't find out until I looked at the scoreboard. There was confusion on the field, and the referees finally ruled that Fenner had not caught the ball in bounds. And as a result, we won the game on the last play of the game, a hard-fought game, and there was a lot of jubilation. Nobody that I know of thought he was in bounds. The controversy is always the next day, when the photos come out and people start arguing. There were front page photographs. On in the Tallahassee paper supposedly was a shot of Fenner catching the ball with both of his feet in bounds. It was a major controversy.

"But right after the game, we won, and we celebrated. We thought we might end up losing, and we ended up winning. And that's all that mattered.'

Larry Smith: "I caught a pass for a touchdown against FSU, which was something I felt good about. But it all came down to the end and that final drive. The defense was on the field, and we were sort of helpless, just standing there watching. They threw a long pass, and Lane Fenner went up and came down, and the referees said he was out of bounds. After the game many people from Florida State said he was inbounds. I have no idea. From what I recall it was sort of inconclusive. But it was an exciting, thrilling game. It was fun to be part of.

"Our next game was against North Carolina State, and I remember that we were favored, but we didn't play as well as we should, and it took us a long time to wake up. Then we finally woke up and pulled out the game on a touchdown from Steve to Richard Trapp. Richard had a big day.

"Richard is just a great athlete. I don't think there's anything he can't do. He was billiards champion of the University of Florida. He won the over-40 national ping-pong championships. A few years ago he won a tennis championship. He played professional baseball and football. I don't know any sport he's not accomplished in."

Richard Trapp: "We went to Raleigh to play North Carolina State after that, and with only a few minutes left in the game, we were tied 10-10. All through the game Steve had problems overthrowing me, because the field was slanted on each side, and it threw him off by about six inches. It took him almost the whole game for him to finally get on the mark. And with only a few minutes left, he hit me on an 'out' pattern, and I made a good fake on my defender after I caught the ball, really faked him out pretty well, and I ran in for the winning touchdown. The play went about 40 yards.

"I remember running toward the sideline, stopping to catch the ball, and with my back to the defender, faking inside like I was going to stop and go back to the inside. He took the bait, and he stopped and took a little step inside, and I just swung back around and went outside, and he never touched me. I had to outrun the safety and ended up scoring. The play came at the right time.

"We then beat LSU pretty badly [28-7]. Everyone had a good game. Back then LSU was one of the best teams in the SEC."

Larry Rentz: "I remember when I played at LSU's stadium for the first time in '66, I was a sophomore, and coming out of the tunnel I could hear these two big, huge Bengal tigers. They were in cages right there a foot away… and I remember the noise level there was totally incredible. But Steve and the offense quickly got the score to 28-0. I was amazed at how totally silent the stands were as compared to the first quarter. It was quite a drastic contrast."

Richard Trapp: "Our record was 6 and 0, and Auburn came to play us at Florida Field.

"The night before our home games the whole team would always spend Friday nights in Micanopy, a little town outside of Gainesville. We'd take a bus out to the Howard Johnson's Motel and watch a movie and have a team meeting and go to bed.

"And every Saturday morning Tom and Glenn and I would watch cartoons on TV. This one morning we were lying in bed, and we had never watched this one cartoon before. We looked at each other and said, 'Oh, my God.' We knew we were late for the bus.

"Sure enough, we ran out of our room, and the bus had already left for the game. We were in a state of panic. We went to the front desk only to be told that the bus had left a half hour before. Obviously, no one checked the rooms.

"We were about 25 miles from the stadium, and we had no ride, and Tommy and I were the only two flankerbacks on the team. We had no choice but to try to hitchhike back. We were standing out by the side of the road, when we saw a Florida highway patrol car come speeding toward us with their lights flashing. We got in the car, and he drove to Gainesville with his siren on the whole way. By the time we arrived, the campus was wall to wall traffic. Everybody had to move out of our way as we came in.

"We snuck into the locker room. When we got there, everyone else was already out on the field taking pre-game warm-ups. We started getting dressed real fast.

"I remember Coach Kensler came into the locker room as we were dressing, and he said, 'Boys, I don't want you guys ever to do that again. Get out there, and let's don't tell anybody that you're not here.' That's all he said. That's all he had to say. My heart was beating a hundred miles an hour.

"The Auburn game turned out to be the highlight of the season. Auburn led at the half on two bad plays. They had a long [89-yard] kickoff return for a touchdown, and an even longer touchdown [91 yards] after we fumbled and one of their linebackers picked it up and ran it in. On that play I was on the other side of the field running a pass pattern, and I looked and saw him pick up the fumble and start to run with it. I had to be forty yards from him when I took off, and I had to run the whole length of the field from one side to the other on a diagonal slant while he was running down the sideline, and I almost was able to tackle him. I dove for him on about the five yard line and got his ankle, and he just was able to stumble into the end zone. And I remember the coaching staff being very complimentary for giving that effort. To even have a chance of getting him from where I started was pretty amazing, so they were real happy about that."

"We finally caught up in the fourth quarter. It fact, the game was tied [27-27]. We had fourth down. There was very little time left. The field goal was longer than what Shade Tree [Wayne Barfield] was used to kicking. We called timeout so the coaching staff could figure out what to do.

"Are we going to try to run or pass to get a first down, or what? One of the coaches mentioned that Spurrier had done some field goal kicking in practice. He said, 'Do you think Steve could kick this thing?' Then Spurrier jumped on it. 'I can kick that, coach. Of course, I can kick that.' And he convinced them to let him do it.

"And when he went out there to make the kick, I remember thinking that we probably had as good a chance scoring this way as anything else. I saw him kick in practice, and I knew he had kicked field goals this long. I remember feeling at the time, Hey, we have a good chance at this. This is what we need to do. I had confidence. I was thinking, We have a decent shot at this."

Larry Rentz: "It was out of the range of Wayne Barfield, our fantastic extra point and short field goal kicker. Bill Carr snapped it, I held it, and Steve kicked it. It was kind of a knuckler, low, but right through the middle of the uprights. A couple of years ago a reporter from the Sun Sentinel called and said that he had spoken to Steve, and Steve told him I had the laces toward him and the ball on a slant. In other words it was a bad hold. But I don't remember it that way. But it makes for a good story. So I'll let him tell his own version of it."

Larry Smith: "I had fumbled to give Auburn an opportunity to score a touchdown that let them tie us up. It was very discouraging to have done that, and fortunately we got the ball back, and we started marching, and we got the ball down to the 40-yard line. Steve had never kicked in a game. Steve told Coach Graves he could make it. Coach Graves said, 'Kick it.' And he kicked it, and we won the game, and that was essential in his winning the Heisman Trophy. It was just a wonderful turn of events for us.

"It was unbelievable. I don't think it surprised me. I can tell you it sure didn't surprise him."

Richard Trapp: "It barely made it over, but it went right square through the middle of the goal posts.

"And that caught the fancy of the nation and probably earned him the Heisman award at the end of the season."

Ray Graves: "I had heard before the game that Steve had told some of the players during breakfast that he dreamed he kicked a field goal to beat Auburn. And what happened, Steve passed to Tommy Christian on third down, but it was about a yard over his head. I didn't know what he was thinking, but Steve was always thinking. There were rewards out there for what he was thinking and what he was trying to execute. But I was going to send Barfield in to go for the field goal.

"The quarterback or captain could wave in or off a player, and Steve waved Barfield off. I thought that maybe he was going to go for a first down. He had about four yards to go, and it was a long field goal, 47 yards. So then he lined up, and he later said he had a special shoe with a zipper on it made for him to kick field goals, and they threw it out there to him, and he kicked the field goal.

"Afterward he said, 'Coach, I knew you were going to send Barfield out, but I figured it was a little out of his range, and if I got back and kicked it, they would figure it was a fake and they wouldn't rush.' And he didn't fake it, and he kicked it! Some people tell this story a little different, but this is what I remember.

"I often wonder what would have happened if he had missed it. That would have been catastrophic. Barfield was second or third in the NCAA in field goals. But Steve had this teammates thinking he was going to complete a pass or kick a field goal or punt, or whatever he was going to do. He gave them that confidence. You know, chemistry is so important in team sports, particularly where you have so many involved. It's interesting to think back. What if he had missed it? And it didn't go over by much, but that was a classic moment, and his timing was perfect. It was the week before the voting for the Heisman Trophy. The game was covered nationally. That was what got him the Heisman Trophy."

Richard Trapp: "After beating Auburn, we were ranked 7th in the nation. It was the highest ranking a University of Florida team ever had. If we could beat Georgia and Tulane, we could win the SEC championship for the first time ever.

"And we went out and lost to Georgia [27-10], and they beat us far worse than the score. They beat us pretty bad. We couldn't do anything. During the game Spurrier was making up plays in the dirt like it was a sandlot football game. He'd say, 'All right, Richard, I want you to do this.' He'd diagram a play in a dirt spot on the grass. Nothing was working. Georgia had a great defense. Jake Scott was one of their defensive backs. They had another All-American who played in the pros for years.

"The main thing was that they were very well prepared. They just somehow knew in advance exactly what we were doing. And that was probably the worst loss of my football career. We could have done big things if we had won that game.

"We beat Tulane badly [31-10] in the next game, and was invited to play in the Orange Bowl on New Years' Day."

Larry Rentz: "After we accepted a bid to the Orange Bowl, we played Miami, and I remember the 'Canes coming up to Gainesville knowing we had already accepted the bid, and they were absolutely as high as a kite. They beat us up physically. The were big, and they were tough. [Miami won 21-16.]

"That was such a letdown for us. It was a very low point. Ted Hendricks played defensive end for Miami. Ted and I grew up together in Miami. We were the same age and had competed against each other since Little League. He came over after the game, and we shook hands. Politely he said something like, 'I always told you you should have signed at U of M with me.' I said, 'Well, it ain't over.' It was just one game."

Larry Smith: "Miami was the best team we played all year. That was a close game, and we had a chance to win it. We didn't feel as bad about losing that game as we did the Georgia game because we felt Miami was a very good football team. Miami ended up in the Liberty Bowl, so they must have had a pretty darn good team."

Richard Trapp: "Losing to Miami wasn't that tough of a loss. It certainly was nothing like the Georgia loss. It wasn't an SEC game. We already had our bid to the Orange Bowl. Don't get me wrong—we hated to lose, but we all played a good game, and we were looking forward to playing Georgia Tech in the Orange Bowl."

Larry Rentz: "We went to the Orange Bowl, and Larry Smith stole the show. Larry and I roomed together our freshman year. Then I got to know him as a football player. He was probably the best all-around running back I had ever known and seen. He could do it all. He played five years with the Los Angeles Rams. He could run and block and catch the ball. He was a special running back."

In the second period Florida was behind 6-0. From his own 6 yard line Smith burst through an opening in the line and scampered 94 yards for a touchdown. It was a highlight of the modest back's distinguished career.

Larry Smith: "I was very fortunate. I got good blocking and got lucky. We were down at their end of the field, backed up. We were trying to move the ball out a few yards so we could get some room to punt. We just ran our standard lead play off-tackle. Since they all knew we were going to run into the line, everybody was up close to the line. Everybody blocked real well, and I popped through, and nobody was there. I kept looking back to see if anybody was going to catch me, and it happened so quick, nobody was there.

"I was fortunate and went 94 yards. So it was one of those fluke short-yardage type players that once you get through the line, there's nobody else there to tackle you."

Richard Trapp: "Larry was very fast for a big guy, and he broke through the line, and as he was racing the safety to the goal line, his pants started to fall off. He was running, holding the ball with one hand, and with the other hand trying to grab his pants. It's pretty funny now. To this day he denies that his pants were falling off, but they were. When you speak to him, tell him everyone says his pants were falling down. Larry says the story is a figment of [The University of Florida SID] Norm Carlson's imagination.

"Larry's long run was the highlight."

Larry Smith: "Back then I had those plastic hip pads that you wore inside your pants. I think what happened was the plastic hip pads were riding up, so it was an optical illusion that my pants were sliding down. Everyone tells me I ran the touchdown with my pants down but you can't run with your pants down. They were sliding a little, but it looked more dramatic than it was.

"I attribute all the attention to Norm Carlson, our public relations man, because he got a lot of attention for me and the team, and it got a lot of play in the newspapers after that. That was just Norm doing a good job."

At the end of the Orange Bowl game, which Florida won 27-12, Larry Smith was named the MVP of the game.

Larry Smith: "Winning that was quite exciting, yes. Things turned out nicely. I remember we just had a lot of fun down in Miami for a week. The Orange Bowl committee took great care of both teams, and we just had a marvelous time the week before the game. And after the game we stayed over a day, and they had a party for us at a country club. So they really made it a fun experience for both teams, win or lose."

And at the end of an outstanding 9-2 season quarterback Steve Spurrier won the prestigious Heisman Trophy, the award given to the nation's best college football player. It was an honor that signalled to everyone that the University of Florida indeed had come of age as a national football program.

Larry Rentz: "At the end of the year Steve won the Heisman award. It made us all proud. Mostly of Steve, but of our school too. Because in those days, Florida always had respectable teams, but it had not been known as a football powerhouse. So that put the school on the map as far as football. All of us were very happy for Steve."

Larry Smith: "Everyone was rooting for Steve to win it. He was a real team guy. All the guys who played with him still root for him. Yeah, he was the leader. I don't know of anyone who didn't respect him or like him. So when he won, we were elated. Everybody was elated. It was a big deal, but I don't know if we were as aware of how big a deal it was then as we do now. Something about being 19 or 20-years-old and not being quite as aware of some things as you should. But everyone was extremely happy for him, and he certainly earned it. He took that team to a little bit higher heights than we could have otherwise achieved."

Ray Graves: "Norm Carlson, who was our public relations director, is one of my closest friends. I brought Norm back from Auburn from the lovely village of Plains, and Norm's a legend. I'm sure Norm's handling Steve's publicity had a lot to do with his being named the Heisman Trophy winner. One thing I remember was that he worked with Steve on his acceptance speech.

"I gave Steve all the credit, and Norm did too, and Norm was the one who suggested to him, 'When they give you the trophy, why don't you give it to the president of the school?' So when they handed him the trophy, before Steve said a word, he said, 'Dr. Reitz, come up. This trophy does not belong to me. This belongs to the students and the university of Florida.' And he handed it to him.

"It had never happened before, and then after that they decided to give one to the player and one to the school. They do that today. And they finally gave Steve a second one. They said, 'Steve's exactly right. The trophy belongs to the school.'"

Steve Spurrier was drafted by the San Francisco 49ers, and spent most of his career as a backup quarterback to the great John Brodie. In 1972 Brodie was hurt, and Spurrier threw for 18 touchdowns in his most productive season. In 1976 Spurrier was the quarterback for the inaugural season of the Tampa Bay Bucaneers.

In the fall of 1977, Steve was finished as a pro athlete. When he returned to Florida in 1990 as head coach of the University of Florida, few knew that before he left, he would take the Florida football program to unimagined heights, including a National Championship in 1996.

twenty-eight

Richard Trapp's Famous Run

In 1967 a rebellious kid from Miami by the name of Steve Tannen joined the Florida Gators. Tannen was smitten with Princeton and Duke, but when a close friend and teammate decided to go to the University of Florida, he figured he would too. Good thing. Tannen ended up as an All-American defensive back before his career was over, and he would go to have an illustrious career playing pro football for the New York Jets.

Steve Tannen: "Because I wanted to be a doctor, I went to Duke on a recruiting trip and was quite taken with the place. They had a great medical school.

"But Wayne Griffith, a guy I played football with in high school, was also on that trip, and he decided he wanted to go to the University of Florida. I said, 'You know, I liked Florida too.' I told him, 'My dad went there. If I can make a name for myself in the state, it might help with my medical practice. I'll go to Florida too.' So I went to Florida, and we were roommates.

"Freshman year was great because I got to play wide receiver, a position I always wanted to play. Except we had some trouble at defensive back, and I ended up playing a little defense as well. We played four games and went undefeated. It was the only time that a freshman team at Florida had ever gone undefeated.

"And then in spring ball they decided that we had a whole slew of receivers and not many defensive backs, and they switched me. At the time I saw there were a lot of receivers—of course, I always thought I was the best one. But at that time of my life I was cocky enough to think I was the best anything. So I said, 'Yeah, sure.' First of all, in those days you didn't say no. The coach says, 'We're going to make you the waterboy.' You say, 'Where are the cups?' It's not like today. So I switched over, liked it, did very well, and started as a sophomore in a defensive backfield that was older than me. The other three were Bobby Downs, Bill Gaisford, and Tommy Hungerbuhler."

Another player who switched positions was defensive back Larry Rentz. Though he had been an outstanding quarterback in high school, Rentz knew he wasn't going to take Steve Spurrier's job and became a starting cornerback. In 1967 the coaching staff switched the versatile Rentz to flanker when they chose strong-armed Jack Eckdahl to be the Gator quarterback. But in the second game of the 1967 season against Mississippi State, Eckdahl went down with an injury and the relatively unknown Larry Rentz came in and ran the offense.

Larry Smith: "Larry was a great athlete, like Richard Trapp. There was nothing Larry couldn't do, whether it was golf or baseball or tennis or football. He was a tough player and very quick. To give you an idea of how quick he was, we used to tease him about being able to dodge raindrops."

Richard Trapp: "Larry was an incredible athlete. He was a little guy, skinny, even smaller than me, maybe ten pounds lighter. Larry ended up in the pros with the San Diego Chargers."

Larry Rentz: "Steve Spurrier was gone, and Florida was looking for a new quarterback, and Jack Eckdahl a lefty, a year behind me, and I, started out head-to-head in competition in summer camp. Early on in the pre-season, the coaching staff selected Jackie, and they wanted me to play flanker, which I did.

"We opened the season against Illinois [a 14-0 win] at home. It was hot as hell. I can remember Jackie having a good day, and I caught a couple of passes.

"We beat Mississippi State, and then against LSU Jackie tore up his ankle. I remember him going down. I remember worrying because he was writhing in pain and holding his left ankle.

"I was visiting with Jack in the hospital that night, and apparently the coaches had leaked to the press that he was not going to be able to play the next week against Tulane. The press was there, and they kind of sprung it on me.

"'Well, how does it feel to be the next quarterback?' I said, 'What are you talking about?'

"I had a week to get ready. It wasn't that hard. I had been playing flanker-back, so I was familiar with the offense. I had to relearn the offensive scheme from the quarterback's point of view. Fred Pancoast was the offensive back-field coach, and I would meet with Fred after practice in the afternoon and go over the game plan.

"Heck, I had a lot of talent behind me. I had a Graham McKeel, a fantastic blocker, at fullback. I had Larry Smith at tailback. He had Richard Trapp as flanker back. I had Jim Yarbrough at tight end. Hell, all I had to do was hand off to Larry Smith or throw a five-yard pass to Richard Trapp, and he'd do the rest. So it was pretty simple."

After Florida was clobbered by LSU 37-6, the team travelled to New Orleans to play Tulane. The team was strengthened by the return of wide receiver Richard Trapp, who had suffered from mononucleosis and had missed most of the first three games.

Larry Rentz: "I remember the Tulane game because everything seemed to click [Florida won 35-0]. I would hand off to Larry [Smith], and he'd gain ten yards. Occasionally, I'd hand it to Graham, and he'd do the same. Throw a little down and out to Trapp, and he'd turn it into a forty yard gain. It was almost too easy.

"Our next game was against Vanderbilt [Florida won 27-22]. That was a tough game, a very hard-fought game. I remember thinking, 'This sure as hell doesn't feel like Tulane. This is getting tough.' I remember a throwback pass to Larry, and I scrambled for a short touchdown.

"We played Auburn next, up there. Auburn was just beating our ass physically. [Auburn won 26-21.] Everybody was moaning and groaning in the huddle. I was the punter, and Auburn had blocked two punts right up the middle and turned those into touchdowns.

"They got in front of us, and all of us were in shock. I remember throwing to Trapp all the time. Richard must have caught a dozen passes. He was so good. I would throw a pass that was off, but he would catch it. He made a quarterback look good."

Steve Tannen: "Next was Georgia, and THE play I remember that year more than any other was against Georgia. Richard Trapp made this amazing catch and run [52 yards for a touchdown]—just an amazing thing."

Larry Smith: "That run was something. Something like nine or ten guys on defense touched him on that play. It was really an incredible, incredible effort. The funniest part about it was that the defensive back coach for Georgia was Billy Kinard, who had been the defensive back coach at Florida a few years before. As Richard was running down the sideline at the end of the run, there are people who swear that Billy Kinard was chasing him."

Larry Rentz: "We played the University of Georgia in Jacksonville. We won it by a point [17-16]. Let me tell you about one run that Richard made. If you haven't seen it, get the tape. This was literally a five-yard pass. Trapp then ran from one side of the field to the other. He ran from the right to the left and then back toward the middle. The play went for fifty two yards and a touchdown.

"All the players and the coaches were watching the film, and there were something like nine Georgia players who had a shot at him, and he scored. It is still the single most unbelievable run I have ever seen."

Richard Trapp: "I had the best game of my college career against Georgia. In the last quarter we were behind 16-7 with maybe three minutes left in the game. We were nine points down. I caught a little curl pattern over the middle, and I ended up scoring a 52-yard touchdown. It was on national TV, and Keith Jackson was the announcer, and he has said on several occasions that that was the greatest run he had ever seen.

"I recall knocking a lot of people out of the way trying to score. I got through a lot of Georgia players. It gets better every year, you know. Someone said that seventeen tacklers missed me. I don't know, but I got past a lot of defenders, and I ended up scoring on the play.

"It's funny, I was at home watching a rerun of Cheers fifteen years later, and in the show everybody was sitting around the bar watching a football game, and they were all cheering, and on that TV they were showing my run.

"That got us to 16-14. We held them and got the ball back. It was to be the last time we were going to have the ball. And I remember catching a third-down play, for 26 yards, and I made a nice run. I got by two or three guys to get down into field goal range."

Larry Rentz: "With [34] seconds left in the Georgia game, Shade Tree Barfield kicked a [31-yard] field goal to win it, 17-16. His name was Wayne, but they called him 'Shade Tree' because he was kind of a slow-moving, just cool guy. He loved to fish and hunt. He got that name because nothing shook him. As long as he could hunt and fish and play ball and have passing grades in school, he was happy.

"I was the holder, and as soon as a kicker kicks it, a lot of times you have an idea how well he hit it from the sound, and it sounded good, and I looked up, and it was perfect. Shade Tree knew it was too, and he hardly finished his follow through, and he was jumping up and down, knowing it was going to be good even before it was."

Larry Rentz: "Kentucky was next, and I remember that one because I got speared and broke about four ribs. They had to wrap me up tight."

Richard Trapp: "We beat Kentucky [28-12], and then we suffered a tough [21-16] loss to FSU. That day we went up and down the field [Florida gained more than 500 yards on offense], and I remember catching a ball deep in FSU territory, and after running with it a little bit, fumbling, and FSU recovering.

"I also remember returning a punt, and I had gotten by everyone except the punter. All I had to do was get by him, and I would have scored, and he tackled me. I remember those two plays that didn't help."

Larry Rentz: "I played in the Florida State game, and we lost that game because Kim Hammond ran the same play twice [41-yard passes] and scored twice.

"Even then, the Florida State game wasn't our big game. We were more up for Miami and Georgia. They would get up for us more than we'd get up for them. I never sensed anything special about the Florida State game, but I always sensed something special about the Miami and Georgia games."

"What I remember about the Miami game was the exchanges between myself and Ted Hendricks. Ted was so good, and his arms were SO long. I remember trying to run around him on an option, and he got me.

"And so at the end of the season we lost to Florida State and Miami, and as a result, the entire season was a disappointment. I wasn't satisfied. I'm never pleased. I was looking forward to the next season."

Richard Trapp: "The last game of my career was against Miami, another tough loss [28-13], and in that game I was tackled and cracked three ribs. It was late in the game, and I was taken to the hospital. I was supposed to spend the night there, but a bunch of my teammates came down to the hospital and talked the nurses into allowing me to get out of the hospital. I had to promise them I'd go to my hotel room and lay down. It was our last game, and we were not going home until the next morning.

"We were staying in a real nice hotel in Miami, and I lay down on my bed, and we had a big party that night in my room. I really had a good time, even though I had cracked ribs, which is very painful. You can't laugh or breathe deep, but they gave me pain pills. I remember everyone having a good time. We had drinks brought to the room, and we signed trainer Brady Greathouse's name.

"The next day we got on the plane. Brady, who's a great guy, came up to me and said, 'You know, Richard, I must have had a great time last night.' The guy didn't drink. I expected him to be mad, but he wasn't at all. He just grinned and walked away.

"I was drafted by the Buffalo Bills. I was the first pick of the third round. I was 'Rookie of the Year' there, but the team had a bad year—we had three coaches my rookie year—and the new coaching staff felt they needed to make changes, felt they needed more defense, and they traded me to the San Diego Chargers for a couple of defensive backs.

"I was traded to New York in 1970. Joe Namath was the quarterback, but that was the year of the strike, and I ended up playing pro baseball that year. I had been drafted by the New York Yankees in the first round, but didn't play. The Cincinnati Reds talked me into playing baseball during the strike.

"I played in the Florida Instructional League. My first base hit was off Jim Lonborg, who had pitched with the Red Sox in the World Series. He was rehabbing.

"The next year I played football for the Philadelphia Eagles and got hurt again. I separated my shoulder and missed about six games. Then I played in Canada and broke my leg. Meanwhile, I had passed my law boards, and I came back to Orlando to practice law. And I'm still here."

twenty-nine

A Humiliation by Georgia

Steve Tannen: "I remember spring practice my junior year, we were scrimmaging. The second team offense was on the field, but the backup kicker, Jimmy Yarbrough, a huge guy, about 6'6, 260 pounds, who played for the Detroit Lions as a tackle for many years, was the starting tight end, so he had the same color jersey on that I had.

"He kicked the ball. I caught it. I broke a few tackles, and I sped down the sidelines. I was going to have a 70-yard touchdown. All I saw in front of me were the same colored jerseys as me. Jim didn't realize he had on the same color jersey as me. He came running full steam at me. He figured I was going to try to avoid him at any second and he was gonna look like a fool, but I didn't move because I figured he was on my team. He just plowed into me, and he broke my collarbone in half. I was laying there. I didn't know what hit me.

"When I tried to get up, I couldn't. They gave me a shot of morphine right on the field. I was done for the rest of spring practice.

"In a way I didn't quite fit in with the political side of organized football. Players were a lot more right wing. I'd say they were 65/35 right wing, and the coaches, deans and anybody else who had anything to do with football from peewee to professional were 80/20 right wing.

"In '67 I went to a moratorium on Vietnam on the square on campus, and I was the only guy on the team that was part of it. I went and heard Jane Fonda.

"It wasn't very militant. The faction was anti-war, pro-civil rights, and I would have been one of those people 'cause that was my bent, but we didn't even protest when it came to civil rights. When I think about it—I played on a college team that didn't have a single black athlete under scholarship until I was a senior. There wasn't a black on the field. At that time schools like Alabama, Mississippi and Tennessee had all integrated. Florida was one of the last, maybe THE last school to have a black athlete on scholarship.

"One year I came to summer practice, and I had to have three haircuts in three weeks because they thought my hair was too long. I was thought to be a 'Hippy.'

"But at school we had good old boys who loved to drink, stay out late, break curfew, and chase women. They were the guys who didn't give a damn for the rules. As kooky as I was, I pretty much obeyed the rules."

Larry Rentz: "In 1968 we had another highly publicized and highly touted team. It was supposed to be 'The Year of the Gator.' In '68 our class was used as guinea pigs for Dr. Cade's Gatorade experiments. He would come out to practice and take blood samples. He would have us drink all kinds of liquids. He was in the experimenting process.

"At the time he was also experimenting with the padding inside the helmets. He had these black tubes, and he had them filled with water. That was the actual inside cushion of the helmet.

"I always thought Dr. Cade was your little old mad scientist type. I say it affectionately, because he was a nice guy. He would do anything for you. He was just so dedicated to the University of Florida and its players. He was trying to help us.

"One of our new defensive ends was Jack Youngblood. His teammates would kid him, because he spent a lot of time in the weight room getting stronger. He was good, steady, and reliable, but each year he worked harder and harder and harder. He continually improved himself. I thought he was a good, solid player, but not nearly as good as he turned out to be."

By all rights, Jack Youngblood should have gone to Florida State, but the area scout, a coach by the name of Bill Parcells, was certain that the boy was too small to play college football. After a brilliant college and pro career, Youngblood has been named to the Pro Football Hall of Fame. He has never let Parcells, the celebrated coach of the New York Giants, New England Patriots, and New York Jets, live it down.

Jack Youngblood: "I grew up in the Panhandle of north Florida, a little town called Monticello. My dad owned a gas station. I started playing football as a youngster. It was the thing to do in the South. Back then I played all sports, football, basketball, and baseball.

"As a senior I was 6'4", 190 pounds, but when it came time for the colleges to sign me, no one came. Bill Parcells came and scouted our team for Florida State. He went back to Bill Peterson and said there were a couple of kids who could possibly play college football. Coach Peterson knew of me, and he asked, 'What about the Youngblood kid?' Parcells said, 'Coach, I don't think he'll ever play college football.' So on his recommendation I did not get a scholarship offer to the school closest to me—Florida State was twenty-five miles away.

"Dave Fuller was the baseball coach at the University of Florida, and he scouted me. Thank goodness he saw my potential. The conversation was literally this—I remember it to this day: During the championship celebration, we were jumping up and down all over the field because we had just won. I had my girlfriend under one arm, and I was hooting and hollering out there in the middle of the field, and right there in the middle of all that excitement, somebody pulled on my other arm. I turned around to look, and there was Coach Fuller. I didn't know him from Adam's cat. He said, 'Jack, congratulations. How would you like to play football for the University of Florida?'

"I said, 'Yes, sir.' There was no hesitation on my part. I honestly didn't think I would get the opportunity to play at the next level.

"I had made plans. I was going to go to junior college and go into continued education. My father had died when I was ten. My mother raised the three of us, two sisters and myself. She didn't have the economic ability to send me to a big school. So I had made plans to go to North Florida Junior College, which didn't have a football team. My football career would have been over.

"As soon as I was recruited at Florida, I decided I wanted to be the very best that I could possibly be. So what do you do in that situation? You try to take the physical asset that you have and make it as good as you possibly can. I started to try to find out all the information about what I needed to do to get bigger, stronger, and faster. I learned from Coach Hall and some of my teammates that I needed to start weight training, which back then was unheard of.

"In fact, some of my teammates thought I was making a BIG mistake. The concept was that I was going to be a body builder, and I would become muscle-bound and wouldn't be able to move.

"I designed a weightlifting program for myself that would make be big and strong and fast to play the game.

"I was just trying to be the very best I could be. I gained fifteen pounds every year. I went from 215 my sophomore year to 230 my junior year. By the time I was a senior I weighed 245.

"When I came to Florida, I was a middle linebacker. I was going to be the next Dick Butkus. My hero was Frank Manuel of Tennessee, who was on the cover of Sports Illustrated my senior year of high school. I wanted to be on the cover of Sports Illustrated my senior year of college like Frank Manuel.

"But they came to me and said, 'Young man, the days of you standing up are long gone. We are going to make a defensive end out of you.' And I was depressed. It literally broke my heart for a week. I was thinking to myself, What am I going to do down there. I don't know how to play.

"As a defensive end, you're not involved in calling the plays. You're not the captain on the field. You're not coordinating the defense like I did in high school. I wondered, What are they doing to me? I'll be lost.

"Then you realize, All right, if you want to play, you'd better be as good as you possibly can. Learning to play defensive line was a challenge at first, but I continued to get a little bit faster and a little bit quicker.

"One of the things that was kind of interesting was that I had kicked and punted in high school. They asked me if I was interested in doing that, and I said, 'Yeah, I can do that too.' So I went out and did that. I kicked extra points and field goals and was the backup punter my freshman year.

"Freshman year we were fairly successful. We went 3 and 1. We beat Florida State. We beat Miami. We lost to Auburn. But beating Florida State was the critical game.

"I was a sophomore in '68, and I played defensive lineman and kicked off and kicked extra points and field goals with an old square-toe shoe straight ahead!

"So I was the one who kicked off in the opening game against the Air Force. It was my opening play. I kicked the ball to Curtis Martin. We had scouted him and knew he was quick. I was wound up like an eight-day clock. I'm a sophomore, and I'm out there, and I'm involved in the first play of the whole season. Bang! I kicked the ball, and I was playing safety, because that's what kickers do. I kicked it off, and I was thinking I'm going to go down and try to make the tackle. That's the defensive mentality. And bang, Martin comes back up the field, and he just flew by all of us. [Martin ran 100 yards for a touchdown.]

"I thought, Oh my gosh, this is no way to begin a career. It was six-zip, and the clock hadn't even started yet! I thought, Oh, geez.

"But luckily, we had a better football team than the Air Force did at the time, and we made it a battle. It went back and forth. It was a high-scoring football game, and we won [23-20] in the final minutes. And somewhere in that whole deal, I kicked a 43-yard field goal. That was in Tampa Stadium. It was my first and longest field goal of my kicking career. And, in essence, it won the game. Yeah! I had to do something to make up for the six points they had put on us at the beginning."

Larry Rentz: "Against the Air Force at the new Tampa Stadium, it was a really windy day. The wind was really swirling. I remember having a hard time throwing the ball and punting into the wind."

Steve Tannen: "I had a good game against Air Force. I returned a punt for a touchdown. I was always fighting with the coaching staff, because I had blocked numerous kicks—at one time I held a record for the most blocked kicks, punts and extra points, seven in my career—and half the coaching staff wanted me on the line of scrimmage, and I wanted to be back there catching the ball. So sometimes I was up, and sometimes I was back.

"I remember I ran it back for 64 yards, and it was kind of thrilling, because we were playing in Tampa Stadium, which was new, and it was the first game of the season, and you tell yourself, 'I can run back ten this year.' But I doubt that I ran back another one.

"We defeated FSU in the next game on a run by Larry Smith. I gave him a nickname that made absolutely no sense: 'Goofy Grape.' He was the antithesis of me: he was a hard, hard worker, never said a word, never complained, always dressed perfectly, always had perfect manners. I was more of a rambunctious kid, more of a rebel, kind of a loudmouth and a practical joker. Larry was pretty straight, but he was a great guy. I always liked him. And he was a hell of an athlete. I hated spring practice whenever I had to tackle him."

Jack Youngblood: "Our next game was against Florida State up in Tallahassee, and we won [9-3] on a run by Larry Smith, who was one of the tough guys. Larry played hard all the time. You knew you had a heck of a player on your football team. Back then kids tried to emulate those veteran players, the players who were ahead of them on the team. They literally looked up to them. Larry was the kind of player all good players wanted to be like.

"On defense, I was getting better, though I didn't realize it at that point. I had learned and had the knack of getting off the football and getting up the field after the quarterback.

"We were playing a 4–3 scheme, which was a little different from other schools. It allowed me to use all my physical assets.

"My defensive coordinator was Gene Ellenson, yeah! We loved that man! We would literally go to war for him."

Larry Smith: "It was a tough football game. Florida State was good then. Coach Bill Peterson was taking them to the top. It was a rock 'em, sock 'em defensive battle. We got down close to the goal line and ran a lead play. We blocked everybody except Chuck Deeson, who was this kid I knew because we had played against each other in the high school All-Star game. I was fortunate to get in for the score."

After Florida defeated Mississippi State 31–14, they beat Tulane 24–3, before losing to North Carolina 22–7.

Steve Tannen: "We played North Carolina in the rain, and I remember several things about that game: we went up there ranked in the top ten in the country. And it just poured. It was very disheartening that we couldn't get anything going. My father, who flew to all my games, sat in a trench coat through the whole game and was soaking wet. When I came out of the locker room at the end of the game, he was standing there dripping wet to say hello and see me onto the bus to the airport.

"He walked around campus, found a dormitory, went in the basement, took off all his clothes, threw them in the dryer, then put his clothes back on and flew home to Miami.

"We lost that day. It seems that every time we had a shot at some kind of national momentum, we would have a game where we'd lose because of a terrible amount of mistakes."

Larry Smith: "We were in the top ten, and North Carolina was the worst team in the country. It had been raining for a week. We went out there, and I must have fumbled the ball eight times, and they beat us. Of course, they didn't fumble it once. I don't think I'm exaggerating—I know our team fumbled a bunch.

"We had high expectations for that team that year and when we lost to North Carolina it was clear we weren't going to fulfill those expectations, and the fans were disappointed."

If the Gator fans were upset at losing to North Carolina, their disposition didn't improve the next week when Florida played weak-sister Vanderbilt to a 14-14 tie. Making things worse, fullback Larry Smith severely injured his Achilles tendon.

Jack Youngblood: "We went to Nashville to play Vanderbilt, and I remember they had lined the field in blue with blue chalk. I thought, This is really different. It gave you the sense it was going to be real cold out there. And it WAS cold, and we were not used to that. We were used to 70 degree weather."

Larry Smith: "They had a field that was real hard. I was planning to go for a ball, and my arch gave way, and I sprained my arch. It was very painful."

Larry Rentz: "Larry Smith's injuring his Achilles tendon was a terrible loss. Larry Smith was so good that our entire offense was planned around him. So at the time he was hurt, our entire team and coaching staff had depended on Larry too much, psychologically and otherwise. So his injury had a devastating psychological effect on us. I know he was limping for months."

Without Larry Smith, Florida lost the next game to Auburn 24-13. Coach Graves was frustrated.

Jack Youngblood: "The SEC games were very critical, and Georgia, Auburn, Tennessee and Alabama were the perennial powers. We had not been able to get into that elite, into that cream of the crop level. Yeah, it was frustrating. No question about that. Because our players were just as good, but for some reason they played better than we did."

Before the Georgia game, Coach Fred Pancoast landed in the hospital with appendicitis. With the offensive and defensive players sniping at each other, Coach Graves decided to switch his coordinators. He moved Gene Ellenson to offense and switched Ed Kensler to defense. But the move only made the situation worse, and Florida lost to Georgia 51-0.

Larry Rentz: "Auburn beat us [24-13], and then going into Georgia, Coach Graves made Gene Ellenson, the offensive coach, his defensive coach, and he made Ed Kensler, his defensive coach, his offensive coach. I had no clue. It was the strangest thing. All of us were saying, 'What the hell's going on?' It was like we were in a daze about the coaching switch. We couldn't make any rhyme or reason out of it.

"It was a total disaster [Georgia won 51-0], and I don't think any of us understood the logic behind it.

"I had always respected Coach Graves. He's a fine man and a gentleman. But he was not your hands-on coach. He was kind of up in the tower. He may have thought it was a good change, to try to shake up people, and it did.

"We were losing [42-0] at the half, and I can remember in the locker room one of the coaches asked me to play quarterback. For whatever reason, I stood up and said a few words, something like, 'If any of you guys want to quit now, just stay in the locker room.' I wasn't nice. Because everybody was kind of slumped over and had given up.

"I don't know…I just thought somebody needed to say something and I did. And obviously, it didn't help. I can recall All-American Jake Scott ran back punt after punt, and I was kicking the punts. Everything clicked for Georgia. They just couldn't do anything wrong.

"But it was a disaster for Coach Graves. I don't think anybody could explain why, other than to try to do something different, and it didn't work.

"That Georgia game….it had to have been years and years and years and years since Florida had been massacred like that. It was total devastation."

Steve Tannen: "The coaches made a strange switch, and we ended up getting beat badly. That game was played in the rain, and it was so bad that when you were on the bottom of the pile, you were blowing bubbles. That game was the height of embarrassment.

"Late in the game Georgia took its All-American defensive end, Bill Stanfill, and put him at quarterback, and they moved the ball. It was just horrific. When you get beat 51-0, it's pretty bad. Oh God, I don't know what happened to us."

Jack Youngblood: "That was the worst defeat of my entire football career.

"There was logic to what Coach Graves was trying to do. We were not involved in those decisions, but we were thinking that the head man was trying to put the right people in the right place to make everything work. With Coach Pancoast being ill, logic dictated that Coach Ellenson, being the defensive coordinator, should be able to call players against defenses. And

Kensler, being an offensive line coach, ought to be able to call defenses against offense schemes.

"But it didn't work out because of timing, execution, and the elements. It rained that day very hard. Literally you could not see the top ten to fifteen rows of the Gator Bowl. I don't know what those people were seeing when they looked down at us, because we couldn't see them.

"It was just an onslaught. I mean, Georgia just ran the ball up and down the field, up and down the field. They just dominated us."

Larry Smith: "Coach Graves was just trying to change the chemistry. I'm not sure it really made any difference. They were just playing well, and we weren't. I have never been back to a Florida-Georgia game. It was not a fun experience."

Ray Graves: "When we lost to North Carolina in the rain, the offense was blaming the defense, and the defense was blaming the offense, and it just felt like I ought to do something. You don't know exactly what's going on in the locker room, but you get a feeling. And I got the feeling it was time for everyone to look at the other side of the coin, so I changed staffs and told the players. I said, 'This is my decision, and I want you to know that.' And it was a decision that could have cost me my job, I'm sure because in the game against Georgia, they completed more passes in the rain during the game than they did warming up. Towards the end of the game it was 48-0, and the Georgia center, who had never kicked a field goal before, kicked one to beat us 51-0, and I have to say that I hated Georgia as much as Steve Spurrier did. We were talking, when Steve was named coach at Florida, I told him, 'If you ever get a chance to beat Georgia 50-0, win one for the old coach.' We laughed, because we were sure no one was going to beat Georgia 50-0, but later [1995] we did [by 52-17] in Athens, and he called me. He said, 'I'm thinking about you.'

"And during the Georgia game I could see John Reaves and Tommy Durrance and some of the freshmen walking up and down the sidelines, and I knew the morale was there. And we won the next two games against Miami and FSU.

"But morale is very important. The cheapest thing in the world is to make excuses. And after the Georgia game I put the coaches back where they were supposed to be. But that was a calculated risk. You make good decisions. You make wrong decisions. That one didn't work."

Led by Larry Rentz, Florida rebounded the next week with a 16-14 win over the University of Kentucky. Florida then hosted Miami in the finale, and when Larry Smith ran in for a touchdown on the final carry of his outstanding college career, Florida won the game 14-10, ending a 6-3-1 season.

Larry Rentz: "We beat Miami, and our fullback, Tommy Christian, had one hell of a game. He had two 50-yard runs. He scored and Larry Smith scored to put our points on the board.

"Finally, we had beaten Ted Hendricks."

Larry Smith: "Miami was a very good team, and it was a nice turnaround, especially nice for me because on my very last carry for the University of Florida, I scored a touchdown to win a game. So that was a nice way to end a career."

Steve Tannen: "We beat Miami to end the season at 6-3-1, which wasn't too bad considering the losses—Georgia, Auburn, and North Carolina. The 14-14 tie with Vanderbilt was bad enough. It was a good season in that we beat Florida State and Miami. In those days it was important within the state to beat Florida State and Miami."

Larry Rentz: "After my final game, I was kind of burned out from football. I had started playing at the Boys Club in Miami at age 6. So I didn't want to go into the pros. I had never even thought of it. However, the San Diego Chargers drafted me. I thought, 'If you don't go out for at least a year, you'll end up regretting it all your life.' So I went to camp as a defensive back.

"Sid Gillman was the coach. John Hadl was at the end of his career. Lance Alworth, Bambi, our wide end, was unbelievable. And Gary Garrison was the first-string flanker back.

"I was on the taxi squad—I don't know why—and I was activated for several games. Gary got hurt, so Sid pulled me from defense and put me at flanker. So I was kind of a utility player. I could have played defense as needed.

"But after that season, there was a players' strike, and I told myself that I didn't really want to play any more. The money was great—they paid me a $20,000 salary.

"I called Coach Gillman and told him I was taking an early retirement. We wished each other well.

"In 1973 I started at the Allen Morris Company. We develop, lease, manage, buy, and sell, office buildings mostly. We are constructing our 78th office out in Carlton Gables. It keeps me busy."

Larry Smith: "I wanted to play pro ball, and I had contact from some teams. I knew I was going to be drafted in the first round, but I didn't know by whom. I was taken by the Los Angeles Rams.

"I played five years with the Rams. My rookie year we actually went 11-0 before we lost our last three games. We went to the playoffs that year but we stopped short of the Super Bowl. Roman Gabriel, our quarterback, was the MVP of the league. I played with Deacon Jones and Merlin Olsen. My last few years Jack Youngblood was there. I also played with Johnny Hadl when he was MVP.

"After five years George Allen went from coach of the Rams to the Washington Redskins, and he traded for me. George Allen was a fascinating fellow. He was ahead of his time in many ways, totally obsessed with winning football games. He was something. In Washington I played with a whole host of characters, Sonny Jurgensen, Billy Kilmer, and Joe Theismann was a rookie.

"My last year in Washington I broke my hand, my foot, and my leg. I was just getting too injured. Playing any longer didn't seem to make any sense. I was making a nice wage, but nothing like they make now. I wasn't at the point in my career where I was going to be getting better, so I thought I'd better find another way to make a living.

"I came back to Tampa in '76. I had graduated from the University of Florida and gotten my masters in business, and I went to work locally in the banking business. Then I went to work for the Tampa Bay Sports Authority for a couple of years. Then at the ripe old age of 30, I decided to go to law school. I attended Stetson Law across the bay in St. Pete, and when I was 34, sort of late for the business, I started practicing law. Now I'm a real estate lawyer. I help people buy and sell property."

thirty

The Super Sophs

In 1969 Coach Graves was blessed with one of the finest sophomore classes ever recruited by the University of Florida. The biggest fish in the school was a new quarterback, a high school All-American from Tampa, a tall, husky pure passer by the name of John Reaves. Luckily for Florida, Reaves lived two streets down from Larry Smith, who was four years his senior. In part because of his idolization of Smith, Reaves was a tried and true Gator fan. All he needed was an invitation.

John Reaves: "I was recruited by Florida, Florida State, Miami, Tennessee, Georgia Tech, Notre Dame, and Purdue, but I always wanted to be a Gator, so my mind was pretty much made up. I'd grown up listening to Gator games on the radio. And Larry Smith was kind of a hero of mine. He grew up on the next street from me, and he went to Florida. And Steve Spurrier was also an idol. So I always liked the Gators, and when I started getting recruited, I did look around—I was intrigued by Florida State's passing game. I visited Florida State and Tennessee—but I kinda always loved the Gators. I still do. I was going to Florida no matter what.

"Don Brown, an assistant coach, recruited the Tampa area for Florida. And Fred Pancoast, the offensive coordinator, came down some. And Coach Graves came to my house. He was very nice. I was thrilled to be courted by people like that. Bill Peterson for Florida State came by. So did Doug Dickey of Tennessee.

"It was different back then. Boosters could recruit you, and I started getting recruited in June of my junior year, and I could have gone out to dinner every night with a booster from a different school, but I was tired of it, and I committed to Florida in December so I could concentrate on basketball, baseball and track the rest of the year.

"When I arrived in Gainesville, freshmen weren't eligible to play on the varsity. You were really a scout team for the varsity. We had an excellent group of freshmen, Carlos Alvarez, Tommy Durrance, Mike Rich, Andy Cheney, Robert Harrell. We really put on a good show. I remember the first time our first-string offense scrimmaged the varsity's second-team defense, we scored on them at will. They were real shocked. They didn't realize how good our players were.

"Some of us really could have helped the varsity that year [1968], because they were loaded except for some positions. They didn't really have any wideouts, and they struggled at quarterback all year. They went back and forth between Jackie Eckdahl, Larry Rentz, and Harold Peacock, and only threw two touchdown passes in 1968.

"So some of us freshmen really could have helped them, because they had all those linemen—Guy Dennis, Jim Yarbrough, Jack Youngblood, Jim Hadley, and Steve Tannen in the defensive secondary. We could have sprinkled in there and helped, but we couldn't because of the rules.

"My freshman year Gatorade had already been invented. In fact, when we had our first water break, they gave us Gatorade, which I had never had before. It was the original potion, which wasn't sweet. But it was 120 degrees, and it sure tasted good.

"They told us we could go over and have Gatorade at the break, and a bunch of us freshmen went over there. You got a paper cup with ice and Gatorade in it. I finished mine and tried to sneak a second one, and there was a senior defensive lineman, Lloyd Thurman, who said, 'Hey, freshman, what do you think you're doing taking a second Gatorade? Put that down.' Larry Smith was standing there, and Larry said, 'Shut up, Lloyd, or I'll kick your ass.' I thought, Thank you, Larry. So that was my introduction to Gatorade.

"I knew Dr. Cade, the inventor. He also was the inventor of the helmet with water in it, but it was too heavy in its concept. He used my wife-to-be, who was a student at Florida then, as a model for that helmet. He put it on her and hit her over the head with a baseball bat. That's why she married me—she got hit over the head with a bat."

Jack Youngblood: "In '69 we began practicing, and Dr. Cade was working on his Gatorade experiments. He tried to kill us all! That first stuff was lethal! At first it was thick and had an aftertaste, and it was all brand new to us. We'd never had anything like that. Water with salt in it was the closest thing we ever had.

"They were constantly working on the formula, trying to make it work from a scientific standpoint, while at the same time trying to make it taste better. They kept diluting it down, trying to make it taste good enough that you could get enough of it into the body to make it work. That was the trick.

"When you came off from a series during practice, they'd give you water and Gatorade and what-not. I remember it was a hot, hot August day, and Mike Kelley came off the field and went over to grab a Gatorade. He chugged the thing, and he fainted right there among us. We said, 'Damn, the Gatorade killed him!' We were all standing around looking at him, going, 'The boy is dead!' What happened was that he got real hot and drank that cold drink, and it just shocked him. And we were blaming it on the Gatorade."

"Dr. Cade began experimenting with Gatorade my freshman year. The four years I was there were the four years he was experimenting. When they first started giving us the stuff, it was like syrup. Then it started to look like milk. They had an old Chevy Suburban drive around the practice field, and on the back of this truck they had cup holders, a hundred cups of the latest concoction. We would drink it.

"I remember one time we had a scrimmage on Florida Field where half the team got Gatorade, and the other half got nothing. It was very hot in Florida Field. It's down in that hole, and the humidity is high in Florida. I think I lost eleven pounds. I was one of the guys who got nothing.

"I remember Dr. Cade was also working on a stronger football helmet. He enlisted Bob Brown, what we call a B-team player, a big guy, a weightlifter but not that great of a football player, in his experiments.

"Riddell was the number one helmet maker at the time, and they made suspension helmets. Dr. Cade had this idea that you could fill tubes with water and put them in the helmet, and they would give a better cushion.

"He had Brown put on the helmet, and he'd hit Brown over the head with a baseball bat. And Dr. Cade would put the helmet on, and Brown would hit him over the head with a baseball bat. One time Dr. Cade knocked Brown out, 'cause the helmet didn't work very well.

"Dr. Cade was an interesting guy. Then he went through a big fight with the university, because when I was a senior, he sold the rights to Stokely van Camp for a bunch of money.

"One of the things I remember, when you watched film, the coaches would run the projector forwards and backwards, backwards and forwards, so you would see the same play over and over and over again. One day we were watching films at practice, and Coach Graves, who would meander in and out of the offensive and defensive meetings, came into the defensive meeting as we were looking at a play. Nobody had noticed he was in the back of the room. On the screen in the background was the Gatorade truck. You could see it drive slowly across the back part of the frame of the picture. And running this play back and forth as they did, you could see the truck go backward and forward, backward and forward, forward and backward. Nobody thought much about it, but after watching this for about two minutes, Ray, standing in the back, said, 'We better go on to the next play before we run that truck out of gas.'"

John Reaves: "When the spring of '69 arrived, I was trying to win a job. They split up the team in the spring. The majority of the seniors were on the other team. A bunch of us freshmen and a couple of rising juniors and seniors played with us, and we won 48-6, which was a shock to a lot of people. The coaches hinted they'd like me to hang around during the summer to work out, so I did. I stayed in Gainesville and worked on the stadium crew that summer. Back then the stadium had wooden bleachers and painted stripes to mark the seats. Our job was to sand off those fifty-year-old paint lines and make the seats narrower, so they could cram more bodies into the stadium. We then would burn the numbers into those new seats in the 110 degree heat. Can you imagine that? I'll never forget the guy who was in charge of our crew. The college got every penny out of him. He was there at eight sharp, took a half hour for lunch, and quit at five. He smoked a pipe all day long. If it rained, he would not quit working. He would just turn his pipe upside down and work through the rain. Eight of us burned 63,000 numbers in those new stands.

"But we didn't mind. We were having fun. We were 18, 19 years old. Who cared? We had a job. I was poor as a church mouse anyway, so any money I could get was a boon to mankind. They paid us minimum wage, $1.35 an hour.

"When the '69 season began, I was alternating at quarterback with Jack Eckdahl, the senior incumbent who had been an All-American at Gainesville High. Jack's dad was a professor of physical education at UF. He was a fine player but he had broken an ankle, which had limited his abilities. We went through two-a-days, and the coaching staff named me the starter.

"We had a scrimmage two weeks before our opener. I'll never forget, we played against the same combination of freshmen and B-teamers, and this time we won 93-0. We had Carlos, Cheney, Durrance, Rich, Robert Harrell, Jimmy Barr, myself, and Richard Franco, the placekicker. Eight true sophomores were starting on the varsity. I said to myself, Man, we might be pretty good here. It's hard to hang 93 points on the board no matter who you're playing.

"Under Coach Graves' system, he gave me some leeway. There was some trust. They would signal either pass or run, right or left out of a formation, and I would pick a play from a variety of plays. We had spent the summer learning and watching films, and when the season began we were ready to roll. We didn't have that good a running game, so we were more of a pass-first, run-second kind of team. We would set up the run with the pass. It was new. All our runs were draws and split-back sweeps and counters that were off the passing game."

Steve Tannen: "That summer I was in Gainesville going to summer school. John Reaves and I got to be real good friends. We played football during the summer, so I knew we had something special.

"When the season started, we were picked by Playboy or Street and Smith as one of the worst teams in the nation. They didn't think we'd be any good because we had a lot of sophomores on the team, Mike Rich, Tommy Durrance, Fred Abbott, Carlos Alvarez, and John on offense. On defense there were Jack Burns, defensive tackle Bob Harrell, and defensive back Harvin Clark.

"Houston was picked as the number one team. They had a wide receiver, Elmo Wright, who made dancing in the end zone famous. I had to cover him, and I had a good day.

"And on the third play from scrimmage, Reaves threw a 70-yard pass to Carlos, and we jumped out to a 7-0 lead, and everybody was shocked.

"It was quite something. Reaves and Carlos had big days and got big ink. We ended up winning the game by a big margin [59-34].

"When you've got a sophomore quarterback and a sophomore receiver, and they did things people didn't think they could, they thought, 'Either Houston is totally overrated, or Florida is totally underrated.' Or they figured Houston let down because they were such favorites. So we really didn't know what to think, although at the beginning of the game everyone on a team thinks they can win. And nothing happened in the game to convince us otherwise. By the end of the game we thought we were something special. We had beaten the pre-season number one team. No one was looking around the room thinking, 'Who are we?' Everyone thought, 'We did our job. We played good. We're a good team.'

"We didn't know how good we REALLY were until about the fourth game, when we saw the way Tommy Durrance could run, the way John could throw, and how Carlos could catch. Then we started thinking, 'We have a DAMN good team.'

Jack Youngblood: "Houston was ranked number one in the country. Houston was a big school from Texas. We had never played them before. They were highly touted. When they came in, it looked like they had brought three hundred players. It was like the Greeks and Romans.

"We held a team meeting the Friday afternoon before the game, and when we were through, we could see them out on the field doing their walk-through. We eased out to get a little peek to see what their team looked like, and they all had on red sweats, and they were everywhere, and we were thinking, my gosh, did they bring all of Houston with them? Where are they coming from?

"A unique thing happened the Friday night before the ballgame. We had a team meeting, and normally the offense goes one way and the defense goes the other and they have individual game plan meetings. Coach Graves said, 'No, we're going to do it all together. The defensive coaches are going to tell the offensive players what we're going to do to Houston, and the offensive coaches are going to tell the defensive players what you're going to see from a game-plan standpoint.' I will never forget it. Coach Pancoast stood up and told us, 'We are going to score on the third play of the game.' We went, 'Right! Right!'

"It was incredible, because we were sitting there yelling, filled with emotion. The adrenaline was pumping a little bit. And we all believed it.

"The next day they won the toss. We kicked, and we went out there, and we shut them down. We stopped that Houston option. Houston had some All-Americans. I had to play a big, old tight end who was an NFL recruit, and I began thinking, Shoot, I can play with these guys. I'm gonna whip his fanny!

"And we stopped them and made them punt the ball. I remember the excitement of going out there and sensing that what we were doing was working. That creates energy and excitement—momentum. When things start working, it feeds the energy.

"They kicked the ball back to us. John got the ball. He threw down and out to Carlos. Again he threw down and out to Carlos. And we scored on the third play!

"Literally we were watching this and going, 'Wow!' That's when believing in what you're doing, believing in the scheme and what the coaches are trying to get you to believe in and how to play becomes a big part of the success.

"We led at the half by thirty [38-6]. It was one of those games where you think, Don't wake me up. Let this dream continue. Pinch me. Is this for real?

"John and Carlos had been highly recruited, big school high school athletes. You know they had been top dogs on campus, and they came in, and of course quarterbacks have that air about them. Carlos was very quiet, a demure sort of fellow. He was studious and very bright and at the same time very athletic. You could see Carlos' athleticism on the practice field immediately. And you could see the talent in John. He was 6'4", 200 pounds, and he had that natural air of a quarterback. He could throw the football a country mile."

John Reaves: "In the opener against the University of Houston, yes, sir. We hung 59 on them. Houston played man-to-man. They would line their defensive backs about five yards off the receivers. They played in the Southwest Conference, where hardly anybody threw the ball. Shoot, they didn't know how brilliant Carlos was as a receiver. On the third play of the game we called a bomb, and he ran by his defender. He was ten yards behind him before he knew what hit him. I got lucky, and laid it on him, and Carlos went 70 yards for six.

"In the second half I threw a 47-yard touchdown pass to Tommy Durrance. Tommy was a freshman with us, an excellent running back, a good receiver, a good runner, a good blocker and smart. He was a great player for Florida. He made All-SEC, and he still holds the SEC record for most TDs in a single season, 20. Of course, I'd tease him that we'd pass the ball down to the one, and he'd jump over.

"We kinda exploded after that. Everything went right. It was one of those great games. [Against Houston, Reaves finished 18 for 30 for 342 yards and five touchdowns! He was named the national Back of the Week in his first college game ever.]

"I thought, Man, this is easy. We were on a roll."

To prove the 59-34 win over Houston wasn't a fluke, the next week Florida bombed Mississippi State by the score of 47-35 as Reaves completed a dozen passes to Carlos Alvarez and threw for 326 yards.

John Reaves: "That was a shootout! Carlos caught twelve passes in that game. Oh, he was fearless. Carlos was a Cuban refugee. His dad was an attorney in Havana, a very intelligent man. He came over to north Miami, and he opened a dress shop. He named it after his daughter Annie. Then they had three boys, all of whom became attorneys. Carlos was a real good running back in North Miami. When I got to the high school All-Star game that summer, Carlos played running back on our team, and I threw him a touchdown pass out of the backfield in that game, and we beat the North 14-13. He exhibited great pass-catching ability in that week or two of practice.

"When we got to two-a-days as freshman at Florida, the coaching staff move him to wide out, and he was a natural. Carlos ran precision routes. He had great hands. He was fast. He ran a 4.5 forty, was quick, was tough and had great hands. And he was a tireless worker.

"The thing I liked about Carlos from freshman year on, we'd say, 'All right, let's go out and work on the route tree.' Those were all the routes in the playbook. And we would go through every route on both sides of the field, and if it wasn't perfect, either the throw or the route and catch, Carlos would come back and say, 'Let's do it again.' All I was doing was taking the drop and throwing. He was running his butt off. In thirteen years of college or professional football, I never had another end like him. Consequently we got so good that even if he was double or triple covered, we could still connect. You talk about quick-outs, slants, curls, outs, corners, posts, or streaks, we just had it down. So it was hard to stop him—hard to stop us. He was brilliant."

Florida State came next. This was more a defensive struggle as Florida forced three interceptions and two fumbles in a 21-6 win over their arch-rivals. Florida's veteran defensive front four, Jack Youngblood, Robby Rebol, Bob Harrell and Bob Coleman, forced two fumbles and three interceptions.

Jack Youngblood: "We kept sacking them. I sacked their quarterback myself four or five times. This was the in-state rivalry. We were really up for this one."

Steve Tannen: "We gave up 35 in the first game and 34 in the second. I guess our defense was a little suspect. But as the year went on, our defense stiffened. In our next game, we beat FSU [21-6]. When I was in college and we played Florida State, you definiately wanted to beat them, because you would say, 'God, we can't lose to Florida State. It was only twenty years ago when they were a girls' school.'

"Our defensive line consisted of Bob Harrell, Robby Rebol, Bob Coleman, and Jack Youngblood. They had a big day.

"When Blood came to the Gators, he was a skinny kid. He was tall, weighed about 195 pounds. He was a Good Ole Boy, sort of a cracker, a northern Florida guy with a southern drawl. Nice and easy, but very athletic. As a football player, you see strong guys, and you just never know what to make of it. Maybe a strong guy can do one thing really well. But an athletic guy can do everything, and that's what Jack was.

"Robby came up with me. He came up as a fullback, and they moved him to middle guard or defensive tackle. He didn't want to do anything but play football, so it was really great for him. He was a 'tough as nails' kid, pretty strong, pretty big. Bobby Coleman was like Larry Smith, really quiet. He was tall and quick and fairly big, so he worked out well there. We had a couple of other guys play defensive end, Dave Ghesquiere, probably the number one defensive end with Youngblood on the other side. Harrell was the other defensive tackle, a strong tough guy too. Mr. Pretty Boy. He was always dressed to the nines. He wasn't great, but he was a good, solid ballplayer.

"Our linebackers were Mike Kelley, Tommy Abdelnour, and Mike Pahalach. Tommy Abdelnour we called 'the Sheik' because of his Arabic blood, was probably 5'7, maybe weighed 210. Mike Palahach came out of Hollywood, Florida, never started until his senior year, worked as hard as anybody. He would have loved to have played pro ball, but he went on to become a lawyer and now is a District Attorney. Kelley was the most athletic of the linebackers.

"And we had a great secondary. Skip Albury at free safety, Jack Burns at strong safety, Mark Ely at one cornerback, and me at the other. Mark, Skip and I were the same age. We had a good, solid group."

John Reaves: "Florida State was very good. And we held them to only six points. They had a brilliant defensive effort that game.

"We began to feel that we were a great team—we were all full of ourselves, and that's when we almost got upset by Tulane in Tampa Stadium [Tulane led 17-0, but Florida pulled it out 18-17 after Tommy Durrance scored a touchdown and John Reaves completed a pass to Carlos Alvarez, who was suffering from leg cramps, for a two-point conversation]."

Steve Tannen: "We should have beaten Tulane by twenty points, but somehow we didn't come to play. It happens, you know. The psyche is such a big part of the game. Something happened, and we couldn't get it together until late in the game. We won it with two minutes left to go."

John Reaves: "There was an interesting play during that touchdown drive. We came to a critical third and eight. We were on the fifty, and I looked over to Coach Pancoast, and he said, 'You call it.'

"Well, a play popped into my head, a simple play called an 8-3. It was a weak-side curl to Andy Cheney. Sure enough, they about quadruple-teamed Carlos, and Andy ran a curl, and there wasn't anybody near him. I threw him the ball, and he ran down to about the five.

"It just shocked them. We scored, and we needed two points for the win. Tulane was playing a zone, and Carlos slithered between two defenders, and I kinda threw it up in the air, and he made a great grab, dragged his feet in there, and we won. Carlos was something."

The next opponent was North Carolina.

Steve Tannen: "North Carolina was next. We weren't too happy about what they did to us the year before, and we beat them pretty badly [52-2]."

John Reaves: "North Carolina had upset us the year before when Larry [Smith] had a tough time with some fumbles. So we were mad, and we put a pretty good whipping on them. And that was NOT me who got caught for the safety—thank you very much.

"Everything went right that day. We hit a bomb early on them to Carlos. We had a really good game plan, and played a really good game, offensively and defensively."

After a 41-20 win over Vanderbilt, Florida's sixth straight victory, the Gators traveled to Auburn to play the seventh-ranked Tigers. Sports Illustrated sent a reporter to interview John Reaves and Carlos Alvarez. If Florida won that day, the two sophomores were going to appear on the cover the following week. John Reaves did set a record that day, but not one that he is proud of.

Steve Tannen: "We played Auburn for the SEC championship. Coach Ellenson decided before the game that our theme song was going to be, 'Dream the Impossible Dream.' Because we had been picked as the worst team in the nation, and we were 6 and 0. So we were ready to kick ass and take names, and we thought we were good. We played that song on the bus as we drove to Cliff Hare Stadium, where they had a jinx. We had never won at Cliff Hare Stadium. So we were trying everything we could think of not to mention it, but everybody knew about it.

"We got up there, and things didn't go well. We didn't play terribly—the game was fairly close [Florida lost 38-12]. But they had nine interceptions, a college record, and every time we'd get back in the game....

"It's a hell of a lot of a game to be giving away. And it kind of brought us back down to earth."

John Reaves: "Yeah, that's when I set the record—still standing—for interceptions in one game—nine. I played awful, and somebody told me the reporter from Sports Illustrated left at halftime. It was just one of those awful games. A nightmare.

"It sounds like an excuse, but Auburn actually played a different coverage against us. Back then, most teams played a three-deep zone or a man-to-man with a free safety.

"Against us, Auburn played what's called a 'cover-2' defense with two safeties and five defenders underneath and four live rushers. And they could really put the heat on you with those four. I've been told that the 'cover-2' defense was invented that day. Their defensive coordinator was the famous Bill Oliver.

"It was a defense they had never used before. They had five defenders underneath instead of the usual four with two guys deep, and they played it to perfection. I threw the ball right to them, because I wasn't expecting them to be there.

"It was humiliating and embarrassing, to say the least."

Auburn was led by its All-American duo of quarterback Pat Sullivan and receiver Terry Beasley.

Jack Youngblood: "Beasley ran by me so fast I didn't know a white boy could run that fast. They ran a reverse, and I played it perfectly. I came up the field, and I did my responsibility. I was supposed to check the back side and look for a reverse and then pursue. And here he came. And I mean, he just flew by me and was gone! He was that much faster!"

Steve Tannen: "We had a pretty good thing going until we went to Auburn. We had the 'Super Sophs.' The 'Super Sophs' were happening."

thirty-one

Coach Graves Steps Down

The disappointment of the loss to Auburn spilled over the next weekend, as Florida led Georgia 10-0, fell behind 13-10, and then rallied to a 13-13 tie.

Steve Tannen: "The next week we tied Georgia, and that was a real disappointment. The year before we had lost to Georgia 51-0, and we were looking to get even. We probably had a far superior team.

"We went ahead 10-0, and so we were getting back to normal, and maybe everyone was thinking, 'Now we're playing like we know how to play,' and maybe thinking like that makes you complacent.

"When people talk about rivalries, Florida-Georgia was a different kind of game. We had a chance to win on a field goal at the end of the game, and we didn't get it. That's why the tie was so disappointing. We could have won the game. To start out 6 and 0, and then get beat with nine interceptions and then tie somebody, it really brings you back to earth. It takes all the momentum out of you, and you have to start building it up again, which we did."

John Reaves: "We still had a hangover from the Georgia game. We were a better team that Georgia that year, but we ended up tying. We missed a chip shot at the end of the game that could have tied it. I wasn't the holder, John Schnebly was, and Nick Sinardi's snap was low, and John juggled it a litle, and Richard Franco missed short. Sniv normally did a great job, but he juggled that one, and the kick was low.

"We should have gone undefeated in '69, but we didn't."

Florida recovered the next week and defeated Kentucky 31-6.

John Reaves: "I remember Harvin Clark, a sophomore defensive back, returned the opening kickoff for a touchdown. We were ahead 31-0 at the half, and we didn't score the second half. We kinda shut down. We just worked on the running game the second half. Coach Graves was not the kind of guy to run up the score."

Miami was the final regular season game, in Miami, and Reaves & Co. swamped their rivals 35-16.

Steve Tannen: "Miami had a history of having good nationally ranked teams. They had George Mira, Don Bosseler, John Morellavich, and Pete Banaszak, just a lot of guys.

"I always wanted to beat them, because that's the only college team I ever saw as a kid. I wanted to catch a pass against them. I had to convince the coaches that I could play wide receiver. The coach said, 'Okay,' and Reaves and I were friends, and we worked out some plays.

"But before the game I was taping up my arm, and I asked a guy named Paul Maliska to cut the tape for me, and as he cut the tape, he almost cut off the top of my thumb. I had to have stitches, and I couldn't play receiver. I was pretty disappointed about that, though I was happy we won."

John Reaves: "We had a thriller down there. Carlos caught a bunch of passes, about fifteen. It was a lot of fun to beat the Hurricanes."

Steve Tannen: "We finished the season 8-1-1. It was the best record Florida ever had until that point. And we got to play Tennessee in the Gator Bowl.

"By this time all the rumors were flying that Doug Dickey was going to be the new coach of the Gators. He was the coach of Tennessee. We all wanted Gene Ellenson to be coach. We thought he'd get it, because he had been assistant head coach so long. He was a good friend of Ray's. We all loved Geno, so we got behind him and tried to do as much as we could so he could be the coach. That's why we were real happy to beat Tennessee in the Gator Bowl. And yet they still hired Doug, so it was probably a fait accompli anyway. It was probably done before the game.

"We went to Daytona to train for the game. While we were there, they let us drive on the speedway. We had our cars, and a lot of us had fast cars. We were supposed to stay behind the pace car and drive a couple laps to see what it was like.

"Well, that didn't last too long. Dick Kensler was a coach, and he had his son on the team, and he had a really fast AMX car, a really fast car, and he was zooming around, and I had a Camaro, and Palahach and I were in my car, and Reaves had a Dodge Charger, and he was blasting around, so we got a little chewing out for that, but we had fun. We probably went 120. It was great, fun, real fun."

The team's reward for their glorious 8-1-1 season was a trip to the Gator Bowl to play Tennessee, the SEC champions, coached by former University of Florida quarterback Doug Dickey. Coach Graves had informed Florida president Steven O'Connell that he wanted to step down after the '69 season, but neither O'Connell nor Graves wanted to make it official until they could get Doug Dickey, President O'Connell's choice as the next Florida coach, to commit to leaving Tennessee and coming to Florida. The problem O'Connell and Graves had was that one week Dickey couldn't make up his mind. One day he was coming, the next he was staying.

During the week before the Gator Bowl game, Coach Graves told the players that it looked like he was going to step down as coach after the season. The players were surprised, to say the least.

Jack Youngblood: "It was kind of strange. It was numbing from the standpoint of, 'Ooh, what is this all about?' Then from a young players' standpoint, you say to yourself, Well, if he's going out, then let's give him a great ride out. Let's go play our hearts out for him. Let's go win this thing."

After Graves made his announcement, Doug Dickey informed Florida president Steve O'Connell that he had changed his mind and was staying at Tennessee. As a result, in the clubhouse right before the Gator Bowl game, Steven O'Connell met with the football team to tell the players that Coach Graves would remain as coach.

John Reaves: "At the meeting President O'Connell actually laid his notes on my shoulder as he told the team, 'Contrary to what you're reading in the paper and hearing, there is no substance to these rumors that Coach Graves is leaving. Have a good game. We'll see you.'

"We said, 'Okay!' and we went out and beat Tennessee."

The 14-13 win over the SEC champs was one of the bigger upsets in Florida history.

John Reaves: "Tennessee was loaded. They had a great defense, with Jack 'Hacksaw' Reynolds at middle linebacker. Steve Kiner was an outside linebacker.

"I remember early in the game we had a third and one, and we called a quarterback sneak. I said, 'I'm gonna take a step back, and I'm gonna ream it in there as hard as I can.' On the snap I took a step back, and I reamed it, and Hacksaw Reynolds was standing there. I tried to run over him, and he hit me so hard that I got up and could see stars! I said to myself, I ain't gonna do THAT again.

"I made the first down, but man, did he lay a whack on my head. We ended up beating them. Carlos caught a touchdown. We blocked a punt, and Jim Kelley scooped it up and ran it in.

"At the end we led 14–13, and we could have scored again. We were on their two at the end of the game. I let the clock run out. They were all yelling at me, 'Let's score again.' I said to the boys, 'We have to play them again next year.'

"I wish we would have scored. I look back and think, We should have scored again."

Steve Tannen: "One of the things I remember most about that game was that I blocked a punt, and Mike Kelley picked it up and ran it in for a touchdown. Then I hit a guy and forced a fumble, and Mike Kelley recovered it. And Mike Kelley got the Most Valuable Player of the game.

"After we won the game, we got a good ring, and we ended up eleventh in the nation. Back then, they didn't play for the national championship. It was never talked about. Maybe the SEC championship, but never the national championship."

Jack Youngblood: "We won the game, but I remember afterward thinking about the coaching situation. I wondered, Somebody tell me what's going on. Give us a clue as to what's happening here.

"Two days later I got a telegram saying that Doug Dickey was taking over as head coach for Coach Graves.

"That affects everybody, because there are huge question marks. You have a system and a comfort level with the coaches. What is going to change? We had just come off one of the most successful seasons Florida had ever had, and you wonder if this change is going to upset all that.

"And the other question was this: if Coach Graves is stepping down, why can't Coach Ellenson take his place? We were big time fans of Coach Ellenson. We would have loved to have him carry on our tradition. All we could do was express our opinion. We were 19, 20 years old. We spoke up for Coach Ellenson, but it turned out to be a symbolic protest."

When each of the players received telegrams two days after the Gator Bowl game that Coach Graves was indeed stepping down and that Doug Dickey, whom they had just beaten in the Gator Bowl, was coming to Florida as the new head coach, the players were confused and angry.

John Reaves: "I didn't know what was coming down. Neither did Carlos. Some of the guys campaigned for Gene Ellenson to be the next coach, but it was too late. They had already cut a deal with Dickey."

The reason Ray Graves told President Steven O'Connell that he only wanted to coach one more year was that his duties as athletic director were becoming more and more time-consuming.

Ray Graves: "I was meeting with alumni and faculty reps when I should have been coaching. The womens' program was coming, and it was getting to be a challenge. We had some capital improvements, buildings that had to be built, and my mind was too much on being an athletic director. I told President O'Connell I was going to have to make a decision. I told him I thought the two jobs were too much. I said, 'After the '68 season I might think about '69 being the last year. It'll be a good time. We have some good freshmen coming in. I won't be leaving the next coach with a real challenge.'

"I think he agreed with me. We didn't talk about it much. He said, 'I'll tell you what I'll do: I'll consider it.' And he mentioned Doug Dickey as my successor. Doug's father was a member of the Florida faculty, and he and President O'Connell were good friends, and Doug had played quarterback at Florida, and he was winning at Tennessee, and he thought Doug might be interested in coming back."

Red Mitchum: "Steve O'Connell, and Bert Kibler, who was very much involved, were on the search committee to find a new coach. During that summer O'Connell was in North Carolina, where he saw Doug Dickey at the golf course. The words I recall Steve telling me were that he said to Doug, 'How'd you like to come home?' He didn't say anything about coaching football or anything. Doug said, 'That sounds very interesting to me.'"

Ray Graves: "He talked to him, and Doug WAS interested in coming back, though in '68 Doug Dickey's Tennessee team ended up conference champions."

The problem that Coach Graves faced was that Doug Dickey kept changing his mind over whether or not to leave Tennessee.

Ray Graves: "There were times when Doug Dickey was not interested. The president would say to him, 'Let's don't make any decisions now. Let's think about it.' Doug came over and visited with President O'Connell during the Gator Bowl [Florida was playing Tennessee], and that wasn't good. I always said that it was as hard to resign from the job as it was to get the job because Doug was back and forth. He was conference champions, so he had it made at Tennessee. The irony of the whole thing was that we ended up beating Tennessee in the Gator Bowl, and that was a mistake for the future. We had a goal line stand that was something, and we beat them, and then just before Tennessee left to go back home Doug told O'Connell he had changed his mind and he was staying at Tennessee.

"O'Connell called a board meeting right after the game, and they asked me, 'Would you consider staying on another year?' I said, 'Well, the only thing bad about this is that I told the players that I was probably resigning.' I hadn't made it definite, but I told them, 'If anything changes, I'll be in touch with all of you.'

"I said, 'I'll stay on.' And then I went back to Gainesville, and on the plane back Doug changed his mind again. He and Bob Woodruff, who was the Tennessee athletic director, got into some argument, and Doug decided to come.

"President O'Connell called me at the house and said, 'Doug's coming.' I said, 'Boy, this is really embarrassing. These players are all going on holiday, are scattered.' I said, 'I'll send them all a wire to their homes.'

"That was about as messy as you can get, and the worst thing about it was the players. Doug came down, and he was changing the offense, and the players weren't happy with his coaching philosophy, and that was sad too. They were thinking, Ours is better than yours. We beat you. It was bad.

"I wanted to be in there with Doug and help him and maybe sit in on some of the staff meetings about personnel, but Doug said, 'No, I don't want you anywhere close to them. The worst thing is to have to follow you. Stay away from my coaches and players.' I said, 'I don't know that that's the best thing to do, Doug.' I felt for him in many ways and couldn't help him.

"The kids had wanted Gene Ellenson—I recommended Gene Ellenson.

He would have been the logical one to assume the job—but the decision had already been made by President O'Connell to hire Doug. It was cut and dried. There weren't any options."

While Ray Graves retired as coach at the end of the 1969 season, he remained as the Florida athletic director until 1980. He worked hard to give women equal opportunity in athletics, as mandated by Title IX, and he oversaw construction of new facilities. When the lion's share of the work was completed, he decided it was time to step down.

Attending his retirement luncheon was George Steinbrenner, the owner of the New York Yankees and a fan of Florida football, and during the lunch Steinbrenner asked Graves to come to his office and talk to him about a job opportunity. "I just bought the Tampa Bay Downs," he said. "Meet me out there for lunch."

When Graves arrived at the track, he saw Steinbrenner and former football coach Lou Saban, a Steinbrenner employee, sweeping with brooms. "Grab a broom, and let's go to work here," Steinbrenner said to Graves. Later Steinbrenner asked him, "Why don't you come to work for me? Be vice president of public relations for Steinbrenner Enterprises." Graves asked, "What will I do?" Steinbrenner told him, "You can work with the collegiate programs. I have to put weight rooms in at Grambling, Ohio State, and other schools. We'll set up some scholarships. Why don't you work with the youth program in Tampa, the Boys and Girls Club? And I want you to lobby for me in Tallahassee." Who could say no to the esteemed Ray Graves? Says Graves, "Democracy is the best form of government, but it's expensive."

Graves worked for Steinbrenner for eight years before retiring after a minor argument. Graves told Steinbrenner, "Our friendship is worth more than anything."

Says Graves, "I enjoyed working with George. I really did. He does so much good that you never read about, locally and statewide, the Florida Orchestra, the Boys and Girls Clubs, and I could tell you some terrific things he did that he asked me not to tell anyone. I tell you, I enjoyed working for George."

Graves is now retired. He lives on a golf course in Tampa with his wife Opal. He is a content and happy man.

Steve Tannen was a consensus college All-American his senior year. He was drafted by the New York Jets, became a teammate of Joe Namath, and was named to several pro all-star teams. He moved to Hollywood to try to make it in the movies. He then worked as an artist for a while until he joined a friend's construction company.

Steve Tannen: "I started thinking about the pros after my sophomore year, when I had a really good year. The Dallas Cowboys started sending me literature. I met with Gil Brandt. After my junior year, I figured that's where I was going.

Larry Smith had come back to school after he had been a first-round choice the year before with the Rams, and we ran into each other. I told him I wasn't going to sign for less than fifty grand, but I did.

"One of the biggest things about the draft was that I had no idea the Jets were going to take me. So many other teams had spent time with me, coming to my apartment, giving me tests. They would time me, give me psychological tests. And Dallas was always sending me tons of stuff.

"On draft day I was in my apartment, and I got a phone call from Bubba McGowen, receivers coach at Florida. He called me and said, 'I have the New York Jets on the phone. Do you have an agent?' I said, 'I'm going to use my Uncle Willie,' a lawyer who lived in Gainesville. Uncle Willie helped players negotiate their contracts.

"And what I found out later was that Uncle Willie wasn't much of a negotiator. He didn't do too much fighting for me. When they offered a contract, he said, 'I think it's good.' I said, 'Wait a minute. Aren't we going to negotiate?'

"I got $35,000 from the New York Jets for signing. I was the 19th player picked in the country. The money is different now, but I didn't want for anything. I lived in New York City, and I had fur coats, but it wasn't anything I could retire on like today.

"At that point in my career, people were comparing me to Joe Namath. He was Broadway Joe. I was Subway Steve. Because I was flamboyant and wore crazy clothes and had long hair. In fact, the one who gave me that name was Steve Spurrier. He was playing with the 49ers.

"I had known a guy who was friendly with Namath, had some business dealings with him, so one of my biggest moments was that I went down to Ft. Lauderdale after being drafted to meet Joe.

"We became friendly, but it was always a strained relationship. We used to drive to work together because not many players lived in the city. We hung out. Later on we had a falling out.

"The Jets were were world champs in '68, [when they beat the Baltimore

Colts in the Super Bowl in January of 1969.] Then in '69 they went all the way to the championship and lost to Kansas City. So I came to them when they were very impressive, when Joe Namath had put the AFL on the map.

"It was the first year of realignment in the NFL, and we had unbelievably high hopes, and we went 4-10 my rookie year. During the year we lost about twenty major guys to injuries. It was a rough experience.

"I played for the Jets for six years, and my last year I was injured and didn't play at all. I wanted to go someplace else, and they wanted me to go someplace else. But then they hired Lou Holtz, and Lou brought back a guy named Walt Michaels, who had been my defensive coach when I started with the Jets and who left after Weeb [Ewbank] picked his son-in-law, Charlie Winner, to succeed him. When Walt came back, he told me to come back and talk to Lou Holtz.

"I was excited Walt was back. I went in to see Lou. He said, 'Steve, the coaches want me to keep you, but I got nine problems on this team, and eight of them are black'—He was inferring I was the ninth problem. Who knows why?—'and if I keep you and let the other eight go, they'll call me a racist.' I said, 'Lou, you ARE a racist.' And I walked out of the room. Two days later I was traded to Oakland.

"I didn't pass their physical, because I hadn't properly recovered from the shoulder surgery, even though the Jets had passed me.

"I took the physical and failed it, and they called Al Ward, the general manager of the Jets, and he said, 'Come back to New York.' I was in Oakland. I said, 'I'm driving to Los Angeles, and I'll call you in a couple of days.' I figured my shoulder wasn't in that great shape, and I decided to retire."

thirty-two

Ruffled Feathers

When Doug Dickey temporarily changed his mind about coming to Florida for the 1970 season, the confusion left a vacuum of anger and resentment that would haunt him during his ten-year coaching tenure. The assistant coaches and players started a movement designed to pressure Florida president Steve O'Connell and the search committee to hire Gene Ellenson instead of Dickey. What they didn't know was that O'Connell had committed to Dickey and that their efforts were fruitless.

Red Mitchum: "The assistant coaches began organizing against getting a new coach. They didn't even know they had contacted Dickey. They petitioned to keep Graves and have him come back. Or they wanted Gene Ellenson, an assistant coach, to have the job. And they tried to get Carlos Alvarez to unionize the players, which is the worst thing I ever heard of.

"It got to be such a turmoil that when they did hire Doug Dickey, he came in like the guy in Li'l Abner with the cloud hanging over his head. And Ray Graves stayed on as athletic director, and it was just a confusing time for Doug and for everybody. It wasn't easy for Doug the whole time he was here. It was really tough."

The choice of Doug Dickey seemed a logical one. After all, he had quarterbacked the University of Florida for three years in the early 1950s. He had climbed the college coaching ladder to the top when he was named the head coach of the University of Tennessee in 1963. In 1969 he led Tennessee to the SEC championship, when he was offered the job at Florida.

Doug Dickey: "We got off to a bad start with the press. There was a lot of emotion for Gene Ellenson to be the coach. They didn't make that offer to him. They made it to me. When I took it, it was now sour apples with a certain number of people.

"We overcame that, got over it. We had one senior class in 1975 that won more games than any senior class in the history of Florida at that time."

With the coming of the 1970 season, the Florida players had to cope with a new coach, Doug Dickey, who had been the head man at Tennessee. Dickey began wedged firmly behind the eight ball. Florida had beaten his team in the Gator Bowl the year before. Most of the players fervently wanted Gene Ellenson to replace the departed Coach Graves and were resentful he was not the successor. And Doug Dickey turned out to be distant and hard to reach. Dissension and unhappiness were in the air when the new football season began.

Jack Youngblood: "He's the head man. That is the name of the game. We had to figure out how to make the best of this and make it work. We knew Dickey had had a successful program at Tennessee, and we were hoping that would carry over here.

"The fact we had beaten his team created a certain amount of ill will among our players, which was a juvenile type of thought process, but that was what was going on."

The switch to Doug Dickey didn't affect the defensive players nearly as much as the offensive players. Dickey's forte always had been defense, and he brought with him as defensive coordinator a coach by the name of Doug Knotts, whom the players grew to admire.

Jack Youngblood: "We realized we had a decent group of guys, and we could play, and we carried on because Doug Knotts came in as defensive coordinator. He continued with the four-three defensive scheme, so our scheme stayed basically the same. The big concern was whether Doug Dickey was going to come in and try to change John Reaves, Carlos Alvarez, and the offensive scheme. That was the big question."

John Reaves: "When the 1970 season rolled around, Coach Dickey was in charge. He was kinda like Tony Dungy had been with the Tampa Bay Bucs—he believed in defense, special teams, and your offense not trying to do anything but avoid mistakes. You have a running game, eat up the clock, and take advantage of turnovers for scoring opportunities.

"Under Coach Graves we had been the total opposite. We were 'bombs away.' We were like the Desert Storm. You go in with an aerial assault and bring the ground troops in later.

"We had a few great defensive players, like Jack Youngblood, but we didn't have a lot of them. In fact, our sophomore year our defense wasn't rated very high in the SEC. In my junior and senior years, they were ranked last. So that system of Coach Dickey's didn't work too good when your defense ranks last in the league."

One of the stellar defenders in addition to Jack Youngblood was a linebacker by the name of Fred Abbott, whose nickname was Catfish, because he had come from rural Florida and was a country boy.

Fred Abbott: "Don Brown recruited me from Florida. Our '68 freshman class had the Tampa area. The big recruit at the time was John Reaves. My freshman class had five or six All-SEC players in it, and one consensus All-American, Carlos Alvarez.

"We still had freshman football, and that year we played four games. You go from being a big dog in high school to being a scrimmage dummy, so the only thing we had were these four games. For freshmen, these were big events.

"I was getting ready to start on the varsity as an offensive tackle in '69, and the week before the opening game in Houston I got clipped in a scrimmage. I was in a cast about six weeks, and they decided to red-shirt me up until the Gator Bowl. I traveled with the team because they thought eventually I would pan out and become a player. It was Florida against Tennessee, and before the Gator Bowl game they came to me and said, 'If this game is very close, we may play you. If we don't play you by halftime, we will red-shirt you.' Fortunately I didn't have to lose a whole year and play in that game. Talk about seeing a 19-year-old cry if they had put me in that game! If they had asked me, I would have gone in, because that was the mindset, but it would have been very bad for me. All my contemporaries were superstars, and for that '69 season I was on crutches on the side-lines. That was a frustrating year to have to watch everybody play.

"When I arrived for spring practice in 1970, Coach Graves was gone, and Doug Dickey was the coach. There was a tremendous amount of resentment or anger or disappointment or just the feeling of unfairness among the players.

Gene Ellenson was the spiritual soul of that team. He was literally the emotional leader. I can remember one night before one the games in '69 Coach Ellenson took the football team to the athletic offices, and we watched a movie together. We were in there watching *The Battle of the Bulge*, and he stopped the movie in the middle of the battle, and he said, 'This is not really the way it was. We were over here, and the Germans were over there.' He had fought in the Battle of the Bulge, and it made the hair on the back of your neck stand up. That's the type of real-life stories and experiences he bought with him, and people would run through brick walls for him, particularly the defensive players.

"Everybody liked Gene Ellenson, and then because of that Gator Bowl game, they might have been the SEC champs, but they got whipped there. So what compounded all of that was the fact that we now had to do it the way they did it at Tennessee. It was, 'Forget about what you did. It's gonna be the way we do it.'

"I don't think you could have had a worse situation. In fairness to Doug Dickey, whoever the powers that be that made that decision did a terrible job of handling it. Right before the Gator Bowl game, Steve O'Connell, the president of the university, walked into the locker room and the exact quote was, 'I don't care if your grandmother told you there's going to be a coaching change. It's not true.'

"And two days after the game we got a telegram that said, 'Congratulations, your new coach is Doug Dickey.' They sent one to everyone at home. Everyone had left Gainesville.

"The opening game in 1970 was against Duke. I switched positions and started playing linebacker. I had signed to play middle guard at Florida, and then they decided they could use my talents better as an offensive lineman, because they had a need at tackle. But then when Dickey came in, he had been known for defense and great linebackers, and I assume this is what happened, but I think it's accurate: Doug Knotts, the defensive coordinator, took the people he wanted in order to create an outstanding defense. This was an era when the champions had great defenses and would win games 10 to 7.

"The year before Florida played a 5-2 defense, and Tennessee played a 4-3, which had a middle linebacker. In other words, the middle guard became the middle linebacker. Being a stand-up linebacker is significantly different than being a middle guard who's down in a four-point stance.

"Coach Knotts was literally used to dealing with the creme de la creme at linebacker. He had just left three All-Americans at Tennessee, Jack

Reynolds, Steve Kiner, and a guy named Walker. I think he was frustrated trying to be everywhere and dealing with the changes.

"Against Duke, I had to cover an outstanding fullback, one of their best players. Pass coverage also was new or foreign to me. For me, it was a struggle." The season opener against Duke was a nail-biter, a 21-19 win. Tommy Durrance scored twice on plunges, and Carlos Alvarez returned a punt 67 yards for a touchdown, the first time he ever tried it.

Jack Youngblood: "Tommy picked up the mantle from Smitty [Larry Smith] of being the tough running back. He didn't have Larry's size, but he had the attitude, and he had the skill. He was one of those tough kids.

"In that game Reaves did some throwing to Alvarez, but it wasn't like it had been before under Coach Graves. But they did have some success."

John Reaves: "Carlos was a great punt returner, incredible. He was such a natural, like that movie with Robert Redford. He went for 67 yards to give us a big [21-6] lead, and then we had to hold on by the skin of our teeth.

"At the end of the game Mike Kelley recovered a fumble on our four, and we squeaked it out.

"That game was when we finally smelled the coffee. I could see, 'Hey, this ain't gonna be the same deal anymore,' because we were running the ball two out of three plays. Coach Dickey obviously was a great coach and had had a great deal of success at Tennessee, but he ran a control-the-clock offense, and when he came to Florida, we only had two passing routes, the all-curl where your two wide-outs run down and curl and your backs run flats. Also he had the hitch, where the guys would run five yards and stop. That was it. So we went from having a passing game with twenty-five plays in it out of different formations, to one with two plays.

"Our offensive line had graduated everyone except one guy, and we had replaced them with guys weighing 220 pounds, so we weren't ramming the ball down anyone's throats. It was kinda like 'smell the coffee.'

"After a while I said, 'Coach, we need to get more patterns in here. We're not going to be able to run the ball on people like this. These guys are too small, but they can pass protect a little bit, stand in their way for awhile anyway.'

"Coach Dickey called around and got more patterns, and we put them in, and we started moving the ball a lot better. It was a tough transition. A lot of guys were upset. Coach Dickey wasn't the friendliest guy in the world, so it estranged a lot of players. And the coaches would make statements in the papers like, 'Well, these aren't our boys. Wait till we get our boys in here,' and guys would hear that or read it and not even want to play."

Fred Abbott: "The Duke game was my debut as a linebacker. After that game, Doug Dickey and I had some disagreements. It was primarily a difference in style. Ray Graves and Gene Ellenson were personable. Their approach was that we were like a family. I needed that to deal with the environment. That's how I motivated myself, that these were all good people, and we were all doing this thing together for a reason. And Coach Dickey's style was entirely different. It was very standoffish and not very personal. That was tough for me. And I left the team briefly.

"I went back to the boondocks from whence I came and pondered my future. I was one of those guys who needed a scholarship to go to college. Vietnam wasn't an issue, because I had a high lottery number. But if I was going to continue my education, the only way to do it was on an athletic scholarship.

"A friend of mine named Alfred McKeithan, a real gentleman, came and talked to me. He said, 'Are you going to clean fish for the rest of your life, or do you want to go to college?' That was a no-brainer. He interceded for me and went and talked to Doug Dickey and asked if I could come back. Dickey said that if the team was in favor of it, it was okay. They had a vote, and I came back. When I returned, I moved back to offensive line and played tackle, where I was more comfortable. The next year I started at offensive guard. My senior year they switched me to linebacker."

thirty-three

Integration

In 1968 Ray Graves made the decision to integrate the University of Florida football team.

Ray Graves: "When I was an assistant coach at Georgia Tech in the early 1950s, we were going to play Pittsburgh in the Sugar Bowl. Pittsburgh had one black player.

"The governor of Georgia told the president of Georgia Tech, 'You can't take Georgia Tech to the Sugar Bowl because Pitt has a black player.' Boy, I'll tell you. It worked out that the legislature and all of them got together with the governor, and they finally agreed to let Georgia Tech play, since it was out of the state.

"In 1968 I decided we needed to start recruiting black players at Florida. I knew they were good athletes, and some of them had started playing on other southern schools. I talked to the staff. We just wanted to make sure we could get boys who could stay in school and remain eligible.

"The only reservation I had was the question: Can they pass at Florida? Listen, I'm telling you, you bring some of these boys in from the boondocks, from these little towns—they would have the grades and the right courses, but they didn't have the background. I was scared about bringing them in and having them flunk out.

"George Levy was the one who told me about this kid, Leonard George. Leonard's father and mother were schoolteachers. I came down, and he was the first black player I recruited. He's a lawyer now in Tallahassee. He was a good athlete, but he didn't play too much. He was a good student. I was proud of him.

"The other black athlete, Willie Jackson, at first couldn't get in. He was ineligible academically, so some of the boosters lent him money to go up to

Valley Forge, a prep school in Pennsylvania, and the first game he ran for two touchdowns. They said he was fantastic. I went up to see him on a wintry day. It was sleeting. He came out in his uniform, and he looked like an athlete and a man. He was a good one. And the pressure was on him.

"Willie was something. He tried harder than anyone, but he wasn't quite as good as we thought he'd be because he tried TOO hard. He dropped more passes than anyone I ever had. His senior year he caught one and ran for a touchdown, and all of us gave him a standing ovation. Of course, it was a good move bringing him in, because his wife gave birth to Terry and Willie Jr., and those children became great players. They were a great family. I'm still close to them. Willie is in Jacksonville. He works for the city."

Willie Jackson: "In high school I was just playing football to play football. It was something to do, and it was enjoyable. I liked it, and the fans liked it, and we just had fun doing it. It was just something to stay away from the streets, stay away from the house. I looked at it as an after-school program— something to do. I didn't have to run home and get in trouble or have to do a lot of work when I got home. College wasn't even a thought.

"But Fernando Storch, who had gone to the University of Florida, and some of the coaches saw football as an opportunity for me to go to college. I had turned 18 before September of my senior year, so I was ineligible to play any more high school ball. So all through my junior year I was enrolled in a study program to prepare myself for college, and when the fall came one of the coaches had a friend up in Wayne, Pennsylvania, and I went to Valley Forge Military Academy for a year because there were no age restrictions there.

"It was exciting and different. We practiced in a Quonset hut because it was so cold. The guys weren't as tough and fast as they were in Sarasota. I was competing at running back with a returning player who was supposed to be the greatest thing. I came in, and we worked well together, and I scored a couple of touchdowns, made some pretty good runs, so it worked out well for me.

"And at Valley Forge I also did well academically. You didn't have anything to do but go to school and drill. They made us go to study halls. So you'd go to class, you'd study, and you got individual attention so that you understood that it was important for you to do your part and do what you were supposed to do. It helped me raise my grade level a bit.

"At the end of the year Fernando knew I had committed to Florida. But I did make a visit to Ohio State. It was a good opportunity, but the airplane ride was rocky. I was trying to be brave, but we would hit air pockets, and I was freaking out. It was my first experience of a bad plane ride.

"I met Woody Hayes and his son, a great defensive back. He was the one who took me around and showed me a pretty good time, but as I arrived, the campus was knee-deep in snow and the roof-tops were covered with snow. It was white all over.

"At the time I thought I was better off being in Florida than being up there in all that snow. That's what really steered me to Florida. I felt I'd rather have liquid sunshine than a lot of snow.

"I was contacted by Jack Eibner, who was the Florida running backs coach. He was really, really impressive. I really enjoyed him and liked him. He was impressive, and I would learn a lot from him. I learned to play and enjoy the game under his tutelage.

"One of the things they told me was that I had a chance to be the first black to play for Florida. They said, 'You could be a pioneer. You can come and play and make it possible for other blacks to come here.' Because at the time the notion was that blacks couldn't play sports and do the academics at the same time at a major college. He told me, 'We need more blacks to be with us.'

"My challenge was do something for the blacks—for mankind.

"At the time there was another black player they were recruiting, Leonard George of Tampa Douglas. In fact, we became roommates. He was the first to sign a scholarship to play for the University of Florida. I had to wait for the ACT scores to come in during the summer of '69, so when I enrolled I couldn't play my freshman year. So Leonard George was the first black to play with the Baby Gators as a freshman, but I was the first black to play on the varsity.

"When I arrived freshman year, the campus was very segregated. There were only fifteen black faces. It wasn't that hard, because we were there to get our education, but the social part could be hard. We kind of stayed away from the fraternity parties. If we wanted a social life, we would go outside of the college fraternities. At that time the community didn't want to accept you because they figured you thought you were better than them, so I guess it was kind of antagonistic. But we were just people trying to get along and do what we were supposed to do. It was hard to have a good social atmosphere.

"But eventually it became more amicable. If you go to class and meet friends on campus, and maybe they take you into their circles. It was okay. We would all congregate in Tiger Hall, which is where we had most of our classes.

"Coach Graves stepped down after the '69 season. I had never played under him, never had any contact with him my freshman year, other than the time he invited me to come to Florida. Under Coach Dickey the players had to do off-season training—we had never heard of that. Under Coach Dickey, we were working out all year long, and a lot of them didn't like all the running and the weightlifting. Their attitude was, 'We just beat you [in the Gator Bowl]. Why are you coming here and trying to tell us what to do?' The feeling of most of the older players who already were here was, 'Is this necessary?' They didn't like the new rituals. And they wanted to have more time to themselves.

"With me, I didn't know any different. It was something new to me. I was there to play football and enjoy myself. I was perfectly happy to do it if that's what Coach Dickey wanted me to do. I accepted everything, even when the coaches punished you by making you run up the stadium. It was all in fun and all about you. You made it happen yourself. They wanted you to train because it would make you a better player. If you wanted to be one of the best, you had to go through the training. It wasn't like it was a great chore to do. It was fun.

"The first game of the season was against Duke in Jacksonville. I could feel the exhilaration as I ran out onto that field. All the people in the stands didn't make any difference to me. What was on my mind was, Am I going to do what I'm capable of doing? Am I going to be a success? My major focus was to just go out there and play football.

"I didn't play much in the game, but I played, and it was okay. It was good to be out there. Our quarterback was John Reaves, and John kind of adopted Leonard and me. He said to us, 'If you need anything, come to me.' John had a car, and so Leonard and I were always going to him to get his car and run around the city.

"John was a real good guy. He didn't have any prejudices. If he did, he kept them hidden. We would always go to him for things, and he would be receptive, even if we messed up—if we borrowed his car and kept it for awhile. And on the field he treated us like any other player. I thought it was a good relationship. I never had any problem with him. We never had any words. Because at the time we did what the coaches and the quarterback told us to do. You just went out and played football."

According to John Reaves, Jack Youngblood, and Fred Abbott, the integration of the football team was smooth and easy.

John Reaves: "There was no problem at all. Nothing. I had played at Robinson High School with several black teammates. I would think just about every player on the team did too. So it was no big deal to us."

Jack Youngblood: "It didn't change anything. They fit right in. Both of them were good kids. They were freshmen, new kids, and freshmen had a position. They had to learn the ropes too."

Fred Abbott: "I was there when Leonard George and Willie Jackson joined the team. I know them both well and consider them friends. I don't think there were any problems from the athletes' standpoint. If there was a problem, it was the older alumni. I don't ever recall there being a problem, but that's easy for me to say because I'm white. From their perspective, things may have happened.

"We beat Mississippi State [34-13] in our second game. Willie Jackson caught a couple of long passes. I thought Willie had incredible size for a receiver. I thought he had tremendous potential. We also had Leonard George, who had started at halfback, but fumbled in a game, and the coaches switched him to defensive back. I just thought, Here are two guys who have some talent and who are gonna play and help us. At that point in time the better black athletes had gone out of the South to play at places like Michigan. So to me, anybody who could help us win was okay."

thirty-four

Unhappiness

Before the Mississippi State game, an outspoken John Reaves told one reporter that he "felt like a robot," because Coach Dickey no longer gave him the play-calling freedom that Coach Graves had given him the year before. Nevertheless, against Mississippi State, Reaves opened the offense up enough to throw for 249 yards in the first half alone. Willie Jackson caught passes for 53 and 40 yards. Tommy Durrance scored twice on plunges, and Carlos Alvarez and Mike Rich each scored touchdowns.

John Reaves: "It was a dumb thing to say. But it was true, the year before I had a lot of play-calling flexibility. But against Mississippi State, we opened it up a little bit. Another factor was the heat. It was 110 degrees down on the field. At one point the coaches said, 'Let's try to score early before people die.' And we got ahead of them, and in the third quarter, I'll never forget, I go to the line of scrimmage to take the snap, and one of their defensive tackles said, 'How do you guys play in this shit?' It was so miserably hot, they wilted." [Florida won 34–13.]

Alabama, Bear Bryant's Crimson Tide, was next. It was no contest as Bama rolled over Florida's undermanned defense 46–15.

Fred Abbott: "Alabama was next, and we lost badly. The most important thing that happened was that between '69 and '70 the offensive line had graduated. Not many people realize this, but four out of five of those linemen had been starters, although one of them was a converted linebacker who had started on defense. The only lineman who wasn't a long-time starter in '69 was a player named Todd Griffith. When the offensive linemen graduated and left, we had to start from scratch. That was the number one difference between

1969 and 1970. Number two, with regard to Alabama, their talent was three deep. Bear Bryant just had too many thoroughbreds, and Florida was hurting for offensive linemen. John Reaves, Carlos Alvarez, and Tommy Durrance were tremendously skilled players, but that and fifty cents will buy you a cup of coffee if you don't have a good offensive line."

John Reaves: "We played in Tuscaloosa on the Astroturf. It was another 110 degree day, and they had the heater on in our locker room, which made it even more uncomfortable.

"Jack Youngblood was out with an injury that day and didn't play. He was our whole defense, and without him they were killing us up front. Alabama had John Hannah and Johnny Musso running that wishbone. I'll never forget the noise. They would snap the ball, and you would hear this ble-e-e-e-e-ew. You'd see our whole defense get knocked back about eight yards, and Musso would run six or eight yards. Our offense hardly ever got on the field.

"At the end of the game we drove down to the two, and I handed off to Leonard George, and he fumbled, and the next week Doug Dickey moved him to cornerback. He was a good running back. He was quick, but he made that one mistake."

Jack Youngblood, badly injured in the Duke game, returned to the team before the North Carolina State game. No one could believe it. The initial diagnosis was that he would miss the remainder of the season. Instead, he was back after missing only two games.

Jack Youngblood: "I had suffered a knee injury on the kickoff for the second half of the Duke game. I had a running start, so I was getting down there making the play. I got double-teamed. Somebody hit me low, and somebody chipped me from the high side and tweaked that right knee.

"Initially we thought it was gone. This is another incredible story: They wrapped it up, and the doc on the sidelines said, 'You're done for the night. They wrapped me up and they said, 'Let's get him to the hospital now. I was put in a trooper's car. Troopers would escort us anywhere we went around the state. I was taken to the hospital in Gainesville before that game was over.

"They were ready for me when I arrived. They got me all checked in. They scheduled me for surgery. I had a sleepless night thinking I would have to have an operation the next morning and that my football career was over.

"Doc came in the next morning, did an exam on my knee, and said, 'This is a miracle. Last night you had no ligaments holding your knee together. This morning you do.'

"As far as I'm concerned, this was the closest thing to a miracle to ever happen to me. He did not operate. He said, 'I don't know how this happened. I thought you had a torn medial-collateral ligament.'

"He said, 'All we are going to do is immobilize it, put you in a splint, and two weeks from now we'll reevaluate you.'

"I gimped around for two weeks, and they went and played Mississippi State and Alabama. We beat Mississippi State, and I was looking forward to playing Alabama with Johnny Musso and John Hannah.

"I had looked forward to playing in that football game, and they didn't take me on the trip, so I decided to get a couple of close friends and our girlfriends, and we went out to a friend's lake house on Cowpen Lake in Gainesville. They had a ski boat and a bunch of food, and we had a tailgate party, and we were listening to the game. We were getting hammered by Alabama. I mean, all you could hear was 'Musso and Hannah doing this,' and I was just beside myself.

"I said, 'To hell with it. I've got to test this knee. I've got to see whether I can play or not. I said, 'Give me a ski.' I took the splint off, got on the ski, and I skiied to test my knee…and it held up.

"I jumped on the slalom ski and slalomed and said, 'If I can do this, I can play football.'

"The next week I started practicing. I played against the University of North Carolina State. The whole game I was concerned about being able to play. There were some tenuous thoughts there. Will it hold up? Can I play? I had practiced, but practice is not playing. It held up."

In the game against North Carolina State, a 14-6 win, the Florida defense stood out. Florida had seven interceptions, a team record, including three by John Clifford.

Jack Youngblood: "John was a wild man. He was a defensive back who played like a rover, an instinctive football player, an overachiever type. John played hard all the time. He would take a risk and make a play."

Fred Abbott: "We had seven interceptions against North Carolina State, three by John Clifford. There were a bunch of guys from Coral Gables who came to our team, John, Randy Talbot, Ralph Ortega, Glenn Cameron, an incredible bunch of people from one high school team.

"During that North Carolina State game, the fans were booing John. Think about it. I don't know of anybody who had a better beginning to their careers than John and Carlos [Alvarez]. And he was struggling and sputtering in '70."

John Reaves: "I couldn't hit the broad side of a barn that day. It was just one of those days, like a pitcher going out there walking everyone. I was perplexed, because normally I'm fairly accurate. I just couldn't hit anything that day. I was booed by the fans, but I deserved it. I threw some bad balls—overthrew, underthrew, throwing wide…"

Willie Jackson scored the first touchdown ever scored by a black player for Florida against the North Carolina State University in the 14-6 win. Halfback Tommy Durrance hit him with a four-yard pass.

Willie Jackson: "The play was called and it worked. It was a great opportunity."

Florida then played FSU in a game that Florida dominated so completely that at one point the Gators led 31-7. Dickey made wholesale substitutions and curtailed the offense. At the end it wasn't quite such a runaway. The final score was 38-27.

John Reaves: "FSU scored first after a fumble, and we tied it up on a long [a school record 81-yard] pass to Jim Yancey, an excellent tight end who made All-SEC that year. He ran an end route, and one of FSU's defenders slipped or fell, and I hit him, and he went the distance. It was one of those freak plays."

Against FSU, Willie Jackson caught an 18-yard touchdown pass from John Reaves.

Willie Jackson: "They were struggling for an identity. They hadn't done the recruiting and gotten the great players who they let go to other states. So that gave us an opportunity to play and win, because they didn't have the talent at the time.

"The rivalry with FSU wasn't intense for me and wasn't for most of the other players. FSU was more of a girls' school as opposed to a powerhouse football team. Beating Florida State was something we expected to do."

John Reaves: "Willie had a lot of talent. He could jump out of the building. He would jump up in the air and make a one-handed catch four feet over his head, but then he'd drop one right on the numbers. So it could be a little frustrating.

"But against Florida State we had a 38-7 lead, and they put in Gary Huff, the third string quarterback, for his debut. Gary threw three touchdowns to Barry Smith late."

Fred Abbott: "Florida State was THE rivalry, and you just didn't lose to FSU, including when you were a freshman. There was a tradition that if you did lose, they would shave your head bald. You just could NOT lose that game. If was like you were on a religious crusade. To me that was the game that epitomizes college football. It didn't matter what the respective records were. It mattered what your state of mind was. It was always the game for me. I laugh at myself because after my senior year I went to the Senior Bowl and played with Gary Huff, James Thomas, and Barry Smith. I had all this intensity playing against them, and I discovered they were guys just like you, me, John and Carlos. But when I was there, it was war.

"All those FSU games stand out in my mind. In 1970 we won big [38-27]. What I remember most was watching Carlos catch a ball on the dead run by grabbing the back half of the ball. In other words, the ball was past his hands, and he reached out and caught a long pass John threw with his fingertips on the back end of the ball."

In a 20-0 win against the University of Richmond, tailback Duane Doel scored all three touchdowns. But Florida did not score until there was less than a minute remaining in the first half.

John Reaves: "Yeah, that was frustrating. We weren't real fired up for the game. It was the University of Richmond, and we were flat. We finally got going. Still, it wasn't an exhilarating performance by us at all."

Fred Abbott: "In the beginning of that game Richmond was playing tough, and some Richmond guy got his leg badly broken, and that took the wind out of their sails. After that, it got to be an easier game. But in the beginning, they didn't know they were supposed to get beat."

Florida flew to Knoxville to play quarterback Bobby Scott and the University of Tennessee, Coach Dickey's former stomping ground. The Tennessee fans were particularly hostile to Dickey and his Gators. The reception was harsh. The Volunteer fans booed Coach Dickey unmercifully, as Tennessee stomped the Gators, 38-7. Scott threw for 385 yards, a Tennessee record, and Florida ended up gaining a total of eight yards on the ground.

Fred Abbott: "It was Doug Dickey coming back to his alma mater to play Tennessee. When we went out onto the field before the game, the Tennessee fans threw oranges at us. They booed us. Doug was persona non grata, along with us. In that game Bobby Scott threw for two touchdowns, and the biggest difference again was our offensive line. It had been decimated, and they won [38-7]."

Jack Youngblood: "Tennessee had an outstanding football team that year. Bobby Scott was a terrific quarterback. I remember one time we chased him, and I got to him, and all I came away with was a handful of jersey. I was holding a whole number 12 in my hand. They were wearing those tearaway jerseys."

John Reaves: "We didn't play real well, and they were pumped with Dickey leaving them. They thought he had screwed them over, and when we ran out onto the field, the fans bombarded us with oranges. They threw a lot of them. I guess they imported them. It was NOT a good game."

In the next game against Auburn, the Gators suffered their worst defeat in the history of Florida Field, a 63-14 loss.

John Reaves: "They played a brilliant game and clobbered us. Pat Sullivan and Terry Beasley were awesome. They had a brilliant kind of game against us, the kind of game we had against Houston the year before. They scored four touchdowns real quick, and aside from a long touchdown pass I threw to Carlos, it was very humiliating."

Fred Abbott: "What was the score? [Auburn 63-Florida 14] Late in the game it was out of reach, and Florida sent in their second team, and I refused to leave the field. I was on a mission. I sent the guy who they sent in to replace me back to the side-lines. I played the whole game. I was not one of those people who was prone to throw in the towel."

Willie Jackson: "We just had a letdown. Those two teams were the premier teams in the SEC at the time. We were just struggling to get the quality of players Auburn had. The reason we were getting beat the way we were was that we didn't have the athletes they had."

Jack Youngblood: "There was nothing we could do to stop Sullivan. He'd roll out and find the receiver and made a miserable day for us. This was a loss that killed any chance we had for a bowl appearance. But that's the SEC for you."

In the next game against Georgia, Coach Dickey stifled John Reaves' passing. In a 24-17 win, Reaves didn't throw a pass until 20 seconds were left in the first half.

Willie Jackson: "In the prior two games, John didn't throw the ball very well. He threw quite a few interceptions. And Coach Dickey decided to work on other aspects of our game, which was the running game, the power game. If we could reestablish that, then we would be able to throw better. If there was something between Coach Dickey and John, we never knew it. No one told the team they were making any changes. He was such a leader, and he established himself as a great quarterback in the league and the nation."

John Reaves: "We had been pounded so unmercifully the last two weeks that we were playing Georgia very close to the vest. Thank goodness, playing that way Georgia didn't race out to a big lead, but they didn't.

"I was running the veer, which was the offense Dickey brought with him from Tennessee. You had split backs—a fullback and tailback behind the tackles. They call it a 'pro backfield.' You take the snap and put the ball in the fullback's belly and ride him for a step, and you read the man outside the tackle. They all block down. If the defender goes up field, you let the fullback have it. If the defender goes to tackle the fullback, you pull the ball out and you either keep it or you pitch it to the outside back on the line of scrimmage. So it was an option. I was not a very good option runner.

"I was 6'3", 205 pounds, could run a 5-flat forty, but I could step up and throw the ball and sprint out and head quick feet. But I was no Tommie Frazier. You need a running back playing quarterback for that offense. It's the kind of offense Nebraska plays. That's what Doug Dickey preferred.

"After running the ball most of the time, we trailed in the game 17-10.

Finally, I got permission to pass, and I hit Carlos on a throwback post. He split the defenders and ran it in for a 48-yard touchdown.

"Then we got it back, and I got hit and fumbled at our 35, so I'm in the jar. I was over on the sideline really down. And they drove down to ice the game, had a fourth and four and on the four, and Jack Youngblood ripped through their whole offensive line, smashed the quarterback and the running back at the same time, caused a fumble, and recovered it on our five."

Jack Youngblood: "The goal line stand won it for us. I can remember them driving down the field. They had two good running backs, and they were just trying to pound the ball down the field and were going to win the game. We just bowed our necks and they fumbled, and somehow I just managed to get my hands on the football—somehow."

John Reaves then brought Florida from behind in the fourth quarter to put the Gators ahead 24-17. It was the highlight of a very unhappy season for most of the players.

John Reaves: "We then went ninety-five yards in two plays. I threw two passes to Carlos, the same pattern on both plays. It was a throwback post.

"In his sophomore year Carlos caught eighty-eight passes in ten games. After our sophomore year, he ran on the track team and hurt his knee. They couldn't find out what it was. They thought it was gout, didn't know what the heck it was.

"He couldn't run on it. It was swollen up, and he was in serious pain. In his junior year he didn't practice during the week but played in the games, and he caught forty-four passes. On two legs he caught eighty-eight passes. On one leg he caught forty-four. Also, in 1970, as I said, we didn't work much on the passing game, and that hurt Willie more than it hurt Carlos.

"We ended up beating Georgia 24-17, a very good win considering the thrashing the previous weeks."

In the Kentucky game, John Reaves threw for three touchdowns, including a 70-yarder to Willie Jackson with only 29 seconds remaining in the half. It was an important play in a 24-13 comeback victory.

Willie Jackson: "I caught a couple of passes in that game. On the touchdown run, I made a lot of little moves, a move there, and a couple of missed tackles to gain a few more yards and score. It was in the paper. They showed how I ran, so it was memorable because they made such a big deal out of it: John was back, and we were back on the winning track—and I was one of the bright spots that helped make that happen."

Fred Abbott: "The Georgia game was like a fistfight. All the Georgia games blend together. You just go toe to toe. You were going to get hit from the first play to the last play, and everyone out there was trying to knock you out, and you were doing the same thing to them."

The final game was against the University of Miami. With a 7-3 record, if Florida won, there was a strong possiblity of a bid to the Liberty or Bluebonnet Bowl.

But the ball took some funny bounces, and Florida lost 14-13.

Fred Abbott: "They told us that the Miami game would determine whether we went to a bowl game or stayed home. Of course, we weren't in contention for a major bowl. You're talking something like the Bluebonnet Bowl. Before the game somebody asked me what I thought, and I was trying to think of a diplomatic way to say that if we weren't going to a major bowl, it's not worth missing Christmas and not being with your family. So what I said to a reporter was, 'Well, if you go to a bowl game, Santa Claus doesn't know where you live.' Dickey was not happy about that. So much for my one shot at diplomacy.

"We lost that day, and a couple weeks later I went to a Christmas party in Jacksonville, and I met one of the Miami players, a guy I had played across from, and we sat and talked, and he said, 'You guys ran up and down the field all day long, but couldn't score. You were supposed to win and you didn't.' I said, 'That's exactly the way I remember it.'

"But I'm going to tell you about the end of that game. I remember seeing John throw a pass to Tommy [Durrance], and I remember seeing Tommy drop it, and Tommy generally was a pretty damn good receiver. It wasn't a hard pass. It wasn't a long pass. Here's a guy who's normally sure-handed and one of the most dependable offensive players when I was there, and he just drops the ball, a catch he would make 99 times out of a hundred.

"Then there's a chip shot field goal right at the end. My roommate, Jim Getzen, held the state high school record at Florida for the longest field goal for many, many years, if not decades. He kicked a 52-yarder for Newberry High School, about 13 miles west of Gainesville, a school even smaller than mine.

"He and I were bosom buddies because we were probably the two biggest rubes on the team. He came out for a chip shot. The ball must have been on the fourteen yard line. We were at home, the last game of the season. He missed it. Time runs out. The game is over. We lose a game we were supposed to win. We don't go to a bowl game.

"Here come these little kids, eight, nine, ten years old, running out onto the field. They're big fans, win, lose, or draw. At that time you could jump over the fence and run onto the field. They would come out and ask for your wristband or chin strap. I was walking off with Tommy Durrance and Jim Getzen, and this kid came running up to Getzen. I thought, This will be good. The kid will cheer him up, ask Jim for his chin strap. I was an arms-length away. The kid approached him and said, 'Number ten. You suck!' And he ran away.

"I thought, Man, what a cold-blooded kid. I thought, Man, this is a hard world we live in.' We laugh about that story, but I don't think Getzen ever kicked again. That was pretty much his career, which was sad. The next year another came in and did most of the kicking. I don't think Dickey ever forgave him.

"Dickey didn't say anything after the game. He was not much of a speaker. I don't think there was anything to be said. People were not excited about going to a lower bowl. That was the general sentiment, but I don't know anyone who was not going to give their best at Florida Field.

"But again, the way we felt about Dickey didn't help things. Juxtapose how we felt about him compared to how we felt about Coach Ellenson, where people would run through brick walls for him. It's one of those intangibles. I don't think it rises to the level of consciousness. For some people it may have, but it damn sure didn't help, that's for sure. You've got enough adversity out there on the field where you don't need it on the sideline."

Jack Youngblood: "I wasn't happy with the season. I wasn't happy losing that game to Miami. It was the last football game I was going to play in, with us not having the opportunity to play in a bowl game. I wasn't a happy camper either."

John Reaves: "Coach Dickey came in before the Miami game and announced, 'If we win this game, we're going to the Liberty Bowl.' Our record was 7 and 3. I swear some of the seniors didn't want to win that game, because they didn't want to play one more game under Coach Dickey. They hated him. There were only five or six bowls back then. It would have been huge, going to the Liberty Bowl to play the Colorado Buffalos, but no bowl.

"Personally, I was extremely disappointed that we weren't going. First of all, I hate to lose. I didn't want to lose to Miami. And on top of that, it cost us a bowl game. Heck yes I wanted to go. I wanted to play."

At the end of the 1970 season Jack Youngblood was honored when he was voted onto the college All-American team. He flew to Los Angeles, where he appeared on the Bob Hope show along with the other honorees, Jim Plunkett, Dan Dierdorf, and Jack Ham.

He was drafted in the first round by the Los Angeles Rams, and after a stellar career was voted into the Pro Football Hall of Fame. Today he is an executive with the Arena Football League.

Jack Youngblood: "I was totally surprised that I was chosen first team All-American. I was very honored to be included. The experience of going out to L.A. and meeting all those players was incredible. What great guys! That was a heck of a class. And if was country come to town for me, because the furthest west I had ever been was Jackson, Mississippi. I hadn't been to any big cities, and I can remember flying into L.A. on that airplane and looking down, and you see city for forty-five minutes before you land. I thought, My God, this is huge! I wonder if someone is going to be there and pick me up and take me where I'm supposed to go? We landed, and they had made arrangements, of course. It was quite an eye-opener, being on television for the first time with all those players and being introduced in front of the cameras. I met Bob Hope a few minutes before the show. He was a very personable guy. It was a total fantasy type situation.

"I was asked to come down to the *Gainesville Sun* on draft day so they could do a piece on the draft. My information was that I would go around the fifth or sixth round. But I had played in the Senior Bowl in Mobile, and I was named defensive player of the game, and I'm watching Jim Plunkett go, and Dan Pastorini went, and I'm watching all those players you had read about, and the phone rings, and someone comes on and says, 'Jack, it's coach Prothro of the Los Angeles Rams calling.' It was a coach from the Rams. I had no clue he was. I didn't know who the Rams coaches were. I wondered, What is he calling me for? Who is this guy? I had no clue, really.

"Pro football literally had been something that had been a fantasy on television. Going on and having an opportunity to play at the next [professional] level was a fantasy. I literally believe God has a plan for you, but if you don't listen hard sometimes, you don't understand what the plan is. I wasn't listening very hard. I had no clue I was going to have that opportunity. So you make plans to carry on with your life. I took a job my senior year to be a banker. I was going to Atlanta to become a banker.

"Prothro said, 'Youngblood, we're thinking about drafting you.'

"I said, 'Okay, thank you coach. That is awfully kind of you.' What do you say? I didn't even know who I was talking to. The thought ran through my mind that one of the guys back at the dorm was messing with me.

"And I hung up the phone, and sure enough, over the teletype came the announcement, 'The Los Angeles Rams, with the twentieth pick, has chosen Jack Youngblood, defensive end, the University of Florida.' Seeing it in print was astonishing! Absolutely astonishing.

"I didn't have an agent. I had a friend who was a lawyer represent me, but essentially the Rams said, 'We'll offer you this much,' and you said, 'Fine.' I had a three-year contract for $21,000, $23,000, and $25,000. In fact, I had the offer to go to the Bank of America for exactly the same money.

"My choice was easy. Yeah. My heart's desire was to keep playing, though when I realized where I was going, I figured it would be a short-lived deal. Where are you going to find a place to play with the fearsome foursome, including Merlin Olsen, Deacon Jones, Lamar Lundy and Rosie Grier? You think to yourself, Do I have a chance of even having the opportunity to play?

"I joined them, and Deacon and Merlin took me under their wing and taught me how to play the game at that level. I learned how to play consistently, how to play on every snap. You have to play every snap like it is the only snap of the game. The game could hinge on what you do on that particular play.

"I played pro ball until 1984. I played in Super Bowl XIV. The Pittsburgh Steelers had won two already. We had been close so many times. Having the opportunity to finally get there was a tremendous experience. And we were ahead at the end of the third period, and with six minutes left in the game, John Stallworth made a tremendous catch for a touchdown to beat us.

"When I retired in '84 it was one of the most difficult decisions I ever had to make. It would be like telling a doctor after he got to the highest level of surgery that he could not do this any more after the end of the year. It's a tough decision.

"But you have to evaluate yourself each year, and if you no longer can play to your expectations, it's time to step down. I could have played three more years as a specialist. In fact, John Robinson, the Rams' head coach, asked me if I would go in and rush the passer on second and long, third and long.

"But I was used to going in at the coin toss and playing until the final gun, and that was the only way I knew how to play. I can't sit on the sidelines. I told them, 'You have to respect that in me.'

"I moved to the front office and started doing television and radio. I did that for five years, and then I moved to the administrative side of the World League up in Sacramento. After that, I came down to Florida and ran the arena franchise in Orlando. I moved to the league level, and I am working out of Chicago with the Arena Football League.

"We're growing, and we're growing up. We're trying to be the developmental aspect of the NFL. And the other satisfaction I got was being elected into the Pro Football Hall of Fame.

"You'll never find anything as satisfying as competing. Very few people can play at the elite level. Like I said before, I firmly believe God has a plan for you. You have to try and understand what that plan is and stay within those boundaries. It is amazing."

thirty-five

The Florida Flop

The 1971 season began with a 12-6 loss to Duke, a two-touchdown underdog. John Reaves was intercepted three times. Duke wasn't very good, but kicked four field goals to win.

John Reaves: "We had had a lot of injuries prior to that game. Tommy [Durrance] was hurt in preseason practice. Carlos [Alvarez] was hardly practicing at all. His injury never healed, and he hurt the other knee too. [Andy] Cheney had hurt his knee against Miami the year before. So in 1971 our wideouts were all sophomores, Joel Parker, Hollis Boardman, Willie Jackson. Really, our whole team was sophomores—and me and Fred Abbott. Our starting running back was Lenny Lucas, a true sophomore.

"Our defense wasn't very good at all. We were tenth in the league out of ten teams. So we opened up and lost to Duke. It was horrible."

Fred Abbott: "I don't know, it was one of those things like you wake up and you're in a bad dream. It was a game we were supposed to win. One thing: Carlos had gotten worse. He wasn't practicing at all and just playing in the games, and that's hard. Number two, I'm not sure the offensive line had gotten much better. They were still looking for answers that hadn't arrived. I don't think the average football fan appreciates how important the offensive line is. What I really remember was after the game thinking, It's over. What happened? How could this happen?"

A 13-10 loss to Mississippi State followed. Florida had six turnovers, four interceptions, two which bounced off the shoulder pads of receivers, and two lost fumbles.

John Reaves: "It was bad. I remember the score was 10-10, and Mississippi State missed the field goal, but we jumped offsides. So they got another shot at five yards closer, and he made it. That's how they beat us. And we had a ton of dropped balls. I don't want to defend myself, but the young guys were dropping balls in addition to our not working on our passing game like we needed to.

"Coach Dickey was not a friendly guy. You never talked to Coach Dickey. But my position coach, Jimmy Dunn, was very friendly, a good guy, and Lindy Infante was our running back coach, a good man. I was okay with the situation. I was hanging in there, trying to do the best we could."

It was the first time since 1947 that Florida had lost its first two games. In those two games John Reaves had thrown seven interceptions. Willie Jackson, now his prime receiver with Carlos Alvarez out, thought he knew why.

Willie Jackson: "When Carlos got hurt, and it changed our offense. I don't know why, but they didn't throw to me until it was third and long, and the defense knew it was coming to me and they would have double coverage on me. And John would try to force the ball in there. It just didn't work."

Florida's nemesis, Alabama, was next, and once again the Gators took a pounding, this time by 38-0. Bama ran for 363 yards, as Johnny Musso ran for 97 yards in 21 carries and scored four touchdowns.

John Reaves: "They clobbered us again. It was awful, a terrible thing. Alabama was fighting for the national championship running that wishbone. They were an incredible team.

"Chan Gailey played later in the game. The new head coach at Georgia Tech was my backup. He threw two interceptions. Because after the game they tried to give me credit for his interceptions as well as mine. I said, 'Thank you very much. Those weren't all mine.'"

Fred Abbott, who recovered sufficiently from a concussion to remember the details of the 38-0 rout by Alabama, had to try to stop Bama's All-American back Johnny Musso.

Fred Abbott: "That sucker was like a runaway train. But Johnny had some great people playing with him, not the least of which was John Hannah. That was like someone saying, 'Here, catch this refrigerator' and on the other side of it is a jet rocket. You had to first catch the refrigerator and then find out where the rocket was. I remember them running the sweep from right to left, to the right, to the left, and the other thing was that Alabama had depth. You'd go two or three series, and all of a sudden here comes somebody who's clean and new, not dirty, winded or tired. They had phenomenal talent, two-deep at most positions."

Tennessee, the twelfth-ranked team in the country, was next.

John Reaves: "Governor Ruben Askew gave us a pre-game pep talk. He came in to pump us up. I don't remember what he said, but I recall that he and Dickey looked a lot alike. They could have been brothers.

"We could have won it. We could have been sitting 3 and 1, but we lost three close ones."

Florida kept Tennessee at bay for the first half. It was 13-13 at halftime. Then the Vols' Phil Pierce threw a touchdown to Stan Trott to win the game 20-13. It was Florida's fourth loss in a row.

Fred Abbott: "I just remember thinking that we could have won that game. But we must have been snake-bit because we lost it. At that point you start to second-guess everything and everybody. After hearing from the press and the fans, it was like getting hit in the head with a 2-by-4 and waking up in hell.

"Football is such an intense physical, adverse experience that the only positive reinforcement is winning. Not the only, but the main. You've been through two-a-days, you're getting hurt and dinged, and you go through a lot of excruciating physical pain, and your primary purpose is to win. And when you don't, there's not much that's fun about it."

The team travelled to Baton Rouge to meet LSU. The Gators lost their fifth straight, a 48-7 mauling by the Tigers.

John Reaves: "We were struggling, down in the dumps. We got clobbered by Bert Jones and company. It was awful."

Fred Abbott: "I would say that Baton Rouge was the toughest place that I played on the road. There are various theories why that is. One is that they only play night games, and the story I heard is that the fans show up in the morning and they start drinking, and by the time you get there, they are roaring drunk. And they would throw things at you like whiskey bottles.

"And the truth was, they had a heck of a football team. That year Bert Jones whupped it on us pretty bad. At that point we were questioning ourselves in regard to what was happening and why we weren't winning. Coach Dickey and his staff were feeling the pressure. You could tell by looking at their faces. They weren't any more used to losing than we were. All the guys in my class came from a 9-1-1 team. Everybody was struggling, and you didn't have to be a rocket scientist to know that the reason they brought Dickey to Florida was to win. And when he didn't, there were no happy campers anywhere."

The next game was against Florida State. The Seminoles were 5-0, the Gators 0-5. FSU was heavily favored. The game was played in Gainesville, and in this game Florida provided the high-water mark of the season when it broke its losing streak with a 17-15 win.

Fred Abbott: "That was probably the most intense, emotional experience I ever had in a football uniform. Everybody looked at everybody else on the team and said, 'There are a lot of reasons why we're 0 and 5, but we're not gonna be 0 and 6. It was nothing but people believing in each other. We didn't have anything to lose and had everything to gain. Our backs were against the wall. That was the game in which Jimmy Barr made an incredible play. He intercepted a fumble in midair and ran it back [26 yards] for a touchdown. I can remember the play like it was yesterday.

"Jimmy Barr was one of six quarterbacks that were signed in my class who once they had their 'come to prayer meeting' he was converted to a defensive back. Jimmy was an incredible athlete, a wonderfully nice guy, a good student, and he got hurt later in a non-football accident and it ended his career.

"Watching Jimmy was like watching a deer in a forest. He just reacted instinctively. He was in the right place, picked the ball off, and he was gone. And it was like a nuclear bomb was dropped on the Seminoles. It's one thing to fumble. It's another to have it picked off in mid-air. It's yet another thing to have the other team score."

Florida State closed to 14-7, but kicker Richard Franco kicked a 42-yard field goal to make it 17-7.

With three minutes left in the game FSU quarterback Gary Huff threw a six-yard touchdown pass. When they made the two-point conversion, the score stood Florida 17, FSU 15. When FSU regained control of the ball, everything was on the line. When Florida held, the Gators had their first win of the season.

Fred Abbott: "I don't think it gets any more intense than that. And FSU was every bit determined as us, because at that point they had lost eight or nine in a row to Florida. They had never beaten us, and we knew we just weren't supposed to lose. It was one of the games where unless you willed it, it wasn't going to happen. As a rivalry things never got more intense. That was it, that was all it was: if you didn't give it all you had, you weren't supposed to be there."

John Reaves: "It was good to get a win on the books, after losing three close ones. Finally, we won a close one."

Carlos Alvarez, out most of the season with arthritic knees, returned for the Homecoming game against the University of Maryland. On the opening drive John Reaves hit Carlos three times.

John Reaves: "He finally got enough strength in his legs to be able to help us. It was wonderful to have him back. And Tommy Durrance also returned. He had been hurt before the opener. He had dislocated his elbow in a goal-line scrimmage the week before the opener, and he scored [from the 7] at the end of that first drive."

When Reaves hit Tom Durrance with a 7-yard touchdown pass, Florida had a 27-23 lead. Maryland then marched down to the Gators' one-yard line, where the defense valiantly held.

John Reaves: "Can you believe that? That game was a seesaw battle, back and forth. We'd score, they'd score. We'd score, they'd score. They were a running team, three yards and eat up the clock, but we were chucking away, throwing the ball pretty good. We finally went ahead [27-23], but there was plenty of time left for them to score.

"We kicked off, and they went back to the same old plan—three yards here, four yards there, moving down the field. Then on the one they fumbled, and we win the game."

Fred Abbott: "It proves there is a God."

All-Americans Pat Sullivan and Terry Beasley were next, and again Auburn won big, by 40-7.

John Reaves: "Oh, they clobbered us again. How humiliating! Coach Dickey pulled me out in the middle of the game, but it was just as well.

"We should have pulled Coach Dickey, because before the game he came into the locker room and said, 'John, we're kicking off. What do you think about an on-side kick to start the game?' I said, 'I don't know.' He went ahead and did it anyway, and they recovered, and they stormed right down the field and scored. So we should have pulled Coach Dickey.

"Once again our sophomores dropped a lot of passes. We had that happen all year. It was inexperience and lack of work on the passing game. If you're going to be good at something, you have to work on it, and we didn't have the linemen to run that power running game."

Willie Jackson believed that he knew part of the problem that Florida was having: there weren't enough black athletes on the team. In addition to him and Leonard George, Florida had recruited two more in 1970 including halfbacks Lenny Lucas and Vince Kendrick. Jackson saw that other colleges were recruiting large numbers of black players. He felt that for Florida to be competitive, the Gators would have to do the same.

Willie Jackson: "We lost to Alabama [38-0], Tennessee [20-13] and LSU [48-7], all established teams who had players. We had lost too many players to graduation.

"We beat FSU, but we had expected to do that. But we had to struggle to beat them [17-15], and we struggled to beat Maryland [27-23] at Homecoming. We were going to have to make a good effort to recruit great [black] players at the University of Florida so we could compete. The good-old-boy thing, where you played because your dad had played, wasn't going to work any more. Alabama had Ozzie Newsome, a great tight end and other [black] players. Tennessee had lots of them. Dickey had recruited a lot of black players before he left there, and when he got here we told Coach Dickey he needed more black players at Florida.

"I remember when I was recruited, one of the stipulations was that Florida would double the number of black players each year. So the first year there was Leonard and I, and the second year we added two black running backs, Vince Kendrick out of Miami and Leonard Lucas out of Daytona. That really added to our attack. From there Florida kept adding blacks to the team, players like Nat Moore, and we got some defensive backs from around Gainesville, and after we got all these black players, that's when we really started to make an impact in the league."

Florida then went to Athens, Georgia, and were trampled 49-7, as the undefeated Bulldogs gained 288 yards on the ground. Before the game was over, Dickey again took a battered John Reaves out. His receivers had dropped at least eight catchable balls.

Willie Jackson: "I'm sure John was discouraged. We were losing to one of our biggest rivals. All of a sudden, he gets jerked out, and at the time I'm sure he thought, I'm the best you've got, and you're taking me out? What's the deal?' We can't see it all. We don't know what's going on, and I'm sure the coaching staff saw something we didn't see. He may have been mentally not into the game or a little jittery. He might not have been as prepared as he was capable of playing.

"The game was out of reach, and they wanted someone else to come in and play, to get some game experience."

Florida rebounded against Kentucky. John Reaves starred, throwing 18-25 for three touchdowns and scoring one himself in a 35-24 victory.

John Reaves: "It hit Carlos with a [56-yard] touchdown to ice the game. We hit the bomb on them. Carlos came over and said, 'I think we can beat them deep.' We talked Coach Dickey into letting us throw a deep ball, and he got behind them and caught it for six. It was a little bit of the old glory. Tommy [Durrance] also had a good game." [Durrance gained 99 yards on the ground and also caught five passes for 63 yards and a touchdown.]

Fred Abbott: "Tommy was nothing flashy, but he was tough as nails. Tommy, to me, was the most dependable ball carrier I saw while I was at Florida. He wasn't a Johnny Musso, but I would take him. From the beginning of the game to the end, I don't care how many times he got hit or how hard he got him, he was always back in there. We had some other incredible running backs in our freshman class including a guy named Harvin Clark, who once scored eight touchdowns in one high school game. Harvin got moved to defensive back. Carlos had been a tailback in high school, and he was moved to receiver. There were some incredible talents who came in there, and when it was all over, Tommy Durrance was the guy who was there play-in and play-out. I have seen Tommy get hit by six guys, knocked upside down, laying on his head, look like a totem pole that was inverted, and he'd get up and go back to the huddle and ran just as hard the next play. He was unreal. He was phenomenal."

After the game John Reaves went to the press to dispel reports that there was a rift between him and Coach Dickey.

John Reaves: "Coach Dickey had asked me to do that. I was being politically correct."

The final game was against the University of Miami, a game that would be remembered forever. The highlight came when John Reaves was 13 yards shy of beating Jim Plunkett's NCAA record for passing yardage in a career. Miami had the ball as time was running out. Florida, which was ahead 45-8, needed to get the ball back for Reaves to get his record. What to do?

When Miami ran a play, every Florida player dropped to the ground, allowing Miami to score. Miami kicked off, Florida got the ball back, Reaves completed several passes, and he got his record. But there were ramifications. Coach Dickey was derided nationally for the play. And an embarrassed University of Miami never forgave Dickey and Florida for pulling a stunt like that. At the end of the game Miami Coach Fran Curci refused to shake Coach Dickey's hand.

John Reaves: "Let me tell you what happened. Harvin Clark was the senior co-captain. Harvin was the starting corner, a good football player. We were ahead 38-8, and we stopped them with about five or six minutes left in the game, and they punted. Harvin returned that punt 67 yards for a touchdown. It was a great run. I remember him hurdling some guys.

"Harvin ran over to the sidelines right after he scored, and he said, 'Hey, I'm sorry.' I said, 'That was a great run. Are you kidding me? Forget about it. We'll get back in there.'

"On the sideline they were reporting how many yards short I was of breaking the NCAA career passing record. Somebody in the box told the coaches I needed eight more yards to break the record.

"All of a sudden, Miami mounted their only drive of the night. They had players. They had Chuck Foreman, Tom Sullivan, Burgess Owens, and Michael Barnes. They were running the wish-bone, getting three, four, five yards a pop, and pretty soon, the clock was eaten up. It was down to only a few minutes, and Harvin started to get nervous.

"Harvin began running over to Coach Dickey between plays. He said, 'Coach, let them score. John isn't going to have time to break the record.' Dickey said, 'No, we're not doing that.'

"Now our fans were up in the Orange Bowl, chanting real loud, 'Let them score. Let them score.' I was just taking it all in. I wasn't saying anything.

"Harvin ran back over again. 'Coach, let's let them score.' 'No.' Harvin came over a third time, 'Coach, we gotta do something.' There wasn't much time left. I don't know how much. He said, 'All right, go ahead.'

"Harvin ran back into the huddle and told the defense, 'All right, this next play we're gonna let them score.'

"They said, 'How are we going to do it?'

"Well, on the snap everybody fell on the ground. And the runner ran it in.

"So we got the ball back, and I hit a pass to Carlos, and we set the record. And after the game we all ran down and jumped into the pond there at the end of the stadium.

"Fran Curci was the Miami coach, and he's still whining about that. Just joking. I see him around town here in Tampa and we kind of joke about it.

"It was never intended to humiliate or embarrass Miami. We didn't know what we were doing. It just happened. It was one of those things.

"I was glad to have broken the record, but I didn't know whether I was pleased or not. I didn't think there would be consequences, didn't know that there'd be discussion of whether I deserved it or not because of the way it happened. Afterwards, of course, Curci complained about it, and Jim Plunkett, whose record I broke, said he didn't think it should count.

"They didn't have a lot of commentators back then. They didn't have ESPN. But I remember hearing Joe Garagiola say he didn't think the record should count.

"But it was nice of my teammates to do something like that for me. Let me tell you about those teammates. This season I was inducted into the Florida/Georgia Hall of Fame. I went up to Jacksonville to a banquet. Nine of my freshman brothers showed up. Andy Cheney, Carlos, Durrance, Harvin, Richard Kensler, Bruce Cutright, Gene Conrad, Fred Abbott, and David Peete all came to the induction ceremony. That's what it's all about."

Fred Abbott: "Then after the gun sounded, there was a grand finale to the game: they had a big tank at the end of the Orange Bowl where they kept flipper when the Dolphins played there, and we all went and jumped into the tank. We did it just to celebrate a frustrating year. Just the idea that all the craziness was over. It was just we were glad the season was over. Don't forget this season was somewhere between Catch-22 and One Flew Over the Cuckoo's Nest. There is not much difference between playing football and being a tail-gunner on a B-52 bomber. It makes about as much sense."

After the 1971 season John Reaves played in the East-West Shrine game and the Senior Bowl. He started eight games his rookie year with the Philadelphia Eagles, but for much of the remainder of a pro career that ended in 1987, he was a backup. Reaves entered coaching, but when he found the ritual of getting hired and getting fired too tough on his family, he decided to stick to real estate and stay home in Tampa.

thirty-six

Bowden to McGriff

In 1972, for the first time freshmen were allowed to play on the varsity. There was another change that occurred in 1972: Doug Dickey recruited twelve of the finest black athletes in the state of Florida, a declaration that the days of segregation in southern college football was over. Among the twelve were Don Gaffney, a talented option quarterback, a linebacker named Sammy Green, and a defensive end named Preston Kendrick, the brother of halfback Vince Kendrick, who had come to Florida the year before.

According to Fred Abbott, the black players fit in smoothly.

Fred Abbott: "Everybody was there to compete, and there were some phenomenal talents there, and I don't know of anybody having any problems. In '72 I was a redshirt senior. I was captain of the team. I would have known if there were problems.

"In 1972 drugs were a far bigger problem in Gainesville than racism. I don't know of any player who was a regular drug user, but I know the coaches were concerned about it. I'm such a redneck that where I came from, being stoned meant you were drunk. It had a different meaning in Gainesville.

"I'm telling you that I didn't see racism as a problem. Most players who are competitors don't care whether you are green or red or purple."

Before the 1972 season defensive coordinator Doug Knotts asked Fred Abbott if he would switch from offensive guard to middle linebacker. Knotts told Doug Dickey what he wanted to do.

Fred Abbott: "Dickey said, 'We'll give him four days in spring practice. If he establishes himself, he can play linebacker. If not, he's going back to the offensive line.'"

Abbott did fine, and for the entire 1972 season he starred as linebacker, the first in a long string of outstanding linebackers developed by Dickey and Knotts. At the end of the year Abbott was named to the All-American team.

Also on the roster was a short, but confident and cocky wide receiver by the name of Lee McGriff. At 5'9", 145 pounds, McGriff was considered too small to merit a college scholarship. Even Coach Dickey told him to his face that he was too small. But McGriff, who summered in Gainesville, had worked out with John Reaves and Carlos Alvarez, and he was convinced he was good enough to play for any college program. McGriff's father, a track star at Florida, was a friend of athletic director Ray Graves, and Graves told McGriff that if he came to Florida as a walk-on, he would get special consideration. McGriff would not only go on to become one of the finest receivers in Florida history, but he would play in the pros and later coach at Florida.

Lee McGriff: "By the time I got to high school, I was stepped in the lore of the University of Florida. My own father had been captain of the track team. Uncles galore went to Florida. For years Florida football games were part of my youth. Though my mother moved us to Tampa, I got to see my father quite a bit, and we'd go to football games. So I had a passion for the University of Florida. My first hero was Larry Libertore, then Larry Dupree, Richard Trapp, Jack Card, a 150-pound linebacker who I loved. Loved him. Bobby Downs was a defensive back. I knew the players from Tommy Shannon to unknown guys like Marquis Baeszler, and Steven and Mark Ely. Bruce Ely was one of my early friends through junior high school, and he had two brothers playing at Florida, and that was just terrific.

"Then in high school my close friends were Jimbo Kynes, whose father was Jimmy Kynes, and he introduced me to Bubba Wertha and Bobby Gruetzmacher, a defensive back during the Golden Era. They were all buddies and still are.

"My heroes were Florida players. They weren't New York Giants or Chicago Bears or Washington Redskins. They were Gators.

"Even though I led the area in receptions, I did not lure much college attention because of my size. I was 5'9", 145 pounds at the end of my senior year. And I could run a 4.5 forty. I could run good. I had interest. I almost got a scholarship at Miami, almost got one at Auburn, and a couple of small colleges who I wasn't interested in. I thought I had a scholarship offer out of high school from the University of Richmond. I was told I would be contacted in a week and that he would need a decision, but he never called me back. I don't know if I would have taken it, but college is expensive, and I was considering it.

"But there is no question my heart was attached to Florida football. I ended up as a walk-on at Florida.

"I arrived in Gainesville in the fall of '71 as a freshman. It was the last year of freshman ball. Miami had rejected me, and Auburn had rejected me, but Ray Graves' staff knew me well and knew my dad very well, and if Ray Graves had remained the head coach at Florida, he very likely would have offered me a scholarship.

"But in 1970 Coach Dickey came in. The twist is that Doug Dickey grew up in Gainesville, went to P.K. Young High School, and my dad was the head football coach and athletic director when Doug was there. So when the transition came, my dad talked to Coach Dickey. He said, 'Let me tell you about my son.' He said, 'Let me talk to Lee. Let me come over.'

"I went to see my dad over the Christmas holidays my senior year. Coach Dickey said, 'I'll come by, and let's talk.' I was very excited. Coach Dickey sat in my dad's living room and said, 'Lee, I heard a lot about you, but I see that you're just not big enough to play at the University of Florida. It looks like you need to mature a little bit. Maybe you ought to try junior college, and then we'll talk about it.'

"So he shot me right in the heart.

"I'll never forget the look on my dad's face, because he had no idea that was coming. So Ray Graves, who was still the athletic director, called me up and said, 'Why don't you come to the Orange and Blue game, and let me talk to you.'

"After the game was over Ray Graves and I sat in the stands, and he said, 'Listen, I know the kind of athlete you are, and this is where you belong. I know you don't have a scholarship. You need to come and walk on. I'll talk to Coach Dickey.'

"That's when I made up my mind to come to Florida, not that I wouldn't have arrived at that at some point and paid my way, but at least I was invited. So that fall I came to Florida, and my roommate was Jimbo Kynes, which was nice. They roomed me in Yan Hall.

"There was then, as there is now, such a thing as a 'preferred walk-on.' I was invited. And from that first day, I was on a mission. I was excited, determined, never sure what I was up against but always ready to take on the worst.

"Florida had signed two Parade All-Americans that freshman class, Ward

Eastman from Peoria, Illinois, and Rick Roselle from St. Pete Dixie Holland. They were 6'2" and 6'4", and I beat them out. Rick was a good athlete, but sometimes he didn't like to practice very much. He was a little lackadaisical.

"Our freshman receivers coach was Fred Goldsmith, who later became the head coach at Duke and other places. Fred saw how well I was doing from the first day.

"I remember about a week and a half into it, there was a day in practice when Fred Goldsmith had had it with Rick Roselle. He tried to insult him as badly as he could by saying, 'If you make one more mistake like that, I will take that guy—and he pointed to me—'and I'll put him in front of you.'

"And within minutes Roselle did it again, and Goldsmith put me in front of him on the depth chart, and I never let go, and I ended up leading the freshman team in receiving.

"Our biggest game that year was against the University of Georgia freshmen, and I caught ten passes for 170 yards and three touchdowns. David Bowden was throwing the passes. David was a star. After that game, Coach Dickey came to the locker room—and these are the things you never forget—and he found me in the shower, and he said, 'This spring, you get a scholarship.'

"So it was a wonderful year. I ended up leading the freshman team in receiving. I really did catch a lot of balls and score a lot of touchdowns.

"And David and I developed a close relationship from the beginning. I loved David Bowden. He was good. If he had played under Steve Spurrier or in a different style offense, his name would still be in the record books."

The opener in 1972 was against SMU. With John Reaves gone to the pros, Chan Gailey started at quarterback. SMU led 21-0, when early in the third quarter Dickey replaced Gailey with David Bowden, who as a Florida freshman broke all the passing records of Steve Spurrier and John Reaves. Bowden, who finished the game 15–28 for 193 yards and two touchdowns, could only close the gap to 21-14. Among those glad to see Bowden get an opportunity to play was Lee McGriff, the backup to Willie Jackson, and Bowden's roommate.

Lee McGriff: "When the season began, I was Willie Jackson's backup. The coaches said to me, 'You're doing a wonderful job pushing Willie Jackson to make him a better player.' I wanted to strangle them, because I wasn't interested in making Willie Jackson a better player. I was trying to figure out how to beat him out. So I spelled Willie whenever they wanted me to. And the same time I tried to remind myself from whence I came, that I was back in Tampa Stadium on scholarship in a Gator uniform. That wasn't altogether a bad experience.

"From the time I was a freshmen, I would have bet that Chan would have ended up a successful coach, because of the kind of person he was, the way he went about his business. He was dedicated, hard working, respectful, intelligent, loved what he was doing, was responsible, had all those qualities.

"I certainly wanted Chan to succeed, but I was rooting for my battery-mate, my next-door neighbor, David Bowden, who played a significant role in the good things that happened to me since I got to Florida. I loved it that David finally got his chance."

David Bowden: "I had loved Steve Spurrier from the time I was a kid, and also Ray Graves' whole outlook on the game. In '69 the Gators had John Reaves and Carlos Alvarez, and they were lighting up the field under Coach Graves. My beloved Gators. In high school we were doing the same thing. Throwing the ball—just the openness of it.

"My senior year I got scholarship offers from all the Southeastern Conference schools, and I got one from Nebraska.

"I got a handwritten letter from West Virginia from the head coach there, Bobby Bowden, who wrote, 'David, I'm sure we're related. Ask your daddy if he's kin to any of the following:' And on the back he had traced out the family tree, and that's when I found out I was kin to Bobby Bowden. So I've loved Bobby Bowden ever since, but nobody wanted to go to West Virginia.

"I went on recruiting trips to Duke and South Carolina. Paul Dietzel was the football coach at South Carolina and Bobby Richardson was the baseball coach. I thought it was unbelievable that he was the coach. My whole childhood was spent on Saturdays watching [the New York Yankees'] Moose Skowron, Bobby Richardson, Tony Kubek and Clete Boyer. If I hadn't gone to Florida, I would have gone to South Carolina. Playing baseball for Bobby Richardson—think about it.

"But I already was a die-hard orange and blue. I remember sitting in church on Sundays and being so upset because the preacher would go past twelve o'clock. The Florida football highlights started at 12:30, and I wanted to see Tommy Shannon and hear Coach Graves talk to Dick Stratton. And then, of course, when Spurrier came to play, I was locked down. I had clippings of Steve Spurrier all over my walls. I would have been 10 years old when Spurrier began playing, and I fell into it. I thought he had a neat name.

"When I was a sophomore, Bubba McGowan and Rabbit Smith walked into my locker in Tampa and handed me a card that said, 'The Florida Gators are watching you, buddy.' I was stoked from then on. I figured that college would just be an extension of my high school career, an extenuation of joy. I figured that once I got to the University of Florida, we'd be winging it all over the field.

"Ray Graves left after '69, and Doug Dickey took over as head coach. Coach Dickey was a very good recruiter. He has a very direct way of speaking. He was persistent. When he arrived at your house, he gave a very lordly persona, which was pretty impressive. And he had a straightforward demeanor, which you've got to give him credit for.

"I arrived on campus in the fall of '71. I played on the last freshman team. Doug Dickey was the varsity coach, but the freshman team was a separate entity. We were more like the tackling dummies in practice. And we played about six freshmen games.

"My freshman year Don Deal was the coach, who would just throw it. We were throwing the ball like crazy. Coach Deal utilized our passing plays a lot more than Coach Dickey would. We broke all the freshman passing records of Spurrier and Reaves. It was so far, so good.

"The other thing that happened in 1970 was that Florida agreed to accept black players. My sophomore year of high school, everything was still segregated. By junior and senior years, we had black players. Have you seen '*Remember the Titans?*' That was our high school. Kathleen was supposed to be the county redneck school where nobody was going to be able to get along, but it proved to be no problem. Some of those guys are still my best buddies. Their head coach from the black school integrated with us. He became our offensive line coach, and he was just a sweet guy. He was rough and tough, but it was easy.

"And I'd have to say that we didn't have any trouble adjusting at the University of Florida either. At the time I was there, we had marginal teams, and I'd come back to Polk County and all the time I heard, 'You guys would have had a better team if you could have gotten along with the blacks,' but I do not see that. There was a lot of controversy because Dickey wouldn't play me, but it wasn't any racial thing. I still love Jimmy DuBose like my brother. I would kill for Vince Kendrick. Those are great guys.

"I got the chance to play in the season opener against SMU. We were trailing 21-0 when I went into the game.

"This is a great memory: Me and Nat Moore were both sitting on the bench. Nat came from Miami, and during that preseason, Nat and I usually were on the second team, but I could see right away that he was my best guy who could catch the ball. I remember Nat and I on our knees, leaning on our helmets on the side-line over in Tampa looking at each other going, 'I'm ready when you are.' Nat eventually showed what he could do.

"Nothing against Chan, and this would be an ongoing thing we didn't understand, but it didn't seem that we were really pressing the issue trying to get our offense unwrapped. Doug Dickey would continue to try to knock them down and mash them, to a point of fault, we all felt.

"When I got in in the fourth quarter, we threw every down. We zoomed up and down the field and made two scores and made it close, and the fans were going wild. It's one of my greatest memories. I loved that night. But life got harder after that."

In the opener against SMU, Doug Dickey also subsituted a junior college transfer named Nat Moore at fullback. In January of 1972 Bob McAlphin, who coached basketball at South Dade Junior College, told Dickey that Moore wanted to play football again. Moore had starred at the University of Tennessee at Martin, became homesick, sat out a year, went to South Dade, and now wished to return to the big-time. Assistant coach Lindy Infante saw films of Moore and recommended him. When Moore began playing at Florida, he was not even listed in the press guide or the Florida–SMU program. But quickly the players saw that Nat Moore may well have been the best player on the team.

Against SMU, David Bowden and Nat Moore brought Florida back to within a touchdown.

Lee McGriff: "You scratched your head over Nat Moore. When Coach Dickey signed the guy, Nat hadn't played football in two years. He was a junior college basketball player and had been driving a pastrami truck. When he showed up, you could tell he was quick. Then put him at running back.

"Nat was a kind of cocky guy. He showed up as a junior, and you thought he had some talent, and then after you saw him in a game, you said to yourself, 'I never realized….'"

Fred Abbott: "Nat Moore was a transfer from Miami Dade. He was a basketball player. To this day when I see Nat, I call him 'Mr. Quickfeet.' He had the quickest feet of any athlete I've seen anywhere. He wasn't big, but he was quick as a cat. That whole year Nat was our entire offense. He was a godsend."

David Bowden: "I started the next game against Mississippi State. It was at Florida Field, and it was hot as hell on that astroturf, but we won [28-13]. I was a sophomore. I remember thinking to myself as we broke the huddle to go to the line of scrimmage, 'I have made it. All the games I've listened to on the radio, and I am now here.' It was third quarter before we completed a pass. Willie Jackson caught an out-route. I was stoked to be a Gator.

"We were behind in the third quarter when Vince Kendrick ran 52 yards [through a hole in the left side of the line] for a touchdown. It always makes the quarterback look good when they catch a little short pass and run a long ways. I like those. Then Nat scored on a reverse to ice it."

Lee McGriff: "Vince and I became lifetime friends. Vince came from an extremely poor Miami family of ten children. He was tough and strong, and had nice, quick feet and could move. He was very quiet and one of the kindest hearts you'll ever know. Whenever he did something good, you'd say, 'Well good. He's a good guy who deserves it.'"

For the first time in Florida history, blacks were winning ballgames for the orange and blue. The players handled it easily. It was harder for some of the alumni.

David Bowden: "Even after I left college, those [traditional] alumni were still struggling. When I would come back to Polk County, the guys who had the money, who were a little older, didn't change when it was time to change. They thought we were getting overrun with blacks, that Dickey was playing the blacks. But as players we didn't feel any animosity at all.

"We changed as the country changed. It was a microcosm. And the Vietnam War was going on, too, man. It was different from when Steve Spurrier was the quarterback, and he walked around campus and everybody loved the guy. When I was quarterback in '72, there was a faction of students on campus who saw us not as the Florida Gators, but as 'the pampered brood of athletes.' We felt that a little bit. The anti-war people were standoffish. They saw us as spoiled brats. So while there were still bunches of students who loved the Gators, it wasn't all warm and glowing. And at the same time

Coach Dickey wasn't warm and glowing. We still felt like we had to prove ourselves to our own coach who we never felt really came over to be 'our guy.'

"I don't want to come across as too harsh on Dickey, but I had grown up with a wide-open Gator offense, like Spurrier runs it now, recognizing that 18, 19, 20 year old guys are fallible, so let them loose, let them have some fun. But Coach Dickey saw it from a military perspective—we need to have the biggest, strongest, meanest guys, and that's how you win football games. That was different. I never felt close to the guy, and I know a bunch of my buddies felt the same way, especially on the offense.

"Several times my junior year, he would start his pep talk, and he was prepared to win the game 3-0. Lee McGriff and I would look at each other and just hang our heads. We wondered, What are we going to be if all we do is kick a field goal this game?' Later Carlos Alvarez came out and said that he's killing the offense, that he has no imagination. We kind of felt that too. Cause if we started with a game plan, even if they stopped us, we kept running the game plan. It was sickeningly apparent."

FSU was next. Fred Abbott decided the team needed a pep talk. At their motel in Perry, Florida, he gave it to them.

Lee McGriff: "Fred Abbott was a fantastic captain. There weren't many seniors in '72. Fred truly was a leader to us. Fred is obviously a very bright guy, and back then he was very well spoken. He could stand up and talk, and he was passionate. He could get you fired up.

"He stood in front of us and talked about being a Gator and beating Florida State. It turned the mood passionate and got people thinking about what they needed to think about. Fred was a guy who I always wanted to respect me. If Fred Abbott respected me, I felt like a very worthy person."

Fred Abbott: "Doug Knotts, the defensive coordinator, came to me, and he said, 'Fred, I don't think this team is ready to play. Is there anything you can do about it?' I said, 'Sure. You guys get on the bus and leave us in here.' We closed the door to the meeting room, and I just said with about fifty thousand expletives added, 'If your heart isn't in it, stay here, and we'll pick you up on the way back.' I didn't want anybody coming out of the room if their heart and soul wasn't into winning the game.

"So real quietly everybody got on the bus. We went up to Tallahassee."

David Bowden: "I remember we took the bus to Tallahassee, and we stopped halfway to eat breakfast. We got off, and Fred Abbott called the whole team over for a team meeting on the side of the road. It was his finest moment. Fred had left Florida in his sophomore year because it just wasn't fun anymore. But then he came back. I was in high school when that happened. But he was a Gator. We could sense that he was 'our guy.' He was a big, strong dude, played linebacker. He was another one who didn't feel the acceptance we all wanted from Coach Dickey and some of his staff, though some of the staff was wonderful. Don't get me wrong.

"But on this day Fred rose above everything. He said, 'We're going to win this game because we are the Florida Gators.' It was just a fire up. 'We are the Florida Gators!' It pervaded everything, man. It was great."

Lee McGriff: "We were in that old locker room of Florida State before the game. It was like an erector set. You could hear the tom-toms beating and the place clamoring. They created a pretty good tension. For those of us who had not played in an FSU game before, it was pretty intimidating.

"We came out of the locker room. We were trying to wait it out, to let Florida State run onto the field simultaneously, so they can't boo you out of the stadium. You could have cut the tension with a knife.

"The FSU team ran out onto the field through one of their banners. The first guy through the banner tripped, and a few guys tripped over him and fell to the ground. So we started to laugh. That just did it. Everybody lightened up. And then we beat their butt. I've always thought that was a significant moment, because it put us in the right place mentally."

Fred Abbott: "We were picked to lose. In fact the headline of the Tallahassee Democrat read: 'There ain't no way.' That's the game we set a school record. The defense had ten turnovers. [Florida recovered six fumbles and intercepted four Gary Huff passes.]

"Ralph Ortega was the outstanding player that day. Ralph is and was a great player. He was a sophomore. He's part of that group of Coral Gables players I talked about earlier. He was just a phenomenal player. You knew he was going to be an All-American as a sophomore.

"We beat them 42-13. When we blitzed, it was a thing of personal pride to get the sack. When Doug Knotts called a blitz, he expected and believed we were going to get a sack. When he called it, you would see that proverbial possum-eating manure grin on everybody's face, because we knew we were getting ready to turn loose. We knew we had to make things happen defensively to give our offense some help. I have a picture of Gary Huff on his knees and me and three of my defensive buddies standing over him after he had been sacked."

Lee McGriff: "The defense was flying around, knowing them around and intimidating the living fire out of FSU. Gary Huff was rattled. His receivers were rattled. They'd come across the middle, and they'd get hit. Years later Barry Smith, an FSU All-American, became a teammate of mine at Tampa Bay, and he told me, 'Damn, I didn't want any part of that ball.' Our defense had their attention. A lot of those turnovers were caused by intimidation."

The 42-13 romp over bitter rival FSU also proved a great day for quarterback David Bowden.

David Bowden: "What a day! They had started the season early and were 5-0 at the time we played them.

"There was a capacity crowd, and a beautiful playing surface. Doak Campbell had grass—that artificial surface on Florida Field was rough—so before the game I was stoked. I felt so at home with any game we had on grass. I was ready to play, man. I think we all were—playing on that grass. We were going to get those Seminoles. We had read the Tallahassee Democrat. The sports guy on Friday predicted, 'No way.' That was the title of the article, 'No way Florida State's not going to win this one tomorrow.'

" But we got on them early, and then the defense sacked him a bunch of times. Fred was great, and Ralph Ortega was outstanding.

"I loved Ralph, loved all those Coral Gables guys, Glenn Cameron. I roomed with a guy named Randy Talbot who was from Coral Gables. Back then it was one of the top high school programs.

"Anyway, we recovered a bunch of fumbles [6] and made some [4] interceptions, and we won the game big. And after the game my grandmother sent me the Atlanta Constitution, and I was picked as the SEC Back of the Week for engineering the drives for touchdowns. When you score that many points, it really looks like you've done something, even when a lot of times you're just handing the ball off, but go ahead!"

thirty-seven

Preston Kendrick Steals a Flag

The next opponent, Alabama, was ranked third in the country. Florida was outmanned, as Bama won 24-7.

Lee McGriff: "Before the game I would not look at Bear Bryant, because he had reached legendary status, and there I was on his field. I glanced at him once, and I thought, I'd better pretend like he's not here. Bryant was bigger-than-life to me.

"Nat Moore had a good game. He didn't make any touchdowns, but he made some long runs.

"It was hot that day. On the bus after the game a bunch of guys were folded in half from cramps."

Fred Abbott: "We were big underdogs against Alabama. We played in Tuscaloosa. and we went out, and for the first ten minutes the score was 0 to 0.

"Just before the half, Nat breaks loose for a fifty yard run, and he gets to the five yard line. It's first and goal on the five, and we're looking to score and take the lead. We're fired up. Our defense is playing their hearts out.

"They were so excited, they didn't know what substitutions they wanted to make or what play they wanted to run. Doug Dickey gets a delay of game. So now it's first and ten. We don't score. We go in at halftime, and it looks like a bomb has gone off, because we've been playing our first team defense the whole game, and they've been rotating people.

"We went out for the second half, and they just wore us out. That year the defense was Florida's forte. The offense was young and still trying to find a quarterback and a seasoned line. So the defense did everything they could, and Nat Moore wasn't enough to make it happen. We just ran out of gas and eventually got worn down.

"But for me and everybody else, it was a thrill to be on the field with Bear Bryant. And the reason I think college football is a better game than the pros is that sometimes you can beat the better team if you've got a bigger heart and a bigger will. Against Alabama that day, we run what we brung, but it wasn't enough."

Against Mississippi in Oxford, the Florida defense was dominating. Florida won 16–0, quite a feat considering that Ole Miss' quarterback was Norris Weese, a slick operator. On the way to the game Lee McGriff was struck by a long trip through cotton fields. He wondered how the vista was affecting his black teammates.

Lee McGriff: "I'll never forget the bus ride to the game. I remember the deafening silence—the team was focused as we were going through miles and miles of cotton fields. I remember looking at some of those black guys, thinking, Man, these guys can feel this. They don't like where we are. How in God's name does Ole Miss recruit a black player, with those fans waving that Confederate flag and coming through those cotton fields?

"Without it ever being said, I always perceived that part of where our steam came from in that game was that bus ride through those cotton fields."

David Bowden: "It was a crisp, cold day. Chan and I alternated at quarterback. I threw a touchdown. Coach Dickey was using the same system Coach Spurrier uses now: when one guy's throwing bad, he puts in the other one. But I didn't like it. Even though Chan Gailey is a wonderful guy, I don't want to be taken out. There was no animosity between Chan and me. Of course, I thought I was better than him, and he probably thought he was better than me."

In the Ole Miss game, Nat Moore scored his seventh touchdown of the season. He gained 142 yards on 16 carries.

David Bowden: "It's uncanny the way some guys could play. Take Lee McGriff, a little, short guy who could fly. He knew how to get open on a pass pattern. Nat Moore was the same way, and he knew how to make people miss him. It's why people love sports. Looking at Nat, you wouldn't think the guy was a big-time ball player. He was 5'9", 185 pounds. But try to tackle him. And, like McGriff, he knew the game. And that part of the game during the Dickey era was left untouched because all he wanted were pounders. We never went into the intricacies of how to beat the defense. We didn't change plays at the line of scrimmage unless there was a cold, hard, easily recognized fact. Whereas now a lot of coaches give the quarterback the freedom to walk up there and call something different if he sees something that might work better."

Fred Abbott: "Again, against Ole Miss, Nat was it. [Moore scored his seventh touchdown of the season.] He was spectacular. Everyone was keying on him. There would be times when he would get trapped by two or three defensive players and really get the crud knocked out of him, but for a little guy, he was tough.

"We were playing for a shutout, particularly late in the game. To win the game is one thing. To win it by a shutout you defensively have done everything you've been asked, and you know the worst that can happen is to end in a tie.

"I can remember late in the game, Ole Miss was driving, and everybody was saying, 'Let's preserve the shutout.' We did. Everyone was excited. For us the shutout was important.

"After the game was over Preston Kendrick, a black guy who played end on the defense with me, said to me, 'Catfish, I'm gonna get you a souvenir.' Now Ole Miss was one of the teams that had not integrated or didn't have more than two black players. And Preston jumped over the fence and went into the stands. I looked at David Poff and said, 'What is this crazy guy doing?' We didn't know why he was going up there, what he was doing.

"He ran up in the middle of ten thousand Deep South people in the end zone, of which I'm sure some were racists, and they're looking at this guy in an orange and blue football uniform running into the stands, and there was a guy waving a Confederate flag. Preston snatched the flag out of his hand, and he ran back down the stands onto the field and gave it to me. He said, 'Catfish, here is a souvenir of this day.' I still have the flag in my closet. And believe me, if Preston had gotten in trouble, every one of us would have gone up there to help him. That is a true story. If you think it takes courage to play football, what do you think it takes to run up into the Ole Miss stands and grab a Confederate flag when you're the only black person there?"

The next game was against Auburn. Doug Dickey sent Fred Abbott onto the field for the coin toss.

Fred Abbott: "As you are now completely aware, Doug Dickey and I didn't have the best of relationships. But after my sophomore year we pretty much buried the hatchet, but we still didn't have what you'd call a personal relationship. We made our peace.

"In 1972 I was the captain of the team and would go out for the coin toss. Before the Auburn game, Doug Dickey came over to talk to me, which was unusual, because normally Doug Knotts would come and talk to me and tell me what he wanted, whether we wanted the ball or wanted to kick off and which goal we wanted to defend.

"But before the Auburn game, Dickey came over, and this was an unusual event. I was one of those guys who had to get pretty fired up to play, and the apex of my getting fired up would be right before we went out onto the field. And here came Coach Dickey, and I had to do a double take.

"He said, 'Fred, what do you think we ought to do if we win the toss?'

"I said, 'We ought to take the fucking ball and stick it down their throats.' Cause I was in hyperspace, way out there.

"He said, 'All right, if we win the toss, we'll kick off.' And he walked away.

"I thought, 'What the hell did he ask me for?'

"We won the toss. We kicked off, and Auburn went eighty yards and scored on the first drive. I was thinking, God, wouldn't it have been great if WE had scored first?' Give the ball to Nat Moore three times and maybe something would happen."

The game came close to being one of the greatest upsets in the history of the University of Florida. Against Auburn in Gainesville, Florida trailed 26-0 in the middle of the second quarter. The game appeared to be a rout, but Florida closed to 26-20 and came within inches of scoring the game-winner.

David Bowden: "Other than Alabama, Auburn was the class of the conference back then. They were big and strong. They had this running back named Terry Henley who would just run over you.

"They led 26-0, and then we came roaring back. I remember rolling out of the pocket, fearing for my life, and this was another thing about Nat Moore: he knew how to get open. Nat was out in the flat working his way back between defenders, and I just shot the ball to him, and he went whoosh and took the ball 52 yards for a touchdown.

"Then we had a safety, Jimmy Revels, Crazy Jimmy Revels, a free spirit who ran an interception back [79 yards] for a touchdown, and after we closed it to less than a touchdown, we had several chances but couldn't score again.

"They made an interception on me late in the game. I remember it like it was yesterday. We had practiced the play all week. It was sprint right, and Willie Jackson was going to do a fly route. We'd sprint right, stop, throw back, but at this time we were closer to the west sideline, so we ran the play sprinting left where you had to stop and wheel around and throw back. It was a jump ball at the end, and they picked it off. If I had put a little more on it, Willie might have got it and took it in. Now it's a great memory. It was heartbreaking at the time."

Fred Abbott: "For me, I thought it was going to happen. We had never beaten Auburn, and I thought, This is finally going to happen, and we just came up six points short. I would have loved to have left there with one in the win column against those folks.

"There was no love lost between Florida and Auburn. In '69 Florida was rated the number one party school by Playboy so all the Auburnites, who were more rural people, thought they would show us because all we knew how to do was party and not play football.

"But this year Sullivan and Beasley were gone, and I thought this was going to be the year we beat them.

"For me, it turned out to be a heartbreaker, though the good part was that of all the guys on defense, there wasn't one who wasn't playing his heart out. I was thrilled to be part of a defense that played like that."

The most disappointed player on the field was Lee McGriff. He had worked his tail off, and he was losing playing time to Hollis Boardman. McGriff made up his mind that he would do whatever it took to win the starting receiver's job.

Lee McGriff: "I was so angry after that Auburn game that I could not accept what happened. After that game, I was not fit to be around human beings. I talked to my dad about it. I said, 'I can't live like this.' He didn't say much. When you're dealing with somebody who's not rational, you let them see if they can diffuse themselves. After I carried on a bit, he said, 'What are you going to do about it?' He said, 'I understand how you feel, but you're gonna have to do something. You can quit. You can pout. Or you can do something.'

"So I made up my mind that I would go to practice in a way that was so extreme that even if the team went out without pads, I was wearing pads. Even if it was half-speed, I was going full-speed. Even if we weren't in contact, I was making contact, blocking downfield, whatever.

"We practiced Monday, which is usually a light day, and of course the team was kind of dragging, but I was in another gear. I'd have gotten noticed anyway, but under those circumstances, I REALLY got noticed.

"At first it irritated them. 'What are you doing?' The players I was doing this to didn't think it was too funny. So I got into a couple of fights with the defensive backs.

"Then we did some drills among us receivers, a little blocking drill that was meant to be lighthearted, so I went up against Hollis Boardman and the others, and before you knew it, I was going at them, and we got into another little tussle.

"Don Deal, the receiver coach, came up to me after practice. He said, 'What the hell is wrong with you?' I was emotional. I said, 'I will never sit on that bench again.' He looked at me like I was out of my mind.

"And I went about it that way every day. Sometimes they would say, 'Why don't you back off?' But I didn't. Thursday was another light day, with the team going out for a little run-through, and I was the only idiot in pads, going full speed.

"Coach Dickey was up in the tower, and a couple of times he called down to me, 'Lee McGriff, this is Thursday. Stop it.' But I didn't. He came out of the tower and called me aside. He fussed at me and said, 'Hey, you're gonna hurt somebody, and that's not okay.'

"He was mad at me, and I had no idea how I left it, but I started the Georgia game. And I started ever since. It was bizarre, but I was a walk-on with a sinking feeling that it was all slipping away, and it changed me. It changed me forever. I put me in another gear forever. So we went to Georgia, and we lost another close game, and even though I was terribly disappointed and wanted to win that game, it was a turning point for me personally."

Georgia was next. Coach Dickey started Chan Gailey against the Bulldogs because he had grown up in Georgia. As it turned out, so had David Bowden.

David Bowden: "Chan started that week because Chan is from Georgia. I remember sitting on the bench before the game wanting to shout, 'Hey coach, I'm from Thomasville, Georgia.' But anyway, that's the way it worked out. I was miffed. I only played a little in that game."

Florida led 7-0 in the fourth quarter until Georgia completed a 44-yard long bomb to tie it. Then Florida fumbled late in the game and with 46 seconds left, Georgia kicked a field goal to win it.

David Bowden: "We had no offense. You want to know what I remember after that game? Chan fumbled twice during that game, which happens day in and day out. The next morning I woke up and I read in the Jacksonville paper that 'Bowden says, when asked why he didn't start, that at least I didn't fumble twice.'

"My heart was ripped in two. I was ready to kill somebody. I got on the phone and said, 'Chan, have you read the Jacksonville paper?' He said, 'No Dave, I haven't.' I said, 'Well, buddy, if you read it, it says I said, "At least I didn't fumble twice." I swear I didn't say that.' He said, 'David, if I would have read it, I would have known you wouldn't have said it.'

"Isn't that great? I love the guy.

"I kept the writer's name in my mind for years, but it matters not now. We can't harbor resentments, can we? It makes us bitter people."

Coach Dickey returned David Bowden to the starting QB role against Kentucky.

Lee McGriff: "Coach Dickey always wanted a quarterback who could run. David was a non-runner. David was a thrower. At this time everyone in college was running the option. David couldn't run the option. I mean, David was mobile, but he was no runner. Doug Dickey wanted a runner. He didn't have one, so he had to play David, but he never embraced him.

"But David could play. He was so accurate, and he had such a great sense of timing. David was second in the SEC in passing that year behind Bert Jones. And he was fighting for his life.

"In fairness to Coach Dickey, it was the times. It was the way football was played. David was far from the prototype of what most teams were looking for, but despite that, David still could be incredibly effective. If was frustrating to me that they were trying to suppress or demote David. For me it was wonderful playing with David."

Against the Wildcats, the sophomore had a career day, hitting 11 of 19 passes for 161 yards and two touchdowns in a 40-0 Homecoming rout of the Wildcats at Florida Field.

David Bowden: "Kentucky played a three-deep zone, so if the quarterback and the receivers run curl routes and posts upon a fake, they are there all day. One of my fondest memories was a play I did change at the line of scrimmage that resulted in a touchdown to Joel Parker on a post pattern. Joel was a big, great-looking guy who could run. We should have thrown to him more. But there was a lot of joy against Kentucky that day."

Fred Abbott: "I was a couple years older than David, but I liked him because he seemed like a very down-to-earth guy. He's one of those guys who really doesn't look like an athlete, but he's got an intense competitive spirit. He was a high school All-American. I remember he was much more mobile than our other quarterback, Chan Gailey. David could roll out and throw the ball. Everybody on defense was hoping that each game the offense would mature and get better, and it certainly happened for David in that Kentucky game."

In that game the Florida defense made six interceptions and recovered three fumbles. Tyson Sever ran a punt back 71 yards in the 40-0 rout.

David Bowden: "Tyson was one of my bestest buds. And his little brother, Glen, was a good receiver who would have made a big difference the next year if he hadn't gotten hurt. But Tyson was great. He was a very reserved, old country boy who loved Randolph Scott movies. And in the Kentucky game Wayne Fields had a couple of interceptions. Fields was something. He was, man."

Fred Abbott: "That defense I captained in '72 had fifty turnovers for the season. And it was all younger players. David Poff and I were the senior citizens, and good God, there were three All-American linebacks, and one of them was sitting on the bench getting ready to take my job.

"We needed a goal line stand to preserve our shutout against Kentucky, and that's when the adrenaline and testosterone are pumping and their highest. Kentucky got to the one, but that's all. It sounds trite, but they talk about having an attitude check. I was the guy who called the signals, and I'd look at every one of those guys and I'd say, 'This is it. They are not getting in.' They'd look at me and say, 'That's right. That's what we're gonna do.' And everybody would give more than they had. We had two small defensive tackles, guys who were too little and too small and too inexperienced, but if you were in a fight, that's who you'd want with you. We stopped them."

The LSU game was played in Gainesville. LSU was ranked eighth in the country and were big favorites. That day it rained heavily.

David Bowden: "More people talk about that game where I live in Polk County than most any other. It was a torrential downpour the whole game. The water was so deep, the old-timey dugouts on the sidelines that are hardly used any more were full of water, up and overflowing. The field was crowned, so it wasn't like that on the field. But ask anybody. It was something.

"We played LSU to a 3-3 tie against Bert Jones. Nat took a long pass down the sidelines in stride, and they ran him down on the one-yard line, and this is a point to reflect on—agony and ecstacy are so close. Nat was tired, so they took him out, and they put Andy Summers, who roomed with Tyson right next to me, and Randy [Talbot], one of my most beloved buds, in the game to make this little one-yard plunge. They hit him, and he fumbled. That hurt him. That means it hurts us all.

"And at the end of the game Fred and the boys got in a big fight with the LSU players. I wasn't in on it. I stayed away from the rough guys. LSU was miffed because they did not expect to be tied or to lose coming to Florida Field."

Fred Abbott: "We were about a thirty-point underdog, and Bert Jones was coming to town. We didn't have any offense, and he was averaging about forty points a game, and they were pushing him for the Heisman Trophy. Proving there is a God, along came a monsoon that was a great equalizer.

"When we came out to play that game at Florida Field, two things stand out: one, it was one of the few times the stadium was not full, but the people who were there were Gator fans, and they were soaked through and through. There were already about eight inches of water standing on the sidelines. So when they announced, 'Here come the Gators!,' we came out of the tunnel to warm up, and I went and jumped into the water, did a belly flop, rolled over, and got completely soaked. I thought, That takes care of that.

"And the second thing I remember had to do with the coaching. During the game Nat Moore broke loose and ran down to about the five yard line. We were close. And they took Nat out of the game and put in a player by the name of Andy Summers. He came into the game cold and he fumbled.

"It was still zip-zip. LSU was driving, and time was running out. They got down close to our end of the field, and there was less than a minute left. They lined up to kick a field goal. We got in the huddle, and I said to these two little defensive guys I've been telling you about, Hitchcock and Lacer, 'John, you take the center and move him to the right. I don't care how you get him there. David, you take the guard to the left, and I'm going to line up in the other slot, and right before the ball snaps, I'm coming right between you guys.' They said, 'Okay, Fish.' And they did, and I blocked that field goal try. I got my hand on it, and it barely went over the line of scrimmage, and that was the game. Otherwise it would have been one of those Auburn games, and we would have lost. I have a picture of that play hanging in my office. A photographer from the *St. Pete Times* took the picture and sent it to me. That's one game I remember very well.

"And at the end of the game there was a gang fight. We weren't backing away from anybody.

"It had something to do with race. One of the LSU players said something to one of our black players, Vince or Preston Kendrick, used a disparaging remark, and it was on. We were all fighting.

"That wasn't the first football fight we'd be in. We had one in that Richmond game. We had one in the FSU game. Those are your brothers. If anyone takes them on, it's like the Three Musketeers.

"But LSU was incredibly frustrated because we were supposed to get our butts whacked by thirty points, and we ended up tying them 3-3. I remember thinking, Bert Jones is NOT going to win the Heisman today."

Florida had another fine game when it defeated Miami, led by fullback Chuck Foreman, 17-6. Florida led 3-0 after three quarters on a John Williams field goal. Nat Moore ran for 103 yards, and Fred Abbott and the defense sacked the Miami quarterback ten times.

David Bowden: "What a boring, hot game, but we won, didn't we? It was pitiful. Neither team could do diddly. In that game I had the longest run of my career, fourteen yards. Other than that, I remember no highlights. I remember the misery of nothing working on offense."

But against the Florida defense, led by captain Fred Abbott, the vaunted Miami offense would do less.

Fred Abbott: "Chuck Foreman was one of the first big running backs who could run and carry the mail. He was every bit of 6'3" and was close to 220.

He was a big guy who could fly. Our position was that you had to stop him before he got flying so every time Chuck Foreman got the ball, everyone on defense targeted him. We knew if Chuck Foreman ever got loose, it was trouble, so the way to deal with that problem was to never let him get loose.

"In that Miami game Wayne Fields made another interception for a [54-yard] touchdown. Wayne weighed 190 pounds, and he was only one millisecond behind Nat Moore in quickness."

In a season filled with heartbreaking games, perhaps the worst was the four-point loss to North Carolina. In the final minutes David Bowden threw a pass to Willie Jackson that would have been the winning touchdown, only to see the ball hit Jackson on the pads below the waist and fall away.

David Bowden: "We were playing on grass again in the Gator Bowl once again. I felt connected to God and his earth, and we threw the ball up and down the field.

"With seconds to go, Willie J. was crossing the goal line, and it bounced off his hip. That was one play…in the course of things, guys get open, and you throw over their heads, so…but then we got another chance. We had the ball on way down the field with time running out, and we go whirling down the field like the Florida Gators that I remember in my mind when Steve Spurrier was the quarterback in the Sugar Bowl."

Bowden passed 23 yards to Willie Jackson, then threw a 35 yarder to Jackson down to the Carolina 9. After an incomplete pass, there were 32 seconds left in the game.

David Bowden: "We threw slants, which was my forte. I threw two to Willie that he should have had, but he didn't get them. On the last play I remember them being all over me, and our hope was to run them out from there, and Vince Kendrick was going to go in the flat. I barely got it off, and from the ground, I saw Kendrick catch it in the end zone and get busted out of bounds. But the referee said he was out of bounds when he caught it.

"We all thought he was in, and the call cost us the game. But it was a great offensive game, Carolina and us."

Fred Abbott: "Everybody played their hardest, but it just wasn't meant to be. I can remember very much not wanting to leave the field on a losing note. I was a fifth-year senior, and I was playing football on a Saturday and I got my degree the next Wednesday, so there were better days ahead."

Lee McGriff: "The game came down to the wire. At the end of the game David threw a pass that I thought was going to me, and I broke for the ball and never saw Vince Kendrick, who caught it, and I will tell you to my grave that Vince caught it, landed on his feet, and he was plenty in bounds. The refs ruled he was out of bounds. I could not believe it wasn't a touchdown. If it's a touchdown, we win the game.

"All of us were plenty upset. Vince was upset. It was one of those games that would have been absolutely thrilling to win. And for me to have a game like that not put the exclamation point on it with a win…it was the dream I had always wanted."

Florida finished the 1972 season with a 5-5-1 record. With a little luck, the record could have been much better. For David Bowden, it was the best of times.

David Bowden: "Wonderful. I'm playing for the Florida Gators. My name is now with those of Tommy Shannon and Larry Libertore. I felt the crest of the mountain was close by. It was our sophomore year, and all of us were young. We had very few seniors. We were gonna be the difference. We were gonna put the program over the top next year—just wait."

For Lee McGriff it was a season of promise.

Lee McGriff: "That was the last game of the '72 season. I had caught a handful of balls, but not as many as I had hoped. Things were happening, and I was catching passes. I may have made the best catch of my career in the North Carolina game on a post pattern. It was a thirty-yard play where I didn't even think I could get anywhere near the ball, but I dove, and look what I found when I landed on the ground on my head. It was my first touchdown of my career. It was a back-and-forth game, so it was a touchdown that mattered."

For Willie Jackson and Fred Abbott, their college football careers were over. The future was ahead of them.

Willie Jackson: "Back then you played, and you were hoping for the best.

It was an experience I looked forward to, because I never thought I would go to college. When I was in college, I never thought I would play in the NFL. But you had to go to college in order to play in the NFL, and once I did that, I thought that maybe I would get an opportunity to play in the NFL. That became an aspiration.

"I got drafted by the Los Angeles Rams in the 11th round. Tank Younger came down to Florida to talk to me about signing with them. He said I would have been drafted higher, but that when they spoke to the coaches, they said, 'He's a good athlete, but his work ethic is not that good.' And after that, I had a little animosity toward the Florida coaches for saying that. I felt they should have only said positive things about their players.

"Looking back, I felt that the pros would say anything just to get you on the dotted line for less money if they can. At that time everyone was getting shafted. I signed for about $32,000. That's all you got at the time. Plus a couple of little bonuses.

"The experience was great. I played with James Harris and Ron Jaworski, and Lance Rentzel and Lance Alworth. That was one of the reasons I didn't make the team. They had to keep those veteran players, as opposed to good quality athletes coming in for the future.

"The next year I tried out with the Houston Oilers. I played during the pre-season, and after that I went to the World Football League and played for the Jacksonville Express. I got my knee bummed up, and that was it for me, because it took a long time to get out of the cast and then try to work my way back into shape. It was really hard.

"I was in Gainesville working out, trying to get my knee right, and I was working as a mail carrier for the University of Florida, and for a few years I was also putting insulation into houses. They had a new foam insulation, and I would put it into attics. And then there was a new football team in Jacksonville, the Firebirds in the United States Football League, and I made the team and played, but there wasn't any money to be made. I decided to stay in Jacksonville, and I did some insurance work, and then I left and went to the Jacksonville Marine Institute, which was for youth offenders, and now I have a position with the Mayor's Council on Fitness and Well Being, and for the last ten or so years I've been a Senior Rec Leader with the Parks Department.

"My son Terry also went to the University of Florida, and he broke quite a few records there—passes caught, touchdowns. Terry ended up playing with the New Orleans Saints and the San Francisco 49ers, and he made more money signing than I made in my whole career.

"But at the time I was coming out of school, you played pro football for the enjoyment of the game, not because you were going to get a whole lot of money."

Fred Abbott: "I was very much interested in playing pro football, and I got to play in the Senior Bowl. I got to meet Gary Huff, James Thomas, and Barry Smith. I was the only player from Florida, plus a lot of other guys from the SEC including Chuck Foreman. It was fun to meet and play with them. Plus you got a paycheck. The South won, and we each got $1,500. It was great. We got to play for pro coaches. Weeb Ewbank and the Jets assistants coached us. Walt Michaels was on the staff, and I liked playing with him.

"Before the draft the news got out that I had had a spinal fusion between my junior and senior years. I was projected to go somewhere between the first and third rounds, and I was picked fifth by the Vikings. Chuck Foreman was their first pick that year.

"I made the final cut, but I was their sixth linebacker, and they were going to put me on the taxi squad. But it was fun. I got to scrimmage against Chuck. Fran Tarkenton was the quarterback. The Vikings still had the Fearsome Foursome with Alan Page, and Roy Winston, a linebacker from LSU, helped me tremendously. Jeff Siemon was their middle linebacker. He'd been the number one pick from Stanford the year before, and he helped me tremendously. He did everything he could to help me make that ball club, and I did everything I could to get his job.

"After we broke camp and went to Minneapolis, I got a call from Don Shula of the Miami Dolphins. I went to see Bud Grant, our coach. If Doug Dickey was conservative, Bud Grant was the next universe over to the right.

"Bud said, 'We have to renegotiate your contract. We really don't need a sixth linebacker,' which was bullshit. I said, 'Well, I'll tell you what, Coach Grant. Here's my playbook. I'm outta here.' His mouth dropped open. I walked out the door, came back to Gainesville, and I signed with the Dolphins a week later. I taxied there for half a season, and this was the year they went undefeated. Bob Griese was there, and Larry Csonka and Jim Kiick, and Paul Warfield, and the 'no-name' defense. Nick Buoniconti was their middle linebacker—that's whose job I wanted, but I wasn't going to play unless somebody got hurt.

"When Larry Little and Bob Kuechenberg both got hurt, Miami needed to pick up a guard, and I was put on waivers, and the Philadelphia Eagles picked me up. I taxied there the last half of the season, and then came back home and on TV watched my former teams, Minnesota and Miami, meet in the Super Bowl. That year I made $7,500 on the taxi squad, not bad money.

"I was claimed by the New York Giants and Bill Arnsparger. I was in the best shape of my life. I was fired up about finally getting a chance to play. I flew in to Manhattan and met with Wellington Mara and Leon McQuade, who was infamous for being tight. He wore the same pair of shoes for forty-five years!

"I asked for $50,000, and Wellington Mara said I wasn't worth it, and I said, 'I'm outta here,' and I flew to Jacksonville, where I signed a contract with the Jacksonville team in the World Football League, guaranteed for $150,000.

"Two days later Bill Arnsparger called. He said, 'What are you doing?' I said, 'I'm playing football for Jacksonville.' He said, 'You can't do that. You have an NFL contract.' I said, 'Talk to Wellington Mara. He said I wasn't worth it.'

"He put me on hold, and he came back and said, 'There's no problem. We'll pay you what you want.' I said, 'It's too late. I'm already playing down here.'

"I was one of three players who had guaranteed contracts. It was more fun playing on that team, because we had a lot of players from the South and the SEC. The second year I played, we had George Mira on the team. At one point they brought Ted Hendricks in, but they didn't sign him. It was all the guys I had played against. Larry Gagner, who played at Florida, was on that team. We became great buddies. It was just a blast. I signed for a third year in 1975, but I tore up my knee.

"It happened on a sweep. I was the middle linebacker, and the outside linebacker got knocked down, and it was me and the tailback and two pulling guards. I got the tailback on my shoulder and was leaving the ground with him when both of the guards hit me. I had all my weight and 220 pounds of running back on my shoulder, and it was like listening to a broom handle break.

"One of the part of owners of the team was an orthopedic surgeon, a guy named Bill DeCarlos. He said, 'Your leg is in so much spasm, we have to put you to sleep to find out how much damage was done, but we think it's a real bad sprain.' As he leaned over me, the anesthesiologist was putting the mask over my face. He said, 'By the way, if your knee is worse than we think, we're gonna go ahead and operate on you.' I hadn't signed a consent or anything.

"I woke up. He was in the recovery room. He said, 'I got some good news and some bad news. The bad news is you'll never play football again because you tore all four ligaments and both cartilage.' I said, 'What's the good news?' He said, 'The good news is you'll be able to walk.'

"He was right, but at the ripe old age of 51 I'm going in for a total knee replacement.

"From there, I went to law school at the University of Florida. I did some color commentating with Otis Boggs. Then Charlie Pell came, and Otis got one of those Ray Graves retirement deals. Otis was out. Then I became a father and a busy trial attorney and retired from the radio after seven years."

thirty-eight

Bowden Bears His Cross

Ray Graves began the recruiting of black players to the University of Florida, but it was Doug Dickey who realized that for Florida to be competitive, he needed to recruit as many top black athletes as he could. In 1972 he brought in twelve excellent black players, led by Nat Moore, and in 1973 he promoted one of those twelve players, Don Gaffney, to become the backup quarterback for the Gators behind David Bowden.

Jimmy Dunn, who had succeeded Dick Dickey as the Gators quarterback in the mid–'50s, was an assistant coach at Florida under Ray Graves in 1963. The following year he was hired by Doug Dickey to coach the quarterbacks at Tennessee. While there, Dunn helped Dickey recruit the first black player at Tennessee, a player by the name of Albert David, from Alcoa, Tennessee. Dunn recalled Dickey's position on segregation during an era when Jim Crow ruled in the Deep South.

Jimmy Dunn: "Coach Dickey and I talked about [the policy of segregation]. He said, 'It's wrong. It hasn't happened before, but we need to recruit the best possible football players we can recruit, and it doesn't matter whether they were white, black, yellow, or green. Just get us the best players. If we're going to win the SEC or the national championship, get me the best players.'

"They had been recruiting black players on the West Coast and in the Big Ten, but not in the South. Dickey was a pioneer. He was a great football coach. But he was too nice a guy. He could have done some things at times to help him under the Ws and Ls, but he chose not to. He took the high road every time, when he could have dipped down. So he never got the credit he deserved.

"When Dickey and I came to Florida from Tennessee, Willie Jackson and Leonard George were there. In 1973, Don Gaffney took David Bowden's job at quarterback. The media was trying to create a situation of discord that really didn't exist. They tried to make it that there was a quarterback controversy, and any time race was mentioned, this was something that was not taking place inside the team. Definitely not. Players know players' capabilities, and it doesn't matter what religion or race, they just want to play with the best possible player at that position to help their team. We NEVER had anything racial on our football team.

"Don did feel some fan backlash from some fans. But he played extremely well. He did good for us. He was a great addition to our football team, and my experience with him was he was first class all the way. And he was a great competitor. He did not like getting beat. I remember one time we played tennis, and I won, and I remember that more than any football game he played. Cause he did not like getting beat, and he did not like getting beat by me."

Don Gaffney: "I grew up in Jacksonville. My dad, George Gaffney, was a baseball player early in his life, and then he became a printer. He played minor league ball at the Negro League level. I grew up around ballplayers.

"When I was growing up, Jacksonville was segregated. We have to talk about that, because it will explain a lot of why my passion was the way it was. Understand that I was a Florida Gator fan, even though the Florida Gators didn't have any black players. I rooted for the Gators because that was the state of Florida's team. I would watch the Ray Graves Show almost every week. I could name every Florida quarterback in succession.

"I had watched Florida football more than any college football because of Coach Graves show. Remember, television was not that extensive back then. If you didn't catch Lindsey Nelson, you didn't get much college football. But I always wanted to be a Gator.

"I used to work the Gator Bowl games selling cokes. I would work the first half, and then watch the second half. You'd find a seat no one was in and watch. My brother Derrick and I and a lot of guys from the neighborhood would do it. It was fun. That's the only way we could get into the game. We couldn't afford a ticket. We weren't an upper middle class family, but I didn't come from the ghetto either. I was fortunate. My father worked real hard. I had four brothers. I was at the top, and then Derrick and Warren, Reggie and Johnnie.

"I remember when I first read that Leonard George and Willie Jackson were coming to Florida. I remember reading in the paper how they were on their way to Gainesville, coming down I-75 from Sarasota in Willie's case and

Tampa in Leonard's. The story was they were late reporting because they couldn't get transportation.

"I don't think Willie was ever given his just due, considering the pressure the guy had on him. I mean, you have to understand Florida football, understand the South, understand the Southeast Conference. None of us had to deal with the gravity of the pressure Willie felt.

"When I began playing football, I was groomed to be a quarterback by guys in the neighborhood. We had so many great athletes where I grew up. A lot of them never got the opportunity to play at the college level. I happened to be the first black quarterback at Florida. I NEVER thought that would happen to me. I had thought by the time I became a senior in high school, the Gators would have at least one. Heck, black players were beginning to pop up at colleges all over the country. I vividly remember Condredge Holloway at Tennessee. It wasn't hard to remember the black quarterbacks from our era because there wasn't but a handful. Condredge Holloway was the first one.

"Ironically, one of the things that made me passionate about Doug Dickey when he came to recruit me was that he had recruited Holloway.

"I'm not sure what would have happened to me if Willie and Leonard hadn't been at Florida when I arrived there, but I do know this: I had an advantage because Doug Dickey was there. Doug Dickey showed that if you had the ability, [color] didn't matter. He was gonna go with the best player. And nobody gives Doug Dickey any credit for that, and I think that's sad. I tell you something else too: I'm not sure I would have made it if I didn't have a coach with the character that he had. And the patience he had. I was blessed to have him and Jimmy Dunn.

"I was actually recruited by Doug Knotts, who was the linebacker coach at Florida. He recruited this north Florida area. He was the first Gator coach I met, the one I talked to an a regular basis. This was an unusual situation: we're talking about a school that plays in a traditional conference in the South in a region of the country where you don't see many blacks, especially at quarterback. Holloway was the first black quarterback to start, and I was second. But strangely enough, it didn't mean a whole lot to me, I didn't see it the way it was because I didn't understand. But there was continuous discussion about it, at home, at school, with my dad, with my coach, and other people were having it about me. It's one of those things I remember: that there were A LOT of people involved.

"During this period colleges were allowed to give an unlimited number of scholarships. The [Proposition] 48 Rule didn't come in until after I got there. They kept telling me they had a big recruiting class [of black players] coming in, but I didn't realize they weren't kidding until after I got there.

"I was the first Viking to play at Florida, which brought dismay to the people in my community who were traditional black-college-type people. They wanted me to go to a black school, Florida A&M, Bethune-Cookman, Texas Southern, Tennessee State, and they called me 'traitor' for going to Florida. They predicted I wouldn't make it there. But there were also black people who were critical of me after I made high school All-America. They said I probably could make it at a black school because I wasn't a Joe Gilliam [Tennessee State] or Doug Williams [Grambling] -type quarterback. That bothered me a little bit. But the pressure on me to go to a black school was intense. A lot of people didn't speak to me for years because I didn't go to a black school.

"When I arrived in the fall of '72, it was the first year that freshman were eligible to play on the varsity. I got to play as a freshman.

"We played a freshman game against Auburn. That same week the varsity was playing SMU in the season opener. Dickey told me, 'Don, you're going to Tampa with us [to play SMU]. You've earned that." I couldn't figure out why, but I knew some freshmen were going. I knew Wayne Fields certainly was going to play, and Sammy Green was going and so was Jimmy DuBose. I didn't understand it, but I was excited. I was looking forward to watching the game from the sidelines. That's what I did. I saw Alvin Maxson, this great running back, and we lost, because we didn't have a great team that year at all.

"We went to Tampa for the SMU game, and they roomed me with David Bowden [who is white]. David had usually roomed with one of his buddies. And David was great. I would have been more comfortable rooming with another black player, but I didn't have a problem. David was busy getting ready to play the game, and I was just happy being there. It was my first trip. David would say, 'What can I do to assist you?' I was a freshman. He was a superstar. We didn't have much to discuss. We didn't have any words or any problems. I didn't think it was right, but I understood what they were trying to do. [Integrate the team.]

"I remember the first time I stepped on a college football field: we were playing Alabama in Tuscaloosa. Coach Bryant was there. I was in awe. I had just seen him in the Cotton Bowl. Here I was with the Florida Gators. Just a few months earlier I had been at Raines High School. We were getting killed, and

I got in for a couple of plays. I didn't throw a pass as a freshman. I was there. I got to hand the ball off in three games. Each time it was to Jimmy DuBose.

"I have to say the students were absolutely wonderful to me. Overall the players were too, because they thought I was a pretty nice person. I only had trouble with one player. It happened the first day of practice on the field with the Gators freshman year. We were practicing taking snaps, and the rotation might have been David Bowden, Chan Gailey, and I—there were a lot of quarterbacks—we recruited Robbie Ball, Glenn Fevers, Mark Newman, and me—all four quarterbacks who played in the North-South high school All-Star game, but I was the only black, and the first one. And I got to the stage before any of those guys. Who would have thought, huh?

"I could throw the ball pretty good. I was convinced I could play. I wasn't worried about that. I stepped into the rotation, I took a snap from our center, Mark King, the biggest center I had ever seen in my life, and "he'd have liked" to have broken my hand. I'll tell you he hit my hand, and I fumbled, and Mark turned around and said, 'If you can't take the damn ball, don't get down there.'

"What do I do? Do I do what I did to my centers in high school, take control? It wasn't my team. But I was a quarterback, and quarterbacks are supposed to have leadership ability. Do I do what I see David Bowden do? David Bowden didn't take that kind of stuff. My freshman year Bowden was the SEC passing champ. While I was being recruited I watched him throw the ball all over the place to Lee McGriff. I read all the articles that David was going to be the next great Gator quarterback. But I wasn't in David's position.

"Here was a situation where you ask yourself, What do I do? I was afraid. If I had been Willie Jackson, all by myself, I might have been in a real bad situation. But others had come the year before, including big Mike Stanfield, and he pulled me aside and said, 'Look, if you're going to be a quarterback, step in there like a quarterback and do what you're supposed to do. You cannot be intimidated by anybody. You're in a tough situation because you're black, Don, but you've got to understand it's going to be like that.'

"Coach Trammell told me, 'The greatest thing you can do is go out and beat these guys.' Then you can get around all the talk, that name calling, the spitting on you. When you've got teammates, black and white, who are tough, who are going to stand with you, you minimize that junk. And when you're good, you minimize, and then eliminate, the junk. Once I reached a point where I became very confident of who I was and what I was doing, I became a tough player to deal with."

At the start of the 1973 David Bowden was the starting quarterback.

Don Gaffney: "David was the guy—in high school David was known as 'The Lakeland Legend.' He broke all kinds of records. David could throw it, man. He was a great second baseman as well. I wanted to be a baseball player too, like David, like Condredge Holloway. But I had to concentrate on academics, and I couldn't play baseball too. I had to make dern sure I stayed ahead academically."

The opener in 1973 was against Kansas State, a 21–10 victory. David Bowden threw three touchdowns, to Nat Moore, Lee McGriff, and Glenn Sever.

Lee McGriff: "In '73 I was a starter from the beginning and really the focus of the passing game. David Bowden was clearly the quarterback. I was excited to death. We played Kansas State and I scored a touchdown. I thought, Man, this is it. This is college football. This is what I dreamed of."

David Bowden: "We played Kansas State at Florida Field at night time, which was pretty neat. I hadn't ever recalled seeing a Gator game at night. And we spanked them. I threw three touchdowns. I remember after the game Coach Dickey was asked about my performance, and he said, 'Well, we're gonna have to wait and see what he does against the really good teams.' I still hold that in my craw a little bit, but I'm sure he didn't mean it the way it came out. But I was a 20-year-old kid thinking, Gee, Coach, couldn't you have said, 'He really tore them up.'?

Don Gaffney: "I rode the bench the whole way. What I remember most about Kansas State was that they wore purple jerseys. Nice color.

"Glenn Sever made some big plays in that game. David had a big game. I stayed close to David every time he came to the sideline. He wore number 5, and I wore number 8. I watched his demeanor. Coach Dunn always was calm. Coach Dickey was calm with his quarterbacks. Coach Dickey was a fun guy to be around. I always watched coach-coordinator-quarterback relationships, trying to learn what I was supposed to do in those situations, and I watched David, and David was always calm. He would talk to Coach Dickey on the sidelines, and he was always calm and winking. David is just a good guy. I always wanted to ask him so badly, 'What did you see? How did you do that? Why did you do that? And I'd ask him, and he would always tell me. David was so polite."

The next game was against Southern Mississippi. Florida was a heavy favorite but only won by 14–13.

David Bowden: "Southern Mississippi, which just about beat us, had proved through the years that they could beat just about anybody. They were no pushover, but we went into the game thinking they were gonna be."

Don Gaffney: "We had them at home, and we were supposed to beat them by more. This was when the wheels were beginning to come off for us. We struggled in a game we weren't supposed to struggle in."

The Southern Mississippi squeaker was followed by four losses in a row. The first was to Mississippi State, 33–12.

David Bowden: "The next week our world was turned inside out. We went to Jackson to play Mississippi State. Going into that game, I was way up in the stats, and so were Nat and Lee McGriff.

"All week we're reading in the papers that the passing game is finally here, that Bowden, who led the conference last year in passing, has made himself prevalent, and it's going to be onward and upward. And then Mississippi State stuck it up our ass.

"We got to the stadium, and forty thousand Mississippi State fans were ringing cowbells. Cowbells were not outlawed at the time. Rocky Felker was their quarterback. He made every correct decision you cold think of. It was awful—they just swamped us. Humility returned.

"Nat got hurt on the second play of the game and couldn't return, but it wouldn't have mattered. The basic defense is a five-two, and you know where they are coming from. Mississippi State ran a four-four. It was wicked. We didn't get much done on offense. And their guy, Rocky Felker, played the game of his life, man. So humility is a wonderful thing. You need a dose of it every now and then. But there was nothing I could have done. You can't throw the ball on your back. I'm telling you, they were all over us."

Don Gaffney: "I did get into that game, my first SEC game. All I was trying to do was not fumble. I felt like a big guy now. It was my first time playing at Florida Field, and I played my first game and threw my first pass, which was incomplete.

"I remember that Nat Moore hurt himself on the second play of the game. Nat was my stability. He was new, too, but he was so intense and reassuring. Nat was playing because Lenny Lucas had gotten hurt. Nat was so fast.

"One of the things that helped me was being on the field with another fast guy, because I was fast. So instead of me having to slow down, I had a guy who was just as fast. Nat wore this ugly number 39. Nat had just got there too, and he was hungry. He broke a punt in the SMU game. He was beginning to make big plays for us. Nat was becoming a superstar.

"When Nat got into his groove, he gave us a different level of speed. Before Nat, Wayne Fields might have been the greatest athlete I ever met. Wayne was as good as the guys I had played with at home, and I had played with Bob Hayes and Harold Carmichael. Wayne made All-American as a freshman.

"Nat was a truck driver and a basketball player. Nat could have played basketball at Florida. He could shoot pool with anybody. He came into a tough situation. Nat had a daughter. Nat had been driving trucks. He wasn't very tall. He was a very, very mature person—a hard, hard worker. Was he a hard worker? Ooohhh.

"He and Vince Kendrick were good buddies, and it helped me being as young as I was to be in the lineup with those two guys."

At the end of the Mississippi State game, Gaffney threw a pass from his own five yard line. The ball was intercepted and run back 95 yards for a touchdown.

Don Gaffney: "I was trying to make a play. I wanted to throw my first touchdown. The score was 26–12 Mississippi State. Coach Dickey had told me, 'Go in and make something happen.' I was trying to do that. It was a bullet-type pass, and the defender stepped in front of it, and immediately somebody knocked my lights out. I got hit. I tried to get up, and I got hit again. I realized then that this is the big time. You either perform or get off the stage.

"Afterward Coach Dunn told me, 'If you throw an interception, you make dern sure you make the tackle.' That's when I learned you have to keep your head in the game at all times. I realized I was trying to force the ball, and the guy stepped in and picked it."

Lee McGriff: "We were out of sync with our running game, without Nat and Vince. It was terribly disappointing, because we believed we were headed for something big. Any time you think you're going to have a great year, and you suffer your first loss, it gets tainted right there. The first loss is always hard to take. But I'd have to say I wasn't convinced we were in for doom and gloom, because I figured Nat and Vince would get back pretty quickly."

McGriff was wrong. Moore and Kendrick didn't play in the LSU game, and Florida again lost, 24-3. During the second quarter quarterback David Bowden was injured, and Coach Dickey replaced him with Don Gaffney.

David Bowden: "Against LSU, the game was close, and I remember taking this lick to my sternum. I went out of that game."

Don Gaffney: "The game was played in Baton Rouge, and I was beginning to get more and more comfortable. I was beginning to feel good. But the pressure was on. I was learning the lesson of big-time football: you either perform or someone else is right behind you. I HAVE to perform. I have only said this to a handful of people, that my playing away from Florida Field presented less pressure and more of a challenge, because I was on the road where other people would see me. When I came on the field at Mississippi State or LSU, their players never said anything to me. They wouldn't even say hello to me. I'm a sophomore. Condredge Holloway started as a sophomore of Tennessee. Eddie McAshan was starting at Georgia Tech as a sophomore. I knew that Florida would lose patience with me if I didn't produce. They were giving me a chance at quarterback as a sophomore, and Coach Dickey was getting criticized for doing that. Coach Dickey, Coach Dunn and I had a lot of meetings. Coach Dickey told me, 'I don't care how many mistakes you make, Don, you've got the goods to play in this league and be as good as anybody.'

"I rededicated myself. I told myself I would learn every play, learn everything about the other team's defense, and I'm going to think like I thought when I was in high school: every time I step out onto that field, I can make a play.

"Against LSU I came in when we were behind, and we made a charge in that second half, and man, it felt good. I began to feel a groove out there with the players. There were a lot of sophomores inserted into that LSU game in the second half. This was a very young team.

"When I looked around that huddle, I was looking at the guys who came in with me. These guys had anointed me their leader. I felt, I'm looking at MY team now. David was off the field, and I was on it, and I felt that when I stepped on the field, the team became mine.

"Now I was going to let my athleticism take over. I began to run more and feel more comfortable. I began to throw the ball the way I was comfortable throwing it."

Alabama was next. It was mid–October of 1973, and there was unrest on campus. David Bowden remembers the discord. He also remembers sneaking out of the athletic dorm the night before the Alabama game in Gainesville to watch the Allman Brothers band.

David Bowden: "We were there the day the National Guard walked up Thirteenth Street with their battle shields on. There was a protest, and people were sitting in the streets. We all ran down from the stadium where we were housed, all the way to Thirteenth Street to watch. I quickly came running back after I saw the meanness of the scene—how they rooted those people out of the street. Gainesville's always been pretty volatile. Are you familiar with the Gainesville 8? They were arrested for possible insurrectionist activities. It was a tumultuous time.

"Socially all the athletes—the football and baseball players—would drink at the same spots, and we'd have our own private parties. We were pretty insulated.

"The coaches didn't want us hanging around with the hippies, even though some of us were hippies deep down inside to a certain degree. I mean I was. Revels was. Everyone who had that, 'Let me out of here' mentality. I was crazy about the Allman Brothers, man.

"I remember before the Alabama game my junior year, I was married, and before the game you're supposed to stay in the dorm, but the Allman Brothers were playing at 11:30 at night. So I snuck out of the dorm, got in my car, made it home, watched the Allman Brothers and then drove back to the stadium. How stupid is that to endanger your place on Florida Field to go watch the Allman Brothers, but I did. Think of the hell to pay if I'd have been caught coming back into the dorm. 'Yeah, coach, I went to watch the Allman Brothers.' This made perfect sense to me. And it was worth it. Oh yeah, they were hot. One Way Out, Baby."

The Alabama game turned out to be Florida's third consecutive loss, this time by 35-14. David Bowden started and threw two touchdown passes, to make the score 14-21, and then 'Bama blew it open.

David Bowden: "As players we thought we were going to beat Alabama. I certainly did. And we played them good. We trailed 21-0, and we scored twice, and we would have tied the game....We had a play where I sprinted right, knowing that McGriff was going to run a post corner. I pulled up, looked back, and McGriff was breaking free. We had brought in a flanker to block, and just as I was ready to throw, he got bowled over, and the guy hit me. We didn't get that play off. And we were so close to tying the game.

"Then they pulled away from us."

Don Gaffney: "When I went into the Alabama game, Coach Dickey gave me a play to run. When I went in, we were changing game plans. It was more of a spread-out game, more a veer game, more of a play-action offense to take advantage of my speed. Because I could get outside. I could move and throw.

"Coach Dickey said, 'Don, read that safety. If he goes one way, you go the other.' I came to the line of scrimmage. I was standing tall and taking my time. I was doing what I'd seen other quarterbacks do.

"The safety went one way, and we went with a play-action, and Lee McGriff ran a beautiful route, and I shot it to him. Eighteen yard gain. Boy, I felt so good. It was so easy.

"Vince came into the huddle, and he said, 'Coach said run the same play.'

"While we were huddling up, Hollis Boardman, a tall flanker, said, 'I was open. Throw me the damn ball.' I said, 'Lee was open too.' He said, 'Throw me the damn ball.' I wanted to say, 'Hollis, get out of here. Don't say nothing to me,' but I didn't say that.

"Lee came back. He didn't say a word to me. I was told, same play, same read, same execution. What did I do? I threw it to Hollis Boardman. And Woodrow Lowe picked if off and ran it in for a touchdown.

"Lowe took off running, and I couldn't catch him. I was in the end zone, and I remember Alabama players running by me, celebrating. I walked by Lowe and said, 'You will never, ever do that to me again.' He looked at me and smiled. I had screwed up because I did something stupid. I knew I was wrong.

"Coach Dickey asked me what my read was. I said, 'Safety did the same thing.' He said, 'Why didn't you go to the same place.' I started to speak, but then I stopped. I wanted to protect Hollis.

"Later Coach Dickey found out what really happened. Guess who told him? Mike Stanfield. Mike had told Nat, and Nat told Wayne. All the black players sat down with me. The guys said, 'Hey man, if you're not going to be a quarterback, we are not gonna support you. If you're scared to be a leader, scared to do your job, we will not support you. We are trying to help you.'"

Lee McGriff: "Without Nat, it forced me to have an even more prominent role in the offense, because we were trying to throw more. At that age you're thinking, 'Well good, give it to me. I'll make up for Nat.' But you still need to run the ball. What was becoming evident was that speed was becoming an issue. Vince was a pounder, and the other backs were just not cutting it.

"At this point there was talk of Coach Dickey's job, and this does affect you, but you're a little bit in a cocoon as a player. You know it's out there, but you don't lose sleep over it, because we didn't believe he'd really get fired. But the chatter was not good. Here we were all of a sudden with two SEC losses."

Ole Miss was next on the schedule. Coach Dickey, undecided whether to go with an erratic David Bowden or a green Don Gaffney at quarterback, elected to go with the veteran.

Lee McGriff: "Right before the game David and I were walking out of the locker room before we ran onto the field. We stopped at the water fountain together, and we were talking. Coach Dickey came up, and he grabbed David by the arm, didn't try to get him away from me at all, and said, 'David, you're starting this game. If you win it, you keep your job. If you don't, we're probably gonna have to make a change.'

"It was like somebody drained the blood out of David. Obviously David can't win the dang thing all by himself. So David went into the game with that thought.

"Ole Miss was a formidable opponent. It was a good game. We were throwing the ball around again, and we were in the game, and we were down, but we made a drive late in the game to go ahead. I caught a long ball to get us down there. It felt like we were going to pull it off."

With Nat Moore still injured, Florida lost its fourth in a row, 13-10. The three-point loss was the fourth in a row in a season in which Florida had been picked to finish 11-0 by Playboy magazine.

In that game David Bowden had fourth and five with 1:26 left in the game on the Ole Miss 33. Thinking he had made a first down, he threw the ball out of bounds to stop the clock. The gaffe turned the ball—and the game—over to Mississippi.

Lee McGriff: "I caught a long ball, got us close, and we scored, went ahead, and we think we've got it because our defense is good. I never had a scary feeling. We thought if we had the lead with not a lot of time left, with our defense on the field, it'd be over.

"So Ole Miss drove the ball on a couple of fluke pass players, and I mean fluke. They were ugly passes where somehow someone ended up with the ball. Then on third or fourth down and less than two minutes in the game, Ole Miss threw it into the end zone. Randy Talbot was right there. He slapped the ball like a volleyball. That's how 'on the ball' he was. He just slapped it away—straight to an Ole Miss player. If Talbot had just let the ball hit him in the head the game would have been over. But he decided to be adamant about it, and he slapped it, and he slapped it to an Ole Miss player for a touchdown! And that was the winning margin.

"Now we've got the ball, and we're going down the field again. I'm excited. This is our chance to shine. Here we go. David hit me on a pass on third down short of the first down marker, but David and I both think we made it. We were hurrying back to stop the clock. David threw it out of bounds, not realizing it was fourth down. He thought it was first down. So did I. And that was the end of David Bowden. It broke my heart."

David Bowden: "Four plays earlier I had taken a wicked sack, and my head was never clear afterwards. Even though we completed a couple of passes to get down to make it fourth and five.

"I'm fuzzy on the whole episode. I never told anybody about that because I didn't want anybody to think I couldn't take that lick and keep on going. So it's pretty fuzzy. So I threw a pass out of bounds on fourth down, and that's a cross I've had to bear my whole life. Jimmy Fisher and I are really good buddies to this day, and we both have crosses to bear, man. We bear it.

"But we didn't realize it was fourth down. We relied on plays being shuttled in to such an extreme degree that you pretty much lost the facet of keeping up with the game—that's the quarterback's responsibility. Don't get me wrong—but I don't think ANYBODY realized it was fourth down. I didn't.

"I remember Dickey tried to get a play in, 'cause I remember him sending [tight end Hank] Foldberg in, and as I was up at the line of scrimmage and the clock was ticking down, it was a fake dive Y across. I remember thinking at the time, I'm supposed to call that at the line of scrimmage.

"Cause if you say, 'Y across,' they're gonna know who you're going to try to throw the ball to.

"It's a haze. I was a little woozy. All I remember is Vince Kendrick—I love him to this day—after I threw the ball, and I turned around to walk back to the huddle to go again, Vince grabbed me right in the stomach and said, 'DB, I think it was fourth down.' Isn't that sweet? Heartbreakingly soft spoken.

"Yeah, it hurt. It hurt for a long time. However, life's full of those deals. Most of them don't happen in front of sixty thousand people.

"After the game Coach Dickey said to me, 'Don't let it get to you. We lost the game earlier. You can't put it on one play,' which we all know to be true. So he was decent about it. He sure was. There were a lot of ways he was decent. I'm sure he's a good man. I love his kids. I coached one of his kids. It's just that offense wasn't his thing, and it was MY thing."

After the fourth down pass debacle, boos reigned down from the stands. Doug Dickey met with Florida Alumni President Witt Palmer and Athletic Committee member Red Mitchum. They talked about his job. Dickey announced he was staying. He had four more years on his contract. During the week before the Auburn game, Dickey made major changes. He elevated two of his black players, quarterback Don Gaffney and tailback Vince Kendrick, to starter. When Florida went to Auburn, David Bowden was standing on the sidelines.

David Bowden: "It hurt. I knew he was going to play more, but I didn't know I wouldn't play at all. The throes of heartache, but looking back on it, it was a learning experience. Coach Dickey played Don Gaffney, and Don did good. But I was thinking, I would have done good too.

"Give Don Gaffney credit. When he got the chance, he played well and then we began to win. We even got to a bowl game."

Don Gaffney: "I kept telling myself, Just keep working, and you'll get another chance. I was learning, getting better. I would study all the time, watch films, study, watch more films. My dad would not let me get down on myself. After every game, my family was there. It's one thing I had going for myself.

"David hadn't gotten into his groove. He was SEC passing champion, and we needed to throw the ball more."

Lee McGriff: "David is a great guy. It just ate him alive. The press turned acid. We had an open date, and we were going to Auburn after that. Florida had never beaten Georgia in that stadium, so it looked like the season was just going to be a disaster. People were fussing at David for making that mistake. It's happened before. It's happened since. Jimmy Fisher did it a couple years later. It was one of those things that was just a tragedy. And the truth is, if we had scored a field goal or a touchdown, that wouldn't have happened. We were going down the field without a problem.

"The press and fans were on Coach Dickey. At this point rumors were flying because it looked like this might be a 4-7 season, and they might fire Coach Dickey. And Coach Dickey decided to roll the dice. He decided to start Don Gaffney at quarterback.

"Later I coached on Coach Dickey's staff, and he told me he did it because of the speed issue. It was all about getting the ball outside and resurrecting the running game, because Don Gaffney could run. David Bowden could not. Don Gaffney could run the option. David Bowden didn't. So he put Don at quarterback and made Vince Kendrick the tailback. That was Coach Dickey's solution to jump-starting the running game."

Don Gaffney: "The fans were all over Coach Dickey, and some of the things they said, man, it hurt so bad, I just felt so bad for Coach Dickey because Coach Dickey took a chance, man. He brought in a lot of black players. He brought in a black quarterback. He was trying to play the best guys, and some players just weren't ready for that kind of change yet.

"After the Ole Miss game, Fred Abbott, our captain, a great captain, a great player, he and John Lacer and David Hitchcock, called a meeting of the whole team. Without anybody saying, 'Look, we've got a black/white problem, the gist was, We're in this together, all of us. We're all Florida Gators, and we've got to represent ourselves as well, and if you don't feel like doing your best, do everybody a favor and leave.'

"I was really proud of Fred, because I knew he was hurting. He was hurting for us, for Coach Dickey, for the program."

thirty-nine

The First

After the 1973 Ole Miss game, there was a two-week break in the schedule. By now Doug Dickey was beginning to feel the heat of a disintegrating season. In 1971 his record was 4-7, followed by 5-5-1, and so far '73 had started out 2-4. The alumni were getting ugly.

Dickey, figured that if he was going to get fired, he was going to get fired doing things his way, and he decided that against vaunted Auburn he would feature the running offense and start two blacks, Don Gaffney at quarterback and Vince Kendrick at tailback.

Don Gaffney: "We had to change things. We knew we had some problems. They were saying, it's gut-check time.

"We were getting ready for Auburn, a top team. We had never won there, and it was going to be nasty. We knew that. This was not the best situation to get ready to start in. I watched the films of Auburn, and they were big and mean. They were a top team, a bowl team, coached by Shug Jordan. I was thinking, this would be a good one to sit out. 'Cause Coach Dickey never said I was going to start.

"A couple of days after the Ole Miss game, Coach Dunn and Coach Don Breaux came to me and said, 'We want you to take every other snap in practice.'

"I had never done that before. And in addition to quarterback meetings, the coaches had private meetings with me. I called my dad and said, 'I don't know. Something strange is going on here.'

"I figured by Friday they would let me know I was starting, but nothing. Friday we got into the stadium, and we went through our drills, and David and I were both with the first group. Chan Gailey, the third-string quarterback, said to me, 'When you're in there, watch me between every play.' I said, 'Okay,

Chan.' He said, 'I'm going to give you the key. Look to the sideline after every play. Watch me. I'll know the play before it gets there, before the guy brings it in, and I will be giving you your key.'

"He said, If you come up to the line of scrimmage, and it's a bad situation, I will let you know.' They gave me exactly one check-off play, a run.

"Going into the game Coach Dickey told me, 'Don't worry about checking to a big play. Just try to keep us out of a bad play.' That was simple.

"After the Friday workout, we went back to the hotel, and I called my dad. I said, 'I think I'm gonna start, but I don't know.' He said, 'Did they tell you?' I said, 'No, sir, but I have a funny feeling. They're going to have to tell me sooner or later. I'll let you know.'

"When I called back Saturday morning one hour before the game, I told him, 'I still don't know. But I know I'm going to play a lot.' Because they had put plays in the offense that I ran and David didn't, a game play designed for what I do. But I didn't really know. They had told me nothing. And the other players were wondering too. "We got dressed, and we went out to warm up. At this point I figured I wasn't starting, otherwise they would have told me. I even saw David talking to Coach Dickey like he normally did.

"Then a strange thought occurred to me: Maybe they were setting me up to fail so they could say, 'I gave him every opportunity.' Then I got scared. We went out onto the field, and Sammy Green, my roommate, said, 'Don, you've got to be starting.' I said, 'I don't know.'

"We went through our warmups, and I decided to put it out of my mind, not to worry about it. We went back into the locker room, and Coach Dickey went into his spiel about what we needed to do, and he said, 'Father Mike, come on up.' Father Mike came up to say our prayer like he usually did.

"It was five minutes before the game, and Coach Dickey was holding a football in his hand, and he said, 'Don, you got it.' The idea was that he didn't want to give me any more pressure than I needed.

"As they were introducing the players and we were coming out of the dressing room, Wayne Fields said to me, 'All right, Don. This is what we've been waiting for.' He said, We!

"We went down the tunnel going into the stadium. I said a prayer like I normally did: 'Lord, just let me do the best I can do.' And for the first time I realized the significance of being the first black quarterback starting at the University of Florida, only the second in the Southeast Conference, one of the few in America. This was the first time a black quarterback started a game at Jordan-Hare Stadium. All of a sudden positive vibes started coming over me. I kept remembering Coach saying, 'You don't have to make big plays. Just try not to make bad plays.'

"We were outside, and Coach Dickey said to me, 'Are you ready for this? This is what you've been waiting for.'

"I said, 'Yes sir, I've been waiting for it.'

"In the back of my mind I thought, I've been waiting for this my entire life."

Lee McGriff: "We went up to Auburn, and you could cut the tension with a knife. Nobody expected us to win. Auburn had a good team. We have this young quarterback who has athletic ability, but he seemed like the jitteriest human being you've ever met in your life. I thought, Oh God, how is he going to hold up? For me, I was thinking he had a strong arm, but Lord knows, sometimes he wasn't very accurate.

"Some funny things happened before the game. Jimmy DuBose was a sophomore. The night before the game at the evening meal, Coach Dickey would always ask a senior to say the blessing. This night he asked DuBose to say it. The place went deathly silent. Jimmy DuBose absolutely froze. When he finally spoke, he said, 'Dear Lord,' and then his voice cracked. Everyone tried not to laugh, but it was hard. About five minutes later the next thing that came out of his mouth was, 'Thank you for bringing me back to Auburn, Alabama.' Later he said he had never been there before, and Auburn had not recruited him, but he was thanking God for bringing him back to Auburn.

"All the guys fell out over as he stumbled and fumbled over the blessing.

"Then Coach Dickey, who never told a joke, told a joke. Just the fact that he tried to tell this joke cracked everyone up. Everybody got loose. And we beat them for the first time at Jordan-Hare Stadium.

"Several memorable things happened in that game. First, I always threw up before every game, but I didn't throw up before this one. It was weird. We went in at halftime, and I drank a grape soda. We got the ball to start the second half. I ran out onto the field, got into the huddle, and I threw up grape soda all over the shoes of our tackle, Mike Williams. He was squealing like a girl when I was puking on his shoes.

"They called the play, and he ran up to the line, and as I'm buttoning my chinstrap, he has purple puke all over his shoes.

"Then at the end of the game Burt Lawless, whose dad played for Auburn, was jumping around so much we could barely get him into the

Coach Robert Woodruff and Angus Williams
COURTESY OF ANGUS WILLIAMS

Red Mitchum
COURTESY OF SCOTT MITCHUM

Angus Williams
COURTESY OF ANGUS WILLIAMS

*Coach Woodruff with
Lauren Broadus
& Angus Williams*
COURTESY OF ANGUS WILLIAMS

Charlie LaPradd
COURTESY OF CHARLIE LAPRADD

Jimmy Dunn
UNIVERSITY OF FLORIDA
SPORTS INFORMATION

Frank Dempsey
COURTESY OF FRANK DEMPSEY

Don Gaffney
UNIVERSITY OF FLORIDA
SPORTS INFORMATION

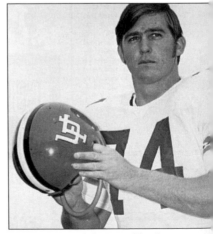

Jack Youngblood
UNIVERSITY OF FLORIDA
SPORTS INFORMATION

John Reaves
UNIVERSITY OF FLORIDA
SPORTS INFORMATION

Ray Graves
COURTESY OF RAY GRAVES

Willie Jackson
UNIVERSITY OF FLORIDA
SPORTS INFORMATION

Jimmy Fisher
UNIVERSITY OF FLORIDA
SPORTS INFORMATION

Coach Ray Graves with Steve Spurrier/COURTESY OF RAY GRAVES

Steve Spurrier
AP/WIDE WORLD PHOTOS

Larry Libertore
UNIVERSITY OF FLORIDA
SPORTS INFORMATION

Larry Smith
UNIVERSITY OF FLORIDA
SPORTS INFORMATION

John Brantley
UNIVERSITY OF FLORIDA
SPORTS INFORMATION

Wayne Peace
UNIVERSITY OF FLORIDA
SPORTS INFORMATION

Ricky Nattiel
UNIVERSITY OF FLORIDA
SPORTS INFORMATION

Kerwin Bell
UNIVERSITY OF FLORIDA
SPORTS INFORMATION

Kirk Kirkpatrick
UNIVERSITY OF FLORIDA
SPORTS INFORMATION

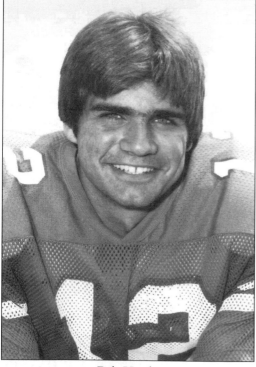

Bob Hewko
UNIVERSITY OF FLORIDA
SPORTS INFORMATION

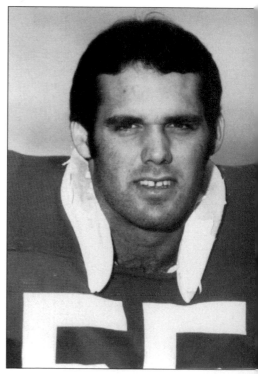

Scott Brantley
UNIVERSITY OF FLORIDA
SPORTS INFORMATION

Danny Wuerffel
THE TAMPA TRIBUNE

Emmitt Smith
THE TAMPA TRIBUNE

Shane Matthews/UNIVERSITY OF FLORIDA SPORTS INFORMATION

Terry Dean/UNIVERSITY OF FLORIDA SPORTS INFORMATION

(l-r) Coach Ray Graves, Gary Froid and Steve Spurrier/COURTESY OF GARY FROID

huddle. Between plays Coach Dickey was yelling at him, 'Burton Lawless, get in the huddle.' He was like a wild pony we were trying to get under control, because we didn't need to do something stupid and get a penalty or turn the ball over or have to punt. Burton just acted like an idiot, and we were all yelling at him, 'Get in the damn huddle and let's run this play so we don't lose the game, for God sake.' That's how it ended."

The Auburn game of 1973 turned out to be one of the great wins in the history of the University of Florida. The game began when defensive lineman John Lacer forced a fumble. Vince Kendrick scored to make it 6-0, and then Don Gaffney hit Joel Parker with a touchdown pass to make it 12-0. Auburn only scored at the end of the game when Gaffney was hit, fumbled, and Auburn recovered for the lone score.

Don Gaffney: "We were on our first drive, and Coach Dunn told me we would score on this play if we called it. I'll never forget, the moment before I threw him that touchdown, Joel told me, 'Just lay it out there, and I'll get it. Put it high.'

"It was a play-action to Vince [Kendrick], and Vince was an intense player, and Auburn bought the run. The safety bit like he was supposed to, and I had so much time, and man, I could throw with anybody.

"Joel ran a perfect post route, and all I had to do was throw the football to him, and it was like it was in slow motion. It was that easy. And from that point on, I realized I could play this game.

"Our entire sideline lit up. We were up on Auburn at Auburn, and we had a tremendous defense, and our game plan was to control the ball. I was not going to throw interceptions. I was not going to get sacked. I was not going to fumble. We were going to control it by giving it to Vince and getting five yards at a time and throw mostly on second down. We didn't want to be third and long. We wanted third and short.

"On that play we scored in the third quarter of the Auburn game, it was an option play going left, and I went down and being quick, I jumped on the defensive end very quickly, went right at him. I gave him a body fake and flipped it back to Vince, who crashed into the end zone.

"I regret a mistake I made when we were running out the clock at the end of the game. We were ahead 12-0, and we were running an option play deep in our territory. My idea was if I slow the play down, delay it and make the pitch real late, that will slow things down. I don't know what I was thinking. I was hoping the defensive end would jump and then come back at me. I tossed the ball late, and their defensive end, a big guy named Ken Burnish— he wanted to hurt me anyway. He was angry. I had had a wonderful day with him all day long. I don't know why I kept underestimating this guy. He was an All-American type player. When I flipped the ball, he hit it, and the ball flew, bouncing, bing, bing, bing, bing, bing, and I had a moment to recover it, and Auburn recovered, and Auburn scored off that and got a two-point conversation.

"Up to that point I had done everything we had planned to do. I knew what I did that play was not right. I was so upset I began crying in the locker room after the game. I went to Coach Knotts to apologize. The defensive guys had played their butts off and I blew the shutout. They didn't deserve that. They deserved to beat Auburn for the first time at Auburn with a shutout. And it was my fault they didn't.

"Despite everything else, I felt bad, but realistically, part of that was having to overcome a lot of stuff that had happened, and then messing up, giving people who didn't like me a chance to criticize. But more than that, it gave those who didn't like Coach Dickey an opening to criticize him for taking a chance on me. Because our team deserved better, and he deserved better.

"Today Kordell Stewart plays quarterback for the Pittsburgh Steelers and no one thinks anything about it. He's just another football player now. But back then it was different. The pressure on me was incredible.

"Afterward reporters asked me about the Gator jinx against Auburn. I said, 'What jinx? I didn't see any jinx. The sky was beautiful. A wonderful crowd. We played Auburn, one of the premier teams in the country.' They said, 'Well, Florida has never won here.' I said, 'I wasn't on those teams, and neither were these guys, but everybody who has ever played for the Gators can rejoice in this victory.'

"When we got back to Gainesville, they gave us a tremendous reception. I couldn't believe it. I was shocked. There were thousands waiting at the airport when we got there. We rode the bus back to the stadium, and when we got there, there were people there. Sammy Green and I went to our rooms, and then we walked across the street to Baskin-Robbins 31 flavors—the owner gave us banana splits for free—and it was late, and we went to sleep. Where else were we going to go? It was one in the morning."

The 11-10 come-from-behind win over Georgia in 1973 was one of the greatest wins in the history of the program. Georgia led 10-3 with 9:36 left in the game. Florida had the ball on its own 20. Don Gaffney passed to Lee McGriff to get the ball down to the Georgia 17, and then he threw him another pass that McGriff caught leaping in the end zone. Florida trailed by one, 10-9.

Lee McGriff: "There was a cold wind in our face, and the place was electric. Here was another game coming down to the wire. There were times when it looked like the drive was going to die. There was a third down pass to me that was way off the mark, but I was hit too soon, and Georgia was called for interference to get a first down. There was another long ball on third down that I dove for and caught to get us down there.

"Don was throwing. He hit Joel Parker on another critical third down for a first down. Now we were down at their end of the field, down near their twenty. It was third and eight, and we called a screen pass to Vince Kendrick, a perfect call, a perfect throw. And Vince dropped the ball. He could have walked into the end zone.

"At that point the place was insane, and it was looking like it wasn't going to happen. On fourth down, I was supposed to go to the back of the end zone and then come across the middle on a curl pattern. I was going down the right side, curling back right to left. Don threw it, and this was an out-of-body experience. Somehow you were going to make the play. The defenders were hanging on. The ball was high. It just happened: I made the play. Touchdown."

Don Gaffney: "Lee McGriff was just an incredible football player. He just needed an opportunity to make plays. During the course of the game, Lee was my conscience. He would talk to our team. He would keep everybody going, and so I didn't have to worry about doing that. There was a lot of hoopla about my coming home, but I couldn't rejoice in that unless we won.

"The fact that we won at Auburn showed we could win in a tough place. We had done something incredible. Georgia had gone and won at Tennessee.

"We took the opening kickoff, and we scored first on a field goal. They came back and scored ten straight points, and they took the lead on us. We were moving the ball up and down but didn't cash in. Both defenses were playing well.

"I thought our next-to-last drive was going to be our last drive. We were in a bad situation because we had to go into the wind. I hated to have to come from behind with the wind in my face. I had played in the Gator Bowl many times in high school, and that wind off the St. Johns River can get tough, particularly late in the evening. So I had experience throwing into the wind, so I wasn't worry. But I was concerned about us executing in general. We were playing well, but we kept killing ourselves. Our next to last drive turned out to be our best drive.

"We got a break on a pass interference call, that gave us the ball near the 25, and then I threw for 30 yards to Lee.

"We had an incomplete and two passes for no gain. We had a fourth down. You can see how the drama was building. I decided that Lee was going to catch the ball regardless. You can't lose going to Lee McGriff.

"On fourth and five, we went to a twin look toward my left, giving me the wide side of the field. It would have been more natural to go to the right side, but I could throw pretty good. That helped my offensive coordinator. He could go both ways with me. I could roll. I could run. The whole idea was this: 'Don, I'm gonna give you two guys to your left, and we're gonna get you on the corner, and we're gonna send James Richards and Vince Kendrick to block the defensive ends. The idea was for me to get on that corner and jump five yards into the end zone. I once saw Condredge Holloway do that, and in my head I was going to make that play. Holloway could jump five yards. I later learned I couldn't. When I broke to the outside, the play opened up beautifully, and there was Joel Parker. He's tall and a great target, and I couldn't resist. I threw the ball running to my left, and I hit him, and he swallowed it up, a super play, and we got a first down on the 20.

"The next play was J.R. [James Richards] on an option. We came with the same counter-option play that I fumbled on against Auburn, and this time instead of taking a chance, I went down. No gain.

"There was an offsides penalty, and then a dropped pass—Vince went in motion, and I threw it to him a little low. Now we're fourth and eight. Here we go again.

"Believe it or not, we did this without timeouts. McGriff went to the right. I dropped back, and this time the Auburn defensive end looped. I would have done the same thing they did: try to keep me inside and don't let me run. So they looped. I could feel him when I stepped back into the pocket. I got ready to throw, pumped, and I saw McGriff coming across. There were so many Georgia players there. I just let it go. He had three or four defenders, but I threw it away from him. Lee would practice this. He would work on his diving catches daily.

"When the safety bit, he was backing up. He was the guy in front of Lee. Lee was dragging across the back of the end zone one yard inside the end zone. We had a deeper pass on the other side. When the safety backed up, Lee hooked to his left. When he looked to his left, I threw to his right. By the time the safety turned around, Lee was on his right side. I threw the ball away from the safety's right, and it sailed a bit and got away a little bit, but Lee went up and got it. He made an incredible, incredible catch for a touchdown."

Doug Dickey decided to go for two to defeat Georgia. One play would decide the game.

Don Gaffney: "I was looking to the sideline, and I saw Coach Dickey put two fingers up, but I went to the sideline anyway. Coach Dunn told me we were going for two. We had worked on two plays, and he told me we were going to use the one with Kendrick in motion. The idea was to throw the ball where we had not thrown it all day. That was to Hank Foldberg Jr.

"The first read was to Vince, if he was open. We knew he'd catch it. The second read was to Hank, and the third was for me to run.

"We sent Vince in motion, which left us with one fullback, James Richards, and Jared blocked backside. When I stepped back, I immediately looked to Vince. The safety and linebacker were both on him. When I looked up, I was thinking scramble because we're talking three yards. I figured the worst case scenario was to scramble and figure something out, find a way. I had been running the ball pretty successfully against Georgia that day. I looked up, and the safety and linebacker jumped Vince, and Henry was wide open. He was just there. I made a mistake and threw it hard and low. I was always told that when you throw it down the middle to throw it high, but I forgot I was throwing into the end zone. So I threw it right into his breadbasket, and Hank is 6'6", and he caught it and folded it up like he was catching a baseball. He has huge hands. I never thought he'd drop it. I never even thought about that. We took the lead 11-10."

Lee McGriff: "Of course we went for two. A win was all that mattered at that point. Look at where we had come from. And there was no overtime. A tie would not have done much good to save Coach Dickey's job.

"On the two-point conversation I ran a quick post, and I was thinking it was coming to me, but Hank [Foldberg] did his little deal, just dragged over the middle, and Don found him and threw a low ball, and Hank came up with it. My God, that place—I can feel the ground tremble forever. It was a wonderful moment."

Don Gaffney: "Unfortunately the game wasn't over. Georgia was one of those 'never-say-die' type teams. Vince Dooley was that kind of coach. After we scored the two points to go ahead [with 3:48 left in the game], we kicked off. They had time, and they started moving the ball really fast. It was really frightening the way Georgia could throw the football. Then their running back broke one on us. At the end of the game Allen Leavitt, their field goal kicker, lined up to kick a 60 yarder.

"Leavitt had been deadly. He had made some big kicks. But remember I was telling you about the winds in the Gator Bowl. It was a swirling wind, and when he lined up to kick it, I said to myself, 'With the finish we just had, there's no way he's going to make it.' I was also thinking, If he makes it, we're going to have to go out there and get right at them. Coach Dickey had called the offense together, just in case. We were ready. We were going to go into our two-minute drill. It would have been my first time running the two-minute drill in live competition.

"He kicked it, it had the distance, but it missed. And when he missed it, it was unreal. We went back onto the field and ran out the clock. I remember standing in the huddle at the end of the Georgia game running down the clock. I was standing there, seizing the moment, thinking, This is unbelievable.

"We ran the ball into the line a couple of times, and the game was over. That was it. Afterwards what I remember was the joy in Coach Dickey's voice. We went into the locker room, and the reporters asked Coach Dickey, 'We play Kentucky next week. What can you do to follow what you've done the last two weeks?' He told them, 'You'll just have to pay your seven dollars to come and see.'

"These were two of the most important victories Florida probably ever had for a lot of reasons. People ask me about them all the time. I'm really amazed that there are people who remember those moments. One guy, a Gator fan for forty years, told me it was the greatest thing he had ever experienced."

Homecoming against the University of Kentucky was next. Florida led 20–3 behind the play of Don Gaffney, but Wildcat QB Sonny Collins closed the gap to 20–18. Wayne Fields, who had three interceptions, picked off a pass with six seconds left in the game to save the day.

Don Gaffney: "It was a big stat day for a lot of players. We gained five hundred yards in total offense. But it took an interception by Wayne Fields to end it.

"Kentucky had Sonny Collins at quarterback. He had a great game against us. Here you had a sophomore in Sonny and a sophomore in me. There were a lot of sophomores on that field. It was a close game. The play Wayne made saved it for us.

"I remember him going up in the air. The ball was thrown toward the corner. He caught it inside the five, and then he broke a fabulous run. I remember that more than anything I did in that game.

"The other thing I remember occurred on the second play of the game. We were running the veer, and we go on this sprint-out, and I kept the ball. I went out of bounds on the Kentucky sideline. The defender hit me late. Coach Curci was standing there, and he said, 'Kill him. Kill him. I told you I was gonna get you, Gaffney. I told you I was gonna get you. We're gonna get you.'

"I went and told Coach Dickey. Curci was mad at me, because when he was at Miami he recruited me. I went to Miami for the Miami-Florida game, and I found myself rooting for Florida, and Coach Curci didn't like that. It was the only trip I made without my parents, and I hated it. Coach Curci wanted to know why I wanted to leave early to go back home. I told him I had made up my mind. He asked me which school. I told him, 'Florida,' and boy, did he get angry.

"After I returned home, Coach Curci sent me a bill asking me to pay for a $24 in phone calls I had made from Miami to home. He was the only coach who got angry with me. I told my teammates about it, and after the game Coach Curci wouldn't shake my hand."

Lee McGriff: "I had one particularly memorable catch. It was deep and I jumped up and caught it. It wasn't a touchdown, but it was a good day. It was Homecoming. It was Kentucky. It was SEC, and now we've won three in a row, and wow, we're beginning to feel better."

Miami, a strong defensive club, was next. The game was played in the Orange Bowl. Florida came away with a 14-7 win.

Don Gaffney: "What I remember about the Miami game was that for some reason we were not very hyped. We couldn't get up for them, because Florida State was around the corner. We had had a big emotional win over Auburn, a big, emotional win over Georgia. We had a scare against Kentucky. When we went to Coral Gables, Miami was not the Miami of today. They had a great defense, had some great athletes on that team. It might have been the most physical game I played that year. For some reason I just could not solve their defensive scheme. It was the first time I was confused. I did not have a tremendous offensive game, but I was able to hit Joel Parker for a touchdown pass.

"This was the year of the 'November to remember.' It was the first time Florida had ever defeated Auburn, Georgia, Kentucky, and Miami in one season, and we won all those games in the month of November. And this was after going five weeks without winning."

Florida State was next, and the Gators were merciless in a 49-0 romp.

Lee McGriff: "We owned them. We threw it, we ran it, we stuffed them. It was just one of those days where you thought you were king of the mountain. We humiliated FSU, and we really enjoyed that."

Don Gaffney: "We just took it to them. Nat Moore had recovered from his ankle injury, and we were trying to showcase him. For our big guys, Nat and Vince, it was all about statistics, and we were able to run up many statistics. We were rolling that day. Florida State could not have stopped us if we had played fifty quarters that day.

"During the game Coach Dickey took me out. He said, 'Don, you don't have any stats. Come on, little man, stand over here with me.'

"Coach Dickey asked David [Bowden] to go into the game, and he wouldn't. He was vehement about it. I was standing next to David, and I looked at him, and I could see how dejected he was. It was hard for me to gloat, because I understood his pain. Coach Dickey took me out, and David wouldn't go in, and we put Chan Gailey in.

"Chan was wonderful. He had coached me through all I was going through, and he helped me. And Chan could throw the ball. Remember, Chan had played behind John Reaves. Against Florida State, Chan threw for two touchdowns."

David Bowden: "We were ahead of Florida State 35-0 at the half. Florida State had a pitiful team. Coach Dickey came to me and said, 'You've got it starting the second half.'

"I said, 'Coach, I don't want to go in with the score 35-0.' I'm harboring bitterness at this point. I remember telling Coach, 'I'm gonna play baseball. What's the point? Let one of the younger guys get in there.'

"And that caused quite a flap. And again, to Coach Dickey's credit, he didn't make it a 'You're outta here' kind of deal. I think that deep within him he understood the hurt."

After the defeat of Florida State, Florida's fifth straight victory, the Gators were invited to the Tangerine Bowl. Many of the players didn't want to go. They wanted a more prestigious forum, or nothing at all.

Lee McGriff: "Probably half the team didn't want to go. They either wanted to go to a bigger bowl or a more exotic situation than Orlando, or they'd rather not do it. Some guys felt, 'We finished in a blaze. We're on a roll. We don't want to go to the Tangerine Bowl.' That was never my sentiment, not at all. My feeling was if I could have played football in somebody's backyard, that was A-OK with me.

"You know when you put it to a vote, and the head coach is there, and you have to raise your hand or not raise your hand in front of the coach, you don't want to be seen as the guy who didn't raise his hand... so we voted to go."

The Tangerine Bowl game usually was played in Orlando, but the directors of the event figured they could sell an extra 20,000 tickets if they played the game in Gainesville, and so the game was moved there.

Lee McGriff: "They were in financial trouble. They were revamping the Orlando Stadium, and so they brought the game back to Florida Field."

Their opponent, Miami of Ohio, was undefeated and underrated. An injury to Don Gaffney ruined the Gator game plan.

Don Gaffney: "I was healthy. I felt good. We were rolling. We had won five straight. We were training in Orlando, and then something happened to my back. I'm not sure how I got hurt, but it was bad enough that I couldn't practice. I could barely turn.

"We thought it would clear up in time.

"On game day the temperature was 26 degrees. It was the coldest I've ever been. I played perhaps a quarter, but I just could not bend over to take a snap. And the game plan was geared to me, so we were in trouble.

"Robbie Davis came in, and he hadn't gotten many reps. He did a real good job under really tough circumstances. Robbie could throw the ball. We called him Snake, because he reminded us of Kenny Stabler.

"We lost the game 16-7 because we didn't perform on offense. If you look at the statistics, there was nothing there. The game plan had been structured around speed, and the things I could do: the sprintout pass, and now we couldn't do that. I couldn't even stand up."

Lee McGriff: "Don wasn't playing well, and Coach Dickey went to Chan Gailey, and Chan didn't have a good day, and then he went to Robbie Davis, and Robbie struggled, and then he came to David. He was desperate. We were about to lose the game. The running game wasn't working, and we needed to throw it. I could have told you that in the first quarter, but he waited until the fourth quarter.

"David ran on that field. I was in the huddle. I was all teared up. I loved David. We had some wonderful moments. I thought he'd never see the field again. I was happy for him, happy for me, because I knew what we had to do when he came in the game. I knew he and I could make it work. And we went right down the field. I was emotional that whole drive, because I was thinking, You know, damn it, here is your guy. At worst, mix in Gaffney with Bowden, but why did you ever just throw David Bowden in the trash can? He was just too good a thrower.

"We ended up losing, but I'll always feel like we ran out of time because if David could have played longer, not only was the ball going up and down that field with David Bowden, but we would have won that game."

David Bowden: "We took a vote on whether or not we wanted to play in the Tangerine Bowl because it seemed a little beneath us. We were there, but I don't think we were totally focused. Miami was undefeated that year, and they came ready to play.

"I finally got to play in the Miami of Ohio game in the fourth quarter. It was nineteen degrees. What I remember most after coming into the game after not playing for five games is seeing the looks on my offensive linemen's faces. I carry that in my heart. Not that they were glad to get rid of Don. Just that I had been there before, and they were glad to see me.

"I went in and played well. I threw a long pass to Nat. It was similar to the very first game I played against SMU. Miami of Ohio was ahead of us all game long. I finally got in, and we raced up and down the field. So my beginning and end were very similar, but this time they wound up beating us."

And so the 1973 season ended, not with a bang, but with a whimper. But for Don Gaffney, it was a year of opportunity, learning, and success. He had taken a dispirited team and made them winners again. And he helped make the transition from a mostly white team to an integrated one smooth and easy.

Don Gaffney: "I thought it was extremely rewarding. It was exciting at the same time. There were no tremendous disappointments. There were moments where I learned things about life and about myself, because there was a great deal to learn about life there. And I did."

For David Bowden, the season could not have been more of a disappointment. It had started with promise, but the fourth-down gaffe in the Old Miss game in effect ended his college career. When he returned in the spring and saw that he no long was being counted on, he decided to concentrate his efforts on baseball.

David Bowden: "My junior year, I went to spring practice and saw that I was fourth on the depth chart behind Gaffney, Chan Gailey, and Jimmy Fisher. I didn't feel I had much of a relationship with Coach Dickey, so I decided to focus on baseball.

"He called me on the phone and said, 'David, I want you to come be like our late-inning relief pitcher.' Which I should have done, because that's what he saw me as, and that was when we had our best moments on offense. But I said, 'No, Coach, I'm gonna focus on baseball.' He said, 'Well, okay.'

"I played four years of Gator baseball. I was an infielder. My senior year I played third base. Twice I made All-SEC, and I got drafted by the Detroit Tigers.

"Out of high school I had been a second-round draft pick and was offered forty grand. Gene Campbell and Ed Catalinas, the director of player personnel of the Tigers, came to the Holiday Inn in Lakeland, and Catalinas said, 'David, you've got a swing made for our park.' He told me to go home and think about it.

"I came back and I said, 'Guys, I love you guys for drafting me, but I'm gonna play for the Florida Gators.' I turned it down because I wanted to run out of that tunnel at Florida Field. So the second time around, I was 21 years old, and they don't give you much money.

"I got a regular signing bonus, went to Lakeland, played a bit at Montgomery and then got released."

After his release Bowden went into the insurance business, but after three months he determined he wasn't ready to give up football. He was offered a combination baseball and football coaching job at Buchholz High School in Gainesville and coached for seven years. His baseball teams won six district titles.

He also became heavily involved in music. He would teach school, go to practice, take a nap, and head for the local bar where his band played rock and roll and country music at some of the premier gigs in Gainesville, including Lillians and The Lone Star. An afficionado of Dickie Betts of The Allman Brothers Band, Bowden played in the band for almost eight years.

Then in 1984, his dad took sick. The music wasn't interrupting his life, but the life surrounding it was. He needed to get away.

David Bowden: "My dad was ill and didn't have long to live. And that wake-up call came from perhaps the Almighty. I told the bar I was leaving to be with my dad.

"Looking back, I was all-blessed. It was all good. The heartache involved prepares all of us—ain't nothing easy, you know. You've got to get over it."

forty

A 7-1 Start

Don Gaffney: Going into spring practice in '74 Coach Dickey decided we would experiment with the wishbone offense. We couldn't figure out why until we saw he had signed a great freshman running back class. We had so many great running backs. We had a great fullback in Jimmy DuBose coming back, James Richards coming back, and Andrew Wade, and we got Robert Morgan, Larry Brinson—great, great speed. We had Wayne Fields, one of the first two-way players. Wayne was still playing running back. He could play everything. He was an All-SEC safety.

"We got Willie Wilder and Earl Carr and Tony Green—my God, look out! I never had anything like Tony, other than David Hopper, who I had played with at Raines High School and who went to Texas Southern. Tony was phenomenal, tough and fast. Now I had a player on the field with me who was as quick as Nat Moore or Wes Chandler, and faster.

"So we had a great big stable of running backs with size and speed and savvy and toughness. And we had a quarterback who could run extremely well.

"We also had some tremendous linemen, which would become known as 'The Family.' We had Jimmy Ray Stephens, Robbie Moore, Joe Loper, Mike Williams, and Mike Stanfield had one more year with us. You're talking of a team that has some offensive fire-power galore.

"The question now is, What do you do?

"I didn't want to go to the wishbone. I was hoping we wouldn't do it. In the spring we studied the way Texas and Oklahoma ran the wishbone, and we were having fun with it, and we looked very good. We had SO much speed."

Lee McGriff: "Coach Dickey decided that he would run the wishbone offense, and I was scared to death of what that was going to mean to me.

Other teams ran the wishbone. Alabama was a wishbone team, and they had a receiver, Wayne Wheeler, who was an All-American. So I tried to find the good side of it. And it did turn out to be a good thing for me, but at first I had an uneasy feeling."

In 1974, Doug Dickey was promoted to the varsity a sophomore quarterback by the name of Jimmy Fisher. He had come to Florida as a thrower, but when Dickey decided to switch his offense to the wishbone, Fisher knew he would have to adjust. He lifted weights in an effort to become faster and stronger. He was going to have to run more, and he would have to be big enough to take a hit.

Jimmy Fisher: "I grew up in Temple Terrace, Florida, a suburb of Tampa.

"I was recruited out of high school mainly in the South. I got a letter from most of the Southeastern teams, Georgia, Georgia Tech, South Carolina. The most impressive person who recruited me was Jim Donnan, who was an assistant coach at Florida State. Nevertheless, I wanted to go to the University of Florida.

"Doug Dickey was the coach, and Jimmy Dunn, the offensive coordinator and quarterback coach, who also happened to be from the Tampa area, recruited me. Jimmy was my position coach. And Jack Burns, a graduate assistant, also recruited me. Jack is now the offensive coordinator for the Atlanta Falcons.

"I arrived in Gainesville in the fall of 1972. It was the first time freshmen were eligible to play on the varsity. It was an interesting time in college, because they were just beginning to restrict the number of prospects they could sign. Right before that period, knowing the restrictions were coming, most schools signed A LOT of kids. So when I came to Florida, we had a full-fledged JV team. We played in four JV games, but our main job was to be the scout team and run the plays of the opposing teams. We had ten or eleven quarterbacks. It's not like it is today when you're only four or five down the list. We had a TREMENDOUS number of kids on our team. You would come in and you could be eighth or ninth, and it would look hopeless.

"I can remember my freshman year when we played Alabama. I was in the stands and I remember they started coming out of the tunnel, and they just kept coming. It was amazing. It looked like an army. There must have been three hundred players! And when they subbed, they actually sent in a whole second team with a quarterback. They didn't have enough room on the sidelines.

"I was quarterbacking the scout team but about three weeks into my freshman season, I broke my ankle when I was tackled by Ralph Ortega and Glenn Cameron, two All-American linebackers. I ended up sitting out the rest of the season to the very end. I tried to come back, but I couldn't.

"We were running a split backfield, and we threw the ball 20 to 25 times a game, but my sophomore year Doug Dickey decided he had the horses and the people to put in the wishbone and make it work, so we all went there. That was an interesting contrast to what I was. I became an option quarterback. We had some guys who were absolutely wonderful throwers. People will never know his name, but we had a quarterback by the name of Mark Newman. He was 6'5", 220 pounds from Bel Glades. Mark won the state title two years. Until he came to Florida, he was in front of me. I mean, if you had to put the mold together, he was destined to go to the next level. But at that point we went to the wish-bone, and he became relegated to the scout team, putting on a show for the offense. It was really a traumatic thing for a quarterback to have to change over. Looking back, Mark Newman was a victim of a trend in college football.

"Back then, the wishbone had been very successful. Oklahoma dominated. They would bring in whole platoons. Alabama had the bone going. It was very successful, and Florida was catching on to it, but it was at the end of the cycle, because once the restrictions came in and you only had four or five quarterbacks, you couldn't subject your quarterback to that much punishment. The defenses were figuring out that if you take away the brains—you know what I mean—[he means that if the defense beats the quarterback into a mushy pulp], the thing doesn't work any more. That really was what stopped the wishbone in college football.

"But the end wasn't yet in sight, and once Coach Dickey put in the wishbone, we were destined to run a lot more. First of all, you had to get faster. You had to get tougher. You had to grow a little bit, but it really limited your chances of getting the reps necessary to become a pro quarterback. So that was the transition I had to go through. Luckily, I hung in there and had just enough foot speed and just enough whatever it took to barely hang in there.

"I wanted to be on the field, and so I put in a lot of time trying to get bigger and stronger. When I arrived, I weighed 170 pounds. I was 6'1" and thin. I started lifting weights and eating regularly and working out, just for survival purposes. I knew I would have to reinvent myself. Because you have to run.

"When the '74 season began Don Gaffney was our quarterback. Don and I were friends. We got along great. Don was very talented, and he could run. He had a lot of quickness. People don't realize what a strong arm he had too. He was a real gentleman to me, and I was to him. We were competitors, but we always kept it there. I'd come in and spell him. Sometimes he'd come in and spell me. But he was designated as the starter."

Florida opened the season at home against a talented University of California team. Coach Dickey used eight different running backs in the 21-17 win. James Richards ran 72 yards to score the winning touchdown with only seconds remaining. During the game Don Gaffney was booed whenever he took the field. A certain segment of the traditional corps of Gator fans was not happy with Coach Dickey's decision to play a black man at quarterback.

Don Gaffney: "We had not played a game, and I was being booed before we even got on the field. Before the game a subtle threat [against his life] was even made against me. I guess that came with the turf. You don't know what to do. You don't know how to take that.

"Coach Dickey talked to my father and to me. He didn't think it was serious, but we had to make a decision. I decided I was not going to let it affect me. I was going to do what I was supposed to do. I just felt so much inward disappointment. I really felt ashamed wearing the orange and blue, because I just didn't think this was the way people saw us, especially after I had proved that I belonged here.

"During one of our talks, Coach Dickey told me, 'Don, if the people who booed you walked past you on the street and you didn't have a Gator uniform on, they wouldn't know who you are. It's not you personally.' And that meant a lot to me. It didn't change the fact I didn't like what was happening, but it certainly helped me to deal with it. I dealt with it. It was hard. It was real hard to be booed on the field like that, and there was no reason for it. We hadn't even kicked off yet.

"We went up against the University of California, a team that had Steve Bartkowski at quarterback and Chuck Muncie at fullback. I was looking forward to what we could do."

Affected negatively by the overt racism, Don Gaffney was shaken, and he did not perform well against California. Florida trailed 17-14 with three minutes left when Jimmy Fisher went into the game and led the winning drive.

Don Gaffney: "Jimmy needed to go in because I had a couple of bad series. I just didn't feel good. I tried to shake it off, but I couldn't. I was affected by the booing and the death threat. That was very unfortunate, but I was. Now I had to search myself."

Jimmy Fisher: "I remember when I got the call. I had had a good spring, so I knew I would get a shot if something didn't go quite right. It was playing home, and it was a great day. That was my first taste of college football. I was on the field, and everyone was there with me. And I got fortunate. They had a couple of defenses that they gave me that they didn't give Don. Sometimes it's just a matter of timing. Lee McGriff was one of the receivers, and I remember him being open a couple of times. And Jimmy DuBose scored the winning touchdown and our defense stopped them at the end."

Lee McGriff: "The name, The University of California, didn't strike fear in the hearts of Florida fans in the Southeast, but that was an outstanding team. They had Steve Bartkowski, Chuck Muncie and [Steve] Rivera, and they ended up going to the Rose Bowl that year.

"California was ahead late in the game, and I ran a post pattern, and Jimmy threw a strike. Two guys hit me in the chin, and I caught the ball, and we were down inside the ten. When Jimmy DuBose ran it in, that became a big win."

Don Gaffney: "We won the game, but we were not happy. We're troubled now, all over again. On the way back to Gainesville, I remember thinking all these things. I said to myself, This is all I need, another dern quarterback battle. I thought, I have to leave. Doesn't it ever end? Will there ever be acceptance?

"But a strange thing happened: we got back to Gainesville, and we had a quiet week. In the press they wrote about the controversy: who is going to start?

"Early, Coach Dickey said, 'Don Gaffney's our quarterback.'"

The Maryland game was played in Tampa. Back in 1974, black players were not as readily accepted as they are today. Local high schools were just beginning to integrate. A contingent of local rooters made it clear they preferred their own Jimmy Fisher to Gaffney. For the old timers, the new Land of Dixie would take some getting used to.

Don Gaffney: "When we got to Tampa, things happened to me that were not very pleasant. It was kind of rough. We had signed a quarterback from Tampa by the name of Jimmy Fisher. Jimmy is a very good person. Tampa wanted to see Jimmy play. There was a crew of fans from Polk County, where Jimmy is from, called the Polk County Crew, big-time Gators, traditional Gators, and they were not convinced a team with me at quarterback was the type of team they wanted to see.

"Black quarterbacks were not readily accepted. Even more than I want to admit. And we realized that for the first time in Florida history, when I stood in the huddle, I was standing with more black players than white. And I can say that the white players were just Gators—they didn't care. Lee McGriff didn't care. Jimmy Fisher didn't care. All we wanted to do was win.

"I knew if this was going to work, I was going to have to make it work. I was gonna just have to bite the bullet and get stronger, and things would work their way out."

Against Maryland, Gaffney and Fisher alternated. The press called it a controversy. Coach Dickey made it clear to Gaffney that he was the starter. He told Gaffney that Fisher also was going to play, just in case something happened to Gaffney and he needed him later in the season.

Don Gaffney: "I was the starter. I was never not the starter. I'd go a couple of series, and he would bring Jimmy in just to give him a chance to see how he could do. And he was doing okay.

"He was a freshman, and I was a junior, and the talk now was that Jimmy was a better passer. Jimmy was supposed to be the next John Reaves. The Polk County crew was thinking that all Gator quarterbacks should come from that area.

"But whenever we got the ball inside the ten, I was back in there. When we were near midfield or in Maryland territory, Jimmy got in to get his feet wet, just in case we needed him later in the year. That was the rationale as it was presented to me. I didn't like it, but that's the way it was being sold.

"You can't play with two quarterbacks. I don't know whether Coach Dickey was trying to appease the white alums. I hate to think that. Remember, his job was on the line. It was, 'Don, you've got to bite the bullet.' Of course, we beat Maryland [17-10]."

Three times against Maryland, Florida had to come from behind. Florida trailed at the half 10-7, when David Posey tied the game with a 49-yard field goal.

Jimmy Fisher: "David Posey was one of my dear friends. We roomed together with some others. David's dad was a teacher at a Boca Raton prep school, where he and his brother wrestled in high school. They were tough kids. The thing that made David different was that David was a tough kicker. Everybody knew that and respected him for it.

"David was fortunate in that our offense was producing a lot of opportunities for PATs, because we scored a lot of points. When he left, he held a lot of records. Now, of course, they've all been broken. A lot of records were broken after Spurrier showed up.

"But If you look at the great teams, they want leadership and they want people they can depend on. Good teams really respond to quarterbacks and to kickers they can depend on, who are with them and who aren't afraid to mix it up. Posey was that kind. He got a lot of respect—a lot of respect."

The star of the Maryland game was freshman back Tony Green, who ran 11 times for 178 yards, including a 76-yard touchdown run. Tony Green would take the Florida offense to a new level.

Jimmy Fisher: "To have a freshman actually contribute and be a part of the win was something that was happening during this period. Tony Dorsett [at the University of Pittsburgh] was the first freshman to really make an impact. But there was also this feeling of, Wait a minute, doesn't he have to pay his dues? Doesn't he have to go through what we had to go through? You know what I mean? Because when I signed, it was understood that you had to spend your time on the scout team. You had to do your hard time, and then you'd get your chance to play on the varsity. With Tony, that was the first time a kid could actually make an impact—right now. And Tony got a lot of instant notoriety early for that.

"But the bottom line was that we wanted to win football games. That was number one."

Jimmy Fisher won the Maryland game 17-10 when he threw a 17-yard touchdown pass to Lee McGriff late in the game.

Lee McGriff: "All my life I wanted those situations to come down to this. I knew Jimmy would throw it to me. I knew how he felt about me. So I knew he was going to give me the chance to make the play. And he did.

"I caught the ball right near the goal line, and I remember pushing myself in to get on across there. It was a major thrill."

Don Gaffney: "After the Maryland win, I knew something was wrong with us. We were not the offensive juggernaut we were supposed to be. Our wishbone was supposed to be dangerous. We knew we could run it, but something was wrong.

"Elements of the press were traditionalists. There were still reporters who felt bad that I had replaced David Bowden. Looking back, I can see that the problem was that the press was attempting to divide the team.

"The discord was subtle. The traditional Gator fan would come to games and say things like, 'Gee, it's good to see a white quarterback again.' That was a quote that appeared in the Florida Alligator. I've got the clipping."

Mississippi State came to Gainesville the next weekend. Gaffney and Fisher split time, and the Gators came away with a 29-13 win.

Don Gaffney: "We scored 29 points. We had Tony Green [who caught a 15-yard touchdown pass from Gaffney], James Richards, and Larry Brinson but the key was Jimmy DuBose. Jimmy and I had a perfect understanding of each other.

"Other than the offensive line, the key to the wishbone is the understanding between the fullback and the quarterback. It's got to be natural, like you were one. They have to think the same way, to feel the same way.

"When Jimmy was in the game, we ran the traditional wishbone more and threw the ball less, which I didn't like because I came out of a throwing program, but we were running the wishbone so well, and we began to feel its power. We were beginning to roll. We began to dominate games."

Jimmy Fisher: "Mississippi State had a tailback by the name of Walter Packer, who was fantastic. Could he run! We held him to 29 yards. We had an excellent defense. Doug Knotts was the defensive coordinator. Dickey brought him down from Tennessee. His forte was making All-American linebackers. That's what he prided himself in. And Ralph Ortega and Glenn Cameron were two of the best.

"When I was a freshmen, I just idolized them. They were being touted as All-Americans, and when I played against them, they just scared me to death. I mean, they were both animals."

Don Gaffney: "We hosted LSU, a team that had beaten us [24-3] the year before, and this was a different Gator team than that one. This time we blew them out [24-14]. Offensively, we just destroyed them. We could have scored at will. Our own mistakes kept the score from being worse. We had turnovers. We were stopping ourselves.

"We would drive up and down the field, and three times we had [David Posey] field goals instead of touchdowns. Here again, I felt I knew why this was happening. In the middle of the game we would change things to make our 'traditional' fans happy.

"We were at that stage: were we gonna be a 'traditional' Florida team. Or are we gonna change things? Are we a wishbone team? That's NOT traditional Florida. But then again, their quarterback was not traditional. So now all of a sudden the Gator fans can't identify with this ball club. This is a part of Gator history we tend to shy away from talking about. And I guarantee you, if I were doing this book about any of the southern schools, it would be exactly the same.

"This happened. This was the way it was. This was a transitional period, and here we were, a team with SO much talent. But we had more black players than Florida had ever had, and we had white players who were wonderful players and great guys. And Coach Dickey was a good man. We knew it always seemed he was under fire. There always was somebody criticizing him. Always criticizing, and he was a good man.

"There was all this talk that 'his players are not disciplined.' You know why? Because he allowed black players to be themselves. He was really a good man, a wonderful man, and a hell of a recruiter. Because every time we talked to a kid who he wanted, we'd say, 'Hey, man, Coach Dickey is wonderful.' That's why Florida signed so many good players. And at the time other Florida schools may have benefited, because the coaches would say, 'Florida has so many black players, the white players don't get a chance to play.' I know Florida State benefited from this during that period.

"All we could do was go out and play our best. We led the SEC in offense. We had a great defense. But that year we just couldn't win over our own fans, and we certainly couldn't win the press. The year before we beat Auburn, but that was nothing. The year before we won the last five games in a row, but that was nothing. There was always somebody saying something negative in the papers."

After Florida won its first four games and its ninth win in a row, the Gators flew to Nashville to play underrated Vanderbilt. The team was listless, and the Commodores won in an upset, 24-10.

Don Gaffney: "We could have won ten games in a row for the very first time, but against Vanderbilt, there was no emotion. We were just beat. When I say beat emotionally, I mean we were taking a pounding over and over. We did not play well at Vanderbilt. We couldn't believe they had beaten us. I don't think they believed it when it happened. That just was not supposed to happen."

Lee McGriff: "Steve Sloan was the coach of Vanderbilt, and he was kind of an innovative guy, a chance taker. We went up to Nashville, and it was cold, so we were out of our element a little bit. We were flat.

"And the less worthy our opponent was, the more conservative Coach Dickey would play. Sometimes that would leave us feeling flat, and that's not an excuse, but it worked that way. Rather than do what Steve Spurrier did to inferior opponents—go out and rip them, and run reverses, and crush them, we would run the dive, run the sweep, and we never threw the ball early. We'd punt, play defense.

"We did that against Vandy, and they hung on. They had a tight end, Barry Burton, who had the game of his life. He even ran a reverse tight-end pass. They made some big plays and got some points. Somehow our defense wasn't our normal self.

"Not until late in the game did we start throwing. And when we started throwing, we got going. Too late. Oh my God, I was sure we were going to take it all that year. And we could have. That was just heartbreaking."
The Gators then travelled to Tallahassee to take on Florida State. This time they had no trouble finding their enthusiasm.

Don Gaffney: "If you can't get up for Florida State, then you're not breathing."

Don Gaffney started against the Seminoles. He ran the wishbone to perfection, with the offense gaining 357 yards on the ground. A 36-yard run by Gaffney ignited the offense, and his 63-yard touchdown pass to Alvis Darby clinched the 24-14 victory. By the end of the game, nary a boo could be heard for Gaffney.

Don Gaffney: "I like to think that long run was the best play. We had shut down somehow. Finally, I just decided I was going to make a play. I dropped back—it wasn't a draw—I just decided to take off with it.

"One of Florida State's defenders came up to hit me, and I hit him and spun off, a 360, all the way around, and I ran for 36 yards. It got us going, got us excited."

But FSU hung tough, and Florida was only ahead 17-14 when Gaffney completed the game-clincher.

Don Gaffney: "Late in the ballgame Coach Dunn told me, 'Don, there'll come a time when FSU will gamble. They like to bring their safeties up and ignore the throwing game. When you see them walk that safety up, you're going to know it. I don't care if we're on our own one yard line. Check to Blue 63.' This was a pass to our tight end, Alvis Darby.

"Coach Dunn and Alvis and I had talked about this play for weeks. Alvis would tease me about it. He'd say, 'You keep saying that. I hope they go and put Fish in the game.' I'd say, 'Be quiet.'

"He also told me, 'If we ever do it, we'll do it against Florida State.' Alvis had a sprained wrist, and before the game Alvis told me, 'If you throw me that pass, remember my wrist is taped, and is hurting. Don't throw the ball real hard.' I said okay.

"I never thought it would happen, but we got in the game, and it was tight. We were backed up, didn't have a whole lot going, and it was third and one. I called a run by Jimmy DuBose. I knew we could run the one yard and keep the drive going.

"Then I saw the safeties, and I checked to 'Blue 63.' The safeties ran in, thinking Bose was coming. Everybody was going after Jimmy.

"I came up quick and threw to Darby. He was extremely fast for a 6'6" tight end. When I hit him fifteen yards down the field, nobody was going to catch him. They were just completely stung. [Darby scored on a 63-yard touchdown to make the score 24-14.]"

Lee McGriff: "Darby was unbelievably open. It was one of those perfect calls. Darby reached out and caught it with one hand, bobbled it, and I was wanting to shoot Darby at the time. I was running my route as he was running his, and I saw the whole thing. When he started bobbling that ball, I thought, Oh, Lord, but then he got it and took off for a 63-yard touchdown. It was a huge play."

Jimmy Fisher: "That was a huge play that year. That pretty much secured Don's position, because we beat them and beat them up there. I wanted the play to happen with me in there, but it didn't, and that's fate."

Duke was the guest for Homecoming. Don Gaffney was gaining confidence and winning support from the Gator fans. His presence had taken some getting used to, but his talent and success was beginning to win over the skeptics. Against Duke, Florida scored 30 points in the first half. On the third play of the opening drive, Gaffney darted around left end and pitched out to James Richards, who ran 68 yards for a touchdown.

Don Gaffney: "J.R. and I had a relationship. Coach Dunn and Coach Breaux were always preaching the importance of maintaining that relationship. Coach Hatfield was the backfield coach, and he would say to me, 'Your backs are going to stay with you, Don, because they'll get some crumbs.' Which meant that we could break the option upfield, and I could still pitch it out to the back. He called them 'getting crumbs.' He would tell the backs, 'We have a quarterback quick enough to stay with you, who can get upfield quick, so you backs always keep running. Don't stop when you see him break the run. The ball may come to you.'

"And that's exactly what happened with J.R. I was ten yards upfield, and I pitched it to him, and he took it the rest of the way. When he turned the corner, he was gone.

"That day we had a big game, and that wishbone was awesome. We began to realize, 'We've got a weapon we can use because we do it so well.'

"And after the Duke game, I knew I was playing with a great football team. We were going to go places. We were going to do things, and now I was the man. I had the support of everyone. The critics were getting off me."

Lee McGriff: "It was Homecoming, and there was complete dominance. The first half we were having fun, throwing the ball, running the ball, [scoring 30 points]. Then in the second half Coach Dickey got conservative and let the game die. It's not that he quit, but he just didn't do anything to continue to try to put pressure on Duke and score.

"It was just his style. It was part of the seventies style. It was a glorious Homecoming day, and we were running on all cylinders, and it was clear to me I could have a big day. And I scored a touchdown in the first half, and then in the second half he just shut it down.

"You want to be a team guy, and I didn't let this show, but I was leading the SEC in receiving and the Duke game was a chance for me to roll up the yardage. Some receivers, including my own son Travis, put up huge numbers but it wasn't until the nineties under Spurrier that you kept doing what you do, letting it rip no matter what the score was, setting records. Coach Dickey didn't do that."

Undefeated Auburn, fifth-ranked and the top defensive team in the country, was next. The game was televised regionally on ABC. The wishbone offense, led by Don Gaffney, was almost perfect. [Florida won 25-14.] The next day in the papers, Don Gaffney was credited in the papers with "running the wishbone like he had invented it."

Jimmy Fisher: "Don had a good game. At that point Don had weathered the challenge, and he was starting to gain more confidence. Cause when you rotate, there's quite a bit of pressure to perform right now. I know I felt that pressure. You need to make something happen this series or you may not be playing the next one. We had both gotten used to that feeling, but at this point in the season Don was commanding the option a bit better than I was. He made some great pitches against Auburn. Don had unbelievable flexibility. He would twist and make yards."

Lee McGriff: "It was a huge game. It was a televised game. They were top ten [fifth]. We were top ten [actually 11th]. It was another perfect, beautiful fall, a wonderful day to play. In that game Don threw me a [7-yard] touchdown pass, and that was the first time Auburn had been scored on that season by a touchdown.

"It was a play action play. I went to the back of the end zone and did a little gyration and then curled toward the post, and Gaffney hit me right on the end line."

That day against Auburn, Jimmy DuBose carried 25 times for 143 yards in a 25-14 win that gave Florida a 7-1 record and assured it a bowl appearance at the end of the season.

Don Gaffney: "We were beginning to feel like it belonged to us. By now, the team was mine. There was no more rotating quarterbacks, no more question about it—this was Don Gaffney's team. And I began to take over.

"I was beginning to think I was [Oklahoma quarterback] Jack Mildren reincarnated. We had a big, tough fullback, Jimmy DuBose, a dominating, speedy offensive line, and a quarterback who could hit the corner and go.

"We scored 25 points against Auburn, but we could have scored as much as we wanted to. But Coach Dickey didn't believe in doing that. He didn't like doing that to anyone."

forty-one

A Sugar Bowl Loss

Going into the 1974 Georgia game, Florida boasted a 7-1 record and was ranked sixth in the country. Georgia scored two points when Jimmy Fisher slipped in his own end zone trying to pass. It happened early in the game, and it was the only series Fisher played.

Jimmy Fisher: "I remember sitting on the sideline the rest of the game hoping we wouldn't lose by one point. What happened was this: back then the Gator Bowl field was high, and you weren't sure what kind of shoes to wear. It's always been that way. We would bring with us different types of cleats.

"It was one of the first plays, a sprint out left on our own three, and I was a pretty good sprinter for a quarterback. I could turn my shoulders.

"Anyway, the defensive end rushed up the field so I couldn't get around him, and I stopped and squared around and tried to find someone open, and when I stopped, boom, there went my feet. Two points.

"God, I felt terrible. The field was always a factor. I had to sit there and live through that one. We lost, 17-16, right?"

Despite outgaining Georgia in rushing yardage 420 to 263, Florida trailed 17-10 in the final minute of the game when Don Gaffney scored on a four-yard run.

Don Gaffney: "This was one tough football game from the outset. Vince Dooley was a tremendous defensive coach. The wishbone has its advantages, but late in the season, great defensive teams learn how to defense it with odd fronts. The Auburn defense was bigger than Georgia's, but Georgia was faster. They played a 'bend but don't break' defense, and sometimes we would get impatient and make a serious mistake.

"That game we made more turnovers and negative plays than we made all season long. We seemed to stop and start, stop and start. We were extremely excited about beating Auburn, and we were awarded a Sugar Bowl bid, which came as a complete surprise to me, but it was wonderful. We were right at the top in total offense, and we were a strong football team in every way, shape, or form. We had a great deep threat in Wes Chandler. We had so many athletes, including my brother Derrick, who was at Florida with me.

"We came out really aggressively, but Georgia went up on us, and we had to abandon the wishbone.

"We scored in the last minute, and the way we scored was beautiful. It was quick, and it was decisive, and it was another advantage when your quarterback can switch from one offense to another.

"We opened the offense up—what people call the 'broken bone.' We would flank our receiver out, or motion out one of our great running backs who could catch the ball. Sometimes we used three receivers. We had Wes. We had Derrick. We had Tony Green and Terry LeCount, a quarterback who was becoming a wide receiver. He was a speed guy.

"Our power game had kind of stumbled around. It had been good, but we didn't do the things we had hoped to do that day. We had a fair game, but we didn't put Georgia away. We had opportunities. We ended up kicking field goals instead of scoring touchdowns. David Posey kicked three. He was really right on that day. But we should have gotten touchdowns.

"It was getting late, and Georgia scored on a drive, and went up 17-10. We now have to throw it. We go into a throwing mode.

"It's great to be a scrambler. On a previous play, I threw the ball when I could have run with it and threw an incompletion. I could hear the coaches yelling, 'Run it, run it,' and I almost got picked off.

"When we made it down inside the twenty, I knew we had been there before, and we had screwed up. I said to myself, 'Don, you've got to win this game. What are you doing?'

"We got down to the four, and I scrambled outside, and I saw two receivers. Lee McGriff was in the back of the end zone. I was going to throw him the ball, and then I decided I would try one of those Condredge Holloway plays where he dove into the end zone. I always wanted that moment.

"I took off and started running. I sprinted into the end zone untouched. I thought it would be a closer play. I ran in with my arms raised. I shouldn't have done that. I should have just gone in and put the ball down. But I raised my arms, and out of nowhere I got blindsided by one of the Georgia defensive backs. When I got up, he pushed me again. He wasn't a dirty player, but that was a dirty play. Lee McGriff had been standing in the end zone, and McGriff stepped up and pushed him, and they got into a shoving match.

"When I got up, I was a little dazed. I was woozy. When I got up, I just didn't know what to do. I remember someone pulling my jersey, calling me. We were going to the sideline, and they said we were going to go for two. That's how out of it I was.

"We huddled up. We had gone over the situation. We knew what we wanted to do. And we had the perfect play called. In retrospect, I really wasn't quite myself. When I took the snap, Georgia came with a corner blitz.

"I was going to go to Alvis Darby, but I couldn't because he got jammed and knocked down. I saw Dub [Jimmy DuBose] where he was supposed to be. I threw the ball, but I didn't throw it well. Nine out of ten times he will catch that ball. But he had to twist his body. Had he caught it, it would have been a great catch. But it barely got away from him.

"I should have thrown a better pass. If he had come open right away, I would have shot it right in to him. But I took the first step, and I looked at Darby, and boom, he got jammed up, and they're holding him, and then I took a second step, and here comes the blitz. On the third step, I threw the ball, the defender pushed me back, but I knew I had enough on the ball.

"But we missed it, and we lost 17-16. We had one more shot, a missed field goal, a long attempt. We didn't have enough time."

Jimmy Fisher: "I'm telling you right now, in my three years at Florida, I should have two SEC rings. We should have been the first Florida team to win the SEC. For two years we were right there for the Georgia game. That was as important a game for us that season as any other."

If the Georgia game was frustrating, the next game against Kentucky was worse. Florida led in the game 17-6, and then turned the ball over seven times. Kentucky rushed for 334 yards in a 41-24 win. It was Fran Curci's first win over Florida in seven tries.

Don Gaffney: "We left our hotel that morning to go to Commonwealth Stadium for the game. The offense took one bus, the defense the other one. The Kentucky fans hung out around the visitors' bus when we arrived to check you out. After the buses were parked, we walked down to the dressing room surrounded by a lot of students and Kentucky fans there.

"As we were walking, I heard someone say, 'This can't be Florida. This must be Florida A&M.' We laughed about that. We decided we would go out and destroy them.

"But of all the games I played for Florida, I think this may have been the only game when we were not in it mentally. We just fell apart. Our sideline was the most chaotic I'd ever been involved with. We had no emotion in the second half. It became frustrating for everyone.

"Kentucky just whipped us up and down that field. Their quarterback, Sonny Collins, just took over the second half. We were standing there in awe watching him.

"It was just not our day."

Lee McGriff: "The defense fell apart, which didn't happen very often. It was a cold day. That was another game where we were ahead 17-6, and Coach Dickey was trying to milk it instead of hammering them—understand, you are getting my perspective. We had lost to Georgia, and we had a pretty good lead on Kentucky, and we didn't seize and rally when we got up on them. Part of the pathway to do that was to throw the ball. There was room to do it. Any defense can take away something, but they have to give something up. If you want to be butt-headed and say, 'Nope, we're gonna do this anyway,' you can get yourself in trouble.

"Even though the wishbone is run-oriented, we had plenty of opportunities. They dared us to throw it. If we did, it worked. He just would not go to the well enough. He played Don Gaffney most of the way against both Georgia and Kentucky. Jimmy Fisher sat on the bench. Our history was that when we struggled and Jimmy came in, there was a spark. This is NOT an anti-Don statement, but when we needed to throw it to win, Jimmy provided the spark. I was very frustrated. I felt, Why not try it? Because Jimmy Fisher NEVER choked."

The final game of the season was against the University of Miami at home in a downpour. The weather, however, became irrelevant as Florida went on to post a 31-7 win over the Hurricanes.

Lee McGriff: "Everybody got refocused. The whole team was huddled right before the game started on the sideline. We were very emotional. I jumped in there and said, 'The rain is going to see who has character, because it's a great equalizer.' Everybody seemed to be in sync.

"I remember it raining, and I remember I got a chance to make some plays. [Don Gaffney threw McGriff a 42-yard touchdown pass.] I remember one time getting the fire knocked out of me when the defender knocked my helmet off.

"I remember feeling that we had a team good enough to win the Southeast Conference Championship, but after the prior two games, we were out of it, and I remember thinking, For God sake, I don't want to lose this last game."

Don Gaffney: "It was the only game where we came onto the field for our warmup and it was already storming. We said they brought their weather with them—the Hurricanes. Even though it rained so hard, we could have scored sixty that day. We were ready offensively. Maybe we were concentrating a little bit more. We had practiced extremely hard.

"Miami was beginning to get good players down there. But we were a VERY good football team, and we knew that. We didn't want to embarrass the Sugar Bowl committee. We didn't want to embarrass ourselves. We felt we owed our fans better than that. We had dropped a game to Vandy we shouldn't have dropped. After beating Auburn and going 7 and 1, we dropped two to Georgia and Kentucky, and the Sugar Bowl folks must have been holding their heads in shame.

"We knew we had to do something outstanding in the game, and we played them, and we defeated them big time. So in this case running up the score was an option. We won 31-7, but it could have been a lot worse. Pete Elliott, the Miami coach, said we were one of the best teams in the country."

The Sugar Bowl was played in New Orleans. The opponents on December 31, 1974, were the Cornhuskers of Nebraska, coached by Tom Osborne and led by quarterback David Humm.

Don Gaffney: "The Sugar Bowl is a big deal, baby, because they didn't have twenty-five bowls back then. Only the big boys got to go to a bowl game. We didn't want anyone thinking, 'Hey, they screwed up putting Florida in there.'

"We were 8 and 3. The only team that ripped us apart was Kentucky. We knew we were a good football team.

"Nebraska came in. They were a powerful team. When I got to New

Orleans, I chatted with some of their players and saw they were disappointed to be playing us. They had lost to Oklahoma, who played in the Orange Bowl against Alabama.

"We were excited. Our disappointment was not finishing the regular season 10-1 or 9-2 at the worst. We figured we'd knock those guys off and go 9-3 and get a possible top-ten finish. All we had to go was play our best game. Then the first [betting] line came out and we saw we were 30-point underdogs! Holy smokes!

"That ticked us off. We couldn't help but talk about it. We felt we were not being respected.

"We took a 10-0 lead, and it should have been 17-0, without a doubt. We were running the option, going on all cylinders. We had a great game plan for them. My job was to handle Nebraska's All-American safety, Wonder Monds, 6'3", a big guy, reminded us of Wayne Fields. During practice our coaches used Wayne to emulate what Wonder Monds did.

"We watched films of every Nebraska game. When we watched films of the Oklahoma-Nebraska game, we noticed that he cheated a lot. When we watched Nebraska play Texas, we saw the same thing. What he would do, when the quarterbacks stepped, he would take off and come at the quarterback or the pitchback. If he did that, you had no chance. We had some backside plays ready for them. Even so, Wonder Monds nailed me a couple times early. I had to make him miss in order for us to do what we wanted to do.

"Jimmy DuBose was killing them inside. That was how we were going to control Wonder Monds. Whenever he came after us in the flats trailing the triple option, if the big fullback broke through, there was no one there to stop him. So now we had Wonder Monds guessing. We had Nebraska in a tizzy. We were killing them with four and five yard runs, quarterback, tailback, fullback, the triple option at its best.

"We didn't throw the ball that many times. We didn't have to. But we had a play to out tight end, Alvis Darby, where we went to the open-side option to give us the bigger field to operate. On that play Wonder Monds would run away from the middle toward the option, and what we did was slip Darby behind him, and it worked perfectly.

"We went on the option going right. I stopped and pulled up, with Darby lined up on the left side. When I looked up, he was wide open going down the middle. He didn't score a touchdown, but the play went for a lot of yards. It was the biggest pass play of the game.

"So we jumped out 10-0 on them. We went on a long drive, eating up the clock, which was our game plan. We came with a pitch to Tony Green, and Tony took it, and we get on the end, and I jump the safety and flip the ball back with a late pitch, and Tony turns upfield, makes one move, and he is gone, high-stepping it down the sidelines and going into the end zone. I don't believe anyone could have executed the option any better.

"And then the ref whistled him out of bounds! We couldn't believe it. We said, 'What? There's no way. And he did not go out. If he had scored, the score would have been 17-0, and Nebraska would have quit. If we get that call, the game was over.

"But then we did it to ourselves. We had first down inside their five, and Nebraska stopped us on downs. How about that! They stopped us on the one. Then Terry Luck, the backup quarterback to David Humm, took Nebraska 99 yards. They chewed up the clock, and they made it 10-7. We were shocked. Because before that our defense had controlled them, but it seemed we had lost some steam."

Lee McGriff: "The worst thing that could have happened to us was that they took Humm out and put a guy named Luck in. They abandoned the pass because that's what David Humm did. They began to run the ball. I'll never forget, we had them way backed up, and they took the ball down the field, and they didn't throw it one time! And they stuck it in the end zone, and now it was 10 to 7.

"When you know you're going after them, there's an energy to that, and if you switch off your offense, you can't always get it going again. If you take the conservative approach, the team knows it, the team feels it.

"When it got to be 10-7, we were dang sure in a game. We made a drive, and Tony Green made a run going to the right side. By all accounts he scored, but an official ruled he stepped out of bounds first.

"We went for it on fourth down, ran the option to James Richards. James is a real good guy and a good back, but we were on Astroturf, and he tried to make a move—he was coming my way, and he slipped. All that was out there was me and the cornerback. He easily could have scored, because I was in his face trying to keep him away from James.

"James gave a little wiggle, and his feet came out from under him, and he stumbled and fell down.

"Then Nebraska kicked a field goal."

Don Gaffney: "We still had a lot of football to play. From that point forward the Nebraska players seemed to turn it up a notch. They were big and fast, and they were coming at us. Nebraska got two field goals, and they beat us 13-10. And that second field goal came after another 99 yard march."

Lee McGriff: "After the game the locker room was like a funeral. We had some really talented players, and it was their last game. Beating Nebraska would have been a huge win, and we had it. We knew we were as good if not better than Nebraska. And from the offensive perspective, I was disgusted with the way we went about it. It should not have happened like that."

Don Gaffney: "It was one tough, tough game, and after it was over we were mentally, physically, spiritually exhausted. And what was more disappointing, people would look at our 8-4 record and say we were a disappointing team. It hurt. The only thing we could do to change people's minds was to win the title the next year. If we didn't win it, the entire four years would be clouded. So we dedicated ourselves to winning it all the next year. We thought we had the schedule for it. We thought we had the team for it."

After graduation, Lee McGriff had his heart set on playing professional football. He could have been a star in the World Football League, but his ego told him to shoot for the stars, the NFL's Dallas Cowboys, a top team led by Roger Staubach. McGriff's pro experience after being cut by Dallas and playing six games for the Tampa Bay Bucs in their first season in the NFL would result mostly in disappointment and heartache. He also found a career in coaching to be more aggravation than it was worth.

Lee McGriff: "What would have been better than to play pro football in Tampa? But that's how it went. And when that was over, my son Travis was born. I had to make a decision about continuing to play, which my heart wanted. But I had a family, and right after I left the Bucs I went into the insurance business.

"I was going good, but I just could not get football out of my system, so I thought, I have to either play or coach. I thought coaching was more stable than playing—I was too stupid to know better—and I decided that rather than go to Canada or Philadelphia or Oakland to play—I had offers—I decided it would be wrong to drag my family around, so I took my first coaching job at FSU with Bobby Bowden in 1977.

"Bobby is wonderful. He's a great guy. And a lot of the guys who were on the staff then are still there. And 1977 turned out to be FSU's breakthrough year. They went 10 and 2. They played Texas Tech in the Tangerine Bowl and beat them.

"Also, the irony of it all, Florida had beaten Florida State ten consecutive times. That year Florida State beat Florida for the first time. I was on the other sideline, so that was quite unique."

Lee McGriff coached under Doug Dickey in 1978 and for Charlie Pell from 1979 through 1982. Pell was a domineering tyrant who badgered and threatened his assistant coaches while pampering his players. At the end of the 1982 season, McGriff decided to get out of coaching.

Lee McGriff: "At that age, at that stage of my life, if I had not crossed paths with Charlie Pell, I probably would not have gotten out of coaching, which long-term, I'd say it was probably better for me that I did.

"Perhaps I would have become a big-time head coach, but at the same time I would not have experienced one-tenth of what I have shared with my wife and children. Hindsight said I did the right thing [getting out of coaching], because all my buddies, including Mike Shanahan, who's at the top of the mountain, have had to move all over the country and make sacrifices and missed a lot of involvement in their children's lives.

"To me, it was just more important to do this."

forty-two

Another Crushing Georgia Defeat

In the 1975 season opener against SMU, Florida performed on all cylinders. Don Gaffney, Jimmy DuBose, and Wes Chandler helped the Gators score 40 points at Florida Field. The team was strong and deep, and the players were confident and hopeful.

Don Gaffney: "We were familiar with each other. We had confidence in the wishbone. We had gone through another spring and another pre-fall, and we felt pretty good about what we were doing. The majority of us had played a great deal, so we were pretty much a veteran team with a lot of young eager players as well.

"In '75 Cris Collinsworth came in. The rest of them weren't premier players in the Tony Green class, but they gave us great depth. They helped us more on defense any anyplace else, and we ended up with one of the best defenses in the Southeastern Conference.

"The thing that got us over more than anything else was the fact that we were experienced. We were very familiar with each other, and we had some bona fide stars. The success of the wishbone is that every play has to look the same. That meant the first option—the fullback, was the key for us on every play. Jimmy DuBose was a legitimate superstar. He was the best wish-bone fullback in the country. Jimmy was a tremendous runner, a great blocker, unselfish, could catch, would do it all. He was the heart and soul of the team.

"Wes was Wes, an All-American, a tremendous big playmaker. The year before he hadn't been used very much, but in '75 he came into his own and gained national prominence as a wide receiver.

"The wishbone de-emphasizes the wide receivers, and we had several very good ones including Wes and my brother Derrick, who were playing the same position.

"In the opener against SMU I was able to throw two long [31 and 42 yard] passes to Wes for touchdowns. We were so devastating with the run that teams had to line up with eight-man fronts. We'd lull them to sleep, and then we threw off the play action, causing the safeties and corners to freeze just for a moment, and we would isolate Wes one on one, and Wes was dangerous. Nobody could cover him, and of course, I was the thrower. I had come to Florida as a thrower, and we stunned a lot of teams, because wishbone teams are not supposed to throw like we could.

"So we beat SMU 40-14, and it wasn't a difficult victory. We were a very, very strong team, and we knew it.

"And then we went to Raleigh to play N.C. State. We went into the game favored.

"We scored on our opening drive. We were good at that, and then teams would adjust. Sometimes we did not put teams away early, and this was one of those nights. And we were ahead 7-0 for a long time.

"The strangest thing happened. We moved the ball up and down the field. We had offensive statistics similar to those in the SMU game. But we kept fumbling the ball. Tony [Green] fumbled, [allowing N.C. State the opportunity to score on a 38-yard bomb to make the score 8-7] and on our final drive late in the game, we were going in for the winning score. We had field position to make a field goal, and we [Jimmy DuBose] fumbled the ball.

"It was a devastating loss for us. Our hats were off to N.C. State. They played us tough, but we just did not play like the Gators were supposed to play. We knew that loss was going to haunt us, that it was going to hurt us down the line, but we had to concentrate on our SEC schedule."

At the start against Mississippi State Florida played listlessly and trailed 10-6 in the first minute of the second half when Jimmy DuBose broke a run up the middle for a 74-yard touchdown.

Don Gaffney: "The play was nothing fancy. It was just us doing what we did best. Again, in the wishbone every play has to look the same, and when teams watched the films of our games, they saw how potent we were. They knew we had Wes and the stable of receivers behind him. You have to pick your poison when you're defensing us. We had tremendous athletes at every position. In fact, the teams that did best against us were the ones who let me run. Some figured that out, and some didn't.

"Against Mississippi State, this was a case where we were going to give them a large dose of DuBose early. And we did. And on this one play Jimmy went right up the middle for a touchdown.

"The other big play was a halfback pass from Tony Green to Terry LeCount [for a 65-yard touchdown]. Terry had played quarterback at Raines High School in Jacksonville, where I came from. Florida was trying to get him on the field because of his athleticism. Terry sometimes caught punts. Terry was still listed as a quarterback, but he was a weapon used a lot of different ways."

After the 27-10 win over Mississippi State, LSU in Baton Rouge was next, never an easy assignment, and Florida ran roughshod over the Tigers 34-6. In the first quarter Don Gaffney threw two touchdown passes, 20 yards to Wes Chandler and 39 yards to Terry LeCount. LSU didn't score its points until the final minute.

Back home in Gainesville, the issue of skin color was fading quickly. The alumni were now used to black men wearing the orange and blue. Black players had proved their worth, had won tough, close ballgames. The blacks could feel acceptance coming. They could feel that most fans were rooting for them, despite the color of their skin.

Don Gaffney: "We finally handled LSU, and we handled them in a large way. More important, the Gator fan club [for this predominantly black team] was growing. The Gators have great fans. They love winning. Like southern football in general, there's a passion there.

"We had gone through this change, and it was such a drastic change. It was going to take awhile, I realized, for them to adjust to me—for them to adjust to us—and for us to adjust to them. It wasn't going to end by the time we left, we knew that. But the important thing was, we were beginning to feel like Gators. The fan base, the media, the SEC, was beginning to change. The country was beginning to change.

"We were a dynamic football team. We didn't have any internal problems at all. There was no one thing, but it had to do with the young players who came in behind us. They had less to deal with. They felt less tension. There was less on their plate. It had been proven that this thing worked. All everybody had to do was play football. The situation for them was entirely different."

Florida hosted Vanderbilt next, and the Commodores suffered a 35-0 pasting. On the first play of the game Jimmy DuBose ran 80 yards for a touchdown. It was 21-0 at the half. The Vanderbilt players said that Florida was a better team than Alabama.

Don Gaffney: "We trounced them, and I think you know why. [The year before Vanderbilt beat them 24-10 in Nashville to mar what should have been a great season.] Of course, we learned a big lesson the previous year: we knew that every time we lined up, we would have more athletes on the field, but that wasn't enough to beat them. We felt bad for our previous team, for the seniors who had left, for having experienced that humiliation.

"This time we were determined to prepare for Vandy like they were Notre Dame coming in.

"They kicked off, and we started on our twenty. We snapped the ball, and I gave it to Jimmy, and all of us carried out our fakes as if we all had the football. That was something we took pride in. That was important to Coach Dunn. He believed every play should look the same. Coach Dickey also preached that. So on that play, when the defenders were coming after us, me and the tailback, they sent all their defenders to the outside, and Jimmy went right through the middle and just kept on kicking.

"Vanderbilt thought they had us defensed, and by the time anyone knew it, the crowd was in a raucous mood, screaming, and as Jimmy headed for the goal line, Vanderbilt still hadn't figured out what was going on. That's the truth.

"Another back who had a great day against Vanderbilt was Larry Brinson. Larry was one of those great running backs who came in with Derrick and Wes. He ran for two touchdowns and caught a pass for another."

Don Gaffney was the starting quarterback as the 1975 season began. While Gaffney led the Gators to a 4-1 record. Jimmy Fisher sat and stewed.

Jimmy Fisher: "I was pretty much resigned to having to sit. I remember being real frustrated during those times. You didn't go anywhere, because if you left, you had to sit out a year.

"I was a wishbone quarterback. We quit getting the big reps, as far as passing. I remember being in the weight room more than I was out on the field throwing, just for survival. You adapted to whatever you had to do. But there was frustration during that period."

The Seminoles of FSU were next up. The game was played in Gainesville. Jimmy DuBose had his greatest day, running for 204 yards on 22 carries. On the second play of the game, Don Gaffney had to leave with a broken wrist.

Don Gaffney: "On the very first play of the game we ran a counter-option. Remember I told you our guys were coached to stay with me when I ran so they could get 'those crumbs'? Well, on the play Larry Brinson cut down their defensive end, and I was free, and I jumped up inside to meet the linebacker and safety, and not only did I get past them, but I drew the cornerback, who was covering Tony, and when all three of them came to hit me, I flipped the ball to Tony. We hit the ground together, and two of them landed on my left wrist. All four of us were lying there, and they were saying, 'We got him. We got him.' I said, 'No, you didn't. It's gone.'

"Joe Kemp, who was from Gainesville, was the Florida State defensive back lying with me. He said, 'Don't tell me.' I said, 'Listen to the crowd.' He looked up, and Tony was on his way. He didn't score, but he ran a long way.

"I tried to push up, and I couldn't. My wrist was limp. One of the Florida State players pulled on my wrist to try to help me up, and I said, 'Ouch.' He said, 'Oh man,' and he helped me up. The other players were pointing to our bench to replace me, but I waved back saying, No, it's okay. I was trying to figure out where we were. We were down at the eight. By the time I ran down there, I couldn't move my wrist.

"We got into the huddle, and I said to the team before the play was sent in, 'Look, we've got to get this thing in right now, because I think my wrist is broken. We've got to score NOW, before I've got to get out of here.'

"It was hurting real bad, and everybody looked at me, asking if I wanted to call time out. I said, 'No, we'll just get this thing in here.'

"My center was Robbie Moore. I said, 'Robbie, look, just pick the ball up and hand it to me, because I can't take the snap.' He said, 'Don't worry about that, Don.' I knew Robbie was going to take the heat from the nose guard because he was making a slow snap, and he did.

"I said, 'Tony, look, I'm gonna hand this ball off with my right hand. Remember how we used to play around, and you'd take the ball like Earl Campbell?' He said, 'Yeah.' I said, 'That's how you're going to take it.' He said, 'Okay.'

"We called a 38-sweep. Robbie softly put the ball in my hand, and I reversed the play and put the ball out there for Tony, and he took the ball like a toss and stepped into the end zone. He was determined not to be stopped. It was the second play of the Florida State game, my last play in the game.

"I left the stadium and our doctor diagnosed it as broken. I stayed on the sideline the rest of the game, went to the hospital that night, and had surgery the next morning."

When Don Gaffney broke his left wrist, Jimmy Fisher returned to the starting lineup. His patience was rewarded. Fisher came in and played the rest of the way, guiding Florida to a 34-8 win.

Jimmy Fisher: "You have to remember that back then Florida State didn't have the ballplayers. We had everybody from the state. Bobby Bowden hadn't shown up yet [at FSU]. Miami was not a factor anymore. Florida got everybody they wanted. So it wasn't a big deal to win that one. There was nothing special. We were just giving the ball to Jimmy DuBose and pitching the ball to the backs, and we would just run around them."

Behind Fisher, Florida defeated Duke 24-16 and Auburn 31-14.

Jimmy Fisher: "Because of the wishbone, Dub became the first 1,000 yard rusher in Florida history. Here's what's cool about the wishbone: you get the ball, you're already on the line of scrimmage so you don't have to run four yards to get back to the line of scrimmage, and if Dub leans forward, he has five yards."

Don Gaffney didn't play against either Duke or Auburn. He dressed for the Auburn game but Jimmy Fisher was sharp, and he wasn't needed in a 31-14 win. In the Auburn game, Jimmy DuBose scored from the three-yard line with 44 seconds left and became the first 1,000-yard rusher in Florida history.

Don Gaffney: "We were very, very excited about that. We were on the road at Auburn, the site of our greatest victory. Jim had a tremendous game. He was becoming our work horse."

The next game, against the Georgia Bulldogs, was for the SEC title. Don Gaffney was healthy again. But Jimmy Fisher had won the two prior games. The question was who Doug Dickey would select to start in the most crucial game of the year.

Jimmy Fisher: "It was an interesting week, because Don had gotten well, and everyone wondered who was going to start. Think about it: Don is from Jacksonville, and he's going back home [the game was in the Gator Bowl in Jacksonville], and Doug ended up deciding on Don. And as you look back at the decision, really and truly, it was the right decision. Number one, he's a senior. Number two, he's going back home. But also, Doug knew I was used to coming into the game if we got in trouble, and he had never done that with Don. So consequently it was a pretty easy decision.

"To be frank with you, I thought I should have started because of the things I had done in big games. I thought the team was with me. But the team was with Don too. I do know when the decision was made, personally it hurt.

"And as the game went on, we didn't have a very good first half. We were losing the first half, and I remember Doug Dickey looked right at me and pointed and said, 'Fisher, you're starting.' I said, 'Okay, coach.' Then I went in, and I didn't do much better. I don't know if I wasn't mentally prepared or what. I don't know what happened to me, but I probably did worse.

"Irk Russell was the coach of the Georgia defense. He was a bald-headed guy who ended up going to Georgia Southern. He was legendary for having great defenses.

"But I didn't respond.

"We lost the game on an [80-yard] end-around. It was a tight-end pass. I was on the sideline, and I remember Gene Washington catching the ball right in front of me and running right by me. All of a sudden I wheeled around, and I saw this guy running down the sideline, and our defensive back squatted, and I knew it was over. They beat us 10-7. We only scored one touchdown. Wow!

"Looking back over my three years, I never lost on Florida Field, first of all. I never lost to Auburn. I never lost to Mississippi State. I never lost to LSU, and LSU was good in those years. I never lost to Miami. I never lost to Florida State. We beat Tennessee the one year I played against them. But I never beat Georgia. I NEVER beat them.

"Georgia was Coach Dickey's nemesis."

"Losing to Georgia was a total disappointment to the team and to the fans. And after reading the papers, we felt like real losers. The big thing at Florida was always, 'Wait 'til next year.' It was about time we won the SEC title. You felt there was something there that you just couldn't get through."

With a minute left in the game Don Gaffney led the Gators down to the Georgia 21-yard line. After three incomplete passes, Florida had fourth and ten. David Posey attempted a 38-yard field goal, but the snap was low, and the kick was blocked. The three-point loss would cost this talented Gator team the SEC championship.

Don Gaffney: "As a boy I sold drinks at four or five of the Florida-Georgia games in the Gator Bowl in Jacksonville, and I played in three of them, and all were tough football games. We didn't have one relaxing game, but in this one, before 70,000 plus people and a regional TV audience, we took the opening kickoff, and we couldn't have been any more fine-tuned. We were clicking. We drove the ball right down, and Tony scored. We went into the end zone, and one of the Georgia players said to me, 'Don't thank yourselves. Thank God.' I mentioned that to Coach Dickey, and to DuBose and a couple of other players. I had no idea what he meant. I mentioned it to my roomate, Sammy Green, and Sammy always had something philosophical to say. He said, 'Don, let's hope we don't have to come back later and even think about that.'

"We moved the ball that day, but we couldn't cash in. We made only one score, and that score was SO smooth. Everything worked. From that point forward, it wasn't a struggle, but we were not making it happen. I don't know why. We had a couple of field goal attempts that went awry. It wasn't raining, but the field was kinda slippery, and that hurt us in the end when Posey tried that long shot.

"Georgia scored on a tight end around late [3:12 was left] in the game. Our defense had just shut them down. We were up 7-0. They came up with this gadget play. They had this fast receiver, Gene Washington. My brother Warren was back there at safety for us. Wayne Fields had been injured. We had Warren and Alvin Cowans, a tremendous free safety. And we had Henry Davis back there. Tony Green, Terry LeCount, and Willie Wilder were among of the fastest guys in the country, and Gene Washington could run with them.

"Georgia faked a run. They ran a dive play, and they gave the ball to the tight end on the end around. We had seen Georgia run that play on the films, so we recognized it immediately. But we didn't think about the third option of this play, where the tight end stops and throws it deep to Washington.

"We were tricked. [Richard] Appleby didn't throw a great pass. Washington had to wait for it, but boy, when he caught it, nobody could catch him.

"And it just knocked the wind out of us. We should have come back, but we didn't. We didn't get it done for our defense. We should have given them a lift by coming back and hitting Georgia with something. But in the fourth quarter, we mounted two long drives that resulted in zero. One was a fumble. And at the end, when David Posey tried to tie the game, the snap was low, and the kick was blocked before he could kick it. If Posey could have made that, we would have had what we needed—our SEC title. We lost that championship by a field goal.

"After the game there were tears. We just couldn't do what we were supposed to do. And since we couldn't, we had to deal with the consequences. The question was whether we were going to just fold or whether we would make something happen. We decided we were going to rebound.

"Our next game was against Kentucky in Gainesville. And in that game we made a statement."

Against Kentucky, Don Gaffney threw for two touchdowns and ran for a third as Florida won 48-7.

Don Gaffney: "The offense was really smooth that day. Tony [Green] scored twice, and Jimmy [DuBose] threw a touchdown pass, and after the win we were given the choice between going to the Gator Bowl or the Cotton Bowl.

"A lot of strange things began to happen within those forty-eight hours. We had a meeting on Sunday, and Coach Dickey said it would be in our best interest to play the loser of Oklahoma-Nebraska in the Cotton Bowl. We were 9-2, but it seemed we were the most disrespected 9-2 team in Gator history. [There had only been two other 9-2 teams in Gator history, in 1960 and 1966. So this was the first 9-2 team in years.]

"But we felt like we didn't get a lot of respect, and when I think about it, we also felt that we hadn't accomplished much. We lost to N.C. State by a point and we lost to Georgia by three points. Had we won those games we would have been 11-0, and you wouldn't have all that hoopla in 1996 under Steve Spurrier for winning the national championship. We would have had it. That was what was most disappointing to the players on the team. We just didn't get it done. We had what it took. We just didn't do it. But that's why they play the games. You make no excuses. That's just the way it goes, and kids have to learn to accept that."

The final regular game of the 1975 season was against Miami in the Orange Bowl. Florida won, barely, 15-11, to give Florida a sterling 9-2 regular season record.

Don Gaffney: "It was a so-so effort. Here again, I could apply the same rationale—no excuse, we just simply were not into it. We didn't play very well. We barely got out of there. We got out on a wing and a prayer. Henry Davis broke a punt [for 63 yards with 3:48 to play]. After he scored, the Miami players were trying to say he was signalling for a fair catch and his knee was down. But he didn't. It was a good play.

"And to seal the victory, Robby Ball had to intercept a pass in the end zone.

"The other thing I remember about the game was that Jimmy DuBose fell five yards short of breaking the Southeast Conference one-season rushing record [of 1,312].

"We had every intention of getting that job done, but for us the fourth quarter was terrible, terrible. Miami was starting to become the Miami we know now. They were loaded with good athletes, and they were just tough defensively. We should have done a better job of calculating that. Jimmy should have gotten it. We were trying. It just didn't happen. But Jimmy didn't care about that. It would have been a great accomplishment for our offensive line—they wanted it."

Don Gaffney only played a short time in the Gator Bowl game against the University of Maryland. His wrist was bothering him badly, and shortly after the game he would be operated on. Don was not effective, and neither was Jimmy Fisher, and Florida lost 13-0.

Jimmy Fisher: "That night the fog rolled in. Don and I went half and half. I was worse than he was that night. Oh my gosh, we weren't ready. We went to the Gator Bowl, and you know how close it is to Gainesville—it didn't feel like a bowl game. And it wasn't really the game we wanted to be in. We were still reeling from the Georgia loss."

Don Gaffney: "I played, but not long. The broken wrist was really getting to me. My hand was giving me problems, and I was getting ready to have surgery. Finally Coach Dickey said, 'Don, let Jimmy have it.'

"It was wet and nasty, not our kind of day. Maryland was up for it. We were not. We can't blame anybody but ourselves for that, but our expectations were a lot bigger than what we got. It was unfortunate. It was immaturity on our part. We really thought we'd get a Big Eight team with some prestige and get a chance to do something dynamic at the end. And it didn't turn out that way. When it didn't, we kind of dropped the ball.

"We were flat. Let's be honest about it. All three bowl games were terrible for me. That was my last collegiate game."

Don Gaffney had been a pioneer. He had heard the booing and the racial slurs, and he had heard the cheers and the adulation. He had taken Florida to within three points of an SEC championship, four points perhaps from a National Championship.

Don Gaffney: "Tracy and I had gotten married in August, and I hadn't had any time to spend with her because soon thereafter I rushed into practice. Football had been everything. I was already accepted into law school, but I didn't want to do that. I was tired.

"It was like running a marathon. At the end, you have a bittersweet feeling. I made it. I really did think I did okay. But for whatever reason, it wasn't a joyful trip.

"Being the first black quarterback at Florida, I had to deal with a lot more. I had to say a lot less. At times I was just trying to hold on. There was a lot of pressure on me and on the coaches. When we played our last game, finally it was over. Now what do you do?

"I wanted to play pro football, but being a realist I knew there weren't that many black quarterbacks. I had that to deal with and also the surgery on the broken wrist. I had to have the pin in my arm taken out. The NFL draft was in February. I was a black quarterback, undersized by the standards of the time, off a wishbone team, with a broken wrist.

"I was not going to be drafted. Canadian teams wanted to sign me, but I wasn't sure I wanted to do that. Really, I was just so tired. I just wanted to get away from football for awhile.

"I went to law school at Florida, and four years later, I was out, and I still wanted to play football. I was a law student wanting to be a football player or a football player trying to be a law student. Anyway you put it, you are leaving something on the field. You had forgot something, something you didn't do, something you needed to do.

"I made it through. It wasn't easy, but I did.

"After graduating, I came back to Jacksonville to practice law. I also played semipro ball with the Jacksonville Firebirds. It was fun. I got to play football again. Jimmy Fisher and I hooked up again.

"I became assistant state attorney, and I started teaching law, and then I got into politics. I was a member of the Florida House of Representatives. I was a member of the city council in Jacksonville. I'm just a private citizen now."

forty-three

Fourth and Dumb

In the fall of 1976 Scott Brantley, one of the most ferocious linebackers ever to play at the University of Florida, arrived in Gainesville. After leading Ocala Forest to the state championship in the 3A division his senior year, he was named the Parade Magazine High School Player of the Year. Every college coach in the nation wanted him. Woody Hayes, Bear Bryant, Vince Dooley, Bill Battle, Fran Curci, Pepper Rodgers and Bobby Bowden were among those who courted him for over a year.

The legendary Bear would call him every Wednesday night like clockwork. Doug Dickey and the Florida coaching staff assumed that Brantley would go to Alabama. But there were other forces at work. Brantley had developed a relationship with Florida defensive coordinator Doug Knotts, and he had also made close friendships with members of the University of Florida's powerful network of alumni, many of whom he met through his father's contacts in the bridge construction business. Brantley had moved to Florida from South Carolina when he was ten, and he loved living in Florida. At the last minute he decided that it made no sense to go to Alabama if he was going to live the rest of his life in the state of Florida. When he announced he was going to Florida, no one was more surprised than Doug Dickey.

Scott Brantley: "As a boy I was a great outdoorsman, loved to hunt and fish, still do, and through my father I met a lot of Gator alumni who owned big ranches, horse ranches, cattle ranches, and who had great fishing pits. When I was in high school Ralph Ortega, who was a great linebacker at Florida, would come down to Ocala and go hunting with us on the weekends.

"I got to know the Craggs family, the McLoud family, and then Coon Dog, Chris McCoun, who's from Ocala. He played with Ralph, and he ended up marrying the daughter of Fred Montsdeoca, who played for Florida back in the '40s. The Coon Dog and Fred's daughter have a son who just graduated from Florida. He was a great special team defensive player.

"Fred Montseoca is among the greatest people in the world. He means so much to the Gator Nation. You think of him and Red Mitchum. I've never been to a Gator game where I don't sit down with Fred Montsdeoca for at least five minutes. It's part of the tradition. It's what I do.

"They are the bloodline, what it means to be a Gator. I meet kids today, and they say, 'I'm going to FSU because I'm a defensive back.' Hey, what the hell is Deion Sanders going to do for you when you get out of football? What is he going to do for you when you're IN football? Not a damn thing. The Montsdeocas, Tommy Cragg, Red Mitchum, Whit Palmer, they were the ones I knew I would have friendships with the rest of my life. That's why I chose the University of Florida.

"I arrived in Gainesville in the fall of '76 as a freshman. I had played in the high school All-Star game, and that's where I met my roommate, Yancey Sutton. Yancey was totally deaf. He had played for Gene Cox at Tallahassee Leon along with Jimmy Jordan, who became the quarterback at FSU. Yancey and I became best friends and roommates.

"People say, 'Wasn't that kind of different?' I tell them, 'Yancey was the greatest roommate you could ever have. He never tied up the phone in four years! If the phone rang, I knew it was for me. His mother would call once a month just to check to see if he needed anything.

"I was a true freshman, and when I went through the whole training camp, I was fourth or fifth team on the depth chart. The opening game of the '76 season was against North Carolina in the Ole Sombrero in Tampa. Late in the first half the starting middle linebacker was screwing up, and the guy they put in didn't do anything, and all of a sudden I heard Doug Knotts' distinct voice, 'Brantley!' I said to myself, What does he want? He said, 'Get over here.' I ran up beside him. He said, 'Get in the game.'

"I said, 'Get in the game?' I had to go in front of the huddle and call the defensive signals. I was supposed to look over to Doug, and he was supposed to give me the signs. But I hadn't paid any attention at the meeting, because I knew I wasn't going to play. I would look at Scott Hutchinson, one of the starters, and say, 'What in the world is he calling?' And he would tell me.

"I started the second half, played the whole second half, and led the team in tackles."

On offense, quarterback Jimmy Fisher was in charge.

Jimmy Fisher: "I finally got to start my senior year. It was all mine. How many times do you still get to be quarterback when you're a senior? You have all these young guys, plus we're in a wishbone, and they are recruiting all these fast guys. So my senior year came, and there still was nobody else who could run that triple option, so they kinda had to give it to me, and Dickey already was on the ropes. He knew, 'Ain't no more rebuilding here, boy. You better get with your best who can make things happen for you.' So he was stuck with me, although I was not the prototype he was looking for. I couldn't run 4.4s [in the 40-yard dash]."

Against North Carolina, Florida trailed by three points with 1:25 left in the game. Behind Jimmy Fisher, Florida marched down to the Carolina two and appeared poised to win the game. But with third and one, no time outs left, and the clock running down, Fisher dropped back and hit Tony Green with a pass in the flat. Green was tackled for a two-yard loss. Wes Chandler had been open on the play, but Fisher hadn't seen him.

The scoreboard, in error, read third down, and Fisher saw that. It was actually fourth down, with seconds remaining. But earlier in the final period Jimmy Fisher had been hit hard and dazed. Perhaps with a clearer head he would have realized he needed to throw the ball into the end zone for a touchdown. When he threw a pass out of bounds on fourth down to stop the clock, the Gators were 24-21 losers.

Jimmy Fisher: "I remember in that last quarter, I got hit. There's no doubt about it, I was a little foggy during the whole last quarter. We needed a last-minute drive to go down there and try to score. So if you look at all the plays I called, we had to throw the ball. Wes Chandler was on the team. Tony Green was on the team. So I was just taking the ball and rather than throwing it downfield, I was throwing it to guys I could see quickly. I was giving it to Tony and throwing quick stuff to Wes.

"We were down near the goal line with less than a minute to go, and there was a penalty or two, and there was confusion. We were trying to get plays off. I got up underneath the center at about the three yard line. I remember looking at the scoreboard and seeing it was third down. Little did I know the scoreboard operator had it wrong. It was really fourth down.

You're not supposed to depend on the scoreboard. And I threw the ball out of bounds to stop the clock, so I could get a play from the bench.

"I remember Doug Dickey running out. I saw everyone running around the field, so I figured I hadn't stopped the clock in time. He came out, and he looked at me and said, 'Fisher, didn't you realize it was fourth down?' I was dumbfounded. I didn't even realize what he was talking about.

"At that point Dickey told the cops, 'You walk that boy in [to the locker room]. Don't let him talk to anybody.' He saw it was such a confusing moment for me. But that happened, and we lost. And we had great expectations that year, and I can still remember that was probably the lowest time of my entire life.

"Here's my senior year, I'm the designated guy, and you do something like that in your hometown, about the worst thing a quarterback can do. Ask David Bowden about that one. It was absolutely the worst thing. So the next week, I just said, 'I gotta go to work here.'

"The next game was against the University of Houston at home. The first five times we had the ball, we opened it up throwing. We scored the first four times we had the ball. [Florida won 49-14.] Then Coach Dickey took me out to give the other quarterbacks some reps. We ended up that day with 615 yards in total offense! And Houston ended up winning the Southwest Conference that year. They got their quarterback problems worked out and ended up coming back. But I remember overcoming perhaps my greatest personal hurdle. The Houston game was absolutely the biggest time of my entire life in my football career. I was so thrilled we could do this, and I was part of it.

"And I credit Coach Dickey. You better believe it. It would have been real easy for him to quit on me. He quit on David [Bowden]. See, at that point no one else was groomed. I was the guy who could run the triple option and make the right read. I could make the decision. So it wasn't so important to be athletic as it was to have the foot speed but also be able to make those throws. He saw that too. And through the rest of the year we bearly beat most everybody. We played a lot of close games. Our defense was marginal, and we had to score more than they scored. We went through the rest of that SEC schedule barely winning."

Florida outscored Mississippi State 34–30. In that game Fisher was cut on the elbow and had to leave the game. Backup quarterback Bill Kynes threw for three touchdowns. On the defensive side Scott Brantley was named SEC Defensive Player of the week.

Scott Brantley: "It was very early in the year, a day game, and it was hot. Mississippi State had a great running back by the name of Walter Packer. At the end of the game they had the ball, and we were in a prevent defense, and they threw a dump-off pass to Packer right in the middle of the field. I was making my drop, and I came up, and he was shaking and baking, trying to elude me and go down the sidelines, and I just squared him up, and boom, hit him and tackled him, and that was the end of the game."

With Jimmy Fisher at the helm, Florida had a string of victories. After defeating LSU 28-23, the Gators played FSU in Tallahassee.

In the fourth quarter Florida had a ten-point lead, and four times FSU reached the Gator fifteen, only to come away with just a field goal. Florida won 33-26.

Scott Brantley: "It was a new era. When I was a freshman at Florida, Bobby Bowden was a freshman coach at FSU. That's when it all started. Bobby Bowden is the greatest thing that even happened to Florida State. Yeah, they have a good theater school, but they ought to rename the university after Bobby. In the early '70s FSU was thinking about dropping the football program, it was so bad. Look at 1972, 1973. So Bobby Bowden pulled them totally out of the fire, and from that 1976 season on, look at what they have done!

"Bobby will tell you he came out of West Virginia to go to FSU for one reason and one reason only: as a stepping stone to Alabama or Auburn, where he grew up. He was only going to be there a short while while he got FSU on course, and say, 'It was fun. Take it.' But he did too good of a job, and when those jobs came open, the timing wasn't right, and he could never leave there now."

In that 33-26 win over FSU, David Posey kicked two field goals including a 54-yarder and four extra points. He became Florida's all time leading scorer.

Scott Brantley: "I was never a fan of kickers but for a kicker, David Posey was a normal guy. In high school, kickers were tight ends and defensive backs who just happen to be able to put the ball through the uprights, but in college you have specialty guys as kickers. Davey was a white guy with a blond afro.

He was number three, a great guy. Kickers are different. They always have been, always will be."

After the opening loss to North Carolina, Florida won six in a row, including a 20-18 win over Tennessee, and and a 24-19 win over Auburn. Jimmy Fisher ran a powerful wishbone offense, as the Gators gained 506 yards. Willie Wilder and Tony Green played impressively, but the star of the game was Wes Chandler.

Scott Brantley: "We had a great goal line stand against Auburn, and I remember making a bunch of tackles, but the one play I recall best was called Chandler's run.

"Jimmy Fisher hit Wes Chandler on a slant route for maybe all of four and a half yards, and I'll bet Wes ran one hundred and eighty yards, zigzagging back and forth across the field, and the only thing that touched him: when he ran out the back of our end zone, that big-ass war eagle flew off his perch and bit him on the back and got flagged for mascot interference! On the highlight film that year, they tagged it as 'Chandler's run.'

"Wes Chandler will probably never be in the pro football Hall of Fame, but he was one of the greatest college players I ever saw. Ask Dan Fouts. Wes is a great, great guy. He's now coaching the wide receivers for the Dallas Cowboys."

The big game of the 1976 season came next against Georgia. Going into it, the Gators had a one-game lead over Georgia for the SEC title. With the defense inexperienced and banged up, there was concern about whether Scott Brantley would be able to play.

Scott Brantley: "The week before that game I suffered a severe thigh bruise in practice. It swelled up, and I lived in the trainer's room with Chris Patrick, the head trainer. All night long I slept in the trainer's room, icing it, applying heat, and they put this God-awful big pad on my thigh.

"I ended up tearing the muscle, and I still have a knot the size of a tennis ball in my quad. But hey, I HAD to play. They put a little juice in there, and it never really bothered me, but I was kind of aggravated about having to play with that big pad."

Jimmy Fisher: "We needed to win this game, or the Kentucky game after it, to win the SEC title. The Georgia game comes up again, and we have to win this thing. I had a real feeling of, 'I wonder if we can get this done or not?' And there was talk about Coach Dickey. People were starting to whisper a little bit. He was a former player, a successful coach at Tennessee, but he didn't have the staying power that some of the other coaches had. So there was talk. You could feel it.

"We had a great offense. Against Georgia we started throwing the ball, and we were moving it around. Jimmy Stephens caught a touchdown. We threw all over the field, and we were ahead at the half 27-13. Man alive, everything felt so good! The offense was clicking. Everything felt so free and easy."

Scott Brantley: "We were actually talking about ring sizes at halftime. We were over in the corner going, 'If we win this game, we win an SEC ring.' It would have been the first time in the history of the school. Then we screwed around and let the game slip away. We didn't score a point in the second half."

Jimmy Fisher: "The second half started. Willie Wilder fielded a kickoff nine yards deep and ran to the eleven. We got the ball, so we're happy. We're going to get the ball first… and what do we do, we start running. Because we were back so deep, we got conservative. We didn't want to make a mistake early. Dickey was a conservative coach big time, man. So we could feel it—that conservativeness. All of a sudden, we just wanted to run it. We went three and out, and we punted.

"And they ended up scoring on our defense, which was real marginal. Our defense was tenth in the SEC that year. Our offense was number one.

"So after they scored, we got the ball back, and we didn't do much with it. And they ended up scoring again.

"Have you ever heard of the fourth-and-dumb call by Dickey? Now Dickey realizes, We have to win these games on offense. So we're on our own thirty, and he goes for it on fourth down.

"Really and truly, at that point I was realizing we had to get some momentum going. I knew it was going to have to be an offensive football game. In my heart I was saying, We're going to win this thing. This is our game. We've got to stay on the field a little longer. Our defensive guys were getting winded. So I remember on fourth and three, the play came in.

"I looked around and said, 'Okay, this is what we're doing.' Then when I got to the line of scrimmage, I almost called time out. I was so close to doing that—just to give Coach Dickey another chance to think about it.

"But remember, he was running most of the plays from the sidelines. If you did something different, you were questioning the coach. Once you got to the line of scrimmage you could change. And I got up underneath, and I looked around, and it wasn't a bad defense. They weren't set up crazy, so the play was still on. They had what we call a 'hard three.' The defensive end was coming at you. So I put the ball in the fullback's belly. I took it out quick because I saw the 'hard three' coming. I flipped it out to Earl Carr, who was 6'2", 225 pounds, an amazing specimen, a great running back from Orlando.

"He got it, and a little defensive back from Georgia came running up, maybe 5'10". Carr put out his arm to stiff-arm him, and the guy grabbed his arm and pulled him down for a one-yard loss."

Scott Brantley: "We had fourth and one on the 30, but when you have a 230-pound Earl Carr in the backfield and you can run him off-tackle or between the guard and the center and all you need is a yard, it isn't that risky a strategy.

"But they ran a pitch to the short side of the field, and them little junkyard dog linebackers, they were 5'10", 200 pounds, and they could run, they ran down Earl Carr going around left end, and that was the turning point in the game. It really was."

Jimmy Fisher: "At that point, we knew we were in trouble. We went downhill from there. The momentum swung. And we lost 41-27. That was the lowest of the low, man. That was it. Tough."

Scott Brantley: "It was quiet on the bus ride home from Georgia. You could have heard a pin drop. But we knew we had a breath of life. We were going to Kentucky the next week. If we could beat Kentucky, we would win a half share of the SEC title.

"Everyone talks about the greatest coach at Kentucky being Bear Bryant. No, the greatest coach at Alabama was Bear Bryant. The great coach at Kentucky was Fran Curci. He had Derrick Ramsey and some great running backs, and Art Still on defense, and Jim Kovach, the big linebacker who played for the Saints and became a doctor. And they were on probation. They couldn't win the SEC, but they sure could screw it up for us. And Fran Curci had those guys jacked up, and they ended up beating us, and we lost all ability to win even a share of the SEC."

Jimmy Fisher: "All we had to do was beat Kentucky, and we'd still have a share. We went up to Lexington, and it was freezing. That's why we don't play up there in November any more. We play it at home. My years were the reasons why they changed. Every time we went up there, it was cold. That day it was freezing. And you've got to remember, if you take Florida kids up to those areas, man alive, it's so cold you're in trouble. There was no heat in the locker rooms. And Fran Curci was the Kentucky coach. He was still mad because of the time Dickey had his players lay down so his Miami team could score, so we could get the ball back and get John Reaves the yards he needed to set the passing record.

"We came out onto the field. We're on the home side—the West side-line. It was a late afternoon game. Kentucky went to the visitor's side—the east side, the sunny side where the sun hits you all day long. So we get in the shade early, and it was VERY cold. I remember the first pass I threw to Wes Chandler. It hit him right in the chest, and it was so cold, he dropped it. Wes was behind all of them, and if he had caught it, we would have scored. But he didn't, and from there on, man, we just couldn't get ourselves together. The offense just didn't do very much.

"But Curci really pulled a fast one on us. Curci really held a pretty good grudge.

"It was one of the most infamous times in Florida football history. We really felt we had really lost something. It was too bad we couldn't get ourselves together for Kentucky. At that point, it wasn't fun any more. That's for sure, because winning the SEC had been our goal for years, and we got so close. Not to get there... our heart was just not there. We were feeling added pressure to make it happen—now. We were living with guys day in and day out and with the coaching staff, preparing for practice, and knowing we had a window that we were in, that it was time to put up or shut up. Even though we ended up going to a bowl game, if we couldn't have it all we felt like we were losers."

After Florida manhandled Rice 50-22, it faced Miami at the Citrus Bowl in Orlando in the final game of the 1976 season. It was Jimmy Fisher's finest moment. He accounted for 366 yards in total offense, running 15 times for 103 yards and completing 14 of 21 passes for 263 yards, as Florida won 19-10.

Scott Brantley: "Jimmy Fisher was a great athlete, one of the smartest, brightest, friendliest guys. He always had a smile on his face. He never said a negative word about anybody. Jimmy was a heady guy who meant a lot to the program at the time. He was just a good athlete who never got the chance to play at the next level."

Jimmy Fisher: "I ended up having a real neat senior year. By our third year we were averaging 7.0 yards per play running the wishbone. Toward the end of my senior year we had a check system in place that Jimmy Dunn gave us. He had made it so simple. Because on a true wishbone you have five and a half guys to the left and five and a half guys to the right, with the fullback right behind you. Using Jimmy's check system we could isolate defenders because we knew where they were going to be. What Jimmy did, he watched how Nebraska began playing Oklahoma, and he took some of those concepts and created the check system. And at some point we led the nation in yards per play. We had Wes Chandler, Derrick Gaffney, Terry LeCount, and my tight end was Jimmy Ray Stephens. I still think Jimmy Stephens is the greatest athlete ever at the University of Florida. He started at three positions in three years at Florida. We had all these receivers so we broke up the bone a little bit. We were able to throw out of it. We took Chandler or Gaffney or LeCount and stuck one of them out and had a split backfield. The fullback still went where he was supposed to go.

"We really had an offense, and I had a great senior year. I led in touchdowns, total offense, all this other stuff, because there were great people around me. And I ended up having my best game in my last game, against Miami. Now how much better can you go out than to have your very best game your last game? I was really fortunate to still be the quarterback, the star, and then have a decent year. Normally by that time you're out in the pasture.

"My last year, 1976, was the first year of the Bucs. The first year of Bobby Bowden at FSU. It was the kind of year that has been forgotten because of some of the things that happened. It kind of ended up like the other two years, but I was proud of what we did.

"We played Miami in Orlando to try to create interest. At this point our wishbone offense was really clicking. We felt like we had the check-off system in place, even though experts thought the wishbone offense was kind of passé in the country at that point.

"In my last game against Miami, I actually set the record for total yards in one game. I ended up running for over a hundred yards and passing for more than two hundred yards, a total of 366. And that was the number one game ever for total offense in Florida history. That went beyond John Reaves, because John was throwing a lot of balls, but the sacks for losses would be subtracted from the total. Of course, since then Coach Spurrier's quarterbacks have had 500-yard games. So my record has kind of been lost. I don't talk about it a lot—there is no reason to talk about it, but I'm the only guy to ever run for over a hundred and throw for over two hundred. I mean, you have to hang on to what you hang on to. So I take it. Because the wishbone generation of quarterbacks is a lost generation. But we didn't have the opportunity to throw forty times a game.

"And the credit has to go to Jimmy Dunn's offense which allowed me to check and actually run the ball a little bit.

"That Miami game was just so momentous for me… there are so many college guys who go through their careers and peak as a sophomore or a junior. Then that senior year, they don't do as well. With me, my best year was my senior year. Most people don't know who I am, okay? I'm not on any of the big charts. We didn't win the SEC. But for me personally, I will always know I can go back and say, 'Hey, you know what, I finished strong. I came back from that first game.' So inside, man, I really have something to hang onto. And I'm proud of myself. It just worked.

"I got real fortunate. You saw where David [Bowden], man, he got hammered. His whole life changed. He was just finished. I see it in his eyes when we talk. I know he harbors some things.

"It should almost be illegal the amount of influence these coaches have over these kids. For years I thought seriously that when kids leave the college game there should be some sort of support group they could belong to for awhile. You're leaving something that your whole identity is tied to. Football can leave some pretty good scars."

Florida was invited to play in the Sun Bowl against Texas A&M on January 2, 1977.

Scott Brantley: "The Sun Bowl was in El Paso, Texas. I thought it was cool as heck to go to Juarez, Mexico, and be wined and dined a whole week. We practiced at the stadium. We had a ball. We had cars to drive. I got a Sun Bowl ring. Every player got a pair of cowboy boots from Tony Lama himself.

"I remember eating Mexican food and getting sick. I weighed maybe 220, but I got sick as a dog, was dehydrated and throwing up, and weighed maybe 205 when the game started.

"It was cold and nice, and we played Texas A&M, one of the best teams in the nation. They had lost a couple of early games, but they put it together at the end, won their last eight or nine, and I don't care what anybody says, they were the best team in the country.

"One of the publications that year was Parade Magazine, and Curtis Dickey, who played for A&M, was named the offensive high school Player of the Year, and I was the defensive Player of the Year, and we were true freshmen starting for our respecteive teams in the Sun Bowl, and that was neat.

"During the game I remember Wes Chandler catching a pass and shaking it in the face of Lester Hayes, who was one of their defensive backs. I thought to myself, Wes, that is NOT a good deal. 'Cause those Aggies were pissed off at that, and they commenced to put us on it.

"They had a fullback by the name of George Woodard. He was 6'1", maybe 275 pounds, and they threw a screen pass to Woodard, and I broke under the coverage and got to him with all my 205 pounds, and when I tried to cut him down, his knee came up and almost shattered my hip.

"I went in, and they injected it right in the locker room, and I asked, 'How long is it going to last, Doc?' He said, 'Til the end of the game, but he didn't count the TV timeouts, so the game took a lot longer, and the later it got, the stiffer it got.

"It was terribly painful. It was the worst thing I ever experienced in my life. But it was the last game of the season, and I would have time to heal, and after they shot it up, after the halftime I went back out there.

"I played another quarter and a half, and the ballgame got out of hand. They whipped up on us pretty good."

Senior Jimmy Fisher didn't have the same enthusiasm for playing in that Sun Bowl game that freshman Scott Brantley did.

Jimmy Fisher: "It just wasn't very exciting. We wanted to be playing for something other than just being in the Top Ten. We had tasted something better, and we wanted to be there. After you lose like that [in the Georgia game], it's tough to get back up. I guess some teams have the ability to do that better than others."

"If in my senior year we had won the SEC, I think Doug Dickey would still be at Florida as coach. Dickey got the offense going, and if he had just gotten over the little hump, he'd still be here today.

"I'm kinda glad I experienced what I did with this team and with Coach Dickey. It made me realize something very important: No matter what you do, how much time you put in, your job depends on eleven Saturdays a year for about three hours, when you have 18 and 19-year-old kids having to perform for you to keep your job. Now that's pretty hairy! A couple of years after I played I thought that what I wanted to do was coach football for a living. I had grown up the son of a football coach. I was working on getting my undergraduate degree and working with Coach Dickey as a graduate assistant. And I decided at that point, there was no way I'm gonna stick my family that way—because I saw all the coaches working on their exit strategies in case it didn't work out. Just knowing everyone was wondering, Where am I gonna be? What's gonna happen? Because once the head coach goes, all the people with him are impacted. At that point I realized I didn't know whether this was what I wanted to do. And I was glad for that, because if I hadn't gone through that experience, I may have had a different perspective.

"When my football eligibility was up after the '76 season, I had to get my diploma, so I hung around for a couple more years, and so I was in town when Coach Dickey was fired.

"More than anything the real start of his downfall came at the end of the '77 season when Florida State came in and beat us at home. We had beaten them I don't know how many times in a row.

"Boy, that happened in our place. That was really mind-boggling that could happen. The next year, 1978, it went downhill from there. We were trying to run the wishbone offense, and we didn't quite have the people to make it work. The quarterback position wasn't real stable, we didn't have a real burner, and the defense didn't do well that year. It was a tough year.

"Charlie Pell was hired and came in. He brought in mostly his own people from Clemson. I never really got to know him too well. At that point I moved out of Gainesville and took work other places.

"I went to Jacksonville and worked with the Athletic Attic thinking that sporting goods might be the answer. I started in the Gainesville area under Jimmy Carnes, the Florida and Olympic track coach. When you leave the university, the first few years you're just trying to earn a living. I did that for a couple of years, and then I came back to Tampa.

"Calgary general manager Jack Gotta came down to talk to me. They were getting players who could run a little bit, like Doug Flutie and Condredge Holloway. They saw me running around and doing sprint-outs and thought they liked what they saw. But then the Washington Redskins' Charlie Waller, who for years worked for George Allen, a real tough old-liner, he liked wishbone quarterbacks because they were old school. Billy Kilmer was on the team, and Joe Theismann so he thought, 'Hey, a wishbone quarterback.'

I went up there and had a tryout with the Redskins, but I couldn't adapt to it. My heart really was out of it anyway. I grew up the son of a coach, and emotionally I knew by the end of my senior year that I wasn't going to get a chance for that next level. I just realized my heart wasn't there any more, and we just kinda parted our ways.

"If a kid ends up a wishbone quarterback in college, who knows if he ever can go on to the next level? Know what I mean? Of course, I look back on it, and I wouldn't trade it for anything. My personal feeling about who I am and what I accomplished—I got real fortunate that I was part of my own little world, and that I really got blessed toward the end of my college career—even though I'm not in the top ten in any of the quarterback categories."

forty-four

The Brantley Brothers

In 1977 Florida needed to find a quarterback to replace Jimmy Fisher. Coach Dickey had to choose between Terry LeCount, freshman Cris Collinsworth, a high school All-American from Titusville, Florida, and John Brantley, the brother of linebacker Scott Brantley.

John Brantley was Scott's older brother, but he did not play varsity ball as a freshman. In 1976 John was redshirted, and in '77 he showed enough ability despite his 5'10" size to vie for the starting quarterback job. It would not take him too many games before he earned it.

John Brantley: "When I was growing up in Greenville, South Carolina, I was a closet Georgia fan. We had a couple of local heroes who went to Georgia. What was funny, the year after I entered Florida, Vince Dooley came to our house to try to recruit Scott, and while Scott was talking to the South Carolina coach, I drive Coach Dooley to his motel, and while we were talking I reeled off his 1964–1965–1966 starting lineups. He sat there in disbelief. He said, 'Johnny, I saw you play against us in the freshman game.' We beat them. He said, 'If I had had any inkling you knew that much about Georgia, we'd have made more of a push to sign you, because it's fun to have kids who know that much about your program on the team.' But my best bet was right up the road at Florida, and I loved going there. I'm still part of the Gator Nation.

"I was recommended to Coach Dickey by Red Mitchum, who has lived here in Ocala for years. Red went to Coach Dickey when it got down to the last three or four scholarships. He told Coach Dickey I was a competitor and a winner, and they took a chance on me, and that's when I made the decision to go to Florida. It was always preached to me that if you were planning to live in the great state of Florida, we felt if you could make a name for yourself, it would pay off if you went to college in Florida. And it worked out.

"I played freshman ball [in '76]. I thought freshman football was a blast. We played four games. We played Auburn, Georgia, Miami, and FSU.

"We had a lot of good coaches. Besides Chan Gailey, we had Jimmy Dunn, who was my quarterback coach for two years. Kim Helton later coached at the University of Houston and in the NFL. Ken Hatfield is still coaching at Rice.

"We were 3-0, and we went up to Tallahassee to play FSU, and at halftime we were winning. And all of a sudden I noticed that FSU had a change of personnel. On the other side of the field FSU was playing some varsity players! We knew they were varsity players because their uniforms were clean, and they were bigger. They were going through a transition period, and that second half they had five varsity players out there, and they beat us the last three minutes of the game. We had a very good freshman team.

"Our coaches didn't care much what players FSU was using. It really didn't matter. They were just out there trying to make the guys who got beat up by the varsity all week better.

"In '76 I was redshirted. That was fortunate for me. Here's where I have always admired Coach Dickey, regardless of what you may have heard about him. He was always up front with anything he told you.

"We were playing Houston in our second game, and we were blowing them out in Gainesville, and about midway in the third quarter, Coach Dickey came up and put his arm around me.

"We were still running the wishbone, but we were going through a transition. We were getting ready to change to more of a standard pro-type offense, and I was a pretty good thrower. He said, 'All right, here's the deal. You can go out there and play the whole fourth quarter, what you have worked for, or you can do what I would like for you to do: take a red-shirt and come back next year and get ready for a pro-style offense, which is better suited for your throwing abilities.'

"I said, 'Coach, that's fine. I'd love to run out there right now, but if it means taking up a whole year of eligibility just to play one quarter, I'm all for red-shirting.'

"So I sat and watched the rest of the game and the rest of the season. I dressed for the non-conference games. I practiced every day to get the varsity ready. And the nice thing about it was that it gave Scott and me the opportunity to play the next three years out of the same class."

Scott Brantley: "Between my freshman and sophomore years I played baseball for Jay Bergman, and I was also practicing football in the spring, and to me they don't mix. I ended up stretching and almost tearing my Achilles tendon on the football field. I landed weird, and they put me in a cast, and it took about two years to get over that, so my sophomore year wasn't nearly as fruitful as my freshman year."

John Brantley: "In '77 we opened the season against Rice. Terry LeCount started the game at quarterback. I was the backup. Terry did his deal, then I went out and did my deal.

"I had a pretty good game. Rice was Rice. They had lost Tommy Kramer and were down a little bit. [Florida won 48-3.] Everybody played pretty well. We threw the ball a little bit, nothing spectacular, a pretty solid win.

"In the fourth quarter Cris Collinsworth went out to do a little mop-up, threw a wounded duck about twenty-five yards, and Gaffney caught it, and the defensive guys fell down, and Derrick ended up running eighty percent of the play. It wasn't even a spiral. It was a fluke thing, but it went 99 yards, breaking the SEC record, so in the record book it says, 'Ninety-nine yards.' Cris will be remembered for it the rest of his life.

"Cris and I are very close. I'm the president of the Cris Collinsworth Foundation, and we talk on a weekly basis."

Scott Brantley: "Collinsworth wasn't even supposed to be in the game. Late in the game they put him at quarterback, and he threw the ugliest pass about four yards, and Derrick made a big catch and eluded everybody for 99 yards. It wasn't as much what Cris did as what Derrick did."

John Brantley: "We played Mississippi State next, a fun game because it was in Jackson. We always played them in Jackson. We never played them in Starkville. In the first quarter, Terry was dazed, so here I was a red-shirt freshman in a really tough situation, because we were playing an SEC team on the road.

"We were still running the wishbone, and my first play was a '29-pitch' to Tony Green. I pitched it out, and heck, Tony went eighty yards for a touchdown. And Coach Dickey even brought it up on his TV show the next day. He said, 'Here's little Johnny Brantley, who supposedly can't run, and he's side-by-side running with Tony Green for a touchdown.' When you've got your adrenaline running, you know, it takes over. Then I threw my first touchdown pass in that game to Wes Chandler, who is the best football player I've ever been around. I hit him on a corner route, and we won the game [24-22].

"Wes was the best. I don't care if we were playing pool, ping pong, anything—people didn't get to see the things he used to do in practice, the one-handed catches. I mean, you name it, he could do it. Wes was just phenomenal. As I've said, he was the best athlete I've ever been associated with.

"With about two minutes to go in the game, we were trying to run out the clock. We called a sprint pass, and I sprinted to my right, and if the receiver is wide open, I throw, and if he isn't, I just run the ball and keep the clock running. Well, I got around the corner, and one of their linebackers grabbed my face mask and bent me back so far I was looking at a size 10 on the bottom of my shoe. He tore some muscles in my back. Fortunately for us, it got us fifteen yards and an automatic first down, and Terry [LeCount] went in there and ran out the clock.

"I was not able to play against LSU the next week, which was an ugly game. I hadn't even changed knees on the sideline, and we were down 21-0. I tried to go in and make something happen, but I was ineffective because of my back. I went in for just one series and came out again. [Florida lost 36-14.]

"The next game was against the defending national champions, the University of Pittsburgh. Without a doubt, that was the toughest team I've ever faced in my whole life. Ten of the eleven defensive players ended up signing with the NFL. They had Hugh Green and Rickey Jackson, who was a sophomore.

"And what was unique about the game was that the defense scored the touchdowns, and it ended in a [17-17] tie.

"It was Matt Cavanaugh's first game back after he broke his wrist against Notre Dame. He wore a soft cast, and he fumbled the ball seven times from center. So we picked up one or two of them and ran them back, and we kicked a field goal, and so we tied them. It wasn't because of the Gator offense, I can tell you that. They flat shut us down. I think I made every highlight film that year because Hugh Green picked me up and threw me to the turf—almost made me look like a rag doll, and that made every All-American show for the next two years. It didn't hurt me any. I'm glad I added to Hugh Green's career. He played with my brother Scott at Tampa Bay. Hugh was a good guy, real quiet but very intense. He got after it."

Scott Brantley: "If it hadn't been for the defense, we'd have got our butt beat. Cause the defense rallied and scored both our touchdowns. Matt Cavanaugh, the Pitt quarterback, had broken his thumb earlier in the season, and he was wearing a soft cast, and we knew he'd have a hard time handling the ball, and we just blitzed him to death, got after him, and we made some big plays that resulted in touchdowns. Without those, we'd have gotten beat."

John Brantley: "Against Tennessee they put in a new I-formation. Dickey just couldn't get it out of his blood. He just couldn't get option football out of his head. It was a transition for everybody, and it was even tougher for Coach Dickey. Because we had so many outstanding running backs with so much speed. In '77 we had six running backs who ran a 4.4 or better. We had Tony Green, Willie Wilder, Earl Carr, guys who could fly. Then we had Wes Chandler and Derrick Gaffney. They were interchangeable. We even put Wes in the backfield.

"I remember we beat Tennessee [27-17]. It wasn't a big blow out. It was a good, solid SEC win. I can remember the last play of the game. Coach Dickey wanted Terry to kneel the ball down. But one of the assistant coaches, I want to say it was Coach Helton, somehow got the word to the huddle to throw a streak pass down the sideline. So instead of kneeling on the ball and ending the game, we threw a bomb down the side of the field. It was incomplete, but one of the Tennessee coaches got upset, and he swung at one of our coaches. Then we went out to the middle of the field, and we had a knock-down, drag-out with about thirty guys out there. I got the smallest Tennessee player over on one end. We were just standing there talking about it, watching all the big guys slug it out in the middle of the field.

"When we went to Auburn, I remember running onto the field, and everyone threw oranges at us, to remind us where we were from, I guess. As we were running out one of my teammates said to me, 'These guys must think we're going to the Orange Bowl.' We got pelted with oranges.

"Terry played and ran option plays. No big deal. I sat, was the backup, and I didn't have a problem with that. I always thought I was fortunate I got a scholarship there. Every down I played for the University of Florida I felt was a gift. I knew I could play, but it's a tough game up there. People don't realize how tough. [Auburn won 29-14.]"

Scott Brantley: "Auburn had a little flankerback, and they ran a reverse, faked one way and ran it back the other way, and I read it, and I met him at the corner, and when I hit him, that whole place, eighty thousand fans, just went, 'Whoooooooo.'

"Right before halftime I hit another guy, and I got knocked out. The fans were all cheering as they were helping me off the field.

"I was going into the locker room, and our head trainer, Chris Patrick, said to me, 'Where are you?' I said, 'What do you mean, where are we? We're playing Georgia. We're in Jacksonville.' He said, 'No, that isn't until next week.'

"I did get hurt, and they beat us pretty good."

John Brantley: "We had a tough week coming off the Auburn loss. At that point Coach Dickey was feeling the heat. That was the week everyone's emotions got caught up. We were playing Georgia next, and he moved Cris Collinsworth to second-team quarterback. Cris had been a highly touted freshman, an outstanding athlete, just a great kid, and he had to find a way to get him into the flow of things. So they moved him to second string, and I wasn't happy with that.

"I came in and looked at the depth chart, and I had gone from two to three. There wasn't any reason for it. I didn't even have an opportunity to be demoted.

"I'm a competitor. I had a red jersey on that week, and my emotions were running high. I said to myself, Man, I'm out here killing myself. I've been starting in baseball. Maybe I don't need this.'

"I got frustrated, and I walked off the field in the middle of practice. I said to myself, It's tough enough to be out here to compete and to be over-looked like that….' And Scott started to walk off too. He was an All-SEC linebacker. He said, 'If he's through, I'm through.'

"We got things calmed down, and the next day I went back out for practice. But everyone knew about it.

"Coach Dickey and I talked about it. Like I said, I admired him. We got to talk, and he told me that Cris Collinsworth, a big-time recruit, needed an opportunity, and that was fine.

"So we went to Georgia, and Terry [LeCount] started the game. He went in and couldn't get anything going, except for one nice pass that Wes Chandler made a one-handed catch for a touchdown. Then Cris went in, and nothing went well. He was a freshman. It wasn't fair to him. He wasn't ready. He'd just been in practice for a week.

"So then I got my chance. He put me in midway through the third quarter, and I quarterbacked the rest of the game.

"Georgia was leading at the half, until we ran a counter play to Wes Chandler. He used his athletic skills to get into the end zone, and we took the lead. The rest of the game we strictly ran the ball and ran it out.

"As second-team quarterback, my center was Doug Schroeder. The starter was a senior, Mark Totten, a kid out of Ohio who was about 6'5", about 310, which was huge. Here was little Johnny Brantley with Totten's rear end up there where I could barely see over my damn face mask. Coach Dickey said, 'All right, we've got to run this time out. Do you feel comfortable?'

"I said, 'Coach, I don't feel comfortable with Totten. I'd like to get Doug Schroeder in there to get the snaps.'

"So he grabbed Doug and threw him in there. That got Coach Helton upset, because we hadn't beaten Georgia for a few years, and I was taking the senior center off the football field. He let me have an earful afterwards, but I just didn't want to take a chance of misplaying the snap. [Florida won 22-17.]

"Hey, what a fantastic bus ride back to Gainesville. That turned the season around for me right there. They figured out Cris wasn't ready. The next week they moved him to defensive safety and right after that, he ended up at wide receiver.

"We played Kentucky, the number seven team in the country, at home. Fran Curci was their coach, and they had Derrick Ramsey at quarterback, and a great defense with Art Still. It was one of those years where Kentucky came out of nowhere with a fantastic team. Terry played the whole game. I didn't play a down. Tony Green didn't play either. He was injured. They beat us 14-7."

Scott Brantley: "That Kentucky team was on probation. They went 9-1 that year, knowing they couldn't go to a bowl game. That shows you the kind of job Fran Curci could do."

John Brantley: "Then we played the Utah Utes at Homecoming. I remember they had a great passer named Randy Gomez who was about 5'8" who threw the ball over the danged place. He had a wide receiver named Jack Steptoe, and I remember he cracked back on Scott and tore his knee up right in front of the bench. I even ran off the bench and jumped on the guy. It was an ugly shot, tore Scott's ligament, and put him out for the rest of the season."

Scott Brantley: "This was when Homecoming used to be Homecoming. They would schedule somebody you ought to beat up on. [Florida was a 31-point favorite.] You'll play hard, but you don't want to get hurt, and hunting season has just begun. We had my pickup packed with the sleeping bags and the coolers and the food. We were going to High Springs to go deer hunting with my brother and a couple of the guys from the team.

"On a pass play, Gomez rolled to our sideline, which was the west side of the stands, and then Steptoe ran a curl route, and I left him because I came in as second contain on the quarterback, and I was flying to the football down toward the sideline, headed to the sideline, looking to the quarterback, when Steptoe ran down and chopblocked me, and tore my left knee up.

"Devastation. I went to the hospital, and they carried me in, and at midnight Pete DeLeCotto reconstructed my knee, and that was a miserable time. I was just miserable.

"I missed the rest of the season. It was the first major injury of my career, and I didn't know how to handle it. I had a full cast all the way up to my crotch. Oh my God, I was so depressed I couldn't eat. I got down to less than 200 pounds, tried to go to class, tried to stay eligible, and through the whole spring it was rehab, rehab, rehab, and in those days it took a lot longer to get back than it does now. And that season was gone—I missed the Miami game and the Florida State game.

"And my brother and them still went hunting. They came and borrowed my keys out of my hospital room. They took my truck and ate my food and slept in my sleeping bag. I missed it, while I was in the hospital having surgery. That added insult to injury."

John Brantley: "Then in the first half against Utah, Terry got clubbed across his face and broke his nose. Here I go.

"I went in, and I had a great game. We were still running the wishbone, and I even ran 62 yards on a play. We had the most [576] total yards in a single game in the history of the University of Florida. Utah was ahead [23-17] when Wes Chandler returned a punt and went all the way for a touchdown. He scored four touchdowns in that game. We were going up and down the field so quickly, and they were too, and that was the sad part: we couldn't stop them. Every time we'd get over and score, we'd relax and come back to the bench, and heck, they'd score again. So it was a shoot-out, a fun Homecoming game that we ended up winning [38-29].

"I started my first game ever against Miami. We went down to the Orange Bowl, and before the game I was nervous. I knew Terry wasn't going to start because he wasn't feeling well. I had a whole week to think about it. Miami was pretty average that year, but ever since John Reaves and the Great Flop and probably before that, they get after the Gators.

"We came out and got going, and we were ahead [17-7], but I didn't do anything special. I had a touchdown pass to Tony Stephens out of Sarasota. I just wasn't going to do anything to lose the game. I had been in a lot bigger games earlier in the year, but I was nervous. You're under a microscope. But we survived and moved on. [Florida won 31-14.]

"The last game was FSU, and it was just a disaster. Wes Chandler got the flu and couldn't play, and everything FSU did that day was just right. That was the game when Bobby Bowden turned the corner at FSU. We had beaten them ten years in a row at that point. That kind of defined their program to where they got some things going.

"Terry started. When I got in, we were so far behind they knew we had to throw the ball. Willie Jones, who hit me on the first play of the North-South high school All-Star game, who ended up at FSU, I was like a magnet for him. Willie Jones just owned me from high school all the way through college. They had our ears pinned back, and they were coming after us, so it was tough. Bobby Butler and the other defensive backs at FSU were tremendous athletes, and since we didn't have Wes Chandler out there to threaten anybody, it was tough to come back on those guys.

"After that loss to Florida State, the alumni were not happy with Coach Dickey, because it wasn't a bad team. The year before we had gone to the Sun Bowl, but we had lost some good players, like Jimmy Fisher, but we had a lot of weapons coming back. There were a lot of high expectations, and we just didn't get it done. And anytime you lose to FSU after beating them for ten years... and at the end of the '77 season we were losing Wes Chandler and Tony Green, so now you really lost a lot, and the team coming back the next year was going to be a VERY young team."

forty-five

Coach Dickey Is Let Go

John Brantley: "In 1978 Coach Dickey brought in Lee McGriff as wide receiver coach and Steve Spurrier as his offensive coordinator. This was Coach Spurrier's first year of coaching. He had come out of a pro setting and hadn't been been in a coaching capacity. But I understand he was like a coach on the field with the San Francisco 49ers and with the Tampa Bay Bucs.

"Steve had been the Bucs' first quarterback in '76, and he was searching for what he was going to do next. It was Coach Dickey who got him into the coaching game. It was probably good marketing—the fans could see 'Mr. Florida,' the Heisman Trophy winner, coming back with an opportunity to get some things going.

"It was fun. You could tell that Coach Spurrier's mind was always thinking. We had to trick people in 1978. We were not big and strong up front. That was one of the problems. For a couple of years we just were not physical.

"We had played Texas A&M in the Sun Bowl in '76, and they just manhandled us. Our specialty players were as good as anybody in the nation. They had speed and quickness. It is what Florida is known for. But we were lacking in size and strength, and to overcome that Coach Spurrier needed to pull his trick plays out of his bag. He had fun. He made practice fun. We had plays where everybody but the center could throw the ball. Heck, we even sat around for twenty minutes trying to figure out a play where the center could throw it, but we never did find a way. So he brought a lot of fun ideas, and he was great."

Lee McGriff: "The start of the demise of Doug Dickey came after the NFL started taking some of our backs, and after a good '76, the team started going downhill. Florida had an off-season in '77, and the fans got very restless saying,

'Look at all this talent, and he can't make it work.' They were all talented, and they could run like the wind.

"In '78 I became an assistant coach for Coach Dickey. The year before they'd had a bad year with all those players who looked like race horses, but they couldn't win many games. They were talking about firing him, and they said, 'You make a change on your offensive staff, and we'll give you another year.' The change was Steve Spurrier and me. We did what we could to revamp the Florida offense, but there wasn't enough time to get it done.

"We ditched the wishbone, and Steve put in the passing game. We won four games. We did some exciting things. After playing with Steve, I now had the chance to coach with him, and he did some things very unorthodox, things you logically wouldn't think would work.

"He would sometimes call a post pattern into the teeth of a zone. All the statistics tell you the tendencies and the right coverages and the percentages, and those tendencies often hold up. But he would make a call, and I'd look at it and think, Oh my God, it's the wrong defense. We're throwing right into the teeth of it, and bam, we'd hit a touchdown. I'd say to him, 'How come?' He'd say, 'Well, you know that guy was sorta leaning that way.' He'd feel things that the normal human can't feel. And he'd get you. He did that more than once.

"Most of the guys on the Florida coaching staff would have told you Steve Spurrier wouldn't have lasted another year in coaching.

"He was loose. He didn't spend until eleven o'clock every night watching tape. He didn't draw up eight thousand plays against every situation humanly possible. He didn't study computer sheets. He didn't do the dogged work that most successful coaches do.

"He would do sacrilegious things like playing golf. Or he would go for a jog before a game. I did that with him. We'd jog and talk and stay relaxed. Steve did not approach coaching as a dogged working business.

"A major experiment was to move Cris Collinsworth to wide receiver. He had come there to be the All-American wishbone quarterback and probably would have been if we hadn't come, but we moved him to receiver. When Steve and I first went to Coach Dickey and told him we wanted to move him to wide receiver, I'll never forget the look on his face. He got mad. He said, 'What are you thinking? Do you understand what we did recruiting this kid?' And on and on. We stuck to our guns, and we had a long meeting with Doug and convinced him, and he said, 'All right, if that's what you guys think you have to do to win, Lee, you get in the car. You go tell his parents. You go tell his high school coach. You go tell them what this decision is.'

"And I did. I went down to Titusville and talked with everybody, and we moved Cris. It was the right thing for Cris and the right thing for us. John Brantley became the quarterback.

"John could throw, and he was competitive, savvy, and crafty. He's a guy you pick on your flag football team who can make plays."

One player who came to camp in the fall of 1978 determined to regain his form after having reconstructive knee surgery was Scott Brantley, who spent the summer in Wyoming working construction, lifting weights, and enjoying the great outdoors.

Scott Brantley: "I had worked my butt off to stay eligible because I did not want to go to summer school, because Doug Knotts' best friend, David Houtz, owned a big ranch in Cody, Wyoming, and I needed to get away. A buddy of mine from high school loaded up my truck, and we drove to Cody for six weeks during the summer. I loved it. We spent the summer away from Florida, away from everything. I was dedicated to the cause of coming back and having a great junior year.

"We fished, white-water rafted, worked at the dude ranch and in construction, and I made good money. We had a ball. I cried when I left.

"I prayed. I wanted to come back and have a great year and get over this injury, and man, I thought my junior year was my best year by far. If that wasn't an All-American year, there wasn't one at Florida. I had 200 tackles that year in eleven games."

Coach Dickey had to choose for his quarterback between John Brantley and a sophomore from Orlando named Tim Groves, another player with relatives in Alabama who had to choose between playing for Bear Bryant or playing in Florida. Like Scott Brantley, Tim Groves opted to stay in the state.

Tim Groves: "I had the opportunity to go to a lot of colleges, but I always wanted to be a Gator. Florida was number one on my list, and when they showed interest in me, I was ecstatic. You were allowed six visits, but I took only three. I went to Alabama to please my mother. We had lived in Alabama, and she was a huge Bear Bryant fan. Bear was there, and I did meet him. He was a very imposing figure. All I remember about that meeting was that he kept asking me questions, and I said three words, 'Yes,' 'No,' and 'Sir.' I could have gone there, but again, my heart was as a Gator. Coach Dickey and Ken Hatfield recruited me and extended me a full scholarship, and I was just thrilled to death.

"When I got to Florida, I couldn't believe how many great athletes the team had. I had been one of the better athletes at Oak Ridge High School, but when I got to Florida, I couldn't believe it: I had never seen athletes like Wes Chandler, Willie Wilder, Tony Green, Terry LeCount, and Derrick Gaffney, and on defense Scott Brantley, Darrel Carpenter, and 'Charlie Horse' Williams. I believe ten guys were drafted into the pros off that team. It's still hard to believe that we only went 6-4-1 with that team in '77. And though I was just a freshman, I could feel the criticism of Coach Dickey mounting. It stemmed from the fact we had such unbelievable talent, and our record wasn't that great.

"Then in 1978, we lost a lot. [With few seniors and little depth, the inexperienced Gators finished the season 4-7.] Doug Dickey had hired Steve Spurrier as quarterback coach. In the spring game of my freshman year we changed our offensive philosophy. We went from the wishbone, where your offensive linemen have to be extremely strong at run blocking and firing out and not letting any seams happen, to trying to throw the ball a little more with Coach Spurrier.

"The biggest thing I recall about Coach Spurrier was his ability to see the field, to see defenses, and to know where the weaknesses were. He could see a defense and design a play that would attack it, and it would work. And he really was able to get Coach Dickey to implement a lot of his offense.

"We all knew what a great college career Coach Spurrier had had. You can't win a Heisman Trophy and be a bad football player. Coach Spurrier obviously was an offensive genius.

"What he did for the whole team was make us feel, Wow, this is going to give us an opportunity to win. That year a lot of seniors graduated and went to the NFL, giving us the chance to compete for their jobs."

When opening day against SMU rolled around, Tim Groves found himself the starting quarterback.

Tim Groves: "We opened the season against SMU, which had a great quarterback in Mike Ford. John Brantley and I were pretty much untested at quarterback. I started that game. We took the ball and marched it down the first drive very well. Then we fumbled. You get a few turnovers, and it changes the whole complexion of the game. We were losing [28-3] at the half, but we had to stay positive and hope we could make some adjustments and come out and play better.

"Johnny got into the game the second half and actually moved the ball pretty well. Johnny could throw the ball. [In the second half John Brantley threw a 60-yard touchdown pass to Tony Stephens.] He wasn't a big quarterback, but he seemed to grasp what Coach Spurrier was saying and understood when and where to throw the ball.' [Florida lost 35-25.]

John Brantley: "They decided to make Tim Groves the starting quarterback. He was out of Orlando, a great athlete, a good-looking kid, and we were playing in Orlando in the Tangerine Bowl, and they felt Tim was the one to start the season. Like I said, I was an overachiever. I wasn't going to blow you away with my physical attributes, but I can throw the ball with anybody. Timmy did everything well. He won the starting position, and started the game.

"Timmy was nervous, and he struggled a little bit. He was in Orlando, his hometown playing against a top ten team, and things weren't going well. So at that point Coach Spurrier came over and said, 'All right, John, get ready, you're in the next series.' So I said, 'All right.'

"I went in and I threw two touchdown passes to Tony Stephens and got us back into the game, but we just had too much ground to cover. We were behind 28-24, and they scored late to make it 35. So it was a good comeback, and I had a good showing.

"Most times you hustle back home, but school hadn't started yet, so that night we stayed in Orlando. About 12:30 at night my phone rang in my room. It was Gerry Spurrier, Steve's wife. She said, 'Coach wants to see you.' I said to myself, Let's see what this is all about.'

"I went up to his room, and he sat me down. He wanted to talk to me. He said, 'I don't care what happens the rest of the year. You're my man. I want to settle on one guy, to concentrate the effort and try to get this thing going.'

"He said, 'Let's move toward that deal. You went in and did some good things. Let's build on those things and go into practice next week.'

"Timmy was in a tough position. He was a sophomore. It was tough. I had gone in and made something happen."

Scott Brantley: "That year SMU had the Pony Express with [Craig] James and Eric Dickerson and a big fat quarterback named Mike Ford. We played in the old Tangerine Bowl, and the lighting was horrible, and they beat up on us pretty good. I did what I was supposed to do, make a lot of tackles. But it wasn't a good start at all."

John Brantley: "The next week we played Mississippi State in Gainesville. We were the underdog, but we blew them out [34-0], and I threw two touchdown passes to Cris Collinsworth. I hit Collinsworth on a corner route for 70 yards. That was our start. [Brantley was 7–10 for 194 yards. Collinsworth caught five passes for 166 yards.]

"Cris had been an All-American quarterback in high school, but he was a runner. We were beginning to see that Coach Dickey was allowing Coach Spurrier to put in a pro-style offense. Instead of running the option, we were throwing the ball more. Cris will tell you he struggled throwing the ball. The college game was tougher than when he played for the Titusville Astronauts. But he was just too great an athlete to keep off the field. Defense wasn't his deal. He had played it for a little while because he had a broken hand. Then they moved him to wide-out, and the Mississippi State game was a coming out party for him. That game I was AP Offensive Player of the Week, and Scott was Defensive Player of the Week. We had a halfback named Calvin Davis, out of Auburndale, who also had a great game. [Davis ran 13 times for 57 yards.] The kid probably never said five words, and he just came out of nowhere to put together a pretty good season.

"We just played well. We got after it. All the years I was there we played well against Mississippi State. I don't know why because Mississippi State and Miami were the two most physcial games we played. We may have beat them, but when you left the stadium that night, you knew you had been in a dog fight. Mississippi State just played hard."

Florida's defense was superb, as the Gators posted an impressive shutout before the hometown fans at Florida Field.

Tim Groves: "Our defense played great. The offense played great. Everything seemed to click. My best memory of that game was that I had one of my longest runs from scrimmage as a Gator. I'll never forget it. Kim Helton was our offensive line coach. He showed me how and what to audible if I went up to the line of scrimmage and the defense had the play stopped. He found this weakness in the Mississippi State defense. I got to the line of scrimmage and I audibilized the play he wanted—it was a down-line option. I was able to cut it up the field, and I ran 56 yards and got knocked out on the one-yard line. I have to give a lot of credit to Coach Helton for studying the game and knowing tendencies and him giving that knowledge to the players."

The next game was a 34-21 loss to running back Charles Alexander and his LSU teammates. Alexander ran the ball 40 times for 156 yards, and Scott Brantley made twenty tackles, including twelve primary stops. The collisions between the two All-Americans rang out throughout the stadium. At one point, Brantley had to be helped off the field. Before the end of the game, Alexander himself had to leave. At game's end the two warriors walked off the field with their arms around each other.

Florida scored on three long plays, a 43-yard pass from John Brantley to Cris Collinsworth; a 97-yard runback of a punt for a touchdown; and a razzle-dazzle play that went from quarterback Larry Ochab to split end Tony Stephens to tight end Ron Enclade for a 48-yard touchdown.

Tim Groves: "The halfback touchdown pass had to have been one of Coach Spurrier's plays. He was always up at the chalkboard devising plays that would have a chance for success. He wasn't afraid to diagram plays like that. Tony Stephens was a great athlete. He could throw the ball extremely well."

John Brantley: "Against LSU I hit an eighty-yard touchdown pass to Cris on a post route. Also in that game Cris had a 97-yard kickoff return. Cris was really starting to take off.

"Then in the third quarter I ran an option, and I twisted my knee, and I had to listen to the rest of the game in the training room. That was tough to do. Timmy went in, and Larry Ochab even played a little. We had just come off a big emotional win over Mississippi State, and we were just flat against LSU [Florida lost 34-21]. Charles Alexander and David Woodley starred for LSU. Scott said Alexander was the best back he ever faced in college.

"Then we went to Tuscaloosa to play Alabama. It was the first time a Florida team had been there in years, and my knee was still bothering me. Timmy started and really couldn't get anything going, so I went in. They did some miraculous things doctorwise. They got my knee ready, and I went in and threw a touchdown pass to Tony Stephens. It was a corner route. And I had another big play to Johnny Smith, a fast kid out of Venice.

"We were right there. [The score was 23-12 Alabama.] But Collinsworth fumbled diving over the goal line—Barry Krauss' helmet hit the ball as Cris was jumping over, the ball shot straight up in the air, and they got it in the end zone for a touchback, and the refs put the ball on the twenty. On the next play they're running the wishbone, they give it to the fullback, [Billy Johnson] and he ran 87 yards for the touchdown. The two plays turned the whole game around. If Cris had jumped over, we would have been ahead 19-14, but instead we fumble, and the kid goes 87 yards for a touchdown. We had them beat, and that was the WHOLE season.

"So we lost, and Alabama ended up winning the National Championship that year."

Tim Groves: "I got to play quite a bit. Take away three plays, one which I was involved in, and we should have won the ball game.

"The play I was involved in took place right before half-time. We were in position to get at least three points. Coach Spurrier called a pass play. I threw a pass, and I got it picked off. We didn't get the three points.

"We got down another time to about the three yard line, and Cris [Collinsworth] fumbled the ball. So that's another seven points we left on the board.

"Alabama had a fullback named Billy Johnson. He wasn't fast, but he was very strong. I remember Jeff Rutledge hitting him on a straight dive, and Johnson ran 87 yards for a touchdown. I couldn't believe that could happen to our defense. Take away those three plays, and we were very competitive in the game."

Scott Brantley: "We played a lot better against Alabama than the score indicated. They had Dwight Stephenson, a All-American center, and Jeff Rutledge at quarterback, and Tony Nathan in the backfield, and two Florida boys, Marty Lyons and Barry Krauss. They were tough, but we could have won that game. We felt pretty good about the way we played."

John Brantley: "Army came to Gainesville for Homecoming. In that game I threw three touchdown passes to Cris Collinsworth [for 18, 43, and 19 yards]. I kept the football from that game. Here again, Cris as a sophomore was starting to build his career. He'll tell you he never had another year as successful as this one. He caught eight touchdown passes, three against Army, just a good Homecoming win, but a game we knew we should win. The game was played on October 21, when they were starting to play cold-weather games up north. It was probably 95 degrees on the astroturf. Army brought their wool pants to Gainesville, and midway through the third quarter they started dropping like flies on dead clams.

"We were in the huddle, and you could hear them getting on each other. They were just sucking wind and cramping up. It was kind of comical, but you sort of felt sorry for them.

"We then played Georgia Tech on Grant Field, which was really getting old. It was Astroturf, and they had duct tape covering half the lines. We should not have lost that game.

"We were ahead 10-3 and had fourth and two on the Tech 2, and I snuck across, and I was WAY across the line. Cris Collinsworth jumped on my back to propel me into the end zone. I was number 12, and he was number 21, and the referee marked the spot off Cris. I was a yard into the end zone. The referee marked the ball based on Cris.

"We were very upset with the call. It was a terrible call. Sometimes you get those on the road. We still should have won the game." [Florida lost 17-13.]

Scott Brantley: "Late in the game, Georgia Tech had fourth and one on about the 50, and here comes the punt team. I was calling signals, and I said, 'We're going to play safe here.' We had a return right, and Yancey Sutton, who could read lips because he is deaf, was looking at Pepper Rodgers on the sideline. He said, 'Scott, Scott, fake punt, run right. Fake punt, run right.'

"I said, 'Get in the huddle, Yancey.' I told everyone, 'Yancey says they're going to run it to the right, so you all be looking for that.'

"They snapped it to the upback, and we stopped them for no gain and got the turnover, and it was because Yancey was able to read the lips of Pepper Rodgers. It made the Paul Harvey Show the next day."

John Brantley: "Again, if we hadn't fumbled against Alabama, if we don't get a bad call in the end zone against Georgia Tech, we've got a pretty good little season going, and we're building some momentum."

Going up against Auburn, the talk in the papers was about Coach Dickey getting fired.

Scott Brantley: "By then speculation had set in that there might be a change. Any collegiate athlete doesn't welcome change. I'm sure it had a bearing on the mindset of the team.

Tim Groves: "You're concentrating day to day on your class study and then you're trying to prepare to the best of your ability for the upcoming opponent. Doug Dickey had been there eight years. What was going to happen to him was totally out of the hands of the players. We're just trying to do the best you can to help the Gators win on Saturday.

"I do remember the night before the Auburn game at Florida Field, someone painted 'Dump Dickey' in big white letters on the Astroturf. It was very, very visible. You're upset someone would do that, but it was also a motivation for us to help our coach. You wanted to play your best for him because of the player/coach relationship, because of the recruiting process, and because you want to see him succeed as well as yourself. We could see the urgency of the coaching staff.

"We beat Auburn 31-7. Johnny played very, very well. He made some great throws. It was a very satisfying with after seeing that on the field. You hate to see that on your home field."

John Brantley: "The Auburn game was the only game I ever sat out the fourth quarter just because we were so far ahead. Everything went well. We came out, and the first play was a counter-option. The defensive end ran up the field, didn't give me any respect, and I ran for 32 yards. On the next play I pitched to Calvin Davis, and he went another thirty yards on a sweep. Then they called the same option play, and I sprinted out to the right, and they had a big boy who played about fifteen years in the NFL for the New Orleans Saints [Frank Warren], and he hit me and jarred the ball loose, and picked up the ball in the end zone and scored.

"So I had scored the first two touchdowns in the game—one for each team.

"We took control right after that. Even in his first year Coach Spurrier was a very good teacher. He really spent the time on the basics and fundamentals. One of the things we learned was any time we looked out to the wide receivers and the defensive back has his back turned to you, you've got man to man coverage. He has him one-on-one. So it was my place to find out where this guy is coming from. Usually they come from outside the end. So I checked off to a man-on-man play, which meant that Cris Collinsworth was going straight for the goal post. I went back to pass. I still don't know where he's coming from. I set my back foot, and here he came—up the middle. So I made a pump motion to throw. The guy jumped up trying to block it. I ducked, and he flew by me. I stepped back up. I threw a post route to Cris running a perfect stride down the middle of the field for a touchdown. That type of play you always remember. That was a big win.

"An article in one of the papers came out before the Georgia game saying Coach Dickey was going to be fired, and that rallied the troops. We should have beaten Georgia. We beat them up and down the field.

"The game I grew up on was the Florida-Georgia game. It was the greatest. The stadium was half Gators, half Bulldogs. You had that cocktail party. There's not a better game to be in as a player.

"We got the ball first, and we drove down and were on about the ten-yard line. I had an out-route to Collinsworth in the end zone, and I was all jacked up, and I threw it, and I hit a girl in the third row of the end zone. He was open, and the adrenaline took over.

"We had a double pass for a touchdown to Collinsworth. Cris was on the left wing, and he stepped back, and I threw him the ball on a lateral, and he hit Ron Enclade, who played tight end, a unique guy and a great athlete, for a touchdown. Ron came to Florida as a quarterback and outgrew the position. Like Collinsworth, he was too good an athlete not to have on the field.

"I also hit Cris down the sidelines on a 33-yard touchdown.

"They led 24-22 with six and a half minutes to go, and they punted to us. Buck Waters came up and fielded the ball about midfield, right in front of our bench and dropped the punt, and they picked it up and ran out the clock. That year we had a great field goal kicker, Berj Yepremian. He was Garo's little brother, left-footed, an outstanding kicker. He didn't miss extra points or anything within 40 to 45 yards.

"With Berj, we knew we had a chance. We just needed to get it. Then poor Tony Waters fumbled the punt, and they got the ball and ran out the clock."

After a very tough 24-22 loss against Georgia at the Gator Bowl in Jacksonville, the press and critics focused on a situation in which Georgia had fourth and one and was going to punt in the first quarter. But the Florida coaching staff sent in the wrong unit, and after being penalized for delay of game, Georgia kept the ball and kicked a field goal—the winning margin.

Tim Groves: "When you are at that level, you would like to think that we could have executed better than we did. You could understand the frustration, even though in the heat of battle things can get confusing. You still would like to think that through preparation that wouldn't happen."

John Brantley: "There was a rally for Coach Dickey when we got back to Gainesville. We were losing close football games. Our minds were on the games. Some of the players had headed up the rally, but I was more upset because we were losing close games.

"We hated to see Coach Dickey leave, but we were a pretty good football team, and we were young. Everyone was disappointed we had lost the Georgia game, but we'd had the chance to win every game that year except perhaps the LSU game. Even the SMU game we got back into, so we had a chance.

"So we flew to Lexington to play Kentucky, and we were disappointed, but we knew we had been good enough to win some of those games. Kentucky had a good little football team. They had won the SEC the year before. They still had Jim Kovach, their All-American linebacker, and some good players.

"We went up on a Friday, and we went out to the stadium for a walk-through. It was a rainy, drizzly day. Come game time, it had quit raining, but everything was still muddy. At the time we didn't wear undershirts under our shoulder pads, so you had a thin cotton tearaway jersey, no undershirt, and a shoulder pad. That's all you needed in Florida because of the heat.

"Game time it was 31 degrees. They passed out long-handles, shirts, warm-weather gear. We were in the new Commonwealth Stadium. The locker room was beautiful. My locker was next to Cris Collinsworth. He was getting dressed, and Cris put his pants on, and he doesn't wear anything but his jock and his pants because he doesn't want anything to impede his running. I did that too. He put his shoulder pads on atop his skin, and here was little, frail Cris Collinsworth putting on his jersey with no undershirt. I said, 'Cris, man, it's 30 degrees out. You're going to freeze to death.' He said, 'We've had a good year catching balls. I'm not going to change anything.' I said, 'Oh hell, I won't either.'

"We went out there, and I froze to death. We couldn't get to the sideline fast enough with the heaters. But we played the game that way.

"I can remember throwing three interceptions in the second quarter. The only guy who was happier than the Kentucky fans was John Reaves back in Tampa, hoping I'd break his record of nine. I was on track to do it. After the third one, Spurrier grabbed me and Cris, and he said, 'What have you got against him? Throw the ball to him. Hell, you've hit every blue jersey out here. Throw it to him.' At the time it wasn't comical. Later on it was.

"We were losing right up to the end. Then I threw a pass to Ron Enclade, and Berj kicked a [38-yard] field goal to win the game [18-16]. Then what made it more exciting, they got the ball back and threw it over the middle, and Scott intercepted and ran off the field holding up the ball."

John Brantley: "Flying back after the game, Coach Spurrier came back in the plane and sat down with me and asked me, 'Where are we going tonight?' He and his wife had met my eventual wife-to-be, and we went out to dinner with them.

"Any times you win in the SEC on the road it's a big win. It doesn't matter who it's against. It was a big win up there. It was one of those that we didn't let get away from us.

"The next week we were scheduled against Florida State. For that game we were in Lake City in a motel. Clemson was playing South Carolina. I told you Scott and I grew up watching Clemson and the Gamecocks because my father's brother went to law school there and lives in Columbia, South Carolina. Steve Fuller, the Clemson quarterback, grew up on the same street Scott and I did. The year we moved to Ocala, Steve moved to Spartanburg, so we kind of lost track of each other. Steve, who was 'Mr. Football' in South Carolina, went to Clemson.

"So we're watching Clemson play South Carolina on the TV, and South Carolina goes up 21-0. I said to my brother, 'Scott, that's what we need to do against FSU tonight. We need to jump on them and take the crowd out of the game.'

"Hell, just the opposite happened. Boom, boom, boom, and we were down 21-0. We started the second quarter, and it was probably the best quarter of football I ever had. I threw five touchdown passes. Two of them were called back. Their backyard is a tough place to play.

"That second quarter, I was throwing passes sidearm and doing everything to make things happen. I even caught a touchdown that was called back. I pitched it out to Cris, and I snuck out the backside, and he threw it and hit me for a touchdown, but they called it back. It was unbelievable. But three of them counted, and that's what mattered. It was 21-21 at the half.

"Then we took the twenty minute break at halftime, and we sat down and relaxed, and when we came back, we were out of it. They took charge of the game, and their fans got into it. We had given our all in that one quarter. We went back out, and we just couldn't get it done. We had a couple of big plays, but Willie Jones hit me in the back. To this day it still bothers me. [Florida lost 38-21.] And as the week wore on, my chest cavity got worse and worse where by Thursday I couldn't even talk."

Tim Groves: "I didn't play that much, and it was a very disappointing loss. Jimmy Jordan was throwing the ball all over the place for Florida State.

"After the game you could sense Coach Dickey was in trouble, just by reading the papers. It was definitely evident that a change was going to be made."

A couple days after the FSU game, it was reported that Lou Holtz was going to leave Arkansas and come to Florida as coach. But nothing happened until the day before the Miami game, when Florida president Robert Marsden fired Coach Dickey. The players, who were not consulted, were puzzled.

Tim Groves: "It's hard to believe you would fire the coach and then expect him to go out there on game day and perform, but the Florida alumni are a very, very vocal group. Again, I don't know.

"What I remember about that game was that John had played well the entire year, and when we got to the locker room, Coach Dickey said, 'Tim Groves is going to start this ball game.' I was surprised, because John had prepared the entire week. I didn't know John was hurt, but as a player, I was elated to get that time on the field.

"I had a great first half. That was probably the best I ever threw. I remember the [37-yard] touchdown I threw to Tony [Stephens]. Tony was another great athlete. We faked a run up the middle, and we ran a take-off, streak route. Tony streaked down the left sideline. I just threw it up there for him to run under and catch. We got a touchdown out of it.

"I also threw two touchdowns to Cris [Collinsworth]. Cris ran great routes to get open. [He caught 11- and 9-yard touchdown passes.] The running game got us within throwing distance. We were up 21-3 at halftime.

"Miami had a running back named O.J. Anderson who really ran well, and my performance in the second half did not help our defense at all. I threw quite a few interceptions and gave them great field position. I put our defense in a bad situation. They came back and won 22-21, and I took that extremely hard, because I had gotten the chance to start and had a good game going, and then my performance in the second half cost us the ballgame."

John Brantley: "We were just little pieces to the puzzle. We were not involved at all. Nobody asked us our opinion. Like I told you, Coach Dickey was always honest with me. That's one thing I can say, and I tell him today when he gets on our radio show each year. He let me know all the time where I stood, and that's all you can ask of a coach. As long as you know where you stand and what your role is, you don't have a problem.

"Going into the Miami game, everyone was loosy-goosy. We wore blue pants and blue jerseys for the first time in Gainesville. I couldn't start because my back had gotten bad. I couldn't bark out signals. The pain was just unbelievable. They even shot me up to try to get me to go. But Timmy Groves went in and did a phenomenal job. He threw three touchdown passes, one to Tony Stephens and two to Cris, and we were up 21-0. We were rolling. We were having fun. Then poor Timmy got a little off track, and he threw [four] interceptions, and there were a couple of fumbles, and they capitalized. And Ottis Anderson, who played for the New York Giants, had some great runs in the second half, and they ended up catching us and winning 22-21.

"Late in the game the coaches pleaded with me to go in, and I tried to go out there for one series, but I couldn't make anything happen. That hit had basically split open my chest cavity the week before. By Tuesday and Wednesday, it was a lot worse than thought.

"After the game all I can remember is the disappointment. I was disappointed we had lost. I was disappointed I couldn't physically play in the game. We had built up a lead we should have held in our own yard, and it was our last game for Coach Dickey, and it would have been a nice finish for him. Our season kinda ended the way it had gone pretty much the whole year. It was a tough little team that tried to do some things. We were .500 in the SEC, but we just couldn't get over the hump that year for whatever reason. It was disappointing."

Scott Brantley: "I liked Coach Doug, but what has been proven over the course of time is that he is best-suited as an athletic director and administrator than head coach. He is a happier, more jovial guy as an athletic director. I love him. He has a great family. I love his sons. He has a great wife, the epitome of the coach's wife. I always enjoyed him and got along well with Doug."

Tim Groves: "After the game all of us just felt disappointment. Not much was said because you knew your head coach had been fired. They hired Charlie Pell to replace him, but we really didn't know anything about him. We were sophomores in college. We were struggling through the season, just concentrating on what you had to do to get wins.

"What I remember is that the coach we kept hearing about was Lou Holtz. We knew who he was. He was at Arkansas. He was the number one choice. I don't know whether negotiations stalled, or he had a change of heart or we didn't meet his demands, but for whatever reasons, he didn't take the job. Charlie Pell took it."

Doug Dickey: "When it slid off, we got into problems my eighth and ninth years. We didn't get the recruiting done that we needed to do. We ran out of quarterbacks and tried to make a transition from the wishbone to a modern passing offense and didn't get enough time to do it. I hired Steve Spurrier my last year to help us do that. We just didn't have the players to get it done. We were a year short. I thought by probably 1981 or so we would be back again, but in those days, as it is today, the people who make the decisions are not very patient, and everybody is scared of the marketing problems. You don't get the chance to rebuild your own program. They were not going to let me do that.

"If we had won a championship in '76 or '77, it would have been different. So that was just the way it went."

forty-six

The Brantleys Go Down

On December 4, 1978, Charlie Pell became the new Florida football coach. Pell's football career began as a player at Snead State Community College in Boaz, Alabama. His coach recommended him to Bear Bryant, and he became a lineman on the Alabama national championship team of 1961. He was a graduate assistant at Alabama in 1963 and 1964, teams that won two more national titles.

After Coach Pell became an assistant coach at Kentucky, he was head coach at Jacksonville State from 1969 through 1973. His record was 33-13-1.

He went to Virginia Tech in 1974, where he was defensive coordinator. In 1976 he was hired at Clemson as Red Parker's defensive coordinator. At the end of the year Parker was ordered to fire several coaches, and he refused, and Parker was fired. When athletic director Bill McLellan asked Pell if he would remain as an assistant to Pat Dye, if he hired Dye, Pell told him, "Hell, no. I can do the job as well as Pat Dye." He got the job.

Clemson was 8-3-1 in 1977 and 11-1 in 1978. Both years he was ACC Coach of the Year. Pell's trademark was lighting a cigar after every victory. A few days before Clemson played Ohio State in the Gator Bowl in 1978, Pell left for Florida.

[Two years after Pell left Clemson, the team was placed on two years probation, the result of recruiting violations under Pell and his successor, Danny Ford.]

Florida's final decision was between Pell and Lou Holtz. Pell received a salary of $45,000 a year.

Said Clemson senior Dwight Clark, "He believed in discipline and perfect organization and he brought unity and togetherness. He puts everything in perspective. He gives us goals that we work hard to achieve, and this year we made all our goals.

"You got a good coach coming your way."

Scott Brantley: "I was team captain, and when Charlie Pell got there, he checked everyone out to see where we stood. After about three weeks, he called me into his office and said, 'Do you know what's going on in your dormitory?' I said, 'What are you talking about?' He started naming names, citing players doing bad things and getting in trouble. He had been there three weeks, and he knew more than I did.

"He was there to clean up the program. He wanted to up-grade. No one improved the facilities more than Charlie Pell at the University of Florida, I promise you. Yan Hall was a piece of crap, and he gutted it, and he turned it into something to be proud of. He put carpet down. We didn't even have carpet in our dorm. He made a nice player lounge, adding TVs and furniture, and he improved the chow hall. He changed the entire environment to what it should be like.

"Coach Pell enlisted the aid of a lot of good people. He went and got Ben Hill Griffin and Dave Thomas of Wendy's and got a bunch of money from them. Coach Pell was the one who spurred them to get involved with the university. That why it's Ben Hill Griffin Stadium at Florida Field. We had a Wendy's weight room with the logo of Wendy's hamburgers on the wall. He was a great guy going and telling the tale and getting these great boosters we have today. He was the one who spurred them to get involved with the university.

"Coach Pell had played for Bear Bryant, and being involved with him was really special. I mean, we worked our asses off. I never in my life saw an off-season program like the one he implimented. We busted our ass two and three times a day to get better, bigger, and stronger.

"Dwight Adams, a defensive coordinator, came in, and Joe Kynes, a red-headed guy who is now linebacker coach at FSU. They came from Clemson with Coach Pell, great people. They were Carolina, good southern—I don't want to say rednecks, but that's what they were. Good ole boys, and I loved those guys. I would do anything in the world for them, so I was in the best shape of my career. I was pre-season All-American in every poll."

Tim Groves: "We had winter off-season workouts, and we got to meet Charlie Pell, the head coach. Talk about a coach who commands effort, a no-nonsense coach. You knew where you stood with the guy.

"And he was an excellent recruiter. The biggest thing I can say about Coach Pell was how he rallied the state—all the Gators, all the alumni. He crisscrossed the state going to Gator gatherings and clubs for all the Gator boosters to start contributing to the program. To this day I firmly believe he built the foundation that Coach Spurrier was able to build on.

"As everyone well knows, we didn't win a ball game in '79, but he kept us positive, stuck to his beliefs, and up until a few years ago, he was responsible for the greatest turnaround in the history of college football."

John Brantley: "When Coach Pell came in, he said to me, 'If you want to be the quarterback next year, I think you need to participate in spring practice. I weighed all the options, and I agreed to skip baseball that year.

"I had a very good spring, and toward the end of the last practice before the spring game, we ran an option play, and I got hit high and hit low, and I broke my leg. I broke the fibula on the outside. Dr. Peete did the surgery, and I still have the plate on my leg today.

"I worked hard all summer. I was running up to eight miles a day. I was doing everything physically to get ready. And when the fall came around, I was ready. I competed. Our first game was against Houston. Timmy Groves was the starter, and I was the backup. Timmy didn't really get anything going, and I went in, and I didn't do anything either.

"It was kind of a crazy game. The defense played well, but the offense didn't get much of anything going, and Houston beat us 14-10. David Galloway, who would go on to play twelve years in the NFL, tore up his knee, which was a big loss, because he was our defensive tackle who controlled the middle."

Tim Groves: "We played Houston in the Astrodome. Houston had a great defense. They had a couple tackles—Hosea Taylor was one of them—who were All Americans. I remember I made a touchdown [a four-yard run], and we took the lead, and I can remember we went for a field goal, and we had a bad snap, and we ended up losing 14-10.

"We were in the game the entire sixty minutes. I felt like we had a chance to win the game. Houston went on to win the Southeastern Conference and play in the Cotton Bowl.

"Under Coach Pell we ran the option that he brought with him from Clemson. It was down-the-line, sprint-out type passes, get to the corner, turn up the field, throw the ball from that. This suited me more than the straight drop-back type of offense."

Charlie Pell's home debut at Florida Field ended in a 7-7 tie with Georgia Tech.

Tim Groves: "I started at quarterback, and we just couldn't get the ball in the end zone. I take a lot of the blame. I didn't make the right reads, or I didn't throw the ball where I needed to throw it, and I just couldn't get it done. I do remember Brian Clark trying to kick a field goal to win the game late, and it got blocked. Their safety just times it perfectly. It was a great defensive effort. You felt like he was up in the air forever.

"The only score we made came when Tim Golden intercepted a screen pass and ran it back [49 yards] for a touchdown. That game led to Coach Pell realizing we had to change our philosophy and get Johnny [Brantley] or Larry [Ochab] in there, and drop them back and throw the ball a little bit."

The game, though, was a disaster, as a head injury would end the football career at Florida of All-American Scott Brantley, who despite only playing two games as a senior, would finish only six tackles behind David Little as the top tackler in the history of the University of Florida.

John Brantley: "The '79 team that went to Houston with Charlie Pell was a very good little football team. It ended up having the worst season, but I'll tell you what, it was not a bad football team. When you lose David Galloway and Scott, there goes your senior class. It just all fell apart."

Scott Brantley: "I suffered a head injury in the Georgia Tech game. I don't even remember the play. I just know what I saw on TV. I was making a tackle on a running back, and I tripped on a seam in the Astroturf on Florida Field, and as I was falling forward, his knee came up and nailed me right in the left portion of the helmet, and it knocked me out. The impact went through my helmet, through the padding, through my skull, onto my brain.

"On TV I saw Chris Patrick, the head trainer, standing over me with Peter Indelicato, the team doctor. And then Charlie Pell came out on the field.

"They put me in the infirmary overnight, and I was fine the next morning. By Monday, I went to class, and they came and got me out of class, took me to the trainer's room and took me over to Shans Hospital for some cat-scans. They found a spot on my brain about the size of a dime.

"The doctor said, 'It's like a bruise on you leg. It won't be there in a week. You might have to miss a game.'

"I said, 'I'm not missing a game. You gotta be kidding me.'

"Then they called another meeting in Charlie Pell's office, and when I walked in, there was my mom and dad, my sisters and brothers, and it was like a funeral. I said, 'What's going on?' Charlie said, 'Because of the injury, you're never going to be able to play football again.'

"That was as traumatic as could be. But fortunately I had the maturity to understand that these things happen for a reason, that though I didn't understand it, further down the road I would.

"I stayed in school, rode it out, and watched as Florida had a dog ugly year. Throughout the whole time, Gil Brandt of the Dallas Cowboys stayed in touch with me. He flew me out to Dallas, and he sent me to neurologists at the New York University Hospital and to a hospital at Johns Hopkins University to see neurologists who specialized in athletic-related injuries.

"These neurologists said, 'You missed your senior year because of this? You're kidding me.' I was happy because it meant I would have a chance to play football in the National Football League.

"I continued to work out, and after the football season was over, I played baseball in the spring.

"Ten or fifteen years later, somebody high up told me that it was Charlie's call not to let me play again. I always wondered why Charlie would never look me in the eye after that. Don't ask me why, but Charlie was Charlie, and Charlie had to make a statement. He'd come into a place, didn't have any recruits, and it's funny how you go 0-10-1 one year, and the next year go to a bowl, and everyone is patting you on the back saying what a great job you've done. That had a lot to do with his decision.

"Think of the ego involved. Maybe I shouldn't say this, because Charlie's dead, and he can't defend himself. But like I said, I knew it was happening for a reason, and if I ever got a chance to play pro ball, it would be with more of an appreciation than I ever had. Not a day went by during my nine-year pro career that I didn't appreciate being able to play.

"I was supposed to be a first round pick with the Cowboys. They were going to draft me with their first pick in the third round, but Tampa took me one pick before that. The Bucs were formed in 1976, and this was the '80 draft. John McKay drafted me, and it was a great experience. I loved it. I played eight years in Tampa. The highlights were going to the playoffs twice, and lockering beside Lee Roy Selmon and being in the state of Florida.

"Once they figured out I wasn't going to die after the first tackle I made at Tampa Bay, everybody bought in that I might be able to play. That was the reward. I had a fun career, though the Bucs had some miserable years, but we had some good years too. I played with a lot of great people, and those friendships were long-lived.

"After eight years in Tampa Bay, I signed with Cincinnati, had my best camp ever, and was going to be on the '88 team that went to the Super Bowl, but I had a sciatic nerve problem, pulled a back muscle, and I was put on injured reserve, and then released and picked up by Don Shula in Miami, but I got turf toe, and so my warrantee had run out. That was it. I retired.

"A friend of mine was starting the first-ever all sports radio station out of Tampa. I said, 'Man, you are crazy. ESPN is one thing, but all sports radio is going to be tough to do.' There were only four in the nation at this time.

"I was a little bit of a pioneer. We took a gamble and started doing sports radio. The station was sold, and now I work for Infinity Broadcasting and CBS Sports Radio and Clear Channel that owns the Gator radio network. I work for both stations.

"I have done the Gator games on the radio for the last five years. This will be my sixth year coming, and I do the Buccaneer games on the radio. And being a part of that fraternity, and being able to come back and watch the Gator games, and now being able to do the radio for both the Gators and the Bucs, I couldn't ask for anything better.

"I also do a four-hour sports talk show every afternoon in Tampa. I've got it down to a science. I could do other things and make more money, but I'd have to live in other places, and I want to live here. Family is important, and I have my family around me, and I have two daughters, one in high school and one in junior high school, and I don't want to leave when they're in school.

"I tell people all the time, 'I thank God every day for heat, humidity, mosquitoes, rattlesnakes, and alligators, because if we didn't have any of those things, every human being in the world would live in Florida.' And they would. I welcome the heat, I welcome the humidity, and I welcome the monsoon from time to time, because all those things will discourage somebody, or they'd all live here.

"Florida has so much to offer. If you love the outdoors, love the water, like I do. This is a very special place. There is nothing like it."

If it wasn't devastating enough for Florida to lose Scott Brantley in the Georgia Tech game in '79, in the fourth quarter John Brantley suffered a freak accident and broke his leg, and he too was lost for the rest of the season.

John Brantley: "Our student section would take those hard plastic tops that go on the soda cups, and at the end of the third quarter they threw them like frisbees at the visiting team.

"I went into the game at the start of the fourth quarter, and on a pass play, I sprinted out to the right, and nobody was open, so I cut up the field. When I tried to cut back against the grain, I stepped on one of the plastic tops, and I blew my hamstring. It was like I had been hit by a shotgun shell. It just blew out.

"So it was Galloway first, Scott second and me third. Though I couldn't walk, I went back into the game to hold for Brian Clark. The score was 7-7, he had a forty-something field goal with [13] seconds left in the game, and I was the holder, and the kick was blocked.

"That was kind of the end of the end for me. Scott and I were lying side by side in the infirmary. Mom was sitting there with us. My hamstring was bad. I had just gone through major rehab getting my leg back, just killed myself to get in shape. Scott had already had knee surgery twice. Scott was told he couldn't play any more. He never played again for the Gators. They wouldn't clear him to play. He wanted to play again, but Florida refused to take a chance on the liability. You can't blame them, I guess.

"It had been a trying time for Coach Dickey, and now this, and it all finally came to a head. You know, enough's enough.

"I went to Coach Pell and said, 'Coach, I appreciate it. I know you're trying to change this program around. I'm a senior, and my leg's not too good. I'm going to get married right after Christmas, and I think I'm just going to go ahead and rehab and start getting ready for baseball.'

"I got married on January 5, 1980, and I played my final baseball season for Coach Bergman and graduated on time. The St. Louis Cardinals asked me to come to camp as a free agent. I said, 'Guys, my legs are so beat up, I just don't have the speed. I'm just gonna move forward with my life.' I went down to Charlotte County and worked with my dad, who built every one of the bridges from Bee Ridge Road in Sarasota all the way to Fort Myers. I was with him about six years, and then I went back up to South Carolina with my uncle and ran his brickyard.

"I had always wanted to live in Florida, so in 1990 I moved back to Ocala, where I needed to be, and got into the insurance business. I have a son in the Marin County Youth Football League, where Scott and I started. He threw eighteen touchdown passes. So we've come full circle. He's kind of a tall, skinny, frail kid, but he's a Gator.

"He's kind of running the track I ran. We've been very fortunate. I've been able to take that Gator experience and apply it to business and relationships. I am so fortunate to be a part of the Gator Nation."

In the 1979 Mississippi State game Florida led 10-7 after the first half on a 15-yard pass from Tim Groves to Cris Collinsworth. It was one of the few times a decimated Florida team would have the lead all year.

Tim Groves: "I remember getting hit on the play. I don't even know how he caught the ball. Cris made an incredible diving catch for the touchdown. But Cris was the playmaker. He was an All-American ballplayer for Florida."

Trailing 24-10, Groves hit Darrell Jones on a 49-yard bomb to get Florida down to the State 19 yard line. But on fourth and two, Groves was sacked for a nine yard loss on a busted play.

Tim Groves: "Darrell Jones was extremely fast. He got behind the defensive back, and I threw it up there, and he ran underneath it. We didn't score when I was tackled trying to find a receiver. Maybe I didn't see the right receiver immediately. Maybe they had on a blitz I didn't recognize. Of course, anytime you're behind and you're trying to score and you get sacked on fourth and two, it's not a good quarterback play. That was very, very disappointing.

"At this point football is becoming very, very difficult, especially when you work as hard as we had worked during the off-season. A lot of people don't realize what goes on the entire year just so you can play on Saturday. You're working hard, you're studying film, you think you have all the bases covered, and you just can't win, it's devastating. It just started to wear on us terribly. It wasn't fun to go to practice. It was the most difficult year of football in my life. What made it even more difficult was to realize that it was my play that was helping us to lose.

"I'm not being too hard on myself. You've got to realize that if you don't make the plays that you've been coached to make, you have to be able to say, 'I could have done this better or done that better.' I felt we had the ability to win, and if the quarterback can't get it done—you have to take responsibility. That's why Coach Pell felt he had to make the change. He came to Florida to win ballgames. He had a lot more knowledge than a 19-year-old about how to do it."

When Coach Pell sought to find a quarterback who could perform better than Tim Groves, against LSU he gave the job to freshman quarterback Tyrone Young. Young was not the answer as Florida lost 20-3.

Tim Groves: "Tyrone was a highly regarded quarterback out of Ocala. He was an All-State and All-American quarterback. Coach Pell was trying to figure out what to do. You've got to give people opportunities just to see what he could do. He was trying to find a combination that could win."

Pell would fruitlessly search for that combination all season long. In the next game against Alabama, the second-ranked team in the country, the Gators were beaten soundly 40-0.

Tim Groves: In that game I was actually on the defensive side of the ball. I was in there for mop-up duty. They had a fullback named Steve Whitman, who weighed about 250 pounds. He ran a straight dive. I went to make the tackle, and he dragged me twenty yards. Getting up, I was so woozy I couldn't see for about two minutes. It was like, Wow, now I know why those guys are the number two team in the country!"

Homecoming was against Tulsa. Coach Pell played Tyrone Young and Larry Ochab at quarterback, but the Gator offense was anemic, and Tulsa won 20-10. The loss, the sixth in a row, gave Florida their worst start since 1946. Florida fumbled four snaps, the pass protection was weak, and so was the tackling.

Tyrone Young was 0-6 passing in the first half and didn't play in the second half. Larry Ochab came off the bench and didn't play badly.

Tim Groves: "On offense we were really in disarray. Trying to get the right pieces to get a win, changing personnel: we were doomed. We could sense the urgency of the coaching staff."

Florida rallied and played an excellent game against Auburn. Johnell Brown, a freshman, started at quarterback for Florida, and the two passes that Auburn intercepted were turned into touchdowns in a 19-13 loss.

In the game six key calls went against Florida. Charlie Pell blasted the officials afterward.

Tim Groves: "Johnell Brown went to Gainesville High School. He was more of a running type quarterback, and again, we were just trying to get a win.

"The best thing I remember about that game was that Auburn had two excellent running backs, William Andrews was one of them, and these guys usually ran for 100 yards in a game, and we held both of them to 60 yards apiece. That was a pretty good defensive effort against a very good running football team."

Georgia was the next opponent. The grind was unbearable. The Bulldogs won 33-10. A 13-yard touchdown from Larry Ochab to Chris Faulkner accounted for the only Gator touchdown.

Tim Groves: "All we could think of was how hard the schedule we played at Florida was. There was never a week off. Again, football was not fun at that time. It was a struggle, not only physically, but it wore on you mentally as well. We worked so hard to achieve a goal, and it was just not there to get. It was very, very difficult."

Coach Pell started Johnell Brown against Kentucky instead of Larry Ochab to get the option attack going. Brown made one first down. Ochab wasn't much better. Florida gained exactly 28 yards on the ground and lost 31-3. Three of Kentucky's standout players were from the state of Florida.

Tim Groves: "You realize you're at rock bottom when a Kentucky team can come in and do something like that to you. Again, it was a very, very difficult time for all Gators."

The FSU game was next. Florida State was 11-0. Florida was 0-9-1. The game was played on a Friday night in front of a national audience.

Tim Groves: "You knew a lot of guys on the FSU roster, a lot of high school buddies. We still had a feeling we could salvage the season by beating them, that we could have some joy. We would have had something to hang our hats on if we could have pulled a major upset. It was such an intense rivalry, and the emotions take over, and all you need are a few positive plays that get you excited, and you forget about all the bad things that have happened, and you believe you can get it done."

But against FSU, Florida couldn't get it done. FSU took a 10-0 lead at halftime and went on to a 27-16 victory.

The final game of the season was against the University of Miami. Against the Hurricanes, Florida scored 24 points, the most they had scored in any game that season. Larry Ochab was outstanding, completing 22 of 35 passes for 273 yards and two touchdowns.

But in this game the defense suffered a letdown and allowed 30 points, as Miami quarterback Jim Kelly strutted his stuff. As a result Florida finished the season 0-10-1. After the Miami game, Charlie Pell blasted Doug Dickey for his poor recruiting. Said Pell, "We paid a tremendous price as coaches and players." He thanked the seniors and told them when Florida got into its first bowl game under his leadership, they were all invited.

Tim Groves: "When I got to Florida, the recruiting was very good. I couldn't believe the number of athletes we had when I came to Florida in '77. Then we started having a couple of down years, and the recruiting pendulum can really swing. And when you have a coaching change, kids don't know what to expect, so Bobby Bowden at FSU, a phenomenal recruiter, had a foot in the door. He could tell a kid, 'Listen, Florida doesn't even have a coach right now.'

"After 1979, the only way we could possibly go was up."

Lee McGriff: "Charlie Pell came in and rehired me as assistant coach in '79. He did not retire Steve [Spurrier]. The two of them could not have lasted five minutes together. Steve was open, loose. There was nothing about Steve that Charlie Pell would want on his staff.

"That year we went 0-10-1, and it was unbelievably horrible, especially doing it under him. We coached our way to 0-10-1. We had better players than that, but he was trying to teach them how to be tough. Our practices were just exhausting. We didn't leave them much steam to play. If we had told the players to make up their own plays, we'd have won two or three games. Like I said, we coached them to 0-10-1.

"But he felt like we were laying the foundation, and we did turn it around big time. Florida football did take a major turn in the right direction and started winning very significantly."

forty-seven

An Incredible Turnaround

After a dismal 0-10-1 record in 1979, Charlie Pell decided he needed to revamp his offense. He hired as his offensive coordinator 27-year-old wunderkind Mike Shanahan, who would later lead the Denver Broncos to Super Bowl victories.

Shanahan's rise was meteoric. He had played quarterback at Eastern Illinois University before having to quit his junior year after losing a kidney. In 1975 and 1976 he joined the University of Oklahoma coaching staff as a teaching assistant, and at age 24 he became backfield coach at Northern Arizona. A year later he returned to Eastern Illinois as offensive coordinator. EIU's record was 1-10 the year before, and under Shanahan the team won the Division II title.

In 1979 he was named the offensive coordinator for the University of Minnesota, and that year the offense set forty school offensive records. It was no wonder that when Charlie Pell went looking for an offensive genius, he picked Shanahan.

Tim Groves: "Everyone talks about how Coach Spurrier is such an offensive genius. If anybody is his equal, it's Coach Shanahan. He's unbelievable in the way he can devise game plans and attack defenses."

Shanahan in 1980 chose as his quarterback, a left-hander, from Pennsylvania by the name of Bob Hewko. Nicknamed "The Baby Snake," because he reminded people of another lefty, Ken "Snake" Stabler, the fabled Oakland Raiders quarterback, Hewko had been recruited by Steve Spurrier during his year under Doug Dickey. He arrived at Florida in 1978, was red-shirted and sat out the '78 season, and was injured in 1979. By 1980 Bob Hewko was healthy again and ready to take over the reigns.

Bob Hewko: "I actually signed a letter of intent with the University of Pittsburgh, which had just won the national championship with Tony Dorsett under Johnny Majors. When Majors left, Jackie Sherrill became the head coach. I committed because they were going to have a passing offense. I liked their offense a lot better than Penn State's. I liked Matt Cavanaugh, the quarterbacks coach.

"But my older brother Alex, who was a lineman, was going to the University of Florida. My brother Eric had also been there. [He lettered in 1976.] Doug Dickey recruited them. In fact, my brother Alex told me not to go because Florida had just signed this All-American quarterback by the name of Cris Collinsworth. Back then he was the big hype.

"I was recruited for Florida by Steve Spurrier. He had just quit playing pro football. I was his first recruit outside the state of Florida. He flew up to Pennsylvania and watched me play a basketball game. What was funny was that I had fouled out by halftime. But he invited me to take a visit to Florida anyway. I took the visit still thinking I was going to go to Pitt, because I didn't know much about Doug Dickey and Steve Spurrier. I knew Pitt was going to have a passing offense. I said, 'What the heck? I'll take a visit to Gainesville.'

"I got off the plane, and I was greeted by a 'Gator Getter.' She was a young, good-looking coed wearing a cowboy hat and a Gator shirt. She was my host for the weekend. I was 18. I got off the plane, really hadn't thought about going, just wanted to see what it was like since my brother was going there, and I had a great time that weekend. I talked to Spurrier, and he told me he was going to put in a wide-open passing offense. I talked to Doug Dickey, and he said, 'We're going to play Cris Collinsworth somewhere, but we don't think it's going to be quarterback.' Because he could run, but he couldn't throw real well. Cris was more an option quarterback, and Florida was putting in a passing offense. Between my beautiful hostess, Dickey telling me about Collinsworth, and Spurrier talking to me, it opened my eyes to Florida. I knew I'd be in the hunt to be their starter, and when I got home I had a different feeling about Gainesville. It kind of switched my mind around. And I thought about being with my brother, which would be nice.

"I was able to get out of going to Pittsburgh because it was an independent school. I still remember, when I made my decision, Jackie Sherrill sat in my living room for about an hour. He couldn't believe it because I had already committed. I said, 'I think I'm going to Florida.' And he wouldn't leave. He sat there, talking to my parents. I guess he thought I would change my mind, but I decided I was going to be a Gator.

"Without Spurrier, I don't think I would have gone because back then they were running the wishbone offense and only threw once in a while. I could run a little bit, but I was more of a thrower. When they brought Spurrier in, I knew I could just drop back and throw it. And when I saw who my competition would be, I knew I had a decent shot there.

"My first year was '78, and when I got to Florida, I found out that I had gotten red-shirted, and I didn't know I was going to get red-shirted. I was 18, and I didn't know what that meant. I wanted to play. When I found out they were doing this, the thought came to my mind to transfer to Pitt. I didn't want to sit out a year. Just to be practicing for a year is kind of boring. I talked it over with my family, and I decided to stick it out. Looking back, it was a great move.

"So I spent '78 studying and practicing, and my first year was '79. Dickey was fired, and Charlie Pell came in, and I tore a cartilage in my knee so I was slow getting into the mix. Charlie Pell's first offensive coordinator was Danny Aldrich. Under his scheme, it was, 'We're going to roll out and look at this guy. He's going to do a twelve-yard pattern. If he's open, hit him. If he's not, run it.' You were not even involved in reading coverages. I thought, This is ridiculous. But because of my knee injury, I was not in the hunt for the starting position that year.

"In '79 Florida went 0-10-1. Charlie Pell was charismatic. He was a great guy, though some of the players recruited by Doug Dickey didn't like him. If it was a close call between one of his recruits and a Doug Dickey guy, Pell would lean toward his recruit. That's politics. But Charlie Pell definitely knew how to build a successful program. His record in '79 was horrible. He realized his offensive scheme was terrible, and he got rid of Danny Aldrich quick. He went out and talked to Gil Brandt from the Dallas Cowboys, and he went out and hired the best guy he could find, Mike Shanahan.

"When I first got the starting quarterback job in the spring game [in 1980], the players started calling me 'The Baby Snake.' [Hewko liked to party like Stabler, who was notorious for his nightlife.] We had a lot of fun, and that carried to the field, because I wouldn't really ever get rattled by anything, and that carried over to the team.

"Mike Shanahan prepared me to start at quarterback. He was the best, as far as a person and also as a coach. If I would audible off during a game and make a mistake, he'd never jump on me. He'd look at it, 'At least you thought that would work.' He obviously respected you when you took a shot at things.

"Our first game of the [1980] season was against the University of California. Their quarterback was Rich Campbell. He could just drop back and throw it, and he had some great numbers against us [43–53 for 422 yards passing]. But we came to play that day all around. Our offense was so confident from what we did during the off-season that I didn't think anybody could stop us. I wasn't even worried.

"I threw two touchdown passes that day. The first one was to Chris Faulkner, who was one of the best tight ends ever. I remember after he scored he got hit hard, and he was laying in the end zone. I came up to him and told him he was not allowed to get hurt that day. So he got up and played the rest of the game.

"And I remember Brian Clark, who was from Sarasota, kicked a 50-yard field goal. He was a heck of a kicker, one of the best Florida ever had. Brian was a really conservative guy, but a fun guy. He wouldn't admit he liked to have fun, but he liked to have fun.

"We scored 41 points that day. [Florida won 41-13.] It was incredible. We scored more points in that game than we did the previous year combined. [Not quite, but Florida did score more points than they did in their first six games combined in 1979.] And again, just the way things worked out, it was a blessing I didn't play at all in '79. I got to watch all that junk on the sidelines. When I finally got a chance to play, it was a good feeling. I was so confident I didn't think anything bad was going to happen."

The ecstatic Florida fans wondered whether the California game was a fluke. Against Georgia Tech, the mostly freshmen and sophomores from Florida crushed Georgia Tech 45-12.

Bob Hewko: "The Georgia Tech game in Atlanta was delayed on account of lightning. I started off, and I missed my first two or three passes. Then the storm came in, and we got to go back to the locker room. I think it was the first time a game was ever stopped because of lightning. It was scary, crazy. The lightning was all over the place.

"We went back into the locker room and just chilled out, got to regroup, and then came out on fire. When we came back out, we started firing the ball, and we ended up scoring forty points in that one too.

"Our defense also played well. Wilber Marshall was a freshman, but in all my years of playing, two guys stand out as the best all-around athletes I've ever been on the same field with. One is Wilber, and the other is Hugh Green, who I played with on the [Tampa Bay] Bucs. They were in the same mold, great athletes, the kind of guys you could have played at five different positions, and they'd be great. Wilber was that kind of guy. He was a game breaker.

"The defense also had David Galloway, who kind of taught me about college football. When I came down from Pennsylvania during the off-season, we were running sprints on our own, not an official practice. I had always been the fastest guy in high school. I was running next to David Galloway, and I was barely keeping up with him, and he was a defensive tackle! I thought to myself, This is unbelievable. I learned about the SEC pretty quick.

"Mississippi State came next, and that was one of the most physical games I ever played in. After the game [which Florida won 21-15], I felt like one big bruise. They had a player named Tyrone Keys, who ended up playing for the Chicago Bears. He was a monster. Those guys must have grown up on the farm. They were huge. They would just destroy you, even if you didn't have the ball. It was such a physical game. After it was over I just remember being out of it. My body was completely gone.

"But we won. We pulled it off.

"It was such a tough game, and people don't look at Mississippi State like that, but I thought we were on our way. We were undefeated. I actually thought it was going to be that same way the whole season."

Tim Groves: "After what happened in '79, to get three straight victories was just wild. A lot of confidence was starting to brew everywhere. We had a bunch of kids, David Little, Dock Luckie, Tim Golden, Cris Collinsworth, Hewko, me, and Joe Wickline, plus a few seniors sprinkled in. People were believing in themselves, believing in the hard work and realizing if we did what the coaches said, if we studied the film and played with full-out effort, things can happen.

"With Coach Shanahan running our offense and Joe Kynes on defense, we were excited to win. Football was fun again."

Bob Hewko: "We played LSU next, at Florida Field. Late in the first quarter we ran a throwback play. I was supposed to roll out to my right, then plant, come back and throw a backside post. Mike Heimerdinger, who is now the offensive coordinator for the Tennessee Titans, was relaying in the plays from Mike Shanahan, who was sitting high up in the stadium. I read the signals, and at first I missed the throwback. If I wouldn't have looked back again, perhaps I wouldn't have gotten injured. Who knows? I wish I had never seen that throwback signal.

"But I looked back, and I saw him make the throwback signal, I planted, and I threw the ball, and when I did, a 300-pound defensive guy plowed into the side of my planted leg. He came off James Jones' block, so it wasn't like he was shooting for me low. All his weight went right into me.

"It was the worst pain I ever felt in my life. My ankle was flat on the ground, and my knee was bent weird.

"I had to have a major operation. I left the field and went right to the hospital, so I didn't see the rest of the game. [LSU won 24-7.]

"If that happened now, with arthroscopic surgery I'd probably miss two weeks. Back then they had to open you up and repair the ligament. I was out for the rest of the year. I dressed for the bowl game, but I couldn't have played. Mike Shanahan said, 'You're part of the team. I want you to be in uniform.' That shows you what kind of guy he was. It was just a point of saying I was still part of the team and was going to be there the next year."

With Bob Hewko out for the rest of the season, Coaches Pell and Shanahan needed to find a replacement and pronto. Pell had recruited well, signing the top four high school quarterbacks in the state of Florida in 1979. One of them was a Lakelander by the name of Wayne Peace.

After Hewko was injured against LSU, Coach Pell played quarterback Larry Ochab for a little while before deciding that the man he wanted was Wayne Peace. Though only a freshman, under Mike Shanahan's tutelage Peace fit into the Florida offense right away.

Tim Groves: "Wayne was a true freshman. He was a high school All-American, very highly recruited. When he got to campus, you could see he wasn't your regular everyday freshman. He was a big, strong kid, and he came in with a confidence about him. Shanahan had a great offense, and Wayne was able to pick it up real quick. He knew where and when to throw the ball."

Tom Shannon: "The guy who really brought the run and gun, or the run and shoot to Florida was Mike Shanahan. He was an offensive genius from the get-go. He had Wayne Peace take two steps back and fire the ball, two steps back and fire the ball, two steps back and fire the ball, drop back five more and throw the bomb. That was when Florida really started airing out the ball."

Wayne Peace: "I was born in Gainesville, and then moved to Lakeland when I was four years old. I went to Lakeland High School.

"I could have gone pretty much anywhere I wanted, but it really came down to Florida, Florida State, and Tennessee. They were the only three schools I visited.

"Johnny Majors was the coach at Tennessee. I'm not sure what the attraction was there, except that I had seen them play on television quite a few times, and I liked the hills and the country, and I thought it would be a neat place to visit.

"Bobby Bowden was the coach at Florida State, and I think the world of him. I liked the way they recruited me—not a lot of pressure, just, 'This is how we are. We'd like for you to be part of our program.' By my junior year I was pretty much signed, sealed and delivered to Florida State.

"Then the summer before my senior year, I went up to the University of Florida football camp. I really fell in love with the campus and the area. I started realizing that Gainesville was so much closer to my parents in Lakeland, that it would be so much easier for them to watch me play at Florida. I thought the world of both schools, but I ended up going to Florida because it was closer.

"Coach Pell recruited me, and I talked to him quite a bit. To this day I think a lot of Coach Charlie Pell. He's a good man. He had an intensity and a fire about him that I respected. As a young man it's sometimes hard to understand, but now that I am a little bit older, I look back, and I remember that he was a guy who would look you in the eye and tell you exactly what he wanted to tell you. So many people will tell you one thing, and as soon as you're gone, say something else. Coach Pell wasn't that way. If he thought I was playing poorly, he'd look me in the eye and say, 'Wayne, you're really hurting the team. You need to step it up.' He didn't sugarcoat things, and I respected that. Sometimes as a player it's hard to deal with, but looking back, I really had a lot of respect for Charlie Pell.

"When the 1980 season began, I was around number four on the depth chart. Bob Hewko, who was a sophomore, was number one, and then Larry Ochab, and then a third quarterback, Mark Massey.

"Our offensive coordinator was Mike Shanahan. What a great man! I think the world of Mike Shanahan. He was young and energetic, and in great shape, and the thing I really liked about Coach Shanahan was he did the things he expected us to do. If we were out running, he'd run with us. I was 18, and he was 25, just a tremendous person who demanded a lot from his players.

"The first game of the season was against the University of California, and Bob Hewko played extremely well. Bob was not a physical guy, but he was a heck of a quarterback. He made good decisions, and he made the best of his abilities. You have to give him a lot of credit, because the year before the team had been 0-10-1, and he just came in and played extremely well.

"In that first game we scored 41 points, which was pretty amazing.

"Coach Shanahan brought in a scaled-down version of the 'run and shoot.' Our offensive line was not very talented or big. We threw the ball on the run a lot, a lot of quick action: one, two, three, get rid of the ball; one, two, three, four, five, get rid of the ball. It was new—no one else in the SEC was running it. It required timing, and every day we had repetition—we worked on your steps and got rid of the ball. The quarterback had to make quick decisions.

"We went to Georgia Tech, and again Bob Hewko was phenomenal. He played tremendous.

"Larry Ochab was the backup. He was a senior. I thought a lot of Larry. He was a gutsy fighter of a guy. He was small, didn't have that great an arm, but just a fighter. Larry was always happy, always had a smile on his face and was enthusiastic. Larry had played quite a bit the year before, and he played most of the rest of the LSU game, and they brought me in toward the end.

"I remember the excitement of it all, being out there on Florida Field, which is really something you never forget. At the same time I was over-whelmed, because I had had very few reps with the first-string offense. But what the heck, here I am, let's give it a shot."

Peace was given the starting nod against Ole Miss, in a game played in Oxford, Mississippi.

Wayne Peace: "We had an open week after the LSU game. Somehow, some way, the coaches decided that rather than spend the rest of the year with a senior quarterback, they said, 'We'll go ahead and finish the year with one of our young guys, give him some time to develop, and let's see what happens.'

"So they chose Roger Sibbald and me. Roger was from Dunellen, a big-time All-State quarterback, a tremendous athlete, one of the other highly touted freshmen. They had won the state championship. I'm pretty sure the reason they settled on Roger and me was that we were the more mobile of the four quarterbacks.

"All week long Roger and I took equal snaps. At the end of the week we had a scrimmage. They told us that whoever did better was going to start the next weekend against Ole Miss. And they ended up giving me the nod.

"I remember I played decent in the scrimmage. Neither one of us set the world on fire. I'm sure the coaches were all thinking, 'Whoa, we are in trouble!' But they decided that if they were going to struggle through the rest of the year, they were going to do it with a young guy at quarterback, and get him experience, because he's going to run the offense in the future.

"We went to Ole Miss with a scaled-down offense. What's funny, when I get nervous, I get sleepy, which I know is weird. We stayed in Sardis, Mississippi, a little, old podunk town somewhere, about a forty-five minute bus ride to the stadium. I got on the bus and right away, I went to sleep. When we got to the stadium, Roger Fisher, our nose guard, had to wake me up. I remember some of their looks. They were thinking, Man, this guy is sleeping? What's going on? But it was just my way of relaxing.

"We went into the game, and like I said, we ran a real basic offense, ran the ball more than we threw it. The passes they had designed for the game were very safe, little short, dinky stuff. We knew we were a better team physically, so I'm sure the coaches' outlook was, 'Hey, let's not give him too much, just get him in a game situation, and see how he responds.' So I didn't have a lot of responsibility, just handed the ball off a bunch, and don't turn the ball over. We won the game 15 to 3. Brian Clark kicked five field goals.

"Coach Pell was pleased. The main thing was, for your first game, just don't make any mental mistakes. Don't turn the ball over, and just let your team win the game. And I did that."

The next game was a 13-0 win over the University of Louisville.

Wayne Peace: "Louisville had a really good defense, and in this game the coaches gave me a little bit more to work with. Once again, we knew we were a more physical team, that we should win.

"The key play of that game was an end-around play. Tyrone Young handed the ball to Cris Collinsworth, and he ran 40 yards close to the goal line.

"I think back to that freshman year: I was 18 years old, not the ideal age for a quarterback. You would prefer him to come in, sit a little bit, learn a little bit before he has to go out onto that field and perform, because it's a lot of pressure and a lot of expectations to put on a young guy. But when you have a 6'6" Tyrone Young and a 6'5" Cris Collinsworth to throw to, both tremendous athletes, all that does is help you. They both played in the NFL, were tremendous athletes. Cris was such a leader. He instilled confidence in everybody. He did it in a quiet way, but when Cris was around, you had a sense of peace and calm, and you felt very good about what was going on.

"We were down near the goal [second and three on the five yard line], and I threw my first touchdown to Cris."

The surprising Gators were 5 and 1, with Auburn up next on the schedule at Florida Field. For the first time the coaches opened up the offense for Wayne Peace.

Wayne Peace: "We knew going into that game that we couldn't out-physical Auburn, that we would need to throw the ball a little bit to win. To me, that was my first really good game as a Gator.

"Their running back was James Brooks, who was tremendous. So for the first time with me at quarterback, we opened up and threw the ball a little bit, and I really felt good about that. [Peace was 12-21 for 156 yards, and scored a touchdown on a one-yard plunge.]"

Against Auburn, linebacker David Little made 21 tackles.

Tim Groves: "This state produces so many great athletes, it just blows your mind. When David Little was a high school senior down in Miami, he was the point guard for the high school that won the state basketball championship. So you've got a middle linebacker who can knock your head off, but who has the athletic skills, the agility, and the speed to be a point guard in basketball. That's just an unbelievable combination. David was a great one. He played for the Pittsburgh Steelers for ten years."

Georgia and Herschel Walker were next. Had Florida won, it probably would have meant its first SEC championship. Despite 238 yards gained by Walker, Florida led with only 1:20 left in the game. But when Georgia scored on a last-ditch 93-yard bomb from Buck Belue to Lindsay Scott, the Bulldogs were 26-21 winners, and the day turned into a bitter one for Florida. Tim Groves, playing defense that day, chased Scott all the way to the goal line.

Tim Groves: "That would have been our first SEC championship. Shoot, every Gator in the world, including us on defense, thought we had that game won. Georgia was ranked number two in the country, and even though Herschel Walker had a great game, we had the lead in the ballgame. We were there to win it.

"There was 1:20 to go. It was third and 11 on their 7 yard line. Buck Belue, their quarterback, broke containment, which meant that the linebacker had to go after him so he didn't run for a first down. So that left a pretty big void—about 12 to 15 yards. He threw a pass to Lindsay Scott. I was right in the line of flight. Our other linebacker was Fernando Jackson, and he missed tipping that ball by just a few inches. He made a great effort just to get that close to the ball.

"Lindsay Scott caught the ball and instead of continuing across the field, he spun back around, and Ivory Curry slipped down, and Scott found a running lane.

"I was pretty fast, but I wasn't a 9.4 sprinter, and Lindsay Scott had that kind of speed. He was off to the races, and we all knew who won that one. [Groves got a hand on him at the eight but wasn't able to stop Scott from scoring.] I was the one who was chasing him, and every year I get some writer from across the state of Florida calling me to ask me about that play.

"If they don't make the play, they have fourth down. That Georgia team, I can tell you, was a team of destiny that year. Great teams win those games. Maybe we just had not reached that level of being a great team. We had made a great turnaround from the year before. To win that ballgame would have been…oh, my goodness gracious! We'd have been SEC champions."

Wayne Peace: "People say 'bitter', but shoot, it's such a great memory to me. Going into the game, we were clearly outclassed. They should have beaten us up pretty good. We installed the four wide receiver offense, and to be honest with you, I was terrible at running it all week.

"Come game day I was extremely nervous, thinking, We've put in this new offense, I haven't really done it well all week, and here I am about to go on national TV against the number two ranked team in America. I'm sure in the back of his mind Coach Shanahan was thinking, Oh Lord, what is going to happen today?

"And the game started, and everything kinda clicked, and we really played a great football game.

"We had the lead, and I remember sitting over on the bench. James Jones was sitting beside me. I remember James and I were shaking hands, saying, 'Man, what a game. What a game!'

"They had third down, were way backed up, and with no time left, they hit a long bomb to beat us.

"It was a tough, tough defeat, but at the same time when you give it your best and you play well against a great opponent, it hurts that you lose, but at the same time, it's not all winning and losing, it's how you played. Did you give it what you had? Did you grow from it?

"And for me that Georgia game was a great experience. People ask me all the time, 'What is the most vivid memory you have?' And I tell them, without a doubt, it was my freshman year, and we were getting ready to play the University of Georgia on national television, and I remember walking out of the tunnel and walking out into the stadium. All my teammates were around me, and they're all jumping and going crazy, and all those tens of thousands of fans—it was almost surreal in that I couldn't hear anything. I could see all the commotion around me, but it was just a sense of calm that I remember thinking, Man, this is what it's all about."

The next game also was a nail-biter, this time with a different result. With six seconds left in the game, Gator field goal kicker Brian Clark came onto the field to kick a 34-yarder to give Florida 17-15 win over Kentucky.

Tim Groves: "Even though we lost to Georgia, we felt we had a very good football team. To keep the momentum going, we had to win that Kentucky game.

"It was tough to get up for it after that Georgia debacle. I remember it being so cold in Lexington. We just didn't play well, offensively or defensively. B.C., that's Brian Clark, saved the day. Brian Clark was one of the better kickers Florida ever had. He put it through there to win the ballgame."

With six seconds left in the game Florida trailed 15-14. Brian Clark came onto the field to try a 34-yard field goal. Earlier in the game he had missed from the 31.

Wayne Peace: "When we played Kentucky, we always played them at the end of the year in that cold, nasty weather. For us Florida boys, that was not a good thing.

"Gosh, it was cold and windy. But going into the game we felt we should win. But we were struggling. We weren't playing well. On the play before the final field goal, I threw a post corner route to Cris Collinsworth. It came off kinda wobbly, and it hit that wind, cause it was real windy that day, and when Cris caught that ball, I'm not kidding you, the ball looked like a damn helicopter spinning. I work with kids, and I tell them, it's not always how pretty the throw looks, it's whether it's caught. That was one of the ugliest throws in my career, but you know what, it was a big completion. Brian Clark kicked a field goal, and we won the game 17-15.

"Brian was a first-class individual, and a great kicker. Lord knows, I put too much pressure on him, because we didn't score as many touchdowns as we should have, and he had to make a bunch of kicks instead. But he's a wonderful, wonderful human being, just real well thought of by his teammates, a such a clutch player.

"Winning that game was very exciting. Now we had a chance to go to a bowl, which was something, especially coming off a 0-10-1 season the year before. At that point it was the biggest percentage turnaround in the history of major college football. And for that we had Coach Pell and Coach Shanahan to thank.

"There were empty seats Coach Dickey's last year. When Coach Pell came in, Florida football was in the pits. There was no money. The facilities were terrible.

"Coach Pell was such a motivator. He came in, raised the money, got the facilities turned around, spoke all across the state of Florida, and got the people excited about Florida football. He could go talk to big people and ask for big money, and get it. In '79, even though we were 0-10-1, people were there cheering and pulling for the team. To this day Coach Pell has not gotten the accolades or the recognition that he deserves. You've got to start somewhere, and I like to feel that Coach Pell and my freshman class had a part in getting Florida football where it is today."

The next game was against third-ranked FSU.

Wayne Peace: "We went to Tallahassee, and once again we were on national television. I hit Tyrone Young with a [53-yard] touchdown pass. We had the lead at halftime, 13–3. Our seniors had never beaten Florida State.

"We were real emotional at halftime, but they came out and shut us out—we didn't score any more—and they scored a couple of touchdowns and won the game. They were clearly the better team. They finished third in the country that year and went on to the Orange Bowl. Even though we lost, we felt good about what we'd accomplished and where we were going."

Tim Groves: "That was another game we should have won. Like I said, great teams find a way to win close games. Maybe at that point in time we hadn't reached that level, because we lost 17–13.

"I remember we kept their quarterback, Rick Stockdale, pretty much in check all day. I can remember that last touchdown pass they had. It just kind of floated up there forever. I don't know why we couldn't get to the ball.

"That loss definitely hurt us, because we felt we had played well enough to win that ball game."

The final game of the 1980 season was at home against Miami. Led by quarterback Jim Kelly, Miami won 31–7.

Tim Groves: "They kicked a field goal late in the game, and Coach Pell was pretty upset about that. He was also upset with the way we played. He was very disappointed after the great run we had, and then to end it on a note like that. It was an in-state rival, and a very bitter loss."

Wayne Peace: "God, they were good. I remember before the game getting up and naming every Miami defender, and they were unbelievable. Six of their starting eleven on defense played in the NFL the next year. Lester Williams and Fred Marion were first round draft choices. They were a dominant team compared to us.

"We took the kickoff and went right down and scored. We led 7–0. Shoot, the rest of the game we didn't have a prayer. They dominated. That was the only game I ever played in my life where I was just getting beat up so bad.

"I remember at halftime thinking, Man, take me out of here and let Roger play. I was getting killed."

"We went to the Tangerine Bowl and played Maryland. We played extremely well offensively. Maryland was a very physical team, but we felt they would try to defense us man to man, and we had Cris and Tyrone, and Cris had a great game.

"I threw two touchdowns to Cris. I remember one of them in particular: We had hit a bunch of quick screens to Cris, and their corners were getting overly aggressive, really coming up and hitting the play in a hurry. We were in the fourth quarter, and I said to him, 'If I shake my helmet, let's fake it.' When the time came, I shook my face mask to him, and he kind of nodded, and sure enough, he took two steps and took a quick turn, like we were going to hit him short again. I pump-faked, and the corner came up hard, and then Cris released, and we hit it for a huge gain.

"We beat Maryland 35-20, and the win ended the season on such a high note. And it was gratifying because it was Cris's last game, and for him to have such a big game, well, he was just so deserving.

"We were the first team in the history of college football went went from no wins to a bowl win in one year. We were 0-10-1 the year before, and then to turn around and go 8 and 4 and win a bowl game, it was just an exciting time."

Tim Groves: "Against Maryland our run defense wasn't very good. They had a running back named Charley Wysocki, and he ran for a Tangerine Bowl record [of 159 yards].

"Cris Collinsworth had another phenomenal game, got MVP of the game, scored a couple of touchdowns. We played well enough to win. That was a satisfying win.

"Just to go 0-10-1 and then to come around and win eight ball games including a bowl game was pretty remarkable. Coach Pell instilled the toughness, the work ethic, the importance of our staying focused. He really turned things around. He rallied the state. He was a dynamic speaker, an excellent recruiter, a tough, hard-nosed guy, but very fair. I really believe he built the foundation for what Florida football is today.

"After graduation I signed as a free agent to play with the Miami Dolphins. To go from high school to college to the pros was overwhelming. Don Shula was the head coach, and Bill Arnsparger was the defensive coordinator. I felt confident I would have an opportunity to make the club, but I got released.

They decided I really had only played one year of college ball at safety, and they were confident in the veterans they already had.

"I was released just when the USFL was being formed, and I played with John Reaves for the Tampa Bay Bandits under Steve Spurrier.

"I was fortunate to have the opportunity to get paid to play football. I played safety, and it was a blast. Coach Spurrier was a great coach, very offensive-minded. They called it 'Bandit Ball.' He is a very, very honest coach. He's very committed to winning, a very, very serious competitor, an honest guy and just an offensive genius. He would see defenses and attack them. He didn't get where he's gotten on a fluke. He's a phenomenal football coach and deserves everything he's gotten.

"What you see is what you get with Coach Spurrier. He expects excellence. He expects you to know your assignments. He expects full effort. When you strive to reach his level, you're going to have success.

"I played one year in Tampa Bay and went to Memphis in the expansion draft.

"The league only last three years. It was a great opportunity to get to play at that level. When it folded, I got out of the football business. I realized I was a dime-a-dozen defensive back. The reality hit me in the face. I said to myself, You have to get a job. I bought an oyster bar in Winter Park, close to Orlando. It's called The Thirsty Gator Oyster Club. I've owned it for sixteen years.

"I have a lot of fond memories, and if I had to do it all over again, I'd go right back to the University of Florida."

forty-eight

Peace and Hewko

When Florida opened the 1981 season against Miami at the Orange Bowl, Coach Charlie Pell had to choose between Bob Hewko and Wayne Peace for his starting quarterback. Pell chose to let them fight it out.

Bob Hewko: "I didn't start the 1981 season. Wayne Peace did. I wasn't mad because the way Charlie Pell and Mike Shanahan explained it to me, it was like quarterbacks 1 and 1a. He said if Wayne was cold, I'd be in there. And I did play in the second half. On the second play I was in I threw a bomb to Steve Miller, and when the ball left my hand I was sure we had a touchdown, but we just missed it. It would have been nice, but it didn't happen."

Wayne Peace: "We were ahead by two points [20-18] with less than a minute left in the game, when [Danny Miller of] Miami kicked a long [55-yard] field goal.

"We were in Miami, and it was a hostile environment down there, and I turned the ball over a couple of times, and I remember thinking I had not played that well, not played to my capabilities, and that bothered me.

"But you had to hand it to the guy. If he can make a 55-yard field goal and win the game with that kind of pressure, boy…

"And anytime you start the season with a loss, it's tough, especially against such a major rival. They were a very good football team."

Bob Hewko: "Danny Miller kicked a 55-yard field goal at the end to beat us, and I STILL hear about that from Bernie Kosar and Jim Kelly. They are always ragging me. I tell them, 'In '82 we beat you guys.' They say, 'Yeah, but you didn't play that day.' It's that kind of routine. It's amazing with those guys. Twenty years later Steve Bono is is still yelling about the high school game I beat him in.

"It was one of those awesome games. It was crazy, and with two seconds left Brian Clark tried to kick a 59-yard field goal. Brian had the leg. I was holding. It just didn't happen. It's just one of those things. It wasn't like a chip shot.

"We lost but we weren't upset about it. It was an awesome game. The Orange Bowl was packed, sold out. It was just an electric game. Unfortunately, we didn't win it."

Wayne Peace: "We played Furman, and we won big [35-7]. Bob Hewko was my backup, and it was a tough deal for Bob, because he was a heck of a good quarterback.

"I was struggling again in the Furman game. I'm sure the coaches were not happy with the way I played, and it only makes sense if one guy is struggling and you have a good quality quarterback like Bob, you've got to give him a try.

"Bob came in and did very well."

Bob Hewko: "The way I looked at it, Furman wasn't much of a team. I was just raring to get in there, and I guess Wayne didn't make some things happen, and they put me in.

"I got into the huddle and I said, 'To heck with this. There is absolutely no reason why we shouldn't be killing these guys.' Which we did. We pulled that out, [Hewko came in and threw two touchdown passes.], and I guess that got me the starting job for the next game."

Wayne Peace: "He pretty much played the whole Georgia Tech game, and we won the game [27-6]. At the time I was mad about it, but it was the right thing to do."

A roaring crowd of 63,876 packed Florida Field to watch the Gators host Georgia Tech, which had defeated mighty Alabama the week before. Bob Hewko passed for over 200 yards, and receiver Tyrone Young caught eight passes for 90 yards and two touchdowns.

Bob Hewko: "I was told I was going to start on Monday, but I kind of knew it during the Furman game. I didn't see any reason why they would put me back on the bench. And that week we had a fun game plan for Georgia Tech. Shanahan gave the ball to us. He let me check off as much as I wanted to. We probably checked off eighty percent of the plays at the line of scrimmage.

"That day I threw a lot of passes [eight] to Tyrone Young. I should have checked off more to him. He could have caught twenty that day. He was open, because there was a mismatch. We would have four wide-outs set, and they would always put this one little defensive back against Tyrone, who is 6'6." It was like a touch football game. I could have called the same play all day, which I almost did, and just kept throwing to him.

"And James [Jones] also had a big day. [He ran 20 times for 92 yards.] The way their defense lined up, if they double-teamed Tyrone, their line would rotate, thinking I was going to throw the ball, and I'd check off and give it to James inside, where a defender left a hole. James had a big game. So it was a game mostly called at the line of scrimmage. It was fun."

The fun stopped the next week when the Gators traveled to Jackson to play Mississippi State. Florida was held to 136 yards in a 28-7 loss. Bob Hewko suffered a knee injury and had to leave the game.

Bob Hewko: "I got hurt again, doing something stupid. That's when I started realizing that I couldn't make the moves I used to make. I was getting chased, and I tried to make a double move instead of just throwing the ball away or going down. I caught my knee in the turf, went down, and that was it for that game. It all came down to my knee. If I could have had a $6 Million Dollar Man knee, nothing bad would have happened. But I kept getting hurt."

Wayne Peace: "Somebody came in and clocked him, and I remember feeling bad about that, but at the same time I was glad to be back out on the field. You feel for your competitor, and Bob was a competitor. We're teammates, but we're competing for the same job, so there is a fine line there. Bob and I were such different people. Bob was a PR major. I was a business major. Bob was very much into being quarterback of the University of Florida football team and promoting that. For me, I felt, let me play, let me go home, spend time with my girlfriend and just stay away from people. So we were different, even though we roomed together on the road, and we remained pretty dang good friends. We didn't hang out together, but we got along very well."

Bob Hewko didn't play in the win against LSU, which was quarterbacked by Alan Risher.

Bob Hewko: "I took Alan on his recruiting visit to Florida. I told him we had so many All-American quarterbacks he shouldn't come to Florida. So he went to LSU. I never understood why they would have quarterbacks take out quarterback prospects. I took out Alan Risher. I took out Bernie Kosar. Why would I tell guys who are supposed to be All-American to come compete against me?"

Florida had not beaten LSU since 1975. The score was 17-0 Florida when LSU reached the Florida 27 with about five minutes left in the game. But Gator defensive lineman Wilber Marshall threw the LSU quarterback for a 10-yard loss, and then he intercepted Alan Risher's pass to seal the win for the Gators.

Wayne Peace: "I can talk first-hand about Wilber, because he was the guy who messed up my back. He was a phenomenal athlete. We came in together as freshman. They had him at tight end, and then toward the end of the year he started playing on special teams, and he was making monster hits on people.

"So in the spring of '81, they decided, 'We have some good tight ends. The guy would be an awesome linebacker.' So that spring during practice they put him at outside linebacker, and he just beat our tackles to death. Every time I turned around, it seemed, I was getting a helmet in the back from him, because he was too fast. He'd run around the corner, and we couldn't handle that. He was not real big, but you did not have a ton of guys who were as strong as him, who could run and jump and move the way he could.

"The summer before my senior year, I ended up having back surgery. I always joked that what led to my back surgery was my taking all those hits from Wilber Marshall all those times in the spring."

The next game was a 15-10 win over quarterback Boomer Esiason and Maryland. Maryland led 10-6 going into the final minutes, when Kyle Knight blitzed for a two-point safety, and James Jones threw a halfback pass to Wayne Peace for a touchdown.

Wayne Peace: "Kyle would be the first to tell you he was one of those over-achievers. He wasn't very big, wasn't very fast, and he wasn't very strong, but come game day, he would show up and play. He was a great, great guy, and a great teammate.

"Mike Shanahan designed the pass that James Jones threw to me for a touchdown. Mike was just tremendous. He was one of the brightest minds. Still is. He was tremendous and just great for my career.

"Maryland ran some kind of odd defense, and we knew that once we got them near the goal line, they always played man to man defense. And in man to man defense, the only player they can't account for is the quarterback. Our fullback, James Jones, was a great, great player. We ran a fake sweep to the right, and when I pitched the ball to him, I waited a few counts, and I swung around to the left. Once James got the defense chasing him, he stopped, pitched the ball over to me, and I caught it for a touchdown."

Homecoming was against Ole Miss. Before the game, as he did most games, Coach Pell gave the team a pep talk. He told them, "I want you to remember the best game you ever played anywhere, and tomorrow I want you to come out determined to play better than that."

Wayne Peace: "He had a different motto pretty much for every game. I just had a sincere, warm respect for the man. I didn't see him a ton after my college days were over with, but every time I saw him, I hugged him."

Florida defeated Ole Miss 49–3. James Jones ran for 73 yards and caught three passes for 42 more, and freshman Lorenzo Hampton ran 10 times for 52 yards. Peace was sharp, and Mike Mularkey caught seven passes for 71 yards.

Wayne Peace: "While I was at Florida, we were blessed with tremendous, phenomenal running backs. James Jones played in the NFL for seven–eight years. He was a tremendous leader, a great athlete, knew everything that went on down on the football field. Lorenzo Hampton was a first-round draft choice and played with the Miami Dolphins. I met Lorenzo when we were in the seventh grade. He's from Lake Wales, from Polk County, where I am from. We started playing against each other in junior high school. We also played basketball against each other. He could do it all.

"John L. Williams was a first-round draft choice and played in the NFL a number of years. Neal Anderson was a first-round draft choice and played in the NFL—we had tremendous running backs.

"Coach Pell and Coach Shanahan were able to recruit them, because they looked people in the eye and talked to him, and people respected them.

Both of them had charisma, where people respected them and wanted to be around them. Pell did a great job recruiting players.

"Mike Mularkey is now the offensive coordinator of the Pittsburgh Steelers. He was recruited to the University of Florida as a quarterback and just grew into a big, ole guy. Mike was one of those who played through injuries. Again, he was not the most physically talented guy in the world, but he played hard and was well-respected by his teammates. He was a fun guy to be around, always smiled and was happy, a neat, neat guy."

Auburn came next, and Florida would have won if not for one particularly egregious call by the officials. Safety Tony Lilly recovered a fumble in the air and returned it 47-yards for the winning touchdown. After the play was over, the officials ruled that it had bounced before he recovered it, and hence the ball could not be advanced. The Gator players swore he caught it in the air.

Wayne Peace: "I remember nothing about how we did offensively. I remember nothing about how well I played. But I do remember Tony, who was my freshman-year roommate. There was a fumble, and the ball popped straight up into the air, and he caught it in the air, and he took it in for a score—47 yards. And the video-tape clearly showed that it did not hit the ground."

Bob Hewko: "Everybody went nuts. It was one of those plays you knew was going to come back and kill you. [Florida lost 14-12.] We had the points in our pocket, and they took them away from us. And that I didn't play was a double disappointment."

The next game was even tougher, a battle against Herschel Walker and the University of Georgia at the Gator Bowl. Walker was being compared to Doc Blanchard and Glenn Davis, Tommy Harmon and O.J. Simpson.

Florida lost 26-21 in large part because of Walker's 192 yards and four touchdowns against one of the nation's finest defenses.

Bob Hewko: "Herschel had our number the whole time. He was absolutely the best back I ever saw. I remember in '80 hearing the hype about this kid. I said, 'No way. He's getting too much press. The kid can't be that good.' And in our first game against him, it was the third play, and he broke it for eighty yards, just ran right through us. It was like, 'Damn.'

"My roommate was Kyle Knight, a defensive back. Kyle went to tackle him, and he knocked Kyle out. The guy was incredible—the best I ever saw."

Wayne Peace: "Herschel was a phenomenal athlete. You couldn't take him down with one guy. You could not depend on one guy to stop the play when he was running. As soon as somebody made a hit, you had to make sure everyone else was there with him. He was a player who could break one at any time."

A 33-12 win over Kentucky followed. Peace was 20-33 for 275 yards and four touchdowns.

Wayne Peace: "I remember that the winner of that game was going to get a bowl bid and the other one was not. So we knew it was an important game. We were two very close teams, and there was a lot of rivalry. But once the game got started, we just kind of steamrolled them. We clearly outplayed them."

Florida State was next. In the previous two years FSU was 11-0 and 10-0. Florida had only two seniors on the team. Wayne Peace had another stellar day, going 20-33 for 275 yards and four touchdowns.

Wayne Peace: "One of the touchdowns was a [26-yard] pass to Mike Mularkey. FSU played some zone defense, but they also played a lot of man to man. They had a strong safety who reacted real aggressively to the run.

"We had been running a dive play to James Jones a lot during the game, and their strong safety was coming up real hard. So for this particular play, we faked the dive—James went flying in there, and the strong safety came up hard, and then Mike released off his block, and I pitched the ball out to him.

"I remember thinking, Yup, he's been suckered up, he's really coming up and making hits, so it is time to use this play. Shanahan called it, and boom, there is was.

"That was a big win. It was unexpected, and we beat them badly [35-3]."

The Gators were invited to play in the Peach Bowl in Atlanta. Their opponents were the Mountaineers of West Virginia.

Wayne Peace: "At the start of the season most of us really thought we were going to do a lot better than the Peach Bowl. To me, it was kind of a disappointing year. We went 7 and 4, which to us was disappointing. We took a team vote on whether to go to the game or not, and the team voted not to go.

"Finally Coach Pell gathered the seniors up and talked to them. The next day, they called another meeting. The seniors got up and talked about their wanting to play in a final game, and we had another vote, and it barely passed."

Bob Hewko: "It took three votes by the team to pick the Peach Bowl. Back then there was a game called The Garden State Bowl. It was in New Jersey, just outside New York City. When the first vote was counted, we had voted to go to The Garden State Bowl. I don't even know who we would have played, but the players wanted to get a week in New York. A lot of the guys had never been there. I would have loved it, because I was from Philadelphia, and I'd have a lot of friends going to the game.

"But Charlie came back in the room, and he started lobbying. He said, 'It's gonna be almost during finals week. You guys don't understand.' He was lobbying us to get us to go to the Peach Bowl. He tried to get some help from the coaches. Jim Rodgers was one of his assistants. Charlie said, 'Coach Rodgers, tell them something about New York.' He was hoping he would say, 'New York is freezing cold and snowy that time of year.' Rogers said, 'It's the Big Apple. It's the best place in the world.' You could almost see Charlie going, 'Oh NOOOO.'

"So we took another vote and again voted to go to The Garden State Bowl. Charlie came back in again. He said, 'It's finals week,' and he was lobbying to stay in the south because it helped his recruiting. On the third vote we agreed to go to the Peach Bowl."

"So we played in Atlanta, and it rained the day of the game. I was in the elevator with Charlie that day, and I said, 'This is my kind of weather. I grew up in that kind of weather.' It was cold, and the rain made it even colder. It was horrible.

"Yeah, West Virginia knocked us off [26-6]. I don't think everybody was fired up about the game. Number one, we wanted to go to New York. Number two, the Peach Bowl was fine, but we were playing West Virginia, and we figured we were the biggest lock in the world. Nobody was fired up.

"I had a different outlook, because I'm from Pennsylvania. I grew up watching Pitt and Penn State play West Virginia. I looked forward to it. Unfortunately, I didn't start that game.

"Wayne started, and he played until there was nine minutes left. I wish I had come into the game earlier. When I came in, I just wanted the guys to have fun and everyone to play some ball, pretty much like all my games. I came in there throwing. We went into a two-minute offense, where I was allowed to call anything I wanted to. We marched right down. I remember calling a play to Chris Faulkner down the middle, and I hit him for a touchdown.

"After the season a group of us were going to to my brother's place in West Palm. Some of the others were going to Miami. Kyle Knight and Mike Mularkey were going to Mike's house in Fort Lauderdale. We were kind of following each other going down 95. I went off at Palm Beach.

"We were going to hook up for a spring break gathering a day later. The next day we learned that Mike and Kyle were involved in a car accident. We couldn't believe it. Mike wasn't hurt, but we went to see Kyle in the hospital. We were young and didn't think it was going to affect his football career. He was cut up, banged up. But the head injury turned out to be bad. When we got back to Gainesville we found out he couldn't play any more. It was terrible. We missed him immensely the next year."

Wayne Peace: "We went to Atlanta to play in a bowl game that most of the players didn't want to play in. We played in God-awful freezing cold weather, and we got our brains beat out.

"For the West Virginia guys, it was like a day in the sun for them.

"When we returned in the spring for practice, Coach Pell had dug this big hole. All the upcoming seniors had to strip the tape off the film of the Peach Bowl game and throw it into the hole, and we had to bury it, and they put a huge rock over it.

"He said, 'We're burying this film. No one will have a record of it.'

"Every day when we went out to practice, we were supposed to touch that rock, so we would remember that that would never happen again."

forty-nine

A Stellar Season

At the end of the 1981 season Coach Pell asked the players to come back for spring practice in top shape.

Wayne Peace: "Not to toot my own horn, but I busted my butt every off-season. To this day I'm a physical fitness guy. I like working.

"Mike Shanahan pushed us all that summer, and he was right there running with us. We'd meet at the track in the evenings—and we later got in trouble for doing this—the NCAA rules said 'the coaches can't do that.' But we would run intervals, and the quarterbacks and receivers threw non-stop. Everybody really worked hard to try to get going in the right direction."

Bob Hewko: "I can tell you something nobody else ever knew: when we came back for spring practice [in 1982], the way Coach Pell explained it, the senior at that position was going to be the starter, and it was his job to lose. At all the positions. I was the senior at quarterback. So I was almost thinking he was doing that for me. I didn't know. But he did it. And the week before practice started, I was playing in a basketball game with Tyrone Young and Timmy Groves and a couple of other guys, and we were playing frat guys in a pickup game.

"I came down on some guy's foot and turned my knee. I couldn't believe it. I just prayed it wasn't anything bad. At the time we didn't tell anyone we were playing basketball. So at the time I said I was jogging and hit a hole. As it turned out, I had torn cartilage. It wasn't serious but it kept me out of hitting in spring practice. So unofficially I got my job back, but I couldn't hold it because I hurt my knee again.

"Then the idea was for me to be ready when they needed me. So Wayne was the starter, and I was there as needed.

"When we began the 1982 season against Miami, we had a record crowd at Florida Field [71,864]. We had an all-new end zone built. It was a beautiful stadium. As far as raising money and improving the facilities, Coach Pell was the best. I'd never seen a guy who could organize things and get people together like he could. He could get you fired up. And the alumni were unbelievable. They were another reason I went to Florida in the first place. I did some research on Florida, talked to my brothers, and it's just unbelievable the support that the Gators have."

Florida opened with a 17-14 win over Miami. Florida trailed by three points with 4:02 left in the game. The Gators were on their own 39 yard line. Wayne Peace brought them victory in six plays.

Wayne Peace: "I remember we liked to run what we called a 'smash route' with Dwayne Dixon on the back side. I took a five-step drop, and we had a primary read on the front, and if there was nothing there, Dwayne would be on the back side. Typically he would be open near the line of scrimmage. I would just dump the ball and try to make some yardage.

"It was an important down, and I dropped back, and nothing was there, and I turned and hit Dwayne, and he shook a tackler and went [twenty-six] yards, which was a huge play when you needed to get things moving.

"Dwayne got down to the [Miami 19 yard line], and then James Jones gained a couple, and [with 1:48 left in the game], we called a '32 Naked' pass, a bootleg naked pass to the right.

"Basically, you fake to the tailback in the flat, bootleg to the right, and your first option is the tight end in the corner. You have the fullback in the flat, and if both of them are covered, then you run the ball. Earlier in the game I had scored a touchdown running it.

"We called the same play, and I remember thinking, 'Man, again? They're gonna be ready for it.'

"It didn't happen real fast. Miami kind of strung the play out, and I was kind of in between—I was thinking, They are really not here. Should I run it? And I strung it out a little bit more, and then James kept moving up the field. I tossed the ball out to him, and he made a phenomenal catch in the corner of the end zone. I overthrew him, and he had to leap, and it was a tremendous catch. Coach Pell's description in Sports Illustrated was, 'Willie Mays Deluxe.' It was a great, great catch.

"It was a huge win. Miami was ranked number one in the country. They were expected to compete for the national championship, and for us to come on our field and beat them in the first game of the season was tremendous.

"And after James made the awesome catch, I was on the cover of Sports Illustrated. It was the first time a Florida player had made the cover of Sports Illustrated.

"Ever since I was a kid, I would get my Sports Illustrated on Thursday, and when I came home from school, I'd read it from cover to cover because I just lived and breathed sports. For me to be on the cover was just really neat. To this day people from all over the country mail me Sports Illustrated covers for my signature. So it was really neat."

The next game pitted 11th-ranked Florida against the 10th-ranked Trojans of USC. The game was on TV at Florida Field. Florida had lost 16 of its last 19 televised football games. Everyone spoke of 'the TV jinx.'

Florida pulled ahead early 14-0, and when the final whistle blew and the Gators came away with a 17-9 win, the players ran a lap around the field. The idea, said Coach Pell, was to share the win with the 12th man, the Florida fans.

Bob Hewko: "I actually looked forward to the USC game more than any other because as a kid living in Pennsylvania, I watched the Trojans play Notre Dame. They were one of the powerhouses, and until this year ['82], we had never had a shot at them.

"What I remember about that game more than anything else was Jimmy Buffett singing the national anthem. We were just totally fired up for this game, just because it was USC on national TV. We knew this game would put us on the map. We were in the locker room, ready to come out onto the field, and we could hear Jimmy Buffett singing the national anthem. It was great, but he's SOOO laid back, it was the longest national anthem I've ever heard in my life. We were ready to power out of the locker room, and Buffett kept singing.

"Then after the game, after we beat USC, Jimmy came into the locker room and he asked me, 'Can you party like the real Snake?' I guess Kenny Stabler and he were good buddies. I said, 'Absolutely,' and ever since then we've been good friends.

"The other thing that happened after the game was that we were in the locker room, and Charlie came in and said we were going to take a victory lap. We all started laughing and said, 'What?' But we all went out and took a victory lap. I don't know why he wanted us to do it, but it was a riot. It was one of those things you'll never forget. We walked out there and waved to the crowd and took a victory lap. Oh, it was nuts. The place went crazy.

"Another thing that happened that day was that Wilber Marshall played himself into being an All-American candidate. We knew how good he was. But this game was on national TV, and it put Wilber on the map."

Wayne Peace: "USC ran the sweep a lot, and in their scheme of things, they did not account for the weak-side linebacker, because not many players had the kind of speed needed to run the play down from the backside. But they hadn't played against Wilber Marshall. Literally there was no one blocking him when they ran the strong-side sweep away from him, and so he would fly behind the line of scrimmage, take the proper angle, and made a lot of hits behind the line before the tailback could turn up. That was just a huge game for Wilber."

After the 17-9 win over USC, Florida was ranked number five in the country. Against Mississippi State, the Gator running backs, Lorenzo Hampton, John L. Williams, and James Jones, helped Florida gain 258 yards on the ground. Wayne Peace was almost perfect going 12-15 for 119 yards as Florida won 27-17.

Bob Hewko: "We had so much talent in '82 there was no way we shouldn't have been undefeated. We were shooting to be number one.

LSU came to town. Wayne Peace and the offense struggled as LSU won 24-13. In mid-game against LSU, Pell pulled Peace in favor of Bob Hewko, but neither had much success moving the ball against the Tigers.

Wayne Peace: "We struggled offensively that game. Who knows why, but they definitely outplayed us that day. They were physical, and I remember we had some plays that we thought would work, and they weren't even close to being right. We just weren't in the right position."

Bob Hewko: "For some reason I always had a knack, even in high school, when I was scrambling, to find someone open. I remember the first series I was in against LSU. In that first series, I ended up scrambling, but instead of doing my usual looking-deep read first, I looked short and tried to complete a short pass. And when I looked at the films, I could see Spencer Jackson twenty yards in the clear open for a bomb. That could have given the momentum back to us, and I missed it. I just didn't see him. I could have killed myself when I watched the films. Why didn't I see him? I always used to see them.

"It's weird about playing LSU. When we played them there, we usually won. At home we'd always be in a nightmare. It doesn't make any sense."

The next game was against Vanderbilt, a supposed patsy in the SEC. Vanderbilt had won exactly one SEC game in its last 35. Florida travelled to Nashville. Twice during the game Coach Pell decided to forego easy field goals for touchdowns Florida never made. The two decisions cost Florida the game, as Vanderbilt won 31-29. Florida gained 540 total yards on offense and lost, but Vandy quarterback Whit Taylor's three touchdown passes were the difference.

Wayne Peace: "Offensively we played great. And defensively we just didn't play well. That was a huge loss because there was no way they were a better team than we were. It was a huge, huge upset. I remember we scored 29 points and moved the heck out of the football."

Bob Hewko: "Vanderbilt had a quarterback by the name of Whit Taylor, who made things happen. I don't know how we lost that game, but we did. I have no idea how. It was a fluke. But that loss took us out of any big thoughts we had."

Homecoming was against hapless West Texas State. Florida gained 783 yards in total offense, including 380 passing yards. The 77 points it scored was the most scored by Florida since the Rollins game of 1924.

Bob Hewko: "West Texas State scored the first fourteen points of the game. They converted two on-side kicks and went in and scored. I don't know how they got through our defense, but they did. We were laughing on the sideline. We looked at them, and half the guys weren't even wearing football cleats. They were so rag-tag. We were thinking, What's going on?'"

"I remember when we were down 14-0 a dog got on the field. The dog ended up going eighty yards for a touchdown! Our crowd went nuts, and I don't know if that turned around the momentum, but we then scored ten touchdowns in a row!"

Wayne Peace: "We were down 14-0, and our fans were booing us. And I'm sure Coach Pell was dog-cussing somebody. We weren't all that upset, because they were just so outmanned. I remember watching them warm up. Some of their players had their pants taped up. And to be honest with you, I'd rather play a Georgia than a West Texas State. Because to me, it's a no-win situation. If you don't beat their brains in, you're considered a failure. And we did beat their brains in. [Florida won 77-14.] We scored at will. [Peace was 15-17 for 289 and three touchdowns by the half.] I was hoping they would take me out for the second half, and they did."

Auburn was next, always a tough opponent. The game was played at Florida Field. The Gators had to face the tandem of Bo Jackson and Lionel James, two Auburn stars who ended up in the NFL. Bo Jackson also played major league baseball. Wayne Peace and Dwayne Dixon started for Florida. Peace was 23-30 for 150 yards, and Dixon caught six passes for 86 yards.

The player who made the difference in the Auburn game was a Florida walk-on by the name of Jim Gainey, who kicked four field goals that day, including two that overcame a 17-13 Auburn lead late in the game.

Florida won the game with one second left when Gainey, a fifth-year walk-on, kicked a 42-yard field goal to give the Gators a 19-17 victory. Gainey was cool as could be, and after the ball went through the uprights holder Bob Hewko hugged him and almost choked the wind out of him.

Bob Hewko: "Jim was one of my best friends on the team. If anything went wrong on the field, Jim was one of Charlie's scapegoats. For anything. It made no sense. Charlie would yell at Jim, and we would crack up, because it was as though it was Gainey's fault no matter what happened.

"But against Auburn there was one second left, and we needed a field goal. Our regular snapper got hurt, and we had a new snapper in there, Mark Hurm, and I was more worried about our snapper than I was our kicker. I told Mark, 'Just get it anywhere near me. Just don't roll it.' And Mark hiked me a knuckleball. And I got it down, and Gainey put it through.

"And Jim is still mad at me because I almost knocked him out after he made the kick. I was the holder after it went through, and I tried to lift him up high above my shoulder, and I lost my balance, and I ended up body slamming him on the ground, and he lost his breath."

One of the toughest tasks Florida had to face each year was playing Auburn and Georgia back to back in the middle of the schedule. Both opponents were bedrocks of the SEC, and it was rare indeed when Florida won both games in a season.

In 1982 Charlie Pell's Gators traveled to Jacksonville to meet Georgia at the Gator Bowl before 80,749, the largest crowd ever to watch a football game in the state of Florida. It was a rout. Wayne Peace got little protection, fumbling three times and throwing two interceptions, and Florida lost, 44-0. Herschel Walker ran 35 times for 219 yards.

Wayne Peace: "There was no doubt in my mind going into that game that we were going to win. No doubt. We felt very good. We were playing very well offensively. We knew we were going to move the football and win the game. And we lost, 44-0.

"It was just one of those weird things in sports. Who knows why things happen the way they do? There is no doubt in my mind that we were a better team that year. At worst, we were evenly matched with them. I was sure we would beat them, and nothing went right. Nothing went right from the get-go.

"We just got our brains beat in. I remember sitting on the bench with James Jones towards the end of the game. We looked at each other, and all we could do was laugh. What the heck happened? We were more embarrassed than disappointed. I don't know."

Bob Hewko: "Georgia was a team that had our number. I was disappointed about that game more than any other. We were playing so bad. I was wishing I would get in in the first or second quarter. Charlie put me in the game with three minutes left.

"The next week I went up to Charlie Pell's office to see him. I said to him, 'Coach, you always said when things weren't going right, if Wayne was cold, I'd be right in there.' He said, 'Bob, you're right. You should have been in there a lot earlier.' And our conversation might have had an effect on how fast he got me into the Florida State game. He didn't hesitate to throw me in against Florida State."

But before Florida State came Kentucky and Tulane. Against the Wildcats, freshman Neal Anderson carried 33 times for 197 yards including a 63-yarder at the start of the fourth quarter. He was just 21 yards shy of the record set by Red Bethea in 1928 against the University of Chicago. Anderson scored three touchdowns in a 39-13 win. In the next game against Tulane, Anderson scored three more touchdowns in a 21-7 win.

Wayne Peace: "Neal came from some little old small town, and he had a real whiny voice, and it was kind of country whiny, so we called him 'Country.' Neal was a good guy, and a good student, well respected by all his teammates, and come game day, the guy had a lot of ability and played extremely well for the Gators and in the NFL.

"Neal was very quiet. All those running backs, with the exception of Lorenzo Hampton, were quiet. Lorenzo was 'big city,' even though he was from Lake Wales. Well, he thought he was 'big city.' The others—John L., Neal, and James, were all very quiet, humble people who let their ability speak for them and really didn't speak much at all."

Bob Hewko: "Neal may have been the most talented back of them all. John L. and James were power backs, and Lorenzo was more of an all-around back—he could run with power and catch the ball, but Neal just had so much talent. He scored three touchdowns against Kentucky and three more against Tulane, and after the Tulane win Coach Pell said we could stay an extra day in New Orleans, because he thought that would be our bowl game. We needed for Notre Dame to lose to the Air Force for Florida to get a bowl bid, and sure enough, when Notre Dame lost, we were invited to the Bluebonnet Bowl."

"I came into the Tulane game in the fourth quarter, and it was another one of those games where you wished you could have gone in earlier. Of course, when you're not in, you're itching to get in. I always thought I could play as well as anybody. That's the nature of anybody who likes to compete.

"But he told me to get in there, and I hit James Jones with a long pass. We played in the Superdome, and I just loved to play indoors. I don't know why, but I did."

Florida travelled to Tallahassee to play FSU. Wayne Peace started the game and ended up setting an NCAA record for completion percentage in a season. His .707 average bettered that of Rich Campbell of the University of California in 1980. But Peace was not sharp against the Seminoles, and

Coach Pell brought Bob Hewko in, and Hewko led the Gators to a long touchdown drive and a field goal to pull out the FSU game 13-10.

Bob Hewko: "It might have been because I was talking to Charlie that week about my not getting into the Georgia game quicker. Because he pulled Wayne pretty quick when things weren't going good.

"I came in, and I ran for a 10-yard touchdown. They sent the play in, and I called time out. I thought I had read it wrong. I wasn't known for my running ability. I was reading a signal from Lee McGriff. It was third and ten and they called an option play. So I called time out. Mike Shanahan said, 'That's what we're gonna call.' And we called the option play, and nobody covered me. I tried to throw it to somebody, but nobody was there. So I had to run. When nobody took me, I just ran it in.

"And Jim Gainey kicked two field goals, and we won 13-10. It was a great game. It was a fun game. It was like a heavyweight fight. At the end of the game we were on the one, fourth down. The crowd was going bananas. They thought we were going to go for it. I went over to the sideline, and Charlie said, 'Take the [delay of game] penalty.' That put us five yards farther back, and Jim kicked a [22-yard] field goal, and we held them at the end.

"Florida State had a bunch of studs. On the field, it was like you were having a fight with those guys. I remember toward the end of the game James [Jones] was banged up. He started limping off the field, and I wouldn't let him go. I told him, 'James, we need you. You're not leaving.' And I pulled him back on the field. He was one of those guys you would go to war with and just love having him next to you.

"I think I had more fun in that game than any other. Because it was one of those fights you knew you were going to win."

Wayne Peace: "Bob came in and moved the team for the winning score. He came in and did a good job. And we were invited to play in the Bluebonnet Bowl in Houston against Arkansas and Lou Holtz."

Arkansas was led by running back workhorse Gary Anderson. Before the game Bob Hewko had some fun with the media and with fellow quarterback Wayne Peace.

Bob Hewko: "A couple of days before the game the special teams bus went to the Astrodome. We had a player, Larry Keefe, a great guy, who was on the special teams. They'd use him everywhere.

"Larry went into the locker room, and he switched the uniforms around. He put on my uniform and he put Wayne Peace's uniform in my locker, and he gave his uniform to Wayne.

"We walked out onto the field wearing the wrong uniforms. We didn't know there was going to be a ton of media waiting for us.

"I walked out wearing Wayne's uniform. The media guys didn't know our faces. Nobody was talking to Wayne because he was wearing number 19, Keefe's uniform. One of the TV networks came up to me, thinking I was Wayne. The guy said, 'You started all these games this year....' I decided to go along. He said, 'How does it feel not to start the bowl game after starting all these games this year?'

"I put on my best Lakeland accent, and I said, 'I'm not real happy about it, but all I'm really concerned about is getting back to Lakeland and doing some hunting.' I figured the guy would catch on, but he never did.

"They ran the piece that night on the news, and Wayne was SO pissed. Everybody was dying laughing. Wayne would probably get mad today if you brought it up. We used to play some good tricks."

Bob Hewko started and threw three touchdown passes to Dwayne Dixon. It was Hewko's first start of the year.

Wayne Peace was furious.

Wayne Peace: "They called me in and said, 'Look, it's Bob's last game. We're gonna start him in the bowl game.'

"I want to say I was happy for Bob, but I wasn't. I'd be lying if I said that. All that week I was furious. I didn't want to talk or see anybody. Just let me go home. I guess you might say I had a little bit of a bad attitude that week.

"I looked upon that as MY team. I'd had a great year. I wanted to be the starting quarterback in that game. If you're going to play quarterback, you have to be competitive, and you have to feel that way. This is my team! I'm the leader of the team! I wouldn't have had the success I had if I didn't have that attitude.

"They knew all week I was upset, which is fine. They left me alone. It was okay. I wasn't a deterrent. Just leave me alone. All right, fine, I'll practice, and I'll sit over there and watch the game, but let's get it over with and let me go home.

"Bob came in and played extremely well, and then I was happy for Bob, because Bob's a good guy. He played well against a very good team. I didn't touch the field. For me that was kind of a lost week."

Florida led Arkansas 17-7 at halftime in the Bluebonnet Bowl, but Arkansas dominated in the second half and won the game 28-24, despite three Hewko touchdown passes to Dwayne Dixon. Hewko was 19-28 for 234 yards and Dixon caught eight passes for 106 yards.

Bob Hewko: "In that game I threw eight passes, three of them to Dwayne for touchdowns. Dwayne was a great receiver to throw to. He could catch anything you threw. And I have to tell you, he can balance a table on his nose. He has a flat nose, and he can balance any table on his nose. Yeah, huge tables. Tell him to do it for you one day.

"At halftime I thought we were going to blow them out, but then Gary Anderson personally destroyed us. And they did stop our offense in the second half. Every time we got the ball, we moved it, but we just didn't get the ball much in the second half. It was a great game to watch. It was a fun game.

"Looking back on it, I think we had more talent than anybody in the country. If there was any team that should have been undefeated, it should have been our team. I mean Lomas Brown, our tackle, is STILL playing with the New York Giants. I don't know how it's possible. He's just doing it.

"After I graduated, I signed with the Tampa Bay Buccaneers in '83. The coach was John McKay. McKay was great, I loved him, but after going through Mike Shanahan's system, our offense scheme was like taking a step ten years back. It was almost like a high school offense. I'd hand the ball off to James Wilder, and that was it. But McKay himself was great. I liked him.

"I bounced around for four years. Sports Illustrated once wrote an article about my making fourteen stops in four years. I can remember the big ones: Dallas and the New York Jets. Dallas brought me in because they were supposed to trade Danny White, and I was going to be the backup to Hogeboom and Steve Pelluer. I was there about six months. But the trade never went through. Then I was gone.

"In between Dallas and New York, there were weekends in Los Angeles, weekends in Cleveland, weekends everywhere.

"In '87, I left football. My first job was working for Caesar's Marketing World, the parent company for Caesar's Palace and all their properties. I got the job by accident. Every year my brother and I would go home for the holidays, and we'd go down to New Jersey for a couple of days to the shore. A friend of mine was working at Caesar's in Atlantic City. He told me Caesar's was looking to open an office in the southeast. 'Would you be interested?'

"I didn't even know what the job entailed. But I knew I wasn't going to play football any more, so I said, 'Yes, why not?' So the next day I met with the vice-president for about ten minutes. I knew nothing about the business, but for some reason he liked me. He had the president of Caesar's fly down to Florida. The next day he asked me, 'What's it gonna take for you to live comfortably in Florida?'

"This was my first job so I didn't know what to tell him. Half a million? A hundred thousand? I didn't know. I called Cris Collinsworth, and Cris was laughing. I ended up saying a number, and he accepted it.

"I was based in Tampa and ran the state of Florida for them. I worked on a lot of their major events in Las Vegas and Lake Tahoe. I worked on a lot of their major events, their fights, and a lot of their entertainment at Caesar's Palace. I had a ball.

"I had that job until Scott Brantley and I started our radio show in Tampa in 1989. Brantley had the show and asked me to join him. We did a morning talk show from 6 to 9 for about three years. Then we switched to the afternoon drive time for a couple of years.

"It was sports comedy. It wasn't supposed to be that, but that's what it ended up being.

"Then a friend of mine, one of the owners of Hooters, asked me what I thought of Arena Football. The Tampa Bay Storm was doing really well. He said, 'What do you think about getting a team in Miami?' I said, 'That would be great.' A week later we bought the rights to the Sacramento franchise, and I became the general manager of the Miami arena football team. Don Strock was our first coach, and the next year I hired Jimmy Dunn. When our main owner decided to sell the team, I had to fire Jimmy and bring in a coach for peanuts. After the third year we sold it. Looking back, selling the team wasn't a great move, because an Arena franchise is now worth $10 million.

"I now have an entertainment company. I work a lot doing sports events out in Las Vegas with the Harrah's properties, and the Atlantis and the Bahamas. I do a lot with Jim Kelly and a company called Pro Access, which represents Barry Bonds and Barry Sanders. I want to stay involved in sports.

"I always told Mike Mularkey that if he ever became head coach, he would hire me as his quarterback coach. The way he's coaching the Steelers, that might happen pretty quick. Would I want to leave Miami Beach to go to Pittsburgh? I probably would. You never know."

fifty

The First Top-Ten Finish

Coach Charlie Pell was a very effective recruiter, and in 1983 one of his best signees was a 17-year old quarterback who lived only ten minutes from campus. A speedster, Ricky Nattiel had always wanted to be a wide receiver, but in high school he had been forced to play quarterback because there was no one better than he to play it.

Nattiel, fearful of airplane travel, narrowed his choice of college down to Florida or Florida State, both an easy drive from home. When the Seminoles told the youngster that they only wanted him as a defensive back, his choice became easy.

Ricky Nattiel: "I grew up in Archer, Florida, just outside of Gainesville. I went to Newberry High School.

"I was All-State my junior and senior years as quarterback, and I was recruited by most of the SEC schools. Not a lot of people nationally had heard of Newberry High School.

"I narrowed my choices to Florida State and Florida. They were the only schools I visited. I didn't want my parents to have to travel too far, and the other reason was that I had always feared flying, and so I could drive up to Tallahassee, and Florida was ten minutes down the road.

"Coach Mike Shanahan was recruiting me for Florida. There was a big group of us who got a tour of the campus. Coach Pell talked to all the recruits. We got a tour of the facilities. But the main guy was Coach Shanahan. He was an awesome guy. He was down to earth, and my parents really liked him a lot. He left a good impression.

"My visit to Florida State was memorable, because the night I got there, I broke out with a severe case of chicken pox. I wasn't even able to leave the room that night.

"The chicken pox hampered my visit, but the other factor was that they didn't want me to play wide receiver. FSU was recruiting me as a defensive back. Jack Stanton, their defensive back coach, was recruiting me. They felt they had enough people at wide receiver. I respected their honesty, because they could have said, 'Fine, you're a wide receiver, no problem,' and who knows what would have happened?

"So I decided to come to Florida, and it was exciting, and it was scary. I enlisted in summer school to get acclimated, and I roomed with Frankie Neal. Frankie was highly recruited and one of the receivers, and he did not mind making that known. He was VERY outspoken and VERY cocky. I didn't know the guy, and he didn't know me, but he made it perfectly clear, 'Hey, I'm gonna be the guy.'

"He didn't intimidate me. If anything, he inspired me. At the same time it made you say to yourself, Okay, this is going to be a different world. This guy is on the same level as I am. He just got here, and Florida has Dwayne Dixon and Bee Lang and Gary Rolle, and this guy is saying, 'I'm going to be out there.' I didn't know whether he wasn't being realistic or whether he just had a lot of confidence in himself. Either way, it was an eye-opener. In high school I was a superstar. At Florida, I wasn't a superstar any more.

"I was glad I went to summer school, because it gave me a chance to meet the other players and get acclimated to the environment, the facilities, with what was to be expected. After the first couple of weeks, I started to get a lot more relaxed, and things started to come a little easier.

"I wanted to make the travel squad my freshman year, so I worked hard during practice. I always worked hard. I worked hard on the field and off the field, lifting weights and running.

"Even so, Coach Pell was hard on me. It was hard to understand, because I was just a kid, and I wasn't used to being yelled at.

"I can remember in one scrimmage before the season started, I was running backup to Dwayne [Dixon], and it was one of those nervous days when I didn't want to make any mistakes. It was getting close to the start of the season, and I didn't want to mess up. And Coach Pell was lurking around, and the scrimmage wasn't going that well, and I was nervous.

"I had stone hands. I couldn't catch a cold. There was a play, a little slant, which would have been a first down, and I dropped it.

"He chewed me out like no other! He yelled at me, ran me off the field. If you were on the first or second team, you wore a white jersey. If you were on defense, you wore blue. If you were on the scout squad, you wore a purple jersey. Well, he made me pull off my white and put on a purple!

"It was that bad. I wondered, Whoa, what do I do now? I was just a freshman, and it was hard for me to comprehend.

"I can remember standing on the sidelines with someone catching passes, and I'm sure I did that the rest of the practice, trying to focus on what had just happened.

"And I knew all along WHY I was dropping passes. It was because I got really nervous when he came around, because I didn't want to mess up. That day it ended up backfiring on me.

"It took awhile to recover from that. I knew it was done out of heat, but it was a devastating blow for me mentally. It was hard for me to recover, and it took awhile.

"Obviously, I was able to recover. When I look back on it, that's just the way Coach Pell was. He wanted perfection.

"I was fortunate—I say fortunate, though I don't really know if that's accurate—that I was not red-shirted. I was determined and motivated to make the travel squad. That's the way I always was: I felt I could do anything if I put my heart and mind into it. At the time I looked at being red-shirted as a demotion. That isn't what it is, but you wonder, Man, aren't I good enough to make the traveling squad? So in my mind, it wasn't so much that I wanted to play, which I did, but making the traveling squad was one of my goals. I didn't want to get red-shirted.

"And I worked my way to second string behind Dwayne Dixon, which as a freshman under Charlie Pell was pretty good."

The 1983 home opener pitted Florida against an excellent University of Miami team. For freshman Ricky Nattiel, his most memorable moment came before the game when he left the locker room and ran through the tunnel toward Florida Field for the first time.

Ricky Nattiel: "The thing I remember most about playing Miami at Florida Field that day was running out of the tunnel. That was the one thing the guys would always tell me about. When you run out of that tunnel and see those 70,000 people yelling and screaming, it's a high you could never, ever forget.

"That was my whole motivation: to play in that game and run out of that tunnel. And it was everything they said, even though I wasn't starting and I knew

I probably wasn't going to play very much, if at all. But none of that mattered. I was on the traveling squad, and this was the first game to start off my college career.

"I didn't play much that day. I did play a couple of snaps. I was playing behind Dwayne Dixon, who was a senior, and that speaks for itself. He was a senior and a proven player, and I was a freshman.

"We weren't supposed to win that day. That was Miami's only loss that year, and they went on to win the national championship. I can remember a lot of Florida bumper stickers at the end of the year: Florida 28–National Champs 3."

In that game against the Hurricanes, quarterback Wayne Peace was almost flawless, an amazing accomplishment considering that over the summer he had undergone an operation on his back.

Wayne Peace: "On July 3, 1983, I had back surgery. I was playing in a pickup basketball game during the summer, and I landed funny, and my back started to really bother me, and my legs were going numb. I knew there was a problem. I went in, and they sent me to Shans Hospital in Gainesville, and they found a herniated disc.

"I said, 'What are the options?' They said, 'We have two options. We can do the old type of surgery where they go in and lay your back open and cut all your muscles, and you're out for the year. Or we have a new procedure that Dr. Bill Friedman at Shans Teaching Hospital has done, and it's been very successful. It was called a percutaneous dischectomy—they go through your side and put a tube in through your intestines and insides, and somehow they take a scissors and cut the bulge in the disc away. The only caveat was that they had never done this on an athlete, only on civilians.

"It was very, very experimental, but I was able to go out and play against the University of Miami in two months time.

"I wasn't nervous going into the surgery, but I was going into the season, because I had pains and discomforts from the surgery, and in the back of your mind, you're thinking, Am I doing severe damage to my back? Am I going to leave the game paralyzed?

"We played Miami on September 8. I had a big flak jacket to protect my back. Defensively we played great, and offensively we did some good things. That was a big win for us to start the year."

The second game was against USC in the Los Angeles Coliseum. For the impressionable freshman, Ricky Nattiel, getting to California was as memorable as playing.

Ricky Nattiel: "I had never, ever been on a plane in my life. That was the very first time. Never been close to a plane. Never wanted to get on a plane. I was scared to fly. It was no secret. I told pretty much everyone that it was my first time flying. I wasn't ashamed of being afraid. I wasn't the only one. Some guys who had flown were still scared.

"Once we got to the airport, I had to accept that we were going to California. So I was a little edgy. We had a layover in Houston, and that broke it up a little. Once I got there, I was fine. I adjust to things quickly.

"I remember the night before the game, I was out with Patrick Miller and a couple other guys, and it was something for a 17-year-old to take it all in, and as we walked down the street, here comes Marcus Allen zooming by us in one of his convertibles. He had the top down, and he was cruising. Marcus had starred at USC, and he knew we were from Florida, and he commented, 'The Trojans are going to beat you tomorrow.'

"That made us laugh and pumped us up."

Florida had the game won with 46 seconds on a field goal by Bobby Raymond, his fourth, but USC, aided by two major Florida penalties, tied it up on the final two plays of the game. What should have been the final play was an incomplete pass just as the clock ran out, but Florida was called for having too many men on the field, and since a game cannot end on a penalty, USC got another chance, and this time it connected for a 25-yard touchdown pass.

Florida was lucky to come away with a 19-19 tie, because USC blew the extra point at the end after a low snap.

Wayne Peace: "To me, that was a huge, huge letdown. To me, we were clearly the better team. We went out there, and we didn't play as aggressively as we should have. We were very conservative. We were playing out in LA, playing USC in the Coliseum. I remember we recovered a fumble towards the end of the second period. Instead of attempting to be aggressive and throw the ball at the end zone, we ran three times and kicked a field goal. I don't know if they were trying to protect my back, but we were not aggressive throwing the ball. At the end of the game we got their long touchdown, and it just…who knows?

"We should have won it. We should have kicked their behinds. We were lucky we didn't lose. I remember being really ticked off that flight home."

Ricky Nattiel: "I got to play in the game and had a few receptions. Without a doubt, that was a game we should have won. It was almost as though USC was playing for the tie and was happy with the tie. Because we definitely outplayed them. And though it was better than a loss, it kind of made the flight home a little bitter."

Indiana State in the rain at Florida Field was next, and Florida did not take the lead against the prohibitive underdogs until the fourth quarter when Wayne Peace drove the Gators 80 yards down the field. He hit Joe Henderson with a 15 yarder to win the game 17-13.

Ricky Nattiel: " We don't care to admit it, but that was a game we obviously were supposed to win, and we kind of took them for granted, and the weather was bad, and they were pumped. They played tough, and they played very well. Once they saw they were still in it, they kept fighting."

Wayne Peace: "If we play them ten times, we beat them by fifty points every time. But this time we barely got out of there alive. We were clearly better, but it was raining and things didn't happen. It was terrible. We were lucky to win the dang thing."

Ricky Nattiel: "Wayne threw a touchdown to Joe Henderson to win it, and so we pulled it out, but Coach Pell really chewed us out in the locker room after the game."

Against Mississippi State, Wayne Peace went 21-34 for 260 yards, placing him in sixth place in SEC history for total yards, right behind Archie Manning. On the ground, the Gators could only gain 63 yards, until John L. Williams broke a run for an 70-yard touchdown as Florida broke it open, 35-12.

Wayne Peace: "That was a game where we finally opened up, threw the ball, and I felt good about it, and I felt we should keep moving forward.

"I have some VHS tapes at the house, and about three months ago my six-year-old son said, 'Dad, can we watch some of your games?' We popped in a tape of that Mississippi State game, and I watched John L.'s run. It wasn't just 'take the ball and run.' He was breaking tackles and making cuts. It was just a phenomenal run."

Ricky Nattiel: "John L. was a running back playing fullback. He was one of the best fullbacks ever to play the game. He had the big wide frame, and he had great footwork. He could bust a 70-yard run, and you were not going to catch him.

"You're talking about a guy well over 220 pounds. He had great hands, he ran great routes, and he was a great blocker. He was going to stick you right in the chest.

"He played a long time for the Seattle Seahawks, and he was the same way. And as in the case of Mississippi State, at any time he could break the game open for you."

The Gators traveled to Baton Rouge to play Louisiana State University.

Ricky Nattiel: "What I remember most about playing LSU was that stadium itself, and how hard it was to play there. We played at night, and even before we got there, their fans were so rowdy. They are obnoxious, but in a good way. They are supporting their team, and when you come into that stadium, you can't hear anything, and it was at night, so you can't see anything.

"There's a big ole tiger in a cage as you come out of the tunnel, a big, huge, humongous tiger right there in this cage, and it's the first thing you see when you come out."

In the LSU game of '83, Florida had one of the great goalline stands in its history. With 2:35 left in the game, Florida led 24-17. After a Wayne Peace interception, LSU had first down on the Florida threeyard line. Two runs cost LSU two yards, and then Wilber Marshall, playing with a broken right hand, intercepted a Jeff Wickersham pass in the end zone and ran it out to the 24.

Wayne Peace: "The thing I remember about that game was offensively we threw for something like 190 yards in the first half, and we really were moving the ball. Then we came out in the second half, and we just shut it down. I remember thinking, What are we doing? Why aren't we being more aggressive and going after this defense? We totally changed philosophies, and it just about came back and snakebit us."

"But Wilber Marshall once again saved our behinds."

Ricky Nattiel: "I remember the goal line stand and Wilber Marshall leaping high in the air to intercept a pass. When Wilber made that play, all hell broke loose on the sidelines.

"For me, it was awesome to be around Wilber. When I was in high school, all you heard was, 'Wilber Marshall, Wilber Marshall.' He came into his own in the USC game at Florida Field the year before when I was being recruited. In fact, I was at that game. That day he really started to make a name for himself."

LSU was sure Florida was going to run out the clock. Instead, Ricky Nattiel handed to Neal Anderson, who broke free for a 76-yard touchdown in a 31-17 win.

Ricky Nattiel: "Coach Shanahan, being the mastermind he was, had to have seen something to call that play. It was a double reverse, and I handed it to Neal, and everybody [on LSU] bit, and I'm sure they were half-shocked that we were doing it.

"Neal was an awesome guy. He was from a small town, like I was. He was really down-to-earth, very tough, and very physical. He always, always, always ran the ball hard. Even if it was a one-yard gain, he ran like he just broke a 90-yarder. He tried to give it his all, and that includes blocking. He was a team player."

Wayne Peace: "He went for 76 yards, and nobody touched him. Like I said, Neal could run. This wasn't a play where he had to break a bunch of tackles, like John L.'s run against Mississippi State. This was catch the ball, hit the sideline, and run. Nobody was anywhere near him. You wonder how that happens, but it does sometimes. Neal was a phenomenal football player, but he's an even better human being. I am proud to say I spent time with him."

In a 29-10 win over Vanderbilt, John L. Williams scored all three Florida touchdowns. Senior receiver Dwayne Dixon was injured going into the game, and his replacement, Ricky Nattiel, made a name for himself when he caught five passes for 54 yards.

Wayne Peace: "Ricky was a true freshman, and it's a major step for a true freshman to make an impact. 'Slick Rick'—we called him 'Slick'—was very undisciplined, and I don't mean that in a negative way—he just wasn't sure of what he was doing all the time. He'd be the first to tell you that sometimes he ran the wrong routes. It's part of the growing process, and toward the end of '83 he started coming on, and he gave us an added dimension we needed. He went on to have a great career at Florida and played in the NFL for several years."

Ricky Nattiel: "It was my first start as a Gator, and it was really exciting to have my name called out before the game. That day I scored on a two point conversation. I caught a short dump pass and scored.

"Though Vanderbilt was my first start, I had gotten some playing time in most games. Wayne [Peace] was a senior, and his man was Dwayne Dixon, which was understandable. It would have been difficult for him, being a senior, to have me, a freshman, become his go-to guy. He knew I was a good receiver, because in order to become the backup, I had to prove myself in practice every day. So I think Wayne developed some trust in me, because I always worked hard in practice.

"And granted, Vanderbilt wasn't the toughest opponent for us, but Wayne was a great guy and an awesome leader. He was never known for having a cannon arm, but he was deadly accurate with his passes. He was smart and rarely made mistakes on the field."

Homecoming was against East Carolina, a game Florida was expected to win easily. Wayne Peace, the most efficient quarterback in Florida history, had his worst day, throwing four interceptions. There were also two fumbles. Florida limped home with a 24–17 win, as Neal Anderson scored two touchdowns.

Wayne Peace: "We did not play well at all. I did not play well. I can't tell you why. They were a feisty team, and they played better than us that day, and we were lucky to win the game."

Ricky Nattiel: "We took them lightly, and they were out there giving their all, because a win for them would have made their season. They had everything to gain and nothing to lose.

"Coach Pell would always warn us about those types of teams. He would say, 'Think of how embarrassing it would be to lose at Homecoming.' As a player, you knew we had a far superior team, that we were supposed to win. Even though your coaches tell you, and common sense tells you, 'Anything can happen,' it's hard not to overlook certain opponents, and there is no question, that took place, and it almost bit us.'

After beginning the 1983 season with six wins and a tie, the Gators were rated fifth in the nation. One of Florida's primary stumbling blocks, fourth ranked Auburn, was next. That day there were three bloody events: A Marine base was bombed by terrorists in Lebanon; Grenada was invaded by the United States; and Auburn defeated Florida 28-21, as sophomore Bo Jackson gained 196 yards, including 55-yard and 80-yard touchdown runs.

Wayne Peace: "I remember thinking, I am watching one of the best that has ever and ever will play the game. He was that good.

"We came out, and we really let them take it to us. They led 14-0 at the end of the first quarter. Then we decided to open up and start throwing it, and we moved the heck out of the ball and scored some points.

"Dwayne caught a bunch of passes [nine], and I threw to Ricky, and I threw some to Bee Lang, whose given name was Broughton and who was teeny, about 5'6."

"We really made a game of it in the second half, and it was a fun, exciting game. And I can tell you I really took a beating in that game. My back really started to bother me. I was having a lot of pain in that game.

"We just started too late. You have to understand, there was a clash between Coach Pell and Coach Shanahan. Coach Shanahan was a very innovative mind who wanted to open up and do things. Coach Pell was the old tradition that we're going to be a strong, tough football team that's going to run the football. For years they clashed, quietly, behind the scenes. But to Coach Shanahan's credit, even though Shanahan and I were very close, he never tried to put me between him and Coach Pell as a go-between.

"Before my senior year Coach Shanahan came to me and told me the only reason he was going to coach that year was because I was there, and he didn't want to leave me on my own my senior year.

"Coach Pell and Coach Shanahan were two totally different people, very good people in their own way, but they had different philosophies on how they wanted to get things done. Coach Shanahan was a young guy with all these ideas, and it just wasn't going to happen in that system."

Playing against Auburn, freshman Ricky Nattiel had his eyes on one man: Bo Jackson.

Ricky Nattiel: "I remember watching film of Bo, and of course I had heard about him, and you read about him. And when he showed up, everything they said about him turned out to be true. God, he was running over guys, and running through guys, and running by guys. Granted he was an opponent, but I was standing there watching him in awe. I really was.

"And we didn't have a pushover defense. That's what made him so impressive. That's when I saw Bo was the real deal.

"Bo was the difference, obviously."

Florida, 6-1-1, met 8-0-1 Georgia in a battle that would determine the SEC championship. Florida had lost five years in a row to the Bulldogs and its alumni were getting antsy and belligerent.

Ricky Nattiel: "This was during the streak when we couldn't beat them. And aside from Florida State, this was the biggest game for us. Georgia was either the first or second rivalry, and we couldn't beat them, and that's all the Florida alumni and the fans talked about, because they were tired of going to Jacksonville and having to deal with losing and hearing the Georgia fans."

Florida made it inside the Georgia ten three times. Each time they came away with field goals. The result was a very tough 10-9 loss.

Ricky Nattiel: "We were pumped up for that game. We were ready to stop the drought, but we had difficulty scoring, and then we lost by a point."

Wayne Peace: "There is an interesting story behind this game too. As I told you, I was having a lot of problems with my back against Auburn—I mean a lot of problems.

"We went into the Georgia game and during warmups I couldn't throw the ball. It literally felt like the bones in my back were rubbing together. All week I was stiff. I went out for pre-game warmups, and I literally had to stop throwing, it hurt so bad. I took a knee and waited for the pain to subside, and I remember looking across the field, and Vince Dooley was looking over at me. I thought, What is he thinking right now?

"I got up and went to Coach Shanahan and said, 'Coach, I can't throw the ball.' He said, 'What's wrong?' I said, 'My back. It feels like the bones in my back are going to explode.'

"He went over to Dale Dorminey, the backup, and said, 'Get ready. You're going to have to play.'

"I went into the locker room and sat there a while. Coach said, 'How are you feeling?' I said, 'Let me give it a shot.'

"The game started, and my adrenaline started flowing, and the pain went away. I played scared but I played the whole game. I threw two interceptions that day, and on one of them I had a clear lane to run, but in my mind I didn't want to get hit because I was concerned there was something seriously wrong with my back, and I didn't want to leave the field on a stretcher. So I made a pass I shouldn't have, and it was intercepted.

"As a result, we struggled offensively, and we lost 10-9."

Ricky Nattiel: "What I remember most was the bus ride back to Gainesville. It was dismal. There was a lot of silence.

"That gave us back-to-back losses. Let's put it this way: It was a tough time in Pell-land."

Kentucky was scheduled next, an easy 24-7 victory to break the two-game losing skein.

Ricky Nattiel: "We had lost two games in a row, and we knew we weren't going to lose another one, and Kentucky wasn't that much of a team. Being as we had lost the two previous games, we didn't take them as lightly as we otherwise would have."

Wayne Peace: "We had an open week, and I didn't touch the field, didn't practice, all week. They kept my bad back real quiet. The press didn't know about it. Before the game Coach Pell came to me and said, 'Look, don't do anything where you are going to endanger yourself. Don't get out and run. We just need you out there to lead the team. Be a leader and let the running backs and the linemen take charge of the game.'

"We threw the ball eleven times [Peace finished 9-11 for just 93 yards.] We were clearly a better team that could dominate and win a game."

FSU was the regular season finale, and against the Seminoles, Florida was forced to open up the offense. That day Wayne Peace had one of his greatest days, going 14-20 for 190 yards, finishing his career with 610 completions, a Florida record, beating John Reaves by seven. Florida won big, 53-14.

Wayne Peace: "I knew nothing about the record until it went up on the scoreboard. I knew I was close, because everyone was talking about it, but I am a very private, personal kind of guy. I played the game because I liked it, because I liked being around my buddies, and I liked competing. Statistics and records just were not very important to me."

Ricky Nattiel: "That win over FSU made the losses to Auburn and Georgia a lot easier to swallow. We actually had a little streak going. We had defeated them in '81 and '82. And against FSU, any time you can blow them out, you do it. You don't call off the dogs in that game."

The 53-14 route over archrival FSU was a happy ending to the season, giving Florida an 8-2-1 record and an invitation to the Gator Bowl where eleventh-ranked Florida met tenth-ranked Iowa. The whole week before the Gator Bowl game, it was miserably cold.

Ricky Nattiel: "We went to Daytona the week before the Gator Bowl game to train, and it was freezing. It was my first bowl experience, an exciting time. We stayed on the beach at a hotel. We were looking forward to it. But it was so cold, nobody was moving. There were no people on the beach. It was awful. It was rainy and cold.

"Before the game there was some jawing back and forth going on between us and the Iowa players. They were also down there training, and we'd run into them in different functions and in restaurants. There were only certain places in Daytona where everybody'd go.

"Iowa's horses were Chuck Long and Ronnie Harmon. They were a pretty good team, but what I remember most was that they were absolutely humongous. These guys were big, eating all that food.

"I remember the night of the game we wore long sleeves, layers of clothes, and the Iowa players were out there with their shirts tied up. I guess they were used to the cold."

Wayne Peace: "It was cold that day, and it was miserable. I'm a Florida boy. We were in Florida, but it was NOT Florida weather. We were right there on the river, and I guarantee you the wind chill was in the 20s that night.

"Iowa was a very physical team, and I was having all sorts of problems with my back. I just really struggled in practice. I didn't feel good. It was one of those games where nothing seemed to happen right, but we were able to win the game because our defense played so great."

Ricky Nattiel: "It was hard to throw the ball, but we won the game, [14-6]. It was more of a running game that night.

"Wilber [Marshall] had a great career-ending game. He was all over the place. I don't think the cold bothered him too much. He knew it would be a running game, and we forced them into a situation where they had to throw a little bit, and we had them coming to the weak side, where Wilber was waiting for them. That was right down Wilber's alley.

"I remember being so happy to get that game over with. I wanted to get back into the locker room so badly."

For the first time in the school's history, the University of Florida had finished in the top ten, ending its season sixth in the nation.

Ricky Nattiel: "Oh, that meant a lot. I was recruited in '82, and that year they did all right ['84], as Pell was starting to build the program, and we were a pretty young team in '83. We had a lot of freshmen, sophomores, and juniors, so we knew with the guys coming back, we were on to something.

"And it was exciting knowing that, because we knew the talent we had. We knew we had our running backs coming back. We knew we had a line. Our defense was young, but solid.

"The two big men we were losing were Wayne Peace and Wilber Marshall, but we had great backups for Wilber. We weren't worried about that. Really, the only position we were uncertain about was quarterback. Going into the next year, we were excited."

With a 9-2-1 record and an impressive Gator Bowl win, Charlie Pell had done everything he had promised.

Wayne Peace: "You have to go back to when we came in as freshmen. The year before Florida was 0-10-1, which tells you the program was at rock bottom. During the course of the next four years, myself and all my teammates and the people after us came together, and we sweated, and we bled, and we cried, and we fought. At the end of my four years, we were the number six team in America. That was a heck of a four-year run. It wasn't the SEC championship, which everyone wanted, but you have to crawl before you can run. We really got that crawling process started."

Wayne Peace didn't get drafted into the NFL, and he signed with the Tampa Bay Bandits to play for coach Steve Spurrier. He and Spurrier didn't get along, and he left football and went into the insurance business in Lakeland.

Wayne Peace: "I was very fortunate. After graduation, I played one year in the United Stated Football League for Steve Spurrier and the Bandits. I didn't like it at all. He and I are just two totally different people.

"First of all let me say, I think the guy has the most phenomenal offensive mind bar none I've ever been around in my life. I would sit there and just be amazed. But I am a feisty, fiery kind of person. If you want to coach me, talk to me, work with me, and I'm gonna bust my butt for you. But don't ridicule me and try to make me look bad in front of other people. You see that with Spurrier and his quarterbacks. He ridicules his quarterbacks in front of the press, in front of other players. You have to have a different kind of personality and mindset to play for him. If you have a feisty kind of personality, you're not going to survive. You're going to be mad at him all the time. So it was not a good experience for me at all. But having said that, I made enough money playing the one year that I could come back to Lakeland and start my insurance business. I own my own State Farm agency in Lakeland.

"Here I am, forty-years-old, and if I want to work today, I work. If I don't, I don't. My life is just great, and I owe so much of that to the University of Florida and the contacts I made while I was there.

"People ask me all the time, 'Don't you wish you were still playing?' I say, 'Absolutely not. I am happy sitting here doing what I'm doing and loving my family and enjoying life.'"

fifty-one

The Last Days of Charlie Pell

Charlie Pell had been under investigation for recruiting and other irregularities since March of 1982 when the parents of a player Pell sought to recruit told the NCAA that he had offered the sister of that player a job if the player agreed to enroll at Florida. Players were questioned about fancy cars, money in envelopes in lockers, selling their free game tickets for cash, and dozens of other infractions. Pell stoutly denied any wrong-doing. When the *St. Petersburg Times* investigated the 1981 team, it found that half of the 140 scholarship or walk-on players associated with that team were in academic trouble. It also found that Pell had a $4,000 slush fund and had enlisted a long list of boosters who provided favors to players. As a result, in September of 1983, the NCAA passed a new rule prohibiting alums and boosters from recruiting off-campus. Prospective recruits were barred from even attending booster club meetings.

Unknown to the players, Coach Pell had submitted his resignation to University of Florida President Marshall Criser on August 26, 1984, five days before the opening game against Miami. The resignation, which was to take effect at the end of the season, was sitting on Criser's desk, as yet not accepted. But as summer was turning into fall, the players knew something was going to happen. Exactly what, they weren't certain.

Ricky Nattiel: "I knew going into the 1984 season that Coach Pell was being investigated. In the off-season we knew the school was under investigation. I started to hear stuff, so I knew it was taking place.

"It was very upsetting, because we didn't know what the outcome was going to be. We just didn't know. We knew it was taking place, and personally I didn't know how it would affect us. Maybe we wouldn't be on television.

We might not have been able to go to a bowl, that type of penalty, but at the time it was all talk. When we found out an investigation was taking place, it was one of those clouds that hung over your head.

"I know it affected Coach Pell, but him being the way he was, he tried not to let it show. He was the type of coach, 'Let's not worry about that. We're going to come together. We're going to stick together. And everything's going to be fine.' Who knows what it was really doing to him inside? I'm sure he knew a lot more about what was going on that we did. Definitely more than I did, that's for sure.

"As a team, we knew we had a good ballclub. We had a lot of talent. Our goal in '84 was to win the national championship. We decided to put our worries about the investigation behind us and go out and play, because it appeared that the way the investigation was going, even if something were to happen, it wasn't going to be decided in '84.'"

Going into the 1984 season, the Florida team had hopes of both an undefeated season and a national championship. Led by senior quarterback Dale Dorminey, Coach Pell and his squad were loaded.

Ricky Nattiel: "Dale Dorminey had been Wayne's backup, and this was his chance to finally run the team. Dale reminded me a lot of Wayne. He didn't throw a deep ball, but he was real smart, and he was a crisp passer. He wasn't going to make mistakes. He was going to find an open guy. Dale had a good touch on his ball, and he was great to play for. He had a great attitude.

"But the Wednesday of game week, Dale got really badly injured. It was three days before the opening game, and we had lost our starter. We thought, Man, what are we going to do now?"

The first game of the '84 season was played in Tampa against one of the country's powerhouses, tenth-rated Miami, coached by Jimmy Johnson and quarterbacked by All-American Bernie Kosar. Starting for Florida was a green freshman nobody ever heard of by the name of Kerwin Bell.

Ricky Nattiel: "Nobody ever heard of him, not even us! Yup, that was the case.

"At the beginning of the year, Kerwin was probably sixth string. He was a walk-on, a no-name. As I said, nobody had ever heard of him. He worked his way up to second-string, and when Dale got hurt, he was the starter. It was a shock for everybody. No one knew what to expect because the season was three days away, and he hadn't had any time to work out with the first team.

"We knew he had the ability. We knew he had the talent. It was just unproven."

After the 1983 season Charlie Pell, knowing he had to find a replacement for Wayne Peace, recruited the four best quarterbacks in the state of Florida. But during practice in the spring a walk-on quarterback by the name of Kerwin Bell began to make his presence felt. Bell had started the year eighth and last on the depth chart for quarterback, but by the end of fall practice, he was second behind Dorminey, a five-year senior. When Dorminey injured himself shortly before the opening game, Bell was named the starter.

For a walk-on quarterback who wasn't recruited by a single college anywhere in the country, it was the end of a wild ride to the top. That Kerwin Bell ended up the University of Florida quarterback for four years was a testament to his skill, determination, and belief in himself.

Kerwin Bell: "I grew up in Mayo, Florida, which is almost half-way betwen Gainesville and Tallahassee, between the Gators and the Seminoles. Mayo is the only town in Lafayette County, and so everyone in the county goes to Lafayette High School.

"Nobody had ever gotten a scholarship from Mayo in any sport in the history of the school so the coaches from the colleges never came by. The only coach who came and watched me play was from Valdosta State. He attended a game and told my coach if the big colleges didn't recruit me or didn't sign me, then Valdosta would definitely want me.

"Neither Florida nor Florida State ever watched me play. They signed players from the big schools. When signing day came, no one offered me a scholarship, not even Valdosta, which is forty-five minutes from my home. If Valdosta had offered me a scholarship, I probably would have gone there. I thank God they didn't offer me a scholarship. The head coach decided to go with some junior college quarterback instead of me.

"Florida State had asked me to come there as a walk-on, but my girl-friend [now his wife] was intending to go to Santa Fe College in Gainesville, and I wanted to be with her, so I took my ACTs and got into the University Florida as a regular student.

"She ended up also getting accepted to the University of Florida, and she was a four-year majorette in the band.

"The main thing was that I wanted to be a Gator. I knew I would be happy at the University of Florida. And I never played a day when I wanted to be somewhere else.

"As a boy I loved to watch Wes Chandler, Cris Collinsworth, Mike Mularkey, Wayne Peace—all the guys I thought were good players who played in the late 1970s.

"I decided to walk on as a freshman in 1983. I was from a small town, and I really hadn't played in big-time competition, so I wasn't really sure of myself. I thought I could compete—if I only played one year, I was going to be happy. I was willing to work to do that.

"I was eighth on the depth chart, right at the bottom. There were six scholarship quarterbacks and two walk-ons. I was number 8.

"The three top quarterbacks they recruited were Pat Pinner out of Lakeland Kathleen. He was 6'4", 195 pounds, a big kid who was the All-South quarterback. Derrick Crudup was a 6'3", 215 pounder, one of the best athletes I'd ever been around. He ran a 4.4 forty. He went on to play five years in the NFL with the Oakland Raiders as a safety. And the third quarterback was a real big kid, a left-hander from St. Petersburg.

"Crudup could really throw the ball, but I knew I could compete with the other two. They didn't throw the ball well, and after that first fall, both of them moved to other positions. Pinner moved to tight end, and the other guy went to the offensive line.

"We had scrimmages at night during the fall, and they would let the young guys play in them, and I always played well, and so it came down to me and Crudup.

"In 1983 I was a redshirt under Wayne Peace. Mike Shanahan watched me in those scrimmages, and when he left Florida at the end of the year, he told some of the coaches that I would be the next quarterback.

"At the start of the 1984 season I was around fifth string. The other four were scholarship guys Coach Pell was going to look at to replace Wayne. He had a duel among those four, and they really went at it. I tried to get reps, but he only was looking at those four.

"In the Orange and Blue game, they split up the squad. Two of the quarterbacks were on the Orange team, and two on the Blue. I was the third-team guy on one of the teams.

"Galen Hall, our new offensive coordinator, told me before the game, 'When you get in there, do your best, because you may only get one or two series.'

"Around the third quarter he got me in. We were behind by a few points, and I led the team on an 80-yard drive, and I went three for three and threw a touchdown pass, which put us up in the game. The guy who caught the pass made a super play, and I can't even remember his name.

"That was my only series. I told people, 'If I could do that every time, I could be Joe Montana.'

"During the summer after the Orange and Blue game, Coach Pell entered me as a 'dark-horse' candidate.

"And right after that game, Valdosta State offered me a full scholarship. They wanted me to transfer. But I decided to stick it out. I thought I could play at the division I college level, and so I stayed during the summer.

"Then one of the four quarterbacks didn't make his grades and failed out of school. He was going to summer school to get his grades up, but he didn't do it, so it moved me up to the top four. When they went into the fall with a four-quarterback race, I was one of the four.

"They graded out after every game, and the week before the Miami game, I graded out second-highest. Dale Dorminey, a fifth-year senior, graded out the highest, and he was going to be the starter.

"Derrick Crudup was asked to move to defensive back or to receiver, and he transferred to Oklahoma and played safety there.

"So I was second. On Monday before we played the Hurricanes, the defending national champions, the coaches announced the outcome of the quarterback race.

"I was happy to be second. The next day we were about ten minutes from the end of practice, and Dale Dorminey was running the option on the goal line. We were wearing shoulder pads and shorts, and you weren't supposed to be hitting, and somebody fell into Dale's knee and blew out his ACL, and that was it for his football career, because he was a senior.

"So then I stepped into the number one huddle, and I began to run plays. At the time I didn't know Dale was through, because he walked off and no one knew it was that bad.

"In the dining hall that night Coach Hall came up to me and said, 'Kerwin, Dale's out for the year, and you're going to be starting in four days against Miami.'

"I was scared to death. I couldn't eat. The food would come back up. I started to watch a lot of film, I prayed, and I did everything I could to try to get ready for that first game.

"The game was played in Tampa. Neal Anderson, the great running back, was my roommate. I think the coaches put him with me to keep me calm. And Neal did the opposite: he tried to scare me, telling me how big the crowd was going to be. Because I had never played a game in front of more than two hundred people.

"I was nervous, especially when we started the Miami game on the four-yard line. Our guy bobbled the kickoff, and we got it on the four!

"But after being out there two or three series, I really calmed down, and we were in the game the whole time. And what defined my career—what gave the team confidence in this little ole redshirt freshman, was the last drive of the game.

"We were behind, and I led them on a 70-yard drive—we converted two fourth-down plays—and [with 45 seconds left in the game] I threw a touchdown pass [to Frankie Neal] that put us one point up. [After the extra point, Florida led 20-18.]

"The play was a regular fade route. Frankie was down on the goal line with a defender right in his face, and Frankie just shook him off and ran for the corner of the back of the end zone, and I lobbed it up to the area—a timing throw—and we executed it great. Frankie was right where he was supposed to be, and so was the ball.

"After that established me, the guys felt, 'Hey, this guy can play.'

"It was my first game, and I thought we'd won it, and then Bernie Kosar took Miami down the field [72 yards in 49 seconds], and he threw a touchdown pass, and we ended up getting beat [32-20]. That was a tough game."

Ricky Nattiel: "Bernie was good. I give him credit. We were playing not to lose. We were in a prevent-type defense. A buddy of mine, Kevin Murphy, who played for the Tampa Bay Bucs a long time, said, 'The only thing a prevent defense does is prevent you from winning.'

"It was awful standing on the sideline watching Miami march down the field. I can remember Frankie Neal and I were standing next to each other, and we kept saying, 'They're going to make a play. They're gonna stop them. Somebody is going to make a play to stop this drive.' And every time we said that, Bernie'd make another completion. It was tough to watch. As they got closer and closer to our goal line, we saw the game slowly but surely slipping away."

After Miami scored, Florida got the ball back for one last desperate try, and Kerwin Bell threw a long pass that was intercepted by Colbert Bain of Miami and then run back for a 59-yard touchdown.

Ricky Nattiel: "After they scored, we were in desperation. We needed to score, and they knew we'd be throwing. They were just sitting back waiting. That was a very tough loss. It was the opening game, and it was a game we should have won.

"But it did a lot for Kerwin, because he had a great game, and it let him know, 'Hey, I can do this.' We hadn't lost to some pushover, and it showed us that even though we lost, we were going to be all right."

In a season of high expectations, the 32-20 loss to Miami was followed by a disappointing 21-21 tie with LSU. Proving that the Miami game was no fluke, Kerwin Bell was an impressive 14-24 for 194 yards against LSU.

Florida trailed 21-14 but with 4:55 left in the game, the Gators tied the score after a 10-yard touchdown run by Lorenzo Hampton.

Ricky Nattiel: "Lorenzo was a mix between John L. Williams and Neal Anderson. He was smaller than John L., but just as aggressive. He ran real good routes, was real physical, was a hard worker, and he had a great, great attitude. Lorenzo was a senior and one of the leaders of the team in '84."

Having already lost once, Charlie Pell decided to play it safe. With the score 14-13, he went for the extra point instead of a two-point conversion.

Ricky Nattiel: "I won't say it bothered us, but I think we would have liked to have taken the gamble. As a player you always want to go for it. But we had lost the week before, and Coach didn't want two losses in a row. Had we won the previous week, the thought process probably would have been different.

"This was our home opener, and I guess he didn't want to lose it. But I think if we had gone for it, we would have made it. As a player, there's a lot less pressure than there is on the coach. I know personally I wanted to go for it."

LSU could have won it, but with 41 seconds left in the game they missed a 46-yard field goal.

Ricky Nattiel: "We had our fingers crossed. Here was the possibility of our going 0 and 2."

Kerwin Bell: "LSU was probably my toughest game in the four years I played. For some reason I didn't play my best. I struggled. I remember throwing an interception, which was costly.

"My primary receivers were Ray McDonald and Ricky Nattiel. Ray made some big plays for us that year. Up to that point, he hadn't played much, but he really came on fast.

"But my most consistent receiver, the guy who did the most for my career, was Ricky. Our names sort of go together in Florida, because that's who I threw the ball to more than anybody, and he always made great catches. Ricky was just a fantastic receiver. He wasn't big, but he was tough, and he had unbelievable speed.

"Ricky and I came in as freshmen. He was a scholarship player, so he played a little his freshman year. That year I red-shirted. But the next three years, we practiced a lot together. I just had a good feel for him. Quarterbacks like certain receivers, and he was a guy I had confidence in and really depended on."

One of the highlights of the 63–21 romp over Tulane was a 60-yard field goal kicked by senior kicker Chris Perkins.

Ricky Nattiel: "Chris was a great kicker. He was very dependable. It was one of those games where you thought, Why not try it? He was kind of pumped to try."

Against Tulane at Florida Field, Neal Anderson ran for three touchdowns, including a 63-yard end around.

Ricky Nattiel: "Neal was real hard-nosed. Every time he ran there was always the possibility of his breaking one."

Kerwin Bell: "Neal was a fantastic athlete. He was big and strong and fast. Neal shared time with Lorenzo Hampton, and John L. Williams was at fullback that year. We had some unbelievable running backs, an unbelievable amount of ability back there that helped me out as a freshman.

And that year we had a great offensive line. Against Tulane, we put up a lot of points."

Against Tulane, Florida gained 302 yards on the ground, and ran up 486 yards in all. The team was becoming the national power everyone had predicted it would be, but the players had an uneasy sense that the Tulane game might be Coach Pell's last.

Ricky Nattiel: "The word was out. The reporters knew what was going on, and they were hounding us about it. Things were starting to get edgy in the camp, not knowing what was about to happen. You hear things are about to happen, but you don't KNOW. You hear he could go down any time. But yet it's not official. You say, it could happen today. And then it doesn't, and then you start to wonder.

"The day after the Tulane game I can remember someone saying there was a mandatory players' meeting in the players' lounge. That's when Coach told us he was going to have to resign.

"He said it was because of the investigation, as a way to lessen the penalty. He said if he continued the penalty would be worse. He said that he would have had to resign one way or the other, either then or at the end of the season, so he chose to resign then.

"I remember a lot of emotion in the room. A few guys cried. Oh yeah, they cried. There was a lot of uncertainty, a lot of emotion going into the middle of a season in which we thought we were going to be able to run the table.

"Now we've lost a game, we've tied a game, and we've lost our coach. There were too many losses going on here."

The word was that the NCAA had been after Charlie Pell from the time he was a coach at Clemson. Apparently, it had caught up with him at Florida.

Lee McGriff, who was Charlie Pell's assistant coach from 1979 through 1982, feels he knows the primary reason the NCAA found out so much about Pell: in McGriff's opinion, some of the long list of assistant coaches whom he had ruthlessly browbeaten and then freely fired had gotten their revenge by turning on him.

Lee McGriff: "I coached for him in '79, '80, '81, and '82. It was unbelievably difficult working for him. He was a taskmaster—an unreasonable, overbearing, intimidating boss. He intimidated the players as well, but he was very good to them too. He made sure they had the finest facilities and the finest this and the finest that. So from that standpoint, he was very good to the players. For the coaches, he was relentless. We just worked ungodly hours. He constantly threatened you about your job. He was a very difficult person.

"I've said it before: if my son ever wanted to play for Charlie Pell, absolutely. If he wanted to COACH under Charlie Pell, I would tie him up to a tree and say, 'You cannot.' Good to the players. Miserable to the coaches.

"He had some great, incredible traits, though. I do want to say that. He was a blink of an eye from being a great, great coach. But his own insecurities and his phobias and paranoia prevented that. If anything went wrong, it was YOUR fault. He was always so afraid that he'd fail. We're talking about an ultra-high level. Looking back, it was that insecurity that got him fired. If he could have relaxed some and trusted some people...but he couldn't, because he didn't trust himself.

"He was forced to quit in the middle of the '84 season. What happened was that he had a pretty ruthless reputation. He left Clemson with the posse right on his back, and when he came here, so did the posse. That seed was planted. They were after him.

"And during my four years, he fired about thirteen coaches. Those firings were pretty ruthless. And these guys came back and got him. He left too many dead bodies on the side of the road.

"On one hand, some of the things he did that were not technically legal weren't so awful. In that business, it's like they say, 'There is honor among thieves.' So the majority of things were relatively insignificant, but the NCAA wanted his neck. I'll always believe that some of those coaches went to the NCAA and sang like birds to get him back for firing them.

"I was able to stay sane because I was at the University of Florida. This was where I wanted to be. Mike Shanahan and Mike Heimerdinger came in, and they have remained great friends. They are wonderful guys and very talented coaches. And we were young. We had the same evil force we were fighting [Pell], and so we had a common bond that brought us together, and we started winning football games."

As Lee McGriff indicated, no single count amounted to a fireable offense, but the NCAA interviewed and searched until it amassed 107 counts against him.

Among the main allegations:

* Ten walk-on players lived free in the athletic dorm in 1980 and 1981.

* An assistant coach promised to help get the sister of a player into Florida if the prospect went to Florida.
* Pell had more recruiters on the road that the eight assistants allowed.
* Pell arranged with a professor to give his students easy grades.
* The university bought a truck for the father of a recruit.
* The players practiced football in the off-season, disguising them as classes.
* Pell's players sold their complimentary tickets to boosters. (A common practice.)
* The players got cash awards from boosters for playing well in games.
* A dozen alums were accused of illegally helping Pell recruit.
* One non-alum, George Steinbrenner, who over the years has made numerous generous donations to the school, was even cited for paying for an eye operation for the mother of a recruit in 1976, and this was BEFORE Pell became coach.

Even though not one of the 107 infractions could be traced directly back to Pell, Charlie Pell elected to step down.

Red Mitchum: "If you want my opinion, I think the NCAA was after Charlie when he came to Florida for what he did at Clemson. I think they were going to get him one way or another regardless of what he did. He had 100 counts against him, but most of them were so trivial—a coach buying a kid a hamburger, a coach giving a kid a ride downtown, everything like that.

"It was so sad."

Rather than stand and fight, Pell chose to protect his assistants and to end the embarrassment for the university, and on September 16, 1984, he abruptly resigned as head coach. Galen Hall was named to replace him.

Said Pell, "I regret the necessity of this action and recognize the drive to win under the circumstances a few years ago led me to make mistakes and to inappropriately delegate authority in some instances. For this, I recognize my mistakes, regret them, and apologize to the University of Florida and Gator fans everywhere. I take full responsibility."

After his resignation, the NCAA reduced the 107 infractions to 59. The NCAA said it would wait until the end of the 1984 season to hand down its punishment.

Wayne Peace: "It was a shame. I hated it. Coach Pell told me one time, 'The only mistake I made in this whole thing was admitting to everything.' He said, 'I even admitted to things I didn't do, trying to protect my other coaches.'

"He said, 'I went to the administration and said, 'I'm the head coach. I'll take the fall for everything. Leave my other guys alone.' After he took the fall, they got rid of the other guys anyway.

"He looked me in the eye and told me, 'That went against everything I've ever been taught. I was taught to fight. I rolled over to take the fall for everybody.'

"I'm convinced that if he would have stayed and fought, he could have coached there for as long as he wanted to, and good things would have happened. It's all water under the bridge now."

Bob Hewko: "Coach Pell was a great guy. He loved football, loved the game. He took a hit for the investigation. He shouldered all the blame, and then he got blackballed, which I don't understand to this day. It hurts me that he wasn't able to get back into the game. Coaches do bad things all the time, and they're back coaching. For some reason, Charlie Pell never got a shot to come back.

"I talked to him a couple of days before he passed away [on May 29, 2001, of cancer at the age of 60]. He told me when he got Mike Shanahan, he would only have him for a couple of years. He knew he was that good.

"It was amazing. He didn't talk about anything but football. He was coughing the whole time, wheezing and coughing. He'd have to take breaks between breaths, and then he'd get back right in the conversation talking about football.

"He talked about Galen Hall and Spurrier. He thought Galen and Steve were really great. He explained to me that when they knew he was going to go on probation, he told Galen how to make up for the loss of scholarships. He said, 'In the state of Florida you can always get talented skill-position players—wide-outs, quarterbacks, running backs. He said, 'The thing you have to do is to stock up on linemen who you can develop. Because you're probably not going to get the top guys, because you're on probation. So you take a ton of medium-level guys who you know can develop on the line. And then when you get off probation, you can fill in with the skill positions later.'

"I don't think Galen took his advice. Galen got to ride a lot of the players who were already there. Then after that it was a big fall-off."

Kerwin Bell: "Charlie Pell was the best coach I ever played under, and I only played three games under him. When I went on to my professional career, if I got cut, he always wrote me a letter, called me and encouraged me. He was a guy who really cared about you as a person. Charlie was such a great person. He and his wife Ward both knew your parents' name, and they never forgot that.

"I tell you, we had some tough characters during that time. We recruited some guys that it took a man to control—to me, half the guys on the team weren't afraid of anybody. If you pointed a gun at them, they weren't going to be afraid. But when Charlie Pell spoke, they listened. They respected him. The way he talked to you, the way he presented himself when he was talking to you, you had to believe that he was the man in charge.

"He was a true leader. Everybody understood that whatever he said went, and there was no ifs, ands or buts.

"We had a five-year reunion with him in '89, and we surprised him. His friends and former players went to see him and Ward. We surprised them with a big reunion.

"He had great charisma, great ability to get people involved, and he helped build the University of Florida. He did a super job of bringing back the boosters and the alumni—getting everybody involved. Coach Spurrier took it to another level, but we all have to remember where it started, and that was with Coach Pell."

After resigning, Charlie Pell sold real estate in Pensacola, Florida. He also had a license to sell insurance, and he worked for a company that recruited and handled employees for small and medium-size Florida companies. Pell would never again be hired to coach football at the college level.

By 1994 he didn't want to live any longer. He walked graveyards, looking at the headstones. He bought a casket. He named his pallbearers.

On February 2, 1994, one day after his 25th wedding anniversary, he drove into the woods near Jacksonville, sedated himself with vodka and sleeping pills, and ran a rubber hose from the exhaust pipe of his car into the back window.

Pell had sent a map to a friend so he could locate the body, and when the friend got there, Pell was standing by the car throwing up.

Asked why he had failed at suicide, Pell said, "I tried too hard."

After he survived he became a spokesman for depression awareness. He moved back to Alabama, and the Alabama Department of Mental Health and Mental Retardation made him a board member.

Then he got cancer. And not even Charlie Pell could beat that.

fifty-two
An SEC Championship is Taken Away

Florida was 1-1-1 when Galen Hall took over for Charlie Pell as "interim head coach." Hall had been an assistant coach at the University of Oklahoma for eighteen years when he was hired by Pell in February to be Florida's offensive coordinator. Becoming head coach had not been in his plans. He had been happy in his job as offensive coordinator.

Kerwin Bell: "Galen didn't have a really strong ego in that he didn't come in and try to change everything. He was a guy who came in and said, 'Hey, this is working.' And he left alone what Coach Pell had set up, our itinerary, the way we practiced, the way we went about getting prepared for a game. Coach Hall just said, 'Hey, let's continue to do what's been going right.' And we went from there. He really made it a lot easier on the players to just continue to play the way we had."

Ricky Nattiel: "When they decided to make Coach Hall the interim head coach, we had a couple leaders of the team who stood up and said, 'This is a time where we're going to have to come together as a team.'

"Galen Hall was very different from Coach Pell and from Coach Shanahan, who were both stern and hard, though Shanahan was stern in a different way than Pell.

"Galen was really laid back, really, really, really easy to just let it all hang out, and for me, I can honestly say that when Coach Hall was named head coach, that was when my career started to blossom. Because that's how I play. That's when I'm at my best, when I feel like, if you make a mistake, that's cool, you come back and do it better the next time. Not, 'Oh my God, oh my God, oh my God. What now?'

"Coach Pell was our leader without a doubt. He was the guy who built the program. He was the one responsible for the players in that room. He was the disciplinarian. He was the one who kept the superstars in line. There was no question about how we got to where we were.

"But from a personal standpoint as far as my performance, when he stepped down and Coach Hall took over, I felt a lot of pressure being released. And I wasn't the only one who felt that way. Once Coach Hall took over, the attitude from the players was totally different. Not necessarily better, but it was a more relaxed environment. Guys started to play that way. And that was another reason for us to come together.

"Me personally, I was a lot more relaxed. I was able to just go out and play football and not worry about making mistakes.

"Coach Hall fell into the position. He was the interim, and basically he went with what we had. He really didn't change a thing. He was the offensive coordinator anyway. He let the defensive coordinator run the defense. He let the talent speak for itself, because we were a very, very talented football team."

Galen Hall turned out to be the perfect replacement for Charlie Pell. The players relaxed and started to have some fun, and they would go on to win the remaining eight games on the 1984 schedule.

The first game under Coach Hall was a 27-12 win over Mississippi State. Ricky Nattiel, freed from the pressure of playing under martinet Charlie Pell, ran wild, returning three punts for 120 yards, including a 67-yard touchdown run. Lorenzo Hampton had a 44-yard TD run, and Neal Anderson had the first TD reception of his career.

On defense, Tim Newton and Alonzo Johnson held the Bulldogs to just 46 yards in the air and only one rushing touchdown.

The next game, against powerful Syracuse University at Florida Field, was a litmus test for the rest of the season, and the Gators passed it easily, shutting out the Orangemen 16-0, the first goose-egging by a Florida team since 1978.

Kerwin Bell: "They were a good team, and I thought we played a good game. We scored early [on a Bobby Raymond field goal]. But our defense played super that day." [They held the Orangemen to only 148 total yards, 47 yards rushing.]

Ricky Nattiel: "Syracuse came to Gainesville expecting to win. They were a very good ballclub. They were pumped. I remember they had a bad-ass cover guy who was supposed to be pretty good, and in that game I took the opening kickoff and ran back a ball about fifty yards to midfield, and we went on to score from there.

"We shut them out. Tim [Newton] and Alonzo [Johnson] and Patrick Miller were outstanding. We were loaded on defense."

The next game was played against Tennessee in Knoxville before 94,016, the largest crowd ever to see a Florida game. Florida scored four of the first five times it had the ball. At the end of the first quarter Kerwin Bell hit Frankie Neal for a 50-yard touchdown pass.

John L. Williams ran for 100 yards and caught four passes for 96 yards, including a 59-yard touchdown. Neal Anderson ran for 178 yards, including an 80-yard touchdown run.

Kerwin Bell: "It was an offensive show, that's for sure. Tennessee had a great offensive team. They had great fans. It was back and forth the whole game.

"I made one of the best throws I made that whole freshman year that day. Frankie [Neal] ran down the sidelines, and he scored from pretty far out.

"At the end our offense made four or five crucial plays that helped us win, because they would come back and score, and then we'd come back and score. John L. Williams finally broke a draw play, made an unbelievable [59-yard] run, and we were able to hold on [to a 43-30 win] at the end. That's a lot of points."

This was an exciting BIG-play offense. Kerwin Bell had a lot of weapons at his disposal.

Ricky Nattiel: "We had three running backs who could have started for anybody, Neal, John L., and Lorenzo. And we had backups like Joe Henderson and James Massey, who also could have started for anybody. We had an offensive line of Lomas Brown, Jeff Zimmerman, and Crawford Ker, the "Great Wall of Florida" is what they called them. It was tough to be a receiver on this team, because how could you not run the ball? All these guys could break it at any time. We could control the football any time we wanted to.

"But when we wanted to throw the ball, we had myself and Frankie

Neal, so we had weapons, and we could score at any time on any given play through the air or on the ground, which is what was expected.

"And when we relaxed and started having some fun, our talent started to show up. We felt, this is where we are supposed to be.

"We felt like we were not ever going to lose a game."

Homecoming was against the University of Cincinnati, a game for running up statistics, and Florida did that, gaining 578 yards all told in the 48-17 win. In that game John L. Williams, Neal Anderson, and James Massey, who subbed for Lorenzo Hampton, each ran for over a hundred yards.

Kerwin Bell: "James Massey was one of the most highly recruited backs. He didn't ever have that great of a career, though he showed flashes—two or three great games in his career. He was a good, tough player, who usually played on the specialty teams. He probably didn't ever get the opportunity that he needed. He was a straight line guy who could really pound it in there."

Auburn and Bo Jackson came next at Auburn in front of a record crowd of 73,397 at Florida Field. Before the game Auburn coach Pat Dye, who himself one day would be ejected from the ranks of college coaching for not playing by the rules, made a comment about "Florida's professional players." The Gator players took notice and seethed.

Ricky Nattiel: "There were allegations that some of the players supposedly were getting paid, but nothing was ever proven. It was just allegations, and Coach Dye made one of those digs, and it became a wall quote. We would take quotes from the opposing teams and pin them to the bulletin board just outside the locker room, and you better believe Coach Dye made the quote board. It was a dig, and the dig cost him."

Behind a massive front four, Florida's arsenal of power runners pounded the Tigers into submission, winning 24-3. The Florida defense was awesome, holding fearsome Auburn to only 117 yards on the ground. Bo Jackson, in his first game back since dislocating a shoulder, could gain only 16 yards in five carries. He then took himself out of the game.

Ricky Nattiel: "We made Bo Jackson quit that game. They absolutely tore his 'A' up. They were hitting him SO hard. It spilled over from the year before when Bo had the big game. Not taking anything from Bo, but our defense was pumped.

"All they talked about was getting the guy, and that had to be the best I ever saw them play, without a doubt.

"Bo was one of the best backs in the nation, one of the best ever, and our guys were hoping Auburn would hand him the football! And every time he touched it, there were five or six guys absolutely tackling him! He carried the ball five times, and then he quit. They said he was injured, but I don't think he wanted to be out there that day. If I had been him the way we were hitting him, I wouldn't have wanted to be out there either. It was that vicious."

Kerwin Bell: "Up until that '84 season, whenever Florida had to go up against Auburn, Georgia, FSU, and Kentucky, Florida had a tough times beating those teams. So I remember when we went into that stretch, everyone said, 'Hey, this is where we can really show what we can do.'

"In the past the team had failed to do that, keeping us from winning an SEC championship. And in my four years, I always felt that Auburn was the closest team to us talentwise. So we knew it was going to be a great game, and somehow, we manhandled them. We didn't hardly have any turnovers, and our defense just played a great game. Bo Jackson was coming off an injury, and he came back and didn't do anything. Our defense shut him out. It was a great game.

"Pat Dye had made a comment about 'Florida's professional players,' and we were all mad about that, and we took the attitude that everyone was against us, that we were the only ones who were for us. We felt like the whole world was against us. Everyone was talking trash about us, saying this and saying that, and from that point on we took an attitude it was us against everyone else. That was our rallying cry the whole rest of the year."

Florida had lost eleven of its previous thirteen games against the Vince Dooley-led Bulldogs. The 'Georgia jinx,' everyone called it. But in one of the biggest wins in the history of the school, Kerwin Bell led Florida to a stunning 27-0 whitewash.

Kerwin Bell: "We played Georgia in the Gator Bowl, and as I was introduced during the pre-game ceremony, I stood there on the field, and my knees were shaking! I could hardly stand up.

"It was just the excitement, with half Florida fans and half Georgia fans in the stadium; electricity was in the air. It was like no other regular season game that I had ever been a part of, so I had to get adjusted to it."

Ricky Nattiel: "We had total control of the game the first half,and we were running the ball extremely well. All three of our backs were having good games. We practiced ball control. We threw it, but mostly first-down stuff.

"When we came out for the second half, we were looking at a chance to win. Of course, we were so spooked by Georgia always finding a way to beat Florida so we never at any time thought it was over. You start by mentioning the Lindsay Scott game. The fans felt the same way. They were excited, but you could tell they were still a little edgy, because they just didn't know.

"But the defense knew. They were pumped and playing well. And with only a few minutes left in the game, as Georgia started to drive, I knew they were really, really pumped on shutting Georgia out."

Kerwin Bell: "We played a great game that day. We really dominated the whole game. We were in total control, and then in the third period, Georgia made a great drive, started taking the ball to us. We were up 20-0, and Georgia took the ball all the way down, and I remember Elijah Williams, a veteran player, saying to me, 'Oh Lord, here we go again.'

"That was the talk that Georgia would always find a way to win. I said, 'We're up 20-0. Don't worry about it.' You could tell Georgia was starting to gain the momentum.

"Our defense then made a great goal line stand, and that changed the whole game around. If they would have scored, you never know what might have happened. Four times they tried to score inside the five yard line."

Georgia had a fourth down on the Florida four. Coach Vince Dooley decided to go for it.

Ricky Nattiel: "Everybody was standing up, and the Georgia fans were yelling, and the Florida fans were screaming, and of course, you couldn't hear a thing in the stadium.

"The Georgia fans saw this as a chance to get momentum on their side, and we were on the sidelines saying, 'Oh God, what is going to happen?' It was the biggest moment of the game.

"We wondered: Is it going to happen again? Are they going to get momentum? And after the play was over, there were so many guys in front of me jumping up and down, I really couldn't see who made the stop, but when I saw our defensive guys jumping up and down and screaming and yelling, I knew what had happened."

Kerwin Bell: "Then the [third] quarter ended, and we went from one end of the field to the other, and as I was walking to the sideline and going to the other end, Coach Hall said, 'Hey, let's run another time, and if we don't get a first down, we'll get some field position and punt the ball.'

"So when I went back on the field, that's what I was thinking. We'll run it three times, and punt. We got into the huddle, and I saw that Coach Hall had signalled a deep pass.

"I asked him to give me the signal again, because I couldn't believe it. We had just talked about what he wanted me to do, you know, 'Let's not make a mistake. We'll just punt if we have to.' And he called for the deep pass.

"It was a big surprise for me."

Ricky Nattiel: "I can recall standing right beside Coach Hall, and after the pandemonium calmed down, we realized that the offense had to take the field. All the guys were scrambling to run out there, and Coach Hall and I were kind of looking at each other, and he said to me, 'Do you think we can throw the ball up on top of them here?' As a receiver, whether we could or couldn't, I was going to say, 'Yeah, I think we can do it.'

"We were on our own four-yard line, and obviously everyone expected us to try to run the ball, to get out of there with some field position and punt it. That was what Georgia probably was thinking as well.

"Coach Hall gave the play to me to take in. It was a 69-route, a simple 'go' route.

"I went out onto the field. I was trying to be as calm and discreet and cool as possible not to give them any indication, because the defensive backs are really, really sharp. They can pick up signals. I was starting to feel a little more mature by then. I knew that if I ran flatout onto the field and acted all excited, they were going to smell a rat.

"So I did my 'I'm bored, I'm depressed' jog out, knowing all along what play we called, and when I lined up and saw the defender covering me seven yards off, I knew it was a man-to-man. I knew they were going to bring the house and try to shut down the run and keep their field position.

"My eyes lit up, though I was still trying to be cool about it. I made eye contact with Kerwin. He knew. We knew we had the coverage we wanted. So it was a matter of executing the play.

"When I started my route, I immediately got on top of the guy covering me, and so ten yards into the route I knew I had him. I was already even with him, and about four yards down I ran right by him. He was beaten real bad. I could tell he was shocked when I went right by him. I can remember when he saw the play developing, he tried to recover, and he stumbled and fell down.

"I kept saying to myself, Please get me the ball, Kerwin.

"As I passed the guy and looked over my right shoulder, I could see the ball coming. 'Oh God, here it is,' and when I made the catch I was right in front of Vince Dooley, right in front of the Georgia bench. As I ran, I could see them out of the corner of my eye. They were in shock.

"And I knew nobody was near me. I started taunting a little bit. From about the Georgia twenty, I started high-stepping it, though I started too soon, because by the time I got to the five, my high steps were getting lower and lower!

"This was one of the only catches in my career where I could actually see the fans. Normally you are so in tune with what you are doing you don't see them. On this play there was no one around, and I could look around. I was running toward the north end zone, and the Florida fans were jumping up and down, and I knew then that this was the nail that sealed their coffin.

"After I scored, the first player to reach me was Lorenzo Hampton. He ran over and grabbed and hugged me. He was a senior, and it was the first time he had beaten Georgia. It was pandemonium.

"People ask me, 'What was the biggest catch of your career?' I'd have to say that one was, because I got in *Sports Illustrated*. They had a picture of me running down the sideline high-stepping. Georgia had had our number, and it was our first time beating them in a long time. It was definitely a boost to my career.

"After I scored to make it 27-0, our fans started to celebrate. You could tell the edge was off. They finally realized, We got this one."

Kerwin Bell: "On that play Ricky ran right past the defender, and he made a great catch and ran for a touchdown. Ninety-six yards! That really fueled everyone for the rest of the game.

"Ricky is one of the fastest receivers I've ever thrown to, and you take your steps, and if he has enough room down the field, if you can just give him air, he's going to catch anything you throw at him, because he's that fast.

"I threw the ball out there, and when I saw him catch it, I didn't know for sure whether he was going to be able to stay in bounds, but then he just ran right down the field. It was an unbelievable feeling to be able to make that play happen. It was not a high-percentage play, but it worked, and we knew then that the game was over and we had it. That was a BIG relief for us."

The morning before the Kentucky game, Galen Hall lost his "interim" designation, when he agreed to a four-year contract to be the Florida head coach.

Ricky Nattiel: "Everyone was pleased. We enjoyed playing for him. He was a player-type coach, and with the talent we had, that was the fit that we needed. We didn't have any disciplinary problems. It was one of those teams where if you just put the players in the right positions, things would take care of themselves."

Florida travelled to Lexington to play the Kentucky Wildcats. Kerwin Bell threw for 183 yards, including a touchdown to sophomore receiver Frankie Neal. Bobby Raymond kicked five field goals as Florida won 25-17 and clinched its first SEC championship.

Kerwin Bell: "The Kentucky game was one of our most hard-fought games. In my four years, they were the team that gave the greatest effort of anyone. They didn't have as much talent as we did, but they always played us tough.

"That's what happened in this game, and it took some great plays by guys on our team to win that game. Bobby Raymond kicked five field goals. He didn't have that strong a leg, but he was very consistent. If it was one you had to have, Bobby would make it for you. Right at the end Adrian White intercepted a pass, allowing us to get out of there with a victory."

After the Kentucky win, LSU still had to lose that day for Florida to win its first SEC championship.

Ricky Nattiel: "We knew we had an opportunity to win the SEC, but first LSU had to lose, and the LSU game hadn't ended when it was time for us to get on the plane.

"I remember the pilot came over the loudspeaker, and he gave the score of the LSU game. LSU had lost, and the plane just erupted.

"And before we could get back to Gainesville, the fans already knew. When we arrived, there were thousands and thousands of fans inside the stadium."

Kerwin Bell: "We had a charter flight, and the pilot flew over Florida Field, turning its wings sideways so we could look down, and I could see that the stands were almost full on one side. That's when we realized this thing was bigger than we thought.

"When we landed in Gainesville and got off the plane, there was a line of people from the Gainesville airport all the way to the stadium. It's probably six or seven miles, and cars were lined up everywhere the whole way. It was unbelievable!

"We got to the stadium, and there were all those people waiting. Then you start to realize that this is a once-in-a-lifetime experience. Of all the things that happened to me at the University of Florida, this is the one I will remember the most. To see all of those people who had rooted for Florida all those years, and to see them so happy, because we had done something Florida had never done before, that was pretty special.

"The whole team went out onto the field and we waved to everyone and shook hands. They had a little program where Coach Hall talked. A couple of players got up and spoke. They played the fight song. It was big."

Ricky Nattiel: "It was a very, very long, fun exciting party and celebration type of night. Wherever you went, people wanted to give you free stuff. Everyone wanted to buy you dinner, buy you drinks. The fans were excited and in awe. They were SO appreciative. This is what the fans had always been waiting for. For the guys, it was as though we had won the Super Bowl.

"My first thought was, I would what would happen if we were to win the national championship? Cause it was right there in front of us for the taking. All we had to do was beat Florida State, and beat the top team in a bowl game, and the national championship was going to be ours."

The final game of the 1984 season was against FSU at Doak-Campbell Stadium in Tallahassee. An inch and a half of rain fell during the first half. In the 27-17 Florida win, Kerwin Bell threw for two touchdowns, and Florida backs Neal Anderson, John L. Williams, and Lorenzo Hampton gained 254 yards rushing.

Kerwin Bell: "It rained so hard, you could barely see the sidelines to get the signals, and the ball was slippery. But we had a great running game. I remember all those guys ran the ball tremendously. And we just dominated them up front. We just controlled them the whole game. It was a pretty easy victory."

Ricky Nattiel had to face a talkative FSU defensive back by the name of Deion Sanders.

Ricky Nattiel: "Deion [Sanders] did a lot of jawing. He was a talker, without a doubt. He taunted every snap. He wasn't a proven player yet, which made him hard to believe. But it was part of his personality. He was good, and he made his presence felt. He wasn't as good as he thought he was, though, and we kind of had our way with him that night.

"What I remember most after the game we were all standing out on Doak-Campbell field—the Florida players and our fans were celebrating. I was talking to my parents, and they turned the sprinklers on us! They tried to run us off the field, because we were so happy!

"We were one game away from the national championship. We were going to play in the Sugar Bowl for the first time, against Miami. We were getting the rematch we had wanted since the first game of the season. Miami was number one, and after we beat FSU, we were number two, and we were going to play for the national championship.

"Going to."

During the week after Florida defeated FSU, the NCAA and the SEC stripped Florida of everything but their jockstraps and helmets, banning the Gators from playing on TV or in any bowl game, thus preventing it even from playing for the national championship.

Ricky Nattiel: "Between the FSU game and the Sugar Bowl, the NCAA reared its ugly head. That's when they dropped the sanctions on us. They said, no bowl games and no television for the next two years. And our SEC championship was taken away from us and was given to Tennessee. Tennessee went to the Sugar Bowl game in our place and beat Miami. We would have beaten them, for sure.

"How could they have penalized us in the middle of the season? That was one of the many, many questions. It was tough to go from such a high to such a low so quickly. We literally were stunned. We walked around like zombies. It was really, really tough for the seniors, because the Florida State game was their last game as a Gator, and they didn't even know it! Imagine that: you've played your last game, and you didn't even know it was your last game.

"It was really, really tough.

"Coach Hall was calm, as always. He told us, 'No matter what they do, YOU are the SEC champions, and nobody can take that away from you. We won it where it counts, and that was on the field.' And that was true. And that became our motto."

On January 13, 1985, the NCAA handed down severe penalties to the University of Florida football program for the 59 infractions admitted to by Charlie Pell. It ruled that two assistant coaches, Joe Kynes and Dwight Adams, had to leave the program. It ruled that Florida would lose fifteen scholarships a year for three years. Florida already had been deprived of playing in the Sugar Bowl for the national championship, but the cruelest blow of all came when the SEC commission voted to deny the 9-1-1 Gators their hard-earned 1984 league championship. The silver trophy, however, still remains in the possession of the university, housed in a glass case for all to see.

Ricky Nattiel: "We got rings anyway. The school got them for us. And we got the SEC trophy too. We never gave it back. We still have it.

"I wouldn't have given it back. But it was tough watching Tennessee go and beat Miami. Because we had beaten Tennessee. We watched that game, and there was no question we would have beaten Miami, and that would have given us the national championship."

Kerwin Bell: "The way we saw it, they knew all the violations from the first of the year. If we had lost to Kentucky, they wouldn't have done anything but add another year to our probation. But they waited until we won it, and then they took it away from us. That's what most of the players were angry about: they kept putting off making a decision until the outcomes were determined.

"I just know we were all really frustrated. We were all disappointed, because we had won it, and we won it without being on probation at the time, and we thought we should go represent the SEC in the Sugar Bowl and start the probation the following year. But that wasn't the way it was, and we just had to accept it."

Ricky Nattiel: "I saw Coach Pell at functions. The last time I saw him before he passed was the night I got inducted into the University of Florida Hall of Fame. He came to the ceremony.

"He never made it known how it affected him. No one ever said, 'Why did you do it, coach?' It was one of those things that happened, one of those personal things that happen in one's career. You go on. It makes you stronger."

fifty-three

Another Amazing 9-1-1 Year

Despite being ineligible for either a bowl bid or the SEC title, the 1985 Florida Gators were determined to show the country that they were a football team to be reckoned with.

Ricky Nattiel: "Going into the 1985 season, we knew we couldn't win the SEC, couldn't go to a bowl, or couldn't play on TV, and it was hard, but we knew we had a good football team.

"Neal Anderson, John L., and Frankie Neal were seniors. I was a junior. So was Kerwin. We still had a lot of talent. We weren't weak at any position. Our role that year was to be the spoiler. We were going to spoil it for EVERYONE ELSE."

In the opener in the Orange Bowl in Miami, quarterback Kerwin Bell put on a passing show that eclipsed that of Miami All-American Vinny Testaverde. Bell completed 20 passes for 117 yards and two touchdowns.

Kerwin Bell: "Probably half the fans in the Orange Bowl that night were Gator fans. This was before Miami really had a big following. But they were a tough team, a good team. I just remember we took charge in the second half and won the game pretty easily.

"I threw a touchdown to Ricky Nattiel. Whenever we needed a big play, Ricky gave it to us. He ran a 4.28 forty, had great hands, and he made great plays all the years I was with him.

"I hit Ricky for a touchdown and John L. Williams caught a pass out of the backfield for a touchdown. I also threw one to Frankie Neal, so we spread it around, because the Miami defense really shut down our running game. We couldn't run the ball at all [Florida gained 53 yards rushing in 40 tries]. So we had to try to throw the football, and we were pretty good at it."

Ricky Nattiel: "Kerwin and I had started to hook up in '84. He, Frankie Neal and I were starting to click. Frankie and I were still roommates at the time. In '84 Bee Lang and Gary Rolle were still there, and one of them would start ahead of one of us, and we kept teasing them, 'You guys are holding us up.'

"Kerwin, Frankie and I were in the same class, and we started to develop a relationship and a trust in each other on the field, and in '85 we were REALLY comfortable with each other.

"Against Miami, I ran a curl route. We were on their 16, and I caught the ball on about the five. We needed to score, and I made a little move, caught the ball, and made it into the end zone. And we beat them in the Orange Bowl [by 35-23]. It was a huge win.

"But after the game, all we kept saying was, 'Man, we can't do anything. No matter how well we do, we won't be able to do anything at the end of the year.'

"But yet, somehow, we were able to tune it out."

Florida hosted Rutgers, a twenty-point underdog, at Florida Field. Florida led 28-7, behind Kerwin Bell's three touchdown passes.

Kerwin Bell: "We came out early against them, and they played pretty good. We were ahead 21-7 at halftime. But we felt like we should have been better, had a bigger lead.

"We went in, made some adjustments, and came out. The first drive of the third quarter we went right down the field, and I hit Frankie Neal for a [42-yard] touchdown.

"Coach Hall felt that 28-7 was a safe enough lead to take me out and give Rodney Brewer some playing time. His first play was a screen pass, and a defensive lineman was standing there, and he tipped it and picked it off and ran it back for a touchdown. It was a freak play, but things started snowballing from there. We had some turnovers, and they scored.

"We look up in the fourth quarter, and it's 28-21, and we're barely holding on, and Coach Hall says to me, 'You have to go back in.'

'I have already cooled down. Now I have to go back in. We were just trying to run out the clock. I got a couple of first downs, and we were getting inside the three-minute mark, and we had a third and eight, and probably our best receiver in terms of having sure hands was Bret Wiechmann, and I threw him a pass—and it hit him in the chest, and he dropped it.

"We punted, and they came back and scored, and they tied the game. [The game ended a 28-28 tie.] I remember walking off the field, and the people in the stands were booing, and it was pretty embarrassing. But that's just the way it happened. Everyone was real down after that game, because we just let one slip away.

"Coach Hall got a lot of criticism for bringing in the backup quarterback too soon. Rodney had a lot of talent; he just didn't have much experience.

"As I look back on it, I really see how important not winning that game was. Going into the Georgia game, we might have been 8-0, and we might not even have lost that game. We look back and say, 'Man, if we wouldn't have tied Rutgers, where could we have been?'"

Against Mississippi State, Florida was tied at the half 20-20. Then on the second play of the second half, Kerwin Bell threw a 83-yarder to Ricky Nattiel for a touchdown in a 36-22 victory. In three games Bell had thrown ten touchdowns. Neal Anderson, who ran for 134 yards and two touchdowns, was 117 yards short of the school rushing record.

Kerwin Bell: "It was right after halftime, and we came out, and I faked a play-action pass to Neal in the backfield, and when I came up to throw, Ricky was running a post route, and I threw it out there. Like I say, he could go and get anything with his great speed. He caught the ball and went the rest of the way for a touchdown. Then we added a couple more scores, and that was it."

Ricky Nattiel: "Bruce Plummer was their top dog at cornerback. He was a real good player, and he got a little arrogant, a little mouthy, and he was starting to take chances. In the right situation I knew I could beat him on a post route, and I brought that to Kerwin's attention.

"Plummer started playing a lot of bump man-to-man, and when we called the play, I knew it would be there. I just had to run a good route.

"One thing about my relationship with Kerwin, if I did my part to get open, he was going to get the ball to me. He had a very reliable, dependable, strong arm. He was precise, and we connected [for an 83-yard touchdown], and it was a turning point in that game.

"Mississippi always played us hard. They were a thorn in our side. It was a dogfight, but we managed to pull it out, and that play was the difference in that game."

Against LSU, the Gator defense had a big night, as Florida won 20-0. It was the worst shutout suffered by LSU since 1954.

Ricky Nattiel: "Neal [Anderson] had a big game that night. He ran crazy on them. And LSU had a pretty good defense. It had Michael Brooks, who was a stud. Neal and the line were the difference that night. It was one of those ball control games. We threw when we had to, but we ran the ball great, and the defense won it for us."

Kerwin Bell: "Our defense played super that game. They got us the ball and great field position, and it was a pretty easy game."

The Tennessee game was played at Florida Field before 74,432, the biggest crowd ever to see a Gator home game. Kerwin Bell faced volunteer quarterback Tony Robinson, who had played high school ball at Tallahassee Leon High School. Experts were predicting a high-scoring game. But Florida won by only 17-10. It's defense, one of the best in the country, was superb as Robinson was thrown for 92 yards worth of losses.

Kerwin Bell: "Everyone thought this game was going to be a shoot out, because the year before we had played a 43-30 game. Tony Robinson had been the Tennessee quarterback, and he threw the ball all over the place. So people were looking for a repeat of that at Florida Field.

"And this game was totally the opposite. Both defenses played great. They really got after us, and our defense stopped Tony. I remember we hit him play after play, really got after him.

"We won 17-10. It was a great defensive game, totally different from what everyone thought it would be."

Ricky Nattiel: "Neal [Anderson] had a big game [he ran for 160 yards]. He broke a long run for a touchdown. Even though the score was only 17-10, we totally controlled the game. We were in TOTAL control. We didn't feel at any point that we were going to lose that game."

Against Southwestern Louisiana at Homecoming, Kerwin Bell had one of his best days, throwing for 296 yards and three touchdowns. He was 15-23, including a 70-yard touchdown pass to Neal Anderson and a 55-yarder to Ray McDonald.

Ricky Nattiel: "Ray was a wide receiver who was in the same class with Frankie Neal, a year ahead of me. Our five main receivers were me, Frankie, Ray McDonald, Gary Rolle, and Bret Wiechmann.

"Ray was very fast. He was from Belle Glades Central, a real good receiver who got caught up in the numbers game. He was real dependable and a playmaker. His son just signed with Florida this year [2002]."

Kerwin Bell: "That was an easy game. It was just one of those games where you just go out there and do your thing."

Virginia Tech was the next victim, a 35-18 loser at Florida Field. The nation's longest unbeaten streak stood at seventeen games. Bell was 14-27 for 180 yards and two touchdowns. John L. Williams gained 153 yards, and Neal Anderson, who was hurt in the fourth quarter, threw a 46-yard option pass to Frankie Neal.

Kerwin Bell: "The best offensive line in the country had graduated the year before, so in '85 we were real young up front offensively, and I got hit a lot. And because our line was so inexperienced, it was a lot harder for our backs to gain yardage. But as far as our skill positions, we were as good as anyone in the country. We had John L. Williams and Neal Anderson, two first-round pro draft picks, and receiver Ricky Nattiel, a first rounder. Walter Odom was one of the better tight ends in our conference. Frankie Neal could have been a first-rounder, but he fell out of school his last year, and still was a third rounder. We had unbelievable talent, and it was just a matter of our line starting to develop later in the year. As we went along, we got better and better. By the end of the year, we became a lot better team."

After Virginia Tech, Florida, ranked number two in the country, met Auburn, ranked sixth-best nationally. Auburn played most of the game without Bo Jackson, who suffered a thigh bruise. Jackson carried just once in the second half.

With Auburn ahead 10–7 in the fourth quarter, Kerwin Bell threw an 8–yard scoring pass to Ray McDonald with 7:18 to play. The defense held on the rest of the way.

Ricky Nattiel: "It was more of a defensive game than anything. No Bo. He got in for one play, but they had Brent Fullwood, who was no pushover. It was a dogfight, like it always is, and somehow we managed to pull it off."

Kerwin Bell: "I tell you, that was the hardest-hitting game I've been in. It was a defensive battle, and they hit us hard, and our defense hit them. Bo Jackson left the game in the second quarter. He got hurt a little and didn't want any more. They were really hitting him. Man, it was just a hard-fought game.

"The whole game they did something with the football in just two series. They scored a touchdown and a field goal for 10 points. The whole game we did something with the football exactly twice, and we scored two touchdowns and beat them 14–10.

"I remember the defense gave us the ball around midfield, and John L. Williams was the key. We ran a draw play, and he ran 36 yards, got us down to the Auburn five. We called a fade route, and Ray McDonald made a great catch. They were covering him one-on-one, and he ran to the corner of the end zone, and I just threw it to a spot, and he made a great one-handed catch.

"And after the game, we were ranked number one for the first time ever by the Associated Press."

Ricky Nattiel: "It was an excited but disappointed feeling all at once. You know you're the best team in the country, but yet you know there's no prize at the end. We knew we were the best team, but when we looked at the schedule we saw our next game was against Georgia, who always was this thorn in our side, so we couldn't get too excited. It added to the pressure.

"Man, we're number one. Can we hold it the rest of the season? It's what we had played for. We asked ourselves, Can we finish the season number one and make whoever they give it to look really stupid? That was our goal."

Kerwin Bell: "We had a lot of media attention. And the players let it get to our heads a little bit and didn't concentrate on the next week's opponent, Georgia. You don't play as good if you don't focus on who you're playing the next week.

"We were doing interviews. And all the talk was about our being number one for the first time in the history of the school.

"And Georgia had played on TV, and we had watched them, and whenever they played on TV they looked really bad. The year before we had beaten them 27-0, and the thought was, We're number one.

"The Thursday before the Georgia game, Coach Hall came to me and said, 'Kerwin, we're not ready to play, you know.'

"I said, 'I feel that too. The team is just not focused on the Georgia game.' Our preparation that week was not good, and we weren't focused, and we went out there and got killed 24-3."

Kerwin Bell: "Georgia came out with two freshmen running backs who ended up in the NFL, Keith Henderson [145 yards] and Tim Worley [104 yards and two touchdowns], and each of them ran for a hundred yards. They kept the ball from us, and on offense we couldn't run the ball against them.

"We did throw the ball well, and we had no trouble going from the 20 to the 20. Georgia had never blitzed that much, so we didn't put check off plays into our game plan.

"But they blitzed us, and we weren't able to handle it. We couldn't check off. We didn't have other plays to go to. We didn't have an answer for it. We weren't prepared to handle it. And either they would hit us for losses, and or I would have to throw the ball away, and we didn't kick field goals.

"Looking back, the lack of preparation on the part of the coaches and players kept us from being undefeated that year. We thought about the Rutgers game when the coach pulled the starting quarterback too soon. And then against Georgia we weren't prepared because of all the attention we got because we were number one. We didn't handle that right. Other than that, we should have won them all."

Florida almost followed its defeat at the hands of Georgia with a loss to Kentucky, but late in the game, trailing 13-12 with a third-and-goal from the Kentucky three, Neal Anderson threw a wobbly pass to Kerwin Bell that could have been intercepted by either David Johnson or Maurice Douglas. But when they collided, the ball fell to the ground, and Florida had a second chance. On the next play Jeff Dawson kicked his third field goal of the game, a nineteen-yarder, and Florida won 15-13.

Kerwin Bell: "At the time I thought it was a good play. We put the ball in a running back's hand trying to throw a touchdown. Neal acted like he was running a sweep, then he stopped to throw a pass back to me. There were two people on me, so he shouldn't have thrown it. But a running back doesn't know that. I remember I dove as hard as I could in there and tried to break it up. Luckily, they dropped the ball. Coach Hall said it wasn't a very smart play, because all we needed was a field goal to go ahead. If they would have intercepted it, that would have been the game. We then kicked the field goal and won the game."

The final game of the season was against FSU at Florida Field. Kerwin Bell was outstanding, throwing for 343 yards and three touchdowns, including a 75 yarder to Ricky Nattiel, an 82-yarder to Frankie Neal, and an 18-yarder to Nattiel. In the 38-14 romp, Neal Anderson became only the second runner in Florida history to break the 1,000-yard mark for a season. Anderson scored the first two touchdowns on the game on short dives. It was the third season in a row that Florida won nine games in a season.

Kerwin Bell: "We were really hitting on the passing game. It was 14-0, a fairly close game, until right at the end of the second quarter when we hit them with three big plays. I hit Ricky with a 75-yard pass for a touchdown—that made it 21-0."

Ricky Nattiel: "Deion was covering me, and I ran a deep post, and I beat him on the post and made the catch. The funny thing was, after I caught it I was running with it, and I knew I was going to score, and I was carrying the ball kind of loose, and at about the five yard line, my thigh knocked the ball out of my hand, and it took one hop off the turf and bounced right back into my hand, and I never lost a stride. It was one of those freak accidents. I was running hard, trying to make sure I got into the end zone, and it was boom, boom, and boom.

"We were having our way throwing the ball all day. We always got pumped up for Florida State, especially with Deion and his talking. I never lost to Florida State. We beat them all four of my years, and Deion was there three of them."

Kerwin Bell: "Then we came right back and held them with about two minutes to go before the half, and as soon as we got the ball we hit them again with a couple more big plays and scored. We had a good four-play spurt there, so at the half it was 28-0."

It was Florida's third-straight nine-win season.

Ricky Nattiel: "Coach Pell built the foundation, and Coach Hall was a good leader. He just made sure the right people were in the right positions, and he guided the ship."

Kerwin Bell: "Coach Hall was a great game planner, and he called a great game, though none of us can take away from what Charlie Pell did as far as recruiting. That was still Charlie's talent. He was the one who brought the people in there. And it was a good program. But you could also see that the probation was starting to be felt, because we didn't have as much depth in '85 as we did in '84, and then in 1986 and 1987, you could really see the depth go away. We started to decline after that '85 season."

fifty-four

Bell to Nattiel

After the 1984 season Lorenzo Hampton graduated, and after '85 Neal Anderson and John L. Williams did the same, along with wide receiver Frankie Neal, who left after becoming academically ineligible. By 1986 the star power on the team was dwindling, and the Gators' success would depend on the health of quarterback Kerwin Bell and his go-to receiver Rickey Nattiel.

Kerwin Bell: "In '84 we had second- or third-string players who were as good as our first-string guys. Then we went on probation and lost fifteen scholarships a year for three years, and by 1986, there were positions that didn't have backups who could play. By 1986 we had Octavius Gould and Tony Lomack, but if something happened to either of them, there were times we couldn't find a running back. And Ricky Nattiel was about the only receiver I had. You could really see the effect of the probation as far as our talent level going down."

Ricky Nattiel: "We were very short of bodies. The probation hit us, and we really began to feel it. They took away fifteen scholarships a year, and this was the last year of it, but I was a senior, and that didn't help me very much.

"We had a pretty good offensive line. It wasn't great, but we still had Jeff Zimmerman. Frankie Neal was gone. He transferred to Fort Hayes State. He needed to go play somewhere where he didn't have to sit out.

"It was starting to get depressing not being able to play on television. For my last two years, 1985 and 1986, I wasn't ever on television. You don't get that national exposure to enhance your career as far as the professional level. Fortunately, the pros knew about me, but other guys, especially defensive players, who might be as good and who needed the exposure, it hurt them a lot. If you have two or three sacks or interceptions, and they don't see you do it on television, they won't know anything about it. That was tough. There was nothing you could do about it. I knew it was right in the middle of my career. I knew I wasn't going to be on TV again, but winning eases the pain a little bit, and we won in '85, but going into '86, we knew it would be a trying year because we lost a lot of talent."

In the opener against Georgia Southern at Florida Field, Kerwin Bell ran for a score and threw a 28-yard touchdown to Ricky Nattiel in a 38-14 win. Sophmore tailback Wayne Williams ran 93 yards, including an 8-yard touchdown.

Kerwin Bell: "Tracy Ham was the Georgia Southern quarterback. Later we would play in the Canadian Football League together. Tracy was a great option quarterback. Georgia Southern had won a couple of 1-AA championships, and they played us tough. But after the first quarter and a half, we started to have our way."

Ricky Nattiel: "We were having our way that day, and it was awesome. We had lost our running backs, and we had lost Frankie, and so on offense it was kind of Kerwin and I leading us to whatever kind of season we were going to have.

"Georgia Southern was always good in their division. They weren't pushovers. They were a decent ballclub, and they had Tracy Ham at quarterback. I had some battles with him in high school. But Kerwin was sharp, and I was sharp, and I was catching everything he threw to me. It was a fun day.

"And after we did that, everybody watched the films, and teams started blitzing Kerwin and double-covering me. So it was good and bad."

The second game was a battle between Heisman Trophy candidates Kerwin Bell and Vinny Testaverde of Miami. When the third-ranked Hurricanes won 23-15, Florida's longest-ever home winning streak of twenty-three games came to an end. In that game Bell was sacked six times for 56 yards in losses. Florida also fumbled four times.

Kerwin Bell: "Vinny and I did a photo shoot down in Miami for a newspaper about the Heisman competition.

"The game was at Florida Field, one of those hot, hot days. It was burning up. Their defense dominated our offensive line, and I got hit all day. We didn't do too much on offense.

"They must have hit me twenty times, and I remember after the game I was doing interviews in the locker room, and I was just so exhausted, and I had a concussion, and I started throwing up and having headaches. They had to take me to the hospital for tests and an IV. They had to keep me overnight for observation because of the concussion.

"So I got hit pretty good that game.

"Miami didn't have a particularly good game either. They couldn't do anything against our defense. But they wound up winning the game. I could tell we weren't the same team as we had been a couple years earlier. We didn't have as much talent as they did."

Ricky Nattiel: "Their game plan was to blitz and to double cover me, because they knew we weren't proven in the backfield. Every team we played the rest of the season did that. It was a matter of how much talent the other team had. Miami had a lot more talent than Georgia Southern."

The lack of depth on the Florida squad was felt so deeply that in the Alabama game a few of the players went both ways. Tackles Keith Williams and Rhondy Weston and nose guard Jeff Roth played most of the way. Alabama, led by linebacker Cornelius Bennett, wore Florida down and won 21-7.

Kerwin Bell: "Guys were having to do all kinds of things. I thought we should have won that game. We didn't play very well, but they beat us. They had Cornelius Bennett, and they also had James Brooks. Mike Shula was their quarterback. It was a game where their defense really controlled the whole game."

Ricky Nattiel: "We battled them okay, but they had Bobby Humphrey, and they had Cornelius "Biscuit" Bennett at linebacker, and that boy gave Kerwin a bruising. It was brutal. Cornelius was an awesome player, and he had a field day. We had nobody to block him. I was glad when the game was over."

A 16-10 loss to Mississippi State followed. In that game Kerwin Bell took another pounding. He was sacked three times, and his confidence was down. Twice he overthrew open receivers downfield. The only Florida touchdown came from the defense.

Kerwin Bell: "Yeah, I got hit a lot. Man, I was beat up. I shouldn't have even played in that game, but I did. After the game I could hardly walk to the bus to get on the plane. It was a tough three weeks."

Ricky Nattiel: "People were learning how to stop us. They were double covering me, and they were sending the house. And that was pretty much their game plan.

"And LSU did the same thing, and in that game Kerwin got hurt. He sprained his knee."

Bell threw three interceptions against LSU before he was injured late in the third period, leaving with a severely sprained knee. He was expected to miss the next four to six weeks. Rodney Brewer took his place at quarterback.

Kerwin Bell: "I went into that game physically drained, and that's probably why I got hurt. Against LSU I was having another rough day. I threw some interceptions. But despite that, we were coming back to take the lead. I threw the ball to Ricky Nattiel at about the ten, and when I did, an LSU guy dove into my knee—late—and tore my MCL. That put me out.

"Rodney came in. We didn't score, and we ended up losing the game [28-17]. During that streak we lost four in a row."

Providently for Florida, the next game was Homecoming against Kent State University. Rodney Brewer, a left-hander, was 13-16 for 230 yards and two touchdowns. Octavius Gould ran for 81 yards and scored three touchdowns in a 52-9 drubbing.

Against Rutgers, Brewer again played well, hitting Ricky Nattiel for a 36-yard touchdown. Gould ran for 102 yards in a 15-3 win. Nattiel was playing with a sore left ankle. During the game receiver Bret Wiechmann was lost for the season with a broken arm, and defensive back Ricky Mulberry was lost with a badly sprained ankle.

Auburn, which was ranked fifth in the country, was next, and going into the game Florida was given no chance at all to beat the Tigers.

The first seven times Florida had the ball, they turned the ball over, and in the middle of the second period Auburn led 17-0 when Coach Hall ordered Kerwin Bell into the game. Bell, injured against LSU and not expecting to play, had not even warmed up.

Kerwin Bell: "I was on the sidelines against Kent State and Rutgers. It didn't bother me to miss those games, but I was NOT going to miss the Auburn game. I just loved being in those games. I had set my sights on returning for that game.

"So we won both the Kent State and Rutgers games, and then we had an off-week, and I came out the week before the Auburn game wearing a knee brace. It was still tender, but Coach Hall allowed me to practice. I thought I could play, but Coach Hall named Rodney Brewer as the starter that day.

"Auburn really got after him, and Rodney made some mistakes. They were really killing him. I remember standing on the sideline thinking that when you are out there in the action, you really don't think about how hard you get hit. The third quarterback said to me, 'Kerwin, I think you may be playing here pretty soon.' And I said, 'I don't know if I want to go in there or not.' If they were killing him, what would they do to my knee?

"Right before halftime, he put me in. I played one series right before the half. I was worried about the knee, and I was throwing off my back foot. We hit a couple of passes, and then we got stopped.

"I came out for the third quarter, and we moved the ball pretty good, but we just couldn't get across the goal line. Even so, we were starting to move the football and to gain confidence.

"At the end of the third quarter we were still losing 17-0, and we started to drive. We changed ends of the field, and then we finished that drive with a touchdown to Ricky.

"Momentum was on our side, and from then on we just felt we could score. We kicked a field goal, and then we kicked off to them, and our defense held them. Our defense had played super all game long. After all the turnovers [seven], we were only down 17-10.

"We kicked off to them, and our defense looked like it was getting tired, and they started running the ball, and they were getting first down after first down. When it got inside two minutes I was thinking, Man, we are not going to get it back.

"Then, all of a sudden, they fumbled. We recovered, and then we had a series where we marched right down the field. Some great things happened. I threw a [five-yard] touchdown pass to Ricky [with 36 seconds left in the game] to make the score 17-16."

Ricky Nattiel: "In that game I suffered a separated shoulder. I was running a deep crossing route about twenty yards across the middle of the field, and

Kerwin threw one that was out in front of me, and I laid out to catch it, and as I made the catch, I found the turf. I landed on my right shoulder, and when I got up, I knew something was wrong. I felt excruciating pain. But we were in the middle of our comeback, and I didn't want to come out. I went to the sideline, and Dr. Indelicato checked it, but there was no way of knowing how bad it was. But I refused to come out. We were coming back, losing only 17-10, and we were driving again."

Ricky Nattiel: "It was third and long, and I ran an 'out' route, and I had to extend myself, and I caught the ball with one hand, and I managed to keep my foot in at the five. Everybody was going crazy, and at this point I didn't care about the shoulder, which I was kind of dragging.

"Kerwin was pumped. Everybody was going crazy by now. Kerwin called a fade route. There was less than a minute left in the game.

"I was lined up on the left side, and we were going toward the south end zone, and the ideal coverage for us was bump man-to-man, which is what we got, so I knew—and Kerwin knew—we had already given each other the eyes—once we got that coverage, he was going to throw it to a spot in the back of the end zone. He throws it while I'm running my route, and when I make my break, I know where it's going to be at that spot.

"He put the perfect height and trajectory on it, and all I did was beat my guy at the line, and I raced to the back of the end zone, and the ball and I got there at the same time, and I made the catch, making the score 17-16." [There were 36 seconds left in the game.]

Kerwin Bell: "At first I thought we were going to kick the extra point. I didn't know we were going to go for two.

"Coach Hall called time out. I came over to the sideline, and he said, 'We're going for two,' and I thought to myself, Oh Lord. We had a play designed for Ricky to run an option route to get open.

"I dropped back, and they covered him, and the pressure came up into my face, so I sprinted to the left and I barely was able to get across the goal line for the two points."

Ricky Nattiel: "We decided to go for two. At this point, why not? It was an easy decision. We could have kicked the extra point to tie, but we wanted to go for the win.

"The play was a quick slant to me, but somehow it got disrupted. Somebody broke through. I remember being in the back of the end zone, trying to get open, and I could see Kerwin scrambling, and I thought of one of those slow-motion films. That play must have taken five minutes to unfold. It was like he was running in mud. Once I saw him break the line of scrimmage, I knew he couldn't throw it, that he had to try to run.

"I was in the back of the end zone jumping and cheering. I probably should have been trying to find someone to block. But I was caught up in the moment. I could see him fighting for everything he had, and somehow he got over the goal line, and man, everybody just went nuts.

"I went over and grabbed Kerwin. I didn't even care about my shoulder. And I went and got it checked and x-rayed, and that's when they determined I had a separated shoulder. It still hurts today, actually, because I was not one for surgery."

Kerwin Bell: "We were ahead 18-17 with very little time left, when Brent Fullwood, who later played with the Packers for a long time, a good running back, took the kickoff and almost broke it. He ran it back fifty yards. Our kicker had to make the saving tackle to win the game. [With six seconds left Auburn's Chris Knapp] lined up to kick a [53-yard] field goal that could have won the game. But it came up short.

"It was a great win for us. In my four years, this is the game most people remember. This and the Georgia game we won 27-0 freshman year, because we hadn't beaten Georgia in so long. But they also remember this one because we had fought so hard to come back."

To prove the Auburn victory was no fluke, Florida the next week went to Jacksonville and defeated Georgia 31-19 at the Gator Bowl, despite trailing early in the third quarter 19-10. Bell was banged up, and Ricky Nattiel refused to miss the game despite the separated shoulder. Against Georgia, Bell threw seven passes to Nattiel, who scored three touchdowns in what was one of the most courageous performances in Florida history.

It was only the fifth time in Florida history that the Gators defeated both Auburn and Georgia in one season.

Ricky Nattiel: "I didn't practice that much the week before the Georgia game, but I wanted to play, and I wouldn't let it keep me out. It was my senior year, and I wanted to have a chance to play at the next level, and not only that, it was Georgia.

"We were struggling, but if you can beat Auburn, Georgia and Florida State, it was a good year. And we had one of them out of the way.

"So they came up with a concoction to put on my shoulder for extra padding, and I strapped it on again."

Kerwin Bell: "Ricky's shoulder still was messed up going into the Georgia game. People didn't know this, but we designed most of our plays to Ricky so he could catch the ball and get out of bounds so he wouldn't get hit. We threw a lot of routes to him going to the outside, and he would catch it and get out of bounds. Sometimes he couldn't, and they'd hit him, but he played the whole game.

"And if you remember the Georgia game the year before, when they blitzed us and we didn't have an answer for them, this time we were prepared. We had a game plan for what to do, and we would go to maximum protection. That left their little cornerback one on one on Ricky. And Ricky killed them for three touchdown passes to win the game."

Georgia had led Florida 16-3 midway through the third quarter. It looked grim.

Ricky Nattiel: "It was me and Kerwin, the wounded warriors. It was one of those games where you make a catch, and you drag your arm to the sideline to take off a play.

"We had freedom to audible if we were given certain coverages, and any time they came up in a bump man-to-man, we would have a signal—he would touch his face mask, or I would touch mine and if he touched his back, we knew that we were going for it. It was an automatic route. And we had that working for us, and I ended up scoring three touchdowns against Georgia that day.

"The first touchdown was a little, short [8-yard] fade route, the same pass I had caught against Auburn. I caught it, and right afterward I fell right on my shoulder."

The second touchdown caught by Nattiel was for nine yards and cut Georgia's lead to 19-17 with 2:10 left in the third quarter. The final scoring play came when Kerwin Bell threw Nattiel a 42-yard bomb in a miraculous 31-19 win over the Bulldogs.

Ricky Nattiel: "We were at midfield, and Georgia kept trying to defend us bump man-to-man. For some reason, Georgia felt they didn't have to double-team me. They felt they were going to beat us handily, and they took us too lightly. I don't know why they'd do that after we had beaten Auburn. They must have figured it was a fluke. They never learned.

"I beat my man at the line again basically with one arm, and my thing was, if I got open and Kerwin had any kind of time, he was going to get me the ball. It was my third touchdown, and we ended up with the victory."

Kerwin Bell: "We hadn't beaten Georgia really but one time in the last eight years. In '85 they upset us, when we had a really good team. So to come back and beat them that year was a big victory for us."

Ricky Nattiel: "It was a very satisfying win, because the year before we had lost in a game where we should have beaten them, and this year we beat them in a year when we probably shouldn't have. We had lost four games in '86, but after beating Auburn and Georgia, the fans didn't care any more. We had a little run going. We had beaten Auburn and Georgia."

With four wins in a row and a 5-4 record, Florida needed a win over Kentucky to assure itself a bid for the Hall of Fame bowl in Tampa. But on a cold day in Lexington, Florida fell 10-3. The ball was slippery and cold, and the offense could not handle the constant blitzing.

Ricky Nattiel: "It was freezing, and that was one of my worst games. I couldn't lift my arm, and it was cold, and for some reason Kentucky was up for the game. I don't know why.

"Nothing went right. I wasn't getting open. I wasn't catching the ball. I was in miserable pain. Kentucky was usually in a double coverage zone, blitzing a lot. They played great defensively. And it was pouring."

Kerwin Bell: "We would have had six wins if we had won, and we would have been eligible for a bowl. Because the last two years we weren't because of probation. A lot of guys hadn't been to one. It was a cold day and rainy, and Kentucky really played well. As I told you, they were the least talented team, but they always played us tough. They got after us, and we didn't do very much on offense. They beat us pretty good."

The Florida State game followed, and Florida was looking for its fifth-straight win over its arch-rival. Rain pelted Doak Campbell Stadium. Late in the fourth quarter FSU led 17-13. All game long the Seminoles had been talking trash. Then Kerwin Bell hit Ricky Nattiel for an 18-yard touchdown pass to win the game. It was Nattiel's final reception as a Gator.

Kerwin Bell: "FSU had Deion Sanders and Martin Mayhew, who talked a lot. The year before Deion was a freshman, and I threw for a ton of yards on him and we scored 38 points. So in '86, it was flooding rain, pouring down, and you could hardly do anything as far as throwing the ball. And they were talking: 'You're not going to throw on us like you did last year.'

"I talked back to them. I told them, 'Guys, if it wasn't raining, I'd be killing you all again. That's the only reason we're not doing anything. The game isn't over, so you all better watch out.'

"Then late in the fourth quarter, Ricky ran a post route, and he beat them for a touchdown. I was just barely getting the ball there. It was so wet, I could hardly throw a spiral. Ricky said the ball was coming in end over end. But he caught it back in the end zone for a touchdown."

Ricky Nattiel: "It was pouring, and it was getting late in the game, and we knew we couldn't run it in. We called a post, and when I went to the line of scrimmage, I was saying to myself, Do whatever you can to get open.

"We didn't know if it would work, but we knew we had to go for it, and we had the perfect coverage for it, man to man, so I ran my route as hard and fast as I could, which wasn't very fast, because I was soaked.

"Just as I started making my break for the post, I looked for the ball, and it was raining so hard I couldn't see a thing. And at the last second here comes this fluttering duck coming through the pouring rain, and I went up and grabbed it for dear life, and I remember making the catch and coming down in the end zone. I was on both my knees, and I threw up both my hands, because I knew that was going to be the winning touchdown.

"I looked up in the stands, and I could see our fans were losing it. There was no way you could have known that we had lost five games that year. No way. It was my last catch as a Gator. It was for a touchdown, and it meant a win over Florida State. It ranks right up there with the one against Georgia the year before."

Kerwin Bell: "If you look at it, I hate to say this, but the weather probably helped us win that game. Because of our probation, they had more talent than we did, but the weather really equalled things out and gave us a chance to win at the end."

Ricky Nattiel: "Nineteen eighty six was one of the most gratifying seasons, because we battled. Our record was only 6-5, but we beat the big three, Auburn, Georgia, and Florida State. And granted there were a lot of guys who didn't get much credit, but as far as the big plays, Kerwin and I were responsible for most of them, no question. It was one of my most gratifying years. It was a good feeling knowing I was the go-to guy and was able to make the big plays when they needed them.

"It was an awesome feeling. The fans treated us like we had won the national championship! They knew the circumstances, that we were on probation. We had beaten Auburn, Georgia, and Florida State, and they were as happy as they had been in '84.

"It was awesome to be able to finish my career that way."

Kerwin Bell: "We finished the year 6-5, and we didn't get invited to a bowl. And at the end of the year Ricky graduated, and we lost more players, and so in '87 we were even weaker."

Ricky Nattiel: "They had me projected to go in the first round of the NFL draft, and as a player, that's what you always hope for. I didn't want to take any chances, so I went to a few workouts, including the scouting combine, which was grueling. They checked my shoulder and knees, and it all held up pretty well. I didn't hide it. It had healed some, and they knew I would have plenty of time to heal. I ended up getting drafted in the first round by Denver.

"I was in Denver from '87 through '93. John Elway was there the whole time. John was a true leader. He was a warrior. He was a big, physical guy who laid it all on the line. You always felt you had a chance when you were on the field with him.

"I played in two Super Bowls. My rookie year in '87 we went and lost to Washington. I was the youngest player ever to score a touchdown in the Super Bowl. It was kind of cool to be starting in a game I had watched my whole life. I also played in our Super Bowl loss to San Francisco.

"I had a cracked kneecap in '89 that slowed me down. I had major surgery in '90, and they put a pin in it. I came back and played on it a couple more years, but I was never able to get back to the top speed I was accustomed to. It was very tough, because I easily could have played another four or five years. Given a fair chance and if I had been healthy, I was just as good as the guys who took my place.

"Injuries happen, unfortunately, and with the players getting as big and fast as they are, every step is important.

"Since my retirement, I've had my hand in a lot of different ventures. I had a travel agency. I had a nightclub. I own businesses. I try to keep busy. I'm involved in a landscaping company. We do custom design and landscaping. Kerwin and I are coaching at Trinity Catholic in Ocala. We took over their football program, and it's going to be a good challenge, because it's a new program. With anything we're involved in, we want to win. We want to win the state championship. This will be our first year as a varsity. We're building it from the ground up."

fifty-five

Emmitt

In 1987, the backup to senior quarterback Kerwin Bell was Herbert Perry, another athlete from Bell's tiny hometown of Mayo, Florida. In large part because of his admiration for Bell, Perry had only wanted to go to one school: Florida.

Herbert Perry: "I was a better baseball player than I was a football player, and pretty much all the southeastern schools including Tennessee, Georgia, Florida State, Miami, LSU, Auburn and Florida wanted me to come and play football and baseball.

"It never really was a decision. Kerwin was four or five years older than I was, and I knew him pretty well. I had been going to games at Florida Field since I was about 12 and had watched his career at Florida. He was going into his senior year when they were recruiting me, and that made the decision pretty easy. I never even went on any other recruiting trips. I wanted to go to Florida if they would give me the chance.

"I met Coach Hall on my recruiting visit. I met him a couple of times when I went to visit Kerwin at school. You had to be real careful. I would go down after games and see Kerwin in the tunnel, but I couldn't associate with any of the coaches because that was against NCAA rules, and believe me, they were very strict about what they could and couldn't do. They didn't want to go back on sanctions. They'd already seen what that could do to a program.

"Galen was a great person and a great coach. What I liked most about him was that he didn't treat anybody any different than he'd want to be treated. If he told you something, it was the truth. I've been in professional sports all my life, and that isn't always the case. He's a fine person, and I respect him to this day as much as any coach I've ever had. When I was at Florida, I respected him probably more so than any coach I ever had.

"Coach Hall took over the team at the wrong time. As good a coach and person as he was, you don't want to take over a team that just went on NCAA sanctions, though you don't turn down a chance to do that. You never know. We might have been able to sweep through a couple of years and then get everything going full strength again and be able to compete.

"And actually, he was on the way to doing that. That team he recruited in '86 was the one that went on to win the SEC championship in 1990. I don't even consider myself part of that. He recruited Emmitt Smith, Godfrey Myles, Jerry Odom, and Brad Culpepper, Tony Rowell, Hesham Ismael, Kyle Morris, Arden Crzyzewski was the kicker—eight or nine of them went on to the NFL.

"When I arrived on campus in the fall of '87, Kerwin and I were already friends. We hung out a lot. He was married to Cozette, who is related to a relative of mine, even though we're not related. Mayo is so small, you'd have to understand the way it works.

"He had a job to do, which was to play quarterback, so it wasn't like I got preferential treatment, but if he saw something I wasn't doing right or something I was having trouble with as far as making reads, he would talk to me. Of the three years I was there, that was the most fun I had, because I didn't feel I was alone."

Kerwin Bell: "After the '86 season, I only had four more hours to graduate. I could have turned pro after my junior year and taken the four hours during the summer if I had wanted to, and people were saying to me, 'You have to think about coming out [applying for the NFL draft], but back then players didn't come out early that much. And I decided I'd rather stay at the University of Florida and play my last year and try to win the SEC championship, even though I didn't think we had the team to do it. I felt it was my obligation to stay and help the university.

"When we returned for the '87 season, we had all new receivers. Because of probation, we had to go with really young guys. They were all really fast, but they had no experience. We had Ernie Mills, who's been a great receiver in the NFL. Ernie was a redshirt freshman who wasn't ready to play. We had Stacey Simmons and Tony Lomack, who had been running backs in high school, great athletes, but who weren't quite ready to play.

"So we went into our first year against Miami with the idea we were going to run the shotgun, that we were going to throw the ball a lot. We didn't really have a running back yet. But Miami had a really great defensive line and they really destroyed us [Florida lost 31–4.] They hit me a lot and slightly separated my shoulder. I had to have IVs after the game.

"Miami also had a great secondary with Bennie Blades and those guys, and our receivers dropped some balls. That was probably the worst offensive game I was involved in. We scored four points on two safeties. That was a BAD game."

The next opponent, Tulsa University, was good for an attitude boost. For the first twenty minutes the Gator offense didn't do much, but then it scored seven touchdowns the rest of the way in a 52-0 romp. One of the six players who scored was a freshman back by the name of Emmitt Smith. In the middle of the first half he ran through the middle of the Tulsa line for a 66-yard touchdown. It was the first in a legendary career.

Herbert Perry: "Emmitt came from a 4A school. As a freshman he was like an old pro. Most freshmen try to prove they are somebody. They are trying to prove they aren't scared of the middle linebackers, scared of the toughest defensive backs. They want to show they are the big dog on campus. So when they get the ball, there is a huge collision.

"Juniors and seniors don't do that. They make their reads, get the ball through the hole, and when someone comes to hit them, they rub off and go down. You don't want to get hurt in practice. You certainly don't want to get killed in practice. But freshmen are out to impress people.

"Emmitt didn't care whether he impressed anyone or not. In practice they'd call plays, and Emmitt would get the ball, but he wouldn't take a hit. He knew what he could do, and so he'd go through a hole, jitterbug a little bit, and he was so patient—he wasn't the kind of guy who took the ball and just took off running—he would sit there, pick a hole, go through it, make five or six yards, and go down. The coaching staff really didn't know how to handle it. They were like, 'What is this?' I remember they actually got on him a couple of times for not hitting somebody.

"But when Saturday came around and he played against Tulsa, he took the ball and went right down the middle untouched. He didn't have to do anything. He just went straight up the field [66 yards] down the left sideline. In practice they always blew that play dead, so nobody had actually seen him run that far. We knew Emmitt wasn't that fast, but in college I never saw anybody run him down. A lot of runners have a fear of the open field, and when they hit it, they don't know what to do. Emmitt never shifted gears, but he never missed a gear. When he hit the open field, he just kept on going like he was going ten yards, and he'd keep right on going for fifty or sixty. He wasn't a breakaway runner, but he was so good at setting people up and getting through holes until he just ate up yards. They said he was too small to play in the NFL, but soon he will break Walter Payton's career yardage record. That was the way he was in college. He wasn't somebody you were scared to death to face as a running back, but at the end of the game he would have 150 to 200 yards, or maybe just 110, but he always made positive yardage. He never took a big loss. He was just smart. And his vision was unbelievable. I've never seen anybody running one way and be able to see a hole on the back side as well as he can. He just feels the football field as well as anybody. He was a professional running back from the first day he stepped foot on Florida Field. You can't say that for many freshmen. Emmitt didn't have Sammie Smith skills, where he was 6'3" and ran the forty in 4.3. He was small. He was short. He wasn't that fast. But he found a way to get yards every time you got him the ball, and he has proven he is one of the greatest running backs ever.

"The other thing I remember about the Tulsa game is that I completed my first pass as a college player. I completed a 15-yard pass to Willie Snead down the left sideline. It was a down and out, and he broke it up the field against a man coverage."

Kerwin Bell: "[Tulsa] was a little, easy team, and it was in that game that Emmitt came in. The starter was a guy named Wayne Williams. Wayne was a pretty good back. He and Octavius Gould had shared time the year before, and both of them were pretty quick and did okay, but neither was the total package. Octavius had size but he didn't have a lot of great speed. Wayne was the speed guy but he wasn't a great inside runner.

"That fall was the first full class of recruits since we went on probation. We got a lot of great players that year. And Emmitt was the greatest of them all. Emmitt was the kind of player you had to see over and over to appreciate. He wasn't big like Neal Anderson. He wasn't superfast like Neal was. He didn't have Neal's raw talent. But when Emmitt got into a game, he made incredible cuts, always got positive yards.

"Emmitt was one of the top high school backs in the country. Everybody wanted him. He was national high school player of the year. And he really got us going after probation. We put him in the Tulane game, and he made a great play and ran [66-yards] for a touchdown, and he scored another touchdown from the one, and he ran for over a hundred yards [109].

"But when you play Tulsa, you don't put much credence in what a player does. To us players, we felt, 'Yeah, Emmitt did good, but it's Tulsa.' To me, when I think about Emmitt, I think about what he did the next week against Alabama."

What Florida did against Alabama was beat them 23-14 at Birmingham in a huge upset. Emmitt Smith, heretofore unheralded, carried 39 times for 224 yards and two touchdowns. Smith had eight runs of ten yards or more. He made five yards more than the Florida record for yards gains in a ballgame, beating Red Bethea's record set in 1940. His 39 carries also was a record, breaking Neal Anderson's mark of 34.

Herbert Perry: "Emmitt was unbelievable against Tulsa; he had a great game, but he didn't play the whole game. The Alabama game was the first game he started, and he basically dominated the game.

"Kerwin also had a good game. We kept the ball away from Alabama. And we did something you can't do against Alabama, something we had never been able to do, which was run the football. If you beat Alabama, you have to beat them passing, because their claim to fame has always been the run defense. That game was on national television, and it was Emmitt's coming out party. I remember one play where he broke down the left sideline for sixty yards.

"I don't think anyone expected Emmitt to do what he did as quickly as he did. Even the coaching staff was surprised."

Kerwin Bell: "We had a special game plan for Emmitt against Alabama. We ran a lot of draw plays, because the Alabama defensive line was really rushing us hard, and we just ran Emmitt up the middle on draws, and he ran for more than two hundred yards. And from then on in '87, we went from a passing team with a lot of young receivers dropping balls, into a running team. We really changed, because of Emmitt.

"I would have liked to have thrown more, but I understood the situation with us not having any receivers. They hadn't come on the way we thought they would. We had to do what we felt we could, though I thought we could have thrown a little more to help Emmitt out some more."

Mississippi State was next, and Florida rolled up 573 yards in a 38–3 win. Smith carried 20 times for 173 yards and three touchdown runs of 4, 42, and 30 yards. His seven touchdowns after three games matched Florida's total rush scoring output in 1986. After the game, a Florida fan yelled, "Emmitt for the Heisman." Said the modest Smith, "That makes me laugh."

Kerwin Bell: "In that game Emmitt had an unbelievable 80-yard run. A defender hit him solid, and he just bounced right off him and went 80 yards [but didn't score]. I've been around a lot of great players, but he made unbelievable plays, and he made them look ordinary. Because Emmitt wasn't flashy at all. He had a great ability to make people miss him and also to break tackles.

"Emmitt is so down to earth. I tell you, he came into Florida Field just wanting to be like everybody else. He had been national player of the year in high school. A lot of times guys have big heads, and they think they're better than everybody else, and even as freshmen they think they run the team. But Emmitt, he was such a team player. He had a good family, was brought up good. Emmitt's just a good guy.

"In the Mississippi game I threw a [34-yard] touchdown pass to Stacey Simmons. Stacey and Ernie Mills could run like the wind. Both of them could run 4.28 forties. They could fly. But they were inconsistent. They'd catch balls and make great plays because of their speed, but then they'd also drop balls. Stacey would have made the NFL if it hadn't been for his hands. He actually got drafted pretty high because of his speed, but he never made it because he couldn't catch the ball with enough consistency.

"Ernie was a really good guy, and I knew that eventually Ernie would be a pretty good player. He was helped out his senior year when Coach Spurrier came, and he became a great receiver his senior year. Then he got drafted and became a great receiver in the NFL.

"He just wasn't ready to play in '87. It wasn't his fault. It was nobody's fault. He shouldn't have had to play that early."

Florida traveled to Baton Rouge to meet LSU, and despite 184 yards and a touchdown by Emmitt Smith, the Gators lost 13–10.

Kerwin Bell: "That was another LSU game where I didn't play very well against them. LSU always was one of those games. I didn't play my best. It was a close game, and we had a chance to win it at the end. We had a drive going, but we weren't able to convert."

Herbert Perry: "That was a heartbreaker. We beat them pretty much all over the field. We just couldn't put the ball in the end zone. We missed two field goals, what with the wind blowing pretty bad there that night. Our kicker, Robert McGinty, kicked himself the whole year over that. We drove down, and we had a chance to win the game, and it was a 27-yard field goal, and we didn't make it. And that was probably the turning point to our season. If we win that game, we might have finished 8-4. Instead we finished 6-6."

After the LSU game, Florida got a breather when it was scheduled to face Cal State Fullerton. In the 65-0 blowout, Emmitt Smith ran for over 100 yards for the thirty-third time in a row including high school.

Herbert Perry: "The seniors that year was the last class that had been able to be recruited at full strength before the NCAA penalties of 1984. And we as freshmen were the first class to be recruited at full strength after the penalties. Emmitt and I were about the only two players who didn't red-shirt. That was the team that won the SEC championship in 1990 with Shane Matthews at quarterback.

"It had been hard because we only recruited fifteen sophomore and juniors where everyone else was recruiting twenty-five to thirty. So we had ten fewer sophs and juniors, and that's huge in college football. And in '87 a lot of the scholarships we did have were tied up in redshirted freshmen, so we didn't have the bodies to be able to compete with schools like Florida State and Miami. We gave them heck, but we just didn't have what you needed to beat them.

"So Cal State Fullerton was a breather. We were to them what Florida State was to us that year."

Florida hosted Temple for Homecoming and won another laugher, 34-3. Emmitt Smith ran for 175 yards. In his first seven games, Smith had run for over 100 yards every time.

Herbert Perry: "They were comparing Emmitt to Herschel Walker and Tony Dorsett, and he looked a lot like Tony, though Tony was faster, so when Tony got a step on someone, he just ran away from them.

"Herschel was blessed with more physical talent, but I don't think anyone has been blessed with the vision or the balance or the first-step quickness that Emmitt had. Herschel ran over people. He was a man among boys playing college football. Emmitt that year was a boy among men. They were a direct contrast."

Kerwin Bell: "We were 5 and 2 at that point, but we weren't as talented as some of the teams we were going to meet later on. We didn't have the same swagger in '87 that we had in '84 and '85, that's for sure."

fifty-six

A Tough Finish

The second half of the 1987 season would turn out as badly as the first half was wonderful, as Florida would lose four of its last five games. The start of the slide began at Auburn. Kerwin Bell was 19-33 for 231 yards but threw no touchdowns. Emmitt Smith didn't score. Two field goals was all the Gators were able to get that day as Auburn won 29-6.

Herbert Perry: "That was not a pretty game. We stayed in Columbus, and then we had to drive 45 minutes before the game. We had actually got things fairly righted. We were 5-2, and the game was big, because that stretch of Auburn, Georgia, Florida State and Kentucky—November was our nightmare back then. You hoped to have lost one game at the most going into this stretch.

"We thought we had a chance to win the Auburn game. But we weren't in the game at any point.

"I remember we had worked on the first play of the game all week long. It was Pro Right I, 252 X, Go. 'Pro Right I' was the formation. '252' was a play-action pass to the tailback—we were going to fake handing the ball to Emmitt, and run an 'X Go' route, which sent the flanker going right down the middle.

"Kerwin dropped back, faked it to Emmitt, he threw the ball to Ernie Mills, who was wide open, and Ernie dropped it. He was open by fifteen yards. And we never recovered from that offensively.

"It was just one of those games where we were really never in it. If we had gotten the first one, we might have given them a game, because college football is so much emotion. We might have been able to take the crowd out of it. But when he dropped that pass, it was just like the wind left us and never came back."

Kerwin Bell: "The Auburn game was a mirror of my whole '87 season. We didn't get much going. It was pretty close late, but then they scored a couple of times at the end."

Georgia was equally merciless. The Bulldogs held Emmitt Smith to 46 yards, and Kerwin Bell was sacked three times in a 23-10 loss.

Kerwin Bell: "They put it to us pretty good. It wasn't a very close game. We didn't play very well."

Herbert Perry: "I was standing on the sideline, and I remember seeing [Georgia's] Rodney Hampton break one up the sidelines and run right by me for about sixty yards. Georgia would have to be considered Tailback U. With Vince Dooley coaching, it was always been run first, pass second. If you're a running back, you want to go to Georgia.

"As a freshman I took over the punting job in the second half of the Georgia game. I stood on the goal line. I was so nervous I don't even remember catching the snap. I punted against the wind, which was blowing terribly that day, and it went 42 yards against the wind.

"I had moved up to second or third string quarterback behind Kerwin and Pepe Lescano, who was a senior along with Kerwin. They were moving someone in to take a few snaps to get ready for the next year, and in one of the games I got to play. For the year I was 3 for 7 for 30 yards."

Florida rebounded with a 27-14 win over Kentucky. In that game, Kerwin Bell threw his 55th and 56th touchdown passes, an SEC record.

Kermit Bell: "The SEC has had a lot of great players, and to have the record for the time was pretty special. I can look back and say at one time I was the SEC leader. Now I'm ranked fifth or sixth. Now everybody's throwing the football a lot more."

Herbert Perry: "Kerwin's people skills are unmatched. To this day, he's just an awesome person. He'll cross the room and talk to somebody. He doesn't avoid anyone. He always has a smile on his face. He's not fake—that's the way he is. He's just happy being himself.

"He loves the game of football. He's still playing it at age 36, which is amazing considering what's happened to him. It's one thing to be in the NFL all those years and be babied, but he has basically had to fight his way year after year.

"At Florida he was eighth on the depth chart, and he fought his way up to number one. He's just a winner, an awesome person.

"I was always in awe of how hard Kerwin and Emmitt worked. I wanted to win, and I wanted to do the best job, but I didn't always put in the amount of work it took, especially at quarterback. It wasn't as big a challenge to me as, say, hitting a baseball. Quarterback is a real headsy position. You have to know the offense inside and out. I knew that offense of Mike Heimerdinger ten times better than I knew any offense after that."

The constant pounding was beginning to take its toll on Emmitt Smith, who twice had to leave the Kentucky game with injuries. But against FSU, which was fighting for the national championship, Smith ran 20 times for 100 yards, and set the season rushing record at Florida with 1,341 yards. The only other freshman ever to rush for more than 1,300 yards were Tony Dorsett and Herschel Walker.

Florida had a 14-3 lead over FSU in the first half. In the second half, Florida could only gain 34 yards, and the Gators lost 28-14.

Herbert Perry: "It's for bragging rights for the state of Florida. It doesn't matter what happens the rest of the year. It makes or breaks your season. If you can beat Florida State, it doesn't matter what kind of year you're having.

"We got up for the FSU game, and we had a chance to beat them. They had a few more horses than we did, and it ended up showing at the end. We got off to a good start, but they basically took over and dominated. If we could have made a couple of big plays, an interception here, a big pass for a touchdown…it just didn't happen that way."

Kerwin Bell: "We played them at Florida Field, and they didn't play their best. They seemed like they were intimidated when they played us at our place. We just felt real comfortable.

"They were more talented than us—by far. We came out and jumped on them early and got the lead—we were ahead 14-0—and I really believe we blew it.

"We got the ball with three minutes to go before halftime on about the 35, which is good field position. I was a senior who had started four years, and I wanted to take the ball and try to score again. A lot of times the last three minutes of the first half is crucial to both sides. I wanted to be aggressive, to try to get a drive going, and get us at least a field goal.

"Coach Hall thought we should just try to run the ball out, to run three times and hopefully run out the clock. To me, that didn't make sense, because nobody says you're going to get the first down anyway of you run it. You're going to have to give them back the all if you don't. And that is exactly what happened.

"We had to give it back, and they wound up kicking a field goal right before halftime.

"I remember walking into the locker room, and everybody was saying, 'Man!' We knew the game was getting away from us, because that was a big momentum change for them, because of what they did right before halftime. They had been down the whole first half, and instead of us trying to do more and really putting it to them, they came back and had the big momentum swing.

"Then they really took charge in the second half and beat us."

Despite the loss to FSU, the 1987 season had to be looked upon as a great success. The reward for Florida's fine play was a trip to the Aloha Bowl on Christmas Day in Honolulu, Hawaii. Their opponents were the Troy Aikman-led UCLA Bruins.

Herbert Perry: "It was kind of exciting. Any time you get a chance to go to a bowl, that gives you something other than pride to play for. And we were going to Hawaii. It wasn't the Sugar Bowl, but it sure beat nothing.

"We had a good time sightseeing, probably too good. We went to see Pearl Harbor. We weren't stupid, but we weren't playing for the national championship. We played a good football game. We just didn't win. We played Troy Aikman. Our defense, which was great all year, sacked him [five times], and he threw a couple of interceptions."

Kerwin Bell: "We went to Hawaii and had a great time. We got there five or six days before the game, and all the players got to ride mopeds all over the island. And we got to play a great team, UCLA, which had Troy Aikman, and fullback Gaston Green, who played in the NFL, and Flipper Anderson, a good receiver who played in the NFL. And they had Ken Norton on defense. He and Aikman later played together on the Dallas Cowboys."

It was 10-10 at the half, and Florida trailed 20-16 with minutes to go. Kerwin Bell was able to march the Gators down to the UCLA 20, but time ran out before they could get any further.

Kerwin Bell: "What I remember about the game is that we sort of gave it to them. We really manhandled them the whole game, and then we gave them a drive, and of the 70 yards they gained, 45 yards of it was in penalties. It was all personal fouls, three fifteen yarders. We hit out of bounds, did things we weren't supposed to. Emmitt had a great game, and we played well, but we gave it away just on stupid things."

Herbert Perry: "We couldn't sustain enough drives. Our weakness was our offensive line. Our wide receivers were young. Stacey Simmons was young; Ernie Mills was young. A couple years before that they had Bret Wiechmann and Ricky Nattiel, some really good receivers. What hurt us most that season was that Kerwin didn't have any seasoned receivers to throw to. We didn't have any deep threats. Stacey could get behind them, but his hands weren't the best in the world, and I don't know how many passes he dropped, but it was quite a few.

"That summed up our year. Kerwin took a beating all year. We had two really good tackles, but they were young everywhere else. If we couldn't run well, we couldn't sustain a drive, because Kerwin got sacked or the receiver dropped the ball. That happens with young receivers.

"Clifford Charlton played a good game that day at linebacker. [He had three sacks.] Clifford was quiet. You never heard him say anything. He was a really hard worker. Jarvis Williams was the team leader on defense, the 'get-up' guy. Clifford never said anything, but 'let's snap the ball and go.'

"In the UCLA game, I had a punt blocked, and that ended up killing us. It was in the second half. It happened quick.

"It was frustrating because the week before against Florida State, they got in there—their punt rush was the best in the country—and it seemed like I was punting between arms the whole game. I'm a two-step punter, so it's not like I take a long time to get it off. I may have taken a quarter of a second longer than normal, but I don't really think so. We were ahead at the time, and they took it in for the winning score.

"We lost 20-16, and that blocked punt ended up being the ball game. It was a pain in the butt because you hated to be part of something that might have cost you the game. It turned the momentum of the game. I was on our fifteen, and that's a tough spot. When you see punts blocked, it's usually inside the twenty, because they have nothing to lose. I may have underestimated their rush compared to FSU's. Maybe I was trying to kick it too hard. Kickers think like that. You run out there, stand on your fifteen, you look in front of you, and there is eighty yards of football field in front of you, and you want to kick it as far down the field as you can. You take one step a little longer than normal, and before you know it, they're there. I'm sure that ended up costing us the game."

Kerwin Bell: "Coach Hall was really mad after the game. I remember him telling the returning players, 'If you're going to play like that, don't bother showing up in the spring, because you're taking everything away from the team when you do things like that.'

"It was my last college game. If I had left after my junior year, I would have been a first-round draft choice. But my senior year I missed four games because of an injury, and my numbers were down because we ran a lot in '87, and I don't know how many touchdown passes were dropped that year—probably ten, so I didn't put up nearly the numbers I had as a sopho-more, and so people thought I had maxed out, and in the draft I was a sev-enth-round pick of the Miami Dolphins.

"I would see Stacey Simmons and Ernie Mills, and they would say to me, 'K.B., man, we cost you millions. We cost you MILLIONS!'

"And I told them, 'Hey, it wasn't your fault. You know you all weren't ready to play.' It's not like they were trying to drop balls. They just weren't ready to play. And I told them, 'You never know, if I had gone out early, I might not have gotten drafted anyway. Who knows?

"I was really upset after the first day, when the draft went four rounds and I wasn't picked. So when the Dolphins called me, I was just glad to go somewhere. Now they keep three quarterbacks and another one on the practice roster, but back then in the NFL teams were only keeping two quarterbacks. And at the time Miami had Dan Marino and Don Strock.

"When they drafted me they told me they were looking for a young guy as a third-stringer because Strock was getting older.

"I had a good camp. Dan Marino was a big help to me. He'd tell me some reads I wasn't making, and he'd always come up and make suggestions and help me as much as he could.

"Right before the season started Don Shula called me into his office and said, 'We're going to have to cut you because we're only keeping two quarterbacks.' But he said, 'You can play somewhere in this league, and I've already called some teams.'

"That year the Atlanta Falcons picked me up off the waiver wire. They made some final cuts, and they released me, but they told me they were going to pick me up again, and they did. I spent my rookie year with Atlanta.

"It was a totally different offense. I never did grasp it. I didn't play because they went with their starters and were trying to win games, so that was a wasted year for me. I sat there and didn't do anything.

"I was a Plan B free agent, and Ray Perkins, the head coach of the Tampa Bay Buccaneers called me and said he wanted me to sign with them in '89. Tampa also had two quarterbacks, Vinny Testaverde and Joe Ferguson, who was a veteran. It was going to be his last year, and Perkins wanted me to come in and be third string for a year and then hopefully I would move up.

"I probably made a mistake signing with them, because right before I signed with Tampa Bay, Lindy Infante, the head coach of the Packers, called me and said he wanted me to sign with the Packers. I was living in Florida. I'm FROM Florida. But as I look back on my career, that might have been my one opportunity, because Lindy was going to camp with five quarterbacks and not one of them was a starter. And instead of fighting for that job, I went to Tampa Bay knowing I was the third-stringer. That didn't make sense, but I was thinking Tampa Bay, not Green Bay. I was young, and I wanted to stay closer to home.

"So that was my one chance, and I didn't take it. Maybe I wouldn't have ended up the guy, but I could have competed for the starting job, instead of winding up third string.

"Tampa left me unprotected, and during the summer of 1990 Lindy called me again. This time Don Majkowski was the starter. I went there and took the physical, worked out for the Packers, and flew home to Gainesville. Cris Collinsworth had a big golf tournament, and Neal Anderson had come down to play in it with me, and the night before Neal and I were playing basketball in Mayo in a game, and I blew out my knee. I tore my ACL, tore everything. I had to have reconstructive knee surgery. That ruined my chances with Green Bay.

"In 1990 Steve Spurrier hired me as a graduate assistant at Florida while I rehabbed my knee, which took six months. I was one hundred percent, ready to go back to play in the NFL in January of 1991, even though I had missed a whole year. Then all of a sudden, a new league called the World League of American Football started up. It was a spring league, and I went to a training camp held jointly by all the teams, and I was drafted in the first round by the Orlando Thunder coached by Don Matthews, a Canadian Football League coach. Don was the all-time winningest coach in the history of the CFL. Our offensive coordinator was Galen Hall.

"I played there for two years, and then I went to the CFL for the first time with the Sacramento Gold Miners. Sacramento was the only CFL team in the states. All the away games were played in Canada.

"When they signed me I was going to be the starter, but then they signed David Archer, who had been with the Philadelphia Eagles, and when Sacramento gave him a lot of money, David signed with us. So I became the backup. Kay Stephenson, who had gone to the University of Florida, was the head coach.

"I was with Sacramento for a year and a half, and that was when I really got involved in coaching. Kay would let me draw up the plays during the week when I watched film of our next opponent, and I'd give them to him, and he'd use some of them. And I'd help him on the sideline.

"Then halfway through the next season David got hurt, and I went in. After the season my contract was up, and the Edmonton Eskimos offered me the starting job for the '95 season.

"I played there a year. Doug Flutie was in Calgary, and we had a lot of big games against them.

"Then Lindy Infante got the head job at Indianapolis, and he brought me to Indianapolis. I was there in '96 and '97. I didn't play much. I had left college in '88, and this was '96, and I had yet to complete a pass in the NFL.

"But Jim Harbaugh got hurt, and against the Philadelphia Eagles, our backup started and got hurt in the first half, and I played the whole second half, and I went 5 for 5 for 75 yards and a touchdown.

"I tell people it only took me eight years to complete a pass and score a touchdown!

"And that was my only action. I didn't play again in '96, and I didn't play at all in '97. So for my NFL career, I'm 5 for 5 for 75 yards. I am the all-time leading passer in NFL history! I have a perfect rating! You can't have a higher rating than what I have.

"We had a bad year in '97, finishing 3-13, and Lindy got fired. Jim Mora became the coach. My contract was up, and they were going to draft Peyton Manning. Meanwhile, Doug Flutie left Toronto to go to Buffalo to get back into the NFL, and the Toronto coach, Don Matthews, called me and asked me to be his starting quarterback in '98.

"In the first pre-season game I broke my left arm and missed the first four regular season games. I came back, and for the last fourteen games of the season I led the CFL in passing. I threw for right at 5,000 yards, had 27 touchdown passes, a CFL record, and had the highest completion percentage at around 67 percent. That's the all-time record for the CFL.

"That was a great year. Then Don Matthews left and went to Edmonton, and Toronto said they wanted to go younger and wanted to run the ball more, and they traded me to Winnipeg for four players.

"We struggled in Winnipeg, because they hadn't won but two or three games. We finished 6–12, but it was a tough year, though we finished strong.

"I came back in 2000 and got hurt. I had to miss five games. When my backup played well, I was expendable because I was making the most money.

"During this time Toronto hired a young guy, Mike Clemons, to be their coach. He was my age, 36, a running back who I had played with. They called him 'Pinball,' and they love him in Toronto. He's been there for twelve years. They asked him to be the head coach and asked me to come back to play quarterback and be the offensive coordinator.

"We started the season 1–7–1, and halfway through the year we redid the whole offense. We went 6–3 the last nine games. So we turned it around.

"I was putting all the game plans in, and then after the season we brought in an offensive coordinator, and I worked with him, and so the 2001 season was going to be my last year. It was my thirteenth year, and I was 36, and I wanted to have one more great year, but I hurt my ankle badly in the first game, tore ligaments, and I missed the first nine games. I came back, and we went 4 and 2 the last six games, but we were out of the playoffs. I was a tough year all around. We were not very good.

"I just got home, and I want to get into coaching. I took a job at Trinity Catholic school in Ocala. They are starting a brand new program. I may do that as a transition before deciding whether I want to coach in college or the pros."

fifty-seven

Turmoil

In 1988 a tall, All-American tight end out of Brandon High School by the name of Kirk Kirkpatrick made the Florida varsity. Kirkpatrick had always wanted to be a Gator, and when his girlfriend also decided to go, his mind was made up. What he hadn't counted on was what a tough time he would have both keeping the girl and making the team.

Kirk Kirkpatrick: "It was easy for me to pick Florida. My girlfriend wanted to go to the University of Florida. That was the main thing, but also, I always was a Gator, so I wanted to go as well. And when I got to Florida, she remained my girlfriend for about six months. The was the most heartbreaking split I've ever had. I guess it was typical: I got to a big school and discovered I was a nobody. I was not a good-looking youngster, and they shaved my head, and I went from being a kingpin at my high school to being a nobody with a shaved head. She discovered there were other people, and she was a pretty girl, and she found out there were guys who were a lot older than me who had more going for them. So, I got my heart broken. It was the first time that had ever happened to me. So it was tough.

"I first arrived at Florida in the fall of 1986. They red-shirted me because I was only 210 pounds. They had a bunch of tight ends who were bigger than me.

"I remember we had Adrian White, Louis Oliver, Carnell Williams, three guys who could really hit who ended being top picks in the pros. They were the starting defensive backfield, and I was on the scout team, so I had to go up against those guys, and they were 22 and I was 18, very timid, and I remember going over the middle to catch passes and getting my clock cleaned a bunch. But it was something you have to go through.

"I was a redshirt freshman, and I played with Kerwin Bell for two years.

He was from Mayo, Florida, and he was a very good quality person. What you see is what you get. He wasn't full of airs. He was very simple.

"He had a great arm. And he was a hard worker. He didn't get distracted by anything. I got to know him better when he returned as a graduate assistant in '90. When you're a freshman, you're too in awe of everybody to get to know them."

But in 1988, Kerwin Bell was gone, and the heirs to the quarterback job were Kyle Morris and Herbert Perry.

Herbert Perry: "Kyle and I were roommates. He was a red-shirt freshman, so both of us were sophomores. We got along great. We were complete opposites. He was a fun-loving, loose kind of guy, and I was straightforward, almost reclusive. I didn't go out. I played baseball and went to school. If I had any free time, I came home. Kyle had the attitude that to be a quarterback, you had to be like Brett Favre, happy-go-lucky, letting it all hang out. I wanted to see something twice before I'd believe it.

"It wasn't an unfriendly competition. We went out there and fought, and he ended up winning the job."

Kirk Kirkpatrick: "Herbert Perry, who played baseball for the Cleveland Indians, Chicago White Sox, and now the Texas Rangers, was quiet like Kerwin, and Kyle Morris was a madman.

"Kyle was a great golfer and a lot of fun to hang out with, but he was a riverboat gambler. He had a rocket for an arm, but too often he liked to throw the ball into double coverage just to see if he could get it in there."

Before the Montana State opener in 1988, quarterback Herbert Perry boasted to reporters that the game would be little more than a scrimmage.

Herbert Perry: "You don't want to insult them, but come on. They should not have been able to stay on the field with us. It's hooking up a four-wheeler to a four-wheel drive truck and having a pull and seeing which is stronger. If the four-wheeler wins, something is wrong with the truck.

"We beat Montana State 69-0, but 1988 was a tough year for me. Lynn Amadee came in as offensive coordinator, and he changed the offense. The year before I had been practicing with the first and second team. Lynn

Amadee was Kyle Morris' godfather, so you can read between the lines. I don't want to say anything negative, but when the offensive coordinator comes in to the first meeting with the team, and the first words out of his mouth are, 'How are you doing, Kyle? How's your father?' I didn't know anything about it. It was like, What's going on? The best I can tell, Lynn Amadee and Kyle's father went to school together. And that year I don't think I got to hand the ball to Emmitt one time the whole season. So it was a little bit different. It kind of took away my love for football. It was a tough year."

Kirk Kirkpatrick: "It was Kyle's first game, and we played a team that was horrible, and I had two catches for 28 yards, nothing great, but we really just crushed them."

Ole Miss came next at Veterans Stadium in Jackson, where Florida won 27-15. Kyle Morris started at quarterback and finished the day 7-15 for 88 yards. Emmitt Smith carried 20 times for 109 yards. One of the game's highlights was Stacey Simmons' 85-yard return of a kickoff.

Kirk Kirkpatrick: "It was my first start. We played at a neutral site in Jackson, and we played pretty well. Stacey Simmons ran a kickoff back 85 yards. Stacey was a freshman brother. He was a speedster, and he had great moves once he had the ball. Stacey's only problem was his hands. If he had had great hands, he would still be in the NFL. So he was more of a running back. He was small, about 175 pounds, but he had great moves and could take a hit, and he could really go."

In the Ole Miss game, defensive back Louis Oliver had seven tackles and broke up three passes.

Herbert Perry: "Louis was another quiet guy. He was a hard worker. He was in the weight room constantly. Kerwin said that when he came to Florida, he was skinny. He wasn't skinny when he left. He was 6'3", 230 pounds, and he could run.

"Louis was the enforcer on defense. You did not want to leave a receiver over the middle with him back there, because he would take his head off.

"I remember in the Orange and Blue game, I misread the defense, and I thought I had a receiver wide open going across the middle, and I ended up hitting number 18 [Oliver] right in the chest, and he took it in for a touchdown. I remember trying to tackle him, and that wasn't pleasant. His senior year he tookover where Jarvis [Williams] left off. He was the guy who would talk in team meetings, and he was the leader. Defense wasn't the problem in '88. Our weakness was offense."

Kirk Kirkpatrick: "Louis, who came from Belle Glade, Florida, was a guy who had all aspects of his life in order. His dorm room was absolutely perfect. He had a 3.5 GPA. He worked out like a madman. He dressed immaculately. He was a very, very sharp, intact guy. He didn't come from much, but he was always very prepared. He was up at seven in the morning, ate breakfast, went to class, then worked out and ran three miles before practice. Louis was very, very on top of it."

Against Indiana State, Kyle Morris, the redshirt freshman, was 15-21 for 299 yards and two touchdowns as Florida won 58-0. Emmitt Smith carried 21 times for 109 yards. In the next game against Mississippi State, Smith led Florida to a 17-0 when in the third quarter he ran 96 yards for a touchdown.

Herbert Perry: "As great as Emmitt was when he began, Emmitt was stronger his sophomore year and maybe a step faster. His vision was God-given. He had a feel for the game few running backs in the history of the game have ever had. He was patient. You couldn't rattle him. Other backs you could rattle, and they'd try to run you over or try to do more than they were capable of doing. Emmitt never did that. He'd let the offensive line do its thing, and he would find the hole. He had a patience and maturity you can't teach. As the game went along, he was still back there chugging along. If you gave him an inch, he'd take a mile, to use an old saying. He'd pick his holes, get three yards, find a little gash there, get four yards, and then pop one fifteen yards. You add that up, and that's twenty-two yards in three carries.

"He was just unbelievable. He was quick. He could go side to side, and it didn't matter. He could be running full speed, and he'd cut on a dime and go the other direction.

"He didn't beat you with his legs. He beat you with his brains and with his eyes.

"You're not going to run over defensive backs any more. If you do, you're not going to last. Everybody wears out. By finding holes and rubbing off guys, he didn't get hit. We didn't have a great offensive line, and he still would run up yards."

Florida's next test was against 14th-ranked LSU and its star quarterback Tommy Hodson. Emmitt Smith had another superb day, rushing for 203 yards and leading the Gators to a 19-6 win. By game's end Smith had run for 2,003 yards in his career. Only Tony Dorsett and Herschel Walker had ever run for so many yards by the fifth game of their sophomore year.

At the end of the game Emmitt Smith predicted that Florida would win the SEC and go on to the Sugar Bowl.

Kirk Kirkpatrick: "It was a typical October day, a little bit hot. Richard Fain had a pick or two for a touchdown. And I had a catch for 12 yards, which was great for me. It was on CBS with Brent Musburger."

The win over LSU was the high-water mark of the 1988 season. The Gators' record was 5-0. They would win only two more the rest of the way.

The first indication that there were problems ahead was a lackluster 17-11 loss to Memphis State, a 23-point underdog. In the final minutes of the game Kyle Morris suffered a broken little finger to his left hand. Worse, during the game Emmitt Smith suffered a knee injury. He would miss the next two games.

Kirk Kirkpatrick: "It was a cloudy, overcast day. We just lost to them, and there was no reason for that to happen. They were horrible."

Herbert Perry: "We had great number ones, but we didn't have a lot of number twos, because of the NCAA sanctions. When our starters got hurt, then it hurt. And against Memphis State, Emmitt was hurt, and Stacey was hurt, and Ernie was hurt. We were down to Willie McClendon, who was a true freshman running back."

With Kyle Morris injured, Herbert Perry made his first start against Vanderbilt. He completed 21 passes for 181 yards, but was sacked three times and threw two interceptions in the face of a fierce pass rush.

Florida was down 7-0, when Perry threw a 29-yard pass to Tony Lomack that took the Gators down to the Vandy three. But there was a mix-up on the play-calling between Coach Lynn Amadee and Perry, as Florida's

Willie McGrady ran the ball into the teeth of the Commodore defense for no gain.

Herbert Perry: "Coach Amadee was calling the plays, and the formation I ran was different from what they called. Plays would not get to the huddle until five seconds before you were supposed to snap the ball. It was a pain in the butt. I had a pretty good game, but we could not put the ball in the end zone.

"Vanderbilt should not stop the University of Florida inside the five-yard line, but they stuffed us twice. If we had had Emmitt, you never know what might have happened. We didn't have Stacey. We didn't have Ernie. We didn't have Kirk Kirkpatrick, our tight end.

"The play calling was interesting. It was not fun."

Without Emmitt Smith to call on, Florida was shut out by Auburn 16-0. By the end of the third quarter Florida had zero yards rushing and less than a hundred yards in total offense.

Kirk Kirkpatrick: "Here's a funny story. Well, it's not really funny. Actually it's kind of sad. Auburn was rated in the top ten, and we were big underdogs, and at our pregame meal some of the players from the '64 team that had beat Auburn wanted to get us all pumped up. They had this little plaque that all of them had signed, and they asked us to sign it too. The plaque said, 'We're going to give our all for the University of Florida, and we're going to beat Auburn.'

"So everybody signed it, and we went and got our ass beat. Brad Culpepper and I laughed that we had ruined those people's plaque. I always felt we had ruined it. It was so bad."

Kyle Morris returned against Georgia but couldn't throw a Touchdown pass. Florida lost again, 26-3. The field goal that Florida did get cleared the crossbar by inches.

Kirk Kirkpatrick: "I remember the Thursday night before the Georgia game Kyle drank too many beers over at Joe's Deli, which is where everyone went to drink beer. Lynn Amadee found out about it on Friday, and he was giving Kyle a hard time. When Kyle played badly on Saturday, Lynn was really mad. He was so pissed off at him that they didn't get along from then on.

"Lynn Amadee was a card. He would come in wearing six shooters. He had been offensive coordinator at Texas A&M, where they had averaged 250 yards passing and 250 yards rushing. He was the hot offensive coordinator, and he came to Florida, and we just stunk! His offense was horrible. He came in talking a lot of BS, and after one year he was run out of town.

"So we got smoked by Georgia. They had a big running back by the name of Lars Tate. The guy was excellent, and we got our ass beat."

Herbert Perry: "Emmitt and Kyle both were healthy for the Georgia game, and they gave me a token start. I went out, and I was three for four for 19 yards. They pulled me, and they put Kyle and Emmitt into the game at the same time after two drives. And basically, that was it for me for the rest of the game."

The week before the Kentucky game, Kyle Morris and Len Amadee fought, and Herbert Perry was given the start at quarterback. Florida trailed early in the third quarter, when Coach Hall put Morris into the game. Morris led Florida to a field goal and a drive culminating in an 8-yard touchdown by Emmitt Smith. The Gators won 24-19.

The FSU game at Tallahassee was the low point of the season, a 52-17 debacle. Kyle Morris and Herbert Perry completed only 6 for 20 passes for 73 yards. Emmitt Smith needed 68 yards to reach 1,000 for the season. He made only 56 before having to leave in the third quarter after injuring his knee.

Kirk Kirkpatrick: "Deion Sanders arrived in a limo for that game wearing a tuxedo. He didn't even take the team bus. It was his last game at FSU, and they just smoked us. They were SO good!"

"I remember the captains went out for the pre-game warmups. Chief Osceola was supposed to come out and throw his spear, but when we came running out, we were so loud, and we ran to the hash mark and we scared Chief Osceola's horse, and he bucked the rider off, so he didn't get his chance to throw the spear. We were so pumped up. We were raising hell. It was the most pumped up I ever saw a Florida team. And what did we lose by? [52-17] That goes to show you how much being pumped up gets you! They just came out and kicked our butts. I goes to show you that talent counts for a little bit more!

"Kyle was very erratic. Like I said, he was a riverboat gambler. And against FSU, we just got absolutely killed."

Herbert Perry: "It was one of their best teams, and it was one of our worst. They were so much better than we. By then, basically the team was falling apart after losing to Vanderbilt, Auburn and Georgia, and eking out a win against Kentucky. To think we started off that year 5-0. You get demoralized. Everyone was beginning to see the writing on the wall, that there would be another coaching change.

"No one with any common sense could actually blame Coach Hall, because we lost Emmitt and Kyle and all our receivers and our tight end, and were down to second and third stringers on a team that didn't have second and third stringers able to handle the job. It wasn't his coaching. That year, 1988, and the next year, Florida was probably the weakest, because of the NCAA sanctions. We had some talent. We just didn't have enough to be able to compete with the big schools. There was a lot of turmoil. And obviously losing creates turmoil. It was NOT any fun."

Despite the turmoil and the mediocre 6-5 record, the Gators were invited to play in the All-American Bowl in Birmingham, Alabama, against Jeff George and Illinois. Thanks to the heroics of Emmitt Smith, Florida emerged with a 14-10 victory.

Kirk Kirkpatrick: "Birmingham is not really the place you want to go to for a bowl. But that's where we went. It was cold and raining.

"The game was played on Astroturf at Legions Field, and on the first play from scrimmage Emmitt took the ball and ran [59 yards] for a touchdown. At this point we pretty much expected him to get 130 yards a game."

Herbert Perry: "It was just a bowl game. It was not a big bowl game. And honestly, by the end of the year I was toast. I felt like, 'This is crap.' I'm a pretty upbeat person, and I try to look at things optimistically, but by that time I was through quarterbacking the University of Florida football team.

"I suppose if I hadn't been playing baseball, I would have come back in '89. But by that time I knew I was going to be drafted in baseball, and so I transferred over to a baseball scholarship.

"They said to me, 'We have Kyle. We have Shane [Matthews]. We just want you to punt.' And so I started the '89 season punting, and the week before the Ole Miss game I had a death in the family, and when I came back I basically lost my punting job, and they didn't tell me about it until Saturday, when I went to run onto the field, and somebody grabbed me by the back of the shirt and told me, 'We're letting Hank [Rone] handle the punting this week.'

"At that point I was completely fried. That was pretty much it. I went and talked to Coach Hall and told him there were three weeks left of fall baseball and that I wanted to go play. He asked me not to.

"I said, 'Coach, that's pretty much it for me.' It was not the way you wanted to end a football career, especially one that you started with high expectations. That was crap, just straight-up crap. It wasn't that I wasn't doing a good job. They told me Hank was a senior, that he'd had a great week in practice, and they were going to let him handle it.

"I still think the world of Coach Hall. He didn't do this. It was the punting coach. I didn't play politics very well, I guess.

"My junior year we went on to the College World Series in baseball, and I was drafted by the Cleveland Indians while I was at the World Series, and I've been playing pro baseball ever since.

"I was accused of being a quitter, and I am NOT a quitter. Five years in the minor leagues, eight surgeries—two shoulder and six knee—proves that I'm not a quitter.

"We had three different offensive coordinators in three years, and I was having great times at baseball and needed to work on my baseball career, because it was fairly obvious that I was not going to play [pro] quarterback on Sundays.

"It's just interesting some of the things that happened."

fifty-eight

Coach Hall Steps Down

The 1989 season began inauspiciously, with the first loss in a home opener since 1971, as Ole Miss was the surprise winner, 24-19. The losers were coach Galen Hall and quarterback Kyle Morris, as Florida fans called for both their heads. Lost in the headlines was a fine performance by tight end Kirk Kirkpatrick and a heroic effort by Emmitt Smith.

Kirk Kirkpatrick: "The home opener was against Ole Miss, and that was my breakout game. I had six catches for 86 yards. I remember we had a third and twenty, and I had a one-handed catch for 27 yards. It was on regionally on TBS, but as far as we were concerned, it might as well have been on nationally.

"Emmitt sprained his knee the first play of the game, but he never left the game. [He ran 26 times for 117 yards and two touchdowns.] Emmitt played with pain. He would pretty much do whatever it took."

Late the Ole Miss game, quarterback Kyle Morris threw across the field, and the ball was intercepted for a 58-yard Mississippi touchdown. The fans booed him lustily.

Kirk Kirkpatrick: "That's what he would do, take huge chances. He would throw it into the flat when there was no reason to do so.

"Whitey Jordan, who came from Wake Forest, was our new offensive coordinator. He was an old coot, must have been 65 years old, a very nice guy. He once coached Eric Dickerson at SMU. Emmitt loved him. Of all the coaches, he was Emmitt's favorite. He didn't have that dynamic an offense, but he was a very nice guy and very much a players' coach, and everyone liked him."

Florida rebounded against Louisiana Tech, 34-7. Kyle Morris only completed six passes but three were 69-, 84- and 44-yard touchdown passes.

Kirk Kirkpatrick: "We played in the rain. They had a fairly good team, but we played well. I caught a pass for 35 yards.

"When Kyle was on, he was excellent. What a lot of people and the fans don't understand is that there isn't much of a difference between a Kyle Morris and a Payton Manning. Kyle's arm was as good as Payton's, but at the time same, Kyle made stupid decisions and Payton didn't. And in a lot of ways, that's huge."

Against the University of Memphis at the Liberty Bowl on a cold night, Emmitt Smith ran 24 times for 182 yards and scored twice in a 38-13 victory.

Kirk Kirkpatrick: "The Liberty Bowl is a miniature of the Old Sombrero in Tampa. It looked exactly the same. They were built by the same architects. The locker rooms are the same. You enter and exit the field the same. It was a little weird."

The Gators the next week traveled to the Old Sombrero in Tampa for a game against Mississippi State. Florida was a 21-0 shutout victor.

Kirk Kirkpatrick: "We had an unblievable defense; we had a horrible offense, which is sort of sad when you have Emmitt Smith at running back. With all the talent we had, we couldn't seem to be able to put the ball in the end zone. We didn't pass the ball. We didn't do much of anything but give it to Emmitt."

Against Mississippi State, the Florida defense was superb. Mississippi State gained only 48 yards in 30 carries. Linebacker Huey Richardson had a league-leading nine tackles.

Kirk Kirkpatrick: "Huey went 6'5" about 245 pounds. He was fast, a great athlete and a great guy, though he's one of the more bizarre athletes you'll ever meet. He loved to watch cartoons and just goof around and be a kid. That's the way Huey is."

Florida's record was 3-1, and against LSU in Baton Rouge, the Gators won again, by the score of 16-13. With only ten seconds left on the clock, Arden

Czyzewski, who had kicked only one field goal prior to the game, booted a 41-yarder one foot inside the left upright to win the game.

Emmitt Smith ran for 117 yards, including a 19-yard touchdown run. After the game Coach Hall talked to reporters with an uncharacteristic intensity.

Kirk Kirkpatrick: "I understand Galen was very emotional after the game, because he knew he was getting ready to get fired.

"We had no idea. We were very surprised by it. We were pretty much shocked by it. We found out the day after the LSU game. We were about to go to our Sunday team meeting, and about ten minutes before we were going to leave, I was watching ESPN, and Brent Musburger came on and said Galen was getting fired.

"As a player, and this is true of any college player, you are always the last to know. They don't care what you think, and that's disappointing, but it's true.

"We had to go into our meeting to hear it straight from Galen himself. I remember him being a little bit sad. He said that mistakes had been made, and that we were going to be fine.

"The reason Coach Hall was let go was over something that had happened a few years earlier. We had a player by the name of Jarvis Williams, who played in our secondary. Jarvis went to Coach Hall and said, 'I really need to pay $500 to my ex-girlfriend because she's raising our child. I'm going to jail and I'm not going to be able to play if I don't pay her.' So Galen made the payment.

"But it was against NCAA rules, and we were put on probation because of it. I have no idea how the NCAA even found out about it. He was doing it to help out his player.

"Coach Hall was replaced by Gary Darnell, who was our defensive coordinator. I didn't know him very well. He was an okay guy, a hard-core disciplinarian."

At the time Galen Hall stepped down, Florida had a 4-1 record. The rest of the way the team was only 3-4. Part of the reason the team fell apart was that two days after Galen Hall stepped down, quarterback Kyle Morris was suspended for the remainder of the season for placing bets with friends on football games.

Kirk Kirkpatrick: "Shane Matthews and two other players were involved in that with Kyle. What happened, they had a bookie in one of the fraternities, and they were placing $25 bets on games. They didn't bet on Florida games.

How can I say this without getting someone in trouble: the father of one of the other players turned Kyle in. The player knew Kyle was betting on football games, and he happened to mention it to his father, who was a very, very strict disciplinarian, a guy who came to every single practice. His life revolved around his son playing for the Gators. When the player told his father that Kyle gambled on a few college games, the information was anonymously given to the athletic director, and then it became public.

"And after Kyle was suspended, we were down to Donald Douglas at quarterback. Donald was a great athlete, but not a very good quarterback."

Florida was able to win its first two games under Gary Darnell, as they defeated Vanderbilt 34-11 behind Emmitt Smith's 202 yards rushing, and beat New Mexico, 27-21, thanks to a super-human effort by Smith, who gained 316 yards, a school record.

Florida led Auburn 7-3 in a defensive struggle, but with 28 seconds left in the game, Auburn quarterback Reggie Slack threw a pass down the right sideline to Shayne Wasden for a 25-yard touchdown and a 10-7 victory.

Donald Douglas, in his first start, carried 12 times for 68 yards. In the air he was 1-5 for six yards.

Kirk Kirkpatrick: "Against Auburn, we gained exactly six yards passing. I had one catch for six yards. I was the whole passing offense that game."

Florida could have won the Georgia game as well. The Gators led 7-3 midway through the third quarter. Florida was driving, and on third and one, when Douglas stumbled, and Emmitt was stopped behind the line of scrimmage, Florida went for it, and failed to make it. Georgia went on to win.

Against Kentucky at Florida Field, Tony Lomack starred for the Gators. The Florida back ran back one punt 45 yards and ran another back 99 yards for a touchdown in a 38-28 victory.

Kirk Kirkpatrick: "Tony Lomack was a running back from Tallahassee Leon, the same school Brad Culpepper went to. Tony was a great running back, but they put him at wide receiver. He had a lot of talent. They just didn't utilize him very well.

"I remember for that game we wore orange pants and orange jerseys. All orange. We looked like Clemson Tigers."

The final game of the regular season was against Florida State University. Emmitt Smith's touchdown against Kentucky had made him the all-time leading scorer at Florida with 209 points. He was named to the 1989 Kodak All-American team, the first non-senior from Florida ever to be named. He would leave with fifty-three Florida rushing records.

Despite Smith's heroics, Florida lost, 24-17.

Kirk Kirkpatrick: "On the first play of the FSU game I could have scored a touchdown. We ran a play for me right up the middle. The play called for me to be covered one-on-one by a linebacker, and when we ran a play-action, the linebacker was sucked in, and I was wide open by twenty yards. Lex Smith was the quarterback, and he overthrew me by twenty yards. It was a national broadcast, and I remember being very disappointed. It was kind of a microcosm of our season."

The Freedom Bowl, played on December 30, 1989, was a dispirited 34-7 loss to the University of Washington. Quarterback Cary Conklin took Florida apart. After Emmitt Smith carried the ball seven times and Washington swept to a big lead, the Florida star took off his uniform and sat on the bench.

Kirk Kirkpatrick: "He took his shoulder pads off and sat on the sidelines. He was pissed off. The offense wasn't blocking for him, he knew he was leaving, and he didn't want to get hurt. He definitely didn't want to play any more."

For several days before the bowl game it was reported that Steve Spurrier was going to leave Duke and return to Florida as head coach.

Kirk Kirkpatrick: "I don't remember hearing anything about Coach Spurrier until after the bowl game. I remember everyone on the plane on the ride home was pretty rowdy, just because everyone knew Spurrier was coming in.

"We knew he threw the ball a bunch. We knew he was a Gator. As odd as that sounds, it's kind of nice when your coach is somebody who played at the University of Florida. I think we should always stay in-house and hire fellow Gators as coaches. As biased as that may sound, I liked that Spurrier was coming in. Emmitt, however, was upset, because he was very loyal to Coach Jordan. He told me, 'I know that Whitey is probably going to be fired. So I'll probably go pro.'

"What am I going to say to him? Emmitt had millions of dollars in front of him. How can I talk him out of that? Know what I mean? So I really couldn't talk to him.

"Coach Spurrier talked to Emmitt a little, but Emmitt said no. But Coach Spurrier is Coach Spurrier. And so if Emmitt is not going to stay, he's not going to stay. Even though he didn't have a huge track record behind him, Coach Spurrier was not going to kiss anyone's ass."

fifty-nine

Steve and Shane

On Tuesday, December 26, 1989, it was reported that Steve Spurrier, the former University of Florida Heisman Trophy award winner, was leaving Duke University to return to his alma mater as head coach. *The Raleigh News & Observer* reported he was offered the job on December 12. Spurrier also was having discussions with the NFL's Atlanta Falcons and Phoenix Cardinals. He signed a five-year contract with Florida for $1.65 million a year.

In the fall of 1977, Spurrier was finished as a pro athlete. Three NFL teams had released him, and he came back to Gainesville with only an offer to sell cars in Ocala or Jacksonville. He was 32, unemployed with a wife and three kids.

He sat in the stands at Florida Field watching Florida play, and he decided he wanted to be a coach. But how to get his foot in the door? He was a golfing buddy of a man named Henry Gray, who was Florida head coach Doug Dickey's lawyer. During a match at the Gainesville Country Club, Spurrier asked Gray to talk to Dickey about hiring him.

After Florida finished the 1977 season 6-4-1, Dickey decided he needed more bang on offense. Dickey's wishbone was becoming passé. Dickey decided to hire Spurrier and give him total control over the offense.

Suddenly in '78, the offense exploded, but Florida still lost more than it won, and to save his job Dickey needed to beat both FSU and Miami. When FSU won, Dickey was out. Spurrier applied for the job, but it was given to Charlie Pell. When Pell did not re-hire Spurrier, he called his old offensive coordinator, Pepper Rodgers, who needed added offense at Georgia Tech. Rodgers' job was in jeopardy, and he hired his former pupil. But Rodgers did not give him the leeway he needed to make the offense work, and Georgia Tech opened the season 1-5-1. Finally, Rodgers relented. Spurrier began calling the plays and implementing his passing philosophies, and Georgia Tech responded by beating Duke, Navy, and Air Force. When Tech lost to Georgia in the final game of the season, Rodgers was fired. Spurrier, who had just bought a house in Atlanta, wanted to stay in Atlanta, but Bill Curry, Rodger's replacement, turned him down. According to a friend of Spurrier's, Curry told him, 'Everybody wants me to hire you, but I have to be honest with you. I don't think you've got what it takes to be a football coach." It was a remark Curry would rue the rest of his coaching career.

Spurrier was out of a job again, but not for long. Spurrier's Georgia Tech offense had defeated Duke, and Blue Devil coach Red Wilson was mightily impressed. Wilson hired Spurrier to be his offensive coordinator, and Spurrier helped guide quarterback Ben Bennett to a career record of 9,614 yards gained.

In 1983 John Bassett, the owner of the Tampa Bay Bandits of the newly formed United States Football League visited Tom McEwen, the sports editor of the *Tampa Tribune*. Bassett asked McEwen who he ought to hire as head coach.

Said McEwen, "Go interview the offensive coordinator at Duke."

"Who is he?" Bassett asked.

"Steve Spurrier. Just go interview him," said McEwen.

Bassett hired Spurrier on the spot to coach the Tampa Bay Bandits in the USFL, and in three years he led the Bandits to a 35–19 record with two playoff appearances in three years.

Jimmy Dunn helped coach the Tampa Bay Bandits under head man Steve Spurrier.

Jimmy Dunn: "One day they announced the United States Football League, that the Tampa Bay Bandits were coming to town, and Coach Spurrier hired me to coach the receivers for him. I had been fired when Charlie Pell came in, and that gave me a chance to get back into coaching.

"The Bandits existed for three years. We were a good team. We were in the playoffs. John Reaves was with us, and Wayne Peace. We also had a real good football player, Gary Anderson, out of Arkansas, who ended up with the Chargers and then with the Bucs.

"Steve's approach to playing offense is that he thinks it's just as safe to throw the ball as it is to hand it off and to run off tackle if you have guys who can throw and who can catch and if they will run the pass routes where he wants them to run to take advantage of the different defenses. And he has the knack of putting the puzzle together with the linemen for the protection. And if his quarterback has protection, he takes pride in that quarterback knowing exactly where the weak spot in the defense is, and he will deliver the ball to that point, and that receiver needs to be there.

"Steve will make a quarterback as good as you want to be. If you don't want to be good, then you're not going to be good. You'll get discouraged. But if you want to be good and you pay attention, he will put you in a position to let you use every bit of your ability, mentally and physically. He'll let you check off the play. He'll give you the opportunity to throw all the screens, throw every pass possible, but you have to perform.

"So his philosophy is that there is no bad field position. Everything is like the middle of the field in perfect weather. A play you call at midfield you would also call on your own two-yard line. And his players believe in that. He does not mind taking the ball straight down the middle of the field out of the end zone. And there are very, very few coaches who would do that. They don't do it because they are afraid of the turnover, afraid of the negative things that can happen, and Steve thinks only of the positive things that can happen.

"Steve changed the SEC. He took the SEC from the wishbone and off-tackle and defensive punting to wide open, best athlete you can find with speed and who can throw and catch."

After the United States Football League folded, in 1987 Spurrier returned to Duke University as head coach, and he built a dynamic offense that so impressed the University of Florida that it hired him in 1990 to rebuild the program.

Who could have predicted that in his first season at Florida he would breathe new life into the team?

One of his first jobs was to find a quarterback. Kyle Morris was returning after his half-season suspension in 1989 for betting on football games. Lex Smith and Dan Douglas were returning, and Florida had recruited a hot young quarterback who had transferred from Purdue University by the name of Brian Fox. But when the 1990 season began, the starter was none of the above. Rather Spurrier chose a quarterback who pretty much had been ignored by the Hall administration, a cool kid by the name of Shane Matthews.

Shane Matthews: "I started playing football when I was five years old. My dad was a head football coach in Cleveland, Mississippi, and I lived there until my ninth grade year, when we moved to Pascagoula, Mississippi, which is on the Gulf Coast and which is the largest high school in the state of Mississippi.

"I played for my dad, Bill Matthews, which can be terrific, but it can also be difficult. When we moved to Pascagoula, the program wasn't very good, and when we arrived, I became the quarterback, and everybody said, 'The only reason he's playing is he's the coach's son.'

"Playing for my dad prepared me to work for Coach Spurrier, because I don't care what level it is, T-ball or Pop Warner, any time you play for your dad there is a lot of pressure. But we never discussed football at home. We felt it on the field. We would discuss basketball or baseball at home, because I played them too, but never football.

"It came down to Florida, Florida State, and LSU. I wanted to play in the SEC real bad. My parents didn't like FSU at all. They didn't like anything about the program. So they said, 'You're not going there.'

"So it came down to Florida and LSU. Baton Rouge is only three hours from Pascagoula, whereas Gainesville is six-and-a-half hours away. But I really liked Florida, and it turned out well.

"In '88 I was a redshirt freshman. I didn't do much my first two years. I kind of got lost in the shuffle. I even thought about transferring back to Ole Miss. I was away from a lot of my buddies, and I didn't get to play. Two of my closest friends had signed with LSU. A couple went to Mississippi State. A lot of my friends who didn't play sports went to Ole Miss. And I had grown up an Ole Miss fan and I had hung around the program for so many years.

"Once you come over by yourself, you don't know anybody, and when you're not playing and things aren't going the way you expected, you kind of want to go back home, back to your roots.

"But when I was growing up, one thing my dad always told me: 'If you start something, finish it.' A lot of kids nowadays, whether it's piano lessons or flag football, if they aren't playing well, they quit. Well, that was never going to happen in my family. So we stuck it out. Thank goodness Coach Spurrier got hired and gave me a chance.

"In '89 I was playing behind Kyle Morris, Lex Smith, and Dan Douglas, and I wouldn't even call it playing. I didn't really do anything. I got lost, big-time, in the shuffle, but my parents wanted me to stick it out and see it through, and I was very fortunate.

"In '89 I got caught up in a betting scandal. Kyle Morris was my roommate, and he and I and a couple of walk-ons from our fraternity were betting on football games. We weren't doing anything different than what other people in college and around the country were doing. We got in trouble, and we had to face the consequences, and then move on. It just got blown way out of proportion. We had to live with it.

"Kyle was suspended for the rest of the season, and then he came back in '90. Kyle was a good guy. He was my backup in '90, and then he transferred to Mississippi College.

"I didn't even know who Steve Spurrier was, to be honest with you. I had no idea. I was back home for Christmas break after Galen was fired. I watched Duke play in the All-American Bowl against Texas Tech with my dad. We watched the Duke offense, and we knew he was going to be our head coach, and he said, 'Hey, this is gonna be a great fit for you if you're just given a chance.' I said to myself, This is perfect for me. Because the offense was very similar to what I did in high school.

"I remember the first meeting Coach Spurrier had with the players in spring ball. He didn't know many of the players. He said, 'Everybody is going be given an equal chance to show what they can do.'

"I really liked him. Like I said, I didn't know who he was. I didn't know he had won the Heisman Trophy. When you live in Mississippi, you don't know Florida history.

"I was very fortunate to get some playing time in some of the scrimmages in the spring. I was the fifth quarterback behind Kyle Morris, Lex Smith, Dan Douglas, and a guy named Brian Fox, who transferred from Purdue. He was Big 10 Freshman of the Year.

"At spring practice Brian broke his ankle, so that moved me up to number four. I played well in the scrimmages and then came the spring game, the Orange and Blue game.

"What they do is divide the team. The Orange team had two quarterbacks, and the Blue team had two quarterbacks. Our quarterback coach, John Reaves, out of the blue started me, and I ended up throwing three touchdowns, and Kyle threw three interceptions and that pretty much gave me the starting job for the fall.

"Spurrier's offense was very interesting to me. I picked it up very quickly, because I'd been around football all my life and I understand the game. Under his system, you not only have to learn the terminology, you've got to be able to know how to attack defenses. To play for him, you have to have a feel for the game. It's a tremendous offense, and once you learn it, it is very easy to run. I picked it up quicker than everybody else, and I like to think I made better decisions, and that's the key to his offense: good, smart decisions.

"I threw my share of interceptions, and sure there were throws I'd like to have back. There are still some games that hunt me. But for the most part I played pretty well."

sixty

Exciting From the Start

Kirk Kirkpatrick: "Spurrier was great right from the beginning. I don't mean to kiss his ass, but he came in with a lot of confidence, and he came in with a relaxed attitude. That was our problem the last three years: under Galen, it was so pressure-packed. We'd be playing Mississippi State, and you'd think it was the Super Bowl because the coaching staff would be on pins and needles, and they'd make us so tight.

"But Spurrier came in and said, 'Hey, you guys are great athletes. There's no reason you can't beat everybody. We're gonna have some fun. We're going to throw the ball around. We're gonna prepare ourselves. We're gonna have some good plays. And we're gonna have a good time.'

"He told us, 'We're going to have a good time. We're going to put points on the board.' He pumped that up. He already knew we had a good defense coming back.

"He said, 'It won't be physical as much as it'll be mental. You are going to have to think a lot, and you'll have to remember your plays and your assignments.

"Our practices weren't physical any more. But they were a lot more mental. And that's where he really excelled. I remember when he handed us the playbook. Everyone thinks Coach Spurrier's offense is so complex. But in reality, the formations come off a basic tree. It's NOT that complicated. It requires common sense. To me, it was fairly easy to learn. There are a lot of different formations, but it's fairly basic. That makes it nice, because everybody understands it and can make adjustments to it.

"He brought us confidence right from the beginning. He came in with a lot of pride. He was always very, very pro-Florida. He said that after the game we were going to sing the alma mater. He was just a great Gator. Everybody was very excited to play for Coach Spurrier.

"Another thing Coach Spurrier did: he picked the right players for the right spots. Shane Matthews was fourth on the depth chart, and he didn't have any more talent than the other people. And he made the plays."

Right before the opening game of the 1990 season against Oklahoma State, five students were murdered on the University of Florida campus.

Kirk Kirkpatrick: "That was absolutely horrible. I remember it because it happened on August 26, my girlfriend's, now my wife's, birthday. That put a big downer on our season from the very beginning, because everyone was scared. You had five gruesome murders. Gainesville is not very big, and each one was a mile or two apart. It was very nerve-wracking. The police were looking for this killer, but for three straight nights some other girl would get killed. Danny Rolling was the guy who did it, but they didn't catch him for two or three months.

"The women on campus were petrified. My girlfriend was scared. If you had a serious girlfriend, Coach Spurrier let you go over to her place and stay the night, which was nice of him, because my girlfriend lived alone. Not that we were living in sin or anything, but I wanted to stay with her because I was worried about her.

"I didn't have a gun, because I'm scared of guns, but I was very prepared. I had a baseball bat. I was ready."

The opening game against Oklahoma State was a stunning inaugural for both Coach Spurrier and Shane Matthews. Florida took the opening kickoff, and without a huddle went eighty yards for a touchdown in six plays. It was a revelation. For the next dozen years, Florida would feature an offensive juggernaut. It would have an offense unique to the history of college football.

Shane Matthews: "Before the Oklahoma State game I remember Coach Spurrier coming into the locker room. It was my first career start. I had come out of nowhere, and Coach Spurrier made me his starter, and a lot of people were skeptical.

"He would always ask me, 'What play do you want to start with?' I said, 'Let's throw a screen or a draw.' I just wanted to get my feet wet.

"He said, 'No, I'll tell you what. We're gonna open with a deep crosser out to Ernie Mills. He'll be wide open.'

"We brought Ernie Mills in motion and ran him on a deep crossing route, and I hit him right in the numbers and gained about thirty yards, and five plays later we were in the end zone.

"We got ahead big-time, and in that game I threw my first career touchdown pass, to Tre Everett, on a deep post route. [It was a 50-yarder.] Tre was one of the fastest guys on the team, another player who had gotten lost in the shuffle under Galen Hall. He and I came in together, and neither of us got to play very much. But Tre was the kind of player Coach Spurrier was looking for: he ran good, precise routes, had good hands and was extremely fast.

"It was a pretty good debut [20-29 for 332 yards, eighth best in school history], and it kind of laid the foundation for the rest of the season."

Kirk Kirkpatrick: "From the very beginning Spurrier would tell us what was going to happen, and it would happen. He would say, 'We're going to run a no-huddle, and we're going to go right down the field.' And we did.

"He calls a great game plan. It was just unbelievable. Everybody was prepared. I remember the day of the game I went to the pregame meal. It was three or four hours before the game, and Coach Spurrier was in the pool because he had just gone for a jog. I swear he was having a beer. He was completely relaxed.

"He said to me, 'Hey, how ya doing? Ready to have a good game?'

"I said, 'Yeah, Coach.'

"He said, 'Alright. We're going to toss the ball around on them.' That's the way he was. He was that confident."

In the 50-7 win, Kirk Kirkpatrick caught several balls, including one that almost went for a touchdown.

Kirk Kirkpatrick: "I had four catches for 50 yards. One catch I took down to the one-inch line, but I didn't score. It was great! It was SO great. We threw the ball around, and we had a good time."

The first true test of the season pitted the Gators against mighty Alabama at Tuscaloosa.

Shane Matthews: "In the first half we couldn't do anything offensively. I wasn't playing real well. They were shutting us down. Will White was keeping us in the game. He had three interceptions. We were down 10-0 until the middle of the third quarter."

Midway through the third quarter Shane Matthews hit Terence Barber in the back of the end zone to make the score 10-7, and then with 'Bama on the Florida 14 with third and five, 'Bama threw into the end zone, where Will White picked it off and ran the ball out to his own two. Florida began its drive from there.

Shane Matthews: "This was one of those games where one of the old Florida teams would have lost. Nothing against them, but I had always heard that Florida couldn't win on the road in the SEC. And with this being Spurrier's first road game in a hostile environment in Tuscaloosa, nobody expected us to win it, but we found a way to pull it out.

"Coach Spurrier called a 'deep post' from the two yard line, and when it came in, I thought, Is he crazy? But he can see things that other people can't, and I ran a play-action pass, and Ernie Mills was wide open, and it was an easy throw. The play should have gone 98 yards for a touchdown, but the turf-monster got him—he tripped on the turf—and he got down to the [Alabama 28]. [Six plays] later, Arden [Czyzewski] kicked a field goal to tie it 10-10.

"And then we blocked a punt and Richard Fain fell on it in the end zone to win it [17-13].

"Richard was a senior. He was one of those DBs who made a lot of big plays that year, a lot of key interceptions. Falling on the fumble was a HUGE play. Richard was a good, solid leader on our team. He played a couple years in the NFL."

Kirk Kirkpatrick: "Will White's third interception in the end zone at the end of the game clinched it. He was only a sophomore, but he was a free safety who liked to play the middle of the field. He didn't come up and lick you, but he was a great centerfielder type. Will had a great knack for the ball. He had three picks that game. That year he was a first-team All-American. And he was only a sophomore.

"It was chaos after we won. It was perhaps the biggest victory Florida had ever had up to that date. We didn't realize it, but Alabama ended up pretty stinky that year. But at the time they were undefeated, so it was a big game for us."

Before the Furman game, Kirk Kirkpatrick was disappointed to learn that because the NCAA had punished Galen Hall for paying child support to the girlfriend of one of his players, Florida would be ineligible to play in a bowl game in 1990 and would not be allowed to win the SEC championship.

Kirk Kirkpatrick: "It wasn't until the Furman game that I found out we had been banned from bowl play and from winning the SEC championship. It was pretty bad, because it was all about Galen Hall paying Jarvis Williams' child support. This had happened was several years before. But we had to pay for it. The NCAA made an example out of us. It was very, very disappointing. I remember being very hurt about that, but what are you going to do? You can't fight something you have no chance winning against.

"I remember we had white shoes, and we painted our shoes black. We were pissed off. Don't ask me what painting our shoes black signified. But when we went out against Furman, we had black shoes, and we decided that the rest of the year we were going to try to win every game and become number one in the SEC anyway."

Against Furman, the Gator defense was outstanding. The offense made a lot of mistakes, including two fumbles and two interceptions. Despite the 27-3 win, Coach Spurrier was unhappy. "We should have scored 50 points," he groused.

One of the stars of the Furman game was tight end Kirk Kirkpatrick, who caught five passes and scored his first touchdown.

Kirk Kirkpatrick: "It was an out and up route, good for 25 yards, and Shane put it right on the money. As sad as it sounds, I scored my first touchdown as a senior. It was exciting, but so long in the making that I wasn't too overwhelmed by it. In fact, I was relieved to finally get it over with. Because before that, that's all I heard: 'You've never caught a touchdown pass.' I was glad to get it over with."

Shane Matthews: "That year Kirk caught more than 50 passes, which is unheard of for a tight end. He wasn't a great blocking tight end, but in Spurrier's system, you don't have to be. He was extremely fast for a player his size. He probably had the best hands on our team. He was my 'go-to' guy. He was a senior who had been through the battles. Here I was a sophomore, and when it was crunch time, many times I looked for Kirkpatrick."

One of the defensive stars of the game was linebacker Brad Culpepper.

Kirk Kirkpatrick: "Brad is still my best friend. He was a very, very hard worker, a very disciplined type of person who gave it his all. Nobody is going to have more heart than he does. A lot of people saw his work ethic and didn't think he had natural ability, but he had great natural ability. He played in the pros nine years. He's the hardest worker I have ever seen.

"That game was a lot closer than 27-3. It FELT closer. And Coach Spurrier was pretty pissed off about that. He really did think we should have scored 50."

Shane Matthews: "Coach Spurrier expects to score a ton of points every time we lace up the shoes. He's a coach who strives for perfection, and a lot of people don't like that, just because they see him throw his visor and scream and yell. But it's all constructive criticism.

"Remember, I was the son of a football coach, and playing for my dad helped me to play for Coach Spurrier, because I could let it go in one ear and out the other. I listened a little bit, of course, but never enough to let it affect me when I played.

"I know there were quarterbacks who found it tough playing for him, but the two quarterbacks who played really well under him, myself and Danny [Wuerffel], we didn't let it bother us."

In a 34-21 win over Mississippi State, Kirk Kirkpatrick caught 7 passes for 99 yards, including a six-yard touchdown pass in traffic. The big tight end, ignored under the prior regime, was becoming an integral part of the new offensive scheme.

Kirk Kirkpatrick: "I'll make no bones about it: I was not a very good blocking tight end. But I WAS a very good receiving tight end. As far as just running my route and catching the ball, I did that better than anybody. And Coach Spurrier did a great job maximizing whatever talent his players had. So if one of his players runs great routes, Coach Spurrier is going to give him great routes to run. He wasn't going to ask me to do a bunch of sweep blocks, because he knew I couldn't do it. That's where he's very smart.

"I was a senior, and Shane was only a sophomore, but Shane and I got very close. He started to trust me, and he just started throwing me the ball a lot."

Senior Ernie Mills also had an impressive game against Mississippi State. The big receiver caught four passes for 118 yards, including an 18-yard touchdown.

Shane Matthews: "I know Ernie was struggling to catch the ball when Kerwin Bell was playing. He struggled so much because they didn't practice throwing and catching enough in practice. When Coach Spurrier got here, that's all we did. And you've got to give a lot of credit to our receivers' coach, Dwayne Dixon, for working with Ernie and making him the player that he became.

"Ernie was extremely fast, and he made some huge catches. His senior year he caught 12 passes and went on to a long career in the NFL."

Against Mississippi State, freshman Errict Rhett carried the ball 25 times for 143 yards, and he caught his first touchdown pass. The Gators had lost Emmitt Smith, but his replacement was showing people he too had great talent.

Shane Matthews: "Errict was not the flashiest runner, but he was a hard-nosed runner and very reliable. He was one of the toughest football players I was ever around. He's also a little crazy. It doesn't hurt when your running back has a little craziness in him. Going into the 1990 season, I don't think people realized how good he was going to be. He had an outstanding career."

Kirk Kirkpatrick: "Errict didn't have the talent Emmitt did, but he was a very hard worker, very dedicated, and he would do anything to get the job done. It was nice, because Emmitt, as gracious as he was, had been the type of player who demanded the ball 25 to 30 times a game. Errict was a freshman. He was so hungry, and that was nice. I don't know how well Emmitt would have fit with Spurrier, though I have a feeling Coach Spurrier would have found a place for him."

Against LSU at Florida Field, Florida led at the half 20-5. Jerry Odom had eight tackles. Dexter McNabb, from DeFuniak Springs, ran for the first touchdown. Shane Matthews threw Kirkpatrick an 18-yard touchdown pass, his third of the season.

Kirk Kirkpatrick: "It was a night game, and we played an excellent game. By the LSU game, we felt we could beat anyone."

Shane Matthews: "Dexter was an integral part of the offense. He was very highly recruited and was very talented. He was your prototypical running back, extremely big, strong, and fast. That year our three backs were Dexter, Willie McClendon, and Errict Rhett—they got most of the carries. If one guy would have played the whole time, it would have put up some HUGE numbers."

After the victory over LSU, Florida was 5-0. More impressive, game after game the offensive numbers were prodigious .

Shane Matthews: "We had Gainesville turned upside down! Actually, the whole country. We weren't ranked in any preseason polls, but after the LSU game, we were ranked tenth. We were getting ready to head to Knoxville.

"That was a nightmare.

"Coach Spurrier always has goals for us, and our number one goal was to win the SEC title first and then go for the big picture after that. If you don't win the SEC, you have no chance at the big title [number one].

"We went to Knoxville feeling good about ourselves. In the first half they got ahead 7-0. Right before the end of the half, we started to drive during the two-minute drill. I threw Kirk Kirkpatrick a wide open touchdown pass in the corner of the end zone, and he dropped it. We would have gone ahead. And that was probably the only pass he dropped his entire career. But he was wide open."

Kirk Kirkpatrick: "It was a corner route, and it went about 25 yards, and I just completely dropped it. I can honestly say it was the only pass I ever dropped in a Florida game.

"It hit me right in the hands. I only had two or three yards to work, and I was worried about trying to get my feet down in the end zone, and I dropped it. We ended up kicking a field goal to make it 7-3, and then they blew us out.

"They weren't that much better than us, but we got behind, and on the opening kickoff of the second half, [Dale Carter] ran one back [91 yards] for a touchdown, and we could never get back on the board."

Shane Matthews: "I threw a couple of interceptions, and it got to be a snowball effect where nothing went right. When it was 20-3, Coach pulled me out and put Kyle [Morris] in trying to get a little spark from him, and he fumbled the first snap, and they picked it up and went in and scored. It just got uglier. They won 45-3. It was a game that taught us a lot.

"Obviously Coach Spurrier wasn't happy. He grew up in Tennessee, so he really wanted to beat those guys.

"The Monday after the game we had to get up at 5:30 in the morning and run the stadium. It was the usual punishment if we didn't go out and play up to our potential. Not only the players did it. The coaches did it too.

"We ran what we called 'the snake.' You run up to the halfway point of the stadium up the stairs, then down, then up, then down, all the way around the stadium like a snake. It's a lot of steps, and you go around twice. It's very tiring, especially at 5:30 in the morning."

Akron was the Homecoming opponent. Florida was merciless, as Shane Matthews passed for 283 yards and three touchdowns before leaving in the third quarter. The final score was 59-0.

Shane Matthews: "We had much better talent than Akron. We took it out on them a little bit. We usually didn't play real well for Homecoming, because you have so many distractions that weekend. But against Akron, we were pretty focused, especially in the first half. We just wanted to get back playing the way we were capable of playing."

Fourth-ranked Auburn came to Florida Field, ordinarily a tough, grueling game, but on this night Florida won big, 48-7.

Kirk Kirkpatrick: "It was Senior Night, our last game at Florida Field, and we were pumped up for the game and feeling pretty good. We had an excellent game plan, and we had an excellent game."

Against Auburn, Shane Matthews was 16-19 for 147 yards, and even though he didn't throw a touchdown pass, Coach Spurrier said that he had played "as good a game as I have ever seen."

Shane Matthews: "That wasn't a lot of attempts or a lot of yards. We usually had more than that, but it was a solid team victory. All three areas—defense, offense, and special teams won that game for us.

"And after the game what Coach Spurrier started having us do was stand in front of the student section towards the south end zone and sing the Alma Mater as a team along with the fans.

"At first we felt, 'Whatever.' But when you've got 90,000 people singing it, it's kind of neat. Especially after you win a game. It feels good."

It had been four years since Florida had beaten Georgia at the Gator Bowl in Jacksonville. Florida had lost 15 of its last 19 games against the Bulldogs. But when Florida continued its incredible run with a 38-7 trouncing of Georgia, everyone realized that Florida was entering a special era of greatness. The past no longer mattered. Anything became possible.

Against Georgia, Shane Matthews was 26-39 for 344 yards and three touchdowns. Florida dominated even more than the score indicated.

Shane Matthews: "Before Coach Spurrier came, Georgia beat Florida almost every time. They owned them. When he took the job, he told the players, 'Number one, we're going to find a way to beat FSU; and number two, we're going to find a way to beat Georgia.'

Because when he was a player, he lost to Georgia quite a bit, and so he wanted to find a way to beat them. And I played well in the Gator Bowl against them every time out. I was playing in the Gator Bowl in the spring of 1990 when I won my job in the Orange and Blue game. Florida Field was being renovated, and we played it in the Gator Bowl The Gator Bowl was good to me."

Kirk Kirkpatrick: "What I remember best about that Georgia game was that when it started, the temperature was about 60 degrees, and by the end it was probably 40 and really cold. It was one of those weird winter days that start warm but end up cool then cold.

"We were pumped up and on a roll. After we beat Auburn, we knew we were going to kick Georgia's butt. The score was 38-7, but we didn't beat them as badly as we should have. I remember Spurrier was a little bit mad because he thought we should have scored 60 points."

In a 47-15 win over Kentucky, receiver Ernie Mills caught eight passes for 136 yards and two touchdowns, his best game as a Gator.

Shane Matthews: "Ernie caught quite a few balls that day. I remember him catching a post in a corner route for a touchdown, and Kirk Kirkpatrick caught a touchdown as well. It was another good effort by every area of our football team. We knew going into that game that we were going to win. We knew we were going to be the top team in the SEC."

After Florida defeated Kentucky, its record soared to 9-1 with only one game remaining. On that day Tennessee lost, so for the third time in Florida history, Florida finished first in the SEC. And for the third time in Florida history, the Gators were on probation and weren't eligible for the honor.

Shane Matthews: "That 1990 team gets overlooked a lot by a lot of fans because we weren't crowned official SEC champs, even though we won it. That irritated Coach Spurrier that they wouldn't give us the official title.

"It had something to do with Galen Hall, and what also bothered Coach Spurrier was that it was something that happened in the mid-1980s, and this was 1990, and they wouldn't let us go to a bowl game, and they wouldn't crown us SEC champs. It still irritates him to this day."

Shane Matthews: "Coach Spurrier has a ritual: any time we win a championship, the whole team gathers around in front of the scoreboard, and we take a picture. After that Kentucky game, that was the first one he took at Florida.

"We were in Lexington, and the Kentucky fans were hostile. They always are. They throw a lot of stuff at you. It was fun knowing we had won that game and that we were going to be the SEC champs in our hearts. It was just a good feeling on the plane ride back home."

Kirk Kirkpatrick: "Of course, we were on probation, so we weren't eligible to win it, and we knew we weren't going to a bowl game, so we decided that the FSU game would be our bowl game."

Shane Matthews: "It was a crazy night in Tallahassee. On the first play of the game, FSU threw an out-and-up. Casey Weldon rolled out, and he popped one to one of their wide receivers, and after our DB bit, the guy went straight down the field and was wide open. So it was 7-0 after the first play.

"The game basically was a shoot-out. They'd score, and we'd cut it to seven, and they'd score again. It was tough on us, because we felt we had a chance to win, but they were better than us that night. The score was 45-30. It eats at you any time you lose to those guys."

Kirk Kirkpatrick: "This was a very, very good FSU team, and Shane had a great day. [He passed for 352 yards.] Shane was a sophomore, very, very wet behind the ears. He had a great attitude about him. He's very laid back, always calm. Shane never gets ruffled. You never think he has that much ability, but he would always surprise you."

Shane Matthews: "At the beginning of the '90 season, Coach Spurrier told all the media people that his quarterback would probably be the All-SEC quarterback, that he would be named SEC Player of the Year, a statement that shocked a lot of people, because I was a kid who came out of nowhere and went on to win all the awards. But in his system, you're going to put up huge numbers. And I had great players around me. If we didn't have a good football team, I wouldn't have won anything.

"I owe everything to Coach Spurrier. If it weren't for him, I wouldn't be where I am today [in his tenth year in the NFL]."

Kirk Kirkpatrick: "Against FSU, which was the last game of my college career, we rolled up 484 yards on offense. They had 487, and we ended up losing, but we just had turnovers that killed us. We had a Willie McClendon fumble and a Dexter McNabb fumble. We were scoring points at will, but the fumbles were turning points for them. It was frustrating for us because we were really moving the ball on them.

"After the game in the locker room, everyone was disappointed. Final games are by nature disappointing just by the fact that the seniors are distraught because they are done. They don't have any more curfews, don't have anything. To have your season and your career done is pretty much frustrating in itself. It's difficult, because while you're playing, you have so much structure. Then all of a sudden, it's 'Okay, you're done,' and you don't have curfew—you don't have anything. You want to stay out until three in the morning? You can do that. And all along all you wanted to do was play football.

"I had pro aspirations. I had had a really good senior year. I really caught the ball well. I ran good routes, was fairly fast, but I was undersized, and I didn't play special teams very well. Someone in my position has to be a better blocker.

"I signed with the Rams as a free agent. I got a $5,000 bonus, and if I made the team I would get $150,000. Back in 1991, that wasn't bad. But I would have played for nothing.

"Playing for the Rams all I can remember was getting my butt kicked. That was pretty much it. I mean, I didn't have a prayer. I was far away from home. I was homesick. That's pretty sad to say when you're 23 years old. But I was. Even though you think you're mature at 23, you aren't.

"The coach was John Robinson. He told me something that was the best information I ever got. It was painful when I got it, and I hated him for a couple of years because of it, but right now I realize it was the best advice he ever gave me.

"He called me into his office and said, 'Kirk, you're a very good receiving tight end, and you might be able to bounce around the league for a couple of years, but you seem bright and smart, and you might be better off going into the real world and getting a real job. If you do that rather than bounce around, you'll be way ahead.'

"That hurt SO bad. My whole life all I wanted to do was play football, and all of a sudden someone was saying I wasn't good enough to play. But it wasn't long before I followed his advice.

"I played for Birmingham in the World League for Coach Chan Gailey, and that was okay, and I played for the Bucs for a couple of games, even caught a touchdown in a pre-season game. And then I got cut, and in 1992 I went to work for Merrill Lynch. It was the best thing I ever did.

"Then I started my own company, which we just sold to a company called Instanet, and they own the company now, and I have a two-year contract to stay on. Then I'm free to do whatever I want. So that was some good advice John Robinson gave me."

sixty-one

Spurrier's First Recruit

When the 1991 season began, Shane Matthews was comfortably ensconced as Florida's starting quarterback. Behind him him was a talented freshman by the name of Terry Dean. An All-American from Naples, Florida, Dean had attended Coach Spurrier's football camp during the summer after his junior year in high school, and he realized that Spurrier knew a lot more about the game than anyone he had run across. In the end Dean had to choose between Florida and Auburn. When he chose Florida, he became Spurrier's first and most important recruit that year.

Terry Dean: "I was recruited by Auburn, Florida State, Miami, and Duke—when Coach Spurrier was at Duke, and North Carolina State. My final two came down between Auburn and Florida.

"Going into my senior year my dad thought it would be a good idea for me to go up to Duke to go to Spurrier's football camp. That was the first time I had any contact with Spurrier. That went pretty well, and then of course we stayed in touch throughout the season. I remember him as having a lot more expertise on passing the ball than I had heard in any other camp.

"He stressed mechanics—where to hold the ball, where to release the ball. He was very analytical on the pass and the physics of the throw.

"And when he got to Florida, I was his first recruit. It was the perfect fit for me. As I learned more about him, I realized and learned that he was a thrilling coach—a head coach and offensive coordinator. It seemed like a pretty ideal situation for a quarterback.

"I graduated from high school in 1990, and I went up to Gainesville to compete for the starting quarterback job. My competition was a junior, Shane Matthews, and Kyle Morris also was returning. It was a wide-open job. And at the time, frankly, I was not ready to be a starting quarterback. It was like going from second grade math to quantum physics in a couple of months. I simply wasn't ready for two years, so I never thought I should be starting freshman year. I knew that Shane had earned the job. He was dynamite. Shane and I were friendly, but we were never friends. But there were never any ill feelings between us. In the opener in '91 against San Jose State, Shane threw five touchdown passes [tying a school record]."

Shane Matthews: "San Jose was one of those kinds of teams that knew they were outmanned, or undermanned, so they blitzed a lot, and we knew that from watching them on film.

"They would come with an all-out blitz, and I would change the play at the line of scrimmage, [and after Brad Culpepper recovered a fumble on the first play of the game], on our first play, I changed the play, and I called a corner route to Harrison Houston, who was starting in place of Tre Everett, who pulled a hamstring during warmups, and he ran a corner route, and I hit him for a touchdown, and I hit him for another touchdown the second time we had the ball. Like I said, this was a team that was going to try to blitz us, and all I had to do was read the blitz, change the play at the line of scrimmage, and let the receivers do all the work. They did, and they beat those defensive backs very easily, which made my throws a lot easier.

"Harrison had a huge day [He caught four passes, three for touchdowns].

"Harrison was a running back coming out of high school. He was only about 5'8", but he was extremely fast. He didn't have the greatest hands—he couldn't catch anything in practice. He dropped balls left and right. But when the game started, he was one of the most reliable receivers I had."

Terry Dean: "Harrison Houston was another member of our freshman class, a super good athlete, a quick receiver. He was an extremely quiet, shy guy who caught onto the system really quickly.

"Another fellow who was in our backfield that year was Errict Rhett. Let me tell you about Errict.

"He was really the first person I met when I got around the football program. My dad and I were in the meal room, and Errict was sitting down by himself, and we went over and grabbed a seat with him. From the first second he was a genuinely nice guy. He's one of the hardest working people I was ever around at the University of Florida. He had a unique trait. When we would practice running plays, he would run full speed into the end zone—every time. Normally a back will run ten yards and come back to the huddle. Errict would run full speed all the way to the end zone every time we handed off to him. I assume he wanted to think he was going to get to the end zone every time he touched the ball. Errict also was totally insane: he was the biggest trash talker I've ever met. He's a character."

Gene Stallings' Alabama Crimson Tide invaded Florida Field. Florida had never defeated Alabama at Florida Field during its entire history. But September 14, 1991, proved that the past no longer would be prologue. Led by Brad Culpepper, Will White and a staunch Florida defense, the Gators shut out Alabama 35-0.

Shane Matthews: "It was only 6-0 at the half. [Arden Czyzewski hit two field goals.] They had a good defensive plan against us. Every time we played Alabama, they always gave us fits. I struggled, but the defense kept us in the game.

"Then, in the second half, we exploded. We found a way to make enough plays in that second half to put some points on the board.

"One of the touchdowns was a pass to Willie Jackson, who was a freshman. Willie is still playing in the NFL. He was probably the most talented receiver I ever played with at Florida. He was about 6'3", 215 pounds, not as fast as most people want their receivers to be, but he was the kind of guy who made plays after the ball was in his hands. Whenever I needed someone to come up with a big play, Willie was the guy I always looked for. He was the kind of receiver Coach Spurrier liked, big and strong. He was a freshman walk-on who came out of nowhere. He's the son of Willie Jackson, who was the first black to play at the university.

"To hammer Alabama like that on national TV did wonders for our football program. We were still laying the foundation, because until Coach Spurrier came, we were nothing."

The Gators, ranked fifth in the country after their impressive shutout over Alabama, traveled to Syracuse to play the 17th-ranked Orangemen. There were missed tackles, blown coverage, and ill-advised passes, as Florida lost 38-21.

Shane Matthews: "We went up to Syracuse, and we really thought we were going to win, though everyone told us how tough it was to play up there. It's a small dome, only seats about 50,000 people, and it's extremely loud and it gets hot in there.

"They ran a reverse on the opening kickoff for a touchdown, and it kind of got the momentum going their way. Their quarterback, Marvin Graves, ran a ball-control offense, where they'd run the 25-second clock down to about two seconds, and we could hardly get on the field offensively. And when we did, I'd throw an interception or something bad would happen.

"It wasn't one of our best games. It certainly wasn't one of MY best games.

"Coach Spurrier was not happy. The next morning we had one of our 5:30 runs."

Florida rebounded with a 29-7 win over Mississippi State in the Citrus Bowl in Orlando. In the first half the Gator defense held Mississippi State to just 86 yards. Brad Culpepper led the defense with seven sacks.

When Shane Matthews threw a 19-yard touchdown pass to Willie Jackson, he tied Spurrier for third place on the all-time career list at Florida with 36. He needed 18 more to catch John Reaves, the Gator's tight end coach, and 21 more to pass Kerwin Bell.

Against Mississippi State, Matthews was 22-35 for 322 yards.

Shane Matthews: "That was a big game for me playing against a lot of my high school teammates from Mississippi. We beat them, but what I remember most about the game was that one of the Mississippi State players broke his leg and had to have surgery, and a week later he died in the hospital. It was an eerie feeling throughout our team the following week.

"That game when I broke Coach Spurrier's career passing record, he was very happy for me. He knew his quarterbacks were going to break a lot of his records, just because back when he played they didn't throw the ball that much.

"He loves for his quarterbacks to break all the records. He was happy when Danny [Wuerffel] broke all my records. Danny and I were both ecstatic when Rex [Grossman] shattered them in 2001. It all comes from the coaching and how he prepares us for the games."

Against LSU in Baton Rouge, Florida played grind-it-out football. Arden Czyzewski kicked three field goals in the first half, and Shane Matthews hit Harrison Houston with a 35-yard touchdown pass to give Florida the 16-0 win.

Shane Matthews: "We moved the ball up and down the field, but once we got inside the 20, we sputtered and couldn't find a way to put the ball in the end zone. That's why we had to kick so many field goals."

When 10th-ranked Florida met 5th-ranked Tennessee, the Gators were seeking revenge for their 45-3 loss the year before. With Tennessee leading 5-0, Florida had a fourth and one at the Tennessee one-yard line. Spurrier elected to go for the touchdown, and Shane Matthews threw a pass to Terrell Jackson. A touchdown pass to Tre Everett, and two short touchdown runs by Errict Rhett followed, as Florida prevailed 35-18.

Shane Matthews: "When we faced Tennessee in '91, we had been embarrassed by the final score the year before, so we were looking for payback. We knew that Tennessee was a team we had to beat if we were going to win the SEC.

"I got sacked for a safety and they kicked a field goal, and when we had fourth and one on the one, Coach Spurrier decided to go for it. He's not the kind of coach who likes to kick field goals, especially when you're on the one, and he doesn't like to punt. He feels his guys can get in there, whatever the play may be. And as a player, I kind of liked that too. You need to be aggressive and try to score as many points as you can.

"We ran a play to Terrell Jackson, our fullback. It was a gutsy call. It was a play-action pass, and they were thinking I was going to run it up the middle, so I faked it, and he was wide open, and I threw it to him.

"Because they didn't let us to go the Sugar Bowl in '90, Tennessee went. So they were the defending SEC champion. Beating them gave us a good feeling. It was a big win for us to stay undefeated in our conference."

Against Northern Illinois, Florida won 41-10, as the Gators rolled up 604 yards in total offense. Shane Matthews threw for 336 yards in three quarters of work. But Coach Spurrier was so upset when Matthews was sacked and pressured in the second quarter, that he put the second team offensive line into the game. When they didn't score in the third quarter, Spurrier became furious. That the defensive line was offsides four times didn't help his disposition.

Shane Matthews: "It's hard to focus for Homecoming games because there are so many distractions, so many parties going on that week. You've got the parade, and there is something going on every night of the week.

"I remember his comments after the game. I don't know if he was talking directly to me or to the whole team about how we was more concerned about going to the parties than about playing the game. That's what he was upset about the most. Because we should have beaten those guys by 50.

"Coach Spurrier is a very competitive guy. What I like best about him, he expects every play to work. As a player you like that. And he teaches us quarterbacks that if the play he calls isn't a good one when you come up to the line of scrimmage, it's the quarterback's job to change it and get the team into a better situation. That taught me a lot about the game."

Florida's most common stumbling block, Auburn, came next. The game was played at Auburn. Willie Jackson, who was a walk-on, got to play in the Auburn game because Tre Everett was injured. Jackson had not caught a single pass before this season. Before the game Spurrier went to him and told him, "Be ready for your big day." By the end of the game, won by Florida 31-10, Jackson had caught 12 passes, second only to Carlos Alvarez's one-game record of fifteen versus Miami in 1969.

Shane Matthews: "Before Spurrier came, Willie wasn't really given a chance. In Coach Spurrier's first year, Willie was a redshirt, and Spurrier spotted him on the scout team. He was killing our defenses, making plays every day. In 1991, Willie was eligible to play, and Coach Spurrier said, 'This guy is too talented to sit on the bench,' and he found a place for him. And once he got in there, he didn't let anybody take his position back.

"Before this game Coach Spurrier predicted Willie would have a big day. He watches tapes of opponents and looks at their defensive backs, and he must have realized that Willie was going to get open no matter what, and even if he was covered, he was so big and strong and athletic, he would come down with the ball no matter what. Coach Spurrier had a feeling this was going to be his break-out game, and he was right."

Against Auburn, Shane Matthews, who usually preferred not to run unless he had to, gained 106 yards on the ground."

Shane Matthews: "Sometimes they would drop nine defenders and only rush two, and that's when I would take off running. I had a 12-yard touchdown run, which is a pretty good run for me.

"Any time you go on the road in the SEC, it can get crazy. Our bench was right behind their student section, and they were throwing Jack Daniels bottles at us. They threw pennies and nickels, and it feels good to get hit with that stuff whenever you're destroying their team on their own field. That was another big win for us."

Despite the fact that it was a bitter cold day in Jacksonville for the game against Georgia at the Gator Bowl, Florida was excited because a win would mean an almost certain SEC championship.

Terry Dean: "The intensity of the Florida-Georgia game seemed a notch above some of the other games. I remember we were on the bus coming into the stadium. Georgia fans were lined up on both sides of the street, and as we were driving in, they were rocking our bus. I just remember it being such an exhilarating feeling coming through that."

Shane Matthews: "Georgia kicked a field goal early in the game, and then we scored on a [13-yard] run by Errict to go up 7-3. We then called a 'cover-2' pass, which spread out the defense, and we had Harrison Houston run a post pattern. We were in our five-wide receiver package, no backs, and I dropped back, and the middle of the field opened up like the parting of the Red Sea, and Harrison ran a good route, and all I had to do was throw the ball down the middle. He made a good catch, and he ran into the end zone [for a 36-yard touchdown]."

Shane Matthews wasn't done. His 61-yard touchdown pass to Alonzo Sullivan upped Florida's lead to 28-3. It wasn't even halftime.

Shane Matthews: "Alonzo was a wide receiver from the Tampa area. He was tall and rangy and extremely fast. He didn't get a lot of action because of the younger players.

"In the Georgia game I hit him on about a fifteen-yard curling route, and he broke a couple of tackles and went straight down the sideline, and nobody could catch him. In the box score it looks like I threw a long pass, but I just threw it fifteen yards, and Alonzo took it the rest of the way.

"I don't know what it was, but we had Georgia's number every time I played them." [The final score was Florida 45-Georgia 13.]

Next up was Kentucky, coached by Bill Curry. When Curry took over the Georgia Tech job from Pepper Rodgers, Steve Spurrier had been the offensive coordinator. Spurrier let Curry know he wanted to stay on, but he was fired anyway. Spurrier always held it against him.

Terry Dean: "Spurrier would even tell us that. He wanted to beat Kentucky more than most because he wanted revenge. And before the game, Brad Culpepper made a comment to reporters that Kentucky was like a 'gimme putt.' You know you're gonna make it, but you're afraid you might miss. That was insightful. I'm sure they played it over many, many times in their locker room." For added incentive, if Florida could defeat Kentucky on this day, the Gators would be crowned official SEC champions for the first time. And there was one other factor:

Shane Matthews: "We still had a chance to play for the national championship. We had to beat Kentucky, FSU, and then we might have had a chance to play for it in whatever bowl game that might have been.

"We prepared for the Kentucky game just like we did for any other game. And at the end of the first quarter we were ahead 28-0. I even caught a touchdown pass!

"It was one of our trick plays where I dropped back, and I threw it to Willie Jackson, and then I ran over to the other side of the field, and he lobbed it over everybody. I ran 30 yards untouched into the end zone. It was my first career touchdown catch. That was fun: running into the end zone. I got to show-boat a little bit—I high-stepped.

"I thought, Man, this is going to be a cakewalk. But it was nothing like a cakewalk. It turned into a dogfight.

"I threw an interception, and the defender ran it down to about the five and then they went in to score. They got within two points [28-26], and then we had a huge drive. [Matthews led a 12-play, 71-yard drive to put the game out of reach.]

"In the drive we had a crucial third and three, and they blitzed, and we got our protection messed up, and I threw the ball blindly over the middle where Errict Rhett was supposed to be, and luckily he turned around and the ball hit him in the stomach, and he fell forward for a first down. That continued the drive.

"Then we were third and goal from the two, and Errict scored on a sweep around left end [to make the score 35-26], and after the game it was just craziness.

"We had players crying. We had guys running around, carrying the cheerleaders' flags around the stadium. It was years and years of all the frustration that Florida fans had suffered for not having an official SEC title. We felt we got robbed the year before. They got all their frustrations out that day.

"I was extremely excited. There were ninety thousand people screaming and yelling. It was a great feeling to be the leader of the team, to be the first quarterback of the first official SEC title. It was just a wonderful feeling.

"Coach Spurrier, of course, was ecstatic. Winning the SEC championship had been one of our goals, and we still had a chance at the big picture—the national title. Miami was ranked number one, and we were ranked number three. We had a chance."

The final game of the 1991 regular season was against Florida State, led by quarterback Casey Weldon, at Florida Field. Going into this game, FSU was ranked number three and Florida was number five.

Shane Matthews: "It was hyped-up to be a shoot-out because both of these offenses had been putting up huge numbers, scoring tons of points.

"Well, it turned into a defensive slugfest. Casey Weldon took a beating. I took a beating. About the third play of the game I got hit high and hit low at the same time, and it caused my knee to buckle. I tore some cartilage. After the game I had to have surgery on my knee.

"Casey Weldon had to leave the game to get stitches. It was the most physical game I had ever played in. I was in a big boot for a week after that game before of an ankle injury, and two days after the game I had to have knee surgery."

It was also a game of bad feelings and trash talking.

Terry Dean: "I remember one play that stands out in my head. They had a linebacker who was one of their vocal leaders. Shane was over center calling out the signals, and this guy and Errict Rhett started mouthing off to each other. Errict got so mad, he started running forward to mouth off at him, and Shane snapped the ball, and we had a procedure penalty called against us."

Shane Matthews: "It was one of the games where neither offense could get going. The play of the game was a scramble out of the pocket. My high school teammate, Terrell Buckley, came up to try to tackle me and left Harrison Hairston wide open, and I hit him, and Harrison went [72-yards] for the game-winning touchdown.

"I don't know what my old high school teammate was thinking. He knew I couldn't run the football very well. He came up and left Harrison wide open, and it was a huge play in the game.

"And our defense came up with the biggest play at the end when FSU had a chance to win it."

Florida won the game 14-9 when safety Will White broke up two passes in the end zone with seconds remaining. Casey Weldon threw for 305 yards, but the Brad Culpepper-led defense prevented him from scoring again. It was the first win over FSU for the seniors.

The 1991 Gators became the first University of Florida team ever to win ten games in a season.

Florida was selected to play 18th-ranked Notre Dame in the Sugar Bowl. Few teams in America have a tradition like that of Notre Dame. From Knute Rockne to Lou Holtz, Notre Dame had always been synonymous with winning football. But for some of the players, making the Sugar Bowl was a letdown.

Shane Matthews: "When we went there, we knew we had no chance for the national championship, since Miami didn't come to play us. We were very disappointed. To be honest with you, Notre Dame didn't have a very good year that year. There was a lot of talk they shouldn't even be in the game."

For others, it was magical to be playing the Fighting Irish.

Terry Dean: "You grow up hearing about Notre Dame. Lou Holtz was the coach. It was something to be playing them. And it was a blast for us. I knew in all likelihood I wasn't going to play, so I had a lot more fun than some of the other guys. It was the first time I had ever been in New Orleans."

Shane Matthews: "We were there to enjoy ourselves. It was the first time Florida had been in the Sugar Bowl in I don't how many years [since 1974]. So we enjoyed ourselves, maybe even a little too much.

"But we came ready to play. In the first half we were kicking their butt. [Florida led at the half 16-7.] And it should have been more than that.

"And then they came out and pounded us in the second half, and we couldn't stop them. Jerome Bettis ran the ball down our throats. [Bettis scored three touchdowns in the fourth quarter.] We were missing some players because of suspensions for missing curfew or not going to class. And I wasn't 100 percent. I was coming off a knee injury, and it was bothering me. [Florida lost 39-28.]

"I was had never been so disappointed in my career after that game. Arden kicked five field goals that day. We didn't kick too many field goals. If we had scored two touchdowns…we would have won that game."

Terry Dean: "I always told people I thought we had the best team in the country that year. If we had stayed healthy, I think we would have clobbered Notre Dame in the Sugar Bowl. But our defensive end, Harvey Thomas, had been in a moped crash. A car hit him and broke his leg. We were missing him. We had lot a lot of people on the defensive line and a couple of people in the secondary. So we were decimated on defense, and in that game we led at the half, but Jerome Bettis just ran wild on us in that second half.

"We should have beaten them. If we had had all our guys on defense, I have no doubt we would have beaten them."

Shane Matthews: "I know Coach Spurrier was furious after that game. He was very upset with the way I played. He didn't say much then. The following spring he brought out the Sugar Bowl film, and we watched it as a team, and he critiqued it over and over. He was very critical, but it didn't bother me. I'm my dad's son. I mean, I am very critical of myself. I'm probably harder on myself than any coach could ever be on me.

"We never should have lost that game."

sixty-two

An Improbable Season

By 1992 Steve Spurrier's recruiting was coming full flower. In the season opener against Kentucky, ten defensive players were in the lineup for the very first time. Word was getting around the state of Florida to the cream of the crop of high school seniors that playing football under Steve Spurrier was going to pay great dividends.

Terry Dean: "Once you found out about him and what he was doing with the program, you were excited to play for him. He's very confident in what he does, and that comes across. As a high school kid, you want to be playing for someone like that."

Florida began the 1992 season ranked fourth in the nation. Shane Matthews was in his senior year, but he was suffering emotionally. That summer his mother had died from cancer, and he missed her terribly.

Shane Matthews: "The July before the '92 season my mom passed away. She developed breast cancer, and they didn't catch it in time, and I'm an only child, and it was rough. My parents had come to every game, and for my whole senior year it was just my dad coming. It was an odd feeling the whole year.

"We were a very young team. We had a new offensive line. That year was probably Spurrier's worst team record-wise [Florida finished the 1992 season 9-4.] But we accomplished a lot for not having much veteran talent. It was probably the best coaching job Steve Spurrier did at Florida, including the national championship team.

"We started off the year in a bad way. We were young with no experience. And we found a way to turn it around."

Florida opened the season optimistically with a 25-19 win over Kentucky.

Shane Matthews: "We felt good coming into the game, because we had beaten Kentucky the year before to win the SEC title. We didn't know how the offensive linemen would respond, but they played extremely well in that game. We had some receivers make some big plays.

Errict, Willie Jackson, and myself basically had to carry the offense, since we had played quite a bit the year before, and everyone else was green. We had Harrison Houston, and we had Monty Duncan and Aubrey Hill, young kids who didn't have a lot of playing experience.

"But it was still Kentucky. We wouldn't know whether we would have a solid football team until we went and played tougher competition."

In the second game of the season the Gators lost to Tennessee in the rain, 31-14.

Shane Matthews: "The rain killed us, because obviously we were a passing team. I mean, it was pouring. Waterfalls were coming down the steps and the stands. There was probably two feet of water standing on our sidelines. It covered my ankles, there was so much water. I remember we had a lot of dropped passes that day. But I didn't play very well, and neither did our defense."

During the Tennessee game star running back Erict Rhett sprained his ankle and was never the same the rest of the season.

On the way home the charter plane hit an airpocket, dropped like a rock, and scared everyone half to death.

Shane Matthews: "We were flying home to Gainesville, and we lost cabin pressure, and while everyone was eating their meal, the plane dropped 10,000 feet. The masks came down, and believe me, I was as scared as anyone. You can imagine how some of these guys who had never flown before felt. It was their first plane ride.

"We had to make an emergency landing in Atlanta. We stayed in the Atlanta airport until they could get us a new plane. I remember Ellis Johnson, one of our defensive tackles, refused to get back on the plane, so our equipment manager, Tim Sain, rented a car and drove him back to Gainesville. Ellis never flew again with the team. He would always ride with the equipment staff on Thursdays. They would pack up all our equipment and drive in a big U-haul truck to wherever we were playing that week. It's a good thing we didn't play on the West Coast or in Hawaii."

During the Mississippi State game, Shane Matthews was intercepted five times, and Florida lost 30-6. With a 1-2 start, Steve Spurrier was not happy.

Shane Matthews: "That was a big game for me, because I'm from Mississippi, and I was finally got to play in front of my friends and family. It was a Thursday night game, a chance for us to show what kind of team we had on national television. And I was in contention for the Heisman Trophy. When I threw five interceptions, that pretty much ended my Heisman Trophy campaign.

"They just physically beat us in every area. Mississippi State has always been a physical team, and that night was no exception. I didn't have a very good night. We had a couple of dropped passes here and there, but I also missed some throws. We had turnovers that killed us, and our defense couldn't stop them. It was a combination of not any one area of our team executing.

"It was just one of those nights when we couldn't get anything going. In order for that team to win, I had to play extremely well, and that night I didn't, and we lost.

"And it was a very hard game to lose, because a lot of my friends and family were there, people who didn't get to see me play live, and this was their first chance to see me.

"I may have put too much pressure on myself in that game, because I was so jacked up to go home to Mississippi and play and try to impress those people. And I fell flat on my face."

Terry Dean: "I played at the end of that game. That game we walked into a hornet's nest. It was a Thursday night game, a pretty electric atmosphere, and they had their cow bells going. It was very loud in that small stadium, and they were ready, especially on defense. They were a pretty good team."

Shane Matthews: "It was tough after that game was over. Usually after a game, my mom and dad would wait for me outside the locker room to greet me, no matter whether we won or lost. This time, only my dad was there. He was there with a bunch of hometown friends, and I was just very disappointed with the way I had played. I felt very embarrassed, because I felt I had let our team down, and I had let down all the people who had come up to watch me play. I felt too embarrassed to show up for classes the whole next week.

I'll be honest with you: I did not go to classes. [Matthews, an excellent student, already had his B.A. He was in graduate school.] I guess I was depressed. I slept until 10:30, got up and ate lunch, then hung out with my girl friend, Stephanie, who is now my wife, until it was time to practice. I was disappointed in how the season had started out. We were 1-2, and I had never been on a losing team before, so it was hard to face."

Terry Dean: "After we lost to Mississippi State, we read what was said about us in the papers, and you're apt to get mad at something that's said about you, but when you go out onto the practice field, that doesn't play any role at all. You're thinking about your job. The time to be concerned is when you hear about it from Coach Spurrier. There is no media pressure that compares to Spurrier."

Shane Matthews: "Coach didn't say much to me right after the game. A couple days later we sat down and talked, and he just told me to relax. He said I wouldn't have to talk to the press the next week, wouldn't have to go to the press conference. We were playing LSU, and he let me get away from the game and try to focus, and the next week we came out and played pretty well."

Against LSU, Shane Matthews threw two key long passes, one to Harrison Houston, the other to Jack Jackson, that resulted in one-yard plunges for touchdowns by Errict Rhett.

Ahead 28-14, Florida had a third and two at the LSU 22-yard line when Matthews twice tried to audible, confusing his teammates and resulting in delay of game penalties. When LSU got the ball back and scored, LSU was back in the game.

LSU had one more shot to tie, but Florida defenders Monty Grow and Lawrence Hatch kept the Tigers out of the end zone.

After beating LSU 28-21, Coach Spurrier was in a foul mood. He benched Errict Rhett and screamed at Matthews for his ill-advised audibles and at his assistant coaches. He accused himself of being a lousy coach.

The next week against Auburn, Florida played one of its better games. The Gators led 17-6 after two impressive drives mounted by Shane Matthews, who was sharp all game long. In the second half the Gator defense stiffened and allowed only a field goal as Florida won 24-9.

Shane Matthews: "He realized he had to take a different approach with this football team, because so many of the players were young. He focuses in different ways, and that week he was pretty hard on us. And we won the game.

"Coach was critical of me, but like I said, it didn't bother me at all, just because I'm harder on myself than he could ever be on me. It was tough, because I was not playing nearly as well as I'd played the previous two years. A lot of it had to do with not playing to my potential, and the other part was that the guys playing around me were younger than the previous two years and didn't have much experience. A quarterback is only as good as his supporting cast."

Terry Dean, for one, never believed that Coach Spurrier's moods had much affect on how well or poorly the team played.

Terry Dean: "I never thought his moods or his criticisms had a strong influence on individual players. I think that's what his intent was, but my belief is you don't motivate people by putting them down or yelling at them or getting grouchy. We played better because we wanted to play better, and we worked harder and got ready for a game. It had nothing to do with being afraid to put Coach Spurrier in a bad mood."

Homecoming against Louisville was next. Shane Matthews was 32-46 for 317 yards and became Florida's all-time passing leader, finishing with 7,605 yards, ahead of Kerwin Bell (7,585) and John Reaves (7,549). After the 31-17 win, Spurrier said that Matthews was the best quarterback in the history of the university.

Shane Matthews: "That was kind of nice to hear, coming from him. He had won the Heisman. He had been the premier player ever to come out of the University of Florida. So it was nice, because he doesn't praise a lot of players too often.

"I think he enjoyed saying that because he had picked me out of nowhere. I came out of—nowhere. He developed me into the player I had become. I think that is what he appreciated the most."

Florida was picking up momentum. After three straight wins, the Gators met Georgia at the Gator Bowl. The team, which had been buried by critics at the start of the season, was back from the dead, and with a 26-24 win over Georgia was back atop the SEC standings.

Shane Matthews shone. He threw for 303 yards, defeating Eric Zeier and Heisman candidate Garrison Hearst. Touchdown passes to Willie Jackson for 9 yards and then to Jack Jackson for 14 yards gave Florida a 23-7 lead. The defense, which was made up mostly of freshmen and sophomores, was improving with each game.

Shane Matthews: "We had no business beating Georgia. They were ranked pretty high [7th], and they were supposed to beat us. They had Garrison Hearst, Eric Zeier, Andre Hastings, and nobody gave us a chance. But we went in there and played extremely well. I always played well in the Gator Bowl.

"We had a couple of drives at the end. I even ran a quarterback draw that I ran for ten yards and a first down, and Harrison Houston made a huge third-down catch to seal it.

"It was another of those good feelings, because we had beaten Georgia for the third time since Coach Spurrier had been there. I was NEVER going to lose to Georgia.

"And we upset them, and it was rare that we were in a position to upset people. Usually we were the favorite. Here was this football team that didn't have a lot of talented players. We just played together as a unit and found a way to win a football game.

"Look at the way the season had panned out. We struggled at the beginning. But the more these guys played, the more experience they gained, the better we got as a football team. The reason we got as far as we did was that every week we improved.

"When we beat Georgia, we were sitting first in the SEC. That was amazing, especially the way we started out, losing two SEC games on the road in the first three weeks.

"One great thing: I never lost at Florida Field. I will always cherish that."

The Southern Mississippi game was played at Florida Field, and the Gators trailed at the end of the third quarter, 20-17.

Shane Matthews: "A lot of that had to do with my not playing real well. It was always one of those small schools that irritated major universities. Southern Mississippi had had huge upsets, and they were trying to pull another one at the Swamp. But we fought back, and we found a way to win that one as well.

"They had a lot of gimmicky defenses, and they were taking away our passing game. I threw two key interceptions that hurt us. We had to find a way to pound it, and Errict was the guy.

"We started [on the Florida 23], and after Errict scored [from the three], we went ahead [24-20]. They had a chance to come back and win, but Ben Hanks, who was an outstanding player, knocked a pass away in the end zone to save it.

"You know, Ben was one of those kids from a rough area who never had a lot. When Ben got here, some people didn't give him a chance because of his grades, but he was a hard worker, a kid who was very dedicated, and he ended up graduating. Coach Spurrier admired him, thought so much of him that he actually unretired his jersey and gave Ben number 11. He wanted Ben to wear his number."

Florida's final home game of the 1992 season came against South Carolina, and at the end of the half the Gators trailed, 3-0. A Matthews dive from the one, and a 36-yard touchdown pass to Aubrey Hill enabled Florida to win 14-9.

Shane Matthews: "It was Senior Day, an emotional day for me, because it was my last home game at Florida Field. Before that game the seniors go out and meet their parents, and it was tough, because it was just my dad out there. We ran out of the tunnel for the last time, and it was my last game in front of all those fans, and each senior was introduced, and my mom wasn't there to hug me, only my dad. So that was tough, and it actually was hard to focus, and the game turned out to be a lot closer than people anticipated.

"We were behind 3-0 at the half. We just sputtered around. But it was a typical 1992 game. We found a way to win. It wasn't pretty, but we found a way to win and move on.

"The winning touchdown was scored by Aubrey Hill, out of Miami, another guy who wasn't highly recruited. Coach Spurrier usually used him in the slot and tried to isolate him on a linebacker. He ran very precise routes. He wasn't the biggest or the fastest guy, but he would find a way to get open and he had tremendous hands.

"So we struggled against South Carolina, but like I said, we found a way to beat them. That was just another step toward our getting to the SEC championship game.

"We beat Vanderbilt [41-21], and that gave us the SEC East title, and we had a little celebration there in Nashville. We took our team picture underneath the scoreboard. It was very gratifying to me, knowing that NOBODY expected us to do what we did, and to be a senior and to be the leader of the team and to carry us to the championship game, it was a tremendous feeling know that this team had come so far."

In the 1992 season finale Florida was defeated by Florida State 45-24, the fifth time Florida had lost to the Seminoles in six years. Junior quarterback Charlie Ward was 27-47 for 331 yards and two touchdowns for FSU. He also rushed for 70 yards. Nothing worked against him. In nine possessions, FSU scored six touchdowns and a field goal.

Shane Matthews, bothered by a sore left knee, finished 15-30 for 175 yards. Spurrier subsituted and put Terry Dean in the game.

Shane Matthews: "It was a rough day for me. My knee was sore, and I also had my right toenail popped off. I had blood in my sock and a lot of blood pouring out of my shoe.

"Charlie Ward was hard to contain. I remember whenever they scored, we would find a way to answer. But then we kicked off, and Tamerick Vanover ran the kickoff all the way back inside our 20 every time it seemed. It was a frustrating game, especially since I was a senior.

"Coach took me out of the game, trying to save me for the Alabama game. Terry went in, and he played well. He showed some spark there. And that got him ready for the following year."

Terry Dean: "I don't remember Charlie Ward as being that good. I just remember their entire team was good. They had a few receivers who were pretty amazing. They were good from position to position. They were a better team than we were."

The SEC championship game was against second-ranked Alabama.

Shane Matthews: "To be honest with you, we had no business being in that game, because we didn't have as good a talent as other teams throughout the league. But we had scratched and clawed our way through some games and found a way to win them. Like I said, that was the best coaching job that Coach Spurrier did while he was here at Florida.

"It was a Super Bowl atmosphere playing in that SEC championship game, and it was exciting to play in it. Alabama was ranked two in the country, and their defense was by far the best I have ever seen in college football. Of their eleven starters, all eleven ended up playing in the NFL. Some of them are still playing today. There wasn't one weakness on defense."

Alabama led 21-7 midway through the third period, when Shane Matthews brought the team back to even.

Shane Matthews: "We fell behind, and everybody thought we were going to get blown out. They figured we were just happy to be there and that we'd lay down. But we came back, and we started throwing the ball and moving it on them, and we tied it up 21-21."

The game was 21-21 with 3:14 remaining, when Alabama's Antonio Langham, crouched and unseen, stepped in front of Monty Duncan, intercepted a short pass from Shane Matthews, and returned it 27 yards for a touchdown.

Terry Dean: "I remember that last play. It was a corner route. The outside receiver runs a curl, and the inside receiver runs a corner. The outside receiver is supposed to hold down the cornerback. But Langham baited him a little bit. He had dropped back like he was dropping into that corner area, and right when Shane started to throw the ball underneath, he broke on it and timed it perfectly and caught it and kept on going—all the way. That was the key play in the game."

Shane Matthews: "We got the ball back, and I was feeling good about myself. We were feeling good as a team.

"But I made a bad read, and a bad throw, and Antonio Langham picked it off and ran it back for a touchdown. And that was the only time in my career that I wasn't able to make the tackle after throwing an interception, because it was not a long pass. It was an eight-yard hitch route, and I just never saw him. That play still haunts me to this day.

"The only good thing about us losing to Alabama was that if we would have won that game, Florida State would have been able to go on and play for the national championship. By us losing to Alabama, we got to knock FSU out of the national title picture. Alabama went on to finish number one in the country.

"But it still was tough to swallow losing that game, being a huge underdog and having a chance to have a monumental upset.

"Langham made a hell of a play, but as a senior you don't expect to make a bad decision like that at that crucial time of the game. It happened, and you have to live with it. And it was hard to live with. I still catch a lot of flack from my buddies on other teams, because they always show the play on TV. Any time an SEC championship rolls around and go into the history of the game, they show that."

As a reward for Florida's 8-4 season, the Gators were invited to play North Carolina State in the Gator Bowl on New Years's Eve. The game was played in a dense fog that rolled in midway through the second quarter and never left.

Errict Rhett, hobbled most of the season, ran 39 times for 182 yards and was named MVP of the game, which Florida won 27-10. Shane Matthews was 19-38 for 247 yards and threw for two touchdowns. It was Florida's first bowl victory since the All-American Bowl in 1988.

Shane Matthews: "It was very, very foggy. It was hard to complete a five-yard pass, it was so foggy. We had no choice but to run the ball, and we gave it to Errict, and he played extremely well. He was the Most Valuable Player of the game.

"My final collegiate pass at Florida was a touchdown pass to Harrison Houston. He ran a post route from forty yards out.

"It was very gratifying to go out and throw a touchdown pass on your last play at Florida. It was such a gratifying year, knowing we had achieved a lot more than what people expected. Obviously we were all devastated to lose to Alabama, but we beat a pretty good N.C. State team, and once the months passed and we could look back on it, Coach Spurrier came to realize that what this team accomplished was pretty amazing. We may not have had the most experienced talent, but we got to the SEC championship game, and that was pretty amazing. I still think it was Coach Spurrier's best coaching job ever."

When Shane Matthews walked off the field for the last time, he held several Florida passing records. He finished with 722 completions, the most ever. He threw for 9,287 yards, most ever at the time. And his 74 touchdowns also were a Florida record.

After a stellar college career, Shane Matthews assumed he was a lock to be a first-round draft choice in the upcoming pro draft. Experts were telling him that he would be the third quarterback taken behind Drew Bledsoe and Rick Mirer. But come draft day, the phone never rang.

Shane Matthews: "I didn't even get drafted. Everybody says it was because of my size. I was only 185 pounds, and I guess I didn't have the arm strength they were looking for.

"I was very discouraged. It was another setback to my career. When you play at a major college like Florida and have success, you feel you can play at the next level. I didn't know what I was going to do, because I had had my mind set on playing in the NFL.

"For two days I sat at home and waited and waited and watched and watched and watched, and I saw all these other quarterbacks I had never heard of get drafted. It was VERY disappointing.

"I got a call from the Chicago Bears. Dave Wannstedt wanted me, and I ended up being the third-string quarterback behind Jim Harbaugh and Tom Willis of Florida State. To be honest with you, I was just glad to be on the roster, even though I was still bitter over not being drafted.

"It cost me a ton of money, and I wasn't happy playing in the cold weather, being that far from the South. But I really didn't have any choices, and I was lucky just to have made the team.

"I've been with the Bears ten years, and I've been cut by the Bears seven times. I was cut after training camp my rookie year, and then a week later they brought me back on the roster for the whole year. So I was with them all of '93, and then I was cut in '94 after three games. They signed another quarterback. So I was out of football the rest of the year.

"I didn't play a down until 1996, the final game of the year against the Tampa Bay Buccaneers. I played in the fourth quarter, and I played extremely well. I had a 99-yard touchdown drive and a 76-yard touchdown drive. I threw my first career touchdown pass to Bobby Engram, and I ran my first rushing touchdown.

"I figured that was going to be the start of my career, and in '97, I signed with the Carolina Panthers. The whole year I was their third quarterback behind Kerry Collins and Steve Beurlein, and in '99 I signed back with the Bears, and I actually was their starter that year.

"Dick Jauron was the coach. I earned the starting job, and had my first career start against the Kansas City Chiefs. We beat them 20–17, and I played really, really well. We got off to a 3-2 start, and I tore my hamstring in Minnesota, and I never got back in there. I couldn't get healthy. I played on and off in 2000 and 2001. I began the season as the starter, but then I tore some cartilege in my ribs and Jim Miller took over.

"In my first game back, we were down 19 points in the fourth quarter, and I brought us back, and somehow we won the game in overtime, and then the following week, I started against the Cleveland Browns, and we were losing 21-7, and we were down 21-14, and with 10 seconds to go, I threw a Hail Mary, and James Allen caught it, and we tied it up and went on to win again in overtime when a defensive back, Mike Brown, picked off a pass and ran it back for a touchdown.

"Those were two of the greatest comebacks in Bears' history, and I had a lot to do with it, and it's nice to know that."

Going into 2002, Shane Matthews continued to hold out hopes that he would get a fair shot at a starting quarterback job in the pros. He hopes to leave Chicago and get his chance. His thoughts wander toward our nation's capital.

"It's a dream," he said. "But it could happen."

sixty-three

Wuerffel and Bowen

In 1993 quarterback Terry Dean was a junior, poised to have a Heisman Trophy-winning season. With Shane Matthews gone, Dean was top dog in town. His competition came from two talented freshman, Eric Kresser and Danny Wuerffel.

Wuerffel was a kid who had moved around from town to town in his chaplain father's nomadic pilgrimage of air force bases. When high school rolled around, the boy was living in Fort Walton, Florida.

Danny Wuerffel: "I played a little football my sophomore year in high school, but I was not a starter. We finished 3-7. My junior year the head coach was Jimmy Ray Stephens, an outstanding high school coach, and we went 8-2, and then my senior year we went 14-0 and won the state championship against Fort Lauderdale St. Thomas Aquinas. We were both 4A schools, the second-largest class. I was voted the USA Today 'Player of the Year.' That year I threw 27 touchdown passes.

"I got a lot of letters from all over the country, but the schools I took visits to were Florida, Florida State, and Alabama.

"I met Coach Spurrier, and one of the things he does to recruit you is to sit you down and play tapes of games, and talk you through it, and try to get young men excited about playing there.

"I was very much impressed. And afterwards, I was more confused, because I would have liked to have gone to all three schools. But I ruled out Alabama, because I felt that even if I got the chance to play there, they were not going to throw the ball quite like Florida State and Florida.

"So it came down to Florida State and Florida. There were two deciding factors for my choosing Florida. The first was that I felt Florida was a better school for my situation. I was undecided in terms of picking a major, and Florida offered the most flexibility. The second factor was that so many of their schools ranked real high nationally. And the third factor was when you look at the statistics Coach Spurrier has with quarterbacks, it was hard to deny that Florida would be a phenomenal place to play. So between the school itself and Coach Spurrier, that kind of won me over.

"I arrived at school in the fall of '92. A lot of guys came in mid-summer for the second summer session, but I did not. I arrived right before training camp. There was no question that I would be red-shirted. Shane Matthews was easily the starter. Terry Dean was going into his third year and easily was the backup. Antoine Chiles was also there, and Eric Kresser.

"Even though I was red-shirted, I traveled to the games and dressed, and I was the signal guy. Coach Spurrier would tell me the play, and I would signal it in to Shane. It lets you get involved in what's going on. You have to learn the game plan in order to signal the plays.

"People watching the game at home on TV got their commentary from Keith Jackson. I got my commentary from Steve Spurrier himself. So often, he would look out to the field, and if Shane didn't do something he wanted him to do, he would say, 'Dangit, you know he's got to look over to the left. Danny, you'd have done it right, wouldn't you have?'

"I had no idea what was going on, but I'd say, 'Yes, sir. I'd have done it.' Whether I would have or wouldn't have, that's what you were supposed to say. It was how his mind worked: when the defense shifted, he was audibling himself as if he were playing—trying to get a feel for the type of things he would want to do in a certain situation.

"Nineteen ninety two was a kind of tough year for us. In all of Spurrier's years there, he has said that was one of the least talented teams he had. We ended up 9 and 4 and had some tough losses, but we also had some big wins. Imagine 9-4 being one of your worst seasons!

"I came to camp in '93, and my competition at quarterback was Eric Kresser and Terry Dean, who was a phenomenal athlete. Terry was as gifted a player as you could be around. He had great athletic ability. He had speed, quickness, was real smart, and threw the ball extremely well.

"We were pretty good friends, and got along real well. He very much had the job, and going into the season I was just trying to be as close to the backup as I could.

"We opened the '93 season against Arkansas State, and Terry had a great game. He threw a couple of touchdown passes, and we had a real good game. I even got in at the end and threw a couple of touchdowns myself."

For one to understand how effective a recruiter Steve Spurrier had become, one needed only to study the career of receiver Paul Bowen. A quarterback and receiver in high school, Bowen had followed Florida football his whole life and wanted to go there. But when he couldn't qualify academically, he went to Potomac Junior College in West Virginia, where he became one of the top junior-college receivers in the country.

In 1993 he transferred to Florida, arriving the same time as Danny Wuerffel.

Paul Bowen: "I red-shirted in '92. One of the wonderful things that was instilled in us at Florida was that we felt we never were going to lose.

"I remember my first day walking in there, I saw Shane Matthews and a lot of the veterans I had seen on television. And there was a sense that we don't settle for being average. We win here. That's what we do. If you don't get the job done, whoever they recruited behind you will.

"I remember when I first arrived, Tre Everett, who was a senior, took me aside and explained this to me. We kind of hit it off, and he would stay after practice and work with me. And Willie Jackson the entire spring the next year would run routes with me. He'd say, 'Hey, Paulie, want to come with us?'

"I would ask them about what they were doing, and they would always take time with me. That was one of the things about Florida: the older guys would teach the younger ones. It's what keeps the bloodline.

"I spent that year getting beat up on the scout team. We would get the varsity prepared for the games. Some weeks it was fun when we played teams that threw the ball. But Vanderbilt ran the option, Kentucky ran the option, and sometimes Shea Showers played quarterback, and sometimes I'd get in there and run the offense, and those big ends would come pound on you, man. Usually I was a wide receiver. Larry Kennedy was the big corner, and Will White, and Lawrence Hatch later played for the Patriots. They were top players you saw on TV, and it was fun to play against them. You get a measure of yourself against them, and it was a big learning curve. In junior college, they teach you about coverages, but it's more about running around and getting open. In Steve Spurrier's offense, you're a piece of the puzzle. If you move the wrong way, you are interfering with what's coming down the road in front or behind you. I got a few lectures about that, because I would be running around yelling, 'I'm open....' not under-standing the whole philosophy.

"Either Coach Spurrier or Coach Dixon would say, 'Okay, Bowen, come here. Look, you need to quit doing this 'cause you're interfering with what's going on.'

"When you're done playing, and you look back—and I coached a couple of years—you understand a lot more what they were trying to teach you. You just marvel at what an intelligent coach Steve Spurrier is. To be able to call the game from the field like he did is amazing.

"I look back. This week my dad asked me if I would have preferred going to Maryland, one of those schools where I would have had an opportunity to play more. But I said, 'You know, if I had it to do all over again, and knowing the outcome, I would still go to Florida because one day I'm going to sit down and tell my grandkids that I played for Coach Spurrier.'

"There are very few men on the planet—Lee Iacocca, Colin Powell, even Bobby Bowden at Florida State, Steve Spurrier, very unique people who come along in life in whatever field they're in, and to be able to have played for someone like that or worked with him or just to have been able to learn from him is very, very fortunate. I'm very thankful for having been put in a position to do that."

sixty-four
Dean or Wuerffel?

Whenthe 1993 season opened, Terry Dean was the quarterback pro tem, and his protoges were two talented freshmen, Danny Wuerffel and Eric Kresser. Of the two, Dean was more impressed with Kresser.

Terry Dean: "Eric Kresser came from the West Palm Beach area. Eric had a cannon for an arm. Danny's was weaker. Danny was always a pretty quiet guy, and he was pretty average. To be honest, I remember thinking that my competition was going to come from Eric Kresser, not Danny Wuerffel.

"My strength was that I was faster and more mobile than the other two. I was always more of a scrambler. It didn't take much to be faster than Kresser. Danny was athletic, a good runner.

"At the start of the season I put a great deal of pressure on myself. I was expected to have a good year. I had waited three years, and I had earned that quarterback job. I was ready to pursue it."

The season opener was a 44-6 thrashing of Arkansas State. In his first start, Terry Dean completed his first ten passes, including a 35-yard touchdown to Jack Jackson and a 40-yard score to Willie Jackson. But Dean learned that he was only as good as his last throw. After an interception, Coach Spurrier yanked him out of the game.

Terry Dean: "I started the game, played well, and threw a couple of touchdowns. The first one was to Jack Jackson, who became my go-to guy. Jack was fearless, had super speed, ran really good routes, and would get open and get to the ball. You put it there, and he was going to get it.

"In the second quarter I threw an interception, and Coach Spurrier took me out and put Danny in. So I sat there on the bench. I thought that was a little odd that someone who had never really gotten any playing time was playing.

"Then in the fourth quarter he brought me back in."

Against Arkansas State, Terry Dean threw for over 200 yards and two touchdowns, and Danny Wuerffel was 6-9 for 100 yards and two touchdowns.

Paul Bowen: "Danny was a lot more even-keeled than Terry. Terry was more the Brett Favre type. He'd get fired up. Sometimes the adrenaline would kick in early in the game, and he would throw it, because he had a hell of an arm. We also had Eric Kresser.

"Between Terry and Danny, Danny was much more even-keeled, and that helped him down the road with Coach Spurrier. Terry and Coach were very similar people, very perfectionist oriented and very driven people, and sometimes when you have two personalities like that—and Terry being young—it doesn't help your situation. Terry and I have talked about it. As you get older you realize things. I used to be stubborn and butt heads with my father or my coach in high school, and it didn't do me any good either.

"And the other thing about Coach Spurrier: it's like playing for Michael Jordan. Coach was a quarterback, and he was very good, and he wants his quarterbacks to be as good as he was. And sometimes very good athletes don't understand why other people aren't as good as they. And some players can't handle that. And some players need a pat, and some players need a kick up the ass, and Coach is not a patter, though I think he's fair.

"Terry was given some opportunities and didn't produce when he was given those opportunities. Look at Eric Kresser. Every spring coach would open it up: 'We have no starting quarterbacks. It's open.' Because of Kresser's arm, Coach wanted to put him in there, but Danny was just so damn good. He completed seventy percent of his passes! What are you gonna do?

"So Terry had to compete with the best college quarterback statistically who ever played the position.

"I think we would have won with either of them. Shoot, we won the SEC. I think if Terry had to do it over again, he would change some things. But that comes with growing up. We look back and think of how we should have handled it."

Terry Dean finished the Arkansas State game with 11 completions in a row.

After the game Coach Spurrier announced that Dean would start in the next game against Kentucky.

Terry Dean: "At that point I had gotten away from the delusion that Coach Spurrier was a father figure. Really, from the get-go, we had a kind of shaky relationship.

"There's no question—he wants it done perfectly. I remember there would be times when I'd throw a touchdown, and he would yell at me if it wasn't the right read and the right throw. It didn't matter what the result was, if it wasn't done the way it was supposed to be done, then he wasn't happy about it.

"He was trying to drive me to be better. But I always thought he was a little bit harder on me than other people. I assume that's the reason he expected a little bit more, that he wanted me to perform better. It was more a head coach/player relationship."

In the 24-20 win over Kentucky, Dean completed his first three passes, for a total of 14 in a row, fifth best in SEC history. Spurrier, with 16, held the record. Dean never knew he was so close.

Terry Dean: "I had no idea. Get out of here!"

But Dean also threw four interceptions in that Kentucky game. Coach Spurrier yanked him, but his replacement, Danny Wuerrfel, threw three more.

Danny Wuerffel: "I tried to top him."

Down 20-17, Spurrier passed up a game-tying field goal and went for the win. Danny Wuerffel gave it to him with eight seconds left in the ballgame when he threw a pass down the middle to Chris Doering in the end zone for an amazing touchdown.

Paul Bowen: "The play before Chris ran a middle route, and he almost made a one-handed catch at the 13-yard line. There were no timeouts left, and I remember thinking, Oh, he dropped it!

"On the next play Danny dropped back, and he looked at number 13, whoever he was, and he shifted over to the left, and Danny threw it just like Coach taught him, and hit him for a touchdown.

"Everybody went bonkers. The crowd went crazy."

Danny Wuerffel: "All of us were playing very poorly. Though I had thrown a touchdown pass to Chris in the fourth quarter, I am not sure why he left me in the game for the last drive. I really hadn't played very well, but Harrison Houston had a great kickoff return, and I threw a couple of passes to get us down the field. With only seconds left, I tried to throw the ball to Jack Jackson out the outside, and the safety flew over the top and almost picked it off, knocking it out of the way.

"Then, on the final play, I called that play again. Coach Spurrier told me to throw it outside to Jack, and as I went to throw it I saw the safety starting to go over there, so I faked it to Jack and threw it down the middle to Chris Doering, and we won, and it was a fun day for the Gators.

"It was a game we had to win, and then it looked like we weren't and then we did, and to come back from behind and win in the last second, it was like we had won the Super Bowl! Everybody rushed the field and there was a pile-on. So it was quite a celebratory scene, despite how we had played."

It WAS a great win for Wuerffel and Florida. It was the beginning of a rough roller coaster ride for Terry Dean.

Terry Dean: "Spurrier wasn't happy. He just kept going back and forth. And then Danny finished and threw a touchdown at the end, and right away I was thinking that that would probably be the last game I started at the University of Florida. It was a low point. It was one of the low points. It was a roller coaster with a bunch of highs and a bunch of lows."

As a reward for Danny Wuerffel's last-minute heroics, Spurrier started him against fifth-ranked Tennessee.

Danny Wuerffel: "What I remember most was that I was really, really nervous that whole week. For obvious reasons. I was a red-shirt freshman. It was my first college start ever. And I was starting against Heath Shuler and Tennessee. That was one of the biggest games for me emotionally, because I was so young, and it was such a big game.

"Nothing stands out in my mind about that game, except for my trying hard to run each play right. I thought Coach Spurrier did a great job calling it. I have to say that one thing that stands out was watching Heath Shuler run to the right and throw a pass to the left for a 95-yard touchdown. I thought that was pretty cool.

"We got ahead, and we were just holding them off from coming back."

After Danny Wuerffel led Florida to the 41-34 win over Tennessee, he starred against Mississippi State, throwing 27-41 for a one-game record 449 yards and three touchdowns. [Kerwin Bell had the old record of 408 set in 1985.]

In the 38-24 shootout, the game was won on a 100-yard kick-off return by Jack Jackson.

Danny Wuerffel: "Coming out of the Tennessee game, I really felt that I had a lot of confidence. We were playing Mississippi State, and they had a quarterback [Todd Jordan] who threw for 300 to 400 yards a game. So it was one of those games that went back and forth, back and forth, and then Jack Jackson's 100-yard kickoff return sealed it for us. But we were moving the ball at will."

Paul Bowen: "That day Chris Doering caught three touchdowns. But the player who stood out in my mind was Jack Jackson. The Wednesday before the game at practice he got hit at the goal line by Lawrence Wright. He ended up hitting the goal post and popping out his shoulder. Then against Mississippi State, he was able to play, and he took the kickoff and ran it back one hundred yards!

"He caught the ball, and he came up and broke to the left on the sideline, and boom, he jetted and was gone. Of course, when he did that, we were all jumping up and down. That kind of took control of the game right there. The year before they had beat us up pretty good at their place."

In the middle of the Mississippi State game, Coach Spurrier, angry that the starting defensive unit wasn't stopping the Bulldogs, began pointing to the second string defensive players standing at the sidelines and yelling at Coach Ron Zook, "Put one of those guys in. Put anyone in."

Paul Bowen: "That's another thing about Spurrier: his assistants do very well. He teaches people how to be successful. Spurrier does that, and so does Lou Holtz. Spurrier reads a lot of books, and one of his heroes is John Wooden [the famed UCLA basketball coach]. He always gave us quotes at practice.

"I remember one of my favorites: Coach Spurrier said, 'You fellows, you all watch golf, right?' Half the guys said they did. He said, 'Who's won the most money on the PGA in its history? Does anyone know?' No one did. The answer was Tom Kite. He said, 'Who has won the most majors?' Everyone knew that one. It was Jack Nicklaus. He said, 'See, fellows, you can't take the money to the grave, but titles never go away.'

"He was always giving you these things to think about. Our playbook was filled with poems and quotes from literature or on Vince Lombardi or John Wooden, things he wanted you to think about. When you're 19 and you read them, you go, 'Whatever. Throw me the damn ball.' But as you get older, you begin to understand what they are trying to instill in you.

"A lot of his players have done well since then, whether they went to the pros or not. Guys like Dexter Daniels, David Bernard, and Larry Kennedy are doing really well in their lives outside of football. A lot of it comes from upbringing, but a lot of us don't come from families that teach us about business or life. Spurrier is always trying to teach you about the patterns of life to be successful, no matter what you're doing. If you apply them while you're playing, you will be successful. If you apply them after you're playing, you will also be successful.

"Coach Spurrier always talks about working hard. Being persistent. Sometimes it's difficult to balance everything in life, but when you're around someone like him for four or five years, whether you buy into everything he says or not, you are who you associate with. If you hang around drug dealers, you're going to deal drugs. If you hang around people who make money, you're going to make money. Hang around people who win, and you'll win. It rubs off. A lot of guys don't realize that. I know I didn't. Being successful was what was expected of you.

"Every spring before every season Coach Spurrier would sit down with the seniors, and they would list their goals for the season. He is very goal-oriented in terms of what he wants you to do. 'If you want to get here, these are the things we have to do.' Preparation for the week always is very important. Because the games are easy if you do the homework."

After Danny Wuerffel's success in the the Mississippi State game, a glum Terry Dean considered transferring to another college.

Terry Dean: "I don't remember feeling that I was going to quit. I know I felt like doing that, but I don't think I was close to actually doing that. At that point I was pretty sure I was going to transfer."

Fifth-ranked Florida defeated LSU 58–3, one of the worst beatings ever suffered by the Tigers. After the game Spurrier apologized to LSU coach Curley Hallman for scoring so many points. In three quarters of work Danny Wuerffel was 14-20—including his last eleven in a row—for 220 yards and three touchdowns to Jack Jackson, Willie Jackson, and Harrison Houston.

Wuerffel almost didn't play because of back spasms.

Danny Wuerffel: "I was given a shot [of cortisone] before the game. Obviously at that point I wanted to play no matter what, because you don't want to let anyone down on the field, or you may not get back there. So I went out there and absolutely destroyed LSU in their stadium at night.

"One of my touchdowns went to Willie Jackson, who was a very physical, strong receiver. I've been a big fan of his, and I'm surprised it's taken the NFL till last year to really give him a chance. Harrison Houston, who caught one of the other touchdowns, was a real special guy. He was smaller than Jack, wasn't as fast—Jack had blazing speed—but Harrison was very quick. He had lateral speed, and he turned out to be a great player."

"It was a real big game, and I was surprised how easy it was. It was their place, at night, and they were a good team."

The next game, against Auburn, resulted in a 38–35 loss. The game turned on a signal that Spurrier sent to Danny Wuerffel that Wuerffel misread.

With Florida up 10-0, Danny threw a soft pass to the right flank to Willie Jackson. It was intercepted and returned 96 yards for a touchdown.

Danny Wuerffel: "We were ahead of Auburn 10-0, and we were going in to score to make it 17-0. We were on the four-year-line, and Coach Spurrier signalled a play, and I misread it. The play I thought he called I thought was a really, really bad call, but you don't question it.

"I called it, and it was picked off, and [Calvin Jackson] intercepted it and ran it back 96-yards for a touchdown.

"I was really frustrated. And then I came to find out that he hadn't even called that play. We probably would have scored on the play that he called. That was the most frustrating play I can ever remember calling at the

University of Florida. It would have been hard for Auburn to come back from 17-0. It was just a communication failure.

"Coach Spurrier wasn't happy about that, but at that point he was still real positive. Later in the game, they blitzed, and I made the right call, and I got it, and they picked it off and ran for about forty yards. That was another big play in the game.

"That was a shame. That was a real tough game for us."

Auburn won it after the Florida defense held on fourth down and less then four minutes to play, but Lawrence Wright was called for a fifteen-yard unsportsmanlike conduct penalty for smashing receiver Frank Sanders to the ground. A 41-yard field goal gave Auburn the margin of victory. The loss kept Florida from going undefeated and perhaps finishing number one in the country.

Paul Bowen: "Even though Lawrence decapitated the guy, we were surprised when they threw the flag. The ball was just barely over his head when he hit him. If he hadn't hit him that hard, they probably wouldn't have called a penalty."

Terry Dean: "My grandmother had died, and we went to the funeral right after the game. On the way from Auburn back to Gainesville we stopped at Troy State, which is in the middle of Alabama. It was the school I probably was going to transfer to. Coach Blakeney had been the receivers' coach at Auburn when I was being recruited, and I always liked him. He's done a dynamite job there. I visited with the coach there and watched part of their practice and was pretty sure I was going to transfer there."

sixty-five

Dean Bounces Back

The next game was against Georgia in a sloppy deluge at the Gator Bowl.

Paul Bowen: "I remember Coach Spurrier was a little worried, because we were going into a BIG ballgame. Eric Zeier could fling that ball around. If you got into a shootout, you never knew what was going to happen. We had just lost to Auburn, and you didn't know how the team was going to react."

Against Georgia, Danny Wuerffel threw an interception for a touchdown that gave Georgia a 17-13 lead, and Coach Spurrier brought Terry Dean into the game.

Danny Wuerffel: "That easily was the worst weather for a game that I could ever recall. When we went out for the pre-game [warm-ups], your shoes disappeared. At the start of the game it was absolutely pouring. The conditions were really, really tough to try to play in. It was hard to get anything going.

"I don't know how much the game against Auburn led to him making a change in quarterbacks. That could have been. But against Georgia early on, we ran a play, and one of the receivers didn't go where I thought he was going, and I threw an interception. Another play that Coach got upset about, Jason Odom planted his foot and just slipped, so his man got free and with the receivers open, I didn't have a chance to throw the ball very well. And I was having a hard time playing in the conditions, and he made a change, which turned out to be a great change. Terry played extremely well, and got us the lead, and it ended up being a huge win for the Gators.

"It was frustrating, because I didn't think I could play any better under the conditions, so that was a hard way to lose your job."

Terry Dean: "I'll tell you what happened. It was an unbelievably heavy rain. It was the heaviest rain I had ever seen at a football game. There was water standing two inches deep.

"At that point I knew I was going to transfer, and the attitude I had that day was almost one of indifference. Danny had small hands, and he couldn't throw a wet football. I went out there during the pre-game, and I was as loose as a goose, and I just zipped the ball around right and left. Spurrier made a couple of comments about it, and when we got in the game and Danny couldn't hold onto the ball, that's when I came in and had some success. I threw a touchdown and we ended up beating them."

Terry Dean threw a touchdown to Harrison Houston with 1:41 left in the first half to give Florida a 23-20 lead. Keeping Florida in the game were four field goals by Florida kicker Judd Davis.

Danny Wuerffel: "Judd made a bunch of field goals in that bad weather. Judd had a phenomenal career at Florida, and that year he won the Lou Groza award as the nation's best kicker."

With the rain continuing to come down, Dean spent most of the second half handing off to his talented back Errict Rhett, who carried 41 times and gained 183 yards. Florida won the game 33-26.

Terry Dean: "That was one of Errict Rhett's biggest games. He was a workhorse. We were just pounding him for three or four yards at a time, and he just kept going."

To beat Georgia, the Florida defense had to play spectacularly. Time after time the Gators stopped Georgia inside their ten-yard line.

Danny Wuerffel: "To this day, I do not know how Eric Zeier played the way he did in that game. He threw the ball like it was a mini-football with stick-um on it. He was firing the ball and played phenomenal that whole game, and our defense kept stepping up and stopping them."

The game was saved when with five seconds left in the game, Anthone Lott called time out. At the same time Eric Zeier dropped back and threw a pass for a touchdown. Just before the snap, the coaches had noticed that Florida only had ten men on the field, and so Lott called time out, and the play didn't count.

Danny Wuerffel: "We were ahead 33-26 with only [five] seconds left. Zeier had the ball down near our goal line [on the 12]. He dropped back and threw a touchdown pass, but it didn't count because Anthone Lott noticed we only had ten men on the field and called time out. They blew the whistle, but a lot of people never heard it. Anthone obviously called time, because he didn't move on the play after it was started.

"When play resumed, Zeier threw a pass into the end zone to Hason Graham, and Lott was covering him, and even though the ball went high over Graham's head, a flag was thrown, and Lott was flagged for interference, and the ball was placed on the two-yard line with no time left. Zeier threw another pass, and this one fell incomplete, and that was a huge, huge day for us."

Terry Dean: "It was such a bittersweet moment. You just go from such highs and lows. You're on top of the world and then the bottom of the world, and suddenly you're kind of back on top, but you're wondering how long that's going to last."

It lasted for another week as Terry Dean started against Southwest Louisiana at Homecoming and threw for 448 yards and six touchdowns, three to Jack Jackson. Mike Bianchi of the *Gainesville Sun* called Dean's performance "the most amazing passing performance in Gator football history." Dean was modest about his accomplishments.

Terry Dean: "I had such an emotional roller coaster experience. This was one of the fun times. I remember they were in a man-to-man defense, did a lot of blitzing, and if you haven't got the athletes to cover our receivers, it's just pitch and catch. They were wide open. And our line was going to block their line without much difficulty.

"We just had some phenomenal guys, guys who are still playing today in the pros. We had Jack, Ike Hilliard, Reidel Anthony, Jacquez Green, Fred Taylor, Jason Odom, who retired last year, and Kevin Carter and Ellis Johnson on defense."

Paul Bowen: "I caught my first pass against Southwest Louisiana, which is now called Louisiana Monroe. We were way ahead, so Danny Wuerffel and I got to play a little.

"Coach Spurrier called a play, and Danny looked at me and gave me a little hand signal, and I ran a little hedge, and he swung it out to me, and I did my best to make sure I didn't drop it.

"We were all very competitive, and that game Jack Jackson caught four touchdown passes, and obviously Jack was a little different than I was."

Danny Wuerffel: "I was excited for our team, but as a human being I also really wished that that had been my opportunity to be out there. They blitzed every down, and you gotta throw it, and you're going to put up those big numbers, and I would have loved to have been the guy doing that. But I was the backup, and I was doing everything I could to support Terry."

In the third quarter against Southwest Louisiana, Terry Dean's luck seemed to have run out. On a pass play, he was tackled, and he landed on his shoulder and had to leave the game. Danny Wuerffel came in and went 8 for 10 for 64 yards and a touchdown.

Terry Dean: "It was my throwing shoulder. It popped out a little bit and strained those ligaments in there, and it was pretty tender for a while. It was frustrating. I had just mounted a comeback and had a great game, and then I was out a while."

Danny Wuerffel started against South Carolina, who led 17-0. But Wuerrfel brought the Gators back in a 37-26 victory. Considering he didn't get much of a night's sleep, it was quite an accomplishment.

Paul Bowen: "South Carolina fans called Danny at the hotel all night. They kept calling him in his room and waking him up. He finally pulled the phone out of the wall. But he was awakened two or three times that night. The hotel wasn't supposed to let calls go through, but you know the South Carolina fans. Sometimes they get a little overzealous."

Florida trailed South Carolina 26-23 late in the third quarter.

Danny Wuerffel: "One of the plays that stands out in that game was a really gutsy call by Coach Spurrier. We were in the third quarter on our own two-yard line, and he called a wide receiver screen. The defender was pressing Jack

Jackson, and I was really nervous to throw it, because if the DB saw it coming, he could have intercepted it right there. But Jack caught it, broke a tackle—actually six or seven tackles, and he ended up running [73 yards]. That was a really big play in that game."

Terry Dean: "Jack ran for a 73-yard gain, until a kid from South Carolina was able to run him down. Not too many people could do that to Jack.

"Jack is a little guy (5'8"), about my height. Jack was a very confident individual. When Coach would discuss the upcoming game, he would say something to the media about the oppostion, 'You have to watch out for this receiver or that receiver.' And Jack would look over and say, 'That guy wouldn't be the sixth receiver on this team, Coach.' And Coach would just laugh."

At the end of Jack Jackson's 73-yard run, he was tackled late, and the referees added fifteen yards for a personal foul. Two plays later Errict Rhett scored from the eight to give Florida a 30-26 lead that they never relinquished.

Danny Wuerffel: "Errict was one of those guys who went full tilt. He hit the hole hard. He was a guy I really liked, and I really appreciated him as a person. And it would be safe to say he was also a little crazy. Errict was always talking, though I wasn't always sure what he was saying. He was fun! He was always open too! No matter what, he would come back to the huddle and say, 'I'm open. I'm open. Throw me the ball. I'm open.' And he'd be no more open than anyone else."

Terry Dean returned from his injury to lead Florida to a 52-0 rout against Vanderbilt. In this game both he and Wuerffel ended up being benched.

Terry Dean: "I had thrown a touchdown, ran a touchdown, and caught a touchdown, then threw an interception and got benched. Wuerffel came in, and he threw an interception, and he got benched."

Danny Wuerffel: "I remember wishing I could have started that game. I was feeling the worst game I played was against Georgia, and that was under tough conditions, and then we went and played South Carolina, and we won that, a big game. But at the same time, it's not fair to lose your job to an injury, so Terry started. Coach Spurrier is the type of coach who is concerned with HOW you are doing things. Are you doing them correctly? Are you doing them HIS way? More so even than judging you against your opponent.

"So if you're not making the right reads or the right calls, he's going to be upset, and I'm sure that was why Terry was benched, and then he pulled me out too, and put Terry back in."

Terry Dean: "I came back in, and then I got benched again. In that game I got benched twice! It got so bad that if you made one mistake, you were sitting on the bench."

Eric Kresser played quarterback against Vanderbilt in the fourth quarter. He threw a 67-yard touchdown pass to speedster Daryl Frazier.

Terry Dean: "Daryl was a track star who didn't have any hands. He was fast as blazes, but just couldn't hold onto the football. But he DID hold onto that one."

Florida State was next, and for this game Spurrier started Danny Wuerffel.

Danny Wuerffel: "The week after the Vanderbilt game, Terry voiced his frustration with going in and out. Spurrier felt I deserved the shot. I felt I had played fairly well. I was 11 for 18 in the first half with a touchdown and no interceptions.

"We ran a funky play in a drive right before the half. The ball was snapped, but none of the offensive players moved. I guess the center snapped it early. So the whole defense took off after me, and I ran around and ran around and got my knee twisted up, but I finished the drive and finished the half, but something was wrong. The knee would give out, but I could stand.

"So Terry started the second half, for two reasons I think: my knee was hurting, but I think he also wanted to make a change."

Paul Bowen: "Danny got hurt [he sprained his knee on the final drive of the half], and he was out the rest of the year. Terry came in and flung it around. It's nice to know you've got somebody as a backup who would be starting at most programs in the country.

"We knew Terry could come in and make plays. We came back that game, and the place was jumping.

"I remember Bill Gaines and Kevin Carter knocked down two of Charlie Ward's passes in a row, and on third down, Warrick Dunn swung out, and Kevin missed batting that one down by less than a foot. Dunn caught the pass and ran [79-yards] for a touchdown. If Kevin would have knocked that thing down, we would have won. [FSU won the game 33-21.]

"Florida State was so talented. [Heisman Trophy award-winner] Charlie Ward was so elusive. We'd have him under wraps, and he'd slip through and all of a sudden, they'd make a play. Those are the things that kill you."

A day after the Florida State game, Danny Wuerffel had season-ending surgery.

Danny Wuerffel: "I had some torn cartilage and I had partially torn my ACL in my knee. I had played fairly well up to that point, I felt, but that year that was all she wrote."

That left Terry Dean to run the Gators in the SEC championship game against Alabama and for the Sugar Bowl game against West Virginia. Terry Dean had survived his benchings and had finished the season on the field. Lesser men wouldn't have survived. Dean, in fact, flourished, as Florida went on to win their final two games.

Terry Dean: "Of all my good memories, the Alabama game was probably the best. I had grown up in Alabama, and when you grow up in Alabama you are either for Auburn or Alabama, and my dad was an Auburn fan, so I grew up always wanting to play for Auburn, and so I was for Auburn and I grew up hating Alabama. From as little as I can remember, the family would get together and watch the Alabama/Auburn game, and I just developed a severe hatred for Alabama.

"And in that game I threw a touchdown to Aubrey Hill, and then I ran for a touchdown early in the game."

Paul Bowen: "We played Alabama at Legion Field, and I remember Auburn had a plane flying overhead with a banner saying they were the true champions. They were 11-0, but they were on probation.

"We led by a point in the third quarter, when Shane Edge kept a drive going by running 20 yards with a punt. Shane could boom that ball. He was a great athlete from Lake City who could dunk a basketball. He noticed that the Alabama defenders were taking off at him, and so he just tucked the ball and took off running. That wasn't something the coaches called. He just did it.

"On the periphery, Spurrier doesn't like that stuff, but I'll tell you what: deep down he likes guys who aren't afraid to take risks. In order to do great things in life, you've got to stick your neck out a little bit. Edge was that type of kid. He took the risk. Of course, if he hadn't made it, he probably would not have punted again.

"So Shane tucked that ball down and took off and picked up a first down, and we went down and scored. Terry hit Harrison on the next play on a post for a touchdown. We took the momentum of the game."

Terry Dean: "Shane said he got a bad snap and didn't feel like he could get the punt off, so he ran it. Shane Edge was not your typical punter. He could two-hand slam a basketball. He could do a 360 slam. He was a pretty spectacular athlete. He sure took a huge risk."

On the very next play Terry Dean faked a handoff to Errict Rhett and threw a 43-yard touchdown pass to Jack Jackson.

Terry Dean: "The thing I remember about that one was that it was a pass-action play. I dropped back, had Jack open on the deep post, and threw it, and when I let it go, I knew I had overthrown it.

"It came out clean and had a little extra zip on it, and I just knew I overthrew it, and he put it in fifth gear and got it and took it to the house from there. It was exciting. That was one play that made all the bad stuff feel a lot better."

In the fourth quarter Florida had a second and 31 from its own 24, and Terry Dean threw a 33-yarder to Willie Jackson for a first down, and seven plays later, Errict Rhett scored from the two to help put away the 28-13 win over Bama. Dean had completed 20 of 37 for 256 yards and two touchdowns and proved himself to be a winning quarterback. The biggest test of the season would be against third-ranked West Virginia in the Sugar Bowl.

Terry Dean: "West Virginia was trying to make a case for being the national champion. If they had beaten us, they thought they had a pretty legitimate claim to it.

"We came in there, and they scored first. Errict Rhett had a great game. I threw for [255 yards and] a touchdown. I remember Monty Grow put a hit on their quarterback, Darren Studstill—I played with him in the World

League—that knocked his helmet sideways, and it was over from there. When Monty put the hit on him, it was over."

One of the key plays in the Sugar Bowl game was an interception by Lawrence Wright. His return included a backward run, and two sharp cutbacks. The 52-yard touchdown broke a 7-7 tie and turned the game around.

Errict Rhett rushed 25 times for 105 yards and scored three touchdowns in the 41-7 Florida rout.

Terry Dean: "We scored two TDs early in the second half, and we just put Errict to work again. I loved Errict Rhett, oh, no question. We were different people, and we didn't hang out. I was into school, and he wasn't. We were just from different backgrounds, but I would go into battle with him any day."

The win over West Virginia was the first major bowl win for Florida since 1967. It was also the eleventh win of the year, the best record in the history of the University of Florida.

sixty-six
From Heisman to Hell

Paul Bowen: "We had a lot of new skill kids in '94. I had a really good spring, and I'd won the receiver award in the spring. We weren't deep at receiver. Monty Duncan didn't play that year because of an injury, and Willie Jackson and Harrison Houston had left, and so in the spring there weren't a lot of receivers around, and Danny and Terry had to throw it to somebody, and I had a really solid spring. They gave me a nice plaque.

"I thought I was going to get more playing time than I ended up getting. When the fall came around and the freshmen arrived, there were Ike Hilliard, Reidel Anthony, Jacquez Green, Travis McGriff, and Nafis Karim.

"If you're a receiver, you want to go where they throw it. We were fortunate to get these guys to come here. I remember in the first fall scrimmage, Reidel caught three touchdown passes against the first-string defense.

"I remember we were in shorts and helmets, and Ike Hilliard came across on a middle route—you run down about fifteen to seventeen yards and you come right across the middle. It's a pretty easy throw, and whoever was playing quarterback threw behind him, and in stride he caught the ball with his right hand, spun all the way around, and kept going, and the two linebackers came up and hit each other, and Ike was gone.

"I remember looking around thinking, Where did they find these guys? But my second thought was, I'm glad they are on our team.

"We could have had Randy Moss too. I met him when he came on a recruiting trip. He was tall and skinny. I talked with him because he had played junior college ball in West Virginia. We were out one night, and we talked for fifteen minutes. I remember him being a very confident kid. You see so many kids on recruiting trips, All-Americans from wherever they come from.

"Randy first went to Notre Dame. I don't think he ever attended Notre Dame. He got into an altercation, and was put on parole, and Notre Dame dropped him. And then he got in trouble at Florida State, and he violated his parole, and Florida State had no choice but to drop him. Then he went to Marshall.

"I never faulted anyone for giving kids second chances. When you're young, you do stupid things."

Another newcomer was a powerful freshman fullback by the name of Jerome Evans. At 6'1", 210 pounds, Evans had the right size and perfect temperament to be the unsung blocker for his quarterback and for the headline-grabbing tailbacks recruited to the team, Elijah Williams and Fred Taylor.

Jerome Evans: "I grew up in Arcadia, in southwest Florida, about an hour and a half southwest of Tampa. I started playing football in a little Pop Warner league called the DeSoto County Youth Athletic Association. I played all the way through little league, junior high school, and went to DeSoto County High School.

"I was recruited hard by Florida State, Ohio State, Georgia, and Florida, and also by Kentucky, South Carolina, and Michigan. I reduced it down to Florida, Georgia, Clemson, South Carolina, and Kentucky.

"The place I wanted to go to was Florida. I loved to watch Errict Rhett all through high school. Also, my senior year, Florida beat Florida State in Tallahassee. Also, Coach Spurrier is a celebrity in Arcadia. People love Florida—it's a Florida Gator football town. One Tuesday, Coach Spurrier called me up. He said, 'I'm going to be in your area, and I'd like to stop by and meet you and meet your mom and dad and your family.'

"Arcadia probably has 8,000 people. He rolled up into town, and the whole town knew he was coming. I had a mob of people outside my house. He parked, and he came inside and introduced himself to my mom and dad. The other coaches came too, and they were like your family almost. They were walking around the kitchen, and Coach Spurrier asked, 'What are we having for dinner?' They ate my mom's cooking, and he talked to my mom, and my mom fell in love with him.

"After dinner, we sat on the couch, and Coach Spurrier said, 'Mrs. Evans, if you let your son come to Florida to play for the mighty Florida Gators, I'm gonna treat him like one of my own.'

"That was pretty much it once he said that. It was signed, sealed and delivered I was going to Florida.

"When I arrived in Florida in the fall of '92, football was like boot camp. It was unreal. You wouldn't think a human body could do some of the things we had to do. And the thought that no one was as tough or as strong or as good as me went out the window real quick.

"Practice was a thousand times harder than any game. Kevin Carter was a starting defensive end when I was there. My freshman year I was a scout on offense, and we had to go up against the first-team defense. I was a guy who played hard. I know we were just the scout offense, but it was my job to get the defense ready for the coming game.

"Coach Spurrier, I thought, was a straightforward guy, a great coach who knows the game. He's got it down to a science. If you line up a certain way, if you're playing a certain defense, he knows what the weakness of that defense is. He knows how to exploit it. Whether we actually do it is another story. If we need a big play, and they are giving you the flat, sometimes you need to try to let your man just outdo their man. He knows the defense. He knows the offense. And my first impression of him was that he would tell you what was on his mind no matter whether you like it or not, whether it's good or bad, no holds barred. Everything's fair game, and if you screw up, he's going to let you know it, no matter who's listening and who's around. No sugar on top.

"In '93, my freshman year, I traveled to all the games, but I didn't get in unless we were ahead 45-0. I finally got to play in '94."

When the 1994 season began, Florida was ranked the number one team in the country in all the pre-season polls. This was heady stuff. Florida had never in its history been so highly rated.

Terry Dean: "When 1994 began, for the first time ever people said that Florida had a shot to be national champions. No question we had the best team in the country that year. We were loaded from top to bottom. When the season began, we were ranked first, and that was for the first time in Florida history.

"It was a neat time. It was a fun time. We were very aware of the fact that we were the number one team in the pre-season. And proud of it. And frankly, we were."

Danny Wuerffel: "After four or five years of having a topnotch program, this leads to more recruits. We started stacking some players and having some depth.

"When we started the season against New Mexico State, it was exciting because we were ranked number one, and everybody was fired up. We were getting a lot of press, and everyone was proud."

In the season opener against New Mexico State, Terry Dean made the country take notice when he went 20 for 30 for 271 yards and seven touchdowns, four of them going to Jack Jackson.

Terry Dean: "The New Mexico State game was like the Southwest Louisiana game the year before. They were playing a lot of man-to-man coverage. Our freshmen were some of the finest receivers ever to play college football. At that time they hadn't established themselves. They were still learning the ropes. Reidel Anthony was always blazing fast and a bigger receiver. Reidelwas a burner. Ike Hilliard developed into the better receiver. He ran better routes and understood the position better. Jacquez Green was a surprise. He was a very quiet, very small guy who hadn't caught anyone's attention at that point. Travis McGriff was part of that group, even though he didn't play that day. They all went on to the NFL and made a lot of money. So it was pitch and catch. We just marched up and down the field. We would do whatever we wanted at will on those guys."

Jerome Evans: "Terry Dean had a gun. He was very confident. He was similar to Coach Spurrier. He was very smart, had great physical attributes, and he knew the offense. I don't think he knew it as well as Danny. When Danny and I were freshmen in '92, I'm not going to say Danny knew it better than Shane Matthews, but he knew it just as well.

"After we were on campus two or three weeks, Coach Spurrier would say, 'Shane, what are you thinking here? What's another good play to check to?' And Shane would say, 'Blue Z.' He'd say, 'That's a decent one. Danny, what's another one?' And Danny would call a play, and Coach Spurrier would say, 'That's the one I was thinking of.'"

In 1994 Errict Rhett was gone, drafted into the pros. Replacing him were two talented backs, Elijah Williams and Fred Taylor.

Terry Dean: "Elijah was a scatback. He was smaller than Fred. Fred was more of a power back. Elijah was a good receiver out of the backfield, not a guy on fourth and one who'd you want to pound the middle. Both were extremely talented. Elijah was with the Atlanta Falcons, and Fred is with the Jacksonville Jaquars. He was All-Pro two years ago. Fred's a solid NFL player."

Jerome Evans: "We had Terrence Foy, Elijah Williams, and Tyrone Baker, three of the top tailbacks in the state—all three came to Florida that year. Tyrone had the most potential of the three. He was the fastest, most gifted tailback beside Fred Taylor. Terrence Foy would have been a great tailback at Florida, but he got into a little bit of trouble. He was a guy who just never stayed out of trouble. In Coach Spurrier's system, if you don't follow the rules, you're probably not going to be there very long.

"If you didn't go to class, Coach Spurrier would sit you down quick. If you didn't have a certain grade point average, or if you missed study hall, he would sit you down fast. And if you came out and had a couple of practices that weren't up to par, he'd sit you down. He would say, 'You have to earn your way every day.' All positions are up for grabs—every day.

"We would watch game film every Monday after a game. He'd sit in the offensive meeting, and the defensive coaches would be in the defensive meeting. Coach Spurrier would sit there, and he'd go through every play—slow motion, rewind it, watch each play maybe fifteen times, look at each player. If you did something well, he'd say, 'Good job on that play.' Or say, if a guy missed a block, he'd say, 'What in the hell are you doing on this play?' He'd turn around to the player and say, 'Be honest with me. You didn't really want to block him on that play, did you?' It was, 'Oh man.' It was all constructive criticism, but come the next game on Saturday, you tried to make every play as perfect as possible, because you knew the films were coming up the next Monday.

"If you got your clock cleaned, they would replay it a hundred times, and he'd ask you what you were thinking or doing.

"After a particularly bad game, he'd watch the film with the whole team sitting there. Sometimes it was brutal. And he didn't spare anyone. I remember my freshman year going through the tapes and watching Shane Matthews, our Heisman Trophy candidate, make a bad play, and he didn't spare him. It was, 'Tell me what you were thinking right now.' He'd go through the checklist, his drop, his keys, where his eyes are supposed to be. He was supposed to be going over everything in his mind, and Coach Spurrier would ask, 'What are you thinking now? What are you thinking NOW? Who are you going to throw the ball to?'

"I once heard Danny Wuerffel say that when Shane Matthews went into the NFL he said that if Coach Spurrier were ever to become an NFL coach, he would destroy teams. Because the way the offense works, you'll call a play in the huddle based on the way they line up, the way they're playing you, and it could all change without anyone ever saying anything.

"For instance, say Coach Spurrier tells a receiver he has a '9 route.' If they play bump and run, he's to do one thing. If they're playing off him, he has to do something totally different. The receiver has to see that, and the quarterback has to see that, and if they're not on the same page, they don't hook up. If the defense is trying to disguise a certain coverage, as long as the receiver and the quarterback both see what they're doing, we're going to have them. Little do they know he's going to run a different route. It's pretty neat."

As terrific as the backs were in '94, the receivers were even better. In the New Mexico State romp, freshmen Ike Hilliard and Reidel Anthony each caught touchdowns and impressed with their raw talent.

Danny Wuerffel: "Ike was a phenomenal player. He was young then, but he combined great speed, size, and he was very physical. He had big legs, and he was not afraid to run into guys and make things happen. The play he is remembered for most occurred in the Sugar Bowl his senior year. He caught the ball in the air going full speed, landed on one foot and stopped, and both defenders went by him. He spun the other way and scored. My ACL would still be laying on the field if I had done that!

"Another freshman, Reidel Anthony, was another great player. He was more of a Jerry Rice type of receiver. He was tall and smooth, wasn't real physical, more of a glider. He ran precise routes, and he had great speed. We had some GOOD freshmen.

"Everyone can figure out who the talent is, but the trick is getting them to come. It's important to communicate with them, but you also have to have something to offer. Spurrier's record of coaching quarterbacks and receivers and making them successful speaks more volumes than anything. When you're in a place that's successful, you get to move to the next level. Coach Spurrier has a phenomenal offensive mind, and he could teach you the game. If you're someone with athletic ability and you come to play for him, you'll be in good shape."

Though Florida went on to defeat New Mexico State by the score of 70 to 21, when the polls came out the next week, Florida was ranked number two behind Nebraska. In the next game against Kentucky, a smashing 73-7 victory, Terry Dean threw for 201 yards and four touchdown passes. In five quarters of play, Terry Dean had thrown 11 touchdowns.

Terry Dean: "I also had one called back on a holding play. At that point Spurrier just wanted to pound [Kentucky coach] Bill Curry so badly. You knew you were going to get a chance to throw some touchdowns on them." Florida led at the half 31-7. Dean started the second half by throwing a touchdown to Reidel Anthony.

Terry Dean: "That was a particularly sweet game, because that was the game in which I lost my starting job the year before. And after we beat Kentucky, I felt like Superman."

The game was also a gratifying one for Paul Bowen. After all the hours of practice, he was able to get into the Kentucky game and score a touchdown, even though he was sick with the flu and a fever.

Paul Bowen: "That game got ugly. We were just doing what we do. Coach put a lot of the backups in. We got on a roll, and Kentucky kind of laid down.

"I was out on the field. We were down on about the fifteen, and I was flexed out in the tight end spot. I was matched with a linebacker, and in the huddle Eric Kressler called a play, and I told him, 'Throw me the ball. I'm gonna be open.' So we lined up, and I ran my route, and I'm looking for the ball because I figured I was wide open. Looking at the film, I saw that if he would have thrown it, the safety would have decapitated me.

"But Eric got flushed out of the pocket, and I just rolled with him, and he put it on a rope right at me. I caught it for a touchdown and didn't think much of it. Having scored as many touchdowns as I did in junior college and high school, I figured I would be getting a lot more. When I caught it, Ike jumped on top of me. I tossed the ball to the referee and went to the sideline. I wasn't gonna go nuts and a draw a penalty, because I was fortunate just to be a part of the team.

"Now as I look back, I wish I had thrown the ball up into the stands in celebration. Or I should have kept the ball. But I just handed it to the ref. But it WAS exciting. It's neat when you work hard and something good happens.

A lot of people I played with never even got a chance to have a ball thrown to them. But I thought there'd be more along the way."

Florida was ranked number 1 when the Gators travelled to Knoxville to play Todd Helton and Tennessee. Helton was the quarterback on the cover of the football magazines, but that day Terry Dean outshone the Volunteers' hotshot, going 14-19 for 261 yards and a touchdown en route to a 31-0 rout.

Terry Dean: "Going into the next game as we went to Tennessee, we were cruising. We were playing like the number one team in the country should play. We went up against Todd Helton and Peyton Manning, and we had a really good game. We were good on both sides of the ball—offense, defense, and special teams. The final score was 31 to 0. You normally don't get a chance to go into that stadium and shut those guys out. But that was a special game.

"I remember on the first drive we got down inside the 20, and I had an interception. I went to throw the ball, and a guy on the line tipped it, and it popped in the air, and they intercepted it.

"It didn't faze me at all. I threw a pass to Jack [Jackson], and it also was tipped on the line, but this time Jack caught it, and he ran it in for a touchdown. And I remember hitting Chris Doering a couple of times across the middle.

"It was funny: everybody used to joke that Doering was Weurffel's guy and Jack Jackson was my guy. That certainly wasn't by design. I don't know why it worked out that way. The difference between Danny and me was that I would take my chances. I would throw downfield, the deep pass to Jack, and give him a chance to go get it. Consequently, I threw some extra interceptions. Doering was more the sure-handed, underneath guy. Danny's nature was to take the sure completion and go to his guy."

Jerome Evans: "It was the first game in Tennessee's new stadium, and we wanted to beat them. We had them down 31 to zip, and I remember they got an interception at the five yard line. We had taken our defensive starters out, and they were all upset because the offense had thrown an interception. They begged Coach to put them back in. So he put all the starters back in, and it was first and goal on the two, and they shut them out. It was great."

Danny Wuerffel: "That was a huge win. We absolutely dominated that team that night.

"I wasn't starting, but I was secure in my role. I wished I could have been playing, but I understood it was important for Coach Spurrier to pick a quarterback and stick with him. He was sticking with Terry, and Terry was responding."

But against Ole Miss, Terry Dean's old bugaboo, the interception, reared its ugly head. Though he threw four touchdowns in the game, giving him an incredible 17 after four games, he also had three picks, including one that was picked off and returned 63 yards for a touchdown to tie the score at 14-14.

Terry Dean: "Joe Lee Dunn was their defensive coordinator. He was supposed to be their guru for defense, but we jumped on them pretty good, though I did throw a couple of interceptions

"But right before the halftime, I threw a deep streak to Aubrey Hill. He went 40 yards, and they signalled touchdown. Then they waved him off and put the ball at the one-foot line, but by then time had expired. But I remember I did throw a few interceptions, and they were bringing people from all over the place, and I was sacked three times as well, and Coach Spurrier was jumping on me more than I had seen him jump on me before. And at that time I began to wonder what was going to happen to me."

Despite the lopsided victory and all of the touchdown pass against Ole Miss, Coach Spurrier was unhappy and upset with Terry Dean's play.

Jerome Evans: "If a quarterback makes mental errors, Coach Spurrier becomes irate. And the next week he's going to go over it and over it and over it, and if a player doesn't take constructive criticism very well, it could crush him. If his confidence is hurt because Coach gets on him for not making the right decision, it'll get to him.

"Coach doesn't stand for it, and he doesn't care who you are or what your records are or what you've done in the past. It's unacceptable. If Terry threw three interceptions and one was run back for a touchdown, Terry got it. We probably watched that film for three hours. And Coach has a memory you wouldn't believe. He remembers the good plays, but he doesn't forget the bad ones. And if you make bad decisions in your life, he doesn't forget that either. Once he gets something into his head, it's real hard to get that out of his head."

Danny Wuerffel: "It had a lot to do with his decision making. Again, Coach Spurrier was very high on doing things his way. What Coach Spurrier REALLY hated was interceptions, especially on first downs. Because you're giving up two more tries. Even on second down, he thinks interceptions are silly. Although a third-down interception is bad, it's more justified."

So while Terry Dean was being criticized behind closed doors by Spurrier, at the same time the newspapers were starting to tout him as a Heisman Trophy candidate.

Terry Dean: "That's when the Heisman talk really started kicking up—that week [after the Ole Miss game]. I was the number one candidate."

The next game was against LSU, a 42-18 win. But Terry Dean's play against LSU did not please Coach Spurrier.

Terry Dean: "You would think that would be a good game, but it's not the way Spurrier is. And I actually think I had a decent game. I ran for a touchdown, and I threw a touchdown, and I had one interception. [Dean was 20 for 38 for 217 yards and a touchdown.] I was not particularly sharp, but I had five or six balls dropped. We kept trying to work the middle, and we kept struggling with our timing.

"After the LSU game I knew I was in trouble. Spurrier was acting differently toward me than I'd seen him. It's hard to describe the difference. It was just the looks I got from him and the comments he was making. At that point I knew I was on thin ice."

Danny Wuerffel: "In the Ole Miss game and in the LSU game, Coach Spurrier didn't say many things publicly about how he was feeling about how things were going. But he wasn't judging Terry based on the 52-0 score, he was judging him based on how he wanted things to be done.

"When the LSU game ended—whether it was justified or not, or whether it's fair or not, Coach Spurrier was very frustrated with the way Terry was doing things, but yet he didn't say it publicly. I thought Coach communicated that in the meetings. Terry would know, but I could be wrong.

"But Coach Spurrier is trying to win. He doesn't care about statistics or who's in the running for the Heisman Trophy."

Jerome Evans: "I know Coach Spurrier didn't have anything against Terry Dean. But Coach Spurrier and Terry didn't get along. They used to fight. They weren't the best of friends. As Terry said, they wouldn't go on a fishing trip together. But Terry wasn't getting the job done. If Coach put him in a position where he felt uptight, it was his job to be the leader of the team. We weren't being led very well."

In the next game, number-1 Florida faced Auburn, the sixth-ranked team in the country. The year before Florida had lost to Auburn 38-35 on a last-minute interception and runback for a touchdown. In '94, Auburn won 36-33.

The week before the Auburn game started badly for Terry Dean.

Terry Dean: "I came to football practice Monday afternoon after class, and I was watching film in one of the coach's offices, when Spurrier came in and asked the coach to leave so he could talk to me alone. I figured he was going to want to talk game strategy or go over what we were going to do against Auburn. But as soon as he closed the door, he cussed me up and down. He said I was not doing what I was being coached to do.

"He said, 'If you don't get this Heisman talk out of your head, you're never gonna play here again.' He told me that if I played badly against Auburn, he was going to bench me.

"When he left, I was in shock. After practice I called my dad and said, 'I think that's it. I think I'm done.'

"Spurrier was our quarterbacks coach, but that week he didn't work with us at all. He didn't talk to us all week long. He sent John Reaves, the tight-end coach, over to work with us, which was unheard of. I knew it was over.

"On Friday, the day before the Auburn game, we had our walk-through at the stadium. On the way out, he came over and told me again that if I played bad, he was going to bench me.

"And it became a self-fulfilling prophecy. I knew that I probably was going to play bad. I knew that that was gonna be it for me.

"I never had my head in the game. I never was there. I threw a bunch of interceptions, and he did bench me in the second quarter. After that game, that was about it for me."

Jerome Evans: "Errict rushed for 150 yards and made another 100 yards receiving. They couldn't slow our running game down, but we didn't have the best game plan, and we threw a lot of bad passes. Coach Spurrier took Terry out in the second period, and put Danny in, but he did have a choice? I don't know. It's his job to put his team in the best position to win. And whether his quarterback is going for the Heisman or not, if he's having a subpar day, it's his job to get the best player on the field that day. We all knew Coach Spurrier wasn't playing favorites. He was trying to put our football team in the best position to win. I thought it was the right decision.

"Danny was calm. He was cool. He was collected. The team respected him. He made good decisions. He may not have been the most gifted athlete, which isn't to say he wasn't a good athlete, because he was. He was like a coach on the field. He was a student of the game. If a defense played a certain way, he knew what play to call, and he knew what each player had to do to make that play work.

"He made some mistakes. He made bad throws. But that's part of being a human being. Danny was a great guy, and he was a great football player, a great talent, a great person. I can't say enough about Danny."

Danny Wuerffel: "Football is a funny game. I've played games where in one half we couldn't complete a pass; there was a game I played in Europe where I threw four touchdown passes. I wasn't doing anything different, it was just the way things fell. So I don't know if I was doing anything different that day, or whether things just changed a little bit.

"We did some things, and they started working. We scored. I threw three touchdowns. We had been well behind, and we got a chance to be in it and go ahead. So that was real exciting."

The shame of it was the all the offensive firepower was wasted when instead of running out the clock, Florida instead threw the ball. Danny Wuerffel threw an intereption that was returned to the Gator 45-yard line. Auburn's Patrick Nix marched the Tigers down the field, winning the game on an 8-yard touchdown pass to Frank Sanders in the left corner of the Gator end zone with just 30 seconds left in the game.

Danny Wuerffel: "We were third and long, and he called the play, and I heaved it down the field, which wasn't, in my opinion, a bad play. It was like a punt. They still had to go sixty yards. But they got some momentum, something was sparked, and in the end they threw it over Michael Gilmore's head, and they caught it for a touchdown, and that was crushing.

"And to make it even worse, we had an open week with all that time to think about it."

Terry Dean: "To tell you the truth, at that point I wasn't paying much attention. But what happened was that Danny audibled and tried to throw it deep, and that stopped the clock, and they got the ball and went down and scored. But really, at that point I wasn't even paying attention."

Danny Wuerffel: "The Auburn game told me that I would be the starter against Georgia, and that Friday, Coach Spurrier told me that I would be starting."

True to his word Spurrier started Wuerffel, who had an 11-for-12 day in a 52-14 win against Georgia. Danny Wuerffel had wrestled the starting job from Terry Dean and never would relinquish it again.

Danny Wuerffel: "I felt real good. We played well and executed well. We had a good day. It was Coach Spurrier's one hundredth win, and after the game he called Coach Graves up on the phone. Apparently, when he played for Coach Graves, Georgia had scored 50 points against him, and he told Spurrier, 'If you ever score 50 points against Georgia, think of the old coach.' So Coach Spurrier called Coach Graves up and told him about it."

It was Spurrier's one hundredth victory, but Terry Dean didn't feel much like rejoicing.

Terry Dean: "There were a lot of hard feelings. I certainly understood the logic; but you don't typically see a change in quarterbacks when the team is still ranked in the top ten. I felt I had paid my dues. I was his first recruit. I took my chances coming to Florida. I felt like I had earned my right to be there. To this day I don't understand why Spurrier was so angry. I don't have a clue."

John Reaves was the receivers coach. He recalled first-hand what happened to Terry Dean.

John Reaves: "Terry started out brilliantly, but then we played LSU, and Terry missed a lot of passes. That irritated Steve. You know how Steve is with his quarterbacks. So we go to the Auburn game, and Terry threw four interceptions in the first half and fumbled a snap. So Steve replaced him with Danny, who played admirably but threw two picks himself in the game.

"The next week against Tennessee, Steve decided to start Danny, and we beat them soundly, and Danny had a brilliant game. At that point Danny had to slip up in order for Terry to get back in.

"At the same time, Terry criticized Steve, which made Steve mad.

"I liked Terry. Terry had good talent. He could run, he threw a beautiful ball, was smart. He was a Heisman Trophy candidate that year.

"I went to Terry a couple of times and said, 'Terry, look, I played for Steve. I know how he is. If you just go tell him you're sorry, you'll get back in.' But he never would do it. Terry had too much pride. So Terry hardly ever played again, which was a shame. And Steve wanted Terry to play again, wanted to give him an opportunity. Away from the team Steve would privately lament about the situation. It was a clash of titans.

"That was something that never should have happened."

Southern Mississippi was the next victim, a 55-17 loser. In that game Eric Kresser came in and starred. He went 7-10 for 214 yards and two touchdowns.

Danny Wuerffel: "I played the first quarter, and Eric played the rest of the game. I'll say this about Coach Spurrier: he's real loyal to the people who are loyal to him. He was sympathetic to Eric, who had worked so hard for many years but hadn't gotten the chance he was looking for to play. So he gave Eric a chance to play."

Homecoming was against South Carolina. Florida won 48-17 to win the SEC East for the third straight year.

Paul Bowen: "A lot of seniors got to start. Coach was trying to get plays for all the seniors. So I had a couple balls thrown my way. Terry got in at the end of the game, and he checked off, and threw me one. It was neat. I didn't think, This is my last game in the Swamp, until it was over. When the final horn went off, I walked around taking a look at the stadium one last time from a player's perspective.

"Then it kind of hits you that this thing is winding down."

It also was winding down for Terry Dean as his quarterbacking days at Florida were over. He dropped from the number one quarterback to number three behind Danny Wuerffel and Eric Kresser. His final opportunity was a sullen, lackluster mop-up performance in the win over South Carolina.

Jerome Evans: "Terry didn't handle it well. What do you expect him to do? He felt he got a bad deal. He felt he was getting shunned. It was his senior year, and when Danny started to do really well, he knew it was over for him. It was like they took the fight out of him. Terry was a good quarterback. He didn't deserve that, I don't think. But he was disgruntled, and everyone knew it. Coach Spurrier went as far as putting him on the scout team. He wouldn't even practice with the offense. He wouldn't even get the game plan. Danny would play, and Eric Kresser would play, and a walk-on might get in, and THEN Terry might go in. Some guys said Coach Spurrier wanted Terry to quit. But Terry wasn't going to quit. He's not a quitter. Terry obviously was upset, but who wouldn't be?"

sixty-seven
Danny's Team

The Vanderbilt game was a breeze. Florida only won 24-7, but it was never at risk of losing the game.

Paul Bowen: "It was cool up there, and it was a tough game. I remember at the end of the game Eric Kresser checked off, and he threw the ball into the end zone, and all the Vanderbilt fans were booing. I remember Coach saying, 'I didn't call that.' Kresser did."

Going into the Florida State game, Danny Wuerffel was sick as a dog. But he had just gained the starting quarterback job the week before, and he vowed he would have to die first before giving up his starting spot.

Danny Wuerffel: "The night before the game I was very sick. I got the flu and vomited six or seven times throughout the night. I felt miserable. I remember feeling that I could have laid down on the bench and gone to sleep at any time. But I wasn't going to step down for the life of me, for obvious reasons."

The Florida State game was a roller coaster. Florida led by four touchdowns in the fourth quarter, only to see FSU fight back and tie the score at 31-31.

Danny Wuerffel: "The fourth quarter was amazing. You'd have never thought any team could have done something like that, and it was absolutely incredible. It was so crazy, I almost wish I could have sat in the stands and watched it. Danny Kanell and Warrick Dunn basically did it. It WAS frustrating. The best thing about it was that it was a tie and not a loss, but it sure felt like a loss, because we had dominated them for so long."

Terry Dean watched from the sidelines.

Terry Dean: "That was one of the wildest games I was ever a part of. We were up by 28 points going into the fourth quarter, and we were sure that for all intents and purposes, the game was over.

"And to be honest, we were lucky to get out of there with a tie. FSU was driving at the end of the game for a field goal when time ran out. Otherwise, they'd have beaten us.

"Seems like it just kind of fell apart, just started snowballing. We got away from throwing and we started trying to run. They kept shutting that down, and then we'd try to throw, and they'd jump on that. They just shut us down. They turned it on instantly. I don't know how that happened."

Jerome Evans: "I didn't play in that FSU game. I got suspended for the most ridiculous thing. I lived in Flavette Hall. They give you a little twin bed, which I hated, because it was so small. When I lived in Yon Hall, I had a full-sized bed, so what I did, I went to the storage closet in Yon Hall, opened it up, put the twin bed in there, and I went and got my full-size bed and put it in my room.

"When the janitor came to spray the room, he saw I had a full-size bed, and he left me a note to switch the beds back. I said to myself, 'Screw that. I don't want to sleep on that little bed.'

"A couple months passed, and he came back, and he was spraying again, and he saw the bed, and I got a letter to go down and see the dean. I thought, You've got to be kidding me.

"They said it was a fire hazard to have the bigger bed in the room, and they said the penalty was to place me on probation. And when you're on probation, you can't participate in extracurricular activities. So I had to miss the Florida State game. Coach Spurrier said I couldn't dress because I was on probation, but he let me come to the game.

"I had to put the little bed back in my room. I'll tell you, it was the most idiotic thing, and I was pissed. I had been practicing hard to play in that game, and you tell me I can't play because I put a bed in my room?

"And we had a 28-point lead in the fourth quarter, and we were so excited about kicking their butt, and then they just started storming back. Oh man, they stormed back. And our offense folded, and the coaches made a lot of bad play calls.

"We played a terrible fourth quarter. It got so bad that when we were on third down, we would punt. We were doing quarterback sneaks on second and six. We couldn't do anything. We were just trying to get out of there with a win, but they had enough time to score a touchdown and tie it up. Every play they ran went for forty yards a pop. We couldn't hold them down. The score was 31–30, ours, and if they had gone for two, they probably would have won it. That was a game I'd like to erase from history."

Florida again played Alabama for the 1994 SEC championship.

Paul Bowen: "The Alabama game was a test of what our team was made of. Tying Florida State was like losing, and we knew the next week we were playing the top, Alabama. They were undefeated going into the game, and they ended up winning the Citrus Bowl."

Losing 22–17 after Bama's Dwayne Rudd intercepted a tipped Wuerffel pass and ran it back 23 yards for a touchdown, Coach Spurrier really pulls out a bag of tricks on the final drive.

His first designed play called for Danny Wuerffel to pretend he was hurt so the Bamans wouldn't suspect that he was bringing in Eric Kresser specifically to throw a long pass.

Terry Dean: "He doesn't really consider them trick plays. We have them in our playbook, and we practice them, and he uses them. It was a planned play. Eric Kresser had a stronger arm than Danny, and he brought Eric in to make that play. I've always said that Kresser won that game for us that day. We were losing at that point and going backwards, and Kresser came in and threw that long pass, and we went down and scored from there to win the game."

Danny Wuerffel: "Eric threw the ball down the field for a long gain, and then I came in and finished the drive to win the game. I found out later that Coach wasn't sure he wanted to take Eric out after that play, because he had a little momentum going, but before he had a chance to think about it, I ran back onto the field, and I'm glad I did."

On that winning drive Coach Spurrier sent in a second trick play in which the linemen all lined up wide of the hashmarks, and Danny Wuerffel threw to Reidel Anthony for a nine-yard gain, though it was inches from being a touchdown.

Danny Wuerffel: "He started pulling things out of his hat on that last drive. It's just a crazy thing he does every now and then. In this one, the tackles line up wide, and he tried to get the defense off-balance for a play or two."

Terry Dean: "If Reidel would have gone towards tackle, he would have run all the way."

The game-winner was a play that went from Danny Wuerffel to receiver Chris Doering behind the line of scrimmage, and then Doering threw a pass to a wide-open Aubrey Hill. With only 5:29 left in the game, Florida went ahead for good, 24-23.

Paul Bowen: "The last ten minutes of practice we always practiced our trick plays, the fun plays. We did it every practice, every day. You might not run them, but they were there if we needed them, just in case. We ran a double-pass play called the Emory & Henry. That's a small college in Tennessee, and Coach Spurrier used to watch them run the play when he was growing up. The quarterback threw a pass out to Chris Doering, who was standing behind two blockers, and Aubrey Hill ran down the field, and Chris threw it to Aubrey down around the two yard line. That was the trick play we practiced.

"We were losing to Alabama when Coach called for the Emory & Henry. Danny threw back to Chris, and he let fly to Aubrey, who was tackled on the two [for a twenty-yard gain], and then Danny hit Chris with a touchdown in the corner of the end zone, and we won the game."

Danny Wuerffel: "We got down to the 2-yard line, and we called a quarterback sneak, but they had it covered, so I audibled with a hand signal, and I threw the pass to Chris. He ran a little quick slant, and I hit him, and we were SEC champs.

"Chris is a great story. He was a walk-on who earned a chance to play. He wasn't the fastest or the strongest, but he had the most heart. He was a real tall guy who ran real precise routes. What I remember most about Chris was that he appreciated being out on the field every minute. Most guys don't appreciate it until after it's over. Chris never took anything for granted. He was living his dream, and it showed."

Terry Dean: "It's tough enough to stop our offense without the trick plays. You put those in and it really gets them confused."

Jerome Evans: "We always work on those little trick plays, and Coach tries to find a spot to run them.

"I remember we practiced this one play at every practice for five years straight, and I've never seen it used in a game. It's called the 'hidden ball play.' He would hike the ball to one of the linemen, and they would give the ball to a running back in some way. After everyone cleared away, he would take off and start running. The defense wasn't supposed to know where the ball was. We practiced it every day, and we've never run it in a game yet. He was waiting for the right moment to pull it out."

In the Alabama game Jack Jackson was hurt, and Reidel Anthony started in his place. In that game Anthony caught eight passes for 105 yards and a touchdown.

Jerome Evans: "That's the game where Reidel solidified himself as a true player."

Alabama marched down the field as the clock was running down. There were 54 seconds left in the game, and Alabama had a fourth and 13 from its own 44.

Paul Bowen: "On third down, they tried to run. Their running back was a good little player who backed up Emmitt Smith at Dallas for a couple of years. They gave the guy the ball, and Keith Council sacked him for a three-yard loss. Keith just beat his man. They were driving at the time.

"That put them in a fourth-and-long situation where they had to throw it. Kevin and the other defensive guys pinned their ears back, and Fred Weary got in and tipped it up in the air, and Eddie Lake caught it and hit the deck.

"We went into pandemonium. It was neat. You never know what's going to happen in those games. We were lucky to win."

Jerome Evans: "He intercepted the ball, and we just went crazy on the sidelines. That was the play when we knew we were going to win the game."

Danny Wuerffel: "That was one of the most emotional wins for me in my career."

The final game was a 23-17 loss in a rematch with Florida State in the Sugar Bowl in New Orleans. Danny Wuerffel threw for a record 28-39 for 394 yards, but he was sacked six times. A Fred Taylor fumble also killed a key drive.

Paul Bowen: "It had been a long season, and we lost the Sugar Bowl game on a fluke play. The ball hit one of our defensive backs on the top of the head, and one of the Florida State guys behind him caught it and ran for a touchdown. We lost by six."

Danny Wuerffel: "I just remember it being a really frustrating game. They did a lot of smart things in terms of how they rushed the passer. All I remember is how frustrating that game was."

Jerome Evans: "We didn't have anything substantial to play for. Nothing was on the line. We weren't up for a national title. Had we won, we would have been ranked a few spots higher. But to our team, the game didn't have any real meaning."

Paul Bowen: "I think the '94 season was a precursor to Florida winning a national title, because we had a bunch of young guys, and we went through a season with a bullseye on our back. After what we went through, two years later it was, 'Hey, this is no big deal.' Although it would have been nice to have won it in '94, it definitely set up to where they could win in '96.

"I remember I was 22, through playing at Florida, and people would ask me, 'What do you want to do with the rest of your life?' And I'm thinking, I just lived my dream. I worked hard and got into the school I wanted to play for, and I was fortunate enough to play for one of the greatest coaches who ever walked this planet. What do you mean, 'What do I want to do with my life?' How many people get to live out a dream?"

Terry Dean did not play a down in the Sugar Bowl game. When it was over, he felt a great weight lift from his shoulders. Though a Heisman candidate, he was not drafted the following spring. He signed as a free agent at a cost to him of millions. But despite the disappointment and potential loss of income, Terry Dean is not bitter and he isn't angry. More than anything else, he is grateful for having had the chance to play football at the University of Florida.

Terry Dean: "I remember when that game was over, I had a cathartic feeling. It was a release of a lot of frustrations. I remember that was a very good feeling—that I was done with football. If was five years of ninety percent frustration and brief periods of fun.

"I didn't get drafted. I went up to the Canadian Football League and played with the Winnipeg Blue Bombers for three quarters of a season. They paid me $80,000 Canadian, which was fine.

"After three quarters of the season had passed, I was either second or third string. They said I either had to go on injured reserve or they were going to let me go.

"I said, 'Okay, let me go.' So I left and went out to San Francisco and worked out with Bill Walsh there. He said he'd bring me to camp with the 49ers if I first got some experience in the World League. In '96 I headed over to Germany, and played in the World League for the Rhein Fire.

"The coach, funny enough, was Galen Hall.

"I returned to the 49ers camp, and while I was over in Germany, they had signed Gino Torretta. So I came back to Florida and played five or six weeks in West Palm Beach with the Florida Bobcats [in the Arena league]. After that, I just said I worked too hard in school not to get ready for life after football, and it was time to get moving on.

"I came back to Naples, and I have been with A.G. Edwards as a financial planner.

"I have to tell you, if I had to do it all over again, I wouldn't have done anything any differently. I'd have still gone to Florida in a heartbeat. I have people come up to me—people I've never met before—and they say, 'Man, did Spurrier screw you.' But I wouldn't change anything for the world. I got a great education at Florida. I met my wife there. I came back to Naples, and I'm doing what I want to do. I have a phenomenal job. If I was going to change anything, I probably would not have bounced around playing professional football for as long as I did. I would have just started right away in my profession. But that also was a great experience, and I certainly got football out of my system.

"I have no regrets whatsoever. I'm not one of those guys who says, 'I wish I had another year.' I got out healthy. I never had any injuries. There's nothing I'd change about it."

sixty-eight

12 and 1

One of the traditions of the Gator Nation is sons of former players coming to Florida to play. Among those sons have been the four Gaffneys, Travis McGriff, son of Lee, and in 1995 the multitalented Terry Jackson, one of two sons of Willie Jackson, the first black quarterback, joined the varsity as a wide receiver.

Terry Jackson: "I grew up in Gainesvile. My father was Willie Jackson, who played with Florida in the 1970s. I attended C.K. Young High School and played for John Clifford, who had played at Florida, since the ninth grade. We were ranked throughout all my years, and my senior year we were number one.

"I played everywhere. I didn't score that many touchdowns, because I played a little bit of fullback, a little bit of wing-back, and some halfback.

"I wanted to go to Florida. My father had played there, I lived in Gainesville, my mother went there, my brother also went there, so I've rooted for the orange and blue ever since I can remember. I used to come and work out with the Florida varsity a little bit, so I pretty much knew all the players. I was acclimated to what was going on at Florida. It would have been hard for me to go to another university and root for the Gators at the same time.

"I did look at other schools. I kept my options open. I visited Kentucky and Duke. I almost didn't go to Florida, because they didn't recruit me heavily until right at the end. I got their last scholarship for that year.

"I was a red-shirt freshman in '94, and I didn't play until my second year, in '95. I began my career at Florida as a defensive player, and then in the spring of '95 Elijah [Williams] and Fred [Taylor] were nicked up and couldn't practice, and in a scrimmage Coach Spurrier said, 'We're gonna give you a shot,' and I went in and ran a draw, and I only ran seven or eight yards, but I made a few people miss, and so he switched me over to halfback.

"Our quarterbacks were Danny Wuerffel and Eric Kresser. Danny was a great competitor. When Danny was back there you pretty much knew you were going to win the game. He was a confident player, and you just felt confident. You knew you were going to be successful on those plays.

"Eric was a strong-armed quarterback. He had a lot of skills—you knew he could light it up, put up some numbers, because he had such a great arm, and in that system, he could make a lot of things happen too.

"It was a pro-style system, and it was my first year on offense, so I pretty much had to learn everything.

"We started the season against Houston [a 45-21 win] at Florida Field. It was the first time I actually came out of the tunnel knowing I was going to play in the game in front of that many people. I scored my first touchdown in that game."

Against Kentucky, in the first quarter Elijah Williams was kicked in the ankle and Fred Taylor separated his shoulder, and red-shirt freshman Terry Jackson was inserted at halfback. The freshman responded by slashing for 138 yards and three touchdowns in a 42-7 victory.

Terry Jackson: "Eli and Fred were switching series, and both of those guys got hurt, so I had to go in. The Houston game had set me up, and so I went into the Kentucky game feeling real good. And the line did a great job of blocking. Anytime you throw the ball as well as we do, you are bound to have some holes, and it was my job to find them and hit them. I was fortunate to be playing in that offense. It was a good time out there being able to make some plays and get the victory.

"Our system is to take what the defense gives you. In that system, if somebody is open all day, or whoever Coach feels can get open on certain plays, that's who is gonna get the ball. Danny ran the system to perfection."

Danny Wuerffel: "Terry Jackson was one of the few players who could play several different positions in college, including running back and linebacker. He was not spectacular, but he was solid, a back who was hard to tackle. Terry was a great football player."

Jerome Evans: "Terry was awesome. He was one of the more physical running backs. He could block. He could tackle. He was a linebacker first. Then they moved him to running back because they didn't have enough guys there. He came over, and he immediately began to contribute."

Another freshman by the name of Jacquez Green entered the Kentucky game and made himself known by blocking a punt to set up a one-yard touchdown by Taylor.

Danny Wuerffel: "Jacquez was the smoothest, fastest guy you'll see. He could run the forty in 4.4, and it looked like he was jogging. He doesn't give the impression he's running fast, but he is, and it's one of the reasons he's so hard to cover."

Jerome Evans: "In '95 we had more younger guys than in '94. We had even more depth. On the defensive line we had more depth. We had Johnie Church, Mark Campbell, David Bernard, Cameron David on one end, Willie Cohens, Willie Rodgers.

"We always had a lot of talent. We always had a team that could have been ranked number one or two in the country, if it hadn't been for a loss to Auburn here, a loss to Florida State there. We played a bunch of teams that had a lot of depth themselves. We didn't have an easy schedule."

The first true test of the 1995 season was eighth-ranked Tennessee, led by their quarterback Peyton Manning.

Jerome Evans: "They had a linebacker named Jess Sanders, who had played for Sebring High School, a school right up the street from Arcadia. We played them in the district playoffs while I was in high school. He graduated two years before I did. So I was really getting jacked up at the thought that on running plays, I was going to be blocking him. I wanted to give him some payback for some of that stuff he did to me when I was a sophomore in high school.

"I remember very vividly, I caught a pass in one of the first series, and I ran him over. I went down the sidelines a few more yards, and he tackled me.

"We were down in the second quarter. We had just run an '80,' a long pass where Danny rolled behind the fullback—me. It was a rollout, and I went to block for him. Tennessee had a guy named Leonard Little, and I blocked him, and he spit in my face. We got down to the two-yard line on the play.

"The play was over, and as I was walking back to the huddle, he ran up behind me and pushed me in the back. I turned around, of course, and started to rush toward him, and as I got close to him, the ref said, 'Watch it, 34. I'm ready to throw the flag right now.' So I just had to take it. Oh my God, I was so upset. I mean, I was about to cry, I was so mad.

"I remember we were getting ready to go in for a score. It was third and goal from the one, and we called time out. Coach Spurrier huddled with us, and he said, 'We're going to run an isolation.' Usually we ran a pass pattern. He said, 'Jerome, I want you to run down, and I want you to knock the crap out of that linebacker. It's gonna be you and him in the hole. We're gonna double down on this tackle, kick him out, the end will turn on the end, and it's going to be you and that linebacker in the hole. Fred Taylor will walk in and score a touchdown. If you don't get a good block on him, he's gonna tackle him, and we're not gonna get back in the damn game.'

"I remember getting so jacked up. I mustered every ounce of strength I had in my body into that one lick. I ran in and hit that linebacker so hard his helmet popped off his head. I ran him over, Fred Taylor ran into the end zone, and when the guy looked up, his nose was all bloody."

Florida trailed 30-14 as the half neared, and then Danny Wuerffel hit Ike Hilliard with nine seconds left to get Florida within nine.

Danny Wuerffel: "We drove down the field and got close [to the 11]. I ran a fade route into the corner of the end zone, and he barely got one foot in bounds. If it had been the NFL, it wouldn't have counted because both feet have to be inbounds. But in college you only have to get one foot in, and Ike was able to do that, and he made a great play.

"That was the beginning of a huge run over the next couple of games."

Terry Jackson: "Ike and I came to Florida together. Ike had a great ability to make plays. He could catch the ball and make things happen after he caught it. He was a tremendous athlete who had the knack for getting open in different spots. He could do everything out on the field. He probably could have played halfback. There were no limits to what the guy could do."

"We went into the locker room only trailing by 30-21. We came back out after halftime, and I remember Coach Spurrier went to the defensive team meeting. He said, 'Okay, guys, we made a bunch of mistakes out there, and this happened, and you guys are playing hard, and you're staying in the game, but I'll tell you what: if you guys go out there and hold their ass, we'll come back out in the second half and we will score EVERY damn time we have the ball. We're gonna score every damn time we have the ball, I promise you that. Just hold them.'

"And we came out, and they held them, and we scored every time we had the ball.

"I have no idea how he knew that. At the half he must have figured out something they were doing, and he devised a plan to attack what they were doing.

"After we beat Tennessee, there was no one else in the SEC who could beat us. After that game, we became number three. The Tennessee game was a game where we decided that this was not a team we were going to allow to beat us. When I was there we felt we owned Tennessee. We knew the guys at Tennessee didn't really think they could beat us."

Danny Wuerffel himself had his finest day, going 29-39 for 381 yards and six touchdowns. Florida was as unstoppable as it had ever been in its 62-37 win over a prestigious opponent at Florida Field. Wrote one reporter afterwards, it was a "symphony of offense that left the 85,105 breathless."

Danny Wuerffel: "That was a big, big turning point for us as a football team, to be able to dominate Tennesssee like that. In fact, I was told Sports Illustrated followed Peyton Manning around all week, and they were planning to put him on the cover.

"When we ended up winning, I got put on the cover. I'll tell you what, if you want to sign autographs for the rest of your life, get on the cover of Sports Illustrated. People mail me that issue all the time!

"At that point that was my best game, and it was a huge, huge win for us and for me. I really felt I was working well with the other guys. And Coach Spurrier was feeling a lot of confidence in me and in the team, and that's what you want as a player.

"Each person has a different relationship with Coach Spurrier. You know he's the coach. You call him, 'the coach.' He's somebody who's intense, but at the same time he can be light-hearted. He cracks jokes all the time and makes people laugh. So you never know what to expect from him as a person, but you ALWAYS know what to expect as a player. He makes it very clear what he wants you to do all the time, and I've always said that I'd rather play for a coach who pushes you to perfection than one who would accept mediocrity."

Terry Jackson: "Ordinarily quarterbacks don't throw for six touchdowns, but under Florida's system, we do.

"We felt by working with Coach Spurrier that if we executed our plays the way the coaches taught us, we would be successful every time we were out there on the field. We had that confidence that we were supposed to score every time we touched the ball from wherever we were on the field."

Ole Miss visited Gainesville, and in the 28-10 victory, Florida only had eight possessions, but it scored on four of them. The key play in the game was a punt returned for a touchdown by Jacquez Green.

Terry Jackson: "Jacquez was really fast. He had been a high school quarterback with a bevy of talents. The guy could make plays. He rushed punts. He blocked some punts. He returned punts. He could do a little bit of everything. Against Ole Miss he ran back a punt for a touchdown, and he also ran a reverse [42 yards] for a touchdown. He was one of those guys, whenever he touched the ball, it could be a touchdown.

"Coach Spurrier ran the sort of offense where you knew you were going to get the ball and have a chance to make plays. Florida is a hotbed for high school football. What high school kid wouldn't want to be in the 'fun and gun'?"

Florida repeated the 28-10 score in its win over LSU. But Danny Wuerffel was sacked five times and he threw three interceptions.

Danny Wuerffel: "That was one of the most frustrating games for me. LSU played a great defensive scheme against us. They pressed our receivers and wouldn't let them get outside. We dropped a half a dozen passes. I didn't play real well and threw three interceptions. I was really frustrated with that game. We should have scored 50 points, but you have to credit the way they played. LSU really played well."

Terry Jackson: "We started the season scoring so many points that it set the standard for how we were supposed to play. But we won the game, and we were happy. But we always wanted to play our best. The goal was to get better each and every game."

After the LSU game, the writers covering the game were lamenting in print that Florida only won the game by 28-10. To an observer it seemed that the writers had adopted Coach Spurrier's perfectionism. To the players, nothing any writer said about the team came close to matching Spurrier's scathing criticism.

Jerome Evans: "We won the game convincingly, but Coach Spurrier was angry. Before the game, a couple of things happened: some guys missed curfew. Other guys had girls in their rooms, and Ike Hilliard had his worst game as a Gator. He dropped a bunch of passes, and he ran a kickoff back fifty yards and someone ran him down. I don't think he started the next week.

"Offensively, we made a bunch of mistakes.

"That game the offense pretty much broke down. I had a bad game. I missed a bunch of blocks I shouldn't have.

"On Monday, we went over the films, and oh my God, that was brutal. While you were in the game, if you made a bad play, you thought about it the rest of the weekend, because you knew on Monday that play was going to be rewound a hundred times.

"The whole offense sat in the room, the lights would go out, and we would watch every play of the entire game. Coach Spurrier pretty much analyzed every position of each's play. If you made a mistake, he would tell you about it.

"Coach Spurrier would say, 'Guys, you have to realize that every play is important. All the way down to the littlest thing. He would point out your mistake and show you why you should have done it a certain way.

"He was constantly coaching and teaching. Another thing too, a lot of teams in the SEC played the same defenses, ran the same blitzes, so when a team lined up in a certain front, when we lined up and saw the linebacker walk up to the line, he would pause the film and say, 'Danny, if you are in this formation, what do you need to audible to in order to make sure that guy is going to get blocked?'

"Even though we had already played the game, he was coaching. He'd say, 'Danny, what SHOULD you have called here?' And Danny would say, 'I should have called this play.' It was constant drilling."

The next serious roadblock for the Gators was Auburn, which had inflicted defeat on Florida the past two seasons. Once again, Florida fell behind 10-0 in the first three minutes.

Danny Wuerffel: "I was really looking forward to playing Auburn, just because of the way the game had gone the year before. [Florida had lost 38-35.] There were a couple of fluky plays, and we fell behind 10-0. We had a fumble returned for a touchdown, and I threw a screen pass that was tipped and intercepted. We got started slow, but then we came back and played really well. We won pretty effectively."

Florida, however, never panicked, and before the half retook the lead en route to a 49-38 victory, only the fifth time in history Florida had won at Jordan-Hare Stadium.

Jerome Evans: "Coach Spurrier tried to instill in his players that it doesn't matter what happens in the first ten minutes of in the first half. What matters who plays the best entire game.

"Sometimes in a game we would go out ahead by 30 points, and he would try to keep us focused, you knew just because you were up by 30 points, on Monday he wasn't going to stop the tape. You know he'd play that tape even if the score was 100-6. He was going to look at each play and wind it back. 'Why are you not hustling here?'

"The whole team would be watching. He had a red dot that he would point at the screen, and if Fred Taylor took a pitch, and dipped his shoulder and ran out of bounds, he'd say to Fred, 'What are you doing right here?' And he'd point that red top at Fred on the screen.

"You didn't think about Coach Spurrier and that red dot while you were playing in the game, but you knew that he was going to watch every single snap, and you had better play one hundred percent every snap, or you were going to hear about it. You couldn't take a play off here, a play off there. You had to play your hardest EVERY play."

In the Auburn game Terry Jackson suffered a shoulder injury.

Terry Jackson: "I separated my shoulder in that game. I ran an 'out' route, and we threw an interception, and I went to tackle the guy, and I hit him on my shoulder, and it separated."

Georgia in Athens was next, and Florida took the Bulldogs apart, 52-17.

Danny Wuerffel was an incredible 14-17 for 242 yards and five touchdowns, three to Chris Doering.

Danny Wuerffel: "That was fun. Statistically that was the best game I ever played.

"But before the game I could not get loose. I couldn't warm up. All pre-game I wasn't throwing the ball well. I tell this story a lot. Before that game I remember praying, 'Lord, I have tried throwing this way and that way, and I have tried to remember everything I'm supposed to do, but nothing is working real well, so I will just hand this over to you.'

"And it ended up being the best game I ever played. I don't usually tell that to people because I don't want them to think God's a genie and you get what you wish for, but there is a great lesson that sometimes in our life we have to get down on our knees and say, 'Lord, in this life the things that I've been trying to do my way are not working out, and so I'm going to turn it over to you, and whatever happens, for good or for bad, it is for your glory.'

"And when I was out there doing so well, I almost had to laugh at the situation. It was interesting. The first touchdown I threw was to Ike, and it was a broken play. I threw the ball late, and it still ended up being a touchdown. There was a defender who I never saw who should have intercepted it, but he was out of position, and I was really lucky.

"On another drive, I actually threw three touchdowns to Chris [Doering], but only one of them counted. I threw one that got called back. And then I threw a second that got called back. Then I threw a third one that counted. That's probably the first time that's happened. That last one I got hit, and I was trying to throw it out the back of the end zone, and he jumped up and caught it! I didn't tell anyone for a year that I wasn't trying to throw it to him. It was my third touchdown pass to him on that drive!

"Chris and I were roommates. Right before we left the hotel room to go to a game, we would listen to Pachelbel's Canon in D to get us in the right frame of mind, and then we'd say a prayer and go to the bus."

Terry Jackson: "I've known Chris [Doering] a long time. I played with him in high school. He was very talented. He wasn't as fast as the other guys, but he really had a knack for making plays. He was a big, tall guy, and he could get open because he was a great all-around athlete who could do everything."

After the Gators 52-17 win, its sixth-straight victory over the Bulldogs, the Florida players didn't even bother to celebrate.

Jerome Evans: "It got to the point where we didn't really consider Georgia a rival any more. The same went for Tennessee. We went out and prepared for them, but we didn't think either of those teams could beat us.

"A lot of teams we played that year played not to lose the game. They tried to play sound football, not make mistakes, keep the game close, and try to win at the end.

"We went out with the mentality that we were going to win the damn game, we would throw the ball all over the field, and we'd take chances on defense."

Northern Illinois was the Homecoming opponent, and Coach Spurrier chose to give Eric Kresser a chance to start at quarterback.

He proved his talent when he threw 26-42 for 458 yards and six touchdowns [in a 58-20 win]. In doing so Kresser broke Danny Wuerffel's school record for passing yardage in one game by nine yards.

Terry Jackson: "Eric had a very strong arm. If he threw you a pass, you better be paying attention because you might hurt your fingers if you aren't focusing on catching that pass. He really had a rocket for an arm.

"And in that game six different players caught touchdown passes. We had a lot of guys who could go out there and make plays—it was just a question of whether you got the opportunity to go out there and do it."

Jerome Evans: "It goes to show you, Coach Spurrier gets guys ready. Eric was capable of leading the offense. He had been there a while. It was Homecoming, and we came out firing right away, and he gave Eric a chance to get in there and show his stuff.

"There were a whole bunch of touchdowns in that game. Even I scored one, and for a fullback to score, you knew we had to score a bunch of points, because that didn't happen very often."

Danny Wuerffel: "I was completely healthy. Coach Spurrier wanted to let Eric play a little out of loyalty to him, which is very commendable. I was thinking I was going to play the first quarter, but the more Coach Spurrier thought about it.... Right before the game he said to me, 'You know what? Eric's never had a chance to start.' He asked me how I felt about it. Of course I wanted to play, but what was I going to say? Eric played and had a phenomenal game. He even threw a 96-yard touchdown to Jacquez [Green].

"I'm not proud of this, but looking back my thoughts were selfish. I wish I had been a more mature person even to have these thoughts: At the end of the '95 season I was real close to winning the Heisman Trophy, and I wish I had had those six touchdowns and all those yards to tack onto my resume. But again, that's not the way you need to be thinking.

"I was really happy for Eric. He deserved it. He had worked hard for a long time, and that was a good day for all of us."

On a cold, bitter night, South Carolina was handed a 63-7 beating. In the first half Danny Wuerffel was 19-24 for 304 yards and five touchdowns as the Gators played perfect football.

Danny Wuerffel: "The memory I have [of the South Carolina game] is a touchdown pass to Chris Doering. At the end of every Friday practice, Chris and I would practice him running along the back of the end zone and me on the 20 yard line, and him being covered, so I would throw the ball about ten feet in the air, and he would jump way up and catch it.

"And against South Carolina, I scrambled to the right, and there were defenders all around him, and I threw him the ball about ten feet off the ground, and he jumped up and it went over their hands and Chris jumped a little bit higher, caught it, got one foot in, and it was one of my favorite touchdowns."

Terry Jackson: "We played at night, and that was one of the coldest games I played in college. It was also very windy. Eli [Elijah Williams] had a very good game. He actually got a concussion, but he came back in, and he did very well.

"We were so talented and so confident, and we had a very high level of expectations. We were confident in what the team could do and believed in the plan the coaches put together. We felt we could go out there and do what we had to do to be successful."

After a 38-7 win over Vanderbilt in a game in which Danny Wuerffel was sacked twice, threw an interception and lost a fumble, Florida State invaded Florida Field. Florida had not defeated FSU since 1991. It was perhaps the 1995 team's finest moment in a season of greatness as Danny Wuerffel completed 25 of 40 passes for 443 yards and four touchdowns, and the offense gained 587 total yards.

Terry Jackson: "FSU was our in-state rival. It's an hour and a half away, and so we knew a lot of their guys. There's a little bit of trash talking. It's a game we know is going to be full-speed-ahead every play. You go in with your 'A' game. It's just that type of atmosphere."

Danny Wuerffel: "That was just a fun game all around. We threw a lot of passes on them and scored a lot of points. [Florida won 35-24.] I threw a [26-yard] touchdown to Jacquez and one to Ike [for 42 yards]. We had a good game and beat them pretty good. I also threw a [20-yard] touchdown pass to Chris. I saw a picture of that catch in a restaurant a week ago. It was something to be able to do that against Florida State.

"In '95 we had a really good offensive line, really solid players. We had Jeff Mitchell, Reggie Green, Jason Odom, and Donnie Young. The linemen played great all year, and with Coach Stephens, they were well-coached."

In the fourth quarter, the Florida defense played man-to-man defense and intercepted Danny Kanell three times.

Terry Jackson: "Our offense was what most people remember most about us, but the defense was a talented group of guys. We had Morris Wright, James Bates, Anthone Lott, and Fred Weary, a lot of good guys."

Jerome Evans: "You were playing a team you really wanted to beat, who had a good chance of beating you. We came into the game saying, We have the talent to beat this team. We can go out and win it. Everyone was jacked up for the game.

"It was an exciting game. Sam Cowart, a linebacker for FSU, became a first-team All-American during that game. We had an offensive formation with no backs in the backfield, and every time we did it, Cowart sacked Danny.

"Finally, Coach Spurrier decided to leave his fullback in the game [Evans], which I loved. We motioned Fred or Eli out, and instead of having a small tailback trying to block a 260-pound linebacker, they had me in there.

"I'd knock him in the teeth, and Danny would throw a strike right down the middle of the field.

"In the fourth quarter, FSU was coming back on us, and we had the ball third and ten, and Coach Spurrier called a delayed screen to the fullback, a play no one expected.

"The receivers ran dummy routes to take the corners with them, and I was so open—the rest of my career whenever Coach would draw up a play, he'd say, 'We're going to get you open like Jerome.' And everyone knew what he meant, because on that play, I caught the ball, and there was no one within twenty yards of me.

"I ran about forty yards down the field.

"It was one of those games that could have gone either way, where they'd miss an interception by a hair, or we'd figure out a way to making something happen. After we won that game, we knew we were going to go all the way."

When the game was over, and Florida finally had defeated FSU, the joy was unrestrained.

Danny Wuerffel: "It was such a big rivalry, and when you haven't won for so long; they had tied us the year before and beat us in the Sugar Bowl; it was such a BIG victory."

On the day number-three ranked Florida defeated FSU, Michigan upset number two ranked Ohio State. As a result, Florida went to the Fiesta Bowl to play top-rated powerhouse Nebraska for the National Championship.

Terry Jackson: "That's what you go into the season thinking about. That's your goal for the season: first the SEC Championship, then the national championship. We were really having a great season, really feeling good about ourselves, and all we wanted was the opportunity to play another great team and have some fun."

To have a chance at the national title, Florida first had to defeat Arkansas in the SEC championship game in Atlanta. It was a cakewalk. Florida won 34–3 for their third straight SEC championship.

Danny Wuerffel went 20-28 for 276 yards and two touchdowns. Florida led 24-3 midway through the third period when Wuerffel hit Ike Hilliard for a 29-yard touchdown. Senior captain and linebacker Ben Hanks then put the game on ice when he returned a fumble 95 yards for a touchdown. At the end of the season, Florida stood a perfect 12-0. It was a new high for a Florida team.

Danny Wuerffel: "We weren't dominating when Ben picked up the fumble and ran for a touchdown. That sealed it.

"We weren't at our most dominating, but we played solid football. We did what we needed to do to win. We didn't make a lot of mistakes. Hey, we won the SEC championship! [For the third year in a row, only the second time in SEC history that a team won in a threepeat. Alabama was the other.]

"It's an amazing thing: the other day my dad was at home, and he pulled out a drawer that had all my watches. You get a watch every time you play in an SEC championship. I had five watches, including four for the years I was eligible. We also got rings for winning it. No Gator before us ever won four. I'm sure of that. [No Gator before Coach Spurrier came in 1990 ever won one.] That's pretty special."

Terry Jackson: "I remember the celebration after the Arkansas game. At that point we knew we were going to go to the Fiesta Bowl and would have an opportunity to play for the national title. It was the first time for the Gators. To go through that whole twelve regular season undefeated and unblemished, that was just a great feeling. That's what you worked so hard for in the off season: to get that opportunity. It was a dream come true for everybody."

After the wipeout of Arkansas, Coach Spurrier handed out four game balls, including one to Jerome Evans for his powerful blocking that kept Arkansas' big linebackers away from the quarterback.

Jerome Evans: "To us, the SEC stood for 'Sausage, egg, and cheese.' Like a McDonald breakfast, a sausage, egg, and cheese biscuit. We didn't want that. We wanted 'the Big Breakfast.'

"Every day in practice we brought it up. We'd stand in a circle and put our hands together, and we'd break by saying, 'NC.' The national championship. All year in '95 we knew what we wanted: to be national champs.

"In '94 we'd say, 'We want to win,' or 'We want to go to a bowl game,' or 'We want to win the SEC championship,' but in '95, every single day of practice, whenever we went out to run or went to lift weights, whenever there was a group of guys together, we'd put our hands in, and when we'd break the huddle, we'd say, 'NC,' or 'National champs.' That was our goal. Nothing else."

Nebraska stood in Florida's way. The Cornhuskers had been national champs in 1994. They were led by backs Tommie Frazier and Lawrence Phillips, who was as renowned for his brushes with the law as he was his considerable running ability. The Fiesta Bowl was the venue. The city: Tempe, Arizona. On the morning of January 2, 1996, Florida was ranked second, the Cornhuskers first. Some of the players were impressed but not awed.

Terry Jackson: "As we watched the films of Nebraska, we could tell they were a very big team, a very talented team that had some skills, but we thought we could match up with those guys and take advantage of those big guys with our speed."

Other players thought Nebraska would be one more pushover like most of the teams Florida faced in 1995.

Jerome Evans: "The very first time we watched them on tape, Coach Spurrier said, 'There is no way we can lose to Nebraska.' Because their defense was so slow, and our offense was so high-powered. We didn't think they could shut us down, and that might have given us a false sense of security.

"Needless to say, when we went out there, they literally whipped our ass on the field. There were the best team we played all year, and they may have been the best team we ever played against ever.

"I don't know if it was lack of preparation on our part—I don't want to take anything away from Nebraska, that was a great football team but we didn't prepare for the game as we had prepared all season. Guys broke curfew, we had girls in the hotel, we had guys going out and drinking, we had a bunch of young guys on the team who distracted the older guys.

"It wasn't just one or two guys; it was everybody. When you're out to win a football game, you have to go out there and conduct business. You have to prepare yourself to win, and we didn't do that. So we got what we deserved. [Nebraska won 62-24.]

"Their defensive line mauled our offensive line. Their defensive linemen took our offensive linemen and drove them back into Danny's lap." [Nebraska sacked Danny Wuerffel seven times.]

Danny Wuerffel: "Their offense was so dominating that we could have scored 50 points and lost. They had Tommie Frazier and Lawrence Phillips, and we couldn't tackle them. They were great that night. [Phillips ran for

108 yards in the first half. Frazier ran for 199 yards and two touchdowns in the game.]

"On defense the pressure they put on us was phenomenal. They had a good game plan, and they played us strong, and they got good pressure, and they made it hard to execute.

"We were frustrated, and they were quite a team. I remember Coach Spurrier saying he didn't think we could beat them if we played them a bunch of times. They were stout. We had a tough time."

Terry Jackson: "Going into the game we felt we could score as much as we had to, but those guys came ready to play. They had been in that situation the year before, and that was our first time. We learned from that, and we took it to the next year.

"Coach Spurrier got up and spoke, and he just said we had to get ready for next year.

"I remember we all felt: 'We'll be back next year.'"

What Jerome Evans recalled was that Coach Spurrier was livid.

Jerome Evans: "Oh my God, I remember being in the locker room after the game. He said, 'A lot of you guys are not going to be here next year. You saw the way their offensive line looked. They don't have a bunch of big, fat guys like we have. I'll tell you what, during this off-season if you damn guys can't lose weight, you ass will be off this team. We're not going to have any big, fat offensive linemen any more. You're going to get down, lose weight, and we're going to be lean, and we're going to be mean, and we're going to be tough.'

"Coach Spurrier was about business. There was always the constant reminder, 'Your scholarship is for ONE year. You renew it every year. The reason we do that is so you earn your way every day. You can't come out here and think you've signed a scholarship, and that's it. If you do not perform, we do not have to renew that thing.' And they don't always. Ninety nine percent of the time they do, but Elijah Brown was the first lineman to be let go. There was a clip in Sports Illustrated that said, 'Florida Lineman Eats His Way Off Team.' Coach Spurrier was not going to stand for it. He said, 'We can't have a bunch of out-of-shape linemen if we're going to win the national championship.'"

sixty-nine

National Champions

Goal-oriented Steve Spurrier was determined to win the national championship in 1996. To do that, he needed a better defense, and so he went out and signed as his defensive coordinator a young coaching genius by the name of Bobby Stoops.

Stoops, a Youngstown, Ohio, native, was an All-Big Ten defensive back at Iowa. He started his career as a graduate assistant at Iowa, went to Kent State, then became the defensive coordinator at Kansas State, where he built the nation's number one defense in 1995.

Spurrier hired him and put the defense in Stoops' capable hands, allowing himself more time to coach the offense.

Jerome Evans: "Bobby Stoops was a players' coach who would hang out and joke around with the guys. If you were around him when he was with a group of players, you'd think he was a player himself. He was really cool, but he didn't take any crap. You knew you had to give him one hundred percent, but he was a guy you could relate to.

"What made his defense so effective was that besides his having great talent, he only had a couple basic formations. When Coach Bobby Pruitt was the defensive coordinator in '95, it was like rocket science. You'd hear, 'Rip, ringo, cover five, zebra, jacko lantern,' and if one thing changes, their responsibility would change. It was so complicated the guys literally had no idea what the hell they were supposed to do.

"Coach Stoops simplified it greatly. Let me put it this way: when you know what you're doing, it allows you to be more aggressive. If you're playing linebacker, and you have all the talent in the world, but you're not sure whether you need to go left or right, you're not going either one of those ways.

"Under Coach Stoops everyone knew exactly what they were doing, and it got to the point during pre-season practice that Coach Spurrier would have to tell Coach Stoops to put the defense in a certain formation so he could run a play.

"We went a whole spring, and maybe we scored two touchdowns on our defense. In '95 teams would score 38 points. You'd have teams having thirteen-play drives. That didn't happen in '96.

"If you compare '96 to '95, you can see that we were much more aggressive on offense—we went for it on fourth down a lot—because we knew our defense was three [plays] and out, or they'd fumble or we'd make an interception. Our defense scored a bunch of touchdowns."

The Gators opened the season against Southwest Louisiana. In the 55-21 win, the Florida defense produced six turnovers and five sacks, a rarity in the Spurrier era.

Danny Wuerffel: "Beginning with our opening game against Southwest Louisiana, we could see the difference in the defense. In that game they were a dominating bunch. They outscored us. [The defense scored four touchdowns. Fred Weary scored two touchdowns on a fumble return and an interception.] It was clear from the get-go that they were going to be attacking and making plays."

After the game Coach Spurrier called the Gator offense 'pathetic.' Even so, Wuerffel finished the day 10-20 for 177 yards.

Danny Wuerffel: "That was a weird game. I never felt like I got into a rhythm, didn't play particularly well, and Coach Spurrier wanted the other guys to play some too—behind me was Brian Schottenheimer and Doug Johnson—so that wasn't great for me."

Jerome Evans: "To be honest, the first two games of each season the offensive team usually got blasted by Coach Spurrier, and rightly so, because the offense is not going to click in the first two games. The first game we're going to be terrible, and the second game we'd be better, and by the third game, we'd better have it right, because Tennessee would be our opponent."

The second game was against another sacrificial lamb, Georgia Southern. Before the game Coach Spurrier forbade Danny Wuerffel, a leading pre-season candidate for the Heisman Trophy, from doing media interviews.

Danny Wuerffel: "In his mind Coach wanted to relieve the pressure on me. I had been up for the Heisman the year before, and there was talk about my winning it this year all through the off-season, and he didn't want it to affect my first game. He wanted me to get away from the media and get back to football.

"I had a hard time convincing him it wasn't a problem, because since sometime during my junior year, I had quit watching TV, and I didn't read magazines or newspapers. I don't want to sound strange, but I avoided doing that until I was out of college.

"I always felt that you either got cocky because they were talking you up, or you got frustrated because they talked you down. So I put the TV out of my room, and I didn't read magazines or papers. At the time it was kind of humorous to me the reasoning behind his not wanting me to talk to the media, but I kind of understood where he was coming from. And for me, it was a pleasure not to have to do it."

In that Georgia Southern game, Wuerffel's lack of distractions paid off, because his performance was breathtaking. He was almost perfect, 15-16 for 267 yards and two touchdowns. When he left the game after throwing a 28-yard touchdown pass to Jacquez Green to open the third quarter, Florida led 42-7. His 78 career touchdowns moved him to sixth place in NCAA history ahead of John Elway of Stanford.

Danny Wuerffel: "I remember being very sharp. Our offensive was explosive. For one, we had a mastermind calling the best possible plays. You know he's designing plays they can't stop. Secondly, you've got receivers and running backs you absolutely can't tackle because they are faster than you are, and if the stinking quarterback can just make a decent throw, that everything should work pretty well.

"My job was to make sure we were using the right play and to throw the ball correctly to the right spot."

Adding to the Gator offense were touchdown runs of 8 and 12 yards by Terry Jackson and the strong right leg of kicker Bart Edmiston, who in the Georgia Southern game kicked his 85th straight extra point.

Danny Wuerffel: "Bart is from Pensacola. He was a great worker and a great kicker. He was one of the best kickers that ever was. He was phenomenal all throughout, though it's sad that he didn't make kicks in a couple of games that were real important, and he never did go on to have the career he would have liked to have had. But he'd go days and days, and weeks in practice without missing a kick. It was cool to watch."

The first true test of the 1996 season came against second-ranked Tennessee at Neyland Field before a throng of 107,608 fans. Florida was fourth ranked. The game pitted two leading Heisman Trophy candidates, quarterbacks Danny Wuerffel and Peyton Manning. It was being called "the most important sporting event in the history of the state of Tennessee."

Danny Wuerffel: "Even though I wasn't reading the papers, I could tell how big this game was by how many people were coming to town to interview me. There was no question that this was a huge game. They had put in extra bleachers, and their stadium was bigger."

Jerome Evans: "Coach Spurrier came and told us, 'This is being called the biggest sporting event ever held in the state of Tennessee.' We said, 'What? They must not have a very big sports history.'

"Tennessee really got worked up over that game. We didn't feel that way. They had a pretty good team, Peyton Manning was a good quarterback, but we knew they weren't going to beat us. We knew as long as we played our game and did the things we did well, the only way they could beat us was running the ball, and so we knew we had a good chance of winning, and we went out there and we were way ahead [35-6] at the end of the first half.

"If you watch the tape of the first series of plays of that game, they kicked the ball off, we got it, and we drove down the field. We were on their thirty-five with fourth down and eleven yards to go, and common sense dictates that you punt the ball. You know what we did? We went for it.

"Coach Spurrier came over, and he said, '14-pass-wide-corner.' It was a one-man route. He sent Reidel out, and he said, 'Jerome, don't go out on this play. I want you to stay in and block. If they blitz, make sure you pick him up. Danny, take your steps and hit him quick. Reidel, get down that field fast. Get your ass down there quick. We're going to score a touchdown on this play.' It was the first series of the game! And we threw a 35-yard touchdown pass, and this is what separated us from other teams.

"After we scored, we felt, Whoa! Before you knew it, we were up 21-0."

After the fourth-down touchdown to Reidel Anthony, Teako Brown intercepted Peyton Manning's first pass, and on the next play Wuerffel threw a 10-yard touchdown pass to Terry Jackson.

Terry Jackson: "I was running a little corner out of the backfield, and the linebacker thought it was a run, and he cheated up. Danny threw a beautiful pass, and I was open in the corner.

"We were pretty hot that first half."

Wuerffel then threw a 5-yard touchdown pass to Ike Hilliard. It has been said that that first twenty minutes was the best football ever played at the University of Florida (and perhaps anywhere else).

Jerome Evans: "Everything we did worked. They couldn't slow us down. I remember we went for it at least four times on fourth down in that game, and we made it every time. And when it was fourth and three, we didn't pass, we ran.

"Oh man, we pretty much took it down. We hit them in the mouth the whole game. In the second half we shut it down, clammed up and played keep-away a little bit.

"Our defense was all over Manning. And you have to give Bobby Stoops the credit. He had had a great defense at Kansas State. His defense was tops in the country at a place like that. You knew it had to have something to do with the coaching. Because they weren't getting the kind of talent we get at Florida, Florida State, and Miami. And they were leading the country in defense."

Danny Wuerffel: "We had some great plays called, and guys made some great plays, and the defense made some turnovers [Florida intercepted Manning four times in the first half].

"They did make a comeback to get close, but in reality it WASN'T a close game. It was 35-21, and then they scored, and then kicked an onside kick, and then the game was over. It wasn't like they were driving and had a chance. It's a shame the final score was 35-29."

After the Tennessee win, Florida was again ranked number one.

Terry Jackson: "By this time we learned that that doesn't mean anything. The coaches were very good about keeping us grounded, reminding us that you've got to go out there and play the game and let that decide everything."

Danny Wuerffel: "By this time you realize it doesn't matter until the end of the year. That kind of stuff is just fun to talk about, but until the year is over… that's the only time it matters."

Against Kentucky, the Florida offensive juggernaut rolled on. Danny Wuerffel was 21-31 for 279 yards and threw for three touchdowns as Florida won 65-0 at Florida Field. The highlight was two consecutive long, twisting punt returns for touchdowns by Jacquez Green.

Danny Wuerffel: "That was a phenomenal day for him. There were some really incredible moves he made. He looked like he was trapped, and he went backwards, and sideways, and forward, and I stood on the stands watching him just like any other spectator, watching his amazing plays. [The first run was for 66 yards, the second for 73.] On the second touchdown, he probably ran 200 yards."

Florida started slowly against Arkansas, leading 14-7 in the second period when the Gator offense exploded, as Danny Weurffel hit Reidel Anthony and then Ike Hilliard for touchdowns.

In a 42-7 win over Arkansas, Danny Wuerffel set a national one-game passing record, throwing for 462 yards [the old record of 457 had been set by David Klingler of Houston]. His first touchdown pass was 56 yards to Reidel Anthony.

Danny Wuerffel: "It was a well-designed play. It's was a deep post, a route we ran often, but we ran it out of a little different formation. We count on the receiver beating the cornerback, and we make sure the safety is no where near him, and when that happens, we have a good chance to score.

"It was only 14-7 at the half, but then in the second half we exploded."

Against Arkansas, Ike caught four passes for 108 yards and a touchdown. Reidel Anthony had nine passes for 189 yards and three touchdowns. Danny Wuerffel threw for 462 yards, a national one-game record, and four touchdowns. Everyone pitched in, Reidel, Eli, Fred, Ike, Jacquez, and Terry.

Danny Wuerffel: "With Ike and Jacquez and Reidel out there, it was hard for anyone to know who to cover."

Terry Jackson: "A lot of players were experienced. They had returned from the year before. Getting the same guys back, having them run the same plays, increased our confidence, and we just continued to get better along with the offensive line until those guys played as well as everyone else. At that point you can't do anything against us."

In the Arkansas game, fullback Jerome Evans' professional football aspirations came to a sickening end. He was severely injured, and though he continued to try to play the rest of the year, he would never again be the star he had been before.

Jerome Evans: "This was the game that pretty much ended it for me. At that point I was in the best shape of my career. I was playing some of my best ball. I knew I would make it big in the pros. Dwayne Mobley, my backup, played in the NFL for a season.

"It was third and short yardage, and I was supposed to block a linebacker to protect Fred [Taylor], and the tailback ran right behind him, and he ran into me and stepped on my ankle some kind of way, and I had strained ligaments, and to this day it still hurts.

"I couldn't stand on my right foot. I had crutches and a big boot, an air cast that held my leg, and I'd come into the training room four times a day, lay it flat, and they'd ice it, and put shock waves through it, and I'd do the rehab where I'd stand on wobble boards, and they would do manual exercises on it, and to this day, it's still swollen. There's a big knot on the side of my leg, and if you look down on the foot, its on the arch, the front part of your ankle, right there in the center."

The Homecoming game was against LSU, a 56-13 win. LSU played man-to-man defense and just could not keep up with Florida's fleet receivers. Ike Hilliard caught eight passes for 145 yards and two touchdowns. Reidel Anthony caught seven passes for 100 yards and a touchdown, and Elijah WIlliams and Fred Taylor each ran for more than 100 yards. Florida gained 625 yards in total offense.

Danny Wuerffel: "What a day! This was one of my favorite stretches of games, and the LSU game was a favorite, because they had done so well against us the year before. They actually didn't play badly, but we executed so well, which was why it was so exciting. When you beat a team that's not as good as you, you don't get a kick out of it, but when you play a pretty good team that is covering pretty well, and you still complete touchdown passes, that's what makes it so exciting. There was a stretch where we hit five or six fade routes where the guys were covered very well, but we completed them anyway. That was pretty special. We had a good game plan, and we played well."

Against LSU, the Florida defense allowed the Tigers only 28 yards rushing.

Danny Wuerffel: "During this stretch, the defense was the difference. When they get turnovers, we get more opportunities to score. You put that together with what we were doing, and we were a well-oiled machine.

After the LSU game, Danny Wuerffel had 92 career touchdown passes, second only to Ty Detmer of Brigham Young University, who held the NCAA record with 121.

Danny Wuerffel: "I didn't think I'd catch him. He played a full four years. I was hoping, though, to finish with 100. I thought that that would be quite an accomplishment."

The next game was an historic win, a 51-10 trouncing of Auburn at Florida Field. Florida scored on its first possession, a 25-yard pass from Danny Wuerrfel to Reidel Anthony, the seventh game in a row they did so. The Florida defense had seven sacks. Wuerrfel was 17-30 for 346 yards.

Danny Wuerffel: "We were on a roll. Our offense was playing so well. The defense was continuing to give us opportunities, and it was a great thing. It really was special to see how excited Coach Spurrier was over the way we were playing.

"And Coach Stoops was doing a phenomenal job with the defense that whole year. He got the most out of those guys. We had Anthone Lott, Shea Showers, Tony George, Fred Weary. They were great athletes, and they were put in a position where they could attack. It was great to see."

After the game Coach Spurrier told reporters, "Danny Wuerffel is the best that's ever played here, that's for sure, maybe the best in the conference, and he may wind up being the best in the country." It was high praise from the Heisman winner.

Danny Wuerffel: "Coach Spurrier and I had a real relationship. It sometimes was good, sometimes bad. Sometimes it was pretty, and sometimes ugly. But I couldn't be more grateful to him as a person, and especially as a coach for all the things he did for us."

On a blustery, rainy day in Jacksonville at the Gator Bowl, Danny Wuerffel was nearly flawless, as Florida defeated the Georgia Bulldogs 47-7. In the first half Wuerffel was 16-23 for 279 yards and four touchdowns. At the end of the day Wuerffel had surpassed Shane Matthews' school record of 9,287 yards gained passing.

At the half, Florida led 34-0. All this without Ike Hilliard and Keith Council, who had been suspended for a game for missing classes.

Danny Wuerffel: "Florida ran a really clean program. Spurrier took great pride on being squeaky clean himself. After I began playing in the NFL, I can't tell you how many players asked me what I got to go to Florida. No one believes me when I tell them I never got a dime to play there. In fact, before my senior year I played golf on a course for free two or three times, and when somehow Florida found out about it, they made me go back and pay and get a receipt to show I had actually paid for those rounds of golf— just to be squeaky clean.

"But that day against Georgia, that was a fun game. We were back in the Gator Bowl, and it was a great game for us. We were still on a roll. We were doing it so often, we were starting to take it for granted. We really, really played well."

On a cold, sunny day in Nashville, Florida came close to losing a game, this one to Vanderbilt. Despite Danny Wuerffel's 100th touchdown pass, Florida had only a 28-21 lead in the fourth quarter as Vanderbilt drove deep into Florida territory, only to have the Gator defense hold. It took a quarterback sneak on fourth and inches, Florida's only first down of the second half, to seal the win.

Danny Wuerffel: "They always played us tough, especially at Vandy. I'm not sure why or how, but they did. I remember they really got after us good that day. But we came out with the win again."

Florida got back on track with a 52-25 win over South Carolina. In the game Danny Wuerffel hit Jacquez Green for a 56-yard touchdown and Reidel Anthony for a 52-yard score.

Terry Jackson: "Reidel was a really, really fast guy. He and Jacquez were two of the fastest players on the team. Reidel and Fred [Taylor] went to high school together from Bel Glades.

"They were tremendous, tremendous athletes. When Reidel got the ball, he could really make things happen. It's what made our offense go. We had four or five guys, when they touched the ball, they could score from anywhere on the field."

South Carolina was the final home game of the year, and Jerome Evans desperately wanted to play in it, his injury notwithstanding.

Jerome Evans: "It was so frustrating. It was the last home game, and I was trying to force myself to play. I had aspirations to play at the next level, it hurt like a son of a gun, so I went out and tried it, and it just wasn't working. I was limping around. I had been rehabbing and getting treatment, and it just wouldn't work.

"The coach said to me, 'Jerome, do you think you're okay to play?' I said, 'Yeah, I'm okay,' so I went in against South Carolina. I should not have been out on the field. I was in for three plays, and then I jarred it, and it felt like somebody literally had ripped the bottom of my leg off."

After the South Carolina victory, the tenth of the 1996 season without a loss, Danny Wuerffel and the rest of the seniors became the winningest Florida class of all time.

Danny Wuerffel: "That was not a great game for us, and I'm not sure why. We were a little frustrated that we weren't smooth offensively. My statistics were pretty poor. [He was 11-34 for 240 yards and threw two interceptions, but two of his completions were the 56-yard touchdown pass to Reidel Anthony and the 52-yard score to Jacquez Green.]

"But the defense played so well, and it was fun. It was also special because it was Senior Day, the last home game, and all the seniors run out of the tunnel, and you see your parents and hug and kiss them and then go play the game, and so I got to hug my mom and dad on the field, and that was nice."

With one regular season game left in the 1996 season, Florida was undefeated up to that point for only the third time in its history [in 1928 and 1995]. Florida's ship was sailing along smoothly. The FSU game at Doak-Campbell

Stadium loomed large. Before the final regular season game of the season, Florida State was ranked number two, Florida number one.

Terry Jackson: "We were pretty high before the game. We were that way every time we played those guys. Both of us were ranked high. Usually we'd be in the top five when we met, so the game always had title implications. So it was a gigantic game. We knew it would mean a lot for the rest of the season. That Florida State team was a great team."

With Florida trailing 17-14 early in the fourth quarter, Danny Wuerffel threw a 26-yard touchdown pass that would have given Florida the lead, but the play was called back on a holding penalty.

Danny Wuerffel: "That was a very frustrating play for a couple of reasons. First of all, the holding call was questionable. But regardless of that, I threw the pass, and then a defensive player took three or four steps and absolutely clobbered me. The ball was thrown, and the referee turned to throw the flag, and he followed the ball and didn't keep his eye on me as he's supposed to. So the worst-case scenario should have been offsetting penalties, but instead the call ended up killing the drive, and we didn't get any points when it should have been something different. That was a huge play in the game, and it was frustrating that it came down to that."

Following that incident, Bart Edmiston set up to kick a 41-yard field goal, but he stepped in a hole, felt a pop in his knee, and he was on crutches before the game was over.

Danny Wuerffel: "I felt bad for Bart, because he was such a good kicker, and he's remembered for things like this."

The Florida defense could not contain FSU's Warrick Dunn, who ran for 185 yards and led the game-winning fourth quarter drive. At the end of the game FSU drove 11 plays for a touchdown. Pooh Bear Williams scored from the one, and Florida fell behind.

Despite being rushed and clobbered most of the day, Danny Wuerffel finished the day with 23-48 for 362 yards and three touchdowns. He completed a 2-yard touchdown pass to Reidel Anthony to get within three points. When an onside kick failed, Florida was a 24-21 loser.

Danny Wuerffel: "So we lost, and it's almost impossible to lose that late in the year and still have a chance for the national championship. So emotionally, in our mind, the ride for the national championship was over.

"It was VERY frustrating time for everyone, including Coach Spurrier. He was down, especially the Monday after. A lot of us were. And it was of the greatest testaments to our character that our football team was able to get over it, and get psyched up again to win an SEC championship, even though at the time we had won some SEC championships, and what we were really looking forward to was a national championship.

"It had all fallen apart, but we had the maturity to come back. A lot of people would have had a hard time getting up for the next game. But guys like James Bates and Lawrence Wright really got in there and got positive again. It was a testament to that group of players."

Terry Jackson: "Oh, we were hurting, but for some reason we still felt we still had a chance at the national championship, that it would happen. Any time you lose late in the season, it's hard to get another chance. So we were pretty upset about that loss.

"We felt we were as good as ever. We definitely felt we should have won that game. We thought we were the better team that year. But playing at Doak and playing Florida State in general, we knew it was going to be a battle."

A frustrated, desperate Jerome Evans attempted to play in the Florida State game.

Jerome Evans: "The thing is, I kept trying to come back. I wanted to play, and then I'd hurt it again, and it would set me back further. I played ten plays against FSU, and my leg was killing me. I made a few plays, but I had to come out. I was so frustrated. I had been through so much, had done all the things I had been asked to do, and for a crummy injury like this, it had crippled me. I could barely move. I couldn't stand on my right foot."

The SEC championship game was played against Alabama at the Georgia Dome in Atlanta. The day before the Gators were given an added incentive when Nebraska, the number one rated team in the country, lost to the University of Texas.

Danny Wuerffel: "I was riding in the elevator with Coach Spurrier the day before the game. We got off at our floor, and all of a sudden the players down the hall started screaming, which upset him because he doesn't like for the guys to be joking around before games. So he went in to yell at everyone, and it turned out that Texas had just thrown a fourth-down pass and had taken the lead over Nebraska, which was incredibly unthought of, which made us one step closer to having a chance at the national championship again.

"Texas did win the game, and that was huge. At this point we were all excited. It was in the back of our minds when we went to play Alabama."

Terry Jackson: "We were in our hotel, and we watched the Texas-Nebraska game. We were rooting for Texas—I think we may have helped Texas win that game. We had all our fingers crossed, and we were watching.

"I remember the play that won the game. Texas had a fourth down, and the quarterback ran a bootleg and hit the tight end to get a first down that sealed the win.

"We were really happy about it, but we still had to go out and handle our business and beat Alabama."

In the 1996 SEC championship game against Alabama, Danny Wuerffel was his usual brilliant self. In the game he threw six touchdowns, an SEC championship game record.

Terry Jackson: "We expected that from Danny. If wasn't out of the ordinary for him to throw six touchdowns. That was just what he did. And he ran the offense really well, and we had some players who could make plays. So we expected Danny to do great."

When Bama QB Freddie Kitchens threw a 94-yard pass to Michael Vaughn, Alabama drew to within three points, at 31-28. Florida needed to respond, and Danny Wuerffel was up to the challenge, as he threw a 21-yard touchdown pass to Reidel Anthony in the left corner of the end zone.

Danny Wuerffel: "Reidel made a phenomenal catch. There were defenders all around him, and he just out jumped them and made a great catch."

Alabama closed to 31-27, and Wuerffel again responded, this time with an 85-yard touchdown to Reidel Anthony.

Danny Weurffel: "We knew that touchdown was a huge momentum swing for them. We got back there, and Coach Spurrier called the play—he actually wanted it completed to the other side, but then he added a tag on the end. Normally, on the back side of the play Jacquez would have run a different route, but he said, 'Put Jacquez on a 'go' route, just in case.'

"Then, as I saw the coverage, I noticed that they were only playing Jacquez man-to-man, and the defender got out of position, and Jacquez ran right by him. I probably didn't throw it more than forty yards, and then he ran the other forty-five. It was a big play."

Against Alabama, Danny Wuerffel threw for 20-35 for 401 yards and six touchdown passes, both SEC championship records. Three of the touchdowns went to Reidel Anthony, who caught 11 passes for 171 yards, both title game records. Florida won 45-30 for the Gators' fourth-straight SEC title.

Danny Wuerffel: "That was just a great, great game. For a long time it went back and forth. Alabama was playing well, and it was another one of those games where we got rolling, and we hit passes, and we kept going. It was a game where we had to keep scoring, as opposed to other games where we were far ahead. We had to keep scoring, and we did."

A week after the win over Alabama, Danny Wuerffel traveled to New York City to take part in the Heisman Trophy award ceremony. He had already won the Draddy Scholarship Trophy presented to the nation's top scholar-athlete. Wuerffel, a public relations major, had 3.7 cumulative grade point average. He also won the Davey O'Brien trophy, given to the top college quarterback, and he was named Player of the Year and the winner of the Johnny Unitas Award. But only one Florida player had ever won a Heisman before, Coach Steve Spurrier in 1966.

Danny Wuerffel: "I was up against Troy Davis again. He had run for 2,000 yards two years in a row, which never happens, and Jake Plummer and Orlando Pace, a lineman from Ohio State.

"It was close between me and Troy, but I won. And my whole family was there, which was a real treat. That night after the ceremony I went into the little lounge bar. The piano player got up, and I went and sat down, and I played and my mom started singing, and we just kind of took it over, and it was fun!

"We had a nice time, and on Monday they had the big banquet. I got up to make my speech, and the first thing I said was, 'I want to give all the glory to my Lord and Savior, Jesus Christ. He's the rock upon which I stand, and I asked that He would forgive my sins for they are many.' And then I thanked all my coaches and teammates, and all the people who were important to me. And they gave me the trophy, which is in my parent's house in Florida."

Terry Jackson: "We were all very happy for Danny when he won it. We thought he had a chance because we had a really good offense and because of all the things he had done. And just the fact that he was such a winner—that's what we thought really made him stand out."

Danny Wuerffel: "If I had to sum up my years at Florida, I would say that I met and got to know some of the best friends I will have in my life. I certainly had great memories with all the guys. What is most special to me was the times we got to spend together. It's what is special about playing on a team. It's great to win a golf or tennis tournament, but that does not compare with winning a football championship, because of the chemistry of the team. Heck, it takes equipment guys, trainers, doctors, coaches, weight lifting coaches, somebody has to book the travel—it's a whole army winning a war over the course of many battles. So to me the biggest thing is the relationship with the players.

"And when I think of Coach Spurrier, I'm just flooded with different thoughts. He's a phenomenal coach. He's a very funny man. He does things differently from any other coach I've ever seen. He doesn't over-labor, doesn't work hundreds of hours. He doesn't take it overly serious when other people do. Yet at the same time he's incredibly intense, a perfectionist in many ways. I just can't imagine having a better time or being more successful. I would have no trouble telling any young player that there's not a better place to play as a quarterback than to play for Coach Spurrier."

On January 2, 1997, the third-ranked Florida Gators met the Seminoles of Florida State University, the top-ranked team in the country, in the Sugar Bowl in New Orleans. Said Coach Spurrier, "It is the biggest game of their lives."

Danny Wuerffel: "We ended up getting another shot at Florida State, but to win the national championship, there was still an undefeated team ahead of us, Arizona State.

"The night before we played the game, Ohio State beat them, so we knew we could win it all if we could win our game.

"I was very into what we were going to do and how we were going to attack them. I was very confident in this game, because Coach Spurrier had put in the shotgun offense. To this day I don't think we would have won had he not done that.

"They were rushing, blitzing, and they had great players. Our line was playing their hearts out, but they were younger and outmatched. When you're in the shotgun, you're five yards farther back, and I can get the ball off before they can get to me. Quite often they still hit me, but I had the chance to throw balls I could not have thrown had I not been five yards farther back. It was a little difference, but with a big result.

"From the shotgun we also figured out how to run a little more, so we could do that as well, but mostly we passed. And on this day, Ike was unstoppable. [Ike Hilliard caught seven passes for 150 yards and three touchdowns.]

"A lot of guys made plays, but Ike caught the touchdowns. He just played a phenomenal game. Florida State tended to be in a man-to-man coverage, and they were very aggressive—it had played to their advantage in Tallahassee, but in this game I had enough time to make some plays, and our receivers made incredible plays."

Florida led 24-17 at the half.

Terry Jackson: "The first half was pretty close. We were popping each other, and nobody was really making that many big plays. We were stopping them, and they were stopping us. Nobody was really in a groove."

An FSU field goal cut the lead to 24-20. Wuerffel threw a touchdown pass to Hilliard, and then from the FSU 16-yard line, he broke from the pocket and ran for a touchdown to make the score 38-20.

Terry Jackson: "We just kept executing and doing the things we had done all year. We had confidence that every time we stepped out onto the field, we were going to win every game. That was our difference. We felt we were the best team and that if we went out there and were focused and executed the coach's game plan, that we could be successful and do whatever we wanted.

"I got a chance to go in there and make some plays near the end of the game to help seal the win. Because the game is never over when you play Florida State. You have to score as many points as you can, because they can score quickly."

The clincher came with 8:42 left in the game when Terry Jackson broke through the middle of the FSU defense for a 42-yard touchdown.

Danny Wuerffel: "We were trying to run the clock out, and they were trying to be real aggressive to stop us, which means that if you can get through the line, you have a chance to go a long ways. And that's what happened. We gashed them."

Terry Jackson: "We were up about fifteen points, and we ran a sweep around the fifty, and I cut back and was open, and I ran for a touchdown. At that point, we knew the victory was ours, and we had our national championship."

Fullback Jerome Evans was able to rest for two weeks before the national championship game against Florida State, and so he decided to give it a try in the big finale. But in football, as in life, for some things don't always work out the way they planned, despite all the hard work and dedication.

Jerome Evans: "I got a chance to relax a little before the Sugar Bowl game, so I felt better. Dwayne Mobley started, but I came in, and in the first series I played Coach Spurrier called an isolation on the right side linebacker named Henry Crockett.

"I ran in, made the block, Fred [Taylor] ran for I don't know how many yards, but when I made contact, I knew I was hurt. I felt like my shoulder had pretty much broken in half.

"It was my senior year, my last game, the national championship game. Do you go to the locker room and not play any more, or do you take a shot at it and keep playing?

"Since it was my last game, I took a shot, kept playing, and that night I went down to Bourbon Street for maybe thirty minutes, and my shoulder was hurting so badly I couldn't have a good time.

"The doctor told me the shoulder came out of the socket. They snapped it back in, and they said what I needed was to insert a pin in my shoulder. That way, if I got hit again, it wouldn't snap out again.

"But I wouldn't get that, because I knew if I did, I would be out of service when it came time to try out for the pros. They said if I could rehab it and ice it, I'd be able to go to the audition. I opted to do that, and needless to say, it was the wrong decision."

Ahead by 52-20, with the clock ticking down, the Florida players began to realize that they were accomplishing something dramatic and unique in the history of the university: they were about to be named the number one team in the country.

Terry Jackson: "After we won, we were just yelling and jumping around, taking pictures—everybody was taking pictures of everyone—just enjoying the moment. It was one of the greatest feelings. We had reached our ultimate. It was what we did it all for."

Jerome Evans: "When we got to the point where we knew we were going to win the game, it was, 'I can't believe it.' My entire career, the reason I came, the reason I went to all those work-outs, the reason I went through all that trouble, was to win the national title, and it was coming to fruition.

"I had never experienced anything like it. That's why I had come to Florida. There is no explaining that feeling. I don't think I can explain it. We were rated number one in the country. We're number one!"

Danny Wuerffel: "Heck, it's hard even to describe. We had been at it for so many years. We'd come close the year before. And the way it happened was so special to me, because we went from being the frontrunner to not having a chance, then to having it again, and it was a testament to the maturity of the guys. So often the things that determine much in life are out of your control. We tend to think we're in control all the time, but that is an illusion. We were given the opportunity, and we had to do our part. And we did, and what a great feeling!

"There were a lot of hugs, a lot of joy, a lot of all the things you do with a group of guys. What was hardest for me was that after the game I was actually running away from reporters who were chasing me. I was trying to find teammates to hug them, but every time I stopped, I would get swarmed with

media people trying to get comments and interviews. I understand they have
a job to do, but it was a time when I was at my emotional peak, and I wanted
to be with my teammates. That was frustrating and somewhat comical."

In 1997 Terry Jackson was injured early in the season. In the fourth game of
the season against Kentucky, Jackson tore his ACL and missed most of the
year. In 1998 he came back and missed five games with an ankle sprain, and
though the 10-2 Gators missed out on the national title, he was a big factor
in Florida's defeating Penn State in the Orange Bowl.

    After graduation Terry was drafted in the fifth round by San Francisco,
where he continues to be an important part of the 49ers offense. Though a
pro, his Gator experience is never far from his heart.

Terry Jackson: "I loved everything about my college experience: the fun.
The friends. The experiences. I had a good time eating dinner with the guys,
or just hanging out with the guys. I cherish the relationships that were built,
something you can't replace, and that's the thing about college: you go off
and leave and do bigger and better things, but at the same time you are always
reminded of those times in college and how much fun you used to have. The
friends you had then. The things you used to do. Things you can't replace.

    "And to win and to have a successful career, that's what anyone who's in
the NFL talks about—they talk about college and how much fun they had.
They talk about their teams. People argue back and forth about who had the
best teams. It happens all the time, every other day. I play with guys who used
to play in the SEC, or we talk to the guys who came from the Big Ten, we
have a Michigan guy on our team, and they say their conference is better
than our conference, and we argue, and it's all in fun—it all stems from the
good time you had in college.

    "Having played on a national championship team, it makes you grateful.
You respect that opportunity and cherish it."

Jerome Evans never got to the pros. He didn't even get a whiff. Draft day
came and draft day went, and Jerome Evans' phone never rang. Then as the
weeks dragged on, he realized that because of his injuries, no pro team was
even interested in him as a free agent. The disappointment was crushing, but
it was a reminder of what can happen when a young athlete sets his sights
on the pros and doesn't leave himself an alternative by getting his diploma.

But Jerome Evans was one of the smart ones. His University of Florida diploma gave him a viable alternative.

Jerome Evans: "On the first day of the draft I watched it on ESPN. On the second day, I sat around hoping, hoping, hoping, but then I thought it was more realistic that I would sign as a free agent. I waited to get a shot. I didn't even get a chance. I never went to camp. Never went.

"No draft, no free agency, no calls, no nothing. I said to myself, I can work and make money. I have a degree.

"Unfortunately for me, my pro career didn't work out, but I don't have any regrets. I just wish I hadn't been injured. But maybe something bad would have happened playing in the pros. Who knows?

"I played football for a great university. I have a lot of good memories. I got my degree. And I have something that very few people have, a national championship. What more can I ask for?"

After Danny Wuerffel graduated, he was drafted in the spring of '97 by the New Orleans Saints. His pro career has been rocky, but he has endured.

Danny Wuerffel: "I came in as the backup, and if you look in my file, you'll see there were about eight guys who I ended up backing up.

"For the first three years, Mike Ditka was the coach. I love Mike Ditka. Oh yeah, absolutely. He's Iron Mike, but he's also a very compassionate and generous and caring person that most people don't know.

"I started two games my rookie year, maybe four the second year, and then I didn't start any the third year. I had a little success, a couple good games, a couple of wins, but for the most part we were a pretty poor team.

"After that in the spring of 1999 I played for the Rhein Fire in NFL Europe, and we won the World Bowl. I started that season and broke the record for touchdown passes with 25. Then I signed with Green Bay, but I didn't play, and last year I was with Shane Matthews in Chicago."

In the winter of 2002 he signed to play with the Washington Redskins. Joining him will be Reidel Anthony, Jacquez Green, and Chris Doering. His coach: Steve Spurrier.

seventy

Spurrier's Bombshell

Winning the national championship in 1996 was a crowning achievement for Coach Steve Spurrier. Unfortunately, it also had its negative side.

Spurrier's problem was that after winning the national championship, the expectations were that he would do it again and again. He knew he had set a ridiculously high standard for himself, an average of 10 wins a year, and he was sure that if his record fell just once, he would face severe criticism. If it dropped low enough, he also knew, he could be fired. It was a bar set ridiculously high for any mortal.

Spurrier, a perfectionist, was a person who always saw a half-empty glass rather than one that was half-full. He focused not on the successes, but on the failures, and he would talk as though it was only a matter of time when he'd be shown the door at UF.

He once said, "If you study coaches and history and cycles of coaches, most all of them hang around long enough that the job chews them up and spits them out." He said it was important that he be able to walk out on his own "instead of somebody shoving you out."

He added, "To have somebody paying you for two or three years to do nothing… I hopefully will never be in that situation." Spurrier was not listening to the applause. His ear was open only to the criticism.

Spurrier knew it had taken a very special set of circumstances to win it once, and with the competition from other Southeast Conference schools as great, or greater, than ever, Spurrier knew how hard it would be to win again. It was possible, but difficult.

Spurrier wondered whether it might make sense to leave Florida on top after his glorious 1996 year. He had talks with Dan Snyder, the owner of the Washington Redskins, and with Rich McKay, the general manager of the

Tampa Bay Bucaneers, about leaving Florida to coach in the National Football League.

After much anguish, Coach Spurrier decided to remain at the University of Florida. After the 1996 season he would sign a five-year $2.1 million-a-year contract, but after each and every season he would debate whether it should be his last.

The years 1997 through 1999 produced records of 10-2, 10-2, and 9-4, incredible numbers for any other coach, but Florida did not win the SEC title in any of those seasons. In 2000 the Gators defeated the University of South Carolina 41-21 to win the SEC East and then only had to beat FSU and Auburn to reach the national championship game. FSU played spoiler, as Florida lost 30-7, ending the Gators national championship hopes. Despite a 10-3 finish, there was some criticism of Spurrier whispered about by disgruntled Florida Gator fans about his inability to beat FSU.

In 2001 Spurrier's team was deeper and more mature, and he was certain Florida would have as good a chance as anyone to win that second national title. In 2001, however, there were two events that moved Spurrier to think about finally exiting college football for the pros.

The first seed of doubt about his wanting to continue as Florida's coach came on November 28, 2001, during a 37-13 win over Florida State at Florida Field.

That day Gator quarterback Rex Grossman led the Gators on three long touchdown drives. For fifteen seniors, it was the first time they had defeated FSU.

Spurrier, in fact, had a record of only 4-8-1 against Florida State, and he was being criticized for his lack of success against longtime Seminole defensive coordinator Mickey Andrews in the papers and by Florida's fans.

So the win was vindication both for his seniors and for Spurrier himself. But after the game Coach Spurrier was incensed at the dirty play of FSU defensive lineman Darnell Dockett.

According to Spurrier, Dockett had tackled Gator Earnest Graham and after taking him down, twisted the fullback's leg so violently that he had to leave the game. Later in the game, according to Spurrier, Dockett deliberately tried to stomp on the throwing hand of quarterback Rex Grossman.

Dockett, who stood at 6'3", 275 pounds, had a reputation for being a bully and a bad actor. As a youth he had been traumatized by life. During the summer after the seventh grade, Dockett walked into his house in Atlanta to discover that his mom had been murdered. She had died from a gunshot wound during a robbery, police said. Shortly after that, his father died.

His uncle, Kevin, took custody of the boy and moved him to Burtonsville, Maryland. The boy, a loner, was often a trouble-maker, and on the football field he had been penalized for rough play in the past.

Spurrier was convinced that Dockett had deliberately tried to injure both Graham and Grossman, and after the game he sat alone under Florida Field and watched game films of Dockett's transgressions over and over. He was surer than ever that Dockett had tried to maim his players deliberately and should be severely punished for it.

Spurrier held a press conference and accused Dockett of being a thug. In response, Darnell Dockett replied, "Who's Earnest Graham anyway? It's not like he's Chris Weinke." He also called Spurrier "a jerk."

FSU's athletic director, Dave Hart, also outspoken, called Spurrier 'a baby," and added, "and he should be punished like one."

Spurrier waited for a defense from the Florida athletic department and from the university. None came. Among the many positive attributes that Spurrier preached to his players was that of loyalty. To Spurrier, who tended to see the world in black and white, you were either for him or you were against him, and when only silence floated down from the halls of academia, Spurrier decided that it might be time to reconsider his position.

On December 1, Tennessee invaded Florida Field for a game that was originally scheduled for September 15. It was postponed in the aftermath of the World Trade Center catastrophe. Had the game been played as originally scheduled, the result might well have been different. Going into the third week of the season, Florida had clobbered Marshall and Louisiana-Monroe, and Tennessee was struggling. The Vols' sophomore quarterback, Casey Clausen, had been spotty, and three of the Vols' top players, including All-American defensive tackle John Henderson and wide receiver Donte Stallworth, were injured and probably would not have played.

Between September 15 and December 1, Clausen's play improved immeasurably, and wide receiver Stallworth recovered from his injuries.

Conversely, Florida had to play without fullback Earnest Graham, who had been injured by Dockett in the Florida State game on November 17.

Going into this meeting against Tennessee, Florida had won seven of the last eight meetings. Florida was ranked second in the AP poll, Tennessee fifth.

Three days earlier Oklahoma State had stunned second-ranked

Oklahoma 16-13. That loss and Nebraska's 62-36 loss to Colorado brought Florida back into the running for the national championship. Wins over Tennessee and in the SEC championship would give Florida a trip to Pasadena and the Rose Bowl to play Miami for the national title.

The Tennessee game was a stomach churner. Before a record crowd of 85,750 who packed Florida Field, Gator quarterback Rex Grossman threw for more than 362 yards, the tenth time in the 2001 season he threw for more than 300 yards. But his two touchdown passes were not quite enough to defeat Tennessee.

Florida scored as time ran out to close the gap to 34-32. Forced to go for the two-point conversation for a tie, Grossman went back to try to find his go-to guy, Jabar Gaffney, but he was covered well, and the pass flew out of the end zone uncaught. Florida's dreams for a second national championship flew out of that end zone with it.

Looking back, it's certainly possible that the World Trade Center disaster indirectly had a hand in the departure of coach Spurrier. Had it not scrambled events, Florida might have won, and Spurrier might still be at Florida. Who will ever know?

On January 2, 2002, Florida defeated Maryland, 56-23 to win the Orange Bowl. In the game the Gator offense gained 659 yards and scored eight touchdowns, a typical Spurrier-led performance. Rex Grossman didn't start, because he had missed curfew and was being punished, but he came into the game in the second quarter and led six touchdown drives.

After the game Spurrier accepted the Orange Bowl trophy by saying, "It's great to be a Gator."

The Gators finished the season 10-2, and yet, among Florida boosters, the season was considered a disappointment.

After the game Coach Spurrier praised Maryland first-year coach Ralph Friedgen, then added, "Whatever you do, if you don't do it next year, you've slipped. If Ralph doesn't win 10 next year, they'll say, 'What's happening, coach?'"

Reporters listened to what he was saying, but no one them understood the full import of his remarks.

The next day, at his beach home in Crescent Beach near Jacksonville, Spurrier invited his friend, sports information guru Norm Carlson, and Carlson's wife, to meet him and his wife Jerri at an Italian restaurant on the beach. When the Carlsons walked in, they ordered a beer. Jerri told Norm Carlson that he should sit down and listen to what Steve had to tell him.

Spurrier showed Carlson a retirement speech. He asked if Carlson would "clean it up" for him.

Spurrier explained that he was quitting at Florida in order to pursue a job in the NFL. The Carlsons were flabbergasted.

The next morning at 9:15, Spurrier called Jeremy Foley on the phone and told the AD he was stepping down. Jeremy Foley was dumbstruck. He was hoping Spurrier was kidding. When he realized he wasn't, Foley began grasping for breath. Foley also knew something else: he had better find a replacement quick, because if he didn't, a lot of the players committed to Florida were going to go somewhere else.

On Friday, December 5, 2002, Jeremy Foley made the official announcement that Steven Orr Spurrier had resigned as coach of Florida. Spurrier remained home in Crescent Beach, where he said in a statement, "I've got the itch. I want to satisfy my competitive desires of coaching in the pros. I need to find out if my style of offense and my style of coaching can be successful with those NFL boys. You think somebody will give me a chance?"

It was as surprising and unexpected as any play he had ever called, including those from his tricky Emory and Henry formation. Spurrier, who had a knack for showmanship, headlines, and publicity, had dropped a bombshell on Gator Nation, on all of college football, whose athletic directors were coughing up added millions of dollars to stop the candidates being sought as a replacement, and on the NFL, where a third of the coaches suddenly become vulnerable to being replaced by a newcomer. Among the franchises rumored to be pursuing him were Tampa Bay, Minnesota, Jacksonville, San Diego, Carolina, Atlanta, and Washington.

The uproar was immediate. Thousands of inches of newspaper copy in papers all over America resulted.

The next Monday Spurrier stood in front of the press. At his farewell news conference, Spurrier told reporters that he had not lined up another job. Not everyone believed him, because they figured him to be more calculating than that, but it was the truth. And it was in keeping with Spurrier's of-the-moment, compulsive temperament.

Spurrier told his audience, "I'm intrigued to see if our style of offense, if my style of coaching, can be successful at the NFL level.

He said, "I would like to be remembered as a coach whose teams were always in the hunt. We didn't win them all, but we were up there fighting for it. It didn't work out all the time, but we came close about every time.

"I would like to be remembered as a guy that never ever was charted with breaking any rules, which in 12 years we never were. I don't know why that is so difficult, but there is a lot of rule-breakers. Not too many now, but there are still a few out there.

"And hopefully, the players, once they leave here, have learned something about how to be a good person and a good citizen, and they'll be successful when they leave here. That's what I hope happens, that our players say they enjoyed playing for me and my assistant coaches."

At his farewell press conference a reporter suggested that the university had not backed him strongly enough after Hart accused him of being a whiner and a baby. Spurrier didn't dispute that. Earlier he had said, "I've been a lone voice. It's sort of been me against everybody else."

It was, he said, just time to go. He figured the program was at the top and that the athletic director would pick the right replacement. The timing was right because it gave Foley enough time to hire the new coach before the new recruits could switch to another school.

Said Spurrier in conclusion, "I'm a Gator and will be for the rest of my life. Only not as a coach."

On Spurrier's resignation to go into the pros, Gary Shelton, a columnist for the *St. Petersburg Times*, wrote, "It's a shame, really. Spurrier had become a fixture in college football, and in Gainesville. If he had hung around a few more years, they would have named elementary schools after him. No NFL town will love him quite so unconditionally. No place will defend him so vigorously, see his side so readily, cheer his name so loudly."

After Spurrier walked away, the big question everyone wanted to know was: who is going to replace him. The first choice was Bobby Stoops, who had led Oklahoma to a national championship in 2001. Stoops was doing just fine at Oklahoma and chose to stay put. Second choice was Mike Shanahan, head coach of the Denver Broncos. He too stayed where he was.

AD Jeremy Foley decided that his short list would include only coaches he knew and trusted, and his next choice was Ron Zook, who had coached at Florida for Spurrier from 1992-1995.

Zook played at Miami of Ohio, began his coaching career at Murray State, Cincinnati and Kansas, where he was defensive coordinator, then moved on to Tennessee, Virginia Tech, and Ohio State where he was secondary coach. He joined the University of Florida in 1992.

The job was rough on Zook, as it could be for assistant coaches under the demanding Spurrier. Zook had started as defensive coordinator, then was demoted to special teams and linebacker coach, where he did a sensational job. After the 1995 season Spurrier offered Zook his old job of defensive coordinator back, but Zook chose instead to jump to the NFL where he joined the Pittsburgh Steelers as special teams coach. He spent three seasons in Pittsburgh, one in Kansas City, and one in New Orleans as defensive coordinator of the Saints under head coach Jim Haslett. Zook's defense played a key role in New Orleans winning the NFC West in 2000. His defense was third best in the league. In 2001 it ranked tenth.

Zook, 47, when he signed a five-year contract, was in the same unenviable position as the men who replaced Knute Rockne, Bear Bryant and Woody Hayes. Spurrier's record was 122-27-1 in his twelve seasons and six SEC championships. How could anyone compete with that?

Said Zook realistically, "Obviously, coming in behind Coach Spurrier is not the best thing to do." He acknowledged that Spurrier had set the bar, and he promised to try to raise it further.

Zook's highest marks come as a recruiter. While he was at Florida, he was able to bring quite a few players from Jacksonville, after years of Florida State getting most of the top players from the area. He talked quarterback Rex Grossman, the runner up in the Heisman award balloting in 2001, into coming back to Florida for the 2002 season. He also convinced most of Spurrier's 2001 recruits not to jump ship.

Zook promised everyone his teams would be as exciting offensively as Spurrier's. "We're going to be an attacking offense. We're going to throw the ball around the ballpark, as Coach Spurrier once said. We're going to score points. That's my style."

When Zook heard the criticism that Florida should have hired an offensive coach and not a defensive one, Zook replied, "As a defensive coordinator, don't you think I know what offenses do that give people problems? You don't think I know what the Rams do?"

To help with the offense, Zook hired as his offensive coordinator, Ed Zaunbrecher, whose powerful offense at Marshall raised eyebrows everywhere. Zaunbrecher's offense averaged 37 points and 505 yards a game, third in the nation, in 2001. (Florida was second with 527 yards a game.) Zook filled his coaching staff quickly, so that Florida would be in full force during the recruiting season.

There was some criticism of Zook's hiring, but Jeremy Foley was quick to point out that his last controversial hiring was basketball coach Billy Donovan, who quickly took Florida to breathtaking heights.

Columnist Mike Bianchi of the *Orlando Sentinel* reminded his readers that the University of Miami had been turned down by Dave Wannstedt and Barry Alvarez before hiring unknown rookie head coach Larry Coker. All Coker did was lead Miami to a national championship in 2001.

Wrote Bianchi, "It's easy to rip Foley, but what's not so easy is coming up with a more viable option. Foley went after two great coaches and was rejected. Not surprising. There's one major problem when you go after great coaches. They already have great jobs."

Said Foley, "I had to go with my instincts about who would be the right fit here. If that calls my own job into question, I say judge it by the scoreboard up there."

Foley has run one of the most successful athletic programs in America. Who would be foolish enough to bet against him?

Said Saints coach Jim Haslett, "He will not let the fans of Florida down."

Said Ron Zook, "You need to have people doubting you. That excites me."

Spurrier, meanwhile, signed a long-term deal to coach the Washington Redskins. He has brought Danny Wuerffel, Chris Doering, Reidel Anthony, and Jacquez Green into the fold. It will be interesting to watch which Fun 'n Gun offense will prove more successful. All of Florida will be watching.

notes

one: *The Early Days*

For the early history of the University of Florida, see *Gator History,* by Samuel Proctor and Wright Langley, South Star Publishing Co, Gainesville, Fla., 1986. On how Florida was nicknamed the Gators, see the *Florida Times-Union,* August 2, 1958.

Interviews with Angus Williams and Red Mitchum.

two: *Love Brings Them Together*

Interviews with Frank Dempsey, Angus Williams, and Loren Broadus.

three: *Fuller Warren's Promise*

When Fuller ran in 1948, the law provided that a candidate could only raise $15,000 for his campaign. Three men, including University of Florida grad C.V. Griffin, the second-largest shipper of Citrus in the state of Florida, raised $450,000 for Fuller's campaign. When Fuller and Griffin had a falling out, Griffin went to the papers and told everyone about the money Fuller had received.

In 1951 the legislature passed a law requiring candidates to report every contribution and expenditure down to the last dollar. [*St. Petersburg Times,* Oct. 29, 1998.]

Warren was investigated by a United State Senate committee led by Estes Kefaufer. Its investigation revealed that one Florida alum, the owner of several dog tracks who had funded the improvement of the University of Florida football team, had been a major contributor to Warren's campaign fund. When Kefaufer subpoenaed Warren, the governor refused to come saying the committee lacked the authority to summon a governor. "I refuse to be exhibited as a sideshow," he said. [See *Florida: From Secession to Space Age,* by Merlin Cox and J. E. Dovell, Great Outdoors Publishing Company, St. Petersburg, FL, 1974. See pages 212-19.]

Interviews with Angus Williams, Frank Dempsey, and Loren Broadus.

four: *The Final Days of Bear Wolf*
Interviews with Loren Broadus, Charlie LaPradd, Haywood Sullivan, and Red Mitchum.

five: *Woodruff Takes Over*
For more on Jim Tatum, see *Onward to Victory,* by Murray Sperber, Henry Holt, NY, 1998.

"He was given one order, to beat Georgia." *The Gators,* by Tom McEwen, The Strode Publishers, Huntsville, Alabama, 1974. pages 160-61.

Interviews with Loren Broadus, Angus Williams, Charlie LaPradd, Haywood Sullivan, and Red Mitchum.

six: *Wild and Crazy Guys*
Interviews with Rick Casares, Joe D'Agostino, Haywood Sullivan, and Red Mitchum. Joe D'Agostino passed away on Christmas Day, 2001.

seven: *A Win Over Alabama*
Interviews with Heywood Sullivan, Rick Casares, Charlie LaPradd, Joe D'Agostino, and Red Mitchum.

eight: *Haddock, Dickey, and Lance*
Interviews with Red Mitchum, Doug Dickey, Tom Haddock, Rick Casares, Bobby Lance, and Joe D'Agostino.

nine: *The First Bowl Victory*
Interviews with Tom Haddock, Joe D'Agostino, Doug Dickey, Heywood Sullivan, and Bobby Lance.

ten: *One-Platoon Disaster*
Interviews with Jackie Simpson, Jimmy Dunn, Bobby Lance, and Mal Hammock.

eleven: *An SEC Championship Slips Away*
Interviews with Jimmy Dunn, Vel Heckman, and Bobby Lance.

twelve: *Dunn and Heckman*
Interviews with Vel Heckman, Jimmy Dunn, and Jackie Simpson

thirteen: *Platooning*
Interviews with Jimmy Dunn and Vel Heckman.

fourteen: *A Year on Probation*
Interviews with Vel Heckman, Don Deal, and Jimmy Dunn.

fifteen: *The First Florida State Game*
Interviews with Don Deal and Jimmy Dunn.

sixteen: *Woodruff Goes for a Tie*
Scott Kelly lost to Governor Hayden Burns by a total of 3,200 votes, one vote per precinct in the state of Florida. Said Larry Libertore, "Had Scott Kelly done two things, spent more time in Miami, and show up on time more often, who knows what might have happened? Who knows you're going to lose by three thousand votes?"

Interview with Larry Libertore.

seventeen: *Larry Libertore*
Interviews with Lindy Infante, Don Deal, and Larry Libertore.

eighteen: *Ray Graves Takes Over*
Interviews with Larry Libertore and Lindy Infante.

nineteen: *A Big Win in the Gator Bowl*
Interviews with Larry Dupree and Tom Shannon.

twenty: *A Lean Year*
Interviews with Larry Dupree, Tom Shannon, Larry Libertore, and Lindy Infante.

twenty-one: *A Devastating Loss to Duke*
Interviews with Larry Dupree, Larry Libertore, Tom Shannon, and Lindy Infante.

twenty-two: *A Big Gator Bowl Win*
Interviews with Jack Harper, Larry Dupree, and Tom Shannon.

twenty-three: *An Upset of Alabama*
Interviews with Tom Shannon, Jack Harper, and Larry Dupree.

twenty-four: *Dupree's Great Day*
Interviews with Tom Shannon, Jack Harper, and Larry Dupree.

twenty-five: *The Coming of Steve Spurrier*
For information on Spurrier's life, see the *Lakeland Ledger* of November 15 and 16, 1996. The articles were written by Logan Mabe and Mike Cobb.

Interviews with Richard Trapp and Jack Harper.

twenty-six: *Steve's Go-To Guy*
Interviews with Larry Rentz and Richard Trapp.

twenty-seven: *Spurrier Wins The Heisman*
Interviews with Steve Tannen, Richard Trapp, Larry Rentz, and Larry Smith.

twenty-eight: *Richard Trapp's Famous Run*
Interviews with Steve Tannen, Larry Smith, Larry Rentz, and Jack Youngblood.

twenty-nine: *Humiliation by Georgia*
Interviews with Steve Tannen, Larry Rentz, Larry Smith, Jack Youngblood, Ray Graves.

thirty: *The Super Sophs*
Interviews with John Reaves, Steve Tannen, and Jack Youngblood,

thirty-one: *Coach Graves Steps Down*
Interviews with Steve Tannen, John Reaves, Jack Youngblood, Ray Graves, and Red Mitchum.

thirty-two: *Ruffled Feathers*
Interviews with Red Mitchum, Doug Dickey, Jack Youngblood, John Reaves, and Fred Abbott.

thirty-three: *Integration*
Interviews with Ray Graves, Willie Jackson, John Reaves, Jack Youngblood, and Fred Abbott.

thirty-four: *Unhappiness*
Interviews with John Reaves, Fred Abbott, Jack Youngblood, and Willie Jackson.

thirty-five: *The Florida Flop*
Interviews with John Reaves, Fred Abbott, and Willie Jackson.

thirty-six: *Bowden to McGriff*
Interviews with Fred Abbott, Lee McGriff, and David Bowden.

thirty-seven: *Preston Kendrick Steals a Flag*
Interviews with Lee McGriff, Fred Abbott, David Bowden, and Willie Jackson.

fifty-one: *The Last Days of Charlie Pell*
On the life and death of Charlie Pell, see the *St. Petersburg Times* of May 30, 2001. See the articles by Bruce Lowitt and Gary Shelton.

Interviews with Ricky Nattiel, Lee McGriff, Red Mitchum, Wayne Peace, Bob Hewko, and Kerwin Bell.

fifty-two: *An SEC Championship is Taken Away*
Interviews with Kerwin Bell and Ricky Nattiel.

fifty-three: *Another Amazing 9-1-1 Year*
Interviews with Ricky Nattiel and Kerwin Bell.

fifty-four: *Bell to Nattiel*
Interviews with Kerwin Bell and Ricky Nattiel.

fifty-five: *Emmitt*
Interviews with Herb Perry and Kerwin Bell.

fifty-six: *A Tough Finish*
Interviews with Herb Perry and Kerwin Bell.

fifty-seven: *Turmoil*
Interviews with Kirk Kirkpatrick and Herb Perry.

fifty-eight: *Coach Hall Steps Down*
Interview with Kirk Kirkpatrick.

fifty-nine: *Steve and Shane*
Interviews with Jimmy Dunn and Shane Matthews.

sixty: *Exciting from the Start*
Interviews with Kirk Kirkpatrick and Shane Matthews.

sixty-one: *Spurrier's First Recruit*
Interviews with Terry Dean and Shane Matthews.

sixty-two: *An Improbable Season*
Interviews with Terry Dean and Shane Matthews.

sixty-three: *Wuerffel and Bowen*
Interviews with Danny Wuerffel and Paul Bowen.

index